CRAN
BR 516.5 .R45
C. 1

RELIGIOUS MOVEMEN

M5/20339

EAST KOOTENAY COMMUNITY COLLEGE

1 1111 00009 1811

DISCARD

D0224740

Religious Movements
in Contemporary America

Religious Movements
in Contemporary America

edited by Irving I. Zaretsky and Mark P. Leone

PRINCETON UNIVERSITY PRESS, PRINCETON, NEW JERSEY

E.K.C.C. LIBRARY.

12.33 B47

October 12, 1982

BR516.5
.R45

Copyright © 1974 by Princeton University Press

ALL RIGHTS RESERVED
Published by Princeton University Press, Princeton, New Jersey
In the U.K.: Princeton University Press, Guildford, Surrey

ISBN 0-691-01993-2 (paperback edition)
ISBN 0-691-07186-1 (hardcover edition)

Library of Congress Cataloging in Publication data will
be found on the last printed page of this book.
Publication of this book has been aided by a grant from the Whitney
Darrow Publication Reserve Fund of Princeton University Press.
This book has been composed in Linotype Baskerville
Printed in the United States of America
by Princeton University Press, Princeton, New Jersey

First PRINCETON PAPERBACK printing, 1977

60-870-482

E.C.C. LIBRARY

WE WISH TO DEDICATE THIS BOOK TO THE MEMBERS OF
THE RELIGIOUS GROUPS WITH WHOM WE HAVE DONE FIELD
WORK. WITHOUT THEIR COOPERATION THIS BOOK COULD
NOT HAVE BEEN WRITTEN.

CONTENTS

THE papers in this volume present the most current empirical and theoretical research on contemporary marginal religious movements in the United States. The movements at the center of the current religious revival are viewed here from the perspective of several different disciplines, with the major concern of this scholarship being twofold. The first is to show what these movements look like, what their goals are, and how they achieve them. The second is to demonstrate the reciprocal effect between them and society: contemporary religious institutions are the products of our own culture and its historical tradition and, further, they are created by individuals who are products of that culture and society.

These new institutions reflect social conditions in the established order. They can be looked at as an index of the personal and communitarian needs of segments of the American population, the success and failure of established institutions in meeting these needs, and the sources, mechanisms, and direction of social and religious evolution. There is no doubt that the current religious revival is a widespread, grass-roots movement in which sectors of American society are organizing institutional support for themselves in order to solve deep personal and social problems. But more than that, they are religious innovations which, in addition to bringing about social change, may represent a new religious adaptation in the continued evolution of religious forms. Moreover, they demonstrate the utility of religion as a metaphor for organizational frameworks and as a vehicle to accomplish a variety of secular goals.

This research is close to problems that many Americans are vitally interested in. We are deeply involved in new religions, and both citizens and scholars treat them as sensitive indices to the state of American society today. With this in mind, one can see that most of the work presented here bridges research preferences and canons of scientific research with social responsibility. The consequences of this produce scholarship based on the empirical tradition of fieldwork coupled with an attempt to assess religious groups dispassionately.

This collection of papers is the result of two research meetings that were organized by the editors in November 1970 and April 1971. The November meeting, a symposium titled "Modern American Protestant

Movements," was held at the American Anthropological Association meetings in San Diego, California. The participants were Lee Cooper, Roger Lauer, Mark P. Leone, Morton Marks, E. Fuller Torrey, and Irving I. Zaretsky. Each member of the symposium presented a paper on the particular religious group with whom he had done fieldwork. The symposium was viewed as the preliminary effort in focusing on issues of mutual concern and isolating the major problems that needed further discussion. The April conference was titled "Marginal Religious Movements in America Today"; the members of the earlier symposium, with the exception of Lee Cooper and E. Fuller Torrey, were also present at this conference, in addition to other scholars. The conference papers were duplicated a month in advance and were made available to each one of the participants. The papers in this book by Professors Allan Eister, Virginia Hine, and Dick Anthony and Thomas Robbins were not presented at the conference; they are included here for the added perspectives they offer on the groups and issues under discussion. These writers were requested to follow the same format in their papers as the conference participants.

The reader will note that the titles of the symposium, the conference, and this volume vary, although all three have addressed the same domain. The differing titles reflect the editors' struggle to find a label that would be conceptually accurate and yet not offend members of the religious groups being discussed. We decided on the current title of the volume because it is benign in tone, and still allows us to pursue a discussion of both the marginal and orthodox aspects of these movements.

The following are the aims of the conference and of this volume:

1. To isolate the major theoretical issues in the study of contemporary religious movements in America in light of current problems and past research.
2. To present heretofore unpublished data on the present-day organization of these movements.
3. To encourage inter-disciplinary cooperation by allowing researchers to benefit from background information collected by various scholars who previously addressed this domain.
4. To indicate the applied nature of current research. As citizen-scholars working within our own society, it may be possible through greater knowledge and understanding to effect positive influence in areas of conflict between these churches, their members, and the larger society.

To provide a sense of how the papers are organized to realize these goals, we outline some definitions and classifications made with participants prior to the conference. Within the scope of current marginal religious movements in America we include the following categories: (1) the churches founded on the margins of nineteenth-century American Protestantism which maintain active memberships today, such as Christian Science, Spiritualism, Mormonism, some genres of Pentecostalism, New Thought Movements; (2) recently founded religious groups such as Scientology, sidewalk churches, Youth for Jesus movements; (3) synchretistic groups based on imported cults such as Santería, Meher Baba, Hare Krishna which are active in many American urban centers. All these churches may be considered marginal, but collectively they represent what Judah (1967) has called the current American Metaphysical Movement.

The topical foci for this volume stem in part from the editors' respective research experiences with Spiritualism and Mormonism and in part from the research problems addressed by the contributors. Our own research over the past several years in this area has convinced us of several points. The emerging religious institutions, when viewed especially from a cross-disciplinary point of view, show the mutual interaction of four important variables. The movements can be seen as the intersection of the established social order and innovative individuals, institutions supportive of particularistic needs, the American tradition of self-help, and the stress resulting from rapid social change. These variables play a part in generating the conditions for new religious movements as well as the revitalization of old ones. Several of these variables are examined in almost every paper in this volume. The uniquely favorable research environment created by this juncture is expressed in the topics considered at the conference and the way they were handled.

We requested contributors to address themselves to one of several suggested general topics: (1) arts, letters, and ethno-musicology related to particular groups; (2) economic foundations of religious movements; (3) culture and personality; (4) legal foundations of religious groups; (5) historical perspectives; (6) role of language in church ritual; (7) doctrinal and ideological foundations; (8) religious ritual including phenomena of mediumship, trance, and dissociational states; (9) social organization of various churches; (10) religious movements in urban contexts; (11) perspectives for fieldwork within American churches; (12) utility of research for social action. Each of the first nine topics has been addressed by at least one paper. Some papers stress ethnographic, case-study material of a particular group or groups, while other papers stress the methodological and theoretical aspects in their analysis. All the papers, however, include a theoretical framework that is related to the general issue or problems exemplified in a specific church group or topic and a presentation of ethnographic data to illustrate the conceptual framework.

It might appear that most of these papers tend toward a secularized interpretation of religion, avoiding theological issues. This is not due to the fact scholars have weighed the theological and belief systems and purposefully tried to secularize their interpretation. Nor do they argue that theology and behavior are not related. Rather, our approach grows out of the fact that the training most of us received in the social sciences tends to focus on the social characteristics of religion and religious groups and less on theology. Ours is an effort to understand the varieties of social behavior within these religious institutions and to point out the relationship of these institutions to the larger society.

The order of the papers in the volume shows a sequential development of ideas to answer basic questions: What is the relationship of religious groups to their surrounding communities? How are these groups organized to fulfill various functions for the individual and his community? What are the communication forms for the transmission of religious beliefs? How do these groups change over time? What research issues do they pose for contemporary scholarship? Answers to such questions are offered in eight topical sections which are based on the content of the papers and the major themes of discussion raised at the conference. Each section is preceded by the editors' introductory comments, which include the themes unifying each section, an abstract of each paper in the section, and the significant issues raised during the discussion of each paper at the conference.

We begin by considering in Section 1 the issues of church and state arising out of the conflicts between the practices of particular religious groups and the norms and values of their surrounding communities. In so doing, the groups are placed within the largest meaningful social unit within whose legal framework they must function. Religious groups wishing to open their doors to the general public and hoping to attain a degree of social stability and permanence have to resolve any legal conflicts that result from their religious observances. The papers indicate the reciprocal impact of this confrontation on the social organization of religious groups and on the tolerance level of the community for religious innovations. All of these groups have tested the limits of the social order on the local, state, and federal levels. They have thus contributed to defining our concept of the First Amendment's free-exercise-of-religion clause.

Having outlined in Section 1 the legal processes through which religious groups exist within their communities, in the following sections we examine particular groups in terms of other social domains.

All of these groups have contributed to the development of an oral tradition composed of such forms as the preached sermon, gospel songs, religious argots, and ritual languages. Section 2 examines how these communication forms are speech events that serve as vehicles for both the transmission of information about the group and as instances of ritual behavior. These speech events often co-occur with a speaker's altered state of consciousness which in turn may effect such states in others. The altered states are uniquely valued by these groups as systems of communication in their own right. They allow participants to validate religious beliefs personally and gain confidence in the rituals of the church.

It is because altered states are so highly prized and cultivated by these groups that in Section 3 we turn to them in greater detail. The concept "altered states of consciousness" represents a continuum ranging from overtly manifested trance behavior to mystical feelings of transcendence to internally perceived but not overtly manifested aesthetic experiences. The papers pay particular attention to the uses made of altered states of consciousness by various groups and the role they play in sustaining ritual behavior and augmenting processes of social change.

Having pointed out some of the communications forms of these movements, we turn to a closer examination of how the groups function for the individual in his social milieu. Section 4 presents a series of papers on the psychological dimensions of various groups. The section begins with a psychohistorical analysis of the current religious revival, the causes for its onset, and its similarity to past revivals. The authors are interested in understanding the cyclical occurrence of such movements within the United States. Some of the papers examine the social pathology models often used to explain these movements, and suggest that models dealing with processual change are more useful in explaining these phenomena. Several groups are isolated for a closer analysis of how they aid the individual in overcoming his problems, their compatibility with community mental health services, and the institutional support they give to their adherents.

The impact of these groups on the individual is not only of importance to individuals, but also of significance to the larger society. Section 5 examines how these groups are instrumental in maintaining the ongoing social order through re-socialization of disaffected individuals or as alternative life styles to those individuals who do not wish to re-enter mainstream society. The papers discuss several Eastern philosophies adapted to alienated Western youth in its efforts to deal with contemporary social crises.

The success of these groups in American society lies in part in their ability to synthesize cultural elements shared by the general society with beliefs and practices which are often antithetical to the given social values and norms. Section 6 analyses the internal system of meanings and symbols used in some of these groups. Mormonism and Scientology are examined from the perspectives of "cultural analysis" to focus on the orientations and meanings they provide for their adherents. These groups have been successful in offering their members prescriptional behavioral patterns that seem to be highly adaptive in daily life. The papers analyze the world view of these groups and the internal social organization which sustains these views through time.

The previous sections treated various religious groups synchronically. But these groups are able to absorb change quite readily. Their success lies in large measure in their ability to be flexible and adaptive, thereby presupposing a steady rate of change. It is with change, both in the churches and in our analysis of the churches, that the next two sections are concerned.

Section 7 turns to the issue of classifying the whole range of churches and movements that currently exist. The papers point out that we need to rethink such classification systems as the church-sect typology, the social pathology model, and the defective individual model, that are usually employed to explain the groups under discussion. While we need synchronic models that account for change and the self-definition of these groups, classification models are needed to address current research interests, rather than those that reify past approaches. In Section 8 the papers deal with processual change. The authors indicate how the groups adapt and evolve to meet the shifting needs of their members and the ongoing pressures from their communities.

The final section is appropriate to the book's tenor: perspectives for future research. It was the opinion of the contributors that we have just begun to examine these phenomena systematically; we need extensive empirical research in some specific areas and on given topics. The directions that this research might take are pointed out in some detail.

In addition to the scholars who generously and enthusiastically participated in the conferences that led to this volume, we, as organizers, and now as editors, have a large debt to the individuals and institutions whose support and generosity have made this work possible. Foremost among the supporting institutions is the Wenner-Gren Foundation for Anthropological Research and its representatives Mrs. Lita Osmundson and Mr. Christopher Dodds. The Lucius N. Littauer Foundation, of New York, provided us our first support, and from the Foundation's director, Mr. Harry Starr, we received warm encouragement. The National Endowment for the Humanities granted us generous support. In addition, costs were borne for one of the conference participants by the Center for Urban Ethnography of the University of Pennsylvania directed by Professor John Szwed. To all of these individuals and institutions we are particularly grateful.

As with any adventure into an unorganized domain like marginal religious movements, the experience and advice of others is indispensable in the successful completion of the project. Among those who provided concrete knowledge and warm support are Professor and Mrs. Norman Itzkowitz and Professor and Mrs. Geoffrey Lewis. In addition to aiding with specific and difficult details, Jeannette Mirsky offered encouragement at times when that resource was most sorely needed. Dr. Wilton Dillon of the Smithsonian Institution gave us much tried advice on many of the details of running a conference. We turned to Professors Elizabeth Colson and Laura Nader for suggestions on specific issues in the planning of the conference. To all these friends our debt is large.

Within Princeton University several resources were made available that led to the success of our conferences and to the publication of this volume. The offices of the Princeton University Conference enabled the pragmatic day-to-day affairs of planning to be done with unusual skill and smoothness. Mrs. Mildred Scott graciously guided the details of planning and running the conference and to her and the director of the conference office, Mr. Edward Hobbs, we are grateful.

Mr. Richard Parmentier, a student in the Department of Anthropology, University of Chicago, and Mr. David Raim at Yale College gave us invaluable assistance in the final preparation of this volume.

For speedy and efficient help with the endless secretarial chores accompanying an undertaking like this, we thank Mrs. Paul Benson, Miss Beverly Fisher, and Miss Anne Mariella at the Department of Anthropology, Princeton University and Mrs. Peter Anderson and the Russell Sage Program in Law and Social Science at Yale Law School.

Irving I. Zaretsky
New Haven, Connecticut

Mark P. Leone
Princeton, New Jersey

The Common Foundation of Religious Diversity

Renewed anthropological interest in the varieties of religious experience has begun to include the churches founded outside the mainstream institutional churches. Current field research in the area of religion comes at a time when some of the most vigorous churches in America are the unorthodox groups tracing their origins in this country to the early and middle nineteenth century. Jehovah's Witnesses; New Thought churches; Mormonism; Pentecostalism, both Protestant and Catholic; Spiritualism; Scientology; Satanism; Spiritism; Occult groups devoted to witchcraft or psychic experiences; imported cults such as Santería, Meher Baba, and Hare Krishna; movements devoted to revival preaching and Gospel meetings; Youth for Jesus groups; and finally sidewalk churches are all experiencing rapid increases in membership today.

These groups produce life styles and personal commitment substantially different from mainline institutional churches, and they are uniquely successful at influencing the life-ways of their members. These religious groups have contributed theological, organizational, and ritual innovations to contemporary religious life in America. They are neither moribund nor concerned with the death of God. Rather, they cater to a reaffirmed religious zeal founded on personalized theologies made to fit the needs of an ever-expanding and diversified following. They provide a framework wherein ecstatic religious experiences for the individual are reintroduced and provided with purpose and justification. They appeal to all age groups; some are especially attractive to young people, and others appeal to senior citizens. While originally drawing from the margins of society in age distribution, economic and social status, they are now successfully making inroads in middle America. These groups have developed religious forms compatible with the pragmatic spirit of contemporary America. They enjoy a kind of hybrid vigor because they are a product of as well as a platform for the intersection of five factors: (1) a greater popular knowledge about secular and religious institutions in overseas communities, a knowledge gained through more travel, public education, and media communications; (2) an intellectual and emotional freedom to invent, borrow, and weld together social forms that were hitherto thought to be alien to and incompatible with the established order; (3) a willingness of Americans to assume, acknowledge, and express their multiple social and religious identities within religious institutions; (4) increased experimentation with the content and form of human relationships and social institutions; (5) an active search for a *weltanschauung* that can cope with and transcend the contradictions inherent in contemporary culture.

What distinguishes the current religious renaissance from previous ones is the fact that the communications media have provided broad-scale publicity on the impact and spread of religious enthusiasm and for the themes and churches that compose it. The great diversity in content and form of current religions is communicated not only in the churches but through special bookshops, movies, records, newspapers, and other media. The message that each of the different media spreads is varied. Television presents stories and documentaries on witchcraft, poltergeists, and psychic experiences. Most of the documentaries have been respectful of participants, even though at times reporters have been openly dubious of the religious assumptions. The emphasis has been on the sensational and unusual aspects of religious experience. Other media, like newspapers, talk about the diffusion of "Religion of Love" and the "Christianization of the World." News broadcasts often report, with benign incredulity, that yet another witchcraft shop has opened and features ritual vestments and products for a variety of occult ceremonies.

It is clear that in interpreting what the current religious revival means, the media have not, nor should we expect them to, given us a unitary view. They have offered us the conclusion that marginal religious groups no longer have a *sub rosa* existence but live side by side with organized religion. Perhaps that symbiosis has always existed, but before we did not have the technology to inform us of the fact as it was happening. We have not had the media as an intrinsic part of popular culture legitimizing a close association with the taboo. The media have not so much created the popularity of religious movements as they have helped to give them a kind of legitimacy through influencing the public viewpoint about them. Through extensive reporting the media have translated eccentric behavior into values and norms viewed as harmonious with society. As a result, a large segment of the population is no longer afraid of pariah status because of religious beliefs. The media for their part have made most people able to realize, "it's here, let's live with it." They have prevented a popular banishment or witch hunt and left any opposition to these movements to formal institutions. This could be one of the most important contributions of the media's role in the current religious scene.

But if the media as a forum have been tremendously influential, they have also been responsible for the diffusion of certain ideas and conclusions about the current religious interest which are not always consistent with the evidence at hand.

First, this has been called a new religious revival, composed of new religions. But perhaps what is new is the pervasive attention it is being given. The roots of this genre of religiosity are well established in American traditions, going back to the colonial period and assuming more modern form in the early nineteenth century. The foundations are American, and the apparatus insuring such revivals is in fact built into the political and economic organization of our country.

Second, neither are these developments regional phenomena. While certain parts of the country—New York State in the middle of the nineteenth century, California, Arizona, and Florida in the twentieth century—have been more receptive to certain cults, they are clearly a national phenomenon. We should not mistake the regional density of cults with the erroneous belief that they appeal only to the native sons of certain areas. Rather, across the country these phenomena are cutting across religious, educational, racial, and ethnic lines. The movement is a kind of religious populism which coincides with the political appetites and aspirations of a large number of people. It is a populism expressing itself in the religious arena. By focusing on one area or state as the cradle of the "lunatic fringe" and the "bizarre," some think we can do away with the need to explain national phenomena. Of course the regional arguments are folly and only speak to a basic prejudice that finds it easier to argue for a mythical ecological determinism. If anything, different regions of this country have been equally alive to religious enthusiasms.

Third, is this pan-regional religious enthusiasm a continuation of political populism in the religious sphere? There is no clear answer, but one might offer the hypothesis that populism in religion began with the institutional churches. As these churches were trying to bolster their position in the community by listening to cries of irrelevance, they preceded the ecumenical movement of Vatican II and the Council for the Unification of Christian Churches. They may have paved the road for ecumenism at the popular level. Coupled with American individualism and eclecticism, the drive for relevance was translated to mean: pick and choose and suit yourself. This may be one factor behind the current revival. Another is that the revival came in the wake of a national interest in solitary, individual experiences of ecstasy. The combination of the two resting on a base of individualism and free enterprise figures in the current religious revival. In a sense, these movements represent the folk ecumenical movement that is willing to choose its religious forms from the reservoir of human inventions, unrestricted by institutional and historic boundaries.

Fourth, one may want to assume a contrary position here and argue that we should not use labels such as "occult" and "religion" and thereby confuse the issue. Such labels merely reify generic notions and do not face ethnographic realities. That reality is that the popular revival is not really a renewed interest in religion *per se* but an interest people have in improving themselves and their life. It is a variant on "how to win friends and influence people," how to bring up your child, and how to do a thousand other necessary human tasks. It is a way of people trying to help themselves, by using a religious system for their experimentations and attempts at self-help. Perhaps it is the popular reaction against a society that offers its tools for help at too high a price, and this is then a way of translating expert knowledge into portable do-it-yourself kits. The do-it-yourself pattern with objects and hobbies of the 1950s is entering the area of self-help and personal orientation in the 1970s. We can describe this as the historical continuity of popular culture which is now making inroads into traditional culture. What complicates the current revival is that the language and trappings of religion are being assumed by many groups that are not explicitly religious but which are open to social experimentation. Therefore, the question is what is the current revival and which groups represent its boundaries?

Fifth, popular involvement with religion cannot easily be explained in terms of the political and social disillusionment of individuals who used to be politically active. While the movements do attract those people, it is unclear whether they are attracting them because of disillusionment or because these people are joiners who participate in everything new on the horizon. What is clear is that these religions as movements are not concerned with national issues; they care about them only to the degree that particular parishioners raise such issues as points of intense personal interest.

It is not a new notion that a religious renascence responds to pervasive socio-cultural forces as well as generates its own impact on social change. Scholars have looked at local contemporary movements within their respective societies to try to explain both the principles governing man's religious behavior and the role of religious institutions within the larger social environment. Within the domain of anthropology and marginal religious movements, as early as 1870 scholars began to investigate and describe groups dedicated to psychic research and the pursuit of occult mysteries. Men like A. R. Wallace and E. B. Tylor frequented Spiritualist gatherings in London beginning in 1872 (Stocking 1970). The London Anthropological Society and the Royal Anthropological Institute devoted several meetings to the considerations of these reports from 1873 to 1898. The product of that investigation gave to the study of religion some landmark concepts and labels, among them "animism." Tylor thought that label was preferable to spiritualism, which had become associated with a particular sect.

Scholars a century ago were no less interested than we are today in such questions as why do such movements arise? where is their social locus? how do they develop through time? In nineteenth-century thought, popular interest in such movements as Spiritualism was explained in terms of evolution. These groups were regarded as survivals from a more primitive era; consequently, they were thought to be phenomena that ought properly to belong to the lower classes. More careful examination revealed however that they in fact enjoyed the participation of individuals from all sectors of the population. More contemporary approaches see the appeal of religious groups—as, for example, Spiritualism—to nineteenth-century England as due to a "crisis of faith" (Stocking 1970) brought on by developments in science and technology and their impact on the individual.

These, of course, are only examples of the continued interest of scholars in explaining particular phenomena in terms of extant models or the dominant social variables of their respective historical period. The emphasis has been on placing particular religious movements in their social context and historical period. The result has frequently yielded greater views of the society and a lesser understanding of the particular religious institution, a point to which we will return below. There are several parallels between nineteenth-century interest in new religions and today's similar interest: that it was submitted to scholarly scrutiny, that the research was partially motivated by rapid social and economic transformations, and that it bespoke a national self-curiosity.

Within contemporary America the current religious revival coincides with economic realities of academic research that demand more research be done at home. It also coincides with the fact that many social scientists have begun to feel an obligation to look at their own society. These factors coalesce to offer fieldwork to scholars and their students in communities neighboring university towns where various religious groups can be found. This is a realistic professional interest since many of the social sciences, particulary anthropology, have traditionally studied religious groups like these and posed questions about them in developing countries. Therefore, the current trend may be seen not only as the rapprochement of the scholar with his citizenry and with national interests, but also as a contribution to comparative studies using data of theoretical import from this country with those from overseas communities.

We assume that the current religious movements are the raw material for religious growth and development. These may be considered mutant forms of religious behavior that with time will be synthesized into acceptable forms and in all likelihood will represent a new establishment from which there may in turn be a new rebellion which might even return to restraint. We should look at these groups neither as islands of pathology nor as the Fertile Crescent for an Aquarian age, but rather as social forms which are the consequences of our own national framework and as representing social processes not inflicted upon us. As a result, we do not share the general American bias that religious segmentation is bad. A unitive interpretation hides too much of reality. We see segmentation and bifurcation as an essential social process behind change and growth.

Characteristics Unifying Contemporary Religious Groups

From the rich domain of modern religious experience we have taken a small sample that we believe is representative and discuss it in some detail. The churches interest us in and of themselves. The specific groups dealt with are Mormonism, Spiritualism, Hare Krishna, Santería, Meher Baba, Pentecostalism, Scientology, Spiritism, Satanism, various forms of witchcraft, Jehovah's Witnesses, and Youth for Jesus. These groups can be individually considered marginal, but collectively they are part of what J. Stillson Judah (1967) called "The American Metaphysical Movement." These groups represent some apparent diversity. Historically they range from Mormonism and Spiritualism, founded in the U.S. in the 1830s and 1840s, to Meher Baba and Scientology, established in the past decade. They range from highly organized and structured groups like the Mormons to very diffuse groups like Youth for Jesus.

We have described these groups by a variety of terms: marginal, radical, pragmatic. These adjectives point to the fact that a group has, or in the recent past had, a conflict with society over an aspect of its practices. Such groups are unlikely to gain legislative support for their claims. They are innovative and are therefore often considered radical, e.g., nineteenth-century Mormonism in terms of communal living and plural marriage, Spiritualism in terms of spirit communication through mediums who offer advice on certain life problems,

Satanists in terms of rituals, Scientologists in terms of using technical devices to diagnose personal ailments, etc . Historically these particular groups have a relatively short history when compared to the mainline churches. Furthermore, their memberships are often composed of ethnic and racial minorities. Each one is composed of a rather small population, though collectively they might reach about fifteen million Americans.

It is difficult to obtain statistical information about these groups for several reasons. They often share the membership of an individual, and one person will belong simultaneously to several groups. Often people do not consider themselves members, even if they attend these churches, but identify themselves by their natal religions. Many of these churches do not have a permanent paid membership but cater to an off-the-street clientele. For these reasons, detailed statistics are hard to obtain and a national census does not help, since many people refuse to identify their religion and, when they do so, do not identify what other group they may frequent.

In attempting to describe the religious institutions and associations encompassed in this book, it has seemed vital to delimit their common elements. It is from these shared features that an explanation of their competence in dealing with contemporary society can be discovered. Marginal churches do appear diverse on the surface, but they do share certain structural features which allow us to treat them collectively. These features are a common base that allow us to treat them as an analytical unit.

1. Most of the churches are offshoots of nineteenth-century American Protestantism. Some are imported religions, and all of these are generically related to groups brought into the United States during the nineteenth century. This is particularly true of the Eastern philosophies. Usually individual Protestants experimenting with various ideas, sometimes under the aegis of revelation, developed most of these religions. Even though some of these groups are not Christian, all encompass the moral teachings of Jesus (Judah 1967: 14, point 5), whom they usually regard as especially enlightened but not divine. Jesus understood his own divinity better than most other men understand theirs; that divinity is common to all men and is the universal emanation of God.

2. Many of the groups have developed from each other through doctrinal and social schisms. The set of ideas developed by Phineas Quimby in Maine in the 1840s and 1850s remained some of the shared concepts for Spiritualism and Christian Science as well as a variety of New Thought movements. Those ideas as incorporated in later groups reappear now in a variety of occult groups.

3. Within recent history these groups have faced persecution from society and attempted to resolve their problems in court. They have often served each other as precedent cases in expanding the limits of First Amendment freedoms. Often they have adapted rituals from one another on the basis of a legal fight. In this respect, each movement has grown on the successes and failures of the others.

4. These groups are organized around charismatic individuals who are believed to have "power" either on the basis of personal revelation or through control of processes to communicate with higher forces. Hence there is an emphasis that the leader is powerful now and ought to be followed on that basis. The leader or founders of brand new churches are usually disaffected Methodists, Presbyterians, Catholics, and others from mainline churches.

5. These churches often have rigid standards for membership and a clear set of rules which, if violated, lead to expulsion. The institutional framework, although not as visible as it is in orthodox churches, is visible to those who make final commitment to membership.

6. Although these churches are often branches of a chartering church, the branches may each have significant variation among them. Belonging to a chartering church often affords legal protection. But often these groups do not seek to band into a large organization but wish to remain small and under the control of the leader. Even when these churches become centralized, local congregations retain a high degree of autonomy.

7. Most of the churches share a membership, especially in the early stages of their growth. Membership is shared because their followers are "seekers" who search out and usually frequent new religious developments and groups. Individuals also join one group after another seriatim, and a Spiritualist today can be a Scientologist tomorrow.

8. These churches proselytize actively and often do not gear their message to special segments of the community. Proselytizing follows from the fact that these are often not the natal churches of individuals; rather, they receive the bulk of their adherents in adult life. The immediate family of a member often does not belong to the church. Like most mainstream churches, these do not consciously recruit new members in a selective way. Anyone is a potential convert. But in statistical fact, as opposed to ideological ideal, these churches cater to narrowly defined and homogeneous groups of people. These may be ethnic groups, age grades, territorial groups, or economic classes. Their pragmatic aspect is often geared to the uniform problems these groups of people bring to them. As a result, they tend to become

service churches. This is different from the greater degree of universalism found in mainline churches.

9. Non-exclusive membership follows from the fact that some of the more radical of these churches deal with only a limited range of the supernatural. To fulfill the whole range of human requirements, it is necessary to seek membership in complementary churches. The clientele of the churches is often transient, as might be expected when the churches deal with a limited range of problem-solving. Also, some of these groups do not offer life-cycle rituals since individuals often want to go to orthodox churches for them.

10. Leaving the church is not regarded as falling from grace, and a person continues to retain his status as being "on the road to truth" even if he leaves.

11. These churches do not have a professional clergy. Clergy may be either self-selected functionaries or laymen chosen by other laymen. A church may actually be the functionary's source of livelihood. There is competition for a clientele and no guaranteed income for the minister.

Among most of the established marginal churches, there is a standard way of involving many laymen in the church organization. One of the latent functions of a lay clergy is the leadership training which men and women receive while in temporary posts as Sunday school teachers, choir leaders, preachers on given occasions, and as members of the whole governing bureaucracy of a church. Lay involvement usually revolves, so that all or most positions of leadership become available to most adult members of a congregation at some time. Because the body of laymen is the whole church, a local congregation and the total bureaucracy above it must be run by them in order to function at all. Further, at the local level a congregation's activities usually proliferate to involve a large number of members. Two complementary processes are involved: laymen must run the whole organization at all levels, and all levels must involve laymen at a sufficient rate to avoid developing a professional—hence, non-lay—cast to its leadership. Because lay leadership is, among other things, a training ground for leadership or at least performance competence in the wider world, churches usually have large ranges of tasks for their people to be involved in, and procession through those tasks is predictable and steady.

Although the clergy is ranked internally, most members of the congregation in good standing have access to those ranks. Any member from young adult on is exposed to a whole range of varied tasks, some of which he may lead but most of which he will participate in as follower. His role will shift from one to the other, and his status will shift through time. There is no great degree of predictability to a member's revolving through the various jobs in a church. A member is therefore trained for flexibility, resourcefulness, and enthusiasm— or generalizing traits as opposed to specific skills.

A revolving lay clergy means that the messages a church gives to its adherents through its spokesmen are going to vary to some degree from man to man, and inevitably the messages will vary through time. There is, therefore, some tailoring of church duties as well as the church's interpretation of the world to the changing circumstances of a congregation.

12. Many of these churches can be characterized as members of the portable ecclesia. They do not insist that there be a permanent locus of divinity. Some prefer to meet on the basis of home circles, bookshop meetings, and independent prayer meetings. This is done partly because of the competition between churches for adherents. The church can be easily disassembled and reassembled anywhere. Sometimes this mobility results from harassment from segments of the community but more frequently from the needs of a mobile clientele.

13. The churches are client-oriented and use a pragmatic theology (Judah 1967: 14–15, point 8) which is changeable and responsive to the existing social needs of their congregations, as well as to what they conceive their potential congregation to be. These groups are specifically concerned with the personal problems individuals bring with them. While individual pastoral care in orthodox churches is above and beyond communal worship, with these churches individual needs are the primary concern and are catered to in the context of the community.

14. Neither the churches nor their members want to withdraw permanently from society, although members may do so for a time. They want to improve their present condition and remain within society. Consequently the churches often translate poor education, lack of skills, or bad habits into behavior that improves the competitive position of the member in society. As a result, the leaders of these groups recognize themselves as gatekeepers to spiritual betterment and to earthly success.

Sometimes explicitly and almost always implicitly, these groups support the existing social structure. Rituals are clearly used in many of the churches to uplift daily life and to return the individual to his occupation. In this sense, groups wish to transform peoples' lives so that they have a greater ability to function in society. They do not produce dropouts; they socialize people back into mainstream society. When Mormons have to shift jobs ten times in a decade, when elderly Spiritualists with fixed incomes find daily expenses climbing rapidly, when urban blacks and Puerto Ricans have to hold three or four jobs simultaneously, then it is to these situations of rapid adjustment that marginal churches match their pragmatic advice.

"God gives freely to all those who recognize unity with him by using his laws" (Judah 1967: 17, point 13). Life is seen as subject to continual improvement in material things. Substantial betterment is usually promised and often delivered both in terms of health and material well-being. With their techniques for retaining and retraining people socially, ideologically, and psychologically these churches have had some success in channeling individuals into higher levels in society than those they occupied before joining the church.

15. These groups do not offer an idealized version of the self. The individual is allowed to pursue the tasks he wants to in the working world. No pressure is set up to realize goals modeled on the life of Christ or the Apostles. The only ideal sometimes seen is to acquire power like the leader's. A corollary to this is one of the key theological traits shared by these churches: the deemphasis of sin and the abolition of hell. Each individual is considered to have a spark of divinity in him (Judah 1967: 13, point 2) and is thus not just closer to God but, in some sense, a real participant in divinity. Sin and damnation are consequently impossible, and because of God's imminence in every man he is everywhere and always concretely present. God is much more tangible for these believers. Because they are so close to God, they feel it is possible to know God's laws and hence to become masters over their own destinies (Judah 1967: 14, point 4).

Because God is all or in-all, it is impossible for evil and its emanations like sickness to really exist. They are either illusions or proceed from our ignorance of our true nature (Judah 1967: 14, points 6, 7, 15). By knowing this, self-improvement and healing become mental and psychological matters for the individual to work out by adjusting his frame of mind. Because sickness and evil are in some sense unreal due to the all-encompassing presence of God, personal salvation is also assured: here and hereafter. There can be no damnation, no judgment, or no real suffering because of the actual imminence of God in all men, now and after death. In a theological sense these religions are ultimately democratic: man is God or, more conservatively, becomes ever more like him (Judah 1967: 16–17, point 12).

16. All the groups have a credo and its exegesis. The credo is rarely referred to, and the exegeses are often done orally and are never written down, thereby preserving the continued authority of the leader and continual change of revelation. Often exegesis will be done by the members and as a result the belief system often becomes eclectic. Consequently, beneath explicit credos, a tremendous amount

of flexibility exists in interpreting doctrine. The degree to which subsurface variation in doctrinal meaning is recognized, however, varies with the church.

Judah (1967: 12–13, point 1) also develops this point. He stresses the reaction against predestination and conservative Calvinism as one of the factors behind the rise of a tradition centered on freedom of the individual to seek his own salvation without a church. He also notes that most adherents of this tradition are unaware of a similar liberal wing in Protestantism.

17. Dogma is implicitly made to fit the need of the congregation. Members are not usually required to testify to dogma but rather to demonstrate that they believe through their actions. In this sense the churches are anxious to show that they are able to offer individualized answers in an age of mass production. The churches see their future growth in terms of fulfilling the need of the clientele rather than molding the clientele to fit the needs of the churches. Marginal churches claim to have a version of the truth, but beneath that claim is a decentralized ideology capable of absorbing change and of generating its own change depending on the circumstances that have been created for its membership by the larger society.

18. The belief in continual, ongoing divine revelation and its interpretation characterizes these churches. Their theologies are subject to public and private renewal, and often frequent renewal. Because the body of official doctrine is in the hands of lay clergymen, men concerned with the immediate problems of the world, frequent change in the doctrinal base can be expected. Different marginal churches place the right to interpret belief in different parts of their constituency. Observed behavior, however, places the locus of interpretive freedom, generally, among the members of the congregation.

19. The de-emphasis on prescribed theology does not mean that these groups oppose intellectual activity. They urge their parishioners to keep an open and a balanced mind, to use common sense. Members are to think through ideas and not accept them unless they make sense. They ask people to test ideas before accepting them, and often the authority for verification is simply personal experience (Judah 1967: 14–15, points 8, 9, 10). They emphasize experience as opposed to theological reasoning, and the ideas they propagate are those pre-tried in the experience of members and leaders.

20. These groups share a common notion of time and view toward history. Most of these groups and their members do not recount their historical roots. The churches always emphasize their newness as a religion. Most of the participants want to stress the difference between their present and their past, not the continuities. The historical aspect

is tied to the fact that these groups attempt to demonstrate that they can answer the existential conditions of man in the present, and, in fact, are uniquely suited to answer the problems of the present. It is considered disadvantageous to refer to past existence because it might give the illusion that the group has derived its answers from the past and is not more attuned to the present than the institutional churches. They are instrumental (pragmatic) and therefore claim to answer individual needs without reference to the institution's history or the person's background. Except for testimonials, personal history is de-emphasized because those who join often want to rewrite or ignore their past, and the pragmatic nature of the church lets them cope with today without worrying about yesterday. Unlike orthodox religions, they believe in a memory-less God for whom today and tomorrow count, not yesterday. In this sense they all share a dislike and distrust of psychology and allied disciplines that compete for helping individuals now. They claim that psychology enslaves a man to retrospection, introspection, and self-involvement.

The churches are not concerned with ultimate causes but rather with how to cure the present. They do not ask "why" questions but only "how" questions; no causality, only deliverance. There is a concern with personnel from an individual's history, not from the perspective of analytical history but to provide examples of people who have meaning in one's life. This is not a primary concern with chronology but with models and reference points for personal motivation.

21. All the churches have one or more ritual elements used to show the supernatural efficacy of the faith. These range through glossolalia, mediumship, trance, visions, possession, and other deeply felt, inexplicable phenomena.

22. All the churches prescribe an inner state for the individual (Judah 1967: 15–16, point 10), but allow highly divergent personal experiences leading to that state. Tolerance for these exists as long as they are neither criminal nor threaten the leadership of the church.

23. An individual's altered state must receive validation through the consensus of the group before he can assume leadership or help others.

24. These groups claim to be not just another competing religion. Through altered states of consciousness, which are their ritual property, they feel they maintain constant contact with the divine. This, they feel, is the basis of all religion. Thus they claim to be dogma-free, unlike orthodox churches, and regard themselves as serving all mankind. This claim is important in understanding the wide array of diversity that these religions allow, the universalism they preach, and their wide appeal to people regardless of background.

25. All the churches use a ritual language during the church

service and in church administration. This language is one of the chief means of pluralizing doctrinal interpretation while unifying the adherents. There is further belief in the mystical power of words (Judah 1967: 17–18, point 14) and their mystical interpretation above and beyond their referential meaning in standard English.

26. In their emphasis on verification through experience many of these groups feel themselves allied to science. This is often reflected in their terminology, as well as in their feeling that they have a way to predict the future. Faith, like scientific results, is not considered a state of mind but the result of direct experience.

Most of these churches deplore the divorce between science on the one hand and religion, ethics, mysticism, and philosophy on the other. They believe they are the meeting point of these two approaches, feel themselves to be interdisciplinary in encompassing both, and feel all these branches of knowing are interdependent, not separate and exclusive. They believe they have nothing to fear from science and can extend its findings by giving them the philosophical and humanistic dimensions often ignored by the scientists themselves.

After presenting this list of shared traits, we must mention several caveats. We have not attempted to celebrate these churches for their uniqueness but rather have attempted to show that they can be regarded as a unit with many shared features. Clearly the features fit these groups differentially. They do not form a perfect grid with each group neatly packed in. The features represent a continuum with each group fitting in a slightly different way and to a slightly different degree.

It is better to group and regroup these churches along various dimensions than to search for a perfect typology. The typology should vary with the problem addressed. And since our interests have stressed social organization, belief systems, and social functions as well as psychological ones, that is what the typology reveals. We have been interested in finding common points along these lines, but other problems would probably find other commonalities within this unified body of phenomena.

Factors in American Culture Generating the Rise of Contemporary Religions

Some of the characteristics unifying pragmatic religions were presented above. To the extent that those traits expose the difference between standard, mainline churches in America and pragmatic or marginal churches, they contain at least a germ of an explanation for the existence of these latter groups. Nonetheless, the sum of the traits does not compose an explanation for why these religions appear when they do, in the form they do. After saying that, then why do we see a religious revitalization like this today?

The comments offered below are aimed explicitly at answering that question solely in terms of the United States. It is not that a general explanatory model applying to the industrialized world could not be built; it is that we have not generalized from the data and generating factors at hand to do that. That has not been our aim.

Initially, it is important to admit that the characteristics listed earlier, while uniting the churches under discussion, are not unique to them. Some of the features are present in institutional churches as well. But it is the features combined with the social, political, legal, and the economic base of our particular nation state that have to be understood as interacting to produce a certain kind of periodic religious revival. It is therefore assumed that the periodicity of revivals is influenced by the structural features of our society. Although we cannot predict the periodicity yet, we can suggest some of the features of our culture where attention might be focused for clues. We think there are five significant areas to investigate. It seems clear that these religious movements often occur in economically depressed areas, in times of personal and social dislocation, in areas that tolerate religious innovation, among ethnic and social groups that promote individualism and competition, and that they often primarily attract women.

To obtain the broadest perspective over these points we have to consider the legal foundations for free exercise of religion. In our country, if a religious innovation incorporated in a church group is to exist and be available to the public at large, it has to avoid continued prosecution. This means that it has to have the support of tax exemption, and its clergy has to have the benefits given to other clergies. It is not that each group innovating seeks this kind of equality, but that it must have it in order to present an attractive alternative to potential members. The direction of Supreme Court decisions has been to subjectify the definition of religion and to move from a consideration of a theistic base for religious belief to criteria like sincerity of belief and deeply held convictions applied to individuals. The result of this trend has been to create the ground work for another reformation. While the essence of the Protestant Reformation was to make every man his own priest, or to give him unfettered access to the supernatural, what we are witnessing today, is a second reformation, the essence of which is to make every man his own theologian. Earlier the channels to God were democratized, but the nature of the deity remained prescribed by the churches. Now it is often up to the individual to define for himself what the nature of the supernatural is. This has been made a possibility within our legal foundations and the individual is now free to decide upon such issues for himself and to act upon them.

But, even if the possibility for theological diversity exists, it does not mean that people will necessarily utilize it. One could argue that the present diversity of alternatives is a logical extension to directions set up at the foundation of this country and that will continue as long as the legal and constitutional frameworks are maintained. But that only begs the question. It shows that there is a potential niche for revivals, but does not explain how and by whom it will be filled.

A discussion of the law raises the problem of state control of certification. As the medical and legal professions became stronger and unified in this country, they formed lobbies which fought to establish the professions' supremacy. This was done in their respective services through state certification which was to be the exclusive seal of competence. Anyone who wanted to compete with them found it very difficult because the state and professions were intolerant of competing sectors. Eventually fewer and fewer people could render these services and this increased the needs of a growing population. As professional services became bureacratized they were less able to serve the specific needs of a diversified clientele and they lost touch with the local conditions that were responsible for certain problems. Individuals who were acquainted with such conditions, for example women who had been part of the local information network within a community, could fulfill these roles, but they could not interfere with the practice of law and medicine. They needed a shingle and that was supplied by religion. The Supreme Court's personalization and individualization of the criteria for what religion is enhanced their ability to create and to be innovative in addressing the problems of the moment in a huge number of community difficulties inadequately solved by the institutions of mainline society.

In this country we have traditionally set the burden of religiosity and piety on women. We have acceded to their "sensitive" nature, and assumed that they were to carry the burden of maintaining the nuclear, God-fearing unit. We have joined to that nineteenth-century notion, the twentieth-century one that they were hysterical, as was thought to be confirmed by early psychoanalytical theory, and consequently known to have pietistic outbursts. The witch trials in Salem dealt with women; there was Ann Hutchinson, and how many others, all the way to the present. Why women? Given that women were part of religious life, and that certain behavior was not regarded as abnormal but considered feminine, it happened that such special behavior sustained innovations in religion, in many cases via women.

This is true regarding dissociation and other altered states of consciousness. Such access to the transcendant can attune an individual to social change and has the seeds within it to short-cut organizational structure and to start new movements. In the nineteenth and twentieth centuries, with industrialization and urbanization, women found themselves in an economic bind. Women had to enter the economy to help support the household, either complementing male income or substituting it in times of family separation. Women often turned to religion and through it to the rendering of personalized service to clients as a way of earning support. Sometimes they worked within a home circle, and often gained a position within the community on their own without reference to their husbands. The important historical fact here is that many groups began by rendering secular services to others. Initially their motivation was not solely religious. Religion simply became an acceptable social form for their activity. They could not operate in the secular world because most had neither the education nor the certification required by the state to render the kinds of services that they performed. In solving these problems and in showing clients how to solve their personal problems, they found an avenue that would short-circuit the whole set of problems. Within a religious context they could easily be ordained a minister and acquire the proper charter to open a church. That kind of certification is given much more easily than secular certification in our society. There must be and is, by virtue of the First Amendment in the Constitution, no governmental control over what constitutes proper ministerial training.

Women are not more markedly active as leaders in the current religious revival than men. This is a divergence from their role in past revivals largely caused by the wide range of activities provided by society now for their energies and demands. Such a range was closed during past periods of religious enthusiasm.

All of these factors coincide with two of our cultural values: individualism and economic competition. As the market closed on small businessmen and as large corporations became involved in controlling the life ways of the individual, fewer people could compete with them. Not only that, public services began to be bureaucratized and ridden with specialization. Within this trend was a natural area for competition. The large services could supply universalistic norms, but were helpless when the needs of some of the population were personalistic, for example those coming out of rural areas as a part of the urban migration. Health clinics, public defender offices, counselling services, job agencies, treated people impersonally and generally could not fulfill all the wide-ranging needs of their clientele. Here then was a perfect place to introduce small services offering to treat individuals and their personal needs. Women became very successful here; helped by their motherly role, they assumed the posture of an understanding sounding board.

The motivation for self-employment and the diverse economic opportunities that religious work offered produced a large set of organizations paralleling the large community services. Most of the religious groups, with few exceptions, did not develop into large corporations. Self-reliance, individualism, competition and free enterprise, produced the wide, diffuse spread of these churches. The churches could not compete by offering identical services, each one had to offer something new. This meant that they had to retain their individualities to avoid competition. The results militated against large-scale union. This made them more vulnerable to legal attack but did preserve the specialized brand of pragmatic Christianity each offered.

What gives the current religious revolution its strength is that it is so typically American and so entrepreneurial. It is the display of the middleman as a religious leader. The loose and diverse organization, the do-it-yourself theology, the preach-whatever-the-market-will-bear attitude are part of the pattern. In historic terms this is part of the genius of America and one of the major characteristics of middleman theology over the past 150 years. The system aids the development by emphasizing Supreme Court decisions allowing greater individualization of belief as part of the free exercise clause of the First Amendment. As a people we have a built-in incentive toward individual frontiers and innovation, and we are reaping the consequences of that tradition today in religion. If it is gone from the small businessman in the economy, it is alive and well in religion. For many people religion was a field for economic activity for a long time, and society simply disregarded it. We shaded it under the tree of disrespect and fraud and claimed it was not nice to talk about religion as economics.

RESEARCH RESULTS

As a result of our own work with the churches and of the scholarship presented at the conference, we have discussed several of the features the churches share; we have attempted to explain why some of the features co-occur, and we have offered some ideas on their recurrence in the past and at the moment. To one degree or another these statements are hypothetical. Consequently, we feel it is important to ask what we really know about these churches. What do we know now that we did not know before?

1. Opposition to religious groups in America is achieved largely through formal bureaucratic agencies charged with the job of social control and conflict resolution.

2. Trance-inducing behavior and other states of mental dissociation were formerly thought to belong to the oppressed, offering them release. We now see them as very common in the middle class where they are used to delineate cultural and social identities and to form new ones. The release offered through trance allows an individual to link himself to a social identity.

3. These religious innovations are not pathologies nor are they usually radical. They introduce moderate change and protect the established social order. They translate the individual's enthusiasm for change into a kind of change that will be tolerated. As a result the majority of these groups sustain the social order; they do not challenge it. They are conservative, although often in radical guise. This is one of the explanations for freedom of religion in America.

While traditional religions provide ideologies, they often do not provide adequate tools or instruments for solving practical problems. These movements, on the other hand, are interested in solutions, not ultimate explanations. They want to achieve competence in the working system. They do not encourage dropping out. They cater to the exploited: marginal farmers, factory workers, elderly women, ethnics in ghettos, urban proletariat. The churches' pragmatism enables members to improve their economic state in concrete ways.

4. For these churches, Christ is an instrument, not an institution. They have democratized the approach to the transcendent by putting the tools to reach it in everyone's hands, and in addition they have democratized theology. This last is their great contribution to the evolution of contemporary religious forms. Exegesis is decentralized and closely attuned to personal, pragmatic problems.

The Churches are concerned with personal salvation—on this earth. Salvation means freedom from personal problems. These movements do not abnegate social responsibility. They focus on individual perfection and offer a path to social responsibility by beginning with the reformation of the self. This tends to reaffirm the existing social order. It is assumed that the individual is the unit of change, not society. The self is condemned as the faulty line in the chain, and this serves as the affirmation of the chain.

5. These movements are American in that they are national, democratic, proselytize without distinction, believe they have a message for everyone and that everyone can benefit from their message. Their

diversity makes them appear as specialized branches of Christianity—which, if true, would be a new type of that religion.

For a society that thought religion a private matter, we see that it is the only place left where social experimentation is possible. It is the folk answer to a system that is over-diplommaed, over-certified, too specialized, and too conscious of where one receives certification. It is the last voice for decentralization and the free enterprise system. What began as an opportunity for women, ethnic minorities, and the economically disadvantaged to improve their condition in society, might end up being the salvation for the whole of society by bringing it back to its roots. These groups are ultimate defenders of the Puritan ethic, not in theology, but in action and performance.

Church and State: Limits of Religious Innovation within the Social Order

CHURCH and State is too restrictive a label, in its traditional legal inquiry into conflicts over religious practices, for the material we wish to cover. The term is borrowed from legal scholarship to help identify a body of literature that deals with at least some of the issues we wish to raise. By church and state we do not mean two unitary structures easily identifiable in jurisdiction. Rather, we view "church" as a diffuse notion used to cover highly structured and loosely structured religious groups, or organizations that operate with a corporate charter from a religious organization. We also refer in that label to individuals' actions, interpreted to be based on deeply-held and sincere conviction, which may or may not be performed in acknowledged religious contexts. The notion "state" is similarly diffused over many different institutions that exercise social control at the local, state, and federal levels: judicial, legislative, and enforcement agencies such as the courts, boards of supervisors, district attorneys, and the police. These agencies are instruments of the state that are significant at different stages of conflict resolution and the building of religious institutions. For example, legislative bodies are significant for institution building insofar as they formulate statutes and ordinances governing behavior; the courts and the police are relevant as remedy agents in resolving explicit conflict situations. Several synonyms for the term church and state would be equally acceptable in delimiting this area of research: religion and society, church and the body politic, religion and state.

When this domain of research is approached through the combined perspectives of legal scholarship and social science, the primary theoretical question is: what are the legal determinants in the evolution of religious forms? More specifically, how do codified law and non-codified group values, when used by state agencies to resolve conflicts between religious groups and secular interests, result in promoting religious development? We are interested in both the short and long range impact of state involvement in religious life: what appears in the short run to be the controlling of a current conflict between a church and its community might result in the long run in promoting some other form of religious innovation.

Our concern with the legal determinants of religious evolution is motivated by the focus of this volume on contemporary religious move-

3

ments. In observing recently founded churches one becomes aware of the importance of understanding the process of building church institutions, namely, the thinking through, formulating and instituting of religious observances which attract adherents but do not invite persecution from the surrounding community. Religious innovators who wish to organize a church to perform services which are open to the public at large and which hope for some stability and social permanence must be well informed about the legal framework within which that church will be viewed should conflicts with the community arise.

In terms of empirical research we need to look at three sources of data: first, the religious innovators' own view of their institutional goals and their understanding of how their religious work fits in with community values and norms. How do individuals structure their innovative religious observances which they think might come under legal scrutiny; how do they view themselves and their community; and, conversely, how do they think society looks at them? How is their worldview accounted for in terms of the social organization and ritual observance of their church institution? A second source of data is the communication channels that exist for the diffusion of information about: (1) the nature of the rules that impinge on the creation of new religious institutions; (2) the remedy agents available for conflict resolution within a given community; (3) the mechanisms that can protect a religious group from altercation with its surrounding community. A third source of data is the records of disputes between a given church institution or any of its adherents and a particular state agency. After we examine our informants' own view of the law and its relationship to their activities, the information upon which they base their world view, and the actual process of conflict resolution on a formal level, we can begin to understand the process of building a church institution and thereby the judicial and legislative determinants of the evolution of religious forms.

In this section of the book we address only one facet of the issues we have outlined above, namely, the formal judicial resolution of conflicts over religious practices which a community finds threatening to its values and norms. Pfeffer and Burkholder are legal scholars who are approaching the question of religious innovation in the context of constitutional issues and court decisions. Thus, religious innovations are placed within the most inclusive social framework within which they must be tolerated. The minority status of most innovative religious groups makes it unlikely for them to receive legislative recognition for what are considered deviant claims. They must depend on the judicial process to vindicate unpopular positions. The legal approach deals with the question of personal freedom and the limits of governmental action with regard to behavior recognized to be motivated by religious belief. How does our constitutional framework maximize individual freedom to believe, act, and advocate within the context of order. These authors discuss the boundaries set in this country for dealing with religion on the formal legal level.

If the legal process is working reasonably well and there is conflict between a religious group and the state, it is to the court precedents that appeal is made. The legal approach is based essentially on the considerations of the First Amendment: "Congress shall make no law respecting an establishment of religion, or prohibiting the free exercise thereof; or abridging the freedom of speech or of the press; or the right of the people peaceably to assemble and petition the Government for a redress of grievances." We are concerned with the first section of this amendment composed of two clauses, the establishment clause and the free exercise clause. On the most theoretical level, the establishment clause is construed as providing for separation of government from religious groups and activities, though the nature of that separation is not fixed. The free exercise clause relates to individual and group behavior and concerns the range of permissible actions motivated by religious beliefs and consonant with state interests. Of course, on more practical levels a different reality may be observed. For example, governmental authorities may determine whether a group qualifies for tax exemption under what constitute, in effect, government's definition of religion or what a church is.

The emphasis on the individual in matters of religion has deep historical and cultural roots in this country. The two major currents are the individualization of the concept of freedom and liberty, and the relationship of the state to religion. The Bill of Rights speaks in terms of the individual, not of groups. In the post-revolutionary period there was a definite fear of individuals combining into various kinds of groups called "monopoly," "establishment," "conspiracy," "factions." Similarly, we have a cultural emphasis on individualism rooted in the frontier realities of this nation and an attitude that the state should not involve itself in religious affairs; this is the separation of church and state. These notions are particularly important to keep in mind when dealing with religious movements that are innovative and new. Most of these groups are individual-oriented. Whether leader or adherent, the individual is regarded as more important than the institution of the church, since any status position can be filled by any qualified person. In these groups, it is often the individual, literally, who starts a movement and through his withdrawal from it can see it collapse. Within the context of the First Amendment, limits are placed on the power of government to act in religious matters. We are concerned with individually committed acts, and with an individual's refusal to perform certain acts, e.g. saluting the flag, when the refusal is based on religious conviction. The current decisions of the courts have individualized the free exercise clause to the point where religion is defined as a deeply, sincerely held belief, with little references to traditional appurtenances of religious forms. Similarly, the court since 1963 has based its decisions in cases dealing with religion primarily on the First Amendment clauses, rather than other constitutional provisions.

Pfeffer argues that in the United States, within the formal framework of the Constitution and work of the Supreme Court, there is no legitimation or formal recognition of a religious group by the state. Religious groups do not have to be formally recognized or registered by the state to enjoy the privileges which religious groups are accorded by the Constitution. Nor is there any delegitimation. In that formal legal sense neither are there marginal or minority religions. Within a constitutional framework all religions are regarded as equal. But in a realistic sense, marginality exists, based not necessarily on theological unorthodoxy but on the tension between religious practices and particular secular interests. This tension results in popular unacceptability of a particular practice of a group, which in turn is reflected in legal and official unacceptability. When a practice of a group challenges and threatens deeply held secular norms, a conflict ensues which is ameliorated to manageable proportions by reason of the group's own change of doctrine and religious observance or by change in secular norms of the community. Thereby, popular unacceptability disappears and legitimation, official or quasi-official comes promptly and almost automatically. Popular tolerance is reflected in the legal tolerance and the legal tolerance reflects the popular tolerance. Pfeffer demonstrates this by reviewing the legal cases of Mormons and polygamy, Jehovah's Witnesses and the salute to the flag, the I Am movement's use of mail to defraud large sums from the elderly, Black Muslims and prison rights, the Amish, and the education of children.

Some might take Pfeffer's point of view and argue that not only is there no marginality and legitimation in a technical legal sense, but there is really no such thing as the Court's attitude to religion. Since we do not have religious law, or ecclesiastical courts to deal with religious questions, one has to view the Court's decisions in cases of church and state as sharing in the general attitude and philosophy of the Court at a particular historical point and within the context of its activity on several fronts, religion among them.

Burkholder disagrees with some of Pfeffer's viewpoints and argues that the wall of separation between church and state is a metaphor which does not accurately reflect social realities. Through their decision making process the courts act in matters of religion, particularly in defining religion. To make this point he eaxmines the judicial responses to unorthodox claims in the name of the free exercise of religion. He traces the historic steps leading to present-day interpretation of the religious clauses of the First Amendment with emphasis on landmark decisions involving representatives of marginal movements. In surveying the contemporary scene he raises some theoretical questions.

Burkholder stresses the question of how much freedom does freedom of religion mean, and, indeed, what is religion? No one clear definitive rationale has emerged in law for adjudicating the limits of religious freedom set by the Constitution. He agrees with Pfeffer that the "degree of tolerance for deviant behavior is determined more by the interplay of long-term cultural values and current prevailing opinion with respect to the behavior in question" than by a genuine concern for granting the fullest expression of religious freedom consistent with reasonable public order. Allied to this issue is the question: What is religion? The law has to be neutral, and the courts cannot probe into the truth or falsity of religious claims. The direction the courts have actually taken requires that the law must be able to recognize religion when it appears before a court. Distinguishing religious activity from other forms of human endeavor is necessary while remaining theologically neutral.

Burkholder argues that an approach useful to the judicial understanding of religion may be gained by adopting some of the analytical tools of the social and behavioral sciences. That framework is appropriate because it is descriptive rather than normative and deals with function rather than essence. It is not useful to talk about religion as if it were an entity, but it is advantageous to look at the religious aspects of a number of different situations. We must also be aware of several levels of meaning of religion: the symbolic, social, institutional, and personal. A classification of the dimensions of meaning would enable the courts to develop appropriate rationales for dealing with the issues encountered at each level. He concludes, "In an increasingly pluralist society, marked by a burgeoning variety of cults, a growing privatization of religious experience, and widespread abandonment of traditional theistic formulations, the task of how to define religion and remain theologically neutral is extremely delicate."

In taking the reader through the history of issues of church and state to the contemporary scene our aim has been to show the social dimension of law and its impact on religion. It is precisely because the groups that we are dealing with are concerned with the worldly problems of individuals and are this-worldly rather than world-rejecting that they have such diverse, untraditional, and secular interests in the life of their parishioners and often use secular means to cope with them within a religious framework. It is the secularity of some of their characteristics that often comes into conflict with the equally secular norms of the state. But also in that sense marginal religions have played a key role in the evolution of constitutional doctrine dealing with religious freedom.

The Legitimation of Marginal Religions
in the United States

In one sense the title of this paper is fraudulent. There is in the United States neither legitimation nor marginal religions, at least in the constitutional or legal sense. From time to time one reads in the press that a new sect or denomination has been permitted to open a church in some country such as Spain or Greece or Israel after acceptance of its registry by the Minister of Religion. In this country no governmental permission is needed to open a church; we have no ministry of religion, and there is neither the need nor the means for official registry of a sect or denomination. The Department of Commerce did issue a Census of Religious Bodies in 1936, but the experiment has not been repeated, and when a proposal was made to include a question on religious affiliation in the 1960 census, it raised such a storm of controversy that the idea was speedily dropped (Pfeffer 1967: 261).

Nor are there any religions that constitutionally or officially can be designated marginal. In our system all religions are equal and none is less or more equal than others, a fact that has not deterred the Greek Orthodox Church from inducing legislators to introduce measures declaring that it too is a "major" religion along with Protestantism, Catholicism, and Judaism. The Supreme Court has often asserted that government may not prefer some religions over others (*Everson* v. *Board of Education,* 1947) and may not, for example, disqualify adherents of non-theistic faiths from the privilege of holding public office (*Torcaso* v. *Watkins,* 1961) or being exempt from military service (*U.S.* v. *Seeger,* 1965).

Yet, in a realistic sense legitimation and marginality do exist. Legitimation may be manifested in many ways: unofficially by something as intangible as the gradual popularization of the term "Judeo-Christian," officially or semi-officially by the grant of tax exemption as a religion, e.g. to the Ethical Culture Society (*Washington Ethical Society* v. *District of Columbia,* 1957) or the Fellowship of Humanity (*Fellowship of Humanity* v. *Alameda,* 1957), or by authorizing its clergyman to solemnize marriages, placing a "No Parking—Church

9

Entrance" at its door, or even by permitting its clergymen to display special license plates on their cars.

So, too, realistically marginality exists. Indeed, probably all religions start in a state of marginality, and if they survive ultimately achieve legitimation, manifested in some countries in the acceptance of registry by the Ministry of Religion, or in the United States and some other countries in any of the ways illustrated above. But the major difference in the context of the theme of this paper is that in the United States theology plays no role either in marginality or legitimation. In Israel, for example, non-Orthodox Judaism is a marginal religion struggling for a legitimation still denied it exclusively on theological grounds. Such a situation is impossible in this country.

Briefly, my thesis is that in the United States marginality is essentially a function not of theological unorthodoxy but of tension with particular secular interests. This tension results in popular unacceptability, which in turn is reflected in legal or official unacceptability manifested in a variety of ways. Once, however, the group's threat to secular norms disappears or is ameliorated to manageable proportions by reason of its own change of doctrine or by change in the secular norms, popular unacceptability correspondingly disappears or is substantially reduced notwithstanding the group's continued adherence to theological unorthodoxy. Legitimation, official or quasi-official, thereupon comes promptly and almost automatically.

The Constitutional Background

Formal relationships between government and religion are not wanting in the United States today, notwithstanding the constitutional prohibition in the First Amendment of laws respecting an establishment of religion. It is commonplace for advocates of specific governmental measures in support of religion to cite such practices as opening prayers by official chaplains in state and Federal legislatures, the presence of "In God We Trust" on our coins and currency, the formula "So help me God" after official oaths, the words "Under God" in our pledge of allegiance, an invocation to the Deity in state (though not the national) constitutions, Presidential proclamations of days of prayer and thanksgiving, and many others (Miller 1953; Gustafson 1970). The precedent for such inventories of governmental religiosity is to be found in an 1892 decision of the Supreme Court wherein it was used to support the proposition that "this is a Christian nation" (*Church of Holy Trinity* v. *U.S.*, 1892). One of the decisions referred to in the Court's opinion was an 1811 case in which a New York court upheld a conviction for blasphemy of one who said "Jesus Christ was a bastard and his mother was a whore." In overruling constitutional objections to the conviction, the New York court said:

> Nor are we bound, by any expressions in the Constitution, as some have strangely supposed, either not to punish at all, or to punish indiscriminately the like attacks upon the religion of Mahomet or of the Grand Lama, and for this plain reason, that the case assumes we are a Christian people, and the morality of the country is deeply ingrafted upon Christianity and not upon the doctrines or worship of those imposters [*People* v. *Ruggles,* 1811].

As late as 1931, the Supreme Court could repeat that "We are a Christian people according to one another the equal right of religious freedom, and acknowledging with reverence the duty of obedience to the will of God" (*U.S.* v. *Macintoch,* 1931), although in a more recent and more ecumenical period, the Court used the same inventory referred to above to support the proposition that "We are a religious people whose institutions presuppose a Supreme Being" (*Zorach* v. *Clauson,* 1952).

These governmental expressions of religiosity and formal contacts between government and religion are fairly universally accepted. Yet, there is an underlying legal recognition that they are possibly inconsistent with the constitutional prohibition of an establishment of religion and the guaranty of the free exercise of religion. Where the contacts go beyond being ceremonial and reach or approach coercion, as in compulsory Sunday observance or prayers in the public schools, they are either justified as secular, as in the former case (*McGowan* v. *Maryland,* 1961), or forbidden entirely as in the latter (*Engel* v. *Vitale,* 1962). Moreover, even ceremonial contacts between government and religion are often explained in terms of secularity, as the defense of Christmas observances in the public schools on the ground that the holiday is no longer religious but has become national, or the defense of "In God We Trust" as our national motto, not on the ground that there is a God who is trustworthy but as a sociological fact that the United States is a nation of people who so believe.

The legal ethos of governmental aloofness from religion has been expressed by the Supreme Court in a variety of ways. The Court has asserted that the First Amendment mandates governmental neutrality not only between competing sects but also between religion and non-religion and even anti-religion (*Everson* v. *Board of Education,* 1947; *McCollum* v. *Board of Education,* 1948). It has held that the Constitution is violated by the enactment of a law whose purpose or primary effect is either the advancement or inhibition of religion (*Abington School District* v. *Schempp,* 1963; *Board of Education* v. *Allen,* 1968).

Most recently, it has stated that the test of unconstitutionality is excessive governmental involvement in or entanglement with religious affairs, and has therefore justified tax exemption of church property on the ground that taxing such property could involve government excessively in religious matters (*Walz v. Tax Commission,* 1970).

Nonentanglement in religious affairs is not a recent innovation of the Supreme Court; it reflects a national consensus going back to Thomas Paine's statement in *Common Sense:* "As to religion, I hold it to be the indispensible duty of government to protect all conscientious professors thereof, and I know of no other business which government hath to do therewith." The historical roots of the consensus are many and varied (Pfeffer 1967: 91). Unlike Latin America, which was populated exclusively by colonists from the monolithic Catholic states of Spain and Portugal, those who settled on the Atlantic Coast between New England and Georgia came from England at a time when the established church faced grave challenges and religious pluralism had become a reality, *de facto* if not *de jure.* The Englishmen who came here were Anglicans, Calvinists, Mennonites, Baptists, Quakers, Methodists, and Roman Catholics, to mention only the major sects. Moreover, among only a comparatively few of them was migration motivated exclusively or predominantly by religious consideration.

By the time our Constitution was written, the bloody religious wars that had for centuries plagued Europe were long over and substantial religious freedom was the rule in England, as of course it was in America. But unlike England, here it was coupled with disestablishment, and by 1787 it was a widespread if not universal consensus that full religious freedom was attainable only in a secular state.

The secular humanism, emanating from Locke and the French Enlightenment, which pervaded American intellectualism during the last quarter of the eighteenth century, was another factor which contributed to church-state separation. So too was the existence of the frontier, where the most practicable church was one in which the only priest was the head of the household and the only source for doctrine or dogma was a portable Bible. Indeed, anti-establishmentarianism if not anti-clericalism was the common tie that rather curiously bound the pietist Baptist of the backwoods and the intellectual humanist of the seaboard. It is significant that none of the first seven Presidents of the United States, which included the intellectual John Adams and Jefferson and the backwoodsman Jackson, was at the time of his election a formal member of any church.

Anti-establishmentarianism was not limited to religion. There was a widespread suspicion of groupings, called variously establishments, combinations, factions, and monopolies, political and economic as well as religious. The Constitution makes no provision for political parties and Washington warned against them in his Farewell Address. Madison, in *Federalist* No. 10, recognized the inevitability of factions, primarily because of unequal distribution of wealth, and looked to government as the most effective means of curbing conflict among them. He asserted that "Security for civil rights must be the same as that for religious rights; it consists in the one case in a multiplicity of interests and in the other in a multiplicity of sects."

By historical accident the Bill of Rights begins with the words, "Congress shall make no law respecting an establishment of religion." (The first two amendments proposed to the States did not receive the necessary number for approval.) Nevertheless the fact that it does so begin is at least symbolic of the anti-establishmentarianism of our constitutional democracy. The Bill of Rights is individual-oriented; as late as 1939 the Supreme Court could hold that its guaranties apply only to individuals, not to organizations, such as the C.I.O. and the American Civil Liberties Union (*Hague* v. *C.I.O.*, 1939). But while anti-establishmentarianism and the individualism of constitutional liberties were applicable to all areas, the framers of the Bill of Rights deemed the major area of concern to be in the field of religion, perhaps because it was there that experience was most recent and most pervasive. And it was in the field of religion that the American experiment differed so radically from Old World antecedents.

Even today there is a fundamental difference between the conceptualization of religious freedom in this country and in many if not most other countries. In the latter, the freedom is conceived as belonging to minority sects or religious groups, often with the qualification that they be officially recognized by the state; it is, in other words, a corporate rather than a personal freedom. In the United States from the very beginning the freedom was deemed to belong to the individual rather than to any group to which he might or might not belong.

The individualization of religious freedom has often been recognized by the Supreme Court. In 1963, for example, it held that the First Amendment protected a woman who refused to serve on a jury because she took literally the command of Jesus, "Judge not lest ye be judged" (*In re Jenison*, 1963). In later decisions, the Court held that young men were entitled to exemption from military service as religious objectors even though the beliefs were in each case entirely individualistic and did not encompass a Supreme Being, at least in the conventional meaning of that term (*U.S.* v. *Seeger*, 1965; *Welsh* v. *U.S.*, 1970).

To such a constitutional scheme of things, concepts of orthodoxy and heresy are equally alien. As the Supreme Court said in 1872:

In this country the full and free right to entertain any religious belief, to practice any religious principle, and to teach any religious doctrine which does not violate the laws of morality and property, and which does not infringe personal rights, is conceded to all. The law knows no heresy, and is committed to the support of no dogma, the establishment of no sect [*Watson* v. *Jones, 1872*].

This statement was made by the Court in a case between the northern and southern wings of the Presbyterian Church which had split on the issue of the church's stand on the slavery question. The Court held that it was beyond the competence of a civil court to pass judgment as to which wing represented the true Presbyterian faith and which was schismatic. In later decisions the Court followed this policy and ruled that the First Amendment's guaranty of the separation of church and state required secular government to keep out of ecclesiastical disputes and theological controversies (*Kedroff* v. *St. Nicholas Cathedral*, 1952; *Presbyterian Church* v. *Mary Elizabeth Blue Hull Church*, 1969).

It is quite obvious that in the constitutional matrix of individualization of religious freedom and governmental aloofness from theological affairs, there is no room for the legitimation of religious groups or movements, i.e. the formal recognition by law of the acceptability of any particular church or faith. Theoretically, every faith is automatically legitimated on its profession, and this is so whether it is espoused by one person, one hundred persons, or one hundred million persons. All stand equal before the law.

American public opinion has been sympathetic to the legal stance of aloofness and individualization. That religion is a private matter is part of the American credo. Tolerance of the widest range of theological divergences is evidenced by the fact that the 1936 Census of Religious Bodies, the only such official census the nation has ever had, listed more than 250 different sects and denominations.

Nevertheless, hostile encounters have not infrequently been experienced by marginal religious movements, either with the law or with public opinion or, most often, with both simultaneously. Broad as are the tolerances of law and public opinion for religious movements, they are not unlimited, and the ensuing tensions may reach the point of traumatic crisis. A study of these encounters, however, reveals that in every case the tension is a function not of the group's theological beliefs, no matter how alien they might appear to be, but of positions or practices which threaten or trench upon strongly held national secular values. When, by reason of change either in the group's position or in national secular norms, the threat disappears or becomes manageable, the legitimation of the group and its acceptance by the general community are practically automatic and generally simultaneous.

With this background we can examine briefly the encounters with the law and the process of legitimation of four marginal religious movements: the Mormons, Jehovah's Witnesses, the I Am movement, and the Black Muslims. The major threatened interests (in the cases of the Jehovah's Witnesses and the Black Muslims there were secondary ones as well) were, respectively, the monogamous family tradition, national loyalty and security, protection of the gullible aged from fraud, and harmonious interracial relations. (Dictates of time and space require that the accounts in respect to both legal encounter and legitimation be limited largely to the arena of the United States Supreme Court.)

THE MORMONS

The first confrontation with the Supreme Court experienced by the Church of Jesus Christ of Latter-Day Saints occurred in 1878 in the case of *Reynolds* v. *United States* (1878). There the Court sustained the conviction of a Mormon under an act of Congress that made it a crime to practice polygamy in any of the American territories. The Court rejected the defendant's contention that he was protected in his practice by guaranty of the free exercise of religion contained in the First Amendment.

> Marriage [the Court said in its opinion], while from its very nature a sacred obligation, is nevertheless, in most civilized nations, a civil contract and usually regulated by law. Upon it, society may be said to be built, and out of its fruits spring social relations and social obligations and duties, with which government is necessarily required to deal. . . . Laws are made for the government of actions, and while they cannot interfere with mere religious belief and opinions, they may with practices. Suppose one believed that human sacrifice were a necessary part of religious worship, would it be seriously contended that the civil government under which he lived could not interfere to prevent a sacrifice? Or if a wife religiously believed it was her duty to burn herself upon the funeral pyre of her dead husband, would it be beyond the power of the civil government to prevent her carrying her belief into practice?

The crux of the decision, as this extract indicates, is that with the theology of a religious group the government may have no legal concern; but where its practices trench upon or threaten such important secular interests as the integrity of the monogamous family or of human life, it may and indeed must intervene for the protection of those interests.

The *Reynolds* decision did not challenge the legitimacy of the Mormons as a religious movement. It held only that adherence to their doctrines did not immunize one from punishment for committing what is generally deemed to be a secular offense. The next case, *Davis* v. *Beason* (1890) went further; it adjudicated the non-legitimacy of the Mormons as a religious movement. "To call their advocacy [of polygamy] a tenet of religion," the Court said, "is to offend the common sense of mankind." Since Mormonism was not a religion, its free exercise was not protected by the First Amendment, and therefore the defendant was properly convicted of violating a law of the Territory of Idaho which required all persons registering to vote in the Territory to take an oath that they are not members of "any order, organization, or association which teaches, advises, counsels, or encourages its members, devotees, or any other person to commit the crime of bigamy or polygamy."

Davis, himself, it should be noted, was not charged with having practiced polygamy or even having taught or counseled it. His offense lay in merely being a member of a group which did so. The decision was therefore a judgment of outlawry, and its logical conclusion appeared later in the same year in the case of *Church of Latter-Day Saints* v. *United States* (1890). There the Supreme Court sustained an act of Congress that voided the charter of the Mormon Church and declared its property forfeited. Since the Church had continued to propagate polygamy, the government had no choice but to bring it to an end.

An interesting incident indicating another aspect of the outlawry of Mormonism occurred in 1879. In that year the Federal government sent a circular letter to the American foreign ministers in Europe, asking them to call to the attention of the governments to which they were accredited the American laws against polygamy, and requesting that they prevent the emigration of professed Mormons to the United States. The governments of the countries to which the request was made replied that they could not inquire into the religious beliefs of emigrants (Stokes 1950).

After the two Supreme Court decisions in 1890, the Mormon Church gave up its struggle. In that year it formally adopted a declaration of submission to Federal law. This declaration, which became part of the Church's Articles of Faith, merits quotation here:

This practice (plural marriage) was established as a result of direct revelation, and many of those who followed the same felt that they were divinely commanded so to do. For ten years after plural marriage had been introduced into Utah as a Church observance, no law was enacted in opposition to the practice. Beginning with 1862, however, Federal statutes were framed declaring the practice unlawful and providing penalties therefor. The Church claimed that these enactments were unconstitutional, and therefore void, inasmuch as they violated the provision in the national Constitution forbidding the government making laws respecting any establishment of religion or prohibiting the free exercise thereof. Many appeals were taken to the national court of final resort, and at last a decision was rendered sustaining the laws as constitutional and therefore binding. The Church, through its President, thereupon discontinued the practice of plural marriage, and announced its action to the world, solemnly placing the responsibility for the change upon the nation by whose laws the renunciation had been forced. This action has been approved and confirmed by the official vote of the Church in conference assembled.

Notwithstanding this proclamation, polygamy still persists among some Fundamentalist Mormons, with occasional encounters with the law. In 1946 the Supreme Court held that a Mormon who took his plural wives across a state border was validly convicted of violating the Mann Act, which makes it a crime to transport in interstate commerce "any woman or girl for the purpose of prostitution or debauchery, or for any other immoral purpose" (*Cleveland* v. *U.S.*, 1946). And in 1955 the Court refused to disturb a state court decision depriving Mormons of the custody of their children because the parents persisted in teaching them the orthodox Mormon tenets respecting polygamy (*In re Black*, 1955).

Despite these rather atypical confrontations and despite the general consensus among Americans denying the authenticity of the Book of Mormon as divine revelation, the legitimation of the Mormon Church was prompt. Presidents Benjamin Harrison and Grover Cleveland in successive proclamations pardoned all convicted Mormons, the forfeited church property was returned, and in January of 1896 the Territory of Utah was admitted into the Union as a State. Today, of course, the Mormon Church is a full and equal member of the family of churches and its faithful occupy high positions in government and enjoy general public esteem.

JEHOVAH'S WITNESSES

Probably no group, certainly no religious group, has had more confrontations with the law than Jehovah's Witnesses. Perhaps because the leader of the Witnesses during their period of major reorganization was himself a lawyer, the group frequently invoked the machinery of the law to vindicate what they believed to be its constitutional rights (Waite 1944). The literature on the subject is voluminous (Manwaring 1962). Our concern here can be only with that aspect of the group's doctrines and practices which presented the major barrier to legitimation and with the deeply-held secular interest deemed by the general community to be threatened by them. This interest was nationalism; the secondary interest of interfaith harmony, threatened by the group's attack upon organized religion and particularly upon the Catholic Church, played a relatively minor role in the struggle for legitimation.

The principal confrontations were occasioned by the refusal of Jehovah's Witnesses children to participate in the common public school ceremony of saluting and pledging allegiance to the national flag, a ceremony which the Witnesses deemed violative of the commandments against having other gods and making graven images.

After several unsuccessful efforts to persuade the Supreme Court to review expulsion of Witness children for refusing to participate in the ceremony, the Court finally accepted jurisdiction in 1940. However, with only Justice Harlan Stone dissenting, it upheld the constitutionality of the expulsion of the children of Witness Walter Gobitis from the public school of Minersville in the coal mining region of Pennsylvania (*Minersville School District* v. *Gobitis,* 1940). The Court's opinion, written by Justice Felix Frankfurter, shows how strongly it felt that the religiously motivated refusal of the Gobitis children to salute the flag represented a threat to the secular interests of nationalism and security.

> National unity [the Court said] is the basis of national security. . . . The ultimate foundation of a free society is the binding tie of cohesive sentiment. Such a sentiment is fostered by all those agencies of the mind and spirit which may serve to gather up the traditions of a people, transmit them from generation to generation, and thereby create that continuity of a treasured common life which constitutes a civilization. "We live by symbols." The flag is the symbol of our national unity, transcending all internal differences, however large, within the framework of the Constitution.

It seems rather far-fetched to suggest that American "civilization" was threatened by the refusal of a handful of children to salute the national flag, yet events following the decision evidenced that the Court's fears were shared by millions of Americans. The Court's decision was announced on June 3, 1940. Between June 12 and June 20 hundreds of physical attacks upon the Jehovah's Witnesses were reported to the United States Department of Justice. At Kennebunk, Maine, their Kingdom Hall was burned. At Rockville, Maryland, the police assisted a mob in dispersing a Bible meeting. At Litchfield, Illinois, practically the entire town mobbed a company of some sixty Witnesses who were canvassing it. At Connersville, Indiana, several Witnesses were charged with riotous conspiracy, their attorney mobbed, beaten, and driven out of town. At Jackson, Mississippi, members of a veterans' organization forcibly removed a number of Witnesses and their trailer homes from the town. In Nebraska, a Witness was lured from his house, abducted, and castrated. In Richwood, West Virginia, the chief of police and deputy sheriff forced a group of Witnesses to drink large doses of castor oil and paraded the victims through the streets, tied together with police department rope. In the two years following the *Gobitis* decision there was an uninterrupted record of violence and persecution of the Witnesses. Almost without exception the flag and flag salute were the causes (Rotnem and Folsom 1942).

Barely three years after the *Gobitis* decision the Court, by a vote of 6 to 3, reversed itself and ruled that children could not constitutionally be barred from public schools for refusing to salute the flag (*West Virginia State Board of Education* v. *Barnette*, 1943). Superficially, the explanation for the reversal lies in the fact that two of the Justices who had joined in the original decision retired from the bench and their replacements took a different view of the issue, and three others changed their minds. This explanation, of course does not really explain much and the more basic causes for the change can only be matters of conjecture. Unlike the case of the Mormons, legitimation did not follow a change in the group's doctrine or practices; it was America which changed, not the religious group.

In part the reversal of decision may have been reaction to the violence visited upon the Witnesses, although by the time of the reversal the violence had largely abated. More likely, it was the post-Pearl Harbor salience of what to the people and to the government was a far more substantial threat to national security, namely the Japanese American community (Grodinz 1949). In the light of the almost hysterical fear of a possible invasion of the West Coast abetted by Asiatic traitors in our midst, the threat to national security or loyalty posed by a few elementary school children was manageable if not too insignificant to be noted.

In any event, the 1943 decision of the Supreme Court was little more than a judicial seal of approval of a legitimation that had already been substantially accomplished. Indeed, the 1943 decision was only an affirmance of a lower court decision which had refused to follow the *Gobitis* ruling and had issued an injunction against the expulsion of children who refused to salute the flag. If there was any one thing which more than others evidenced the legitimation of the Witnesses it was the enactment by Congress in June of 1942, six months after Pearl Harbor, of Public Law No. 623, which, after defining the pledge of allegiance and describing the flag salute, stated that "civilians will show full respect to the flag when the pledge is given by merely standing at attention, men removing the headdress." Since children attending public schools do not usually wear their hats in school, and since adult Witnesses can and generally do avoid situations where the pledge of allegiance is recited, the practical effect of the new law was to remove the major barrier to legitimation. That this official act of the government reflected a national consensus is evidenced by the fact that the measure was introduced in Congress under the sponsorship of perhaps the most nationalistic of large-membership organizations, the American Legion.

Jehovah's Witnesses, unlike the Mormons, eschew participation in public or political affairs and hence do not achieve positions of national eminence. Their militant missionary activities, and particularly their anti-church and anti-Catholic preachings, which have been a secondary obstacle to legitimation, have become somewhat muted. Nevertheless, there has been no change in their unorthodox theology, and despite this, their mass convocations, such as those held in Yankee Stadium in New York City, are fully accepted by the general population and reported by the press with the same respect as that accorded to the more conventional faiths.

THE "I AM" MOVEMENT

Unlike the Mormons and the Jehovah's Witnesses, each of which experienced many encounters with the Supreme Court, the "I Am" movement confronted the Court only once, although, as will be seen shortly, in two stages. The first, *United States* v. *Ballard* (1944), involved a prosecution of the movement's organizers, Guy W., Edna W., and Donald Ballard, for using the mails to defraud. The indictments charged that the defendants had falsely and fraudulently represented "that Guy W. Ballard . . . alias Saint Germain, Jesus, George Washington . . . had been selected and designated . . . as a divine messenger"; that the words of "ascended masters and of the divine entity Saint Germain" would be communicated to the world through the "I Am" movement; that the Ballards had supernatural powers to heal the incurably ill—and that they had in fact cured hundreds of afflicted persons. The indictments charged that the Ballards knew that these representations were false, and that they made them solely for the purpose of obtaining for their own use the moneys of the credulous.

During the course of the trial it was testified that the Ballards had represented that the teachings of the "I Am" movement had been dictated from Heaven to the Ballards who took down and transcribed them, and that Jesus had shaken hands with them. The trial judge instructed the jury that they should not decide whether or not these statements were literally true, but only whether the defendants honestly believe them to be true.

The majority of the Supreme Court, in an opinion written by Justice Douglas, agreed with the trial judge. They held that under the constitutional principle of the separation of church and state and religious freedom, neither a jury nor any other organ of the state has the power or competence to pass on whether certain alleged religious experiences actually occurred. The jury could no more constitutionally decide that Guy Ballard did not shake hands with Jesus than they could constitutionally determine that Jesus did not walk on the sea. The Court said:

> Heresy trials are foreign to our Constitution. Men may believe what they cannot prove. They may not be put to the proof of their religious doctrines or beliefs. Religious experiences which are as real as life to some may be incomprehensible to others. Yet the fact that they may be beyond the ken of mortals does not mean that they can be made suspect before the law. Many take their gospel from the New Testament. But it would hardly be supposed that they could be tried before a jury charged with the duty of determining whether those teachings contained false representations. The miracles of the New Testament, the Divinity of Christ, life after death, the power of prayer are deep in the religious convictions of many. If one could be sent to jail because a jury in a hostile environment found those teachings false, little indeed would be left of religious freedom. . . . The religious views espoused by respondents might seem incredible, if not preposterous, to most people. But if those doctrines are subject to trial before a jury charged with finding their truth or falsity, then the same can be done with the religious beliefs of any sect. When the triers of fact undertake that task, they enter a forbidden domain. . . .

What, in effect, the Court held was that no agency of the secular state, including a jury, may pass upon the validity of religious beliefs or religious experiences. On the other hand, it also held that it was constitutionally permissible to allow a jury to decide whether the Ballards actually *believed* that what they recounted was true, and if the jury determined that they did not, they could convict them of obtaining money under false pretenses.

There were two dissenting opinions, one from what may be called the right, the other from the left. The former, by Chief Justice Stone, argued that if the Ballards obtained money from elderly or infirm persons by stating that through their spiritual powers they had cured hundreds of persons afflicted with diseases and ailments, the prosecution should be allowed to prove that no such cures had been effected. From the left, Justice Jackson urged that the prosecution should not have been instituted in the first place. Few juries, he said, could find that the Ballards honestly believed in something which the jury felt was unbelievable.

The decision of the majority of the Court seems to me to be a pragmatic compromise. Acceptance of Chief Justice Stone's approach would threaten the long-established legitimacy of the Christian Science movement, or would require the exclusion from juries trying Christian Science practitioners for fraud of all physicians, surgeons, nurses, and all other persons connected with the conventional healing professions. Acceptance of Justice Jackson's approach would leave the aged and the infirm at the mercy of charlatans. Justice Jackson sought to meet this fear by the following statement in his dissenting opinion:

> The chief wrong which false prophets do to their following is not financial. The collections aggregate a tempting total, but individual payments are not ruinous. I doubt if the vigilance of the law is equal to making money stick by over-credulous people. But the real harm is on the mental and spiritual plane. There are those who hunger and thirst after high values which they feel wanting in their humdrum lives. They live in mental confusion or moral anarchy and seek vaguely for truth and beauty and moral support. When they are deluded and then disillusioned, cynicism and confusion follow. The wrong of these things, as I see it, is not in the money the victims part with half so much as in the mental and spiritual poison they get. But that is precisely the thing the Constitution put beyond the reach of the prosecutor, for the price of freedom of religion or of speech or of the press is that we must put up with, and even pay for, a good deal of rubbish.

The majority of the Court could not accept either approach; yet it may have felt uncomfortable with the compromise it had adopted, for logically it sanctioned the prosecution for fraud not only of Elmer Gantry but of thousands of real-life ministers, priests, and rabbis who weekly preach the literal historicity of a Bible which they may not themselves accept. In any event, two years later the Court took a step which led to the *de facto* legitimation of the I Am movement. The conviction of the Ballards again came up in 1946, and this time the Court threw out the indictment for an entirely different reason— namely, that women had been excluded from the grand jury which indicted them and the trial jury which convicted them (*Ballard* v. *U.S.*, 1946). The Court's opinion ended with what appears to be a broad hint that it would be wise for the California authorities to forget the whole thing. The authorities apparently took the hint; at least, I have not come across any subsequent retrial or prosecution of the Ballards or their followers.

Yet the decision leaves unanswered the troublesome question of how what is claimed to be religion can be distinguished from fraud and thus acquire legitimation. It is a relatively simple matter for a judge or jury to determine whether or not a certain brick sold for a large sum of money is gold or lead, or whether certain corporate shares are valuable or worthless; it is not as simple a matter to determine whether or not a solicitor of funds to build a spiritualist temple has actually communed with the physically dead.

State courts that have uniformly upheld convictions under statutes prohibiting fortune telling have disposed summarily if not contemptuously of charges that these statutes violated religious liberty; yet one man's fraud may be another man's religion, and vice versa. A jury of Catholic priests would probably have little hesitation in finding astrology to be fraudulent and astrologists defrauders. But a jury of Jehovah's Witnesses would probably have less hesitation in making the same finding with respect to Roman Catholicism and Catholic priests.

The test cannot be what the majority believes. It may well be that the majority of Americans do not believe in the literal historicity of all events narrated in the Bible; that fact does not make defrauders out of fundamentalist preachers. Perhaps the test should be that of time: those faiths that have survived over a long period are religions; those that have not were frauds. This would set up a sort of Darwinian law of survival: all new faiths are presumptively fraudulent and should be so treated; those that nevertheless survive will thus establish their right to legitimacy and to be deemed religions; those that do not will have thereby confessed their fraudulency.

It may be safely said that neither this trial by fire nor the test of numbers accords with what I have suggested is the dual constitutional concept of individualization of religious freedom and governmental aloofness from theological affairs. The conclusion I reach from the I Am case is that the felt need to protect the gullible from fraud is not likely to be a serious barrier to the legitimation of marginal religious movements. The reason for this, it seems to me, is that in this case, unlike the others, denial of legitimation would necessarily result in a confrontation between church and state in the area of theology, a confrontation American constitutional tradition seeks to avoid.

BLACK MUSLIMS

A group that appears to have inherited to some degree the communal animosity formerly visited upon the Mormons and Jehovah's Witnesses is the Black Muslims (Lincoln 1961). These are Negroes who challenge the goal of integration and assert the supremacy of the black race and undying enmity between black and white. They also profess to adhere to the faith of Islam and maintain temples for Islamic worship, although they are not accepted by the recognized Moslem churches.

Because of their racial views and their reported resort to violence (the assassination of a schismatic leader, Malcolm X, was widely attributed to followers of the orthodox leader, Elijah Muhammad), there has been some claim that the Black Muslims are not a bona fide religious group but racial extremists acting under the guise of religion. However, the courts faced with passing upon their grievances against the constituted authorities have generally recognized their status as a religious group (*Pierce* v. *LaVallee*, 1963; *Bryant* v. *Wilkins*, 1965).

Most of their grievances arise out of the restrictions upon their members who are inmates of prisons. In many cases they claim that they are not permitted to practice their religion to the same extent as members of the more conventional faiths, that they are deprived of opportunity to read the Koran, to hold religious meetings, to receive pork-free meals, and to obtain the services of Black Muslim religious advisors. In most cases prison wardens have been making every effort to accommodate Black Muslims in their beliefs as far as can be done without unduly interfering with prison discipline. Where the Muslims have found it necessary to bring legal proceedings, the majority of state and lower Federal courts faced with the issue have held that Muslims could not legally be accorded less opportunity to practice their religion than other prisoners unless their demands present a clear and present danger to the functioning of the prison (*Sostre* v. *McGinnis*, 1964; *Sewell* v. *Peyelow*, 1961). Where restrictions imposed on the Black Muslim prisoners are reasonably necessary to assure effective prison administration, the courts have held that their constitutional rights are not violated thereby (*In re Ferguson*, 1961).

The United States Supreme Court has not yet fully faced the question of the legitimacy of the Black Muslims as a religious movement. It is possible that it never will, for it appears that the process of legitimation is proceeding fairly rapidly and with resistance from the courts which seems mild compared to that encountered by the Mormons and Jehovah's Witnesses. Should, however, the Supreme Court find it necessary to pass upon the question, it may reasonably be predicted that the legitimacy of the group as a bona fide religious movement will be recognized. The reason for this, I think, is that the threat posed by the group to the secular values of interracial harmony and domestic tranquility is of manageable proportions, particularly when viewed in the context of overall Negro-white relations. This is so partly because of the salutary work they perform in prisons, but more importantly because their black nationalism has become almost exclusively theological rather than political and the role of violent militancy has been taken over by non-religious groups such as the Black Panthers.

CONCLUSION

The experiences of the Mormons, Jehovah's Witnesses, I Amites, and Black Muslims have been and are being paralleled by other marginal religious groups. One may note both the Hasidim of Brooklyn and the Old Order Amish of the Midwest. One particularly fundamentalist group within the former believes that since all truth is within the Torah, as explicated in the Talmud and other Rabbinic commentaries, there is neither need nor authority to study other sources. Accordingly, they refused to allow their children to attend not only public schools but also the usual Jewish day schools where both secular and sacred subjects are taught. Instead, they sent them to yeshivahs wherein they received instruction only in sacred subjects, and the language of communication was Yiddish. The inevitable encounter with the state authorities enforcing the compulsory school attendance laws culminated in a Supreme Court action upholding the authorities (*People* v. *Donner*, 1951). Thereupon, the Hasidim, like the Mormons, yielded; they permitted their children to learn secular subjects in the yeshivahs, and they are now a fully legitimated group notwithstanding their retention of old-world garb for themselves and their children, their strict adherance to the Sabbath and the dietary laws, and their use of Yiddish as the language of communication.

The Old Order Amish are undergoing a similar confrontation with the authorities. While they do not object to their children receiving secular instruction up to the age of 14, their doctrines forbid it after that age. Since all states today extend their compulsory school attendance laws to secondary schools, the Amish have faced prosecution for violation of these laws. In Kansas the courts refused to accept their plea of religious conscience, and the United States Supreme Court denied their request to review the decision (*Garber* v. *Kansas,* 1967). In Wisconsin the state's highest court upheld their claim, but the Supreme Court has agreed to hear the state's appeal [1] (*State* v. *Yoder,* 1971). Should it uphold the decision, its action would manifest a change in national secular norms, and legitimation of the Old Order Amish could be expected to be prompt and practically automatic. Should it reverse, the Amish would be faced with the same choice as the Mormons and the Hasidim: conform and achieve legitimacy or refuse and remain unlegitimated.

With the Hasidim and the Old Order Amish the challenged secular interest has been the community's concern with the education of children. With the Mormons it was the monogamous family relationship. With the Jehovah's Witness it was nationalism; with the I Amites, the protection of the gullible from fraud; and with the Black Muslims, the protection of the community from violence. The experiences of these and other sometime marginal religious groups, e.g. the Seventh Day Adventists, the Christian Scientists, and even the Roman Catholics, indicate that non-legitimacy is a function of the threats they present or seem to present to deeply held secular values of the community. Once the threat is eliminated or reduced to a manageable degree, legitimation comes promptly and easily notwithstanding continued divergence from conventional theological norms.

---

[1] Since the above was written the Supreme Court has affirmed the decision of the Wisconsin court (*Wisconsin* v. *Yoder* 406 U.S. 205 [1972]).

"The Law Knows No Heresy":
Marginal Religious Movements and the Courts

This paper is concerned primarily with the dimensions of legally recognized religious freedom as experienced by marginal religious groups. It focuses on judicial response to unorthodox claims advanced in the name of free exercise of religion. We shall first trace the historic steps leading to the present-day interpretation of the religion clause of the First Amendment, with particular attention to the landmark decisions involving representatives of marginal movements. Following a survey of the contemporary scene, we conclude by examining some major theoretical questions raised by the conflict of freedom and order in the realm of religion.

Marginal religious groups have played an important role in the development of the distinctive American understanding of religious freedom. In the list of Supreme Court decisions customarily classified under the "church and state" heading, religious movements outside the Judeo-Christian mainstream are disproportionately represented. The Mormons, Jehovah's Witnesses, Seventh Day Adventists, and the "I Am" cult all figure prominently in the significant decisions that have contributed to the evolving constitutional doctrine of religious freedom.[1]

---

[1] From the beginning of the American republic until 1940, the Supreme Court considered the meaning of the First Amendment religion clause on only six or seven occasions, but in the past generation more than forty decisions of the high court have been concerned with that issue. The body of cases generally considered under "church and state" now numbers more than sixty, but not all of these are grounded in the religion clause of the First Amendment. Some rulings are based on First Amendment freedoms other than religion, or on Fourteenth Amendment concepts.

Certainly a considerable part of this upsurge since 1940 must be attributed to the Court's holding that the "due process" and "equal protection" phrases of the Fourteenth Amendment make the provisions of the First Amendment applicable to the states as well as the federal government. In addition, a number of historical and social factors help account for the frequency of Court decisions in the religion area—judicial activism, growing religious pluralism, sensitivity to civil liberty issues, the expansion of governmental control and activity.

Synopses of most of the cases, through 1963, are found in Stokes and Pfeffer (1964:104–148). Tussman (1962) provides full texts of major Supreme Court

This unusual degree of judicial activity on the part of marginal movements demands some explanation. Let me suggest two interrelated observations. First, the very fact of being a "marginal" group— a deviant from mainstream America—poses the probability that the religious understandings and values subscribed to will give rise to practices that run counter to accepted community norms and thus offer a challenge to established conventions and institutions. An obvious example is the nineteenth-century Mormon view that multiple marriage is a religious obligation. Given a society in which monogamy has been assumed as a bulwark of the social order, the polygamist represents a threat that must be countered by the legal system.

The second observation follows; the minority status of the marginal group makes the expectation of securing legislative recognition for a deviant claim quite unlikely. Thus, the marginal groups have been forced to depend on the courts in their efforts to vindicate unpopular positions. The purpose of the Bill of Rights is to protect minority views, but laws are made by majorities, so the conflict is joined. "The smaller the minority, the more likely it is to need constitutional protection; the greater it is, the more likely it is to obtain the protection it needs through legislative exemption rather than judicial intervention" (Pfeffer 1967: 616).

I. The Development Of Constitutional Religious Freedom

In any attempt to understand American socio-legal phenomena, one must give attention to the symbolic function of the Constitution and its interpretation by the Supreme Court. "Probably nothing in American culture is more 'sacred' than the Constitution, and no group of men has more prestige than the Supreme Court" (Johnson 1960: 349). With no established national church to provide supernatural sanctions and legitimations, with no monarchy to offer a latent symbolic authority, with no homogeneous culture or traditional institutions, the people of the new nation gave allegiance to a piece of parchment. Talcott Parsons has argued that the common value system undergirding the American "moral community" is no longer grounded in

decisions up to 1953. For discussion and analyses of the legal issues, see Stokes 1964, Pfeffer 1967, Kauper 1964, Konvitz 1968, and Kurland 1962.

Apart from the interpretive background on particular marginal groups found in such studies as Braden (1953) and Manwaring (1962), the sources used for this paper have been the specific court cases cited. Acknowledgment should also be given to the survey essays in the annual series of volumes entitled *Religion and The Public Order*, edited by Donald Giannella.

The citation of legal cases herein follows the standard form of title, volume number, abbreviation of state or federal series, page number, and year.

specific religious organizations; with religion "pluralistically and 'privately' organized," basic values are now "embodied in the Constitution and in the official interpretations of it" (Parsons 1961: 46).

As the arbiter of constitutionality, then, the Supreme Court deals not only with law, but with the moral self-understanding of a changing and complex society.

> In the absence of a socially accepted established church the Supreme Court has become the moral censor in our society. Its decisions are not only legally binding, but its opinions have all the normative weight which in other societies would be accorded to canon law and the resolutions of church councils. It must in the name of the Constitution articulate the silences in that document. Possessing both authority and sanctity, it has become the supreme spokesman for the values of society which transcend both self-interest and current politics [Grimes 1964: 31].

The problem of religious freedom, especially as it is focused by the claims of marginal groups, must be viewed in this larger perspective of constitutional government. The cornerstone of religious freedom is found in the First Amendment: "Congress shall make no law respecting an establishment of religion, or prohibiting the free exercise thereof. . . ." According to its preamble, the Constitution was established "to form a more perfect union, establish justice, insure domestic tranquility, provide for the common defense, promote the general welfare and secure the blessings of liberty." Thus, religious freedom, presumably one of the "blessings of liberty" here affirmed, must be considered in relation to the several preceding purposes of government.

In its largest sense, the problem of adjudication in this area is the classic problem of freedom and order:

> Essentially, Americans have always had to reconcile politically two logically opposing principles. On the one hand, the role of conscience to determine the proper relationship of man to God has been held to be the most vital and sacred immunity a man holds in society; on the other hand, the right of society to set the terms and conditions of public peace is unquestioned [Grimes 1964: 33].

When a case comes to the Supreme Court, it represents the failure of the political system to reconcile that opposition at a lower level. The Supreme Court cases are the hard cases, the one-in-a-thousand, the borderline controversies that present matters of judgment and opinion on which reasonable and learned men can disagree. The Supreme Court has in fact had little success in making up its collective mind in its opinions on religion; more than three-fourths of the cases during the past thirty years have included dissenting opinions.

At a time when divergence and pluralism characterize the social reality, and public consensus on the role and meaning of religion is lacking, the Court is faced with tasks of adjudication that inevitably involve it in questions of profound moral and religious significance.

The Court Considers Religion

In the light of these basic considerations, we shall review the Supreme Court's actual performance with respect to religion. The discussion deals almost exclusively with the "free exercise" provision, since the problem of religious establishment does not figure significantly in the cases involving marginal groups.

For a long time, direct confrontation with the constitutional meaning of religion was avoided by relying on the view, based on the principles of Jefferson and Madison, that religion, considered as purely personal belief, is beyond the limits of government action.

> The religion, then, of every man, must be left to the conviction and conscience of every man. . . . We maintain, therefore, that in matters of religion no man's right is abridged by the institution of civil society; and that religion is wholly exempt from its cognizance [James Madison, *in* Blau 1964: 84–85].

In one of the earliest church-state cases to reach the Supreme Court, the fundamental principle was stated: "The law knows no heresy, and is committed to the support of no dogma, the establishment of no sect" (*Watson* v. *Jones,* 13 Wallace 679 [1872]).

Within the same decade, however, the Mormon polygamy controversy required the Court to speak to the limits of "free exercise." After reviewing the historical setting of the Constitution, the opinion reinforced an individualistic, interior concept of religion by quoting Jefferson's belief that "religion is a matter which lies solely between man and his God" and his conviction that "man has no natural right in opposition to his social duties" (*Reynolds* v. *United States,* 98 U.S. 145 [1879]). This led to the conclusion that "Congress was deprived of all legislative power over mere opinion, but was left free to reach actions which were in violation of social duties or subversive of good order." The Court then arrived at the operational distinction between belief and action that has proved so decisive. Justice Waite declared: "Laws are made for the government of actions, and while they cannot interfere with mere religious belief and opinions, they may with practices."

This belief/action dichotomy served as the fundamental guideline for both federal and state adjudication for more than half a century. The principle has been restated and labeled the "secular regulation" rule by David Manwaring: "There is no constitutional right to exemption on religious grounds from the compulsion of a general regulation dealing with non-religious matters" (Manwaring 1962: 51). This approach had obvious practical advantages for the courts, as it avoided any need to investigate the validity or sincerity of religious claims.

The supposedly obvious line between opinion and action, however, is not always clear cut. As Milton Konvitz has pointed out, a Catholic at confessional and a Jew fasting on Yom Kippur are both performing religious *acts*. The Mormon polygamist "claimed that his second marriage was an *acting out of his religious beliefs,* just as performing the Mass is" (Konvitz 1968: 34). Legal convention, however, protected the celebration of the Mass, but prohibited the taking of wife number two. Because most citizens agreed with these views, there was very little sympathy for the deviant minority's claim to divine approval for polygamy. Therefore, in spite of the "no heresy" principle, a few years later the Court could describe belief in polygamy as "the pretense of religious conviction" and convict a Mormon, not for the actual practice of polygamy, but only for being a member of a group that advocated the practice (*Davis* v. *Beason,* 133 U.S. 333 [1890]).

Without denying the governmental prerogative to prohibit certain acts which may be deemed detrimental to the larger public interest, we must recognize here the problem of majority versus minority opinion regarding the nature of "true religion." The sociology of knowledge helps us understand the prevailing opinion that the laws enacted by the majority are more representative of "true religion" than the claims made against them, in the name of minority religion. In spite of protestations of neutrality with respect to belief, the process of adjudication has all too often been influenced by such presuppositions.

Religion or Fraud?

Even the wholly protected realm of belief may come under judicial scrutiny, however, in allegations of fraud. Here the trials of the "I Am" cult present us with a most instructive set of judgments and criteria; the Supreme Court split three ways in a 1944 decision that reveals the problems in dealing with religious claims that the majority of Americans would find highly questionable.

The "I Am" movement originated in the experiences of Guy W.

Ballard, an obscure mining engineer and student of the occult, who claimed to have been visited by the godlike messenger, St. Germain, while hiking near Mt. Shasta in 1930. Ballard was enveloped in flame and color, taken for marvelous spiritual journeys, and initiated into the divine plan of the ages. From this beginning, Ballard and his wife and son were chosen as "accredited messengers" by the "ascended masters," to reveal the "Mighty I AM Presence" to all mankind. Ballard's spiritual experience, published as *Unveiled Mysteries* under the name of Godfre Ray King, did not appear until 1934, but within a few years the burgeoning movement had captured a curious audience of millions, with thousands of devoted followers, and the Ballards were thriving on sales of literature, records, and other cultic materials. Upon the death of Guy Ballard in 1939, Mrs. Ballard announced that "our Blessed Daddy Ballard has made his Ascension" and immediately assumed firm leadership of the movement, although the crisis left many followers disillusioned (Braden 1953: 2257–307).

Legal troubles began in 1940 with a Federal Grand Jury indictment against Edna and Donald Ballard on a number of counts, all related to use of the mails to defraud. After a trial, a dismissal, a second trial and conviction, and a reversal by the Circuit Court of Appeals, the case of *United States* v. *Ballard* came to the Supreme Court (322 U.S. 78 [1944]). The issues in this rather complex case are discussed in the companion paper in this volume (Pfeffer, within).

In sum, Justice Douglas, speaking for the majority, held that no secular court has competence to rule on the verity of religious belief as such, but that the jury was free to determine whether or not the Ballards actually believed what they claimed. Justice Jackson, in dissent, argued that in matters of religion such determinations are highly delicate: "I do not see how we can separate an issue as to what is believed from consideration as to what is believable." Quoting from William James, Jackson emphasized the peculiar nature of religious experience, noting the impossibility of sensory verification. To ask a jury to investigate sincerity, but not truth, in a situation where the essential truth or falsity is beyond investigation, is to ask the impossible. Although many persons claimed to have been duped by the Ballards, other faithful followers testified to their healing powers. And who could challenge the appearances to Guy Ballard, now deceased? Yet, it seems obvious that a jury of average citizens, forced to determine the sincerity of claims quite contrary to their own experience, would be led to a verdict of fraud.

Although he personally saw "nothing but humbug" in the Ballards' teachings, Jackson forcefully opposed the whole effort at demonstrating actionable fraud: "I would dismiss the indictment and have done

with this business of judicially examining other people's faiths." [2]
Jackson's views, even though expressed in dissent, have been restated
frequently by authorities in the field and would likely gain fuller
acceptance today. The guarantee of religious liberty means for many
that neither the truth or falsity of religious beliefs, nor the good or
bad faith with which they are held, can become legal issues (Kauper
1964: 26; Konvitz 1968: 43ff).

The Expansion of Free Exercise

During the 1930s, the Jehovah's Witnesses embarked on intensive
proselytizing activity that included massive door-to-door canvassing,
sound trucks, street meetings, and parades. Their aggressiveness provoked public hostility; communities passed ordinances prohibiting
such activities, or established restrictive licensing policies. But the
Witnesses, inspired by an apocalyptic theology, ignored such restraints
and were arrested by the hundreds (Manwaring 1962: 24–28). The
flood of convictions led the Witnesses to develop an extensive legal
department. Appeals were filed routinely, and were eventually considered by the Supreme Court, but the "freedom of religion" claims
got nowhere. The "secular regulation" rule still prevailed; the courts
were reluctant to recognize a distinctive sphere for the free exercise
of religion.

The breakthrough for the Witnesses came in 1938, with a change of
tactics to arguments grounded on freedom of the press that resulted
in the Court striking down an ordinance against literature distribution
(*Lovell* v. *Griffin,* 303 U.S. 444 [1938]). Subsequently there followed
the notable series of Supreme Court cases dealing with Jehovah's
Witnesses and based on a broad concept of multiple First Amendment
rights of speech and advocacy, which established new rights for the
use of public places, distribution of literature, and door-to-door
solicitation (Stokes and Pfeffer 1964: 118ff).

This recognition of a general "freedom to propagate," however, did
not speak clearly to the question of a substantive and distinct freedom
of religion. An important step in that direction was taken in *Cantwell*
v. *Connecticut* where, in overturning a conviction for breach of the

---

[2] Jackson did recognize the possibility of actionable false representation related
to religion, "as for example if one represents that funds are being used to construct a church when in fact they are being used for personal purposes," but this
of course is a verifiable event.

The actual disposition of the Ballard case, after the conviction was sustained
at the lower level and another appeal entered, involved a second Supreme Court
ruling voiding the indictment because of improper drawing of the grand jury panel.
329 U.S. 187 (1946).

peace by a Witness evangelist, Justice Roberts did away with the absoluteness of the time-honored belief/action dichotomy:

> Thus the Amendment embraces two concepts,—freedom to believe and freedom to act. The first is absolute but, in the nature of things, the second cannot be. Conduct remains subject to regulation for the protection of society [310 U.S. 296 (1940)].

Another significant step was the argument, first advanced in dissent by the "liberal trio" of Murphy, Black, and Douglas, and then as the Court's decision in *Murdock* v. *Pennsylvania,* that Witness proselyting is equivalent to the worship practices of more conventional churches.

> The hand distribution of religious tracts . . . occupies the same high estate under the First Amendment as do worship in the churches and preaching from the pulpits. It has the same claim to protection as the more orthodox and conventional exercises of religion [319 U.S. 105 (1943)].

During this same period, the Witnesses gained a victory over the compulsory flag salute. Justice Jackson's memorable opinion emphasized the preferred position of the First Amendment freedoms, without, however, clearly distinguishing religion. But, by criticizing compulsory expression of belief, and granting exemption from a ceremony that the Witnesses viewed as idolatrous, the longstanding "secular regulation" rule was breached.

> If there is any fixed star in our constitutional constellation, it is that no official, high or petty, can prescribe what shall be orthodox in politics, nationalism, religion, or other matters of opinion or force citizens to confess by word or act their faith therein [*West Virginia State Board of Education* v. *Barnette,* 319 U.S. 624 (1943)].

This series of decisions introduced the "clear and present danger" rationale, developed in free speech and press cases, to the religion context. In *Cantwell,* the Court concluded that the activity of the proselyter "raised no such clear and present menace to public peace and order as to render him liable to conviction." Justice Jackson in *Barnette* declared that the First Amendment freedoms "are susceptible of restriction only to prevent grave and immediate danger to interests which the state may lawfully protect."

These holdings clearly repudiated the secular regulation rule. Further, in both *Murdock* and *Barnette,* the Court recognized the minority conception of "religion"—for the Witnesses, street solicitation is required religious activity, flag saluting is prohibited idolatry. These "subjective" views are set over against the "objective" opinion of the majority which finds the categories of commercial peddling and patriotic ceremony more appropriate. Once again, the definition of religion—"mainstream" or "marginal"—is at issue.

Following upon these precedents, the first clearcut judicial effort to "balance" freedom of religion against the public welfare, in a setting that included issues other than "freedom to propagate," came in 1944. Mrs. Prince, a member of the Jehovah's Witnesses, was prosecuted for allowing her nine-year-old niece to accompany her in selling religious literature on the street, in violation of child labor laws. Justice Rutledge focused the competing claims: on one side, "the obviously earnest claim for freedom of conscience and religious practice," allied with "the parent's claim to authority in her own household"; on the other side, "the interests of society to protect the welfare of children" (*Prince* v. *Commonwealth of Massachusetts,* 321 U.S. 158 [1944]). After giving fair attention to the claims of religion, the Court ruled in favor of the state.[3] Justice Murphy dissented; for him, it had not been clearly established that "a legitimate interest of the state is in grave danger."

These decisions opened the door to the affirmation of a protected sphere of *religious activity* under the First Amendment. If the "free exercise of religion" is to have substantive meaning, apart from mere interior belief and the other freedoms of speech, press, and assembly, there must be situations in which certain religiously-motivated acts— or refusals to act—will be granted exemptions from the prevailing secular regulation. Such claims for recognition may be of two kinds: claims for *exemption* from a positive *requirement* of the state (e.g. military service, jury duty, the flag salute) because of a religiously grounded *proscription*; or claims for *permission* to carry out a religiously conceived *obligation* (e.g. polygamy, snake handling, child labor, sacramental use of wine or drugs) that is *prohibited* by the state.

It was not until 1963 that the Supreme Court decided a case in favor of an appellant solely and uniquely on the grounds of "free exercise" of religion. In *Sherbert* v. *Verner*, the Court held that denial of unemployment compensation benefits to Adell Sherbert, who, as a Seventh Day Adventist, refused to work on Saturday, was an infringement of her constitutional rights; religious freedom was violated in that she was forced to choose between following her religious principles and

---

[3] The opinion took note of the contention that "the street, for Jehovah's Witnesses and their children, is their church, since their conviction makes it so; and to deny them access to it for religious purposes as was done here has the same effect as excluding altar boys, youthful choristers, and other children from the edifices in which they practice their religious beliefs and worship." But, replied Rutledge, "the public highways have not become their religious property merely by their assertion."

thus forfeiting benefits for which she was otherwise eligible, or abandoning a precept of religion in order to accept work (374 U.S. 398 [1963]).

Justice Brennan's opinion took notice of an earlier case, *Braunfeld v. Brown* (366 U.S. 599 [1961]), which held that a state Sunday closing law was not required to grant an exemption for persons whose religious convictions called for a day of rest other than Sunday (although the state was permitted to do this); Brennan distinguished the *Sherbert* holding on the ground that practical considerations in administering the Sunday law would make exemptions unworkable. Justice Stewart, who concurred in the *Sherbert* result, argued that Braunfeld should be overruled.

While the immediate finding of this case may not seem extremely significant, the Court's procedure in reaching its conclusion has established a precedent that one authority calls "the dawn of a new day for religion claims" (Galanter 1966: 241), while another declares that Sherbert "opens up new vistas on religious liberty" (Kauper 1964: 42). The two-stage test for evaluating a religious claim, as set forth in *Sherbert*, asks first if the issue in question imposes any *burden* on the appellant's free exercise of religion. If this question is answered affirmatively, the Court takes a second step. Is there a *compelling state interest* that may justify the infringement? The opinion emphasizes that "in this highly sensitive constitutional area, 'only the gravest abuses, endangering paramount interests, give occasion for permissible limitation.' " As a subsidiary test, the state would need to demonstrate that no *alternative forms of regulation* would suffice to accomplish its justifiable desired ends.

The *Sherbert* doctrine stands as the highwater mark in the Supreme Court's interpretation of the scope of free exercise of religion. It has been widely discussed, challenged, praised, and criticized. Its methodology has been decisive in important decisions of lower courts, affecting both mainline and marginal religious groups, but its full potential impact is yet to be realized.

II. MARGINAL RELIGION AND THE LIMITS OF FREEDOM

The opportunity for testing the evolving concept of religious freedom in the courts arises when persons claiming religious motivation challenge some general regulatory law. Such laws may be of two types:

(1) those which are designed to promote the public health, safety, morals, and general welfare in the exercise of the state's police power and which do not directly limit or restrict the free expression of

ideas; and (2) those which are directed against various forms of expression of ideas and which are justified on the ground of protecting the public peace and internal security [Kauper 1964: 38].

In the following, we examine selected cases involving representatives of marginal religious movements in conflict with laws of general operation.

Drug Cults

American Indians have used peyote from the time of Cortez. The practice was given ritual form over the generations and was institutionalized in 1918 as the Native American Church, a blend of Aztec and Christian elements (Aberle 1966; Slotkin 1956). In 1962 a group of Navajos engaged in a ceremonial including the use of peyote were arrested and convicted under a California law prohibiting the possession of peyote. On appeal, the California Supreme Court reversed the decision, granting immunity on First Amendment grounds (*People* v. *Woody*, 394 P. 2d 813 [1964]).

Justice Tobriner's opinion in *Woody* is a model of judicial reasoning following the *Sherbert* precedent. After surveying the history and practice of the Native American Church, and recounting the all-night ritual observance the Justice concluded that the use of peyote is a "cornerstone" of the cult, its "theological heart." To prohibit the use of peyote is to place a burden on the free exercise of religion.

But is there a "compelling state interest" justifying this abridgment? The state asserted that peyotism had "deleterious effects upon the Indian community" and that to allow religious exemptions to the narcotics laws would lead to fraudulent claims. But the court replied that there was no public record of such harmful consequences; in fact, the moral behavior of the Indians was considered exemplary. As to the possibility of spurious claims, the court noted that the state produced no evidence, and that other states (Arizona, Montana, New Mexico) have amended their narcotics laws to allow exemptions for the sacramental use of peyote by the Indians. In conclusion, the court presented an exercise in balancing:

> We have weighed the competing values represented in this case on the symbolic scale of constitutionality. On the one side we have placed the weight of freedom of religion as protected by the First Amendment: on the other, the weight of the state's "compelling interest." Since the use of peyote incorporates the essence of the religious expression, the first weight is heavy. Yet the use of peyote presents only slight danger to the state and to the enforcement of its

laws; the second weight is relatively light. The scale tips in favor of the constitutional protection.

Other appeals to religious freedom as ground for exemption from narcotics laws have not fared so well. Probably the most famous case is that of Dr. Timothy Leary, arrested in December 1965 at the Mexican border in Laredo, Texas, and charged with illegal possession of marihuana. He was convicted and sentenced to the maximum term of thirty years in jail and forty thousand dollars in fines. On appeal, the Fifth Circuit Court upheld the conviction, holding that Leary's religiously based defense did not justify an exemption from Federal criminal statutes (*Leary* v. *United States*, 383 F. 2d 851 [1967]).

After detailing Leary's academic background, his research in psychedelic drugs, and his membership in the Brahmakrishna sect of Hinduism, Judge Ainsworth set out to refute Leary's reliance on the *Sherbert* and *Woody* precedents. (It was noted in passing that the California case had no binding authority.) The opinion rejected the possibility of a serious burden on free exercise, observing that the Indian peyote exemption was essentially different in that peyote played a central role in the ceremony and practice of the church, whereas Leary's allegedly religious use of marihuana was occasional, private, and personal. The court went on to declare a compelling state interest in drug prohibition:

> It would be difficult to imagine the harm which would result if the criminal statutes against marihuana were nullified as to those who claim the right to possess and traffic in this drug for religious purposes. For all practical purposes the anti-marihuana laws would be meaningless, and enforcement impossible. The danger is too great, especially to the youth of the nation, at a time when psychedelic experience, "turn on," is the "in" thing to so many, for this court to yield to the argument that the use of marihuana for so-called religious purposes should be permitted under the Free Exercise Clause. We will not, therefore, subscribe to the dangerous doctrine that the free exercise of religion accords an unlimited freedom to violate the laws of the land relative to marihuana.

Several distinguished critics have observed that both the findings of the trial court and the appellate opinion reveal a vindictive stance, in the context of strong public feeling about drug use and Leary's role as a "pied piper of turned-on youth." Milton Konvitz deplored the refusal to take Leary's religious claim more seriously, observing that even Mormon polygamy was treated with more deference. Picking up the positive emphasis on personal religion in American life from Tom

Paine and Jefferson through Emerson and Thoreau to recent Supreme Court decisions on conscientious objection, Konvitz suggested that "what the Court of Appeals in the Leary case rejected as merely private and personal, others might select and honor as the innermost heart of that which the Free Exercise Clause protects" (1968: 86).[4]

The use of psychedelic drugs to induce religious experience has given rise to a number of groups calling themselves "psychedelic churches." In 1966, Leary announced the founding of the League for Spiritual Discovery, and sought unsuccessfully to establish its constitutional immunity for the religious use of drugs. Another group, known as the Church of the Awakening, was incorporated in 1963, under the leadership of Drs. John and Louisa Aiken, who for some years had used peyote and mescaline for religious and therapeutic purposes. The Aikens, licensed osteopaths in the state of New Mexico, have filed numerous petitions and appeals to government agencies, to date without success, seeking administrative exemptions similar to those granted to the Native American Church.[5]

One of the more controversial groups, whose members have had numerous encounters with the law, is the Neo-American Church, which was incorporated in California in 1965. Founded by the Rev. Arthur Kleps, known also as Chief Boo Hoo, its basic doctrine is that hallucinogenic substances, particularly marihuana and LSD, are the "true

[4] With regard to "compelling state interest," Konvitz contrasted Judge Ainsworth's eager acceptance of Congress's 1937 position on the evils of marihuana (ignoring considerable contemporary professional opinion to the contrary), with the more objective judicial inquiry into the actual situation, as in *Woody* and the Communist cases before the Supreme Court in the 1950s.

As to the actual disposition of Leary's case, among the points in his appeal to the Fifth Circuit Court was a claim that the marihuana tax law demanded compulsory self-incrimination. On appeal to the United States Supreme Court (which did not consider the religious issue), this count was accepted; Leary's conviction was overturned and a new trial ordered. Found guilty again, Leary was also convicted on possession charges in California in the spring of 1970.

For further comment on the issues raised here, see Phillips (1969).

[5] I would like to acknowledge informative correspondence on psychedelic churches from Dr. Walter Houston Clark, Rev. Arthur Kleps, and Miss Lisa Bieberman of the Psychedelic Information Center in Cambridge, Mass. Miss Bieberman writes: "I think that attempts to organize 'churches' based on the drugs have been misguided and premature. This has been successful only among the Indians where apparently sufficient cultural unity existed to make a real ongoing religious community, based on a mixture of Christian and tribal traditions, possible. . . . I believe the use of psychedelics for spiritual purposes should be considered protected by the First Amendment. . . . If there is to be a religious test for the right to use psychedelics it should be based on individual sincerity, as is done in the case of Conscientious Objectors. . . . Psychedelic drugs are not a religion in themselves, but their use can be part of a religious discipline within the context of a broader faith."

Clark (1969) provides essential background on the psychedelic religious experience and the resulting movements.

Host" and that it is the religious duty of all members to partake of the sacraments on regular occasions.

In 1968, Judge Gesell of the U. S. District Court for the District of Columbia denied a motion, grounded in part on freedom of religion, for dismissal of drug sale and possession indictments against Judith Kuch, averred to be an ordained minister of the Neo-American Church. Noting the difficulty of determining what is and what is not religion, and the obligation to avoid judgments based on one's own values, Judge Gesell nevertheless found that there is little evidence "to support the view that the Church and its members as a body are motivated by or associated because of any common religious concern" (*United States* v. *Kuch,* 288 F. Supp. 439 [1968]). But even were the religious claim valid, the public interest is paramount. The opinion expressed some uneasiness over the balancing act required by the *Sherbert* precedent; Judge Gesell was inclined to leave such functions in the hands of Congress, allowing the courts to work with a simple belief/action dichotomy. In any case, he found a substantial state interest outweighing the claimed religious exemption.[6]

Other Public Health Issues

Certain religious groups with scruples against medical practices such as vaccination have taken their claims to court. Building on the doctrine set forth by the Supreme Court in 1905 that "a community has the right to protect itself against an epidemic of disease which threatens the safety of its members," the public interest has prevailed over religious conviction in the great majority of cases (*Jacobson* v. *Massachusetts,* 197 U.S. 11 [1905]). The continuing efforts of Christian Scientists, however, who seek to substitute prayer for medicine, have resulted in a number of legislative exemptions from public health procedures and health education in the schools. Christian Science practitioners have gradually secured legal recognition, usually in the form of exemptions from state regulations affecting the practice of medicine (Braden 1969: 250–266).

---

[6] After noting such evidence on the Neo-American Church as the church symbol, a three-eyed toad, the official songs, "Puff, the Magic Dragon" and "Row, Row, Row Your Boat," and the church motto, "Victory over Horseshit!", Judge Gesell announced that "the Court finds this helpful in declining to rule that the Church is a religion within the meaning of the First Amendment." The court also rejected the defendant's claim for equal protection along with the Indian peyote cult, and the argument that there is no longer a rational basis for the 1937 Marihuana Tax Act.

Fur further discussion of the issues raised in these cases, see *California Law Review,* January 1968 (entire issue), and "Drug Crime Defense—Religious Freedom," 35 *American Law Review* 3d 939.

A more complicated problem of religious freedom emerges when the issue is not that of balancing personal conviction against public health, but the health of the believer himself. Here we encounter the Jehovah's Witness doctrine that blood transfusions are forbidden by Scripture; the courts have had to decide whether to restrict religious liberty against an individual's will, in order to save his life. When the situation involved a minor child, the decision to overrule the parents' convictions has prevailed.[7] But with a mentally competent adult, the question is more difficult. In view of the honored history of religious martyrdom, ought not religious freedom include the right to commit suicide?

The majority of such cases have been decided in favor of court authorization of blood transfusion, even for unwilling recipients, on ground of the state's right to uphold life (*United States* v. *George*, 239 F. Supp. 752 [1965]). But in a case decided before the Illinois Supreme Court, it was determined that religious practices can be infringed only when they threaten *public* health, welfare, or morals. In dealing with "a competent adult who has steadfastly maintained her belief that acceptance of a blood transfusion is a violation of the law of God," even though the court may consider her beliefs "unwise, foolish or ridiculous, in the absence of an overriding danger to society we may not permit interference" (*In re Brooks*, 205 N.E. 2d 435 [1965]). In concluding, the court quoted Justice Brandeis: "The makers of our Constitution . . . conferred, as against the Government, the right to be let alone—the most comprehensive of rights and the most valued by civilized man" (*Olmstead* v. *United States*, 277 U.S. 438 [1928]).

The Law and The Black Muslims

Another kind of conflict is found in recent cases in which Black Muslims in prison have claimed that they were denied equal privileges in the practice of their religion. Since the Muslim religion includes, in addition to the usual requests for literature, holding meetings, and contacts with clergy, such obligations as pork-free meals and the wearing of beards, some difficulties might be expected. But the problem from the prison administration viewpoint centers more on fears of disruptive activities by members of a movement understood to be dedicated to black supremacy by violent means. Although courts have traditionally been reluctant to interfere with prison administration,

[7] The precedent cases include: *People ex rel. Wallace* v. *Labrenz*, 411 Ill. 618 (1952); *State* v. *Perricone*, 181 A. 2d 751 (1962); *Raleigh Fitkin Hospital* v. *Anderson*, 201 A. 2d 537 (1964). All these cases were appealed but denied certiorari by the U. S. Supreme Court, thus making it reasonably certain that the issue is closed. See discussion in Pfeffer (1967: 699–702).

it is now established that prisoners do have certain rights and privileges and that authorities cannot punish or discriminate religious belief as such, although reasonable measures to maintain discipline are assumed.[8]

A number of the earlier cases questioned the status of the Black Muslim movement as a religion, citing the doctrines of racial supremacy and the intrinsic evil of all whites. In one case, the Muslim Brotherhood was declared a secret organization seeking purely secular objectives within the prison. In another, later reversed by the Supreme Court, "certain social studies" were introduced by the Attorney General of Illinois to show that the "Black Muslim Movement, despite its pretext of a religious facade, is an organization that, outside of prison walls, has for its object the overthrow of the white race, and inside prison walls, has an impressive history of inciting riots and violence" (*Cooper* v. *Pate*, 324 F. 2d 165 [1963]).

But other decisions have established the validity of the Black Muslim religion, relying on the testimony of Muslim ministers and the work of scholars such as Eric Lincoln. A significant recent decision of the U. S. District Court in California ordered that Black Muslim ministers be granted the same privileges as other chaplains at all California state prisons, and that prisoners be allowed to receive Muslim publications (*Northern* v. *Nelson*, 315 F. Supp. 687 [1970]).

Judicial recognition of the Black Muslim faith was also one of the issues in Muhammad Ali's lengthy struggle to avoid induction into the armed forces. In the series of Selective Service procedures, court decisions, and various appeals, Ali (formerly known as Cassius Clay) had claimed recognition both as a conscientious objector and as a minister of the Muslim religion. In 1966, a Justice Department hearing officer concluded that Ali's beliefs were sincere and recommended that the conscientious objector claim be sustained. But the Justice Department advised the Appeal Board that the registrant's refusal to participate in war rested on "grounds which primarily are political and racial" and did not constitute a "general scruple against participation in war in any form." This ruling was accepted by the Appeal Board and subsequently by the Fifth Circuit Court of Appeals, but the Supreme Court, in an unsigned opinion, reversed the conviction. The Supreme Court decision did not respond directly to the question of selective opposition to war, but it did declare that the Justice Department "was simply wrong as a matter of law in advising that the petitioner's beliefs were not religiously based and were not sincerely

---

[8] See the detailed annotation, "Provision of Religious Facilities for Prisoners," 12 *American Law Review* 3d 1276 (1967).

held" (*Clay* v. *United States*, 403 U.S. 698 [1971]). The Court's language in affirming Ali's religiosity may be read as a clear legitimation of the Black Muslim faith.[9]

Black Muslims have had other conflicts with the law that raise religious freedom issues. In New Jersey, Muslim school children who refused to salute the flag, claiming they owed allegiance only to Allah, were barred from school, but reinstated after an appeal to the State Commissioner of Education (*Holden* v. *Board of Education*, 216 A. 2d 387 [1966]). The Black Muslim leader Elijah Muhammad lost his suit against the Flint, Michigan, police department, in which he charged that they interfered with religious liberty by entering a Muslim meeting and refusing either to leave or to surrender their weapons. The appeal was dismissed, on the ground that important public peace and order interests were overriding (*Muhammad* v. *Sommers*, 238 F. Supp. 806 [1964]).

Scientology: Religion or Not?

Several court decisions involving L. Ron Hubbard's "Church of Scientology" raise some interesting issues of definition and judgment. In 1963, the Federal Food and Drug Administration seized and condemned a number of electrical instruments, known as E-meters, and a large quantity of literature from the premises of the Founding Church of Scientology in Washington, D. C. The government claimed that the material was "misbranded," i.e. false and misleading claims were made for the cure and treatment of disease. The Scientologists argued that as a religious movement they were protected by the First Amendment, and appealed the decision.

In a detailed opinion displaying considerable acquaintance with both the teachings of Scientology and the development of First Amendment doctrine, Judge J. Skelly Wright studied the question of Scientology's standing as a religion, recognizing that the area of religious healing has been customarily exempted from the general regulations of public health and medical practice (*Founding Church of Scientology of Washington, D.C.* v. *United States*, 409 F. 2d 1146 [1969]).

Judge Wright rejected the simple views of the religious issue held

---

[9] The question of ministerial status was not touched in the Supreme Court decision. In the 1968 Fifth Circuit opinion, the court applied the test of "whether a registrant, as a vocation, regularly, not occasionally, teaches and preaches the principles of his religion" (*Clay* v. *United States*, 397 F. 2d 901 [1968]). It was observed that Ali continued to list his occupation as professional boxer, even though certified as a minister of the "Lost Found Nation of Islam." Jehovah's Witnesses have faced similar problems in claims for ministerial status, as their view that all members are simultaneously ministers has been subject to evaluation in terms of actual time spent in religious work.

by both parties—the government's claim that religion is irrelevant and the appellant's view that "free exercise" protects from all secular regulation. Holding that the religious question is more complex than this, he surveyed the relevant precedents, from *Cantwell, Barnette, Ballard,* and *Sherbert,* and then posed the question—is Scientology really a religion?

After observing that the church is incorporated as such, that it has licensed ministers, and that the writings of Hubbard give a "general account of man and his nature comparable in scope, if not in content, to those of some of the recognized religions," the court concluded that "the Founding Church of Scientology has made out a *prima facie* case that it is a *bona fide* religion." Thus, the literature setting forth the theory of auditing and the use of E-meters is religious doctrine and not subject to the laws on "labeling," even though some of the statements in the Scientology texts would, in isolation, appear to make questionable claims for curative powers. Judge Wright, however, carefully avoided making a blanket statement: "We do not hold that the Founding Church is for all legal purposes a religion."

In June 1969, the Second Circuit Court of Appeals granted an application for discharge from the Army Reserve for Aaron Barr, who had become an ordained minister of the Church of Scientology. His petition as a divinity student had earlier been denied, because, the Army explained, the "Academy of Scientology" was not found in the official educational directory. The court, however, declared that "it is enough, absent rebuttal, that the Church is incorporated in New York as a religious corporation, that it has a substantial membership and a functioning divinity school which ordains its members" (*Barr* v. *Weise,* 412 F. 2d 338 [1969]).[10]

[10] Judge Moore's decision in this case refers to Wright's "very able opinion" and its ambiguous findings. He comments on the practice of Scientology: "It is not for us to prejudge the benefits, or lack thereof, which may come to members of the Church from being audited while holding in their hands two tin soup cans linked by an electrical apparatus. The use, if any, which the Reverend Barr may make of these E-meters, now released by virtue of Judge Wright's decision, is for the future."

The ambiguous religious status of Scientology is evidenced also in the litigation over tax exemption. The Court of Claims had ruled in 1968 that a large part of the activities of the church were profit-making in nature, and that some of its net earnings inured to the benefit of L. Ron Hubbard and his family, in violation of the Internal Revenue Code. The Founding Church lost its appeal of this ruling, 412 F. 2d 1197 (1969).

Continued government effort to condemn the use of E-meter culminated in a decision of the United States District Court stating that "E-meter auditing will be permitted only in a religious setting subject to placing explicit warning disclaimers on the meter itself and all labelling." Judge Gesell's opinion ruled against any non-religious use or sale of the device (*United States* v. *An Article or Device . . . Hubbard Electrometer,"* 333 F. Supp. 357 [1971]).

III. Toward A New Understanding of Freedom of Religion

This survey of cases has demonstrated the variety of conflicts between freedom and order that representatives of marginal religious groups have brought to the courts. In this final section we shall investigate two basic questions that recur, in one form or another, in every attempt to determine the authority of the First Amendment religion clause. The questions are, in simplest terms: "How much freedom?" and "What is religion?"

How Much Freedom?

If we ask just how the limits of religious freedom are set by the courts, it is clear that no one definitive rationale for adjudication has emerged. The jurists have developed a number of testing procedures —secular regulation, interest weighing, clear and present danger, compelling state interest, alternative means—but only the first of these offers a self-evident approach. In creating the possibility of carving out an exemption from existing legislation for certain kinds of religiously motivated action, and justifying this exemption by balancing religious conviction against public policy, the *Sherbert* formula tended to favor a case-by-case procedure. We have seen how court opinions may vary widely in their application of this balancing technique.

A comprehensive theoretical pattern for the balancing process is set forth in Professor Giannella's model:

> A thoroughgoing balancing test would measure three elements of the competing governmental interest: first, the importance of the secular value underlying the governmental regulation; second, the degree of proximity and necessity that the chosen regulatory means bears to the underlying value; and third, the impact that an exemption for religious reasons would have on the over-all regulatory program. This assessment of the state's interest would then have to be balanced against the claim for religious liberty, which would require calculation of two factors: first, the sincerity and importance of the religious practice for which special protection is claimed; and second, the degree to which the governmental regulation interferes with that practice [Giannella 1967: 1390].

The actual case material, however, suggests that a genuine concern for granting the fullest expression of religious freedom consistent with reasonable public order is often secondary. That is, the degree of tolerance for deviant behavior is determined more by the interplay of longterm cultural values and current prevailing opinion with respect to the behavior in question. Thus, public fears of racial animosity and of the drug subculture have been reflected in the hesitance to grant Black Muslim prisoners equal access to religious ministrations, and the almost total refusal to acknowledge religious motives in the use of prohibited drugs.[11] If the minority view seeking recognition is perceived as threatening, then it is all too easy to fail to give adequate attention to the religious claim.

One may observe that the major judicial efforts at carving out exemptions to secular regulation have tended to emphasize the dimension of worship. It is significant, I think, that in several of the Jehovah's Witnesses cases a generation ago, the Supreme Court argued, almost extravagantly, that door-to-door proselyting is equivalent to conventional worship. Again, the *Sherbert* breakthrough had at its center a conviction about the proper day for worship. Further, the *Woody* opinion emphasized that peyote was used only in the setting of corporate worship. It appears that a strong cultural predisposition to characterize religion primarily in terms of the centrality of worship is operative here.

Unusual ethical obligations claimed in the name of religion have run into more trouble; the idea of slavery or polygamy as a divine command never gained much acceptance in the American ethos. Conscientious scruples, such as those opposed to vaccination or the flag salute, have indeed achieved recognition over the years, but legal exemptions from established norms in order to carry out alleged divine commands are rare. In an age of increasing emphasis on individualized forms of religious expression, however, we may expect more challenges to conventional understanding (Konvitz 1968: 73–106).

What Is Religion?

This paper bears as its title the early Supreme Court affirmation "the law knows no heresy" in order to remind us that in matters of religion, the law is always a neutral observer. The major thrust of the relevant court decisions confirms the principle that judges and juries cannot probe into the *truth* or falsity or religious claims, although there is less agreement about the propriety of inquiry into the *sincerity* of religious conviction, as the *Ballard* opinions indicated. But what about the question of defining "religion"?

In retrospect, it is surprising how little attention has been given to the matter of definition. Although several formulations about religion

---

[11] We may explain the exception for peyote-chewing Indians by observing that, as an isolated ethnic minority, they present no threat to middle America, and can be indulged in their specific behavior. The present narcotics situation may be contrasted with the legislative provisions for making sacramental wine available during Prohibition.

have been advanced in the course of Supreme Court decisions, they have not been widely employed in actual adjudication. Some indeed have argued that the courts ought not attempt to distinguish religion.[12] But the direction the Court has acually taken, in affirming the preferred position of First Amendment freedoms, requires that the law must be able to recognize "religion."

Religion therefore cannot be ignored, nor can the courts simply accept the self-definitions set forth by every claimant. Respect for the meaning of the First Amendment demands a method of distinguishing religious activity from other forms of human endeavor. If, in some circumstances, the law must defer to religion, it must be able to identify it—and yet remain theologically neutral. In an increasingly pluralist society, marked by a burgeoning variety of cults, a growing privatization of religious experience, and widespread abandonment of traditional theistic formulations, that task becomes extremely delicate. The difficulties faced by the courts in some of the cases discussed above bear witness to the problem.

A new approach to the judicial understanding of religion may be gained by adopting some of the analytical tools of the sociology and anthropology of religion. Social science methodology, in its conceptualization of religion, operates within a framework that is singularly applicable to the judicial setting. The social science perspective is characterized by the following factors: (1) it is descriptive rather than normative; (2) it is concerned more with function than with essence; (3) it assumes that religion is a complex phenomenon, embracing a number of distinctive elements or dimensions. Each of these principles has been recognized in some fashion in some of the relevant court proceedings, but they have not been operationalized into a consistent pattern. Since judges are now accustomed to reviewing and adopting the wisdom of professionals in other fields, it seems appropriate to invite them to consider the utility of conceptualizations derived from the social theory of religion.

The actual practice of the courts reveals some implicit acceptance of a sociological and functional method for dealing with religion. With the necessary broadening of the religious category from the theistic, quasi-Christian formulations of the nineteenth century, jurists had to

[12] The First Amendment principle advocated by Philip Kurland argues that "government cannot utilize religion as a standard for action or inaction because these clauses . . . prohibit classification in terms of religion" (1962: 112).

The Supreme Court attempts at definitions of religion are found in *Davis* v. *Beason*, 133 U.S. 333 (1890); *United States* v. *Macintosh*, 283 U.S. 605 (1931); *West Virginia State Board of Education* v. *Barnette*, 319 U.S. 624 (1943); and *McGowan* v. *Maryland*, 366 U.S. 420 (1961). For discussion of these see Burkholder (1969: 94–110).

develop a non-theological, descriptive approach. Two kinds of cases are instructive here—those dealing with tax exemption status and those evaluating claims for recognition as religious conscientious objectors to military service.[13]

Probably the most frequently cited case on tax exemption is that of the non-theistic organization known as the Fellowship of Humanity. The California Court of Appeals, recognizing that the *Ballard* opinion precluded any inquiry into the *content* of belief, declared that the *practice* of religion was subject to factual verification. The court determined that religion includes the following elements: (1) beliefs (not necessarily supernatural), (2) cultic association, (3) a system of moral practice, and (4) organization. Having asserted that the beliefs of the Fellowship occupied "the same place in the lives of its holders that orthodox beliefs occupy in the lives of believing majorities," the court concluded that, by analogy with conventional religions, the Fellowship did qualify as a religious organization (*Fellowship of Humanity* v. *County of Alameda,* 315 P 2d 394 [1957]).

The two major Supreme Court decisions broadening the religious grounds for conscientious objection have followed the same pattern for determining functional equivalence. The test set forth in 1965 was "whether a given belief that is sincere and meaningful occupies a place in the life of its possessor parallel to that filled by the orthodox belief in God of one who clearly qualifies for the exemption" (*United States* v. *Seeger,* 380 U.S. 163 [1965]). In the more recent Welsh decision, the Court declared that even if a registrant does not characterize his own beliefs as "religious," the courts may declare them to be so, if they meet the functional test (*Welsh* v. *United States,* 90 S. Ct. 1792 [1970]). In this series of decisions, the Court has stretched the definition of religion to encompass a wide variety of personal conviction, resulting in considerable confusion as to the limits of such construction.

There now remains no valid test of the content of a claimed religious belief—neither its truth, good sense, comprehensibility, the-

[13] We will not discuss the debatable question of the constitutional validity of tax exemption for religious institutions, beyond noting that the recent Supreme Court decision upholds the generally accepted policies; *Walz* v. *Tax Commission,* 397 U.S. 664 (1970).

A parallel case to *Fellowship of Humanity* is *Washington Ethical Society* v. *District of Columbia,* 249 F. 2d 127 (1957). Both these cases are cited in the Scientology decision reported above. For a discerning discussion of the issue, see Brancato (1968).

Strictly speaking, the conscientious objection cases do not deal with constitutional freedom of religion, but merely with interpretation of the Selective Service Act. The concept of religion set forth in these cases, however, has been articulated in other judicial contexts.

ism, or its acceptance by any organized group. Courts may, at the most, apply general tests of psychic function—or when dealing with institutions, of institutional form and function [Galanter 1966: 264].

As this statement acknowledges, there is a difference between these two kinds of tests, even though the functional approach to defining religion appears in each. The internal allegiance of conscience is not the same thing as an organization seeking tax exemption. That the personal form of religion is of a quite different order from the institutional becomes more obvious when we are forced by today's pluralistic situation to move beyond conventional categories.

Awareness of several levels of meaning for religion is not, however, a purely modern discovery. James Madison's original proposal for the Bill of Rights differentiated religion and conscience:

The civil rights of none shall be abridged on account of religious belief or worship, nor shall any national religion be established, nor shall the full and equal rights of conscience be in any manner, or on any pretext, infringed [quoted in Stokes and Pfeffer 1964: 21].

For the Founding Fathers, there was indeed a latent duality in the concept of religion, which unfortunately was obscured when the word was used but once in the final form of the First Amendment. On the one hand, "religion" is a deeply personal experience, equivalent to "conscience," apparently, as the words were used interchangeably. But "religion" also has an institutional form—the churchly structures that might seek tangible support (i.e. "establishment") from civil authority.

This distinction of personal and institutional dimensions, recognized in the early phases of the constitutional process, may now be extended and clarified further, with the help of modern social theory. The work of Talcott Parsons and Robert Bellah calls attention to the additional analytical differentiation of cultural and social system levels. Bellah described religion succinctly as "a set of symbols that may be institutionalized . . . in a society, or internalized in a personality" (1965b: 171). Religious symbols are basically cultural phenomena, those "symbolic forms and acts that relate man to the ultimate conditions of his existence" (Bellah 1970: 21), which are expressed at the societal and personal levels of action through the processes of institutionalization and internalization.

By conceptualizing religion as a multi-dimensional phenomenon, we allow for distinctive meanings and functions at each of the three system levels of culture, society, and personality. Clarification of these dimensions would enable the courts to develop appropriate rationales for dealing with the issues encountered at each level. Adapting this perspective to judicial problems may appear to complicate an already confused situation. But I contend that the use of such a model for ordering the data of religion would actually make for clarity and consistency in adjudication.[14] Two brief examples from cases already mentioned may help make the point.

Justice Stewart in the *Sherbert* decision suggested that the Court's recognition of a religiously based exemption amounts to an "establishment" of religion that is prohibited by the first phrase of the First Amendment. But by distinguishing levels of religiosity, it becomes clear that one cannot "establish" an individual conscience. To recognize the appellant's claim does not put the government in the position of promoting a theology (cultural level religion) or supporting an institutional church (societal level); it is instead fulfilling the mandate to maximize religious freedom at the personal level.

Judge Wright's opinion in the *Scientology* case demonstrates the difficulty of drawing a line between the religious and secular with respect to the status of organizations. He acknowledged the inherent ambiguity by stating that Scientology may not be a religion for all legal purposes. The use of the analytical process to differentiate the symbolic and the social-organizational aspects of Scientology would clarify the problem that Judge Wright intuitively recognized.

Thus, to push this implicit awareness to the point of making it a consistent mode of conceptualizing the varied expressions of religion is to open up a number of new possibilities in the legal domain. By elaborating the distinctive aspects of the symbolic, institutional, and personal dimensions of religion, and proposing that distinctive judicial rationales may be considered at each of the three levels, it becomes possible to work out alternative resolutions for some of the continuing dilemmas of freedom and order with respect to religion.

---

[14] In my earlier work on the problems of the First Amendment religion clause, I combined insights from Parsons, Wilfred C. Smith, and Geertz (1966) with Bellah's formulation cited above to create a more comprehensive model for definition: *Religion is the expression in human action of belief-attitudes of commitment to that which is conceived as ultimate in a nonempirical sense; these expressions are symbolized in cultural patterns, institutionalized in societies, and internalized in personalities.* This formula enables the distinguishing of religion from non-religion, without resorting to particularistic theologies. Its usefulness in dealing with the issues in court decisions is elaborated in Burkholder (1969: 209–284).

Language in Culture and Society: Linguistic Forms in Ritual Contexts

This section deals with spoken language in various ritual and church contexts. The religious groups discussed are Spiritualist churches, Afro-American churches on the east and west coasts, Afro-Cuban Santería cults in Puerto Rico and New York, independently organized prayer groups in Massachusetts, and independent revivalist churches in Kentucky, California, and Oklahoma. Many of these marginal churches in America have developed an indigenous and unique oral tradition in the form of chanted sermons, gospel and soul music, glossolalia, prayers, and specialized religious argots. These verbal forms are codes which are used by members of these groups to communicate about their social realities and cultural history as well as about their personal and collective identities.

Much of the speech and musical elements prevalent in these churches are now making their way into traditional institutional churches, as older denominations are trying to gain relevance and attract new members. For example "St. Francis de Sales Catholic church in New Orleans has introduced forms of traditional Afro-American music with the church's traditional European music. Physical movement is encouraged. People clap, sway, gyrate, snap their fingers, and pump their legs to the music. Some rise and give spontaneous testimonials, others shout in prolonged seizures of ecstacy" (*New York Times,* August 6, 1972, p. 43). Ritual forms are the crossroads where marginal folk traditions feed into popular culture. These forms might remain identified in the public eye with small marginal groups, but they are becoming diffused into the larger society and employed by a wider and wider audience.

The basic unit of analysis in these papers is the verbal utterance as it is produced in a religious activity. The utterances range from specific vocabulary items to larger units, such as ritual phrases and formulas, to complete ritual sequences such as sermons, prayers, and songs. All the contemporary religious movements rely on spoken language to a greater degree than on sacred written texts. Whether Pentecostal preachers, itinerant gospel singers, or Spiritualist mediums, they believe that the word of God is continuously revealed anew, and each individual who truly seeks can serve as a channel for the divine message. Popular access to divine revelation is one of the main features of many of the contemporary religious groups. But it is not verbal utterances alone that allow an individual to move into closer contact with the transcendent. Spoken language is aimed to produce an altered state of consciousness in the individual. Such utterances become a vehicle for as well as a manifestation of mystical experiences. They are performative utterances. The verbal utterance is both our unit of analysis and the basic unit in the ritual event; it makes the event happen. These performative utterances are produced consciously and purposefully. Throughout the religious activity, the speaker is conscious of the fact that the utterance is supposed to achieve the anticipated goals of his listeners.

The analyses of these speech events draw heavily upon models developed in socio-linguistics, psycho-linguistics, and anthropology. The assumption here is that these utterances are to be understood not only as a system of signs and symbols but as a vehicle of communication. They comprise a system of codes that reveal the speaker's personal, social, and cultural identities and express his degree of involvement and religious commitment to the group. The verbal utterance is regarded as an index of social relationships. Therefore, the papers analyze not only the semantic referents of the utterances but also their form.

The authors of these papers, while interested in describing the particular groups they worked with, are also concerned with the substantive and methodological contributions they offer beyond the specific groups they describe. The four writers are concerned with cross-cultural and comparative research. Rosenberg and Marks are interested in spontaneous chanted sermons and accompanying musical forms. This is an effort to discover principles of oral composition and performance that can be applied cross-culturally; for example, are there cues that mark the appearance of an altered state of consciousness within musical performance that may be shared cross-culturally? Bateson and Zaretsky are interested in comparative studies. Bateson in terms of liturgical renewal occurring in various mainline churches and Zaretsky in terms of shared argots among various churches that make up the American metaphysical movement.

The underlying methodological premise of these papers is that language cannot be studied in isolation from the field contexts in which it occurs. Verbal behavior encodes meaning whose decoding requires our understanding of the rules of verbal performance as well as the functions and contexts of its occurrence. Such understanding is based on a knowledge of the ethnographic realities gained through fieldwork. All these papers rely on data that is derived from particularly demanding field observations, often requiring a great deal of equipment such as tape recorders, movie cameras, and sometimes occurring in churches where the writing down of material is not permissible. Frequently, field workers have to fashion their own research techniques, since they are looking at clues that have previously not been noticed. The major difficulty is that many different kinds of observations have to be conducted at the same time. Since so much of the behavior occurs when informants are experiencing altered states of consciousness, observations are even more demanding. In this type of research, the field worker has to condition himself to watch for many different kinds of metamessages. This requires a context by context observation. The rhythmic structures, physiological reactions, change in vocabulary, and kinetic behavior seen in eyes, hands, and limbs create a many-layered behavioral complex. The labels that we use to describe it, e.g. "altered states of consciousness," have to be understood as shorthand terms for observations that have been made on various levels.

The first paper by Morton Marks poses three questions. What are the signals by which we distinguish rituals from all other communication events in these particular groups? What form must these rituals assume in order to communicate social information? And what social information do, or can, these rituals contain? In answering these questions he proposes a theory of ritual behavior among certain groups in the New World as well as a method of ethno-historical study.

In dealing with the first question Marks is concerned about the relationship between ritual communication and trance behavior. He says that at first he was unaware of the trance element in the music he was analysing. As soon as he began transcribing sermons and song texts, he quickly realized that their semantic content often signaled that trance behavior was becoming part of the performance. The beginning of trance coincided with, and was being signalled by, a set of metamessages, including rhythmic changes, alterations in breathing, and intonation patterns. In other words, it became clear that linguistic and musical structures were not simply stylistic features but were tied to other behavioral domains. This observation was investigated in gospel concerts in the United States and other field situations in Puerto Rico and Brazil. After the musical texts were written out, such performance rules as style-switching and the staggered entry of rhythm patterns were seen. But it still remained to have the performance transcribed to show the interplay among voices and instruments, as well as the procedural aspects of each performance—that is, the way songs would begin in one style and end in a distinctively different one.

In answering the second question, Marks points out that by focusing on performance styles, one has a key to understanding the ritual of marginal religious movements among Afro-American blacks and Afro-

Cubans in the United States. He examines gospel songs as a sequencing of formulas in a performance context and explores this through models from socio-linguistics. Through his analysis he argues that ritual conveys information both in a technical sense and also in the sense of social meaning. Style-switching shows an alternation between African and European styles and their behavioral correlates. Marks analyses the interplay between particular communication forms, the ethnographic contexts within which these rituals occur, and the cultural history of the participants. He concludes that social meaning is generated through the alternation and interplay among a set of codes, and channels of communication, to produce statements of and about cultural identity.

The rituals are not just descriptive and expressive statements. Performers and participants state their personal religious and cultural commitments by fulfilling them on the spot. These rituals implicitly convey information about the world view of individuals and their awareness of the connection between history and ritual structure; for example, in Afro-American rituals, the historical consciousness of ties with Africa is expressed structurally through the Africanization of performance rules such as staggered entry. Marks sees these rituals as rites of passage into altered states of consciousness, which in turn mark statements with unique import. He concludes that we should stop looking at gospel music as an evolutionary step to jazz and view it in a broad New World context to allow us to make statements about connections between ritual forms and historical consciousness.

Rosenberg focuses on performance from a different vantage point. He deals with the spontaneous chanted sermon as heard in southern California's San Joaquin Valley and in Eastern Kentucky, delivered by preachers who were Pentecostals working in a variety of fundamentalist and independent churches. He deals with the chanted performance of the sermons and bases his analysis on theoretical frameworks worked out by psycho-linguistics. Rosenberg discovered that the preacher is not preaching word for word, but rather is preaching in terms of units. Some of the units are memorized and may be short or long. They are articulated within the sermon in such a way that we recognize them as preaching-formulas. Sermons are often very long and hard for the preacher to memorize in great detail. While preaching, the minister draws upon these formulas, fits them into new contexts, and creates new sermons within his oral tradition. He speaks in metrical patterns and the meter allows him to tie together the material he uses for the sermon. It is the meter that is crucial. What is of ultimate importance to the congregation is that the preacher "preach and not teach." If the sermon does not go well, if the congregation is not receiving its anticipated performance, a preacher will often introduce a sequence that he commands well and thus create the feeling that the sermon is supposed to generate within the congregation. Rosenberg highlights the relationship between the sermon and the response it is supposed to evoke in the listener. This issue is also raised by Bateson who is concerned with what she identifies as the numinous quality of ritual, the sense of fusion that people expect to feel from viable rituals.

Bateson's data are based on a prayer group that speaks in tongues, glossolalia, organized by several middle-class white Christians in their early twenties in Massachusetts. This group repeats the format of thousands of such groups around the country, indicating the renewed vitality of independent worship units. Bateson explores the question of the meaning ritual has for an individual.

The analysis comes from her interest in the liturgical renewal that is part of churches like the Episcopal and Catholic. Bateson wonders whether the churches by changing certain rituals are rendering them more or less meaningful for the people. Essentially she is tackling the relationship between theology and ritual. She focuses on language and asks whether individuals look at the semantic meaning of terms which are meant to render a theological statement, or whether they gloss over the separate meanings and simply see the whole as a unit whose purpose is to make them experience certain desired feelings.

Bateson's main argument is that changes in ritual units, i.e. alterations in grammar, syntax, or vocabulary within prayers, transform the way the ritual is perceived by the individual from a single unit into its component parts. The changes may transform a ritual into a theological act. That theological act can become ritualized again through repetition or intensity of experience. She points out that the kind of fusion that occurs when rituals are effective is varied. Sometimes fusion can produce a great deal of excitement and meaning for the individual, and sometimes a great deal of meaninglessness.

Fusion is not created by just repeating rituals in a vacuum. What is important is the context in which it is done. One has to consider the personality of the individual, the legitimation and authority base of the ritual. If the ritual becomes banal, it loses its efficacy; if granted new authority, it can regain its sanctity. The new liturgical renewal is an effort by people to invest symbolic power in certain rituals that have become empty.

Bateson argues that the events that make good ritual and have a numinous quality to them also have a certain unity to them. For example, the creed in Christian churches. Its repetition word by word presents a unified statement, and the experience of saying it, a single act. Few people think of the creed sentence by sentence with the different meanings of each sentence, rather they repeat it as a unit. This is a ritual act; it has a degree of fusion as it unfolds. Bateson describes an activity that is done in synchrony and divides it into its component parts, words strung together into sentences which are strung together to form a single, ritual sacred action. In this analysis she develops her notion of the *praxon* to describe the levels and components of the whole experience.

In his paper, Zaretsky continues the analysis of performative utterances by examining the particular religious argot developed in Spiritualist churches. The research is based on Spiritualist churches on the West Coast and mid-Atlantic states. He points out that Spiritualists use a particular vocabulary as their system of communication. The argot is used by both parishioners and church functionaries during church services, as well as outside the church context in discussing church-related topics among themselves or with interested newcomers. The argot includes lexical items which label every facet of the church life and belief system. This vocabulary is composed of standard English terms which are used, however, in nonstandard ways. The argot meanings of the terms have been created by Spiritualists. Zaretsky's essential argument is that through their verbal exchanges in the idiom of the argot, Spiritualists create the social organization of the church—the roles, statuses, and hierarchical relationships that articulate the church as a social institution. Once a church is organized and a social structure is made explicit, participants within the structure formulate a grammar of rules for the proper and continued use of the argot by both themselves and newcomers to the church. Abiding by these rules, penalizing their misuse, and generating new ones allows Spiritualists to control the structural evolution of the church through time.

Zaretsky points out that the analysis of religious language in the form of the argot is particularly useful in several ways: first, to discover the cultural knowledge that individuals have about their social group; second, to allow investigators to use the linguistic data as indices of social relationships which cannot be easily discovered in situations where a population is anonymous, continually changing, and often unavailable for interviews; third, to isolate the area in which participants in these churches claim to make their most important contribution. The analysis is based upon research methods developed in ethnographic-semantic studies, and further develops those methods by showing how abstract terms may be analyzed in order to gain a clearer understanding of the referents which they label.

All four papers make a contribution toward the further definition of the newly developing area of language and religion. They point out with clarity the need for sound inductive approaches to the gathering of data in field contexts, and the importance of focusing not only on the structure and style of these languages but also on their social and cultural meaning for participants. Religious languages are codes whose decoding depends not only on technical knowledge of linguistic forms but also on an intimate familiarity with the ethnographic contexts in which these languages are used. The analysis of verbal utterances within religious groups frequently allows us to see the linkage between these groups and the larger society of which they are a part. The analysis of language prevents us from looking at religious groups as if they are self-contained entities living in a social vacuum. We are forced to see the connections between a group and its environment through the perspectives of the participants who formulate these communication codes.

Uncovering Ritual Structures in Afro-American Music

1. INTRODUCTION

IN this study I am presenting a theory of ritual behavior among certain groups in the New World. I am attempting to answer the following questions: What social information do, or can, these rituals contain? What form must these rituals assume in order to communicate such information? What are the signals by which we recognize ritual form in communication events in these particular cultural contexts? In attempting to answer these questions, I deal principally with three sources of data: Brazilian Carnival; Afro-Cuban santería; and the sermons and gospel music of North American blacks.

I am paying particular attention to the interrelationships between linguistic and musical structures. There will first be a presentation of the analytic concepts employed in the writing of this study. A discussion then follows which deals with the application of this body of theory to the ethnographic data.[1]

Field observations were carried out in Oakland and Berkeley, California, 1965–1969; in San Juan, Puerto Rico, June-August 1969; in New York City, 1970–1971; and in Belém and Recife, Brazil, July-August 1971.

2. NEW WORLD NEGRO CONTEXTS: STYLE-SWITCHING AND RITUAL

The common historical background for the data is culture contact in the New World between various African and European peoples. Throughout the Western Hemisphere there exists a tremendous variety of groups which may be called "Afro-American." These range from the so-called "bush Negroes" of the Guianas, to various Caribbean groups,

---

[1] For additional information on some of the topics covered in this paper, see the following sources. *Trance and possession behavior:* Lewis 1971, Bourguignon 1971; *style-switching:* Gumperz 1964, Gumperz and Blom 1970; *Brazilian carnival:* Bastide 1967, Real 1967; *santería:* Bascom 1951, Cabrera 1968; *sound and ritual:* Needham 1967; *Afro-American sermons:* Rosenberg 1970; *Afro-American music:* Szwed 1970, Oliver 1970; *Afro-Cuban music:* Ortiz 1965, Howard 1967; *ritual:* Turner 1967, Wallace 1966.

to North American blacks. Each group represents a unique situation of culture contact, and it is my purpose to analyze the communication forms employed in the rituals of several of these in an attempt to formulate a new approach to the ritual behavior of these groups.

Culture contact is reflected in the accretion of styles from various sources, both European and African. These styles represent multiple codes in the communicative behavior of these groups. It is my aim to demonstrate how these codes pattern in relation to one another, and how this patterning reveals underlying social meanings.

I am attempting to deal with culture contact, an essentially historical problem, by applying some of the approaches developed in socio-linguistics and in the broader area known as the ethnography of communication. The application of a socio-linguistic approach to illuminate an essentially historical problem raises some interesting questions concerning the relationship between structure and (ethno-)history, and the expression of this relationship in ritual. This approach is in contrast to the kind implicit in the following statement:

> Finally, the relationship between ethnosemantics and the diachronic approach to sociocultural phenomena through ethnology, history, archaeology and the comparative method deserves comment. Ethnosemantics may be able to develop valid and, within limits, useful descriptions of contemporary social systems, but the linguistic model, even more strongly than the model employed by the British structural functionalists, is inherently incapable of making discoveries about the content of history and the nature of historical processes. If anthropology is to have a diachronic component, that component cannot consist of an inventory of cognitive rules. (Harris 1968: 603)

In setting forth the rules for performance that underlie a wide variety of Afro-American ritual behavior, I am going against such assertions as the above, which contend that ethno-semantics and linguistics-based models in general, with their emphasis on behavioral rules, represent essentially ahistorical approaches.

In viewing certain Afro-American rituals as forms that generate meaning through the alternation between European and African-derived styles, I regard them as structures that express cultural distinctions, rather than as forms that mediate between such distinctions. This manipulation of modes and styles that are associated with different cultures in contact resembles a point made by Gumperz in regard to bilingual situations:

> The rigidity of such co-occurrence rules reinforces the perceptual distinctness of codes. In spite of the underlying grammatical simi-

larities, therefore, the shift between codes has a quality of abruptness which to some extent accounts for the speaker's view of them as distinct languages. Such codes seem ideally suited for communication in societies which stress cultural distinctions, while at the same time requiring regular and frequent interaction. (Gumperz 1969: 447)

This "quality of abruptness" in the switch from one set of performance rules to another is a common feature in many Afro-American rituals, and may in fact be one of their defining characteristics. This sense of abruptness is often created by the use of what has been termed "metaphorical switching," the introduction of codes or performance styles appropriate to one context into a new context. This phenomenon is especially noticeable in situations involving trance induction. This topic is taken up below and is examined in detail in sections 4 and 5.

While "code-switching" is only one device for communicating meaning, I regard it as central in establishing that the structure of certain Afro-American rituals, above all the ordering of their elements, reflects an awareness of the historical situation of cultures in contact. Since switching involves the element of choice between alternate means of expression, it conveys a group's or individual's awareness of the differences between the performance rules of cultures in contact, and between the behavioral domains to which these rules are tied.

By focusing on the empirical content of Afro-American rituals, it may be shown that what is termed "social meaning" arises out of the interplay among elements such as message—form, code, intonation pattern, as well as speech and musical variety. All of these, together with the overt content or the dictionary meaning of messages, act together to generate *contextual* meanings. The socio-linguistic approach, then, emphasizes meaning as conveyed through multiple channels and as analyzable through the interplay among these channels of meaning.

In describing the distribution and co-occurrence rules for various linguistic and musical features in a set of communication events which I am calling "rituals," I am following and expanding these points as set forth by Hymes:

> The ethnography of speaking is concerned with the situations and uses, the patterns and functions, of speaking as an activity in its own right. . . . If several dialects or languages are in use, all are considered as part of the speech activity of the group. . . . One way that patterns of speaking constitute a system is in virtue of restrictions on the co-occurence of elements. (Hymes 1962: 2, 10, 14)

Implicit in this definition is the notion both of a "linguistic repertoire" and "style-switching." The former treats the speech varieties
controlled by individual speakers as a behavioral whole; the latter
refers to the shift between two or more codes, styles, or dialects in such
a repertoire. Both of these concepts have been elaborated at length in
other contexts (Gumperz 1962, 1964, 1967), and they are employed in
this study in the analysis of the data. The connection between these
concepts and ritual communication will be taken up below.

In every instance, the data analyzed represents what I am calling a
ritual event. The basic problem of description here is to determine
whether "ritual events" are fixed entities in themselves which determine
the particular communication forms to be used, or whether these forms
create and structure the events. Before expanding my discussion of
"ritual," I must state my own belief that rituals have empirical content,
and that the study of this content may best be approached through the
application of the socio-linguistic techniques outlined above. One
useful definition of ritual is furnished by Victor Turner. His approach is essentially an expansion of Van Gennep's "rite of passage"
model. According to Van Gennep, rites of passage

> Accompany every change of place, state, social position and age.
> Van Gennep has shown that all rites of transition are marked by
> three phases: separation, margin (or *limen*), and aggregation. The
> first phase of separation comprises symbolic behavior signifying the
> detachment of the individual or group either from an earlier fixed
> point in the social structure or a set of cultural conditions (a "state");
> during the intervening "liminal" period the state of the ritual sub-
> ject (the "passenger") is ambiguous, he passes through a realm which
> has few or none of the attributes of the past or coming state; in the
> third phase the passage is consummated. (Turner 1967: 94)

Turner has expanded the notion of the so-called "liminal" or transitional phase of the rite of passage, and indeed defines ritual in these
terms:

> I consider the term "ritual" to be more fittingly applied to forms of
> religious behavior associated with social transitions, while the term
> "ceremony" has a closer bearing on religious behavior associated
> with social states, where politico-religious institutions also have
> greater importance. Ritual is transformative, ceremony confirma-
> tory. (Turner 1967: 95)

In every instance, the data to be analyzed below embodies a ritual
situation as here defined; that is, what I am calling ritual form applies
to cultures as well as to individuals; it represents in microcosm the

situation of contact and subsequent transition between African and European-derived cultural forms. These transitions are symbolized in the alternation between various styles and/or codes, both linguistic and musical. At the same time, when style-switching takes place in Afro-American cultures, *it creates a ritual setting*, which may be either "sacred" or "secular."

What is crucial for the discussion is that switching is always from a "white" to a "black" style, from a European to an African one. The Africanization of musical and linguistic behavior is one of the performance rules underlying a number of communication events in a variety of New World settings.

To put it another way, style-switching may be said to arise out of culture contact, and it is employed on the symbolic level to express what Reisman has called the "duality of cultural patterning" between European and African forms. His argument is derived from his observations of speaking styles in a village on the West Indian island of Antigua. He noticed that "The alternations between Creole and Standard English . . . are related to the dual patterning of values and cultural and linguistic expression" (Reisman 1970: 129). What is important for the present work is Reisman's demonstration of how this alternation between Creole and Standard English is not simply an "expressive" feature of speaking styles, but is actively employed in generating ritual events:

> An association is set up between argument, Creole, noise, and disorder. Both Creole and argument are referred to as "making noise." This, of course, is negative definition. People take great joy in making noise, as a matter of fact. . . . This is the basis of the symbolism of most village rituals. Meetings begin with a call for Conduct, and descend into "noise" and Creole via argument. In one case, christening parties, there is a ritual argument simply to make sure the inevitable happens. . . . Such a structure is an invitation to general argument, with everybody talking at once and with increasing Creolization of speech down from the chairman's formal English. . . . When the noise becomes too great there will be a call to Conduct and a temporary reestablishment of order. The oscillation between noise and order may thus be seen as tied in part to the alternations between Creole and Standard Language. (Reisman 1970: 141)

These, in turn, are related to the duality of cultural and linguistic expression mentioned above.

This discussion of the meaning of the oscillation between "noise" (Creole) and "order" (Standard English) is approached from a different angle in a later paper of Reisman's. The point he makes here is important for my later discussions:

> On the island of Antigua there are a variety of ways of speaking that Antiguans sometimes call "making noise." I want to call these speech events contrapuntal, in the sense that . . . each voice has a "tune" and maintains it; and that the voices often sing independently at the same time. The essential feature of argument is the non-complementarity of repetition. Each person takes a point or position and repeats it endlessly, either one after the other, or both at once, or several at once depending on the number of people participating. (pp. 2, 30)

In a footnote (p. 40), Reisman observes that the oscillation between "noise" and "order" is probably a widely distributed West African speaking convention. However, in Africa it occurs without its attendant New World meaning as an expression of cultural duality and the symbolic movement between the categories of different cultures. Reisman quotes two examples from West African groups, the first a Jabo (Liberia) drum signal, recorded by Herzog, that gives the command, "Stop ye the noise, speak ye one by one" (p. 40). The second example is from Bowen's *Return to Laughter,* and describes a village meeting of the Tiv people of Nigeria:

> In this case, however, it was quite clear that the two men had brought a dispute for arbitration. At Kako's sign, one began his story, interrupted by questions from all the notables and punctuated by sarcastic comment and injured denial from the other. Soon everyone was saying so much, and so loudly, that no one could hear. Then someone screamed "Shut up! Shut up!" until all had taken up the cry. Then a silence, and the case slowly warmed up to a shouting point again. (Bowen 1964: 51, 52)

Reisman argues that such West African conventions constitute "part of the underlying culture of Antiguan villages" (p. 40).

This point could be expanded, and it could be said that the "Africanization" of behavior, especially in group settings, is an underlying performance rule throughout much of the New World, and that everywhere it is connected with a break from "order," usually represented by European-derived forms, into seemingly "disorderly" group behavior. Frequently, the observer, unaware of these performance rules, may interpret complex collective or corporate conventions as "noise" or disorder, and will ignore the underlying organizing principles and the meanings these can generate.

In the data collected by Reisman, the elements of ritual-as-transition, style-switching, and the building of complex performances all co-occur. The oscillation between "order" and "noise," which is really a multi-level, simultaneous speech event, is crucial for much of the data to be discussed below. While these examples deal with the connection be-tween *speech* styles and ritual events, parallel cases could be cited for performances in other areas of Afro-American culture.

Just as it has been suggested that certain West African conventions underly speech behavior in Antiguan culture, I am suggesting that a particular musical style, widely distributed throughout sub-Saharan Africa, is the source of an important communication strategy in the New World for generating ritual events. A. M. Jones has called this style a "fundamental feature of African drumming and African music in general, namely, *the staggering of the points of entry* of combined rhythm patterns" (Jones 1955: 41; italics in original).

In Africa, this stylistic device is part of musical aesthetics. Thus, if four drums are playing four separate rhythms which in themselves are quite simple, they are staggered in such a way so that their main beats *never coincide*. At the same time, one rhythm pattern may start *near the end* of another. The result of this technique is a high degree of rhythmic complexity, often with triple rhythms cross-beating with duple ones.

As is the case with the West African performance rules or conven-tions cited by Reisman, this musical style *in Africa* does not represent transition from one cultural style to another; it is simply a part of composition technique. In the New World, however, this pan-African stylistic device has been and continues to be employed in Afro-Ameri-can cultures as a communications strategy to represent, dramatize, or bring about transitions (rituals) of various kinds.

An excellent illustration of this point is provided by Herskovits in his description of Protestant hymn singing among a group of Trinidad "Shouters":

> But just as the essential rites of the cult are carried on beneath an overlay of conventionalized decorum, so these "Sankeys" [Protestant hymns from printed hymn-books] also mask more vigorous musical forms. This was disclosed when a recording was being made of "Jesus, Lover of My Soul." . . . After two verses, the singers, con-tinuing the melody, began to change their rhythm, introducing hand-clapping as the tempo became faster, until the hymn was transmuted into a swing idiom which in the proper setting would result in the spirit-possession that was simulated in the sounds made by the singers on the record. (Herskovits 1966: 345)

Here, "Africanization" is expressed on the musical plane by the addition of a complex rhythmic accompaniment to a staid Protestant hymn tune, whose melody line is altered in the direction of a percussive singing style. But, once again, there is more going on than what is conventionally called "expressive behavior." *The change in style is generating a ritual event, namely spirit-possession.* This topic will be taken up in detail below. For now, it is enough to say that notions such as the "thoroughgoing assimilation of Christian and pagan beliefs which has taken place among New World Negroes" (Herskovits 1966: 321), break down when particular performances and rituals are closely studied. It is precisely here that the ethnography of communication approach may be employed in order to arrive at some idea of the significance of the ordering of various codes and styles in particular communication events.

I am using "music" as the place where these various categories come together; chief among these is style-switching and its place as the symbol of transition between cultures, as well as its role in generating different kinds of ritual events.

In the discussion of musical form, the working assumption is that *"song forms and performances are themselves models of social behavior that reflect strategies of adaption to human and natural environments"* (Szwed 1970: 220; italics in original). Therefore, to sum up, it may be said that the central problem is to describe the patterned use of sounds, both linguistic and musical, which reflect and/or actually bring about changes from one social or psychological state to another. The focus here will be primarily on the ways in which transitions may be dramatized in sound, and the way such dramatizations are linked to performance rules in rituals in the United States and in other New World cultures.

3. AFRO-BRAZILIAN CARNIVAL: WHERE THE PRIVATE BECOMES THE PUBLIC

An analysis of the Brazilian carnival is important for the discussion that is to follow in later sections. Indeed, what takes place in carnival is a model, at the societal level, for what occurs on a smaller scale in other New World Negro contexts. The underlying rule may be stated as follows: *In the New World, African-derived performance rules emerge during the liminal or transitional stage in rites of passage; as they emerge, they create the ritual setting.* This formulation will first be applied to a discussion of the Afro-Brazilian carnival and then to a song associated with it.

Carnival is the occasion on which the private behavior and corporate conventions of various Afro-Brazilian private organizations, including cults, secret societies, and voluntary organizations, are put on display in a communal rite of passage. All of these groups comprise a kind of storehouse of ritual behavior, which generally occurs in private contexts for most of the year. On certain fixed occasions, however, these groups come out into, and transform, the public domain.

My discussion is in two parts: the first includes the ethnographic background of carnival in Brazil, and the second discusses the structure of a carnival song that demonstrates how the emergence of African-derived performance rules, transforms, or ritualizes, the setting.

The general features of pre-Lenten carnivals in the New World have been well described by Roger Bastide: "It is the new carnival, with its parades, its masks, its dances, which has triumphed in the southern United States, in all the Antilles, in the Guianas, and in Brazil. But it has preserved its dualistic structure down to the present day—the white man's carnival in ballrooms which charge steep admission prices, and the black man's carnival, in the streets" (1967: 175). It would be a mistake to describe the black carnival in terms of "crowd" or unstructured behavior simply because it takes place in the streets. Outdoor carnivals are highly structured events and are tied to a firmly established base of cults and clubs, some of which have histories of more than three hundred years. Paradoxically, the seemingly public street carnival includes a greater variety of organized private behavior than does the more European indoor celebration.

The Brazilian pre-Lenten carnival is the most elaborate and certainly the best known of all. Like the others, it has a dual nature, indoor and outdoor, white and black. This carnival, and especially its parade, is a liminal event in the sense that it is a "betwixt and between" time when cultural forms are displayed, which would otherwise remain more or less in hiding. Afro-Brazilian private behavior comes out and becomes public, all in a highly organized way. In the process, the public domain, the streets, are "Africanized."

The Brazilian carnival parade may be seen as a transition zone between various cultural styles, European, on the one hand, and African and Amerindian, on the other. This boundary situation has been outlined by Arthur Ramos in his description of the starting place of the carnival parade in Rio de Janeiro:

> Every year, the Eleventh of July Square in Rio de Janeiro receives the avalanche of this collective catharsis. Here, carnival is no more than a pretext. Within a very short time, we witness the recapitulation of an entire collective life. Institutions which are fragmented, crumbling and attenuated: their surviving elements are gathered

together in the "Eleventh" Square. This place is a great grindstone, a gigantic mill which fashions unconscious material and prepares it for its entry into "civilization." We are witnessing an activity similar to dreamwork ("Traumarbeit"): condensations, masks, sublimations, derivations. . . . The "Eleventh" Square is the boundary between black culture and white European culture, a boundary without precise limits, where institutions interpenetrate and cultures merge. (1954: 255–258)

Ramos was a psychiatrist, and it is clear from this passage that he saw the Rio carnival in terms of a psychological model, what he called the "irruption of the 'folkloric unconscious' into 'civilization' " (1954: 257); that is, "old images of the black continent, which were transplanted to Brazil," appear in the carnival procession. Ramos states: "The folkloric unconscious can be considered an archaic, undifferentiated structure, which breaks into the life of civilized man beneath the form of superstitions, survivals, pre-logical values; in a word, folklore" (1954: 258). This psychiatric, or really Jungian, interpretation of the connection between African folklore and the carnival setting only serves to mystify, and it is hardly an adequate explanation of the event.

Roger Bastide has supplied a more acceptable view of the boundary situation between "white" and "black" in the Brazilian carnival:

What is interesting to note is that all the African folklore, on its way to extinction with the arrival of younger generations, and all the [New World] Negro folklore, created by the Church but today forbidden by it ("Congos," "Mozambiques"), refuse to die and persist in the carnival. The royal dignitaries of the [African] religious associations who are no longer permitted to dance in front of the Church, appear in the Carnival in the form of Afoshê (Bahia) and Maracatú (Recife). . . . (Bastide 1967: 175)

Thus, the boundary is almost always crossed in the direction of more African cultural forms.

Bastide comes close to but does not state the private/public distinction I consider crucial. He does mention the African religious associations of the cities of Northeastern Brazil; he does not, however, give a full picture of the extent to which various voluntary associations form the underpinning of the outdoor carnival, and how each of these groups has its own way of "coming out."

A much fuller description of one Brazilian street carnival is supplied by an American ethnographer, Katarina Real, who worked in Recife in Northeastern Brazil (Real 1967). She studied twelve different *types* of carnival associations, which include more than one hundred eighty individual groups (p. 150). Each of these groups has a more or less permanent place in the Recife carnival. Each type of association has its own complex history. Some of them originated in medieval Portuguese guilds which then became the model for carnival clubs for freed slaves, who, in turn, developed and elaborated the guild processions along African lines (p. 25). Part of their procession included steps from *capoeira,* a combat dance from Angola (p. 31).

Another important group in the Recife carnival, the Maracatú, developed out of the processions of colonial Brazil which represented various African "nations," voluntary associations comprising slaves from the same tribe. In time, the Yoruba nation came to dominate this procession, so that the head priestess, or *iyalorixá,* of the Recife Yoruba cult house (*Xangô*), became the queen at the head of the procession which represented the coronation of the Congolese Kings. Here is one example of the fusion of public and private roles in carnival, as well as the fusion of "cult" with popular culture: the head of a public procession is also the titular and spiritual head of a cult group (Real, p. 74).[2]

What is important here is that when each group comes out, it often displays its most sacred and private behavior in public. Thus, one of the "Indian" groups of Recife, the *Caboclos de Pena* ("Feathered Indians"), are members of *catimbó,* a men's secret society of Amerindian origin (Real, p. 90). According to Real's informants, many of them come out in shamanic trance. This behavior is also manifested in the dance of another group, the Tupi Papo Amarelo Indians, which they call the *macumba.* Here, the whole "tribe" is in trance: "If the drum beat is very strong, the people in that line go into trance" (p. 119). Other groups display their cult's or secret society's most sacred objects, such as religious statues or sacred animals.

The carnival in Recife is the most richly folkloric in Brazil, but others follow the same basic pattern. They are all corporate rituals and corporate displays. In the carnival of Rio de Janeiro, one of the most important carnival associations is the *escola de samba,* or samba school. This is a type of voluntary organization formed in the hillside slums around Rio. For much of the year in between carnivals the

---

[2] A very significant parallel to this feature of the Recife carnival is found in the Rio carnival, where the head of some *escolas de samba* (samba schools) are also *pais* (lit., fathers) of the Umbanda religious cult. Structurally, this is the exact parallel to Recife; historically, it represents a later development, since both Umbanda and samba schools date from the post-slavery era. The Rio fusion may be seen as a detribalized version of the Recife situation, where the public-private levels are tied to the African nations of the Congolese and the Yoruba, respectively. Umbanda and samba schools are not tied to any particular tribal base, but instead are seen as "Brazilian" phenomena.

samba schools work out and practice elaborate routines which involve costumes, dance steps, and songs. While membership in these groups is related more to economic status than to "race" or color, many of the members of the schools are black; their music is the *samba de rua,* or street samba, and many of their instruments are of African origin.

The Song: "Pede Passagem" ("Asking for Room")

Like the carnival parade, "Pede Passagem" is a transition zone between two cultural styles. The subject of the song is the entry of the samba schools into the carnival parade in Rio de Janeiro. The song represents this event in musical terms, through the staggered entry of percussion instruments. Style-switching takes place gradually until a point is reached where a dramatically marked crossing over into a different musical style is fully effected. "Pede Passagem" must, therefore, be discussed as a transformation and as a ritual process.

At this point it would be convenient to draw up a chart which represents in schematic form the shifts in style and the changes in setting and social categories which the former shifts symbolize. The column on the left is a list of features which are transformed into those in the righthand column. Each of these contrasting pairs will be examined below:

Bossa nova	*samba de rua* (street samba)
Guitar	Afro-Brazilian percussion ensemble
Indoor	outdoor
Solo	chorus
Song	march
European	African

The text of the song follows; below it is a translation.

Instrumentation	*Text* [3]
Guitar	1. Chegou a hora da escola de samba sair,
	2. deixa morrendo no asfalto uma dor que não quis.
add: *teleco-teco*	3. Quem não soube o que é ter alegria na vida,
	4. tem tôda a avenida p'ra ser muito feliz.
add: *tamborim*	5. Ai, arrasta felicidade pela rua,
add: *reco-reco*	6. esquece a quarta-feira e continua
	7. vivendo, chegando. Traz unido o povo cantando com vontade,
	8. levando inteiro um estandarte, uma verdade,
	9. seu coração

[3] Text and music copyright 1966 by Sidney Miller.

Instrumentation	Text
add: *afuchê*	10. Vai, balança bandeira colorida, pede passagem p'ra viver a vida.
add: *surdo*	11.–20. (Repeat)
(guitar drops out)	

Translation:

1. It's time for the samba school to come out,
2. to let die on the asphalt a sadness it never wanted.
3. Whoever has never known what it is to have joy in life,
4. has the whole street in which to be happy.
5. Ai, it spreads joy through the street,
6. it forgets about [Ash] Wednesday and keeps on
7. living, moving. It brings the people, united, singing
8. strongly, bearing a standard, a truth,
9. their hearts.
10. It comes, waving its colored banner, asking for room to live its life.
11.–20. (Repeat)

To the left of the text I have listed the musical instruments in the order of their entry into the performance. It is important to point out that in the particular version of this song that I am analyzing,[4] the text makes up only part of the song's total message. The song's meaning may be said to be encoded at two levels, it's semantic content and it's musical style. The switching that takes place at the level of the background accompaniment lends the song a significance it otherwise would not have. In other words, it is necessary to analyze not only the verbal sign system (the text), but the musical sign-system (the changes in instrumentation) as well. These two sign-systems converge at the level of a "sound and meaning" relationship which will be analyzed in detail below.

In a sense, the version of this song by Nara Leão reflects the conflict between the social meanings which are attached to two musical forms, the bossa nova and the street samba. The former style appeared in the early 1960's as a reaction to the outdoor, "hot" street samba. The bossa nova was, in fact, an attempt to cool the street samba off, to move it indoors and to sit it down. In sum, the bossa nova movement was an attempt to de-Africanize the samba.

This point was explicitly made in a recent interview with Carmem Costa, a Brazilian samba star of the 1940s. In response to my questions about bossa nova, she replied: "If it's really a dance, show me the steps!" That is, this form was divorced from the kinetic base of the samba as a march or ring-dance, and had become more of a Europeanized concert form.

[4] By Nara Leão, on Philips record (Brazil), 632.787.

As a counter-response to this movement, there has grown up in Brazil a genre known as the protest samba. The label is self-explanatory: these songs deal with social and political issues in explicit terms and use the traditional street samba form as their musical vehicle. The recordings of Nara Leão abound in such songs. In these compositions, it is primarily the texts which convey the protest message. The uniqueness of "Pede Passagem" and its importance for this study lies in the way it uses the contrast between musical styles to generate a social meaning.

The song begins with an introduction by an unaccompanied guitar in bossa nova style.[5] This may be described as muted and "indoor." Lines 1–2 introduce the voice of Naro Leão over the guitar, singing in the vibratoless, lagging style associated with the bossa nova. By line 3, a percussion instrument enters, playing a rhythm known as *teleco-teco,* an important component of the street samba. At line 5, the *tamborim* enters. This is a small, tuneable hand-held drum used extensively in street samba bands. At line 6 appears the *reco-reco,* a box-mounted spring scraped with a stick to produce a rasping sound. At line 8, the *afuchê,* a gourd rattle covered with a network of beads, comes in. Each continues to play its own characteristic rhythm, so that by line 10 a very complex, multilinear rhythm pattern has been built up behind the solo voice. At line 11, the vocalist and guitar drop out, a *surdo* or parade drum is added, and a chorus appears and repeats the entire text over the full percussion ensemble.

The transition from bossa nova to street samba has been effected by a switch which takes place in the background accompaniment and in the carrier of the melodic line. Without this switching, the song would merely remain a statement *about* the samba schools. With the switch, however, the reference of the text, these schools, symbolically enter into the performance. The rhythmically complex, march-based style associated with them gradually intrudes into the originally solo-voiced, guitar-based song.

This switch from a solo to a collective style is directly tied in with the overall Africanization of the performance. To phrase it another way, more African performance rules "come out" and transform the performance. This point is corroborated by Alan Lomax's study of world folk song styles, which he calls Cantometrics. He defines this as follows:

The Cantometric system looks at song performance as a specialized act of communication whose principal function is to organize the

[5] See the Appendix, pp. 117 ff, for the text and music of the songs discussed in this paper.

response of human collectives in ritual or ritualized situations. It views all song performances in terms of three basic models:

1. Well-integrated and highly cohesive group performance in which the participants conform to an agreed-upon communication plan in a highly disciplined and orderly manner.

2. Moderately or poorly coordinated group performances, in which the participants follow the agreed-upon plan, but show a relative degree of independence from it.

3. Solo performance in which a skilled virtuoso dominates the communication space for a period, thus imposing his communication upon his more or less silent and passive listeners.

The extraordinary homogeneity of African song style is the result of the almost universal use by Africans of the first of these patterns— the highly cohesive, complexly integrated song model. Black Africans synchronize their motor and their vocal acts more tightly than the people of other culture regions. The set of song performance traits which facilitate vocal synchrony and produce unified choral performances are shown, in what follows, to link most Black African culture areas [including Afro-America] into a tight stylistic cluster. (Lomax 1970: 188)

Clearly, the transformation of "Pede Passagem" from Lomax's model 3 to his model 1 sums up the style-switching that takes place here and that links together all the features listed above. It is important, however, to go beyond this kind of style trait listing and to reach a conclusion as to what meaning this switch generates.

An action is symbolically carried out in this version of "Pede Passagem." One could say that this action is effected by the calling up or conjuring of one sign-system (the musical style) by another (the text). These two sign-systems then converge or co-occur in the second half of the song. The text may be seen as having an almost magical function: it does not just talk about the samba schools (a *reference*); it causes them to appear in the music (an event). We are close to a distinction between different types of speech forms, those whose primary function is to describe or express, and those utterances which *do* something or actually carry out some action. The latter are referred to as performative utterances (Austin), and we may extend this notion of performative acts in speech behavior into the realm of similarly active or "doing" (as opposed to merely "expressive") features of musical behavior.

So far I have shown how the song's musical form symbolizes an action carried out. It is now possible to say more specifically what this action is, and to relate both the song form and this action to my earlier discussion of the ritual nature of carnival in Brazil.

Perhaps the most significant lines of text in this regard are 6–7:

Esquece a quarta-feira e continua vivendo, chegando.
(It forgets about Wednesday and keeps on living, moving.)

In the pre-Lenten celebration, Ash Wednesday traditionally marks the end of carnival. Many Brazilian songs speak of this Wednesday as a day of sadness, when the samba schools return to the slums and begin preparing the next year's routines.[6]

The meaning of lines 6–7, then, is that the samba schools do not go back "indoors" but instead stay in the streets, traditionally their domain for only the four days of carnival, and make them their own. It could be said that the first part of the song talks about such an event, which the second "transformed" half symbolically carries out. The transition from "reference" to "event" moves the song outdoors and into the street, while the chorus that takes over the melody line become the actors in the ritual of "coming out."

By means of style-switching, the song crosses stylistic boundaries in its movement from "white" to "black"; this, in turn, symbolizes the crossing of a social boundary, from "indoor" to "outdoor." It turns samba schools into a metaphor for what one could call the "structured liminality" that prevails in the outdoor street carnival. That is, the participants in this event are not at all like those ritual subjects-in-transit, described by Turner, who have been stripped of all roles in the liminal period and have nothing (Turner 1967: 98). In the carnival, people *can* "be themselves" while at the same time acting out institutionalized roles.

It is clear, then, that the kind of ritual represented by the carnival, while clearly liminal in nature, is quite different from those analyzed by Turner. The differences are due to the cultural duality present in Brazilian society, and to the boundaries between private and public behavior discussed above. "Pede Passagem" breaches this boundary by linking styles attached to different domains of meaning, and by acting out this boundary-crossing by means of style-switching.

4. "El Santo en Nueva York": Public Possession

This section will be divided into four parts: (1) the ethnographic background of slave religion in Cuba, with emphasis on Yoruba

[6] For example, "Marcha da Quarta-feira de Cinzas" (Ash Wednesday March), by Carlos Lyra and Vinicius de Morais.

ritual; (2) the historical development of Yoruba ritual in Cuba as a result of changes in social organization brought about by slavery; (3) the music of *santería* as the Yoruba religion in Cuba is known; (4) the migration of santería to New York City, and the impact this religion has had on popular culture there. In the latter part of the discussion, the ethnography of communication approach will be applied.

The Ethnographic Background

Cuba, like Brazil and other New World colonies, had a multi-ethnic slave society. The major tribal divisions were among the Yoruba, known in Cuba as *Lucumí,* the Congolese, the Dahomeans, and the Efiks. Each of these groups maintained its own tribal culture, preserved in good part through the institution of the *cabildo* (Bastide 1967: 89). This was a voluntary organization comprising slaves of the same African tribe or "nation." As in Brazil and other parts of the New World, such organizations were a largely urban phenomenon. They served as the source for *santería* and for other African-derived religions and secret societies in Cuba. While African traditions were preserved through the cabildos in an organized way and in urban settings, there is evidence to show that even on the plantations tribal consciousness among slaves of different ethnic origins was maintained through the various African religions.

On the basis of a narrative written by a black Cuban born into slavery in the middle of the nineteenth century, it is possible to get some idea of how well African religious traditions, including ritual language, were preserved by individual slaves even when far removed from any urban institutional framework:

> I knew of two African religions in the barracoons [slave quarters]: the Lucumí [Yoruba] and the Congolese. . . . [The latter] were more involved with witchcraft than the Lucumí, who had more to do with the saints and with God. . . . The Lucumí were at it when you least expected it. I have seen old Negroes on the ground for more than three hours at a time, *speaking in their own tongue and prophesying* [italics added]. The difference between the Congolese and the Lucumí was that the former solved problems while the latter told the future. This they did with *dilogunes,* which are round, white shells from Africa with mystery inside. . . . The Lucumí and Congolese did not get on either; it went back to the difference between saints and witchcraft. (Montejo 1868: 33, 34, 37)

This passage is important for two reasons: it firmly locates two important focal points of Yoruba religion in Cuba, worship of the "saints," Yoruba deities identified with figures from Catholicism, and divination (see Bascom 1952). It also identifies *Lucumí,* the Yoruba language in Cuba, as the prophetic tongue, associated both with divination and with prophetic speech. This latter practice involved belief in "possession" by the deities, and the topic of trance and spirit-possession must now be discussed in some detail.

As pointed out by Erika Bourguignon, who directed a large cross-cultural research project into altered states of consciousness:

> [These altered states] are present in all human societies and un-doubtedly have occurred since [the] earliest times of human exis-tence. They may occur in both normal and pathological forms, and they are subject to modification through learning and suggestion. They represent, in other words, recurrent types of human behavior, available to be experienced by some, to be observed by others. As such, they represent raw materials for potential cultural utilization, much as is the case for dreams. . . . As such, they are available for cultural interpretation and cultural patterning, for possible inte-gration within an institutional, often ritual framework, integration within a world view and a value system. (Bourguignon 1971: 12, 13)

Bourguignon has suggested that the term *trance* be applied to the altered state itself and to its accompanying physiological manifesta-tions. These may include sweating, trembling, and hyperventilation (overbreathing). The terms *possession-trance* and *spirit-possession* should be applied to trance states when such behavior is interpreted as caused by outside, supernatural forces and entities. Trance, then, is an analytic or *etic* category, while spirit-possession is a folk or *emic* one.

In Africa, possession-trance is an extremely widespread belief, and as such is a phenomenon that appears in a wide variety of contexts. Thus, Zaretsky's *Bibliography of Spirit Possession and Spirit Medium-ship* (1967) lists almost five hundred entries drawn from all over the African continent. In another survey of the ethnographic literature dealing with trance and possession, Erika Bourguignon, using Mur-dock's *World Ethnographic Sample* as a base, has reviewed one hun-dred fifty-six societies of sub-Saharan Africa. She found the belief in spirit-possession present in ninety-eight of these groups; simple trance was present in twenty-one, while thirty-seven showed neither (Bourguignon 1968: 352).

For Dahomey, the following has been reported:
[Spirit-possession] occurs regularly among the Nagô-Yoruba . . . during rites for *orisha.* . . . These deities are seen on the one hand as founders of descent-groups, and on the other hand as forces

of nature. People who become possessed by *orisha* . . . in the course of a ritual show behavior of a very disciplined kind. Such behavior is modelled on the traditional picture of the personality of the being who is supposed to be incarnated in them. (Verger 1969: 50)

It is important to point out that Yoruba possession-trance, as a highly conventionalized occurrence, follows strict performance rules. Knowledge of these is generally shared by members of the culture, so that as soon as a possession takes place, the identity of the possessing deity is immediately known to onlookers. As evidence of this, Verger points out:

> As new orisha appear [in the course of a ritual], symbolic objects are distributed to the *olorisha* [literally, owner of the *orisha*] as follows: Ogun Fashina: a pointed cap, two *aja* (hand bells) and a cutlass.
> Shango: a double axe or *oshe.*
> Oya: a fan. . . . (Verger, p. 59)

These are highly standardized symbols, which serve to mark the trance state and to identify the possessing deity. They are mentioned here because they occur in a New World context to be discussed below.

It must be stressed that possession-trance here is not an end in itself. Instead, the "deities" interact with the public, speaking, prophesying and dancing. In fact, these activities do not begin until after the onset of possession-trance. This point is also important for later discussion.

Santería: the Yoruba Religion in Cuba

The religion of santería derives principally from Yoruba sources (Bascom 1951; Cabrera 1968). It passed through the centuries from a tribally-based religion of the cabildo and the plantation to a national one, embracing all colors, races and classes. It was by no means a women's or poor person's deprivation cult, nor one limited solely to Cuban blacks.

It might be said that the current practitioners of this religion have been acculturated to Yoruba patterns. They have maintained a remarkable fidelity to Yoruba traditions in their ritual language (Bascom 1952; Cabrera 1957), systems of divination (Bascom 1952), music (Ortiz 1965), use of herbs (Cabrera 1968), as well as in other beliefs and practices. Possession-trance plays an important part in santería, as it does among the African Yoruba. Bastide has pointed out two important differences in the occurrences of this phenomenon in Nigeria and in Cuba:

> In Nigeria, the worship of the gods (*orisha*) is tied at the same time to the lineages and to the cults; the *orisha* is considered founder of the line and his worship is presided over by the oldest lineage head; this office is transmitted from generation to generation, but without mystical trance. At the same time, certain members of the lineage and also certain persons outside of it who have been called by the deity after a sickness or in a dream, form cult groups, whose members dance in honor of the *orisha* and are possessed by them. . . . However, slavery [in the New World] completely destroyed the lineages. The worship of the family lineage has disappeared. (Bastide 1967: 112); (cf. Bascom 1944)

In Cuba, the Yorubas adapted to the situation of slavery by grouping together in a single organization all the worshippers of all the *orisha*. This was necessary because the social organization that in Nigeria supported separate cults for each *orisha* was disrupted by slavery. The result of this was a new ritual cycle, in which worship no longer consisted in calling one of the deities in particular. Instead, all of them were called, according to a fixed hierarchic order known in Cuba as *shiré* (Bastide 1967: 113). The cycle always opened and closed with an invocation to Elegguá, the Yoruba threshold deity and trickster figure. The consequence of this new ritual ordering was that in Cuba there would be a multiplicity of simultaneous possessions within a single ritual. This was different from the situation in Nigeria, where "everything would stop as soon as someone became possessed" (Bastide, p. 113). Thus, possession rituals in Cuba became highly communal events, and a variety of performance rules would emerge as the various *orisha* began to possess their worshippers.

The Music of Santería

In Cuba, part of what has been termed Yoruba acculturation to Hispanic patterns involved the identification of the *orisha* with saints and other figures from the Catholic religion (Herskovits 1937; Bascom 1951). The deities thus became known as *santos,* and the music employed in the *shiré* sequence became known as *toques de santo;* the whole ritual was called a *bembé.* These were the most public ritual events of santería. Conventionalized possession-trances would take place among initiated worshippers, known as santeros and santeras, in the context of singing, drumming, and dancing. "Accidental" first possessions might also occur at *bembés* among onlookers. They would then have to be initiated at once, in order to "seat" or socialize the possessing deity.

Within the *shiré* sequence, each deity had its own rhythms and melodies, as well as its own style of dancing and moving when manifesting through a worshipper. In the music connected with santería that has come out of Cuba and is available on recordings, it is possible to detect three distinct styles. While it might be argued that these represent different levels of acculturation, they really help to support the private/public distinction outlined in the previous section. They also demonstrate how "switching" occurs simultaneously in linguistic and musical domains, and how it is employed to create a ritual event.

The first style is closest to Nigeria Yoruba drumming, and makes use of a trio of *batá* drums. These are shaped like a "truncated cone, giving two heads of different size and tone" (from notes to "Drums of the Yoruba," recorded by William Bascom; Ethnic Folkways Library FE 4441); they are held horizontally and struck on both ends. These drums, accompanied by a gourd rattle covered with a network of beads (*atchekeré*), various gongs (*agogó*), and rattles (*maracas*), as well as by voices singing melodies with texts in Lucumí, are directly involved in calling down the various deities (see Bascom 1951 and Ortiz 1965).

The second style, it might be argued, is more "acculturated," since songs in this style show the influence of Cuban popular music, and have the same instrumentation as the popular songs. This includes a trumpet section, piano, bass, gong, and drums. While the traditional song texts of santería were always in Lucumí, the more popular-style songs were always sung in Spanish. It could, therefore, be argued that "acculturation" was symbolized here on two levels: musical style and instrumentation, as well as the choice of linguistic code in which the text was sung.

Another way to look at these songs is in terms of a private/public distinction. That is, the musical *form* is public, since it reflects the prevailing popular mode. But this form only masks a private *content,* which deals with what is often a detail from the system of beliefs and practices of santería. An understanding of these songs' content presupposes an extensive background knowledge of this religion.

For the focus of this section, the most significant variety is the third. Songs in this style begin in the "acculturated" or "popular" mode, with Spanish texts, and then shift into a more Yoruba or Lucumí mode. That is, trumpets and piano drop out, *batá* drums are added, and the text shifts into Lucumí.[7]

---

[7] See, for example, "Elegguá Quiere Tambo" (Elegguá Wants Drums), on the recording "Homenaje a los Santos," Seeco Records, 9269.

Underlying this switch is the rule that Spanish and Lucumí comprise the total linguistic repertoire for the practitioners of santería, and that a switch from the former language into the latter, coupled with parallel shifts in musical style, change the nature of the performance taking place. That is, the switch into Lucumí and *batá* drums turns the song into a *bembé*, or possession dance. A song that becomes a trance-event for the performer may, in turn, trigger trance behavior in the culturally conditioned listener.

One illustration of the performance rule underlying this type of transformation may be drawn from the work of Celia Cruz, a santera who is also one of the best-known figures in Afro-Cuban popular music. Like Elegguá, she is a threshold figure, on the boundary between what might be termed "cult" and (popular) "culture." Her recordings always contain several songs to the *santos,* and a recent album of hers recorded in the United States with the orchestra of Tito Puente (also a santero, according to informants) contains four songs to the *santos* out of a total of ten selections.

The opening few lines from the first song on the record will suffice to show the intimate link between "cult" and popular culture, and the underlying performance rules which govern this relationship:

Yo soy Lucumí,
y bailo pa' ti;
yo tengo mi *ache,*
y bailo *bembé.*
(I am Lucumí,
and I'm dancing for you;
I have my *power,*
and I dance for the santos.) [8]

What this passage demonstrates is that Celia Cruz's involvement with santería is not a static item of her biography, but is instead an on-going commitment, the underlying social fact which can transform her public "performances" into public rituals. That is, she can cross the boundary into trance behavior, at which point she is no longer merely "performing" but is showing forth her *aché,* the "power" that she derives from her *santo* (Yemaya, according to informants). Her songs may thus become sacred dances. Depending on the level of background knowledge and involvement in santería on the part of the listener, such performances would have different meanings. For the santero, with his knowledge of the performance rules which govern the showing forth of the deity, these would be rituals which served as

[8] "Alma con Alma," Tico Records, SLP 1221.

the public confirmation of the santera/performer's religious commitments.

"El Santo en Nueva York"

Large-scale Cuban emigration to New York City began in the early 1960s. With it came santería. It has been estimated (Robins 1970) that there are now about six thousand practitioners of this religion in the New York metropolitan area. This figure includes fully initiated members, as well as what might be termed "fellow-travellers," interested individuals who regularly attend *bembés,* and who may go for divinatory "readings."

While the actual number of santeros is rather small, the impact of santería has been felt very strongly in New York among the Cuban and non-Cuban Spanish-speaking population, as well as among a number of American Blacks. Santería-in-exile has become an important cultural focus for these groups, and has played a large part in stimulating interest in African, especially Yoruba, culture among both United States Blacks and large numbers of Puerto Ricans living in New York (Robins 1970).

As one index of this impact, radio stations which had formerly played all-jazz programs switched over to so-called "Latin" (Afro-Cuban) formats. The music of santería began to be played on these programs, often in the form of *toques* taken directly from recordings of the *shiré* sequence. While it could be argued that this is nothing but a commercialization and profanation of the ritual music, it could be said that the merging of "cult" with mass culture picked up new impetus in a new and alien environment. That is, instead of disappearing in exile, santería took on new life by "coming out," entering into, and even dominating certain aspects of popular culture in New York.

For example, cult practices and paraphernalia have been built into performance rules in various ways. Most significantly, possession-trance has become routinized. This phenomenon can occur in formal settings, such as theater concerts, or it can occur in informal settings, such as outdoor public places.

In the summer of 1970, I witnessed a conventionalized possession dance in Central Park. During the summer months, groups of Cuban and Puerto Rican drummers appear on weekends around Bethesda Fountain in the Park. While one of these groups was playing, a Cuban in his twenties began to dance in front of the drums. A large crowd gathered, and from the style of his dancing it was clear to many that he had "gone up with" (become possessed by) Changó, one of the *santos.* Besides dancing, he walked around and gave messages to members of the audience. To anyone unfamiliar with possession-trance and santería, he would no doubt have appeared quite insane. But his behavior allowed anyone familiar with the performance rules associated with the deities to identify the possessing *santo* as Changó.

On a more formalized and institutionalized level, a similar phenomenon is embodied in the figure of La Lupe, a popular Cuban vocalist who became initiated into santería in New York in 1968 (in order to please her *Puerto Rican* audience there, according to informants!). Initiation is known as *making santo,* and it is an elaborate ritual. As part of it, the initiate is required to become possessed by his or her *santo,* who is then permanently "seated" in the initiate's head. According to informants, La Lupe never succeeded in bringing hers, Ochún. But this is unimportant for the argument. What is significant is that during the period when La Lupe was being initiated and was subject to certain restrictions, such as the wearing of white, she made a commercial recording.[9] Its cover bears a picture of her in the dress of an *iyawô,* or initiate. This represents the complete merging of the role of public performer with that of cult priestess. Thus, in yet another context, a segment of private behavior has become public.

It is now possible to tie together some of the threads of argument, and to show how the ritual structure of santería and its diffusion in the New World are reflected in the performance rules underlying an event of ritual communication. The focus of this part of the discussion is a song entitled "El Santo en Nueva York." Its text deals with the exile of the gods and with the changes in ritual observances brought about by the ecological and social differences between Cuba and New York City.

Below is the text, followed by a translation. See the appendix for a transcription of the music:

1. Yemaya e olódę akoyó Yemaya (*Chorus*)
2. El santo en Nueva York, el santo en Nueva York,
3. tiene su ritmo embrujador, y la santera, y el babalawô
4. tienen algo y no es amor.
5. Si te manda Petra, cuando te tiran los coco',
6. que no te tape la letra;
7. si te mira Amada, al tirar los caracoles,
8. te dicen del santo nada.
9. Mira que el señor trae el santo en New York.
   (*Band*)
10. Mira que el señor trae el santo en New York (*Chorus*)
11. Changó, ¿dónde está la ceiba, el álamo y el cundeamor? (tu ve')
    Mira que el señor trae el santo en New York (*Chorus*)

9 "La Lupe es la Reina," Tico Records, SLP 1192.

12. Aqui no tenemo' palma, ni ochile pa' mi, tambo', tambo';
      (*Chorus alternates with leader with same line until the end*)
13. Ni la cal ni la jutía, ni la hierba con olor, qué dolor. (*Chorus*)
          (*Band*)
14. Mira que el señor trae el santo en New York (*Chorus*)
15. Ogunare apreni achi ogwaniye (?), onile pa' mi, Changó, tu ve'. (*Chorus*)
16. Oní abé, oní abé, oní abé, Yemaya Yalode, Changó.
17. Harina con quimbombó para el grandioso Changó, tu ve'. (*Chorus*)
18. Traer el santo en New York, traer el santo en New York, mamá. (*Chorus*)
19. Ogunare apreni achi ogwani 'gwani 'gwani gwaniye, traer el santo en New York, (*Chorus*)
20. Oní abé, oní abé [10]

Translation:
  1. Yemaya e "owner of the river" akoyo Yemaya (*Chorus*)
  2. The saint in New York, the saint in New York,
  3. has a haunting rhythm, and the priestess and the diviner
  4. have something and it isn't love.
  5. If Petra tells you, when they throw the coconuts [in divination]
  6. not to cover up the [divination] figure;
  7. if Amada looks at you, when she throws the [cowry] shells [in divination],
  8. they'll tell you nothing of the saint.
  9. Look, the man is bringing the saint in New York.
          (*Band*)
 10. Look, the man is bringing the saint in New York (*Chorus*)
 11. Changó, where is the ceiba tree, the poplar and the cundeamor [fruit]?
      (*Chorus*)
 12. Here we don't have palm oil, nor pepper for me, drum, drum. (*Chorus*)
 13. Nor white lime nor the [sacrificial] bush rat, nor the fragrant herb, how sad. (*Chorus*)
          (*Band*)
 14. Look, the man is bringing the saint in New York (*Chorus*)
 15. Ogun, chief of the warriors ogwaniye [?], "landlord" for me, Changó, you see. (*Chorus*)
 16. "Owner of the fan" (*three times*), Yemaya "Mother at Outside," Changó (*Chorus*)
 17. Flour with okra for the mighty Changó, you see. (*Chorus*)
 18. Bringing the saint in New York, bringing the saint in New York, you see. (*Chorus*)
 19. Ogun, chief of the warriors [?], bringing the saint in New York (*Chorus*)
 20. "Owner of the fan" (*twice*)

The notion of code-switching may once again be employed as a tool in analyzing this song. Here, the switching between Spanish and Lucumí patterns with changes in musical style. Once again the process

[10] Words and music copyright 1969 by Justi Barretto.

of "Africanization" underlies the performance, with the musical form proceeding from a strongly North American-influenced dance band style, into an *emically* named Yoruba and Lucumí praise song style known as *kasha*.

The opening bars of this song are taken from the *toque* dedicated to Yemaya, one of the most important Yoruba *orisha* and Lucumí *santos*. This line in Lucumí, sung in the style associated with the *shiré* sequence, immediately establishes a sacred context. The band then shifts into a chord sequence which follows standard dance band harmony (lines 2–9). The text in the opening section (lines 2–12) laments the dearth of ritual items brought about by the "exile" of santería to New York. The text also mentions the problem of bringing the deities to speak through two of the forms of divination employed in santería. The first one mentioned here involves the throwing of a whole coconut, and the other, the casting of sixteen cowry shells, the *dilogun* referred to in the slave narrative quoted above (see Bascom 1952 for a full description of these systems).

An instrumental sequence then follows, and at line 10 a chorus enters. The song has begun to be Africanized in two ways: a call-and-response pattern is set up between leader and chorus, and the harmonic structure is simplified down to the alternation between two chords, C^7 and F, every two bars.

From line 11 to line 13, the lead singer enumerates all the ritual items missing in New York. These include palm oil, a basic ingredient in many ritual food offerings. The changes in the ecological setting also resulted in the absence of certain trees, such as the ceiba, in Cuba associated with Changó, the deity connected with thunder and lightning, as well as with strength and virility (Cabrera 1968: 221); absent, also, were many of the herbs known in Cuba. These were employed in folk curing, and the knowledge of them was embodied in an elaborate system of classification, in which each tree, herb, or leaf had as spirit-ruler one of the *santos* (Cabrera 1968).

After line 13, there is again an instrumental passage in dance band style. The chorus returns after this (line 14), and the song style then undergoes another important shift. The leader switches into Lucumí, and begins to recite some of the praise names of several of the *santos*, Changó, Ochún, and Yemaya. These include *onile* for Changó; it is a Yoruba word meaning "landlord." *Oni abé* is probably from *oni abebé*, Yoruba and Lucumí for "owner of the fan," one of Ochún's praise names and attributes, like those distributed in the possession rituals described by Verger. *Yalode* is a praise name for Yemaya, and is from the Yoruba *Iyalode*, literally "mother at outside," a title of the head of women and in charge of the market at Abeokuta, a

Yoruba town in Nigeria (personal communication, William Bascom). While reciting these praise names, the vocalist's song style becomes more percussive and rhythmically complex, employing pauses and repetitions (see lines 15–16 in the transcription). The drums answer the phrases in Lucumí and add to the rhythmic complexity.

The type of praise singing that appears here conforms in detail to a traditional Yoruba practice, both in Nigeria and Cuba. It has been described by Fernando Ortiz:

> This ritual polynomy, or recitation of the different names for each of the gods, as well as those belonging to many of them in the same invocation, is so characteristic that in the Yoruba language there exists a special word to signify this ritual practice: kasha, which is used in the religious songs of Afro-Cuban santería. Thus, in one of the songs to the goddess Yemaya it is said:
>
> > emí odé, omó odé,
> > omó odé, emí odé,
> > káchu, ma má iyá, gbe le yó.
>
> ("Here is what I say, your servant child. Your servant child, what I say: I recite your holy names! Eternal and true mother! Give me health and happiness!") (Ortiz 1965: 190, 247)

Immediately following the praise singing (line 17), the vocalist symbolically makes a ritual food offering to Changó, consisting of flour and okra, "one of the foods that the *orisha* Changó likes best" (Cabrera 1968: 532).

What this shift signifies is that even though drastic changes have occurred in the *natural* setting which render the practices of santería difficult, the *cultural* forms which pay homage to the deities are still intact. Thus, the problems expressed in the first part of the song are symbolically overcome in the second. This is accomplished through linguistic and musical code-switching. The appearance of traditional *kasha* singing is a reaffirmation of the presence of the *santos* in exile and of the continuing desire to honor them.

The most significant aspect of this performance is that it demonstrates the extreme portability of at least part of a whole ritual complex, and that it is performance rules which are the hardiest part of this religion, since they are the least subject to alterations due to changes in locale.

All of this takes place in the span of about three minutes on a recording considered highly "commercial" and one played on radio stations in San Juan, Puerto Rico, and in New York. Again, an understanding of the song's message is completely dependent on the background knowledge controlled by the listener. The opening dance-band format might be seen as a masking device which hides the real content of the song. The code-switching near the end is a type of de-masking, which symbolically reaffirms the ritual by moving away from the "acculturated" format and symbolically, from the problems created in the transplant of the religion to the United States. To further reaffirm the ritual, an occurrence of possession-trance during a live performance of this song by either the vocalist or a member of the audience would put the seal on the song's message, the presence of the *santos* in exile.

5. Afro-American Gospel Music: Shouting for the Lord

In the previous sections, I have dealt primarily with *code*-switching and its role in creating a ritual setting. In the Brazilian song, it is the *musical* code that shifts. In the Cuban example, clear-cut changes in the linguistic code, from Spanish to Lucumí, accompany changes in the music. In this section, I will be dealing primarily with *style*-switching within a single language. That is, in discussing gospel music, I will be looking for what might be termed *channel cues*. These include changes in intonation pattern, rhythm, and breathing rate, all within a single linguistic code. It is these features which create the ritual setting, what may be described as trance-events.

The Ethnographic Background

A linguistically-oriented approach may once again be employed to help illuminate an historical problem. The degree and extent of African retentions in the culture of United States blacks has been a much-debated subject. In regard to Africanisms in the linguistic code, recent investigations into the relationship between West African languages and Afro-American speech by a British researcher, David Dalby, have brought to light a considerable number of African retentions in the lexicon associated with jazz: "Dr. David Dalby has drawn some remarkable comparisons between Wolof words and currently surviving American Negro usage, relating 'jive' talk to the Wolof *jev,* meaning 'to talk disparagingly'; 'hip' to the Wolof *hipi,* meaning 'to open one's eyes'; and the jazz term to 'jam' to the Wolof word *jaam* for slave" (Oliver 1970: 93).

While this lexicon is associated with West African speech and musical patterns in the secular domain, there is linguistic evidence which demonstrates a connection between a West African religious practice and a term widely employed in Afro-American religion, "to shout":

The hand-clapping which accompanied musical performances in all parts of West Africa persisted in the American Negro church;

it was noted as early as the eighteenth century and remained a familiar characteristic of the services of the "Sanctified" and "Pente-costal" churches. In the 'thirties it was still far from uncommon for witnesses to report a "ring-shout"—a shuffling dance in counter-clockwise direction performed by a circle of worshippers which gradually intensified in tempo and collective excitement. In form and character it appears to have been close to the circular dances performed throughout West Africa. Dr. Lorenzo Turner even identified the term "shout" as being identical with the Arabic *saut* used by West African Muslim peoples to mean walking around the Kaaba. (Oliver 1970: 57)

Whatever the origin of the term *shout,* it is perhaps the most common way of referring to trance behavior among Afro-Americans in the United States. It has both a transitive and an intransitive usage; it is both agency and agent. As transitive *agent,* preachers and singers speak of "shouting" a congregation, sending them into trance. The communication events employed here are sermons and gospel songs, which are directly involved in trance induction. Thus, for example, preachers talk about "getting their congregation high" through their sermons. The same is true of the gospel groups known as "house-wreckers." These travel from church to church, "shouting" the con-gregations. The formal aspects of trance-inducing music will be taken up below.

As *agency,* it may be said that when shouting takes place on the individual level among preachers and singers, it is controlled within a communication event of speaking, singing, or a combination of speech and song. As in the Yoruba example mentioned earlier, trance behavior is not an end in itself, but is instead a highly controlled and culturally patterned activity. This behavior is usually productive of a message, often rhythmically complex and in the form of music. Thus, performance rules underlie trance vocalizations, which may occur in a variety of contexts.

The literature abounds in references to trance in Africa as an activity that takes place within speech events and musical settings. Examples could be drawn from all over the African continent, so it appears safe to assume that this relationship is a salient feature of African religious and communicative behavior. To cite one example, a study of messianic movements in the Congo reports that "Spirit-possession became a standard part of the services; when Kimbangu [the messianic leader] would become possessed while delivering a sermon, his initiates would be seized by 'the Spirit' and begin to quake" (Anderson, 1958: 54). Another example comes from the

Ethiopian Church of South Africa, a "nativist" church which combines African and European Christian patterns of worship. The description of the collective conventions here, the interplay between the preacher and the singers, strikingly recalls Reisman's Antiguan examples of "making noise" and "contrapuntal communication":

> The preacher, a fanatical little man in a long black gown, stands behind a table. Two women, one of them the minister's wife, have hymnbooks and lead the singing. They continue to sing even during the sermon, which forces the minister to shout. The preacher works himself up to a high pitch of excitement, addressing his congregation with a word from Gen. 24. . . . The preacher fights with both arms in the air, sobbing, crying, shouting, and groaning, and the others—while singing—listen to this message of the glorious future which is in store for true Ethiopians. (Sundkler 1961: 182–83)

While elements of the Kimbangu cult and of the Ethiopian Church have been introduced from the New World, Anderson and Sundkler, the authors of works dealing with these movements, are at pains to demonstrate the extent to which pre-contact African religious beliefs and practices have been syncretized with Christianity. What is important for the present study is their description of the communication forms employed in these churches, and their co-occurrence with trance behavior. These forms most likely represent, in the context of a different system of belief, the re-shaping and maintenance of pre-contact linguistic and musical practices related to trance behavior. These comprise an underpinning which has apparently resisted change and the new system of belief which has grown up around it.

These two examples from "nativist" African churches possibly represent the mapping of African prophetic speech, produced in trance, onto the sermon, a speech event derived from the European church. The features of prophetic speech have been described in detail for the Gã people of southern Ghana (Fitzgerald 1970), and the description probably holds true for other African groups as well. The speaking style described is controlled by a group of Gã mediums, generally women, who regularly enter into trance in order to receive messages from the gods and convey these to clients (p. 3). While prophetic speaking may involve a switch in linguistic code, "The most dramatic markers of prophetic speech are not, however, the possessed medium's switches in language or dialect. The alternative dialects simply provide interchangeable backgrounds, as it were, against which the prophetic speech style is displayed" (Fitzgerald 1970: 9). What is significant for this paper is that the prophetic style is distinguished chiefly by what I have called *channel cues*. For the Gã mediums' speech, these include changes in pitch, volume, vowel length, glottalization, overbreathing or hyperventilation, repetition of words, as well as various rhythmic effects (Fitzgerald, pp. 10–11). Many of these same features appear in the trance-associated part of Afro-American preaching and singing style, to be discussed below.[11]

Prophetic speech might be termed trance vocalizations in the service of society. In the Gã example, this speech generally occurs in a known language, and the channel cues which mark it as "prophetic" occur outside the core words of the medium's message. At the same time, Gã prophetic speech is managed as a performance that is connected with other aspects of Gã musical culture: "What emerges from listening to the performance of Gã prophetic speech is an impression of deeply embedded rhythm producing patterned pauses, hyperventilation, volume changes, glottalization and other non-standard speech behavior" (Fitzgerald, p. 12).

Again, this description might serve as the model for the markers of trance-produced messages in Afro-American sermons and gospel songs. In these forms, linguistic, musical and trance behavior are patterned together in much the same way as in the African and Afro-Cuban examples. That is, communication events can become trance-events for the "performer"; when this takes place, highly marked linguistic behavior, produced in dissociation, is introduced into the linguistic or musical structure.

It is, however, the differences between the songs of santería and gospel music that reveal an extremely important distinction between the place of trance behavior and possession belief in the two traditions, Afro-Cuban and Afro-American. In the former case, spirit-possession is a completely *overt* category, and is explicitly related to Yoruba traditions. Here, possession behavior is strongly marked on levels other than song style and is tied in with the worship of a pantheon, the members of which have clearly distinguishable characteristics and modes of behavior. In the music of santería, there is often a clear-cut shift into overtly "African" (i.e. Yoruba) behavior: an African tongue, Lucumí, replaces Spanish, and African instruments, *batá* drums, replace more European ones.

In gospel music, the occurrence of trance and possession behavior is marked at a much more *covert* level. There is no African pantheon of deities, and there is no African-derived liturgical language. In a word, Afro-American religion is not explicitly derived from any particular African tradition. Nevertheless, there is a core of performance rules which clearly relate gospel music to more overtly African beliefs

---

[11] It might be pointed out that hyperventilation is to be heard in the latter part of Herskovits' recording of "Jesus, Lover of My Soul," referred to on page 66 above (personal communication, William Bascom).

and practices, such as those embodied in Afro-Cuban santería. Because trance behavior is a covert category in black North American culture, and because it is so highly patterned and institutionalized within gospel music, its very presence has, for the most part, gone largely unnoticed until now.

In santería, a linguistic variable, the switch from Spanish to Lucumí, is one of the signals for the presence of an overt structure, spirit-possession. In gospel music, the underlying performance rules and signalling devices are similar, in the sense that a transformation in style takes place that coincides with the introduction of trance behavior into the lead singer's performance. The specific features of the signals are somewhat different, however. In gospel music, what begins as a *tune,* whose melodic structure does not vary with changes in the text, is turned into *preaching,* a ritualized, trance-produced form of speech which displays many features of the prophetic style described above. In a sense, the occurrence of trance in the analysis of gospel music must be *proven* through an analysis of the changes in the message output of the performer. No such proof, of course, is necessary in the case of santería, where the occurrence of spirit-possession has many more markers, and need not rely so heavily on code-switching as the only means to signal its presence. This strategy is thus relegated to a less important place as a performance rule in that tradition.

On the other hand, style-switching is the most important signalling device in Afro-American trance behavior, and it is possible to "prove" that trance occurs among North American black performers by comparing the alterations in channel cues and message forms of gospel singing-preaching with the results that have been obtained in the analysis of the features of trance-produced vocalizations in other traditions.

In using the term "trance-produced vocalizations," I am employing the findings of Felicitas Goodman, a researcher who has analyzed a considerable corpus of glossolalia utterances in several cultural settings. She defines glossolalia as a "non-linguistic event of phonation which does not involve the intent of linguistic communication" (1968: 2). The connection between this phenomenon and trance behavior is more fully elaborated by her in a later statement:

> We could now give the definition that glossolalia is an event of vocalization uttered while the speaker is in a state of dissociation termed trance. . . . I therefore propose to advance the hypothesis that the state into which the glossolalist places himself, or rather its neurophysiological correlates, drive, as it were, the brain centers responsible for the vocalizations. . . . I am suggesting, in other words, that the glossolalia is an artifact of the trance, it is generated

by it. I am thus hypothesizing that trance is the primary behavior pattern, and as such, it produces organizations similar to glossolalia patterning in breathing rhythms (Umbanda cult), mass trancing of the Shakers and in curative dances of native societies, to name just a few. What the artifact will be, is decided by the respective learning situation or cultural expectation. (1969: 127)

While trance behavior underlies both prophetic speech and glossolalia, it is necessary to emphasize that the former represents a highly-marked speech event, while the latter represents the loss of natural speech in trance, and its replacement by a non-linguistic series of sounds not intended to be communicative. In attempting to relate Afro-American trance vocalizations in speech and music to African models, the difference between the kind of trance-associated communication that takes place in black and white "marginal" churches in the United States firmly supports the argument for an historical connection between the patterning of trance behavior in the black churches and African forms. That is, glossolalia may occur in these black churches, but this phenomenon does not occupy the central position it has in the white churches. In the black churches, sermons and gospel songs are the places where trance is achieved, and they represent a highly elaborated patterning of trance behavior. This is quite unlike the trance rituals analyzed by Goodman, where glossolalia is more or less an end in itself and may be termed trance vocalizations in the service of the *individual*. The crucial difference between the patterning of trance vocalizations is that in the white churches where music is part of the service, glossolalia erupts *outside* the structure of the music itself. In the black churches, trance vocalizations occur *within* and become *part of* the music. At the same time, these gospel songs become the agent in inducing trance in others. Glossolalia does not play a direct role in sending others into trance.

I will first analyze a song in which the lead singer enters into trance, or "shouts," and I will point out the features which mark this state. I will then analyze the patterning of a song involved in trance *induction,* showing how prophetic speech or preaching combines with song to produce a type of "contrapuntal communication" directly employed in creating a ritual setting.

The Songs

The first song to be analyzed is entitled "It Ain't Nothing But Love" and was sung by the Five Blind Boys of Alabama at a church service recorded live in Brooklyn, New York.[12]

---

[12] On HOB Records, 293.

The song is in call-and-response form, with alternation between leader and chorus. For the purposes of this analysis, I have transcribed only the leader's part. See the Appendix for a transcription of the music.

Since it is only the leader, the equivalent of a trained medium or priest, who enters into trance, the main features of speech produced in this state will appear in his part of the total performance, which also includes an instrumental ensemble of organ, electric bass and drums.

The italicized portions of the text indicate an accompanying and very strongly marked constriction of the vocal chords. The words in parentheses indicate the system of responses which the leader sets up within his own performance, and which overlap with the responses of the helpers.

1. When you hear me prayin', it ain't nothin' but love (Lord God)
2. When you hear me prayin' (Yeah), it ain't nothin' but love
3. When you hear me prayin' (Lord Yeah), *it ain't* nothin' but love (*Lord*) love
4. Ain't nothin' but the fire (Good God A'mighty) comin' down from above
5. When you see me shoutin', it ain't nothin' but love (Lord God)
6. When you see me shoutin', it ain't nothin' but love
7. When you see me shoutin' (*Lord* yeah), *it ain't* nothin but love (*Lord*) love
8. Ain't nothin' but the fire (Good God A'mighty) comin' down from above
9. Let me tell you this . . . [Spoken]
10. I'm talkin' 'bout love, boys
11. God gave his only begotten son (Yes)
12. They hung him high, boys (*Lord,* yes)
13. Even stretched him wide
14. They drove nails in his hands (Lord)
15. Pierced the Savior in his side
16. I'm talkin', I'm talkin' 'bout love, boys
17. He did it for you an' me, wasn't that love?
18. The reason I say . . . [spoken]
19. When you see me *cryin',* it ain't nothin' but love (*My* God)
20. When you see me *cryin',* it ain't nothin' but love
21. When you see me *cryin',* (*Lord,* yes) *it ain't* nothin' but love (*Lord*) love
22. Ain't nothin' but the fire (Good God A'mighty)
23. Do you *feel the fire?* (Lord)
24. Do you *feel* the fire? (Lord)
25. *It gets all in your hands* (Lord)
26. *My my my my my feet, Lord* (Lord)
27. *And oh, and oh Lordy* (Lord)
28. I wonder wonder wonder *do you feel it?* (Lord)

29. *Do you feel the fire?* (Oh yeah)
30. Comin' *down* from above (Oh yeah), comin' down from above.

As ritual, this song must be viewed as a process and as a transition, the goal of which is for the lead singer to enter into trance and to produce a message while in that state. The category "trance" is defined in this song as the "fire coming down from above," and it is the lead singer's role to call down and display this "fire" to his audience. Thus, the opening melodic section (lines 1–8) establishes a kind of threshold which must be crossed before trance is achieved. Mixed into this section are elements of preaching style, which will be summarized below.

As with ritual form in general, there is a great deal of ambiguity in the structure of this song. We may contrast musical order, or tune, and musical disorder, or preaching. "In ritual, form is treated as if it were quick with power to maintain itself in being, yet always liable to attack. Formlessness is also credited with powers, some dangerous, some good" (Douglas 1966: 95). The elements of preaching style which threaten the "orderly" tune are a series of responses (Lord God, etc.) set up by the leader and which overlap with those of the helpers; in a call-and-response song they would appear to be formally redundant.[13] The second feature is a strongly-marked constriction of the vocal chords which accompanies various phrases in the text.

The first of these features, the singer answering himself, reflects the form of the Afro-American sermon, a speech event in which the preacher often enters into trance. When this takes place, there are marked shifts in the form, content, and speech style of the sermon. In terms of form, the only aspect to be considered at this point, the sermon begins with statements by the preacher followed by responses from his congregation. As the preacher becomes dissociated, he begins to give his own responses, thus incorporating the congregation's role into his own performance. After each of his trance-produced statements, generally preceded by an occurrence of hyperventilation, the preacher interjects formulaic statements such as "Good God" and "My Lord."

In the Five Blind Boys' song, these formulaic responses appear in the lead singer's statement of the opening melodic sections, before he has reached trance, and before he has fully introduced preaching style. Already, then, the *form* of the trance-associated part of the song-sermon is anticipated: the singer-preacher gives his own responses on top of

---

[13] It might also be pointed out that the overlap between leader and chorus is a feature of African song style retained throughout New World Negro music (see Waterman 1952).

the regular responses of the helpers. In line 1 of the text, for example, the helpers respond by repeating the last words of the leader's line, "It ain't nothin' but love." But the leader's own response, "My Lord," overlaps with theirs. The opening melodic sections, then, are formally ambiguous. Trance *form* makes an early appearance in the song.

In terms of vocal quality, the appearance of a noticeable constriction of the vocal chords suggests that there is a gradual raising of the singer's energy level as he approaches entry into trance. Such constrictions appear in the opening sections of sermons as well, until they finally co-occur with other features of prophetic style in the last sections of the sermon. This vocal quality is probably a universal concomitant of trance vocalizations, since it is characteristic of the glossolalia utterances as well. "A certain threshold must be reached, or a certain energy level achieved before phonation [i.e. glossolalia] is triggered. The concentration of energy necessary to reach and overcome this threshold causes a tensing of the muscles of the throat" (Goodman 1968: 15). In this gospel song, a cluster of constrictions occurs right before the shift into trance style (lines 19–22). Here, again, a feature linking trance and vocal style intrudes throughout the song.

Lines 23–29 consist of trance vocalizations. A basic question that could be asked here is, how do we know that the singer is in trance? Aside from the fact that he is saying so in these lines, there is the evidence drawn from the intonation pattern and certain other channel cues of these utterances. In regard to intonation pattern, from line 23 to line 29 there is a noticeable peaking effect in this pattern, with an ever-increasing differential in pitch between the first note of the utterance and the last. This increases gradually, so that by line 27 there is a leap of almost an octave between the first and second words of the utterance (see transcription in Appendix). Each of these vocalizations is followed by a sudden drop in volume and pitch, marked with the highly regularized response, "Lord."

The intonation patterns of the vocalizations in lines 23–29 are not only strikingly different from what precedes and follows them in this song; they also correspond precisely to what Goodman states is the typical pattern of the glossolalia utterance: "A rather even start in the middle range, a peak at the upper limit, and then a drop, attenuation or decay to the lower limit. The end of the glossolalia utterance *always* drops, and sometimes precipitously, often terminating in a sigh, or becoming so low as to be inaudible" (Goodman, 1968: 12).

It might be said that the underlying *form* of the glossolalia and preaching utterances is the same, but that they exhibit radically different linguistic and cultural patterning on top of this deepest layer of trance vocalization. Thus, the drop or sigh at the end of the glossolalia utterance corresponds to the sudden drop at the end of the preaching, which is "marked" with a response as noted above ("Lord"). The most obvious difference, of course, is that the glossolalia is primarily *sound,* while the preaching consists of linguistically *meaningful* statements.

Another important area of difference which shows strong cultural patterning is in the area of the rhythmic organization of these utterances. Goodman states as a kind of law that there is an "inverse ratio between richness of rhythm pattern and intensity of trance" (1968: 34). This strongly contrasts with the gospel example, which bears a closer resemblance to the Gã patterning cited above. A brief look at the music of lines 23–29 reveals very complex rhythms, which include repetitions, pauses and a rushing effect in line 28. It is probable, then, that gospel music represents a lower level of dissociation than is reached in glossolalia production. Deep trance is sacrificed for the ability to produce and communicate a complex message, in which linguistic content, paralinguistic features and kinetic behavior all combine to dramatize the reaching of the trance state.

Up to this point, I have focused on the relationship between preaching and song style. I have touched upon the clash between sound systems drawn from different domains, the song and the sermon. This clash has a role in trance induction, and the structure of gospel music shall now be examined from the viewpoint of the trancing member of the congregation.

To return briefly to the notion of "contrapuntal communication," the underlying rule there is simultaneity and non-complementarity in the speech activity of several individuals. In gospel music, the underlying rule is to combine speech with *music,* to produce what may be termed *paradoxical communication.* That is, sound sources from different perceptual domains are combined and their boundaries confused in a manner quite similar to the South African example cited earlier, where preaching and singing occur simultaneously but with no apparent relationship to each other.

In gospel, it is not natural speech that is combined with music; it is *prophetic* speech, or preaching, as described above. This preaching is either embedded into or else rides over a welter of background melodic and percussive lines which may be carried by either voices or instruments. When ritual dissociation is entered into within the gospel song, it becomes a trance-event linked to the sermon, and prophetic speech replaces the original melody. In these songs, only the lead singer goes into trance; the deeper this state, the more the melody line is altered by preaching style, generally in the direction of the intonation curve described above.

When the singer "shouts," he often demands a trance response from his congregation: he "shouts" *them*. In gospel, the congregation is encouraged and even commanded to enter trance, to "feel the Spirit." From the view-point of the formal aspects of trance induction, a rhythmic clash is set up between the preaching which transmits these commands and the web of cross-rhythms in which it is embedded. Both the unpredictable speech-accenting of the preaching-melody line, along with the over-breathing which marks the lead singer's phrase and sentence junctures, clash with the regularly stressed background rhythms. The listener is not sure whether he is to fit the preaching into the background rhythms, or whether he is to isolate the verbal message from this background. Perceptual domains and levels of structure are thus made highly ambiguous in the gospel song. It is unclear whether it is song or sermon, since it contains features of both.

The titles of many gospel songs suggest their trance-inducing function, which is brought out in the course of the song. One could make a long list of titles, such as "Come Up to Glory," "Let the Lord Be Seen in You," and "Meet Me Over Yonder."

The latter song has several striking features. One of them is the high elaboration, in the opening pre-trance threshold section, of the overlaps between leader and chorus; all of this takes place over an instrumental background of piano, bass, and drums. These overlaps include not only the system of calls and responses set up by the leader, but also the chorus's role in sometimes completing a line started by the leader. Below I have arranged a few lines of text from this song to show this overlap and to give some idea of the complex relationship between leader and chorus (for the complete text and musical transcription, see the Appendix). In notation, the symbol (X) represents a hyperventilation occurrence, which marks a phrase juncture in the leader's vocal:

(Leader) I remember   (X) I had to hang my head
(Chorus) -member when my mother died   I had to hang my head

(L.)   (X) I heard her say (X) (Oh Lord)   (X) over there
(Ch.) and cry   "Come on and meet me, over there"

(L.) (X) well, come on   (Lord have mercy)
(Ch.) Whoo!   Come on and meet me over yonder

The early appearance of hyperventilation recalls a point made in reference to a group of Jamaica revivalists: "The dancers expel the breath on a deep forward bend and suck it in with a grunting sound as they straighten up. This serves to induce possession-trance; however, it is also continued during the trance itself. . . . It is noteworthy that some of the physiological features of trance may be used to induce the state, by imitative anticipation" (Bourguignon 1970: 94, 101).

The pattern of leader-chorus overlap, hyperventilation, and progressive tightening of the leader's vocal chords progresses in this song until the point is reached where a "crossing-over" takes place. Here, the instrumental background drops out, while the chorus picks up a rhythmic figure from the piano part, foregrounds it and ascends into falsetto (see the transcription in the Appendix. This point is marked with an asterisk). It could be said that the background voices become percussive at the moment of transition.

This song fits the basic theme of ancestor worship, with various kin waiting for the trancer "on the other shore." Trance, then, is what brings the lead singer closer to his departed relatives. Once the crossing-over has been fully effected, every one of the leader-trancer's statements is preceded by a hyperventilation:

(X) I've got loved ones/ (X) they're all gone on before me

This breathing pattern is a *physiological* feature accompanying trance; it is also a feature of *cultural* patterning, which serves to mark trance utterances. At the same time, trance *induction* is involved, because the trancer is inviting his audience to meet him "over yonder":

(X) I want to know from you today/ (X) will you meet me there

Here, then, trance and trance induction are co-occurring phenomena, in a context that could hardly be called "Christian" at all.

On the purely stylistic plane, the introduction of preaching, which coincides with and expresses the trancer's mental state, separates out from the background of falsetto voices and percussion instruments. This recalls a point made by the Brazilian ethnographer, Edison Carneiro, who has stated that the hallmark of African musical style in religious songs is the "autonomy of the melodic line in relation to the music of the percussion instruments" (Carneiro 1964: 140). In gospel music, when melody line is replaced by preaching, this represents the entry of the preacher into the liminal zone known as trance. At the same time, his trance-produced messages clash with the helpers' statements and help send others into this state.

6. "I'M GOING HOME": PERCUSSION AND TRANSITION

The purpose of this section is to tie together some of the themes presented in earlier sections. The focus of the discussion will be two songs, one of them gospel and the other Puerto Rican. They both deal with the theme of "going home," and they employ similar strategies to communicate this transitional or liminal feature. The gospel song includes the element of trance, while the Puerto Rican song does not. Before taking up the analysis of these songs, it is necessary to fit them into a broader New World context.

The Ethnographic Background

The theme of "going home" is widely distributed throughout New World Negro contexts, and in general is derived from the earliest slaves' consciousness of exile, and of their desire to return to Africa. There exists a variety of emic labels that refer to "home." Such terms may appear in sacred or secular contexts, and the only real difference between the sacred and secular rituals which express the movement "home" is in the presence or absence of a reference to spirits or some other supernatural entity.

In general, the idea of going home had at first a quite literal meaning, namely, return to Africa. As the slaves' exile became a permanent condition, this theme lost its literal meaning and went through various transformations, ending up as a theme built into various communication forms. In Brazil, for example:

São Paulo de Luanda, capital of Angola, was the only one among the African ports of the slave trade to remain in the collective memory of the Brazilian Negro. This memory was kept in the [religious] songs of macumba, *Aruanda, Aluanda, Aluanguê*, of capoeira, *Aruandê*, of maracatú, *Zaluanda, Aruenda*. . . . The descendents of Angolans, Congolese and Cabindas and in general the Bantu-speaking African peoples kept and still keep alive the word, in all its enormous emotional significance:

N'Aluanda só se pisa de-vagá ("On Aluanda you must step slowly").

In the course of three centuries, wave after wave of slaves left from the port of Luanda, in slave ships similar to the Castro Alves, bound for Brazil.

These were the Negroes most subject to *banzo* ["the deep and sometimes fatal longing for their native land exhibited in the early days by the Negro slaves in Brazil" (Taylor 1963: 94)].

With the passing of the years, the word no longer designated the port of Angola; it came to embrace, ambitiously, the whole of Africa, mysterious and beloved land of peace which was transformed, for the Negro, into a Promised Land. (Carneiro 1964: 76)

For Haiti, the pattern is similar, with an added, sacred element: It is believed that the *loa*, or spirits, are able to travel back and forth to

Africa at will. In Haiti, the African place name Guinée (Guinea) became a generic term for Africa as "home." To cite one illustrative example, a Haitian dance, *Mambo Ayida*, contains the following verse in Creole:

Mambo Ayida é.
Pral nan Guinee, pinga ou misé m'tende.
Si ou jound bon ouanga wa po'té.

(Priestess Ayida é./ You go to Africa, take care you do not stay, I am waiting./ If you find a good protective charm carry it back.) (From Songs and Dances of Haiti, vol. 3, Folkways Fe4432)

Besides this transmutation of Guinée into a term for Africa, other African place names and tribal designations have undergone a process of conversion into deities (*loas*) and have been incorporated into the *vodun* pantheon:

> In considering the origin of Haitian religious belief and ritual, those African elements which have been retained in their aboriginal purity may be first presented. The importance of the Dahomean and Nigerian elements in the *vodun* cult are self-evident when the deities derived from the peoples of these areas are detailed. It has been stated that the name of one of the important "companies" of gods, Rada, is a contraction of the word *Arada*, which is the name of the Dahomean town Allada. . . . The term *Dahomey* itself also figures in the name of such *loa* as Erzilie Freda Dahomey, where Freda with all consistency represents a corruption of the name of Whydah, a Dahomean seaport. . . . Of the Petro group, Wangol (Roi d'Angole) is obviously Angola, while the designations [of the deities] Ibo and Congo speak for themselves. . . . But all recognition of geographical names as such has disappeared, and they have been transmuted into designations of gods. (Herskovits 1971: 270–71)

The idea of "home," then, having lost its original meaning, became a category in a cognitive system, and going there represented more of a psychological transition than an actual physical movement from place to place. This theme appears in many musical contexts, and probably represents the oldest stratum of New World Negro, as opposed to purely African, music. Thus, a Brazilian author writes:

> The songs [of the Recife Maracatú] affirm even more strongly that we are dealing with an exiled nation. . . . Let us look at this song of the "Old Cambinda Nation" of Palmares, one of the most important rural centers of the state, and as such, naturally a center of

Negro elements directly descended from African parents and grand-parents:

Leader:
O Princess Leopoldina,
Where is it that you're going?

Chorus:
I'm going away to Luanda
To see Senhor Dom João, my father.

(Ferreira 1951: 17)

The notion of ritual-as-transition fits such songs very well. These usually contain what might be called *action texts*, where a movement "back home" is symbolically carried out. One of the distinctive features of such songs is the gradual building of a complex multilinear rhythmic structures which symbolizes the activity of transition.

The general role of percussion as a marker of the liminal stage in rites of passage has been noted by Rodney Needham (1967: 604–614). He points out that noise-makers and percussion instruments are employed universally in such rites. For Needham, however, "percussion" means simply noise, unpatterned, a-rhythmic sound. One of his examples will suffice here:

Marriage rites are relevant, too, for at a European wedding there is a traditional parallel to the Chinese firecrackers: pans—more recently replaced by tin cans—are tied behind the wedding carriage, where they bang, resound and clash like mad. . . . Now this last is a crucial fact which shows a more fundamental correspondence with firecrackers, and with cordite salutations, namely that in these cases there is no rhythm. . . . What counts, therefore . . . is not rhythm, and certainly not melody, but nothing other than percussion. (Needham 1967: 614)

In view of the earlier discussions of the patterned use of sounds to convey "transition," this statement can hardly be said to do justice to the question, and indeed goes exactly counter to the Afro-American examples. Despite his inaccurate definition of "percussion," his point is important for a discussion of the musical examples to follow.

The Songs

The first song to be discussed is entitled "Me Voy Pa'l Monte," or "I'm Going [Back] to the Woods," and was recorded in New York City by a Puerto Rican group led by trumpeter Willie Rodriguez.[14] Like

---

[14] On Fonseca Records, No. 1120. Adelberto Santiago is vocalist.

most of the songs analyzed in earlier chapters, "Me Voy Pa'l Monte" is divided into sections of contrasting musical styles. The difference here is that these divisions and the changes in style they embody are directly linked to a text that deals with transition, the movement "home."

As noted earlier, Afro-Cuban religion and music have exerted a strong influence on the Puerto Rican community in New York City, so it is difficult to say whether the theme of "el monte" is a borrowing from Cuban culture, or whether it represents a widely distributed Afro-Caribbean theme. In regard to Cuba, *El Monte* is the title of a book by Lydia Cabrera that deals principally with Yoruba and Congolese religious beliefs in Cuba. The place of the term in the Yoruba belief system has been defined by Cabrera's Lucumí informants as follows: "We are children of the Woods [El Monte] because life began there; the Saints are born from the Woods, as is our religion. . . . The Orisha are there: Elegguá, Oggun, Ochosi, Oko, Ayé, Changó, Alláguna. And the Eggun—[spirits of the] dead, Eléko, Ikús, Ibbayés" (Cabrera 1968: 13). While "el monte" may also be translated as "the hill," it is clear from the context that it must be rendered as "the woods" or "the bush." This is supported by Cabrera's citation of an Afro-Cuban proverb, "un palo no hace el Monte," or "a [single] stick does not make the forest." Interestingly, this appears to be an almost word-for-word translation of a Yoruba proverb, "igi kan kii ş'gdo," or "one tree does not make a forest" (personal communication, Robert Farris Thompson). The theme of "el monte," then, extends far back into Yoruba oral literature and religious belief. "El monte" is the home not only of spirits, but of the herbs, trees and stones associated with them.

This theme also appears in secular form, often in the phrase "monte adentro," or "back in the woods." This phrase crops up again and again in Afro-Cuban and Puerto Rican song texts. To cite one example, the following line occurs in a recently popular Afro-Cuban song, recorded by Ramón "Monguito" Quián, considered one of the most traditional Afro-Cuban singers now recording in New York City:

Yo vengo de monte adentro con mi sabrosón montuno.

(I come from back in the woods with my tasty montuno.) [15]

It is interesting that the term "montuno," found in the name of the song form "son montuno," is itself derived from the word "monte"; this point is important in considering the switch in "Me Voy Pa'l Monte" into the son montuno form (personal communication, Robert

[15] On Fania Records, SLP 369. The song is "¿Donde Está Tu Montuno?"

Farris Thompson). In this case, the musical form and the text's semantic content are both expressing the same basic message. At the same time, the name "Cimarrón Pa'l Monte" (literally, "a slave who has run away to the woods") often appears on posters advertising dances held in hotels and dance halls in New York City with a mixed Cuban, Puerto Rican, and Dominican clientele.

"El monte," then, in its religious context, is the home of deities, the *orisha*, and of ancestral spirits, the *eggun*. In its secular context, "el monte" means roughly the same as "down home" or "back home" in North American black usage. It is "soul" country, in the popular sense of the word. This double use of the term parallels the "Aruanda" of Afro-Brazilian usage. In Brazil, Aruanda means the land of spirits and "soul" country as well.

The song "Me Voy Pa'l Monte" illustrates Needham's points about percussion and transition so well that it almost could have been the inspiration for this article. The song is divided into an introductory melodic section, sung in unison, followed by a highly percussive sequence in son montuno form, sung in call-and-response style. Separating the two segments is a rhythmically irregular phrase played on cowbell; this phrase marks the transition into another musical style:

The text follows:

1. Voy monte adentro a llevar este dulce cantar a mi tierra natal, a mi tierra natal.
2. Y mis canciones dirán lo que siento por ti, bella perla del mar, bella perla del mar.
3. Voy pa'l monte, monte adentro, (*repeated three times*).
4.–5. (*Repeat first two lines*)
6. Me voy pa'l monte, (*repeated three times*).
   [*Break—cowbell enters*]
   Chorus: Me voy pa'l monte
7. *Leader:* A Puerto Rico me voy
   Chorus: Me voy pa'l monte [*chorus repeats same line throughout*]
8. *Leader:* Y yo me voy a gozar
   Chorus:
9. *Leader:* A mi madre, voy a verla
   Chorus:
10. *Leader:* Que yo le voy a cantar
    Chorus:
11. *Leader:* Yo le canto desde Nueva York
    Chorus:
12. *Leader:* Para que goce mejor
    Chorus:
13. *Leader:* Rico, rico rico son montuno
    Chorus:

14. *Leader:* Para que lo goce bruto
    Chorus:
15. *Leader:* Monte alegre
    Chorus:
16. *Leader:* Que un jibarito va
    Chorus:
17. *Leader:* Cantando así
    Chorus:
18. *Leader:* Diciendo así por el camino
    Chorus:
19. *Leader:* Que yo me voy, yo me voy
    Chorus:
20. *Leader:* Yo me voy pa' el monte
    Chorus:
21. *Leader:* Para gozar, pa' vacilar
    Chorus:
22. *Leader:* Ven, morena linda, vamos a vacilar [*trumpets enter*]
23. *Leader:* Rico, rico, rico vacilón
    Chorus:
24. *Leader:* Oye, mira con Willie Rodriguez
    Chorus:
25. *Leader:* Yo me voy, mi vacilón
    Chorus:
26. *Leader:* Rico, rico, rico, rico sabrosón
    Chorus:
27. *Leader:* Oye, pa' que lo goce
    Chorus:
28. *Leader:* Borómbom, borómbom
    Chorus:
29. *Leader:* Borómbom, borómbom
    Chorus:
30. *Leader:* Bom, bom, bom, bom
    Chorus:
31. *Leader:* Bom, yo me voy, yo me voy
    Chorus:
32. *Leader:* Pa' vacilar, para gozar
    Chorus:
33. *Leader:* Bórom, bórom [*Fade*]

The performance rule underlying the song as a whole may be termed the activation of a metaphor; the first part of the song talks about an action which the second part carries out. In this case, the action is going home to Puerto Rico from "exile" in New York. The theme of going home has been remodelled to fit not the situation of an exiled African nation in slavery, but that of a Caribbean community in cultural exile in North America.

What is significant here is that the place called "home" is being created through the music. More specifically, the switch in musical style changes the setting dramatically. Once again, the switch represents the Africanization of performance rules. These may be summarized as follows: (1) the unison style of the opening choruses switches into call-and-response; (2) after playing the broken rhythms that mark the switch into a different style, the cowbell serves as the unvarying metronome-like base for all the rhythmic variations taking place in the vocal line and instrumental ensemble; (3) the leader overlaps with the chorus; (4) the leader's vocal is made up of many fragmentary formulaic expressions ("para gozar, pa' vacilar"), which are employed as much for their percussive sound as for their meaning; (5) at line 22, an invitation to dance appears ("ven, morena linda, vamos a vacilar"); (6) at line 23, the trumpet section enters, playing a contrasting rhythmic figure, so that five contrasting rhythm patterns are set up among vocalist, chorus and instrumental accompaniment (see Appendix for transcription of music); at lines 23–24, the vocalist "praises" the music and the band leader ("Rico, rico, rico vacilón/ Oye, mira con Willie Rodriguez"). This practice strongly recalls a point made by J. H. Nketia in reference to the use of texts in Akan drumming:

> The common use which is made of language texts as the basis of drumming allows for flexibility in the use of the modes of drumming, particularly in dance situations. So long as there is a musical ground, the master drummer can break away from the fragmentary texts of a dance piece. He is at liberty to make incursions into the repertory of the speech mode of drumming and to change his style from the strict form of the dance to that of the speech mode of drumming in order to give directions to drummers, greet or praise dancers, convey a message of sympathy, or quote a suitable proverb if the situation requires it. (Nketia 1963: 49)

While Nketia is describing drum style here, he has in effect stated the performance rule for the switching that takes place in the lead vocalist's part in the second half of "Me Voy Pa'l Monte." The Puerto Rican vocalist alternates between largely percusive, formulaic, and fragmentary statements and invitations to the dancers and praises for the musicians. Afro-Puerto Rican vocal style, then, reflects and is probably modelled on the style of the West African master drummer, with the voice taking the place of the master drum. This interchange is clearly evident in the closing lines (28, 29, 30, 33) of the song, where the vocalist imitates a drum. The voice thus becomes totally percussive and semantic content is suppressed in order to represent movement or transition.

What all this adds up to is a piece of very complex and very percussive social dance music, the kind that generates great excitement on the dance floor. In effect, the dance hall becomes "el monte" by virtue of the unifying power of the music. The freedom of the vocalist to switch in and out of the musical framework and to greet and praise dancers reproduces the style associated with West African dance rings. This style takes on a different meaning in a New World context, and is quite consciously employed to create a setting of social cohesiveness, accomplished through a change in performance rules.

The second song to be discussed here is titled "I'm Going Home." Its form bears a remarkable similarity to that of "Me Voy Pa'l Monte," while its content demonstrates the way in which the "going home" theme may be incorporated into a trance ritual.

The song begins in an acculturated mode, with a melodic section and a text that deals with "working on the building." This theme is a common one in white country and western gospel songs. In black gospel music, it is used as a metaphor for reaching the trance state. Black gospel music abounds in this metaphorical use of "home" to mean trance. To cite just a few titles, there is "Get Right Church and Let's Go Home," "He'll Let Me Come Home" by the Violinaires, and "There's a Dark Cloud Rising, Let's Go Home," by the Sewanee Quintet. The major difference between the "white" and "black" treatment of this theme is that black gospel singers turn these songs into trance events by introducing trance behavior into their performances, thereby actualizing the metaphor. "Home" thus becomes the name for the liminal state known as trance.

The text follows:

1. *Leader:* Lord, I'm workin' on the building,
   Chorus: Whoo
2. *Leader:* It's a truly foundation
   Chorus: Whoo
3. *Leader:* Oh, holdin' up the blood-stained, yeah, blood-stained banner
   of my
4. *Leader:* Lord
   Chorus: Yeah
   Leader: Lord
   Chorus: Yeah
   Leader: Lord

5. *Leader:* Blood-stained banner of my
   Chorus: Lord
   Leader: But look-a here [*spoken*]
   Chorus: Lord
   Leader: —
   Chorus: Lord
6. *Leader:* I'll never get tired
   Chorus: Whoo
7. *Leader:* (X) of workin' on the building
   Chorus: Whoo
8. *Leader:* I'm goin home, yeah, I got to get my re-
   Chorus: -ward
   Leader: yeah
   Chorus: -ward
   Leader: yeah
   Chorus: -ward
9. *Leader:* I got to get my re-
   Chorus: -ward
   Leader: But listen to this [*spoken*]
   Chorus: -ward
   Leader: —
   Chorus: -ward
10. *Leader:* When you see me cryin'
    Chorus: Whoo
11. *Leader:* (X) I'm workin' on the building
    Chorus: Whoo
12. *Leader:* Oh, holdin' up the blood-stained, yeah, blood-stained banner
    of my
    Chorus: Lord
    Leader: Yeah
    Chorus: Lord
    Leader: Yeah
    Chorus: Lord
13. *Leader:* Blood-stained banner of my
    Chorus: Lord
    Leader: Yeah
    Chorus: Lord
    Leader: Yeah
    Chorus: Lord
    [*Break*]
14. *Chorus:* Oh yes!
15. *Leader:* Lord, I'm goin' home
    Chorus: Oh yes I'm goin' home!
16. *Leader:* Goin' home. Got to see my
    Chorus: [*Repeats same line throughout*]

17. *Leader:* mother, I'm goin' home
    Chorus:
18. *Leader:* Got to see my father, I'm goin' home
    Chorus:
19. *Leader:* (X) Got to see my sister, and my brother, too
    Chorus:
20. *Leader:* I'm goin' home; (X) when I get there
    Chorus:
21. *Leader:* (X) Gonna sit right down, (X) ask my Lord
    Chorus:
22. *Leader:* (X)   (?)   , (X) sit right down
    Chorus:
23. *Leader:* (X) Sit right down, (X) tell my father
    Chorus:
24. *Leader:* (X) How I've been climbin',
             (X) rough side of the mountain
    Chorus:
25. *Leader:* (X) Tryin' to make it in.
             (X) Tell my father,
    Chorus:
26. *Leader:* (X) How sometimes, (X) I'm gonna drink,
    Chorus:
27. *Leader:* (X) Drink from the healin' water
    Chorus: [*Fade*]

In the opening melodic section, the lead singer talks about "going home to get my reward." He begins to hyperventilate (X) quite early in the performance (line 7), and this is a clue that the song is going to become a trance event. When the music switches in line 14, the lead singer begins to enumerate the departed kin that he is going to "see" (in trance). With some changes in vocabulary, this song is conceptually not very far from the Afro-Cuban belief in "el Monte" as the home of the eggun (see lines 24–25). It is clearly an ancestor song, and the co-occurrence of trance behavior, chiefly hyperventilation and constricted vocal chords, with an ancestor theme places the performance in a clearly African tradition. This co-occurrence represents another unsuspected Africanism in black North American gospel music.

As in "Me Voy Pa'l Monte," a percussive vocal style is employed to suggest transition. Here, the background voices shift into a conga-like pattern behind the lead vocalist at line 15 ("Oh yes I'm góin' hóme!"). The leader staggers his entries, so that the first syllable in each of his lines overlaps with a syllable near the end of the chorus' line (see Appendix for transcription of music). The leader also introduces an interesting rhythmic effect in line 20, where the semantic content and the presence of hyperventilation suggest that he is reaching trance: he pauses after the word "when" and lets the background figure come through. He thus introduces a rhythmic variation that crosses with the background figure in a technique quite similar to that of a West African master drummer.

In regard to melody, the vocalist employs one, two or rarely three notes in his vocal, starting at line 15. He is not "singing" in the usual sense, but is using his voice as a percussion instrument. Melody is suppressed for the sake of rhythmic effects. This is a common feature of gospel song style, and the loss of melody may be related to the achievement of the trance state by the vocalist. This flattening out of melody may be taken as another "channel cue" that marks the trance state.

To briefly recapitulate the discussion of percussion and transition, the following points can be made: in "Pede Passagem," the staggered entry of percussion instruments and the resulting Africanization of the musical form is employed to suggest that the music is "coming out"; in "Me Voy Pa'l Monte," the introduction of a percussive style linked with a "returning exile" theme suggests movement to "el monte," while creating it on the spot; in "I'm Going Home," the switch in style coincides with the appearance of trance behavior, so that a more percussive vocal style reflects the psychic state of the vocalist, while the rhythmic clashes set up in the performance may help to produce this state in others.

In all cases, the movement "home" is tied to the introduction of African performance rules and motor behavior. "Home" is created through these rules. These songs, all of them recently recorded, reflect the oldest stratum of New World music, still very much alive. They show how a particular theme may be remodelled to fit different social situations. They also demonstrate the basic underlying unity of performance rules in a variety of New World Negro music.

7. CONCLUSIONS

In beginning this study, I posed three questions concerning ritual in the Afro-American context. These questions are related, and must be answered simultaneously. In posing the first question, I am implicitly arguing against a view held by some anthropologists, namely, that *all* ritual is "communication without information":

> Ritual may, perhaps, most succinctly be classified as communication without information: that is to say, each ritual is a particular sequence of signals which, once announced, allows no uncertainty,

no choice, and hence, in the statistical sense of information theory, conveys no information from sender to receiver. It is, ideally, a system of perfect order and any deviation from this order is a mistake. (Wallace 1966: 233)

Since I do not view Afro-American ritual as mere rote behavior which contains zero information, I have argued against such a view by stating that one of the defining features of Afro-American rituals is the alternation or switching between European and African forms, from "order" to "making noise." It follows implicitly that since switching must necessarily involve uncertainty and choice among alternate modes of expression, it does convey information both in the technical sense and also in the sense of social meaning.

I have attempted to analyze the interplay between the structural features of particular communication forms and the culture history and ethnographic contexts within which these rituals take place. What emerges from this analysis is the conclusion that social meaning is generated through the alternation and interplay among a set of codes and channels of communication, and that one social meaning generated by these rituals consists of statements of cultural identity. Thus, these rituals may be called individual and/or societal statements about such an identity. Switching demonstrates a group's awareness of the differences between the performance rules and strategies of cultures in contact, and of the behavioral consequences of adopting these symbolic forms. Something happens in rituals; they are like performative utterances, and are not merely descriptive or expressive statements. What this "something" is depends on the particular ethnographic context. In earlier sections I attempted to describe some of the possible domains to which ritual behavior may be tied. Thus, in the Afro-Cuban examples discussed, going into trance and receiving one's *santo* or deity becomes part of the social meaning generated in the ritual event. That is, the "performer" is stating his or her personal religious and cultural commitments by fulfilling them on the spot. Thus, going into trance is here like a performative utterance; the performer does not merely talk about a *santo*, he or she receives it. In these rituals, the trance state is generally signalled by a style switch. From this particular example a generalization may be made: when style-switching takes place in a musical context, it signals that an extra-musical event is taking place. In the Cuban examples, this event is the entry of a supernatural entity into the performance, interpreted as spirit-posseession by members of the culture.

Ritual form generates social meaning and carries out actions. At the same time, an analysis of ritual form can be a key to the ethno-history of a group. Rituals implicitly convey information about the world view of individuals and their awareneess of the connection between history and structure. It is very significant that in all the data I have analyzed, the "Afro" component is stressed, and it is precisely this component that carries out the actions implicit in the texts. The Africanization of performance rules is also a performative, since it is this process that creates the ritual setting and/or event. In other words, what I am terming Africanization always carries with it whole domains of behavior and structures not present when the "performance" begins. Thus, the study of the ordering of the elements is crucial; performance rules themselves may be said to have a staggered entry. Performances must therefore be viewed as processes and as totalities whose multiple codes form coherent systems that generate meaning.

In stressing the transitional feature in my analysis of ritual, it is clear that these performance rules, generally tied to an African-derived base, emerge or come out in the liminal part of the ritual. This "coming out" may be a vast communal rite of passage, such as carnival. It is necessary to understand this event, since it may be seen as the model for many other kinds of Afro-American ritual events. Carnival links structural features with culture history. It fuses public and private roles; since it is a procession, it is the very model of a liminal event. It is also a ritual display, since it is in this procession that the various groups display their private behaviors and hierarchies. It is also tied to history, since among its very origins in the New World are included coronations of kings and queens of various African nations or tribal groups.

This is a different view of Afro-American public festivities, which have typically been dealt with either as copies of European counter-parts, or as more or less purely "African" events, and as such as temporary lapses from "civilization," or else as ambulatory open-air museums of bygone primitive customs. While I have dealt principally with Brazilian carnival in this study, the ritual pattern in other areas of the New World is substantially the same. In Cuba, for example, with its multi-ethnic slave society, the different tribal groups were organized into *cabildos*, the equivalent of the Brazilian *"nações"* (nations). In terms of the Cuban carnival, the most important of these groups was the Efik nation, which had preserved in Cuba a secret society known as *Abakuá*. Members of this society, known as *ñañigós*, would come out in full tribal regalia twice a year, at Epiphany and during the pre-Lenten carnival (Cabrera 1969: 37–50). In the cities of Cuba, groups of *ñañigós* who controlled various neighborhood terri-tories, would come out into the streets and would clash with rival groups of Efiks. This ritual combat between rival African groups at carnival time has parallels in Brazil, where rival groups of Angolan *capoeira* fighters would clash in the streets during carnival (see p. 70 above). Other parallels exist in Trinidad and Haiti.

Another feature of the Cuban carnival that parallels the situation in Brazil was the emergence from the Yoruba cult houses of *santeros* and *santeras,* who brought their sacred drums, the *batá,* into the streets as part of the processions. This is equivalent to the appearance of cult objects in the Brazilian carnival described above (p. 70), as well as the emergence of the cult houses there during the processions. These instances demonstrate again how private religious groups or cults, as well as secret societies and voluntary organizations all double as public carnival associations, displaying their regalia and hierarchic organization at fixed intervals.

Even in those countries of Latin America which could hardly be said to have a strong African-derived cultural component, the pattern is the same. Carvalho-Neto has recently shown how in Uruguay the Congolese "nation" known as *Loango* has been transformed into a carnival club, the last African remnant in that part of Latin America (Carvalho-Neto 1965; cited in Bastide 1967: 176). In all these instances, what comes out into the streets is behavior governed by a group of performance rules which are the legacy of a wide variety of African peoples brought to Spanish, Portuguese, French, and English America. These African-derived rules govern linguistic, musical, motor, and religious behavior, and emerge during the liminal zone known as carnival. It is, then, structured liminality that prevails during this event.

In describing carnival as a rite of passage, I have attempted to enlarge the scope of such rituals as first analyzed by Van Gennep. He examined only the passage between fixed social positions and roles within a *single* society, while I have looked at such transitions as they move from the performance rules and social hierarchies of one culture to those belonging to another culture. It is also clear that the kind of ritual represented by carnival, while clearly liminal in nature, is quite different from those analyzed by Victor Turner. Participants in carnival are not stripped of roles in the liminal zone of the carnival parade. It is precisely here where they display them. As rituals, carnivals do something by breaking the boundaries between private and public behavior created in part by the cultural dualities present in New World societies. Carnivals break these boundaries by bringing private styles into the public domain, and by declaring social and cultural identities in the streets.

What takes place in carnival is, paradoxically, rule-bound but liminal behavior. What happens there is structurally equivalent to what takes place in other Afro-American ritual events, especially those involving trance behavior. There, liminality and transition are not expressed as the emergence of private behavior into the streets. Rather, the change is an internal or psychic transition, which often takes place during a public performance. The movement into trance or an altered state of consciousness occurs simultaneously with the emergence of more African behavior, exemplified in one context by the appearance of Lucumí in Afro-Cuban rituals as the language of spirit-possession. Such African performance rules also serve to mark the trance state; this behavior is then interpreted within the culture as possession by Yoruba deities. Trance rituals, then, often take the form of a passage between the performance rules of different cultures. As these rules emerge along with trance, they create a ritual setting, which means that trance behavior may be triggered in others as well. Thus, trance and possession behavior represent at the individual or "micro" level what takes place at the mass or "macro" level during carnival. To put it another way, in trance rituals, altered states of consciousness are the liminal zone into which African performance rules emerge; in the carnival ritual, it is an "altered state of society" that is created as African performance rules emerge into the streets.

In applying the carnival model to the study of Afro-American ritual behavior, other patterns and parallels appear. Carnival is on the boundary between private and public behavior; trance rituals are, as well. Thus, the fusion of private and public roles in the Brazilian carnival (*iyalorixá* as head of the *maracatú; pai de Umbanda* as head of an *escola de samba*) is parallel to Afro-Cuban culture in other ritual contexts. Thus, figures like Celia Cruz and La Lupe are on the boundary or threshold between private and public behavior, just like their Brazilian counterparts. The emergence of what are essentially cult performances into the "popular" or public domain may be viewed as a simple commercialization of cult practices. But the coming out of ritual performances into public, and especially in exile in the United States, points to the fusion of "church" and "community." That is, rituals need a social group ("church") to maintain them, just as social groups need rituals that help give them a cultural identity. Exile, with all its dangers of loss of cultural identity, has heightened the interdependence of ritual and community. Each helps to maintain the other.

The continued existence of African cults and secret societies in the New World is in itself of great interest and significance. What is equally interesting and important is the way these cults have been articulated with the national or popular culture. From preliminary research, it would appear that such fusions of cult and popular culture, especially among the Caribbean community in the cities of the United States, has been greatly aided by the mass media. This points to the portability of ritual forms via recordings, for example, and of the power of these forms in immediately creating the ritual setting wherever they appear.

Implicitly, then, there is a widespread and ongoing cultural process in the New World whereby African cult performances are coming out, often into highly "commercial" contexts, such as recordings and theater performances. Viewed in this light, in a pan-New World context, black culture in North America exhibits structural parallels to what is found in Brazil and Cuba, and probably elsewhere. These parallels may be put into schematic form as follows:

cults	public processions	(Brazil)
santería	public performers	(Cuba)
gospel	"soul" singers	(U.S.A.)

While its African content is certainly less overt than in other black religions in the New World, gospel must, nevertheless, be viewed as the repository of African-based performance rules in the United States. Furthermore, the connection among trance behavior, music and popular culture in North American black society is the exact parallel to the Brazilian and Cuban situations. This argument is supported by the appearance of "soul" music in recent years, and by such figures as James Brown, Aretha Franklin, Wilson Pickett, and many others. It is a cliché by now to refer to the church "backgrounds" of these performers. What must be pointed out is that "church," with its attendant rule-governed trance behavior, is no more a "background" for these performers than is Celia Cruz's identity as a santera a background for her. Thus, soul singers are threshold figures in the same way as their Brazilian and Cuban counterparts. Their performances turn into trance rituals almost indistinguishable from "shouts" in church. The connection between "gospel-as-cult" and "soul" music may seem a bit far-fetched; the proof that there is such a connection comes from within black culture itself. Gospel and soul groups often "cover" each others' recordings, sometimes changing the arrangement, but otherwise preserving the trance-associated features (preaching, hyperventilation, paradoxical communication) outlined in section 5.

Gospel and "soul" music have not received anywhere near the attention they deserve. It is time to stop looking at "spirituals" as an evolutionary step on the way to jazz, and instead to see them as an activity in their own right, tied to a whole domain of ritual belief and practice, linked to other New World traditions. Gospel must also be examined in its relationship with popular culture, namely, its connection with "soul" music. The kind of rapid feedback across what have been presumed to be boundaries between "sacred" and "secular" domains within black culture makes it doubtful that this is any longer a viable distinction in North American black culture or anywhere else in the New World, especially as "cult" merges more and more into popular culture.

In attempting to broaden the domain in which ritual structures may be found, I have discovered that what is termed "popular" music, often dismissed as "commercial" and, therefore, not a fit subject for analysis, does in fact exhibit elaborate patterning, and often communicates basic information about a culture. At the same time, a seemingly "popular" and, therefore, public mode of expression can often encode a meaning whose decoding requires for the analyst an extensive background knowledge and familiarity with performance rules. There are, for the members of a culture, part of his cognitive reality.

The integration of altered states of consciousness or trance behavior into such performance shows how deeply rooted and central this phenomenon is in New World cultures; these states are so patterned and institutionalized within performances of various kinds that they have often gone unnoticed. This is especially true of North American culture. It is only by comparing the structure of gospel with related New World forms and ultimately with West African prototypes that one becomes aware of what is taking place in the music. The possibility exists that the cues that mark the appearance of an altered state within musical performances may be shared cross-culturally, at least within the African-Afro-American sphere. This suggestion is based on some preliminary field work I carried out with Cuban santeros and Brazilian Umbandistas. When I played them gospel songs, they could immediately tell when a singer had "caught a spirit," as they put it. This sharing of cues throughout the New World points to an historical relationship among all these New World cultures, and, of course, to their common origin in West Africa. Here, Afro-American studies point to the need for further research in Africa. One basic question is whether cults are tied to other levels of culture in West Africa, or whether this is a strictly New World development.

The most general conclusion that emerges from this study is the enormous role that African cultural forms have played in the New World in the shaping of national popular cultures. The situation has clearly been more complex than what is usually described by the term "acculturation." This process has generally been viewed as black adapting to white; the existence of multiple codes in the communicative behavior of New World blacks puts this concept in a different light, and calls for a refinement of the theory of culture dynamics in the New World.

The task, then, is not only to search for Africanisms, but to find the place where they are on display, that is, their ethnographic context. Since they often occur alongside non-African content, the meaning of these juxtapositions must be determined in each case.

APPENDIX

I would like to thank Larry Wilcox of Emil Charlap Associates, New York for preparing the musical transcriptions in this Appendix.

PEDE PASSAGEM

© SIDNEY MILLER

-2-   "Pede Passagem"

El Santo En Nueva York

By Justi Barretto

3.

EL SANTO

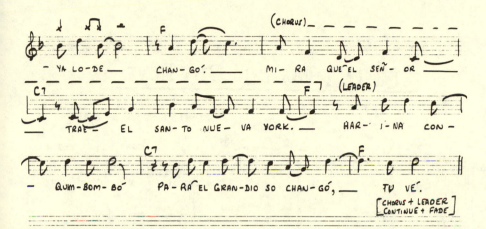

- YA LO-DE ___ CHAN-GÓ. ___ MI- RA QUE~EL SEÑ- OR ___

— TRAE- EL SAN-TO NUE- VA YORK. ___ HAR- I-NA CON-

— QUM-BOM- BÓ PA- RA~EL GRAN-DIO SO CHAN-GÓ, ___ TU VE.

It Ain't Nothing But Love

By the: 5 Blind Boys of Alabama

2.

It Ain't Nothing But Love

3.
IT AIN'T NOTHING BUT LOVE

(OH _ YEAH) _   COM-IN' DOWN ____ FROM A-BOVE   (OH

YEAH,) COM-IN' DOWN _ FROM A- BOVE,   FROM A-   BOVE. ____

Meet Me Over Yonder

By: W. De Shields

"Meet Me Over Yonder"

-4-   "Meet Me Over Yonder"

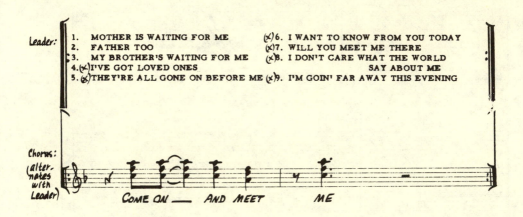

"MONTE ADENTRO"

—3—

RI-CO, RI-CO, RI-CO VA-CI-LON

ME VOY PA'L MON- TE

O-YE MI-RA CON

ME VOY PA'L MON- TE

ME VOY PA'L MON-

WILLIE RO-DRI-GUEZ

YO ME VOY MI VA-CI- LON.

(PATTERN CONTINUES TILL FADE OUT)

I'M GOING HOME

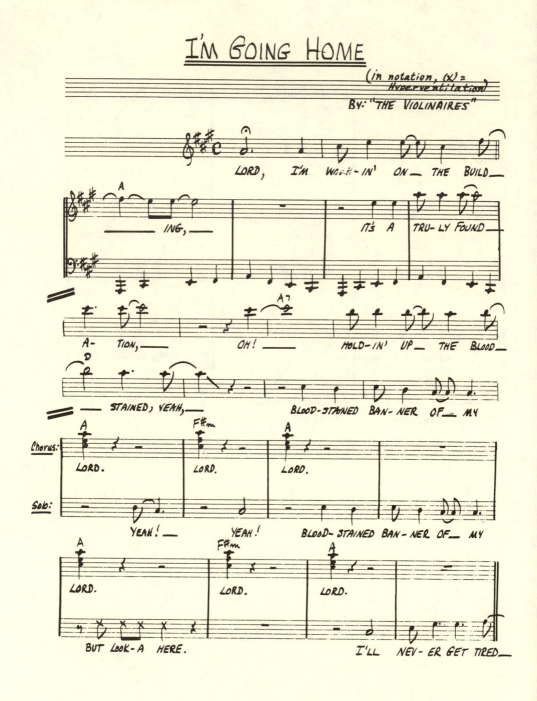

-3-

"I'M GOING HOME"

The Psychology of the Spiritual Sermon

Had it not been for the controversy concerning the alleged oral creation of epic narratives such as the *Odyssey* and *Beowulf*, I would never have sought similar compositional modes in the spontaneous and oral sermons of the rural South and Southwest. The pioneer field work in oral composition, conducted by Milman Parry and Albert B. Lord in the mid-1930s, concerned the talent of the individual singer: specifically, how he is able to perform while composing a heroic song several hundred or even several thousand lines in length. Parry thought that the basic unit of composition was the formula: "A group of words, regularly employed under the same metrical conditions, to express a given essential idea" (Parry 1930). Lengthy epics were constructed, according to this theory, by the manipulation of formulas: such word groups could be recited in different concatenations, and the formulas themselves could be varied by the substitution of one or more words in such a way as to create new formulas by analogy with old ones.

The oral formulaic theory of composition is actually an old one, having been first suggested by a German scholar, J. Kail, in 1889 (Kail 1889: 21–40), and became popular with classicists for many years after. Nevertheless, it is fitting and proper that we acknowledge Parry and Lord as pioneers in this field, as they first field-tested their theories in the "living laboratory" of Jugoslavia. Before their experimentation, Kail's theory was only one among many others; after 1930 the Parry-Lord theory of composition, however much modified subsequently, became the starting point for all researchers of oral composition. The work of these two men has influenced the scholarship of nearly every modern and classical language, of ethnology and psychology as well.

But as Lord, and nearly every writer on oral formulaic matters, has recognized, one of the major problems in dealing with this new concept is the lack of a suitable lexicon with which to describe its phenomena. The purpose of this paper will be to try to describe the process of oral composition as it was found in the "marginal" churches of the South and Southwest in terms now made available to us by psycho-linguistics. If such a lexicon is valid, we will be able to describe precisely not only how the art of the American folk preacher is realized,

135

but how oral composition has taken place throughout the world. Such description is necessary because the lexicon and the categories supplied by literary critics are vague and impressionistic, whereas scientific terminology enables a description of spontaneous preaching in behavioral and causative terms.

In turning our attention away from the audience of traditional heroic songs and epics toward the singer, Parry and Lord did a remarkable thing: they showed us that all the characteristic features of the oral performance which we had long assumed occurred because of the demands of the listener really came about because of the demands placed upon the singer by the nature of his performance. The use of conventional language and the avoidance of novel imagery, the seemingly leisurely pace of telling a story, the "adding style" and the strikingly repetitious character of the narrative—all of these features were the result of the rapid pace of delivery and the necessity of the oral performer to formulate subsequent lines even while he is uttering the line of the moment.

This theory of oral composition was at first widely accepted, and then as widely criticized. In the 1950s Jean Rychner applied the theory to the *Chanson de Geste* and Magoun to *Beowulf* (Magoun 1953). Fifteen years later skepticism was universal, as the work of Larry D. Benson testifies (Benson 1966). The major methodological problem was that Lord compared the songs of the *guslars* which he recorded in Jugoslavia—a genuine oral tradition—with the narratives of ancient Greece and medieval Europe as he found them in manuscript. Correct procedure demands that the first comparison be made with another certifiable oral tradition, so that the principles of composition can be extracted from them. And then, the oral tradition in Jugoslavia appeared to be dying out, perhaps as Lord suggested because of the drive toward universal literacy under the Communist regime.

From my own experience in Jugoslavia—as a tourist and thus neither extensive nor professional—it seems as likely that urbanization as much as literacy is causing the passing of the oral epic tradition. Like many "emerging nations," Jugoslavia is attempting to industrialize as rapidly as possible. There is a concomitant stigma attached to being a peasant or in maintaining the old peasant ways, one of which was the playing of the *gusle*. At the same time both the national and local governments realize the commercial appeal of "folklore," and so nearly every city and town with any sizeable tourist trade sponsors frequent "folklore" entertainments. *Gusle* playing is thus kept alive, but the life-signs are fragile; and an authentic oral tradition is, under such circumstances, impossible.

This, then, is the background of my interest in "marginal" churches. The first services I attended were held in Bakersfield, California, and several small cities and towns in the San Joaquin valley. Every preacher I met during my two years in this region had been born in the South; any California influence on his sermon style or the conduct of the service is negligible. Concerning nearly every attitude of worship, except basic doctrinal issues, services were unconventional. They were marked by an active participation by the congregation in the form of speaking in tongues, possession, ecstatic dancing, clapping, tapping, spontaneous singing and shouting which Charles Keil noted were alien to the "prevailing conception of Protestantism" in America (Keil 1966: 7–8).

Specifically, the kind of preaching I was interested in—whether the preacher be Methodist, Baptist, or Pentecostal—was stylistically consistent, and thus cut across denominational grounds. The preacher begins his sermon in normal, conversational prose. He introduces the passage from Scripture upon which the sermon will be based (the "text"), and then elaborates upon it by describing, often in detail, the relevance of the "text" to its semantic environment (the "context"). Almost invariably his tone and his diction are normal—to him. His voice is clear, and his rhythms those of prose delivery.

But as he gets further into his message for the day—the application of the day's "text" to everyday morals—his voice becomes more tense and more dramatic. He becomes more animated and begins to speak increasingly rapidly. The tone of his voice may become lower in pitch and grating in timbre. As he becomes more excited and more intense his throat constricts so that he is generating more saliva than he can swallow and it is necessary for him to wipe his mouth continually with a handkerchief. This may also be taken as an indication of an altered conscious state.

Most important for the present research is the rhythm of delivery. As the tempo and intensity of the sermon increase the preacher usually begins to chant his lines; a decided tonal center may emerge. The chanting is often well regulated and proceeds, with well-timed ups and downs, to an emotional climax at which point the preacher breaks off and concludes the sermon with several remarks in conversational prose again. During the time that he has been chanting, however, the language is regularized rhythmically, the determinant being the length of time between lines rather than a syllable or stress count. The lines are punctuated by a loud, audible gasp, which is as regular as a drum beat.

Variations of this form occur frequently, although what has been described is the favored style. Nevertheless, some preachers do reach a high emotional plateau fairly early in their performance and simply maintain this level throughout. Occasionally a preacher aims for an emotional peak in the middle of his performance, and then gradually relaxes the tone and rhythm of the sermon. But by far the most popular form, as has been mentioned, is to strive toward a peak which occurs near the end, followed by a gentle denouement.

The preaching style of these men marks them most emphatically as marginal, and this aspect of their service shall be the major concern of this paper. In some locations they are known as "old time country preachers" and are held to be something of a cherished relic of former days. The men who compose spontaneously and preach orally refer to themselves as "spiritual preachers" and will cite Scripture to prove that theirs is the only proper way. Luke 24:49 is one of the favorite authorities: "And, behold, I send the promise of my father upon you: but tarry ye in the city of Jerusalem, until ye be endued with power from on high." The important concept for spiritual preachers is the command to "tarry" in the city, and not to attend a seminary or to get formal religious training. The power of the Holy Ghost from "on high" will endue the chosen with the power: it is not something he can seek or learn from man.

The congregation is an active member, collectively, in the sermon. The simplest way to describe their involvement is to call the service antiphonal, but the actual situation is more complex. In the churches I visited, the preacher and congregation did not respond to each other—which would be the usual understanding of "antiphonal"—but to the performance of the service and to the Spirit of the Lord. Members of the congregation called out, or clapped, or sang as the Spirit moved them: "Amen," "Yes, sir," "That's right," "You tell it, Reverend," etc. The functions of these cries are multiple. The congregation was involved in the performance of the sermon, at times even in its creation. There is a greater bond between preacher and audience than in conventional preaching because they support his performance with such affirmatives as "Yes" and "That's right." The congregation may get more deeply involved in the sermon because they have had a hand in creating its message, and so they are not likely to feel that they are being "preached to" or that the minister is aloofly chastising them. Aggressions can thus be released in this kind of performance rather than being directed toward any person or group.

I visited Black preachers primarily because of their inclination to regularize the meter of their delivery; often the sermon was chanted, and occasionally sung. The language thus produced was close enough to Parry's definition of formula—the "group of words regularly employed under the same metrical conditions"—to make comparison with oral narrative traditions possible. The transcriptions of the sermons of most spiritual preachers do not scan well, there being as many hyper- and hypometric lines as there are standards, but the time interval between formulas is usually quite consistent. This interval is maintained by the preacher himself by an audible gasp for breath, which sounds much like a vehement grunt. His timing is reinforced, however, by the exclamations of the congregation which are keyed to his rhythm: they insure his consistency.

When sermons are to be compared with the heroic songs of Homer or with those of the Jugoslavian *guslars,* or the epics of the *akyn* of Central Asia, the comparison must be made with caution. Sermon formulas are not quite the same as the others: the Homeric unit is marked by a very rigid meter that does not allow for variation; Anglo-Saxon narrative verse alliterates, and its meters are more flexible; the Jugoslavian meter is neither bound to formal metrical patterns nor to alliteration. Nevertheless, the method of composition is close enough to allow meaningful comparisons: in many areas what may be said about the spiritual sermon may be said about the other singers of tales.

Lord has been criticized for his poor linguistic psychology, especially when he tried to discuss the process by which narrative was composed:

> From the point of view of usefulness in composition, the formula means its essential idea. . . . But this is only from the point of view of the singer composing, of the craftsman in lines.
>
> And I am sure that the essential idea of the formula is what is in the mind of the singer, almost as a reflex action in rapid composition, as he makes his song. Hence it could, I believe, be truly stated that the formula not only is stripped to its essential idea in the mind of the composing singer, but also is denied some of the possibilities of aesthetic reference in context [Lord 1965: 65–66].

To begin with, we must assume that the existence of ideas precedes and is apart from their expression in language, the most common expression being in sentences. The formula, the group of words, does not "mean" its essential idea, but is rather an expression of it; and the "essential idea of the formula" does not have priority in the singer's mind, but rather the idea itself which must then be encoded into an acceptable language. Recent linguistic theory holds that the function of language is to convert ideas into sentences: usually we first think of something and then we formulate the syntactic structure and lexicon with which to express it. After the syntactic structure has been generated many of the "blanks" can be filled in, which process transmutes the deep structure into the actual sentence itself, a manifestation of the surface structure. There is also some evidence, however, that in many cases certain key words form the basis of syntactical generation, that prior to forming a sentence we have one or more words already in mind (Deese 1970: 50–51). The encoding process then would not necessarily follow the strict patterning of generation of syntax-provision of lexicon, but could begin with lexical choice. This may well be what happens when the spiritual preacher repeats the same word from line to line:

> What do ya think that ya want
> 35 Why the *rod* of your deliverance is in your own hands
> Stretch out the *rod* that's in your hands
> I don't have a new *rod* to give ya
> I don't have a new instrument to give ya
> I don't have a new suggestion for ya
> 40 I do not have a new plan
> Your course has already been charted by destiny
> Stretch out the *rod* that's in your own hand
> (Rosenberg 1970: 108).

When I first analyzed this passage it seemed that each new line was created by one of three methods: analogy with syntax, similarity of idea, and the use of "key" words as bridges to the following line. "Rod" seems to have been in the preacher's mind when he chanted these lines, not the least because the "person" addressed is Moses, who is about to stretch out his rod to dry the Red Sea. It seems to me now, as before, that when the preacher has formed the "rod of your deliverance" line that the syntax of the following lines will be arranged to include the key word "rod." After a series of three lines (35–37) with "rod," this word is dropped but the syntax and most of the lexicon is retained: "rod" has already served its purpose.

Much has been made of the role of memory in oral performance. Lord thought that the singer "does not 'memorize' formulas any more than we as children 'memorize' language. He learns them by hearing them in other singers' songs, and by habitual usage they become part of his singing as well. . . . The singer has not had to learn a large number of separate formulas. The commonest ones which he first uses set a basic pattern, and once he has the basic pattern firmly in his grasp, he needs only to substitute another word for the key one. . . . the particular formula itself is important to the singer only up to the time when it has planted in his mind its basic mold. When this point is reached, the singer depends less and less on learning formulas and more and more on the process of substituting other words in the formula patterns" (Lord 1965: 36).

Curiously, Lord's description of the creative process sounds much like a metaphor of the generative theory with the important difference that he views language composition as being somewhat mechanical: new formulas are created by analogy with the old, the composition process merely one of substituting a word or a phrase. There is no doubt that occasionally this process does occur. But generative theory shows that given a certain deep structure, an infinite number of surface structures can be generated; the crucial difference is that Lord ties the creation of new formulas (really metrically governed sentences) to a recollection of "the commonest ones." Generative theory enables us to see that the singer is freed from such "memory" and such reliance: what the singer has at his command is not several score or several hundred formulas which he manipulates by word and phrase substitution, but rather a metrical deep structure which enables him to generate an infinite number of sentences in his native meter.

But memory does seem to be centrally involved in the concatenation of formulas, rather than in the creation of the single unit. For instance, in 1967 and again in 1968 I recorded two sermons on the same topic by the Rev. Rubin Lacy which were constructed around Aarne-Thompson Tale Type 1613, "The Deck of Cards." This is a type of "counting song" (Wilgus and Rosenberg 1970: 291) which assigns a religious meaning to each card in the standard deck: the two might be made to correspond to heaven and hell, the three to the trinity, the four to the gospel writers, etc. A brief selection from that sermon will be useful:

And, God
Said there's two ways to go
Heaven
Or either hell
Mister Hoyle
Made a two-spot
He called it a deuce
God from Zion
And put it in the deck
And God
Made the father
Son and the Holy Ghost
Ain't God all right?
And Mister Hoyle
Made a three-spot
And called it a trey
(Rosenberg 1970: 130).

The passage shows several features which enabled Lacy to recall this idea with great accuracy over the years; nearly all of them relate to the fact that the lines are closely connected associationally. To begin with, the "counting song" is built around a familitr sequence of numbers, from one to ten. The song follows that sequence. The description of each card and its meaning rhetorically alternates back and forth: God says or does something and Mister Hoyle responds in some way, in Lacy's version for the purpose of imitating and detracting from Him. Finally, the syntax of each passage on each card is similar:

> So God
> Made a earth
> * * *
> And God
> Made a year
> * * *
> And God
> Made the Father

While the response to God's acts are syntactically and lexically the same:

> Mister Hoyle
> Made a deck of cards
> * * *
> Mister Hoyle
> Made a two-spot
> * * *
> And Mister Hoyle
> Made a three-spot

Lacy had fairly accurate recall of this passage because it was coherent; the sections were related to each other and the progression was natural. He had broken down the sequence into a dozen or so subsections (each one concerned with a separate card) with which he used similar syntax, and then he stitched them together.

The Rev. Elihue Brown of Bakersfield frequently described the birth of Jesus in the metaphor of the Glory Train (Rosenberg 1970: 169), using similar techniques. The story of the birth uses the chronology of a train ride: "Got on the train of nature/ Stayed there nine months/ Stepped off at the station one mornin'/ Stayed right there/ Until God wanted him to come on out/ God was so concerned brotheren/ Till He came all the way to this sinful world/ Came in the shape of a baby/ Wrapped Himself in human blood." It is not length that limits such mannered descriptions—Lacy has a forty-seven

line favorite on the Four Horsemen—but the addition of new information. When the subject is kept within the associational scope of the
recited material, as we have just seen Lacy and Brown do, the string
could be substantially extended. We know, for instance, that humans
can retain only seven or eight words in a random string but several
dozen in a sentence. We are not limited as much by the amount of
information we can process as by the number of symbols we try to
master (Miller 1967: 12, 25).

The trick, then, for the oral performer is to find ways of organizing
his material. Repetition of his material, specifically of certain narratives or exempla within the larger framework of the sermon, will
help him. In repetition the smaller units, whether sentences or formulas, tend to be grouped in the performer's mind into larger segments: hence the strings such as "The Deck of Cards" or the "Glory
Train." Medievalists call such sequences "Themes" and "Type-
Scenes," the former concentrating on the formulaic structure and the
latter on the subject described. If the oral performer can retain, with
reasonable accuracy, a few Themes, his job has been made so much
easier than if he must try to manipulate or create anew several hundred
formulas.

The situation is somewhat analogous to that of computer engineers
who must in an instant grasp and remember the patterns of lights used
to show whether relays are open or closed (Miller 1967: 6–7). Rather
than try to remember an entire string of lights as independent entities,
they think of them as forming patterns of threes or fours. For instance,
one might decide that three lights off would be coded as "0," two off
and one on would be "1," and off-on-off would be "2." Once having
memorized this coding process, the engineer's task is tremendously
simplified; he can look at a string of lights, code it, and translate it
into only five or six code digits, instead of the twenty on the machine.
The same amount of information may be retained when it is coded,
and with practice the technician can further simplify the coding
process, reducing more information to simple code symbols, thus
increasing the amount of information retained without having to
increase the capability of his memory span, which might not be
possible, and certainly would be more difficult.

It is well understood that human memory is limited by the number
of symbols it is required to comprehend, and not by the amount of
information signified by them. In the case of the oral performer, I
assume that the "basic" unit is the formula, what I prefer to think of
as the metrically governed sentence generated in oral performance.
Because of the reasons already cited—chronology of subject, logic,
syntactical parallelism—the performer has an easier time in clustering

formulas together to form a theme. An important point of difference between the engineer and his string of lights and the preacher who is reciting sentences in a story is the degree of accuracy. The engineer demands perfection, while the preacher is not so meticulous. He seems to be working with syntactical and semantic outlines: it does not matter if the "text" varies somewhat from performance to performance. Verbatim memorization is not important because he does not need it to preach; he can improvise, generating slightly new formulas as the occasion arises.

We may speak of bits and chunks, then, only with an understanding of this crucial difference: accuracy. The "bit" corresponds approximately to the metrical utterance, the formula; the "chunk" corresponds to those concatenations of formulas which recur so frequently in oral performance, the theme. It should also be pointed out that the preacher usually recalls the semantic content (a psychological unit) and then clothes it in words. An obvious exception is in the case of the "stall formulas" whose syntax and lexicon are repeated verbatim so frequently that memory must be involved. However, the lexical variation in different versions of the same stories shows that even when the narrative event remains constant, the language often varies.

In *The Art of the American Folk Preacher* I showed how two sermons on the same topic, recited a year apart, used the same four episodes from the life of David in the same order, and how the rest of the sermon was structured around these events (1970: 85ff). The common stories in the two sermons were of David's anointing, his fight with Goliath, his flight to the cave to escape Saul, and his rescue of the lamb. There is little or no episodic overlap in these stories, except for the character of David, a demonstration that variety of subject or information does not hinder the memory; again, it is length. The same principle holds for the generation of sentences: their length does not seem to deter the ability to recall, whereas their complexity—the number of transformations employed in their formulation—intensifies the interference with one's memory (Savin and Perchonock 1965: 348–53).

Whenever a preacher has an idea which he wants to use in his own sermon, or hears a story or a message with the same intent in mind, he interprets—puts it into his own words—and it is his own interpretation that he remembers, and this is what will become the rhetoric of his own sermon. Memory is in these cases a recollection of our own initial verbalization (Carmichael et al. 1932: 73–86). In this single observation we have the basis for the form of oral transmission. Thus sermons tend to change less and less the more they are performed, as the preacher recalls not the initial stimuli but his own mental organization of his information. The process of memorization may well be concerned with the formation of the larger blocks of information we have just discussed until there are few enough blocks to enable the performer to recall all the information (Bousefield and Cohen 1955: 83–95).

One has only to read several lines of sermons that have been repeated and compare them with their predecessors, and then not too closely, to see that "by heart" memorization is never attained; many of the lines are a-grammatical jumbles which dozens of replayings on the tape recorder will not decipher. This is the other side of the communication coin; when Parry and Lord shifted the focus of their research and ours from the audience to the singer and his problems, they left the audience little understood. What they told us about the performer changed our understanding of his relationship with his audience. Here again the congregation of the spiritual preacher is in a position somewhat analogous to the audience of other traditional performances. Like the *guslars* and, presumably, the auditors of medieval epic and romance, the congregations studied were tradition-oriented. They not only expected but demanded to hear the old tales, the ones they themselves knew well. New stories were suspect. This respect for tradition was certainly true of stories from the Bible, there being fewer than fifty favorites.

What the tradition-oriented audience brings to performances is certain expectations: of story (as we have just said), of language (both in lexicon and in formal considerations such as traditional openings and closings), and of the performer's style. The congregation enjoys the sermon more *because* it knows what is coming next. Experiments with audience participation showed that members of the congregation could anticipate their preacher not only in the language that was to come but occasionally in the melody he would use to express it. It is possible that the preacher often takes his cue from an exclamation in the audience. Under these circumstances there is a great deal of communication.

But there were a great many times when the preacher's words were unintelligible. I could not even distinguish the phonemes after repeated tape reruns, and I do not believe that during the service the congregation could either. Yet they continued to respond quite vigorously. I have argued that in this art form the message is the medium (Rosenberg 1970: 40) because the "message" seems to elicit a visceral response to rhythm and melody. But there may be more to the preacher's claims that he is conveying "ideas."

Experiments have been performed in which recorded sentences were played, with a background of noise, so that the sentences could be heard but were not intelligible (Bruce 1956: 245–52). The experimenter told his subjects the topic of the sentences they were about to hear, and then replayed more sentences, again after first introducing the alleged subject. Actually the sentences used for each topic were the same; the interpretation by the subjects differed, however, because each was predisposed toward certain information once he was given a topical introduction. Everyone heard not so much what he wanted to hear but what he expected was going to be said. The decoding apparatus in the brain, in other words, is able to generate sentences to match input, even if that input is imaginary.

In another experiment, sentences with different deep structures but identical surface structures, both beginning with the words "they are" were played to subjects, again with a noisy background (Mehler and Carey 1967: 335–38). The subjects had the most difficulty in identifying the sentences with the altered deep structure, suggesting that the inability to identify the deep structure distorts the accuracy of perception. To return to our noisy church services, it is clear that something is being "understood." It may not be precisely what the preacher is trying to communicate, but it is probably something meaningful to the congregation, possibly something which they could paraphrase for themselves.

The acceptability of sentences is, after all, entirely a subjective judgment (Deese 1970: 30). Poor grammar is quite common in the sermons, not only because of the low level of formal education of the ministers but because rapid delivery often forces mistakes. Take such nonsentences as "But he's a profession in his field," or "He saw the dream, meaning seven years of poordom of no prosperity," or "You know, we as a whole, if we are told to do something, that we don't see any sense in doing that we don't think it oughta be did"; all were spoken during moments of relative calm and were clearly enunciated, and none drew quizzical looks. Communication of some sort was taking place.

Communication also occurs on the level of rhythm: again, the message is the medium. The meter of the chanted sermon line differs somewhat from the stresses placed on the same line in conversation; attention to the musicality of the language forces such a change. Yet usually the pause in the sentence, punctuated by the audible gasp, falls at the end of a major component, a noun phrase or between the noun phrase and verb in a verb phrase:

I heard a fellow Oh Lord
Is the strength of my life
Then whom shall I fear?
And the Lord is my Shepherd.

Clauses tend to be broken at the end of the main clause, which is usually delivered first:

If He hadn't 'a been my shepherd
I'd 'a been gone a long time ago
* * * * *
The Lord is the strength of my life
Then whom shall I fear

We also have evidence that in those cases when the break between components is not so pronounced, as in careful conversation, the auditor tends to interpret the break himself (Fodor and Bever 1965: 414–20). In a particularly interesting experiment, tape-recorded sentences were played to subjects upon which audible clicks had been superimposed. The results showed a marked tendency to place the clicks in the direction of or at the component junctures. The assumption is that even when such delineating factors as hesitation pauses or various inflections are not present, listeners tend to interpolate component boundaries on their own. So, presumably, will the congregation punctuate in their own minds what the preacher fails to do behind the pulpit. Their rhythm, after all, is that of their preacher; during the service they will help him regulate it.

Generally, though, the utterances of the preachers are grammatically acceptable, though their sermon style is marked by a very high proportion of simple declarative sentences. It would be wrong to infer from this that the cause is poor education or even a low intelligence. We know that nearly all adults have the competence to generate very complicated sentences employing several transformations. Only those who are severely retarded or who suffer from aphasia may be reduced to generating simple sentences. Rather, the conditions of performance, particularly the need to generate the next formula rapidly, profoundly influence sentence formation.

Experiments which were designed to test the relationship between the complexity of a sentence's deep structure and the ability of the individual to store it in memory, showed, not surprisingly, that simple declarative sentences produced the least interference (Savin and Perchonock 1965: 348–53). More complex sentences, such as passive voice, interrogative, and negative—all requiring at least one transformation—produced noticeably more interference with immediate memory recall. The project, as noted, set out to determine the relationship between syntactical complexity and the simplest of linguistic operations; my assumption is that the results may be carried further to imply that if the simplest operation, memory, is impeded, then more complex operations, such as generation, would also be subject to interference, and in the same relation: sentences requiring one or more transformations would be more difficult to interpret and create.

Literary critics used to attribute the simplicity of oral narrative diction to the artist's consideration for his audience. This theory held that if the language was too complex, or the metaphors too abstract, the listener would lose the thread of the story. The style of oral epic permitted no such distractions. Now we are certain that the simplicity of syntax comes about because it is easier for the oral performer, in this case the preacher, to compose simple sentences. While there is no evidence yet that simple active sentences have linguistic priority, they may have some kind of psychological priority. This would result if in interpreting complex sentences we first reduced their basic propositions to simple sentences. The evidence for this, however, is still sketchy (Deese 1970: 42–4).

Similar evidence for the ease of processing simple sentences has been deduced from experiments with self-embedded ones. Subjects could read sentences which contained two embedded relative clauses, but they were not likely to say them nor did they understand them readily when they were heard. It was their syntax that made them difficult to understand, and induced a reluctance in people to speak them. Our memories are again the limiting factor: we have difficulty processing self-embedded sentences because it is difficult to remember which of the subjects go with their separated clauses (Miller and Isard 1964: 292–303). The process requires holding the entire sentence in our minds while we sort out the clauses. This is difficult enough for formally educated people who have been coached on interpreting self-embedded sentences, and next to impossible for the oral performer.

The simplicity of the sentences generated in oral performances has other aspects: clauses tend to be generated chronologically, that is, in a way that matches the events the sentences describe. Memory performs better with temporally arranged sentences, and in several cases when the input to subjects was reversed, so that events were not arranged syntactically as they occurred in reality, the interpreted sentence was transformed to correspond to events (Clark and Clark 1968: 129–38). Clearly the events themselves have an effect on the way sentences are organized. The simplest sort of plot structure characterizes the stories in the sermons, a straightforward single-strand narrative, each episode of which is introduced by such formulas as "after a while" and "by and by." The semantic component of speech is what allows us to distinguish between a concatenation of formulas or lines and a semantically related string which we know as the sermon. Each line can no doubt be "explained" in terms of generative theory, and can be described by the vocabulary of psycholinguistics. But the theory does not help us to understand why certain sentences follow others or why certain speakers prefer certain expressions. The desire to be scientific has led us to view the formula as a thing discrete, almost autonomous, almost apart from the man who uttered it. The tendency, quite unintentional, surely, has been to view the oral performer as a manipulator.

Rather, he is creative. Though the quality of his poetry is often poor, the imagery meager, and the meter chaotic, it is a poetry nevertheless. It is worth studying because the way in which the sermons are composed is the way in which the heroic songs of Jugoslavia are created, and possibly because the songs of Homer and the *Beowulf* poet were composed in the same way. And we study the spiritual preacher for his own sake.

Edson Richmond suggests that, like Tinkerbell, folklore cannot thrive unless it is believed in (Richmond 1970: 503–05). That the spiritual sermon still thrives in American unofficial culture among the marginal churches shows that the faith is not yet dead. The preacher performs for his congregation two or three times a week and perhaps for others as often. Yet there is still a congregation to be preached to, still worshipers who help create the sermon addressed to them, and as yet no crippling and widespread apathy; the sermon continues to be preached because there are still people who demand it.

They know something, those people, that we don't: what evaporates when one reads the transcribed sermon. What is lost is what makes the performance vital. Without the congregation's rhythmic responses, without the ecstatic trances, the hand-clapping, and the calls of encouragement to the preacher, the performance is a dead one indeed. The things the text leaves out are the crucial things, the things we should study next.

Perhaps the most profound lesson I have learned from this study of marginal churches is that though they are a counter-culture in the United States, though they are well removed from the so-called mainstream of American life, yet they share many of the same problems and situations as the bards and preachers of medieval Europe, the priests of the later Middle Ages, and the epic singers of Central Asia. This removes them somewhat from the often petty existence of their immediate lives and justifies them not as members of a marginal religious movement but as members of a very large segment of humanity.

Ritualization: A Study in Texture
and Texture Change

In the following paper, I will attempt to use a linguistically derived model to characterize those religious phenomena called *rituals* in terms of *textural* rather than *structural* differences from other types of inter-action. After presenting an emic theory of structure derived from Kenneth Pike, I will derive a heuristic unit of texture, the *praxon*, from a description of the emerging rituals of a charismatic (tongues-speaking) prayer group. The praxonic analysis of texture is explicitly formulated to apply to the development of rituals (or the process of ritualization) through textural changes to be described as *fusion*.

In the study of religious phenomena, a separation is traditionally made between actions associated with religion, called rites, rituals, or ceremonies, and cognitive systems of belief or mythology. Within this separation, theorists have taken different positions as to priority: Robertson Smith (1889) argued that ritual was prior and that beliefs developed to explain it, while Tylor (1871) argued the priority of belief. Others—most notably Levi-Strauss (1966) in recent years—have argued that an analysis of the symbols used in ritual is itself the key to the underlying cognitive aspect.

Implicit in the model derived from descriptive linguistics which will be used here is the principle that it is possible to describe language without describing content, meaning being invoked only contrastively. The present study attempts to describe ritual behavior and the distri-bution of meaning over different units in that behavior, without, however, explaining the content or nature of symbolic meaning. An initial, working definition of a ritual is repeated, customary procedure, associated with religion and involving at least two human participants. That this is inadequate as a definition is immediately obvious; it serves only to focus attention on a set of phenomena, very crudely bounded but useful for the generation of hypotheses. In the following, I will argue that ritual cannot be delimited, that ritualization is a more-or-less phenomenon which may be accounted for in terms of texture, and that ritual is not necessarily associated with religion but that there is a wide overlap between ritualization, the social institution of religion, and the phenomenonological experience variously referred to as

150

"cosmic consciousness" or the "idea of the holy" (Otto 1917). Further, it is implicit in my approach that, although many rites are performed in solitude, they are best explained in terms of an interactive model.

THE STRUCTURE OF BEHAVIOR

The effort to use the techniques of descriptive linguistics to describe the whole of human cultural behavior has been most fully stated in the work of Kenneth Pike (1967). In brief and extremely simplified form, we may say that Pike suggested that two central insights of descriptive linguistics were applicable outside the boundaries of language: (1) the notion of *emic* units, units defined in terms of their contrastive function and distribution within a culturally defined system, and (2) the notion of *levels*. The model then suggests that every stretch of human behavior, say a conversation, is segmentable into emic units at a number of levels. Such a multilevel analysis of a stretch of speech by a single individual, in extremely schematic form, might be diagrammed somewhat as follows. (Level A represents segmentation into minimal units such as phonemes, while the hierarchy might go up to include higher level segmentation involving units hours or even days in duration.)

DIAGRAM

E., etc.

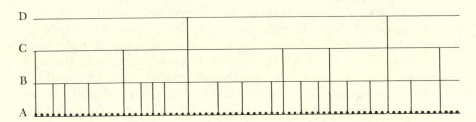

When such a model is extended to include all behavior which is culturally patterned and relevant to communication, it needs to be considerably expanded, and as yet we have no fully adequate model or technique for including body motion and other vocalization with speech. The separation of language from other types of communicative behavior reflects the experience of linguists over the years (Bateson 1968), but ultimately a full analysis of interpersonal codes of culturally patterned communication cannot rest on a sharp separation of modalities. The separation becomes increasingly untenable at higher levels;

thus, for example, a kinesic line (body motion) recording raised eye-brows, lifted shoulders, and outturned wrists, might be separable from a linguistic line recording the separate morphemes of *so what?* but at the next level up these are combined in a single unit in the interaction. The same problem arises from interactions involving several partici-pants: at low levels of analysis, it may be a convenience to describe the participants separately, but at higher levels a single unit may involve two or more actors. Thus, at a low level, a handshake involves two distinct stretches of behavior, but the social event at a higher level of analysis surely involves two persons in a single event. Thus, the units at high levels of analysis, e.g. a "play" in a baseball game, will subsume actions in several modalities and performed by several in-dividuals in a defined context. The physical forms of the units at higher levels will be less homogeneous than at the lower levels, and their duration occasionally equal but generally greater.

This multilevel model may be characterized as the "Dagwood sand-wich" model of human interactions: level piled on level, each con-structed of different ingredients. It has considerable utility for descrip-tion, but has rarely been fully carried out. It also presents serious disadvantages. A number of theorists have maintained that *no* seg-mentary/sequential model is adequate for describing human behavior (Lashley 1951; Chomsky 1957, 1965), a charge which will not be analyzed in detail here except by maintaining that all human behavior has a segmentary/sequential aspect which presents itself for description. Most seriously, this Dagwood sandwich model supposes such intricacy of shared coding that is almost impossible to imagine using it to account for interactions between mother and child, members of differ-ent subcultures, etc. In what follows, it will be assumed that such a model is roughly applicable to the structure of culturally patterned behavior *by each individual,* but that, in considering interactions, we must consider the possibility that the entire structure is not shared but only the divisions at some levels. This leads to the question of whether segmentations at different levels have differential importance, in vary-ing contexts, and it is here that we discover a key to understanding ritualization.

Before moving on, it is necessary to ask about the extent to which the model described above for the structure of behavior includes ritual: Is ritual governed by the same codes (phonemic, tagmemic, kinesic, etc.) that apply to other interactions, such as conversations? The answer is that sometimes, especially in newly-formed groups, the codes are the same, but there is a strong tendency to divergence, with ritual exerting a conservative influence (Latin in the Catholic Church, King James English, the preservation of Sanskrit, etc.) There is even evidence that a divergent code is sometimes preferred. An adequate theory of ritualization must account for these tendencies.

RITUALIZATION IN PROGRESS

As an alternative to considering events in terms of the total internal structure of each level and its position in the hierarchy, I would like to introduce an example and examine it in some detail. During 1965–66 I attended and took notes on the prayer meetings of a group of middle-class white Christians, mostly in their early twenties. A core group of eight to ten, with as many as six less regular attenders, met once a week in an apartment in a New England city from 8 P.M. until midnight or later, for prayer. (A slightly different group, with many overlapping members, met on another night for Bible study, and there was a good deal of other contact in the course of the week.) Sunday church attendance was in mainstream Protestant churches: Lutheran, Episcopalian, Congregational (with fundamentalist leanings), etc. The prayer sessions of this group followed a general pattern, with frequent deviations, which is described in the following. All descriptions are reconstructions from notes taken after the meeting or the following morning, since it was not possible to tape record or take notes during sessions.

1. The evening began with hymn singing, from the Billy Graham hymnal, sometimes lasting as long as one hour. Only a fraction of the hymns in the booklet were used, and these were used on almost every occasion but with no set order. Hymn singing continued until all late comers were presumed arrived and often ended with some member of the group asking, in some exasperation, whether the group should not be praying by now.

2. Even so, prayer was usually preceded by a discussion of intercessions, which often involved descriptions of experiences during the week, non-members of the group for whom prayer was requested, or the reading of letters from friends out of town, perhaps working as missionaries. These discussions underlined both the fact of a network of groups of such "born-again Christians" and their sense of distinction from people encountered at work or school who stood in need of prayer. Here again, discussion was sometimes protracted, until some members again became impatient to get on to praying.

3. The main portion of the evening was approximately two hours spent in prayer, which included a number of different activities.

(3a) Long stretches were spent in silence, with each person praying as the Spirit moved him. During silent prayer, speaking in tongues was often just barely audible from two or three members of the group, a whisper or a murmur, or occasionally soft laughter. Most members of the group either bowed their heads or closed their eyes, sometimes "using their chair as an altar" (kneeling on the floor, and resting the upper body on the chair seat, head buried in the hands). Members of the group varied in their reports of what they were doing during silent prayer, some reporting visions (usually lights and colors) and others reporting distraction (remembering to feed the cat, etc.). A middle group, which I will treat here as typical, reported spending their time in colloquy with God, sometimes in tongues, sometimes in verbal or sub-verbal prayer, sometimes filled with emotion (love, longing, remorse) and not verbalizing.

(3b) At frequent intervals, a member of the group would pray spontaneously, using ordinary English and rather stereotyped phraseology. During such prayers, which often began with an address (e.g. *dear Jesus*) but had no marked ending (such as *amen*), the soft prayer in tongues would cease, and there was a general expectation that others would listen and join their prayer to that of the speaker. Such prayers included "gate-keeping" prayers at the beginning of the session ("Dear Jesus, we just want to thank you for bringing us here and for being here with us . . ."), requested intercessions (e.g. X would pray for Y's brother, who he had said was having trouble in school), and, increasingly, more personal prayers of praise or petition as the evening went on.

(3c) Occasionally, a member of the group would prophesy. Prophecy was usually indicated by a firm, authoritative voice, somewhat more formal and sometimes in Biblical language, and content which stated divine will, often in response to a petition for guidance, but usually reassuring and non-specific. Often the first person pronoun referred to God. Only three or four members of the group prophesied with any frequency, and there was often discussion of members' resistance to speak out when God "laid it on them" to speak, and of the importance of daring to pray for the gift of prophecy and other spiritual gifts.

(3d) Less frequently, a member of the group would pray out loud in tongues, usually then praying for an interpretation, and another member of the group would offer an interpretation in terms comparable to (3c): complete interpretations were apparently the same as prophecies. If an interpretation was not forthcoming, the meeting sometimes broke down in discussions of what to do, since such uninterpreted utterances in tongues were strongly frowned on. If, however, utterances in tongues were sung, there was virtually no demand for interpretation, and tongues were uninterpreted in several other contexts (see below).

Only tongues spoken in the context of unfocussed common prayer were treated as messages meant to inform.

(3e) Intermittently, often immediately after other inputs, someone would say "Thank you, Jesus" or "Praise the Lord." Such exclamations were conspicuously absent after long, wordy intercessions, and were one of the principle sanction-reward techniques of the group. Longer standardized interjections included hymn refrains in which all could join: "All things are possible, Jesus is here."

(3f) Sometimes someone would address the group in a conversational tone. Occasionally this would be to pass on a "Word of wisdom," also a spiritual gift, or to discuss the intimation of a prophecy or interpretation, still incomplete, or to comment on a deficiency in the prayer process ("I keep getting the feeling that this isn't what we're supposed to be doing tonight . . ."). Members raised their heads and came to attention at different rates, sometimes obviously reluctant and wanting to return to prayer, but sometimes such interruptions ended the session. There was a general understanding that prayer is difficult and talk a temptation.

4. Towards the end of the meeting, one or two people would ask to be prayed for with laying-on-of-hands, and several members of the group would gather round their chair, laying hands on the person's head or shoulders or holding hands, praying aloud in English or in tongues without pressure for interpretation. It was in this context that the "baptism of the Holy Spirit" was sometimes granted to newcomers, who then spoke in tongues, or healing occurred, sometimes by proxy. Such prayer was also often requested for help in overcoming temptations or depression.

5. The meeting usually ended with renewed singing, sometimes in tongues (each member articulating according to his tongue but following the common tune). Afterwards, there was sometimes a period of discussion, with soft drinks and cookies, depending on the hour.

A few other general characteristics of the group that may not be immediately discernible from the above should be mentioned: role differences were clearly apparent, sometimes related to differences in spiritual gifts; sessions were not all equally successful and were occasionally regarded as failures; transitions from sections 3 to 4 or 4 to 5 were not always simultaneous for all concerned and some members could be observed only gradually coming out of a light trance. However, meetings were highly decorous, even during section 4, the portion of highest common intensity. Whatever mild states of dissociation occurred were heavily socialized and shaped by the group tradition.

THE TEXTURE OF BEHAVIOR

For testing the structural model, a possible portion of section 3, the main prayer period of the evening, will be analyzed.

A. A period of silence.
B. Susan says, "O Lord Jesus, we thank you because you're really real and you're really right here with us, and we can just feel you here in the room. And, Jesus, we really wish you would help us to pray and help us to love everyone here. . . ."
C. A period of silence.
D. John says, "You know my friend Bill, Jesus, that I've prayed about before. And I know you're looking after him, but couldn't you just give him a sign because he's really having trouble with his exams and he's thinking of maybe leaving graduate school at the end of this term, and . . ."
E. A period of silence.
F. Bill prays out loud in tongues.
G. Ann says, "Thus saith the Lord/ Yea I say unto you/ I am the Lord your God/ and I am a God of Love/ So turn again/ and this is what I want to say to you,/ you should be washed in the blood of the lamb."
H. John says, "Thank you, Jesus."
I. A period of silence.
J. Susan initiates and others join, singing "Jesus is here, Jesus is here, all things are possible, Jesus is here."
K. A period of silence.

At the highest level, of course, the whole evening is a single unit; at the next structural level down, it is subdivided into the five standard sections already described. At a lower level of segmentation, the main prayer session may be segmented, and the above represents one such segment. These different vocalizations, occurring over a half-hour period, seem to group together: Susan acts initially as gatekeeper, John prays for guidance and later his "Thank you, Jesus" accepts the interpreted message in tongues as an answer to his prayer, and Susan's renewed gatekeeping takes the incident as evidence of the efficacy of the group's prayer and as transition to a new passage, closing the "Bill" passage. From the point of view of the group, F (the speech in tongues) and G (its interpretation) are a single event, constituting an answer to John's request.

In applying the structural model to this passage, we can note first of all that there were no gross bodily motions during it, such as to be audible, so that bowed heads and closed eyes were sufficient to filter out body motion from the communication stream. We can focus on the vocal portion, noting as we do so that the "period of silence" has a vocal portion as well, the murmuring or whispering in tongues, which was not resumed between F and H, but was resumed after D (relating to the fact that such petitions do not require an answer, while utterances in tongues do require an interpretation). Thus we can simplify our task by analyzing only the vocal line (treating continuities in other modalities as a transfix), but assuming that, to the extent that techniques appropriate to the vocal line can be applied to other modalities, the same modifications in interpretation might also be appropriate under ritual circumstances.

The structural levels with which we are concerned are as follows.

The entire prayer meeting is *one unit* at the highest level.

It has *five sub-sections* at the next level down, including the main prayer session.

The main prayer session breaks into sections (no set number) of which we are examining *one.*

Our example breaks into *three sections:* B, D through H, and J, with silence as transitions.

At the next level down, B and J are not subdivided, but D-H has three sections: D, F-G, and H.

The next level down is, roughly, the paragraph level. None of our speakers speaks more than one paragraph, and we might split F and G at this level. It is probably most convenient to treat each of these sections, including the sections of silence, as a paragraph.

DIAGRAM 2

Higher levels of organization, fitting the sample section into the structure of the entire evening

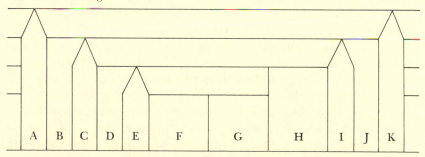

Lower levels of syntactic, morphological, and phonological analysis

(Following the usage of Immediate Constituent analysis with conjunctions, transitional sections are in peaked enclosures rather than boxed. This does not, however, imply that all divisions are binary.)

The sections vary in the applicability of further analysis. Spoken paragraphs have sentence structure, as well as morphological and phonological structure. So, in a slightly different sense, does speech in tongues (indicated only by intonation, see Nida 1964). But the periods of silence, while they no doubt have substructure for each individual, have no common substructure for the entire group.

Strikingly enough, one of the first things we notice about the structural analysis is that it can only be consistently made at all levels if we focus on only one participant. It does not even exist for the group as a whole.

By comparing the different paragraphs, I hope to show what I mean by *texture*. John's prayer for Bill is most similar to ordinary discourse. It includes some facts about Bill that the group may not know, and they must pay attention to follow what is being said. Furthermore, if he knows English and knows the meaning of the separate morphemes, even a newcomer to the group can understand most of what is being said.

At the opposite extreme is the hymn refrain. It is known by heart, so that although it has the internal structure of English it cannot be regarded as being encoded or generated in the same sense as John's prayer. As soon as Susan sings the first word, what follows is highly predictable and others can and do join in. Furthermore, it serves for this group as a kind of doxology, which means that a newcomer, knowing English, does not know what is being affirmed here. The entire unit, like the Lord's Prayer or the Pledge of Allegiance to the Flag, has a meaning, which cannot be deduced from an analysis of the parts.

Between these two extremes stand Susan's opening prayer and Ann's interpretation. Susan's prayer seems superficially comparable to John's, but familiarity with the group shows that her prayer is much more predictable, has much lower information content than John's. It is not memorized but it contains a large number of set phrases: "O Lord Jesus," "you're really real," "help us to pray," "help us to love." These turn up as units again and again in Susan's prayers and seem to be used as wholes, in the classical sense of *clichés;* through repetition and association, they have both acquired and lost meanings for the group in a way different from novel phrasings.

Where cliché is the appropriate word for Susan, Ann's utterance can only be described in terms of the concept of a *formula*. This concept was developed (Parry 1930; Lord 1965) to describe the method of composition of epic poetry and has been applied to many other kinds of materials, including spiritual sermons (see Rosenberg, this volume). Ann's interpretation is made by stringing together memorized formulae, derived from Biblical or liturgical sources, with only a brief transition that one might think of as generated on the spot: "this is what I want to say to you, you should be. . . ."

To use a concatenation model of speech as an example, we can see that while John's prayer might be said to be made by stringing together a large number of separate small chunks, Ann's interpretation, while almost as long and almost as complex from a structural point of view, is made by stringing together a much smaller number of bulky, preformed chunks.

To illuminate the nature of these chunks, we can compare them with a more familiar concept, that of an *idiom*. Hockett (1958: 172) suggests the following approach to the definition of an idiom: "Let us momentarily use the term 'Y' for any grammatical form the meaning of which is not deducible from its structure. Any Y, in any occurrence in which it is not a constituent of a larger Y, is an idiom." Such a definition includes the word *white* in *white paint* but not in *White House,* which is itself an idiom. However, the definition excludes the phrase *White House* in the larger idiom *That man in the White House.* In each case *white* is a single morpheme with a constant grammatical function. Thus, Hockett's definition differs from the common understanding of "idiom" in including the minimal case—an idiom consisting of a single morpheme (since the meaning can certainly not be deduced from the phonological structure.) Hockett ignores, however, the application of the definition to very large units, such as the entire Lord's Prayer. Furthermore, the term idiom is too clearly focused on verbal behavior. Thus, I have found it useful to coin the term *praxon* as an extension of this familiar notion.

In a structural segmentation of a stretch of behavior, we get a multi-level hierarchy of sequenced units in many modalities at each level. In a textural segmentation of a stretch of behavior, I am proposing a *single* segmentation of sequenced units at *different* levels. Praxonic segmentation segments behavior into the minimal chunks, whose meaning is not deducible from their structure, even though this may be very extensive.

Consider one example, the sequence "Let's all say the Lord's Prayer: Our Father who . . . Amen." Structural analysis will give us the full linguistic Dagwood sandwich of this utterance, including a segmentation into a hundred-odd morphemes. Praxonic analysis suggests that it contains seven praxons:

Let	's	all	say	the	Lord's Prayer	"Our Father . . . Amen"
1	2	3	4	5	6	7

It might in fact be reasonable to construct a ratio of words or morphemes to praxons to characterize a stretch of discourse. This ratio would express the difference in texture between the various sections described in the prayer meeting. Utterances consisting of a small number of high-level praxons (high morpheme: praxon ratio) may be called *fused*. Lest confusion arise, however, from the suggestion of what looks like a mathematical expression, I have to point out that the same praxonic structure for an event is not necessarily shared by all participants and may shift rapidly over time. Someone who had never heard the Lord's Prayer before but spoke English would have to struggle along doing his best to deduce its meaning from its structure, just as a new arrival in the prayer group would have to try to understand Susan's prayer. Interviewing and observation allow one to establish rather readily that one sequence is, in general, more fused than another, or that the current tendency is toward fusion (or its opposite, *fission*), or to speculate on differences in degree of fusion for different participants, but this is a far cry from precise quantification.

Conditions of Fusion

A consideration of examples of ritual has led me to the conclusion that ritualization consists in a high degree of fusion, that rituals typically consist of high-level praxons. Since high fusion also seems to be a characteristic of infant experience, this may be related to the numinous, "holy" quality of much ritual (Erikson 1966). A consideration of the conditions of fusion, as related to ritual, seems to match up with a number of well-known facts about ritual. Fusion comes about through (a) addition of meaning, (b) atrophy of components, (c) blurring of boundaries, or (d) hyperregular surface structure.

(a) Addition of meaning here actually refers to a number of similar but not identical processes. The difference between *the white house* and *the White House* seems to lie partly in a greater specificity of the second term, and partly in the addition of a number of special connotations (as in "The White House denies . . ."). *That Man in the White House* has both of these features, as well as an emotional connotation, and we must suppose that the fusion of this praxon was related to the very strong feelings of many people about FDR.

It is the addition of strong emotional connotations that is perhaps crucial for ritual. A couple goes out to dinner, eats certain foods, hears certain music, dances . . . and becomes engaged. On anniversaries of their engagement they may replicate the entire evening, originally a sequence of events, now fused into a whole. The same argument might be made for the Last Supper. Thus a nonce pattern is crystallized into a newly meaningful single unit.

(b) Atrophy of components would seem to be a common property of rituals because of their frequent antiquity. Here the argument cuts both ways: on the one hand, what is there about the religious context that makes people content to say words or perform acts whose original meaning is lost? On the other hand, what are typical effects of repetition over long periods?

A small example of the effect of atrophy of components is given by the phrase *wrack and ruin.* Since few people know the meaning of *wrack,* the term must either mean 'X and ruin' or have a meaning as a whole, 'devastation, decay'. I would argue that 'X and ruin' is unstable, and tends toward either a dropping of the X or an attribution of meaning to the whole. Similarly, the partial or complete atrophy of words such as *art, hallowed,* and *trespasses,* or the fact that such words as *pledge, allegiance,* and *indivisible* must be virtually empty for young children, must contribute to the fusion of such praxons as the Lord's Prayer or the Pledge of Allegiance. In the extreme case, almost the entire structure is atrophied, as in the Latin canon. An examination of all contexts where archaic language is used (poetry, political speeches) might reveal the general basis for a toleration of fused praxons, with all the implications this carries.

(c) Blurring of boundaries occurs through repetition and habit formation, as in driving, when the series of actions involved in starting the car are merged into a single experiential unit, or as when the mumbled words of the rosary are run together. However, the process of blurring boundaries can be forced in various ways, especially by mixing modalities. When words are set to music, spoken in unison, or both danced and sung, only the high-level boundaries are likely to match perfectly, and therefore the structure is only fully intelligible at the highest levels, with lower-level segmentation destroyed. The use of multimedia barrages, especially where these are out of synchrony, as with music combined with random slides and turning strobe lights, presses towards fusion, the "total experience." The use, therefore, of dissonance between verbal and rhythmic line as a cue for going into trance, as in santería ceremonies (see Marks, this volume), can be explained as a sudden impetus to fusion, through a shattering or denial of lower-level structure.

(d) Hyperregular surface structure is a characteristic of artistic production and may be regarded as representing the aesthetic aspect of fusion. In poetry, the poet works over his lines until they are characterized by more regularity than ordinary speech: rhyme, meter, assonance, and alliteration may be specified in a poetic tradition; further study may show consistent but unspecified distortions in phonology, patterns of repetition of morphemes and syntactic surface structures (Bateson 1970). These have the effect that particular words in the poem have a quality of necessity and the poem an overall quality of unity. Furthermore, the poetic process, in which the poet's careful tuning loops back and back through the sequential structure, may also tend to blur grammatical boundaries. Wallace Stevens is an example of a poet who may use the whole poem to make a concerted attack on the individual meaningfulness of his words and their role in the sentence, and many of the lines of Hopkins are enhanced by an ambiguity about what is noun or verb, what is subject or predicate. Similarly in other art forms, such as dance or painted decoration on pottery, what we see is increased regularity and redundancy (Lomax 1966), so that the observer responds to a whole. An excess of this, of course, produces doggerel, so that the problem of the real artist is to achieve just the right amount of hyperregularity and then play with it.

These four conditions of fusion are interrelated in a number of ways, and all relate to traditionally recognized characteristics of ritual in various societies. The addition of meaning is related to the heightened sense of significance and arousal that often attends religious ceremonial; atrophy of components is related to the common antiquity of rites; blurring of boundaries is related to repetition, group performance, and mixed modalities; and hyperregularity is related to the aesthetic elaboration of religious ceremonial. In ritual, we must see repetition and heightened arousal as gradually producing a measure of the other characteristics; in poetry, a manipulation of structure is used to produce the arousal. Thus the two complement each other, but no hard and fast line can be drawn.

Another way of considering the phenomenon of fusion would be to note that a praxon is a minimal structural segment whose meaning is not deducible from its structure, but that different kinds of meaning are appropriate to different degrees of fusion. When we speak of the "meaning" of the entire Lord's Prayer, we are using the term in a rather different sense from when we speak of the "meaning" of the word *bread*. I would argue that the bulkier the praxons of an interaction, the less they are understandable in referential terms. Instead, the communication must be seen as serving primarily expressive and phatic functions (Malinowski 1968). Thus, the language of highly-fused messages, in poetry and ritual, is only in a minor degree referential, and their truth value should not be judged in terms of reference. Further, an unsegmentable (unsegmentable because the parts cannot be determined or because their sum is notably less than the whole) statement is much less subject to contradiction and query than a segmentable one. If one treats *The Lord is one* as four praxons, subject to rearrangement without loss according to the grammar of the language, the statement coexists with a family of related sentences: *Is the Lord one? The Lord is not one. The Lord is six. Moloch is one.* Certainly, the sentence *It will snow tomorrow* coexists with the related sentences *It won't snow tomorrow,* etc. I would contend that the Shema in its ritual use is a single fused praxon, coexisting at a much higher level with a family of praxons such as *Who brings forth bread from the earth.* It is essential to distinguishing the ritual from the theological use of such phrases to see that in ritual they are fused and in theological discourse they are segmented. Recently, the theologians and Church historians prevailed upon the Episcopal Church to try deleting the *filioque* from the Creed, which now says of the Holy Ghost, "Who proceedeth from the Father . . . and with the Father and the Son together is worshipped and glorified" ("and the Son" once stood in place of the dots). The effect is, predictably, fission: turning the recitation of the Creed from a ritual to a theological act, which makes everyone present extremely uncomfortable, having long been assured that this was not a word-by-word matter. On the other hand, if one part of the whole is to be changed without too much loss of sacredness, it is handy to have a temporary fission so that change or substitution occurs in a small praxon, which can then perhaps be re-fused.

From this point of view, the sudden acceptance of complex and sometimes bizarre theologies by new converts is not surprising. In the emotional "white heat" of conversion, such theological discourse is fused and affirmation becomes properly a single act. Converts of this sort can be trapped into word-by-word argumentation about the validity of individual words in the whole which they affirm, but it is a more authentic expression of the nature of their affirmation when they sew Bibles into the lining of a coat or bind verses to their foreheads or chant them in the street. It might even be possible to argue that a difficult theology supports fusion, just as the mixing of modalities switches the santería dancer into trance.

APPLICATION TO THE CONTEMPORARY UNITED STATES

It remains to carry this general analysis back to the problem of the marginal churches, and to suggest some of its implications for the problem of innovative ritual.

The recent increase in new religious groupings in the United States occurs against a background of a civilization which seems increasingly to emphasize fission. Some examples would be the assembly line or the woman who cooks a dish by following a recipe step by step or bathes her baby by the rules in a child care manual. Some applications of "systems analysis" fall precisely into this trap, as exemplified by an architect who complains to me that the "systems analysis boys" in his office want him to break the design process down into steps, each of which he can justify separately, instead of moving toward a total aesthetic conception of a building. Time and motion study represents fission. In the intellectual sphere, communication is increasingly conceptualized in referential terms.

This pressure toward fission can even be observed in the liturgical movements of the mainline churches, which tend to be predicated on the notion that ritual should be intelligible word for word, that repetition should be avoided, and that atrophied components are anathema. If the argument of this paper is correct, they have precisely misunderstood the nature of ritual, perhaps because they are ministering to congregations who have been made incapable of achieving a sense of heightened significance through fusion.

On the other hand, the tendency towards fusion can be observed in many other aspects of contemporary society. Youth culture is characterized by techniques for fusion: rock music, multimedia experiences, drug use, reciting mantras, high stereotypy in expression. Newly arising religious movements, devising new rituals, are in many cases moving towards fusion even while the mainstream churches seem to be moving away. It is in this context, I believe, that we must understand the importance of ecstatic experience in the shaping of new religious traditions, for they are confronted with the paradox of innovating "new rituals" and must rely on emotion or on aesthetic structure as alternatives to time in bringing about fusion.

It is important to see the process whereby new religious movements strive towards the level of fusion that will make their rituals meaningful and numinous for participants in terms of the recurrent rhythms of fusion and fission that characterize the communicative patterns of a society. Fusion and fission fluctuate as each new member learns to participate by alternately imitating and incorporating large chunks of rule-governed behavior and then analyzing these chunks to become the basis for more flexible performance. In periods of change, fusion helps to bridge differences in detail of individual structure (as in the use of silence to bridge the varying experiences of separate worshipers), and yet at the same time fission allows for a tinkering with individual parts without destroying the sense which participants have of a whole. Thus, in the Catholic Church, one of the early strong emphases in liturgical renewal was on the fact that the Mass is composed of parts, which can then be tinkered with while change is localized.

Nevertheless, while praxonic texture must be in constant fluctuation, textural variation in our own society may present a special case. Many individuals seem to have lost the capacity for fused experience and to reject all ritual forms. The inability to experience repetitive material as fused leads to boredom, certainly one of the major ills of our society.

On the other hand, a hunger for fusion drives some individuals to the opposite extreme, and the rise of the marginal religions is perhaps one symptom of their search. Furthermore, the distinction between religious and secular contexts may impose artificial breaks in the continuum of textural types. The heuristic use of the concept praxon may provide a bridge between the structural and the phenomenological analysis of behavior that will allow a new understanding of the role of ritual, seen as part of a continuum.

In the Beginning Was the Word:
The Relationship of Language
to Social Organization in
Spiritualist Churches

"When I use a word," Humpty Dumpty said, in rather a scornful tone, "it means just what I choose it to mean—neither more nor less." "The question is," said Alice, "whether you can make words mean so many different things." "The question is," said Humpty Dumpty, "which is to be master—that's all."— Through the Looking Glass And What Alice Found There

O<small>N</small> Tuesday evening, after a long and crowded church service, Reverend Kelly of the Metaphysical Temple of Spiritual Life, went about her chores closing the church for the night and started speaking about the service that had just ended: "You see, like tonight I had them packed in, I read for thirty-five people . . . did you see those kids trying to test me with those mathematical questions, I tell them Spirit's got more important things to do. And those women over there, sitting in the back, I think they're from [Reverend] Watkins' place . . . and who was that guy sitting on the side? . . . you see, they come here, half the time I don't know who they are. They could be snoopin' around trying to make trouble, or they could be just new and don't know their way around here . . . I can't place them . . . that's why I say, we all in these churches, we have a code worked out, when I give them messages I tell them that *vibrations aren't right* or the *conditions will improve* or that *Spirit sends you love* and *envelopes you with the great white light of eternal truth.* My people know what I want to say to them, we understand one another. And the rest, they want me to say stuff I don't want to say . . . well they can go elsewhere."

Spiritualists use a particular vocabulary as their system of communication. They have adapted standard English into a ritual language, a kind of religious argot. The argot is used by both parishioners and church functionaries during church services, as well as outside the church context in discussing church-related topics among themselves or with interested newcomers. The argot includes lexical items which label every facet of the church life and belief system. The more integral an activity or belief is to the functioning of the church, the more elaborate are the labels applied to it. This vocabulary is composed of standard English terms which are used, however, in non-standard ways. The argot meanings of the terms have been created by Spiritualists and are often not understood by native speakers of English who are unfamiliar with the beliefs, rituals, or social organization of these churches. Because this argot is composed of standard English terms we may view it as phonemically and syntactically one language to all native speakers of English, but functionally as two distinct systems of communication. Non-Spiritualists interpret the argot as an ambiguous, unconventional, and incomprehensible use of standard English. To Spiritualists, however, the language transmits very specific information about church life which the parishioner is able to interpret for himself. On the most general level of Spiritualist meaning, all of the terms in the argot are shared by the formally organized churches. However, superimposed on the shared argot are also some specific lexical items and nuances of meaning that are unique and restricted to individual churches.

Church participants recognize that the argot is both a literal and metaphorical code for communication. They use it purposefully and self-consciously. They recognize the relevance of the medium to the message and are aware that the spoken word is not only a vehicle for religious communication but often its essence.

For the anthropologist language is also a code and a particularly important source of information. Not only does he listen to the content of what is being said but also to the style in which it is couched and the structure in which it is conveyed. The linguistic form often places the speaker in his cultural and social contexts and thus sheds additional light on the content of his communication. Language is a system whereby an individual is able to communicate about others while reflecting upon himself.

But language is not just a symbolic system to be studied for its own sake; it is a key to the understanding of a culture and its social organization. While Reverend Kelly talked at length on that Tuesday evening about the church service, the people, the language, the messages from Spirit, she was telling me much more than just about church problems; she was also telling me about herself, how she related to *her people*,[1] how she viewed herself vis-à-vis them and how she felt about her *platform work*, the on-stage and back-stage realities.

To decode this kind of information I needed to listen creatively. I had to pay a great deal of attention to both the content and the form of the statements. I listened to the language of the church, and simul-

---

[1] At first appearance, and later when helpful, argot terms are italicized.

taneously I had to compare and contrast what I heard with what I had observed. For language as a cultural and social system is revealed as it is used.

In this paper particular attention is paid to the Spiritualist argot for four reasons. First, to indicate how language can be used to tap the cultural knowledge, the cognitive map, that individuals carry in their heads about their social group. Such knowledge allows them to behave in a manner that will elicit anticipated results. Second, to allow the investigator to use the linguistic data as an index of and as evidence for the social relationships and institutional structure within each church and among the various branch churches of the Spiritualist denomination. Third, to provide a research tool in acquiring information about an anonymous and continuously shifting church population with whom interview contact is virtually impossible. Fourth, the argot is acknowledged by church participants to reflect the belief system and social organization of the church. It is not a construct arbitrarily imposed of the data only for theoretical considerations.

The material presented here deals with the Spiritualist movement in Bay City,[2] California. The research upon which it is based has been conducted during the past five years.[3] It has been an unusually long field tour and was aimed to include a comprehensive study of all the extant, formally organized Spiritualist churches in Bay City. There were several topical foci of concentration during fieldwork. However, a systematic and consistent effort was made throughout to collect data on the particular use of language, a Spiritualist argot, within these churches.[4]

[2] All persons and places mentioned have been given fictitious names, and any resemblance between these names and those of actual persons in Bay City is unintentional. The name Bay City is borrowed from Lofland (1966). Since I worked in the same location as he did, I have used his place name for consistency in the literature.

[3] Although this study was conducted principally in Bay City, fieldwork was also done in the New England and mid-Atlantic states, as well as in state and national conventions of Spiritualists. Fieldwork during the past five years has been supported at various times by the following foundations: National Institute of Health Training Grant in Anthropology, grant number GM 1224; Mabelle McLeod Lewis Memorial Fund; Smithsonian Institution post-Doctoral Research Program; Wenner-Gren Foundation for Anthropological Research, grant number 2514; National Science Foundation Institutional Grant administered by Princeton University. I would like to express my gratitude to these foundations.

[4] I would like to thank Professor Elizabeth Colson who advised me during fieldwork and has always patiently and generously discussed with me the various research issues included in this project. I would like to thank Professors Brent Berlin, Paul Kay, William Sturtevant, and Mr. Jerrold Guben, for having made some helpful suggestions in the analysis of the material.

I am particularly indebted to Miss Mary Frederick who worked with me during most of the fieldwork. She helped in every aspect of the research. Without her the work could not have been brought to a successful conclusion.

Within the general term *Spiritualism* fall the activities of a great many churches and splinter groups active in Bay City. Therefore, the churches in this study were chosen not only on the basis of their stated beliefs and religious practices, but also on their organizational structures. All the churches herein described are: (a) legally and religiously recognized as being affiliated with the Spiritualist denomination, (b) regularly convened for religious worship, (c) formally organized as churches, and ((d) open to the public at large. Excluded from present analysis are privately held séances and other spiritualist gatherings, conducted even by ordained ministers, which were not in a formal church or which did not develop out of some church affiliation of the participants. Also excluded were privately held classes of Spiritualist practitioners which were organized to train individuals to offer therapeutic services. In the case of *séance work* and *class work* the use of a religious argot differs from that of *church work* and has to be analyzed independently.

The thesis presented in this paper is as follows: through their verbal exchanges in the idiom of the argot, Spiritualists create the social organization of the church—the roles, statuses, and hierarchical relationships that articulate the church as a social institution. Once a church is organized and a social structure is made explicit, participants within that structure formulate a grammar of rules for the proper and continued use of the argot by both themselves and newcomers to the church. Abiding by these rules, penalizing their misuse, and generating new ones allows Spiritualists to control the structural evolution of the church through time. The social structure of the church has to be viewed and understood in terms of the speech events through which participants in the church: (1) define and make explicit their roles and statuses within the church, (2) test and affirm their mobility within the church hierarchy, (3) perceive and announce their own spiritual development, and (4) establish the context markers of church activity within the larger society.

In pursuit of the above task a study has been conducted to collect data on the use of the church argot through the techniques of ethnographic semantics. The lexicographic analysis proceeded through the following stages: (1) isolating the corpus of terms, (2) glossing each term in its natural speech context occurrence, (3) discovering the overall number of senses in which a term is used, and (4) demonstrating, according to the relevant criteria of the churches, the relationships that exist between terms that label identical or similar referents.

The use of language in the church is a topic of great sensitivity to many Spiritualists, for it deals with some of what is considered the most sacred portion of the service, namely, the demonstration of spiritual communication through mediumship. In my analysis I do not wish either to secularize or to profane these sacred services, nor to engage in a kind of reductionism and say that all mystery is locked within the spoken word. Rather, my attempt is to present a cultural and social system at work through the vantage point of participants in Spiritualist churches.[5]

I. Who Are Spiritualists and What Is Spiritualism?

Individuals who frequented Spiritualist churches during the course of my research were men and women of all walks of life, a cross-section of ethnic, cultural, religious and socio-economic backgrounds. The Spiritualist movement made its goal to attract a diversity of people and "to make everyone feel at home." Partly toward fulfilling that goal, many churches syncretized artifacts and beliefs from various traditions into a religious system that is a kind of patchwork quilt of many other religious systems extant within the United States. The larger churches usually attract a more diversified population than the smaller and more obscure churches. This is in large measure due to the fact that larger churches can afford to advertize their services in the local newspapers and have the financial resources to remain permanently located at a given address. Therefore, they are more likely to receive a diversity of people who are investigating Spiritualism for the first time.

Both large and small churches have a nuclear population that attends it with some regularity and offers continued financial support through love-offerings during the church services. That population tends to be more homogenous and can be characterized by certain shared features.

Many of the nuclear groups are middle-aged men and women who never married or are divorced or widowed. Often they live in apartments in large downtown complexes, or sometimes in hotels catering to permanent residents. Their furnishings are usually cumulative memorabilia of places and times in which they felt more integrated into the fabric of social life. They work at white collar jobs, secretarial, clerical, semi-skilled or semi-professional. Their free time is largely unoccupied. They spend much of that free time seeking companionship. They regard themselves and others in the churches as sensitive people who are "seekers of a spiritual path," "Students of Truth," "pioneers of the Aquarian age" and believers in the equality and brotherhood of men. Most of them have been born and reared in orthodox denominations

---

[5] Some of the material in this essay appeared in *Culture and Cognition: Rules, Maps, and Plans,* edited by James P. Spradley, Chandler Publishing Co., San Francisco, 1972, and those sections are reprinted with permission.

but have disaffiliated themselves from active participation. They regard Spiritualist churches as marginal churches that are becoming recognized by an increasing number of people as the most satisfactory forms of worship.

Church participants speak about and communicate through their behavior an intense sense of individual loneliness. Even those who are married or have a steady companion relate to the church as individuals rather than as couples. Most adherents are looking to fill an empty social space in their life and concomitantly depend on others for advice on problems of job and residential mobility, health difficulties, and issues of daily decision-making. They are caught in a twilight zone of time, in transit between a cherished past and an undetermined future.

In searching for help in decision-making, these individuals turn to Spiritualist churches and to the realm of spirits, who are often the departed relatives or friends of the individual. Such spirits can be relied on for good advice and are also regarded as substitutes for the social vacancies individuals feel in their daily life. Although the churches seem to offer a modus vivendi to their adherents, most participants remain loyal only to a quest for personal deliverance, and are uncommitted to any one religious institution that offers them a means to that deliverance. They are followers of a quest which is punctuated by recurring disillusion with institutional answers. They come to a medium for help, find hope, often lose faith, only to return to another medium to seek anew.

In their quest they are particularly attuned to language, or more specifically to being talked at, lectured to, and verbally managed by a host of religious functionaries. They remain passive observers and absorbers, a kind of captive audience always in groups, always alone.

Spiritualism

Spiritualism is one of the earliest metaphysical movements to appear in the first half of the nineteenth century. In over a century and a quarter of history it has spanned the evolution of amorphous, spontaneous, and often short-lived associations into formally organized, clearly defined, established churches.

Throughout its history Spiritualism has enjoyed some popular interest. Especially in the nineteenth and early twentieth century it offered séances and *physical phenomena* to a great many individuals who were interested in the demonstrable aspects of religion that might approximate scientific proof for personal beliefs. In approximately twenty-year intervals since the Civil War, Spiritualism has experienced a renascence of popularity correlated with national crises of war and economic failure. Such periods of national upheaval and personal disorientation brought to its gates several kinds of people: those who suffered personal loss of relatives who died in wars, those who felt anxiety over their own death and were preoccupied with notions of reincarnation, those who were dislocated and had difficulty in making decisions about life problems, and those whose search for new "spiritual paths" became a way of life.

To all of them Spiritualism brought the message that there is no death, there are no dead, and that death is but a transition to a new dimension of life. After the transition called death, individuals continue to exist in the form of spirits with whom communication is possible through the aid of spirit mediums. Spirits, once they have entered spirit land, maintain an interest in the people still living on the earthplane. Through the instrumentality of the medium in a church service, séance, or home cicle, spirits are able to advise those who seek their guidance on personal problems and to instruct them on how to conduct their daily lives in harmony with God's and nature's laws.

Spiritualist Churches

Spiritualist churches claim the status of a Protestant denomination with religious and legal rights equal to those enjoyed by orthodox churches. Their essential belief is: "Spiritualism is the science, philosophy, and religion of continuous life, based upon the demonstrated fact of communication, by means of mediumship, with those who live in the spirit world. . . ." (*National Spiritualist Association Manual* 1967: 40)

These churches consider their activities to be scientific, philosophical, and religious. The scientific aspects consist of both the manifestations of the spirit world experienced or witnessed personally by individuals and the *demonstrations* performed by mediums in church services or séances. It is through these experiences in the séance room and in church services that the faith of both parishioner and medium is sustained and verified. This faith allows the parishioner to acknowledge the authenticity of the experience. The philosophical aspects are all the pastoral teachings and lectures which involve critical evaluation of the style and content of spirit communication and the conclusions derived therefrom. The religious aspects are conceptualized as the attempt to understand and live by the laws of nature, which are said to be also the laws of God.

All Spiritualist churches in Bay City render two kinds of service to their parishioners. First, there is the medium's *message*, either in the form of a reply to a parishioner's question about personal life problems or in the form of a lecture (sermon) addressed to the whole congregation about the laws for the appropriate conduct of life. Second, there is the *laying on of hands* as a form of *healing* to those who seek such help for physical ailments or mental disturbances. Both messages and healing are part of every church service.

For the purpose of fulfilling these two kinds of service, each church has a staff which is divided into the following categories: *student minister, healer, licentiate,* and *minister-medium.* Any person who belongs to any of these ministerial categories has specific obligations to discharge in connection with which he must resort to specific lexical items that are part of the church argot.

Two characteristics of all the church positions are that they are titular statuses which effect both legal protection for the practice of mediumship and formal division of labor for the church staff. Legally they function to allow a person to engage in counseling or healing without prosecution by the law for fortune-telling. Functionally they serve to indicate specific church jobs and so reduce the conflict and competition for these by the church staff.

The Church Staff

Student ministers are those individuals studying with the pastor in her *development class.* Some of these students are interested in church *work* and in eventually becoming certified as minister-mediums. These student ministers—primarily as part of training—are asked to assist in church work, in giving invocations and benedictions during church services or class meetings. Most student ministers have had previous experience with orthodox churches and consequently employ in their invocations or benedictions traditional Christian terms such as Jesus Christ and Father, Son, and Holy Spirit. These terms are not part of the accepted church argot, where they are replaced by such terms as *Christ Principle, Infinite Intelligence, Spirit World,* and *Angel loved-ones.* However, student ministers are not criticized for their use of orthodox terms and are told that they will do better as they gain confidence as public speakers and begin to use what they have learned in class, namely, the right terminology for church work. Student ministers do not give either healing or messages in public; hence, they are formally restricted from using certain of the church's religious terminology. They cannot claim in public to *see, hear, feel, sense,* or *intuit,* on the basis of which they can minister to the gathered flock. The use of these terms in public is reserved for the properly ordained ministers, whose *psychic* abilities have been formally recognized. Student ministers who insist on using the argot terms reserved for mediums are regarded as a threat to the church and as usurpers of power. They are sanctioned by the pastor, who may refuse to give them a message or may not assign them a church task. In effect, student ministers cannot use in reference to themselves any verbs such as *see, feel, sense, intuit, receive,* or *get* (which imply fully *developed spiritual powers*) or adjectives such as *sensitive, spiritual,* and *psychic* (which imply that the speaker is in contact with higher *forces* and therefore can recognize such qualities). The proper domain of speech for student ministers is the noun category. They may name those things that they have been taught, but they may not communicate, explicitly or implicitly, that they have personally *contacted* these *entities* or undergone these *experiences.*

Healers are charged with conducting the healing service, the laying on of hands, for those who come to them with problems of health or personal welfare. The healers utter public prayers for the general good health and welfare of the congregation at large. Such a prayer is usually phrased in the church argot. Healers, however, do not converse with their individual clients. Their job is silently to lay hands on the head of the client and act as a *channel* for the *healing forces* to flow to the client and restore him to "perfect health." In some churches, however, healers do give messages to their clients during or after the laying on of hands. The message is the same kind that a medium gives to a client. In the case of the healer, however, it is called an *independent reading,* since the client did not submit a question to be answered. In giving this message the healer uses much of the same terminology the medium uses. Healers who give such messages are looked down upon by the church pastor. She considers them to be ministering to the congregation beyond their abilities, since they have not yet been certified as mediums. Most of the conflicts in the church are over precisely such instances where members of the church staff usurp the medium's role and give messages in the church argot to the congregation.

Licentiates have the same religious privileges as minister-mediums, except that they cannot officiate at marriages. Within the church context they contribute to church work primarily in giving lectures during the church service. Normally they do neither healing nor message work. The *licentiate* is a transition title between *healer* and *minister-medium*. However, the certificate of licentiate is useful in that it allows its holder to give private consultations and receive referrals from the pastor when she does not want to deal with particular cases. Essentially, the certificate of licentiate allows the individual to counsel as any church minister would and be protected by law. Licentiates can use the full range of lexical items in the church argot. However, since they do not give messages in church, they do not have occasion to use this argot in public. If they insist on giving messages in public, they can be sanctioned by the pastor. Such sanctions may include her refusal to ordain them as full minister-mediums, or her postponement of ordination indefinitely.

Minister-mediums are in charge of the message work. It is in their province to use the full range of the church argot because they have demonstrated their *mediumistic* abilities and have been certified as mediums. Most churches in Bay City are run by men, although there are exceptions. However, within Spiritualist circles in Bay City it is more common for men to assume the role of *healing ministers* and women to assume the role of *mediums*.

It is a rule of the churches that any person in one level of the ministerial hierarchy can use the lexical items characteristic of any ministerial level below his but not of those above. The ministerial levels are hierarchical, with student minister being the lowest level and medium the highest. Most individuals have to go through each level successively; it usually takes two years from the someone new to Spiritualism qualifies for ordination as a minister-medium. Each church ordains its pastor's students with certificates of the national organization which chartered the church. It is in the classroom where students earn these ministerial certificates that the movement of Spiritualism is replenished, for each new minister-medium can open her own church and continue to train new people.

The Chartering Organization

All the churches in this study were officially chartered by at least one national Spiritualist organization, and all the ministers permanently associated with churches were certified by similar national organizations. Some churches held charters from more than one organization, under the justification that if one organization folded, the church would still be chartered by another and thus be protected by law in its spiritual ministry. Just as individual Spiritualist ministers have to be certified in order to operate within the law, so churches have to be chartered as official Spiritualist churches if they are to offer mediumship and healing. The charter does not vouch for the quality of the services offered, but it does indicate that the churches chartered and the ministers certified by national organizations have met minimum requirements of competency in message work or healing.

The national organizations are all recognized federally, by the states, and locally as Spiritualist associations within whose right it is to charter churches, certify ministers, conduct courses on various aspects of Spiritualism, and sponsor Spiritualist camps. Each national organization does not necessarily have a mother church—that is, one that is regarded as the original church founded by the organization or one which serves as a headquarters for the organization. Rather, there exists a national office for each with a board of directors and officers to administer the business of the organization. The national organization functions with respect to the local churches it charters as a legitimizing agency, not a mother church.

Various national organizations are represented by chartered churches in Bay City, and they vary in belief-system, ritual practices, and the use of certain lexical items within the Spiritualist argot. For example, the United States Spiritualist Association (USSA) does not support any belief in *reincarnation*. Consequently, most of the churches chartered by the USSA do not use the Spiritualist argot developed around the notions of reincarnation which are upheld by other Spiritualist national organizations. USSA churches do not use in their service such terms as *reincarnation, karma, reembodiment*. On the other hand, the Universal Spiritualist Association (USA) accepts the giving of communion as part of the Spiritualist service, using the orthodox terminology associated with communion which is not accepted by the USSA. Since these differences exist between national organizations, a minister usually seeks a charter for her church from an organization whose beliefs are in harmony with her own. For the most important job of the national organization, from the viewpoint of the local church, is to stand by its chartered churches and protect them in case of legal action. Spiritualists point to several cases that occurred four years ago in a neighboring Bay City community. Several individuals who had consulted a medium accused her of fraud and turned to the police for prosecution of the medium. The national organiaztion which had certified the medium provided her with legal counsel and succeeded in having the charges dismissed.

The Medium and Her Church

It might appear from the above statements that the chartering organization tends to stamp its own identity on its chartered churches. This is true only in part, because a minister affiliates with an organization that is compatible with her own belief-system and thus is able to shape her church according to her own image of what a Spiritualist church ought to be. For the most part, national organizations do not exercise any effective supervision over their chartered churches which would force them to adhere to any specified format of service.

In fact, individual churches are really centered around the personalities of their medium-pastors and possess many of the attributes of a charismatic cult. A pastor has opened the doors to her own church, which she has organized according to her wants and which she has legitimized by a charter from a national organization to her liking.

The church is likely to move when the pastor moves and die when the pastor dies. Through time, the medium-pastor attracts clients, who constitute a personal following which the pastor can call *my people*. The pastor's *people* come to church to *receive the message* from the pastor, more so than from any other *medium working* in the church alongside the pastor. Although each church has an official name, all churches are referred to by the names of their pastors. For example, the Metaphysical Temple of Spiritual Life is know as Reverend Kelly's place or simply as Kelly's. This identification of the pastor's personality with the church as *ecclesia* is further indication of the complete and pervasive authority that the pastor maintains over church activities. Although each church has a board of directors or trustees, the pastor is always president of the board. The members of these boards are usually the pastor's spouse, personal clients who come to the pastor to receive messages, or personal friends who are not likely either to usurp power or to impose their will in church decisions.

Most churches do not have paid memberships. But most pastors have followings. The following is not permanent, however. It is customary for Spiritualists to *travel* from church to church in search of good messages. But at any given time each church does have a small nuclear group which attends it with some regularity. In time, the composition of this nuclear group changes. Once any person within the following of a pastor has entered a conflict situation either with the pastor or with another member of the following, he or she usually leaves the church and looks for another medium from whom to receive the message.

The churches share a geographical location. With one exception, the churches are located in downtown Bay City or in nearby commercial districts. Again, with the exception of two, all the churches are conducted in rented premises. The reason for this is that most pastors do not have the finances to buy a building and convert it into a church. Renting an office or an apartment and decorating it as a church is less expensive and is also less demanding of maintenance. Rented premises also allow a pastor more mobility. She may open a church or move its premises with greater ease according to her will.

A final feature of all the churches is that each medium-pastor creates a particular set of meanings to the Spiritualist argot to be used in her own church. Since the churches are grouped in close proximity to each other and also share a population that goes from church to church in search of *a good message,* mediums are highly competitive with one another. That competition is keenly realized because most mediums offer one kind of service, a *contact* with the *spirit world* through a verbal message. In past years when séances were offered to the public-at-large, mediums could specialize in various kinds of séances, such as *trumpet, materialization,* etc. and through these form their individual identities. But now that most spirit communication is done in the church service through message work, there is virtually no service that one medium can perform that another one cannot. Therefore, to impose an identity on her church and to unify a group of parishioners as *her people,* a medium is forced to create argot innovations.

II. TYPOLOGY OF CHURCHES

Having pointed out some of the features common to all the churches, I will move now to consider the three types of churches characteristic of Bay City Spiritualism. These may be distinguished by the following criteria:

1. the nature of the Spiritualist organization which chartered the church and the kind of relationship established between the church and its chartering body;

2. the range of activities the church offers to its parishioners; and

3. the internal social organization of the church.

These variables are significant to parishioners when choosing a medium to follow. These organizational features are also significant in our analysis of the contexts and determinants for the use of the argot within the various churches. I visited and became acquainted with all the Spiritualist churches in Bay City. Long-term research, however, was conducted in only a few churches, which served as a sample. Table 1 presents an overview of the three types of churches in Bay City. Type A includes two churches in Bay City, in this category. I worked intensively with Reverend Cooper's Pacific Spiritualist Church. This church is affiliated with the United States Spiritualist Association of Churches. The pastor of the church and all its current ministers were ordained by this organiaztion. The church proclaims the Declaration of Principles published by the USSA. During church services the USSA hymnal is used, as is the USSA *Manual* for any ceremonies, such as christenings or acceptance of new people into membership. This church participates in the state and national conventions of the USSA and abides by the rules and regulations set by the state and national boards. The church pastor always clearly indicates to the congregation that this church is an affiliate of the USSA, which, she states, is the Science, Philosophy, and Religion of Modern Spiritualism. The church upholds the belief-system of the USSA and does not support beliefs in reincarnation. A relatively strong affiliation with the chartering organization is one of the main characteristics of Type A churches.

TABLE 1. COMPARISON OF SPIRITUALIST CHURCHES

	Type A	Type B	Type C
number of churches in sample	2(1) *	10(6)	8(4)
charter organization	USSA	USL/self-incoroprated	A mother church (usually of Type B)
relationship with chartering organization	strong	weak	intermediate
Religious Activities			
church services	yes (weekly)	yes (weekly)	yes (irregular)
mediumship classes	yes (at medium's initiative)	yes (at client's request)	yes (at client's request
lyceum	yes	no	no
séances	yes (by church pastor)	yes (by guest mediums)	no
Social Activities			
clubs	yes	no	no
social events (bazaars, card parties, etc.)	yes (regular)	yes (infrequent)	no
Internal Social Organization			
paid membership	yes	no	no
hierarchy	rigid	weak	weak
client-medium relationships	authoritarian	egalitarian	egalitarian
client-client relationships	stratified	nonstratified	nonstratified
Beliefs			
belief in reincarnation	no	no	yes
syncretistic beliefs	no	yes	yes
Sources of Spiritualist Argot			
chartering organization	yes	no	no
medium's teachings	yes	yes	yes
client's perferences	no	yes	yes

* Numerals in parentheses indicate number in sample studied.

The Pacific Spiritualist Church offers biweekly religious services and a Sunday morning *Lyceum* (Sunday school) for adults and children. The church further sponsors ladies' and gentlemen's clubs, which work for church-sponsored social activities and which also help sponsor the many and varied church social functions, such as dinners, card games, and bazaars. The Lyceum is frequented primarily by the clients of the pastor. On occasion, however, people new to the church are encouraged to attend, in order to learn more about Spiritualism.

The ladies' and gentlemen's clubs are primarily supported by church members. The church social activities are scheduled throughout the year and are open to the public at large. Each of these activities is an annual event, repeated each year at approximately the same time. This church advertises its services weekly in the newspapers and invites the public to church and social events. The church also offers classes in spiritual development, conducted by the pastor, for persons who request them. Private consultations are available with the pastor and with any of the certified ministers. The pastor offers private séances on a very limited basis.

The Type A church is characterized by a high degree of organization. The Pacific Church has a paid membership of about one hundred eighty persons. All social events and church activities are conducted by the students of the pastor, who are organized into committees in charge of various tasks. Authority over all church matters is vested in the pastor and moves downward to the board of directors and the congregation in pyramidal form. The church occupies and owns its own building.

This church's services attract a congregation of about one hundred twenty individuals, about sixty-five women and fifty-five men. The congregation is composed of some families and couples but mostly of single adults. One feature of this church is the diversity of its congregation, which includes nearly as many men as women and a fair number of families and couples. The membership is overwhelmingly white; while there are no minority-group persons in the paid membership, a few blacks and Orientals do attend services.

Theologically, the church supports the teachings of the USSA and those of the pastor, which are reputed to have been given to her directly from *spirit*. Any beliefs upheld by the congregation which are contrary to those of these two sources are not given public expression.

Linguistically, this church shares the Spiritualist argot spoken within all churches. However, this church is characterized by some uniquely defined terms within the generally accepted argot. It does not use publicly any terminology associated with reincarnation, such as *reincarnation, karma,* or *reembodiment.* Although such terms are current in the general Spiritualist argot, they are not used in the Pacific Church. Further excluded are such terms (and their derivatives) as *psychic, astral, cosmic, astral travel, evil entities,* and *spirit possession.* Again, these terms form part of the shared Spiritualist argot of all churches. Type A churches do not employ the above-mentioned terms for several reasons. First, the strong affiliation of this church with the USSA partially determines the use of language. For example, the USSA continuously emphasizes the use of derivative forms of the term *spiritual* in order to minimally ally Spiritualism with mainstream Christianity. In contradistinction to *spiritual,* such terms as *psychic* or *astral* are shunned because they have a more secular connotation related to some people's talents or abilities, rather than to *church-developed spiritual* values. The USSA further encourages the use of such terms as *medium, counselor,* and *spiritual adviser* for the church staff, as opposed to the more common appellations of *reader, psychic, clairvoyant,* or, in jest, *fortune-teller.* The motivation of the USSA in favoring certain terminology within the Spiritualist argot has been to add dignity to the church staff, so that the public will not treat Spiritualism with the condescension shown to palm readers or road-side gypsies.

Another factor influencing the use of language in Type A churches is the well-articulated teaching of the pastor. Reverend Cooper offers classes to her following in which she defines all the key terms used in the church service. During classwork she explains USSA referential meanings of such terms as *medium, mediumship, healer, healing, communication,* and *spiritual contacts.* In addition, she defines these terms further in light of her own teachings of Spiritualism. In line with her own teachings, she introduces terms which are not part of the official USSA lexicon but nonetheless are acceptable within Spiritualist circles. Examples are *God-consciousness, Godhead, soul-knowing,* and *Mind.* Since this argot is dealt with, albeit not explicitly as an argot, in classwork, and since most members of the pastor's following have participated in her classes at some point in their church affiliation, one can safely say that it is the common language that binds the pastor's following and allows them to assume a unique identity vis-à-vis other Spiritualist churches.

The determinants of the Spiritualist argot for churches of Type A are: (1) a strong affiliation with the chartering organiaztion, (2) the authority and instruction of the pastor, and (3) the social cohesion of the pastor's following. These three factors allow for the development and maintenance of the church argot, and, conversely, the church argot serves as a platform for cohesive social action.

Often terms that are unique to one church (because they are coined or are given a special meaning by the pastor) are known to the Spiritualist community, because all churches share a clientele of *travelers* who attend, consecutively, all churches and thus serve as a channel for the diffusion of the argot. For example, Reverend Cooper was in the habit of using the term *soulmate* to refer to someone's ideally suited mate, either in this life or in *spirit world.* Individuals who frequented Reverend Cooper's church would use the term *soulmate* even at the church of another pastor. Most mediums in Bay

City were acquainted with the term and recognized those who used it as Reverend Cooper's people. Most pastors would not use this term on their own initiative and would employ it only if the term appeared in the question posed by a client. Ultimately, any one church does not have a different Spiritualist argot, but simply a varied degree of use of terms employed by all Spiritualist churches.

Type B Church

Church Type B is the most common variety; there are ten in Bay City. I worked intensively with six of them. An example is Reverend Kelly's Metaphysical Temple of Spiritual Life. Churches of this type are affiliated with national organizations like the Universal Spiritual League, which differ from the USSA in that they allow the teaching of reincarnation and exert less control over their chartered churches. Some churches of Type B have also incorporated themselves as Spiritualist organizations empowered to charter daughter churches and ordain ministers under their own auspices. The Metaphysical Temple of Spiritual Life was originally chartered by the Universal Spiritualist League, but two years ago Reverend Kelly incorporated her church into a chartering organization. Thus, she became effectively the pastor of her own church and the president of her own corporation. When the church was affiliated with the USL, the pastor did not announce the affiliation to the congregation at regular intervals during the church service as is done in Type A churches, for the church upheld its own Declaration of Principles, compiled by the pastor. The hymnals used for church services are Cokesbury hymnals, which the pastor bought on her own. The church service is syncretistic, with Spiritualist elements and Catholic borrowings. The church offers communion services and supports beliefs in several saints. The pastor and several of the church ministers hold ordination papers from several organizations to which they have belonged over a period of years. The church never participates in conventions or business affairs of any chartering organization.

Reverend Kelly's church offers religious services three times a week. The church does not have a Sunday school, and very few of the pastor's followers have young children. Further, the church does not have social clubs and offers only a few church-sponsored social events. These social functions revolve around the holidays of Christmas and Easter and usually occur in conjunction with ceremonies of ordination of the pastor's students to some level of the Spiritualist ministry.

The church offers *spiritual unfoldment (mediumship)* classes with the pastor for a limited number of persons whom the pastor approves. During classwork the pastor instructs her students on aspects of

Spiritualism as they have been written about in various sources. She does not claim to have received any teachings from the spirit world. The pastor gives private consultations and sometimes refers some of her parishioners to her student ministers whom she teaches about counseling. The pastor never conducts séances; for the purpose of demonstrating what they are, she invites guest mediums.

The church does not have a paying membership. The congregation is composed primarily of single adults, mostly women. The average attendance at a service is about thirty persons, of whom twenty-two are women and eight are men. Authority over all church matters is vested in the pastor. Various tasks of administering the church are performed by the pastor and her close friends or students who voluntarily assist her. The pastor's following is not organized into any network of committees for church activities.

Theologically the church presents the teachings of the pastor and any version of Spiritualist philosophy that is either acceptable to the congregation or that is expressed by a guest speaker and which is not defamatory of any other group. The pastor is eager to present materials that she knows her congregation and students are interested in. Consequently, the church teachings appear to reflect the attending congregation more than they do an *a priori* selection of ideas by the pastor.

The church rents its premises and has changed location twice in the past several years. The church is wholly dependent on the pastor for the performance of religious services, since no cadre is organized to conduct services in her absence. Compared to Church Type A, this church is more egalitarian in the relationships that exist between pastor and co-ministers and pastor and congregation. The pastor does not view her role as that of an advocate of Spiritualism, but rather as a minister who is charged with helping her flock in their daily problems. Consequently, the church offers many services, like communion, to those persons who wish it who have broken away from orthodox churches.

Linguistically, the church uses the full range of terms within the Spiritualist argot. Although the church is officially nondenominational, most of its staff and congregation acknowledge themselves to be Christian Spiritualists. In their words, "we go with Christ." Therefore, such terms as *communion* or *Holy Spirit* have been given Spiritualist meanings in addition to their traditional denotations. The church is primarily syncretistic, so it is easily able to adopt terms from other religions or philosophies and add Spiritualist meanings to them. The one exception lies with terms specifically associated with Type A churches. Such terms as *Infinite Intelligence, Mind,* and *Over-soul* are regarded as unnecessary euphemisms for the term *God* and therefore are not used often. Such terms are characteristic of the United States Spiritualist Association; because churches in Type B wish to define themselves as not being part of the USSA, they avoid them.

Churches of Type B do not have a strong affiliation with a chartering organization and do not, therefore, have any external pressures to use a particular set of terms, as do churches of Type A. It is up to the pastor to indicate any limitations on the argot used.

The pastor is sensitive to the linguistic modes of present-day hip culture, and such terms as *vibration, spiritual, meditation, phenomena, reincarnation,* and *karma* are recognized by her as being not only Spiritualist argot terms but also part of the hip culture. The pastor clearly indicates that she accepts various usages of these terms within the church context. The philosophy behind the church is "to make people feel at home," so the full Spiritualist argot is accepted, and additional senses for the argot terms are allowed if they are an integral part of the out-of-church life of the clientele.

Type C Church

Type C includes eight churches in Bay City. I worked with four of them, and I shall use as an example Reverend Gilman's Chapel of Divine Truth.

This church is an affiliate of one of the practicing churches in Bay City which was incorporated into a chartering organization. The pastor and several of the practicing ministers of the Chapel of Truth (as it is abbreviated) have all been ordained or certified by the mother church, which is a variant form of Type B. Reverend Gilman uses the hymnals of the mother church and conducts services on the latter's premises. In effect, Reverend Gilman sublets one evening a week from the mother church for religious services of her own. The church abides by the rules and regulations of the mother church, and those rules are usually enforced. The staff of the mother church has easy access to the premises and keeps a watchful eye on the activities of all sublessees. If conflicts arise between Reverend Gilman and the staff of the mother church, Reverend Gilman's charter can be revoked and she can be asked to leave the premises.

Her church offers religious services once a week and offers no social activities, except for an occasional coffee break after services. The pastor does not offer mediumship classes. Private consultations are available with the pastor, but she does not offer séances. The church is not organized on a congregational basis with a regularly attending nuclear following; instead, the pastor announces when services will be held, and those who wish to follow her attend.

Theologically, the church does not sponsor a uniform and codified body of beliefs. It allows its platform to be used by speakers belonging to a number of metaphysical movements which are variants of Spiritualism, such as Science of Mind.

Linguistically, the church uses the full range of terms of the Spiritualist argot and is not distinguishable from church Type B. The only organizational feature which influences the use of language is the right of the mother church to ask the pastor not to use a term which it finds offensive. If the pastor persists in using it, a conflict will arise and the pastor may be asked to move her church elsewhere.

III. Method and Conceptual Framework for the Analysis of the Lexicon

At the outset of fieldwork I did not know that Spiritualist churches used an argot in church-related activities. I did not begin with a plan to do linguistic research within the churches. But as soon as I started attending church services, I became aware that although I listened intently and everything was said in Standard English, I really did not understand what was being talked about. I kept wanting to ask "What do you mean?" "Can you be more specific?" I soon realized the source of my difficulty; I listened to conversation differently from the way other parishioners were listening.

Many of the parishioners listen for tone, emotion, or metaphor, but not for content. I was listening for specific referents in conversation that others seemed to regard only as stimulation to cathect with their own thoughts, visions, and spirual concerns. My predisposition was to listen for specific, clear referents in conversation. That made me different from other parishioners. It turned out that this bias became my most valuable tool in research. By focusing on content and semantic referents I was approaching the Spiritualist argot from a different direction from that of most parishioners. By paying attention to semantic referents I was brought almost instantanously face to face with the significant issues in the belief system and social organization of the churches.

The status I assumed in the churches was that of participant-observer. I did not conduct the study in the tradition of psychic research. My interests throughout fieldwork were not in *spiritual phenomena*. While I attended every church service, séance, and social function that I could, I did not request messages and submitted a billet only when requested to do so by the medium or her immediate assistants. I was not interested in either proving or disproving the existence of spirits, the veracity of claims to mediumship by any one medium, or the truth of falsity of Spiritualists' notions about the essential nature of man, God, our earthly life, or the immortal future. Nor did I approach this research from the perspective of "experiencing" Spiritualism to discover what it feels like to get a message or to serve as a *channel* for spirit communication. My orientation was to learn and to understand how a group of people, when gathered together to form a relegous institution, organize themselves socially, and how they further utilize their human resources to accomplish their institutional goals successfully.

Once I realized the existence of the argot, I attempted to elicit information about it from several informants. This initial attempt failed for several reasons. First, I was a newcomer to the church, I did not know many people, and my interest in the church was not yet established. My informants were not sure whether I was genuinely interested in learning about and partcipating in Spiritualism or whether I was merely a curiosity-seeker who might mock church practices. I had not earned the trust of my informants. Second, the argot is a secret and sensitive area with church personnel. When I originally inquired about argot terms, I was simply refused information. Third, I did not know what the full range of argot terms was, nor did I know the uses to which language was put in Spiritualist churches, and therefore I was not sure what I wanted to find out from my informants. Unlike anthropologists who go into communities and attempt to discover the native categories for such things as diseases or colors, I was not dealing with objects or concepts that I could say *a priori* Spiritualists would have labels for. One can safely assume that every community will have some terminology for colors, particularly those colors in its natural habitat which involve objects of particular social or cultural import. I did not know which concepts or objects Spiritualists deemed particularly significant and so could not ask informants about their labels. Therefore, participant-observation was essential to first acquaint me with those things that Spiritualists had labels for; then I could attempt to discover the meanings of the labels. Fourth, I realized in the initial phases of fieldwork that all the senses of the argot terms were created through the church usage. Some of these senses are standard to the argot. For example, the term *spiritual* is most frequently used in the sense of "someone who leads a righteous life in accordance with the principles of life, called laws of nature, put forth by a Spiritualist church." But, through creative use of the argot, new senses are given to the standard argot. For example, Reverend Wilkins used the term *spiritual* in the sense of "someone who is psychic, developed to receive spirit communication." This latter sense of the term would have eluded me unless I had observed it in use.

Such usages have to be observed in actual occurrence. To interview informants and to elicit information about the argot yields only standard meanings, such as the first sense of *spiritual*. A substantial portion of the innovative usages of the argot are usually not presented. This was my experience with my informants; the generalization may not hold for other research projects.

Observation in natural speech contexts leads, also, to direct questioning. The replies of informants are then checked against past and subsequent observations of natural usage. These suggest new questions for direct elicitation which allow one to draw a distinction between the idiosyncratic speech of an informant and the standard usage of the terms.

Within the first year's fieldwork with the churches, I was able to learn a great deal about the argot. It was after that time that I began to ask about it in my interviews. I had established full rapport with my informants. I had compiled a list of argot terms. I had discovered what I thought to be the function or role of such an argot, and my objective was to learn what my informants considered the argot terms to be and how they viewed the role of such an argot in church life. After intensive fieldwork, I could use my own knowledge of the church as a foil for eliciting additional information from my informants. The initial period of fieldwork undertaken before any linguistic inquiry could be made was essential in acquiring a personal criterion for judging the linguistic information that my informants were at last willing to give me.

Once the argot terms were collected, I attempted to gloss each term. The glosses allowed me to group the terms according to certain relationships. The linguistic analysis has been primarily used in allowing me to verify ethnographic information that I had collected through observation. It also allowed me to isolate a body of evidence that would be objective, verifiable, and duplicable, to allow other scholars working in the same area to validate certain conclusions about the structure of the churches. Previous ethnographic treatment has been intuitive, observational, and personal. We often times lack the unified body of material that would allow two people to converse about a given set of problems in referring to a common data base.

The focus on language served an additional advantage in this particular field situation. These churches have a constantly shifting population composed of individuals who may come once or twice to a service and never be seen again. The churches further support an ethos of anonymity where it is inacceptable to inquire about individuals let alone interview them. The observer therefore needs a tool that could give him some information about the exact social relationship at any one point in time between individuals in the church. Again language serves that function. For example, sometime after a service, I would ask a medium, "Why did you give her a brief message?" The answer was, "Oh, I know her. She is just a troublemaker. She kept asking me about *karma* and I know that *karma* is Watkins' people. I don't deal with this *karma* business." By identifying a term and observing that the medium gave the individual a particularly brief message, I was able to find out about a situation of conflict that otherwise I would never have known existed. The individuals through their use of an argot reveal their church affiliation, interests, and loyalty to a particular medium.

The methodology used to gather information on this argot has been dictated largely by the sacred nature of this language and by the difficulty of discussing utterances of informants in the speech contexts of church life. I have not been interested in elicited speech, because the quality of information would have suffered. It was my responsibility first to determine the corpus of the argot by itemizing the lexical terms essential to it; then, to isolate instances where each lexical item was used; and later, to gloss each instance of use for its referential meaning and function. I was led to conclude that perhaps the language of Spiritualism and the séance room is the one most suitable for analysis by the field of ethnographic semantics, so haunted by the spirit of "God's Truth or hocus-pocus."

The relevance of ethnographic semantics to ethnography has been in the study of cognition through the semantic organization of lexical aspects of a people's language. Most lexicographic studies made in the context of ethnographic semantics have dealt with cognitive systems which have as a referent some aspect of the physical world which is three-dimensional, like firewood (Metzger and Williams 1966) or color categories (Conklin 1955), or otherwise demonstrable, like skin disease (Frake 1961). While many scholars have spoken enthusiastically about the importance of such studies (Sturtevant 1964; Kay 1970), other scholars have pointed to the limitations in the literature in terms of both the limited data presented and the methodology used (Frake 1961; Burling 1964; Berreman 1966). The various arguments within the field of ethnographic semantics have been reviewed by Colby (1966). Most recently Berlin (1968) has published data dealing with Tzeltal numeral classifiers, presenting a complete corpus of terms in an attempt to overcome some of the limitations for which the field has been criticized.

My research differs from previous studies in the following ways: I did not have a set of categories, an etic grid, to classify the material. Part of the argot deals with referents which have no representation in the material world; the referents are abstract. Such terms as *spirit, spiritual, sensitive, psychic, clairvoyant,* and *vibrations* do not have demonstrable material referents. Furthermore, as conceptual categories they are never explicitly and concretely defined; rather, it is expected that such terms will be understood from observation of their usage in the church contexts. The referents are not mute three-dimensional objects, but often spirits who define and describe themselves to the informants through psychic experiences involving clairvoyance or clairaudience. This means that such spiritual referents can quickly transform themselves, and the dimensions describing them at one point in time do not remain constant and may not be valid beyond a certain time depth.

The ethnographic semantic method of collecting and presenting the data has to be understood for its limitations as well as utility. That method offers only a tool to get fine-grained and detailed data about problems and issues that have often been conceptualized through field observation. In this research area it probably did not produce a major breakthrough in ideas, as much as it provided the detailed nuances that are the evidence for the initial observation. The charts and graphic representations of the data are simply aids in visualizing material that can be also described in prose.

IV. THE ROLE OF LANGUAGE AND THE SPOKEN WORD IN SPIRITUALIST CHURCHES

The Power of the Spoken Word

Spiritualist churches share with other American metaphysical movements, such as Christian Science and New Thought churches, a belief in the inner power and meaning of words. Judah (1967: 17) has clearly identified this belief as one of the defining attributes of Spiritualist churches when compared with orthodox denominations.

> Most metaphysical groups have a belief in an inner meaning of words beyond their dictionary definition—a meaning that cannot be discovered empirically from the standpoint of usage or etymology, but that is revealed intuitively. This is known by a variety of terms, such as the spiritual, metaphysical, or occult interpretation. Each leader of one of the sects may have his own special definitions which often disagree with the explanations of others. A particular metaphysical sect may make use of the Bible, but its exegesis does not exhibit an awareness of studies in historical and literary criticism, nor does its interpretation show any dependence upon orthodox theology past or present. To one not acquainted with this intui-

tional or inspirational method, the interpretation would appear to be allegorical. For the adherent of the metaphysical sect, however, it offers the key to a higher truth, through which the Bible appears in agreement with its particular interpretation.

Spiritualism shares a working lexicon with metaphysical and occult movements and current youth culture. Such terms as *karma, reincarnation, rates of vibration, auras, astral travel, soul flight, psychic powers, cosmic consciousness* are common to several religious groups. Through their use speakers indicate membership in a specific group and express various degrees of involvement in the whole metaphysical subculture. What separates one group from another is the particular meaning given to a term and the rules governing its proper use. An examination of the church argot as a set of utterances exchanged between parishioners and church functionaries has to begin with a particular view toward the role of speech (parole) within the belief and ritual systems of Spiritualism.

Spiritualists speak of the "power of the spoken word" in both the religious and secular spheres. Their claim is that words, once uttered, have the power to create or effect the referent which they symbolize. This belief is conceptualized by the saying: "Words are things; once spoken, they are deposited into the ether and will be picked up by like-thinking people." Once a word has been spoken, and particularly in the idiom of the Spiritualist argot, its referent gains an objective reality, a material manifestation, which it might have lacked prior to being verbally uttered.

The implication of this belief for a church participant is that he must use words very cautiously and self-consciously, because through his verbal utterances he effects both a personal and a social reality for himself and his fellow participants in the church. In the context of the church, an individual must not employ those terms restricted in use to an ordained healer or medium, lest he cause himself to believe that he is personally in contact with spirit forces and also convince his listener that he is an instrument for spirit communication. Thereby he may effect for himself the fictitious status of an ordained minister. In a more secular vein, an individual can affect his physical health through verbal communication. If one person tells another that he suspects himself to have an illness such as cancer or heart trouble, he may in fact acquire the illness or force himself to conduct his life as if he had that illness. Therefore, he must not label such things directly, but use a code name, an argot term. In essence, an individual has to be watchful of his language, so that he does not create for himself and others a reality which could be personally harmful or socially misleading.

The belief in the power of the spoken word does not include the belief that a speaker who utters a word or name gains magical control over its referent. While the uttering of the name of a spirit may put an individual in contact with that spirit, the contact does not imply control or power over the spirit to force it to act in either a beneficial or a malevolent way. In this sense, there are no forbidden words or names, as there are for example in Judaism regarding personal names of God. Furthermore there are no supernatural sanctions for misuse of the Spiritualist argot. While there are social conflicts over the use of terms, they are purely intra-church encounters resolved within the church social organization and never involve supernatural or spiritual remedy agents.

The Role of Speech in Social Organization

As was stated earlier, the raison d'être of a Spiritualist church is to bring the message to its parishioners. Anyone who seeks a Spiritualist church (who is not just a curiosity seeker) does so because he needs some kind of solution to a problem he faces. The mediums working in the church bring the message in two ways. The first is as a response to a question asked by a parishioner during the religious service. This is called *message work*. In the presence of the parishioner the medium contacts a spirit and is given the relevant information about the parishioner's question or problem. The medium then tells the parishioner what this information is. The medium's statements are called the *message*. Second, the medium may bring a message to the whole congregation on how to lead the good life and get in tune with nature's laws, which are God's laws. Abiding by this knowledge is supposed to prevent the parishioner from being defeated by the life-problems he faces. This message constitutes the church's teaching and is regarded as the philosophical portion of Spiritualism.

These two kinds of messages are the essence of any Spiritualist church, and both are verbal utterances exchanged between medium and congregation. It is essential that these messages be in the form of the spoken word because for the parishioner a message has to be an immediate, pertinent response to his problem at the time of the church service. Any reference to a written text within the message is regarded as preaching or moralizing and is not likely to be accepted. The message must be personally acquired by the medium in the presence of the client. On a congregational level, the message as philosophy of life must be revealed orally by a medium through the form of a spirit-inspired address (lecture, sermon, or class work). This verbal style allows the congregation to accept the message as spirit's assessment of the human condition at the moment of the church service; thus the message assumes a public significance and is understood by each person in the congregation to be also personally relevant. For both kind of messages, the personal and the congregational, a religious argot is used.

The fact that the messages are presented verbally and are couched in terms of an argot is also significant to the social organization of the church and has to be understood in terms of Spiritualist belief in mediumship.

Mediumship is an egalitarian concept. It is based on the belief in the *psychic power* or *sensitivity* of an individual to effect a spiritual *contact* with *spirits*. This psychic ability is potentially within every person's grasp, for it is said to be lodged in the divine spark which is innate to every living thing. It is up to the individual who wants to manifest this power to develop himself spiritually.

An individual can develop himself to be receptive to psychic experiences. But if he wants to be recognized for his mediumistic abilities, he needs to have consensual validation from others that he possess psychic powers. That validation is gained either in classwork training with a medium or on the basis of having received ordination papers for mediumship work. Given the fact that everyone could become a medium (or at least sufficiently psychically sensitive to make a spiritual contact with spirits) when a group is organized around the belief and practice of mediumship, there has to be some mechanism that introduces into it order, a division of labor, and a structure. A group that does not create an ordering system, finds itself quickly at the mercy of violent competition and conflict between individuals who try to assert themselves as more psychically attuned than their colleague, as *primus inter pares*.

For Spiritualists the ordering system is the spiritualist argot and the rules developed for its proper use. By implementing a stratified system of church roles and statuses each known by its occupants' use of specific argot terms, Spiritualists are able to maintain a belief in the egalitarian concept of mediumship and an authoritarian, and highly stratified social organization. The Spiritualist argot is used to institute a social organization. It works to structure shifting groups who cater to transient populations. The argot is particularly important to the role of medium-pastor as leader of the group. Within the church structure the medium-pastor becomes the gatekeeper to both church participation and to communication with spirits. She controls the ebb and flow of the number of students who are trained in mediumship. She retains her status and position by defining ever more specifically and idiosyncratically the argot terms and by exacting recognition for these from her students.

She can control the rate of social change within the group by deciding which new terms could be added. If new people who are recognized to be part of a particular subculture want to participate in a church, the medium acknowledges them by adopting the key terms of their subculture into the church argot. And similarly, by forbidding certain terms she keeps individuals who are culturally associated with such terms away from the church, for example hippies.

For Spiritualists the word of God is constantly revealed to man via the mediumship of Spiritualist ministers. The medium reveals to her following "The word" and continues for the duration of her ministry to reveal the message anew. Her presentation is always an oral delivery; the word is seldom transcribed. Therefore, to receive the message an individual must be acquainted with the argot in which the message is couched. To learn the argot an individual must continue to participate in church life and thereby to support the church organiaztion financially and socially. The medium as the revealer of the word has prerogatives about the kind of language in which she will deliver the message; she cannot be questioned about the accuracy or content of the message, because she is considered only an instrument for spirit and not the initiator of the message. Her authority and privilege in the church are recognized by all, because at any time she can refuse to act as an instrument of the message and thus can deprive her following of spirit guidance. Furthermore, her congregation cannot easily refer to any of her past revelations, none of which has been written down, and so there is no binding text to transcend any disagreement within the congregation and keep it unified in the absence of the continuously revealed word of the medium.

Each medium has her own style of speech for delivering the message and is also known for that, as well as for the content or quality of her guidance. The following commanded by any medium is interested not necessarily in Spiritualism as a religion with a body of beliefs, but in the particular medium's version of Spiritualism, her own teachings. These teachings are locked within the argot pattern of the medium. Consequently, there is no unified body of ideas that would cement the Spiritualist churches and transcend the individuality of any one. The result is that there is no theological base to stem perpetual schisms.

The argot does not only have structural impact on a group; it also has symbolic value. Spiritualism does not use any three-dimensional objects to symbolize any of its beliefs or practices. The churches do not subscribe to the use of crosses, figurines of saints, candles, altars, or ritual vestments. In orthodox churches such symbols can be purchased, worn on one's person, or kept in one's immediate environment. These symbols can, among other things, arouse in the individual feelings associated with the church, give him an overt identity vis-à-vis other members of a community, and serve as objects of meditation and silent prayer. Spiritualists consider that words perform for them the function graven images do for orthodox Christians. They claim that they repeat *affirmations* when they want to experience church-related feelings. Or they choose some term from their argot to meditate or pray silently with. Instead of holding an object, Spiritualists say that one should hold a thought or word. Finally, they recognize each other and present their Spiritualist identity to the community by using the language of the church, the argot. Spiritualists underscore the importance of spoken language in church participation because the sine qua non of any Spiritualist ritual is a verbal exchange between a medium and a parishioner. That communication in the form of an argot is the one religious symbol or artifact sui generis to Spiritualism.

Orthodox denominations enjoy a sacred space known as the church. The church building is treated with reverence, whether a religious service is in progress or not. Most Spiritualists do not have a church edifice and consequently cannot claim a sacred space that is physically defined. Since their churches are conducted in rented or sublet premises, they must rely on some mechanism that will distinguish the sacred from the profane for the religious service. Such a mechanism is the spoken invocation and benediction by the church pastor, a verbal utterance in the argot of the church which renders a secular space into a sacred one.

Not only is the spoken word of theological and social importance within the context of the church, it is significant also as a practical response by the church to community legal pressures. The churches have created a religious argot that protects the medium from legal prosecution and allows the client to conclude that the medium is in contact with spirits. The argot is based on a set of terms that are sufficiently ambiguous to allow the maximum selective interpretation on the part of the client. The client is expected to make his own equation between what the medium is saying in the message and what he asked in his billet. Such an ambiguous terminology would not allow a client to lodge a formal complaint against a medium, for he would lack prima facie evidence against the medium. Also, the argot has a set of terms which can be used in the message to indicate that the information really comes from spirits. An example of a message, given on page 199, demonstrates how the argot is used.

What is characteristic about these terms and the way they are woven together into a language is that anyone who is listening to the message, be he a police decoy or a parishioner, never knows what is referred to unless he wrote the billet, in which case he will assume that the medium is referring to his problems. But the rest of the audience is left ignorant of the nature of the problems being addressed. The argot protects the medium. Mediums can and do err in the kinds of information they convey to clients when they are not using argot terms. Mediums can give inaccurate advice, or they can be accused by clients of having given wrong advice. The language is useful in allowing a medium to convey information or to sidestep questions of total strangers whose queries and problems are often unfathomable to her. Finally, the argot allows her to show that she communicates with the spirits. This gives the system of belief a kind of rationale and "logic" which it would lack if answers to questions were given directly in standard daily speech.

The Backstage Language

It seems quite clear from the above discussion that the mediums use the argot in a purposeful, self-conscious way. The discussion pointed out the stratificational elements in how the argot is used and the in-group out-group discrimination it allows. But little has been said about the "backstage" usage of the argot when mediums discuss church-related issues among themselves.

It is natural and expected for individuals engaged in a specialized activity which includes a technical argot, or jargon, to discuss their work with their colleagues and in doing so to use a particular metaphor system in a kind of backstage fashion. Spiritualist mediums are no exceptions. They do discuss their message work with their colleagues, and they do use a particular metaphor system. Many of the mediums have had previous experience with the performing arts in the entertainment field, therefore their backstage talk about mediumship often draws upon that earlier experience. The circumstances in which such conversations occur are usually relaxed, ex cathedra gatherings—for example, meeting for coffee after a service or riding home in a car. One medium might say to another, "Did you see those people they were trying to fool me, but I hit it with them, I really hit the mark that time." Or "I had pretty good odds with that one" or "In message work you got to hold your audience, you can't go too slow or you lose them."

Performers in different entertainment professions share subcultural backstage languages. To some degree the use of that language does indicate that mediums are very conscious of the performance and entertainment function of their services. That function is very often reinforced by the parishioners who clearly state that they go from church to church to watch the mediums *work*. They will speak quite openly about the entertainment value of church services.

However, mediums differ in their backstage discussion of their platform work. If a medium has had a great deal of work experience in theater the more likely he is to revert to backstage conversations. However, if a medium came to mediumship through his quest for "spiritual paths" he is less likely to use any backstage metaphors. The more authoritarian and hierarchical a church social organization, the less frequently will its medium-pastor participate in backstage conversation. The more egalitarian the social organization of the church the more backstage discussions of mediumship take place. The more established a church is the less its functionaries revert to any backstage conversation. They guard the official church argot and reinforce it through usage in every opportunity. However, the less established a church is the greater the frequency of backstage and idiosyncratic conversation.

The backstage conversation serves an important function for the church personnel. With continued success in the performance of mediumship and validation of that success both in backstage conversation and parishioners' response, the backstage aspects become merged with the on-stage realities of the belief of the audience and any skepticism about the performer is transmuted into conviction in the performance. It reifies for the medium the belief that it is not the truth or falsehood of her messages that count, but it is whether she is helping people that is the ultimate criteria of competent mediumship.

V. Church Contexts for the Use of the Argot

At the core of Spiritualist churches are the messages which individuals send and receive. It is impossible to understand Spiritualists without a knowledge of the subtle meanings which are attached to these communication events. But meaning is not revealed from a textual analysis of the messages in themselves. They can only be understood in their context. We have already examined the structural features of the churches and the three types of churches with some of their characteristic argot forms. Now we shall consider the contextual situations in which speech events occur. These include church services, mediumship classes, social events, séances, and private readings (consultations). Then we shall discuss the actual use of the argot, including the persons who are senders and receivers of the messages.

The Church Service

The majority of Spiritualist church services are conducted on weekends. However, some churches meet also during the week, primarily in the evening. Such evening services usually begin around seven-thirty, to accommodate a clientele that commutes by bus. As people enter the church, they find a table by the door upon which are hymnals and two baskets, one for a love-offering (donation) and one for billets (written questions for the medium to answer during the portion of the service called message-work). Most regular attendees of the church prepare billets in the church; however, new people often prepare theirs at home, at work, or elsewhere, in advance of the service. Those who do not know that they must write a question are advised of this by a church secretary, seated at the table, who introduces them to the billet format. This conversation with the secretary is the first contact a client has with the church argot. The secretary socializes newcomers into the terminology of message writing and message receiving. She uses a series of nouns to describe the billet and the message: *billet, reading, message, psychic reading, independent reading.* The secretary further describes to the client how the medium works by using the following verbs: *see, feel, sense, get, give, intuit, read, psychometrize.* Finally the client is told about receiving the message with a set of verbs such as *accept, welcome, recognize,* and *confirm.* The secretary uses all these terms in referring to the work of the pastor of the church. She does not use any of them in an active voice in reference to what she herself can do, even if she is an ordained medium in her own right. This is the pastor's church, and the church staff does not claim to have the same powers as the pastor when speaking to a newcomer. Most newcomers do not understand what the secretary is talking about, but follow the simple instructions of writing down a question to be answered by the medium. If the client returns to the church, in time he or she will learn what the specialized terms mean. The secretary simply uses the church language; she does not define it for anyone. Newcomers show obvious perplexity at this usage.

The client new to the church writes his billet in standard English. Typical billet questions for a newcomer are: Will my rent be raised? Will I be able to pursue my music effectively? Should I stay in Bay City or go back home to Wisconsin or keep traveling, perhaps to the South? However, those who continue coming to the church and who learn the argot used there, learn also to use that argot in their billets. For example: "Just a message please." "Will conditions improve around me?" "Have you a message for me?" "When will I start having phenomena?" "What about vibrations around the office?" "What about my sister's spell?" Such questions indicate to the medium that the client is a regular attendee of Spiritualist churches.

Once a client has submitted his billet, he or she takes a hymnal and chooses a seat. Most individuals do not know others in the church; if they do, anonymity is usually maintained. It is deemed inappropriate to engage strangers in conversation or to pry into others' personal problems. It is these very personal questions that brought clients to the church in the first place, and they are not acceptable topics of casual conversation in the context of the church service or in the few minutes before it begins. Clients usually do not come to church much before the start of the service, so the wait in the church is never very long and is not necessarily conducive to conversation. The mediums do not circulate in the congregation; they are usually seated or standing behind the platform (pulpit), or else they remain in a back room until the service begins.

At the advertised hour the service begins with an invocation by one of the church staff. The invocation contains a series of nominal terms applied to God, such as Infinite Intelligence, spirit force, and over-soul; a series of verbs describing the activity of the spirits in coming to the church to help the congregation; a series of adjectives naming the quality of help the spirits can offer; and finally a series of nouns labeling the problems that the congregation might have brought to the Spirits for a message.

After the invocation several hymns are sung. Hymns are either traditional orthodox ones like "Rock of Ages" or specifically Spiritualist hymns addressed to spirit world. These hymns describe the wonders of spirit world and the joy of the congregation to unite with their spirit loved-ones, and they beseech the spirits to come to their aid. Such hymns employ argot terms which label spirits, describe aspects of spirit land, and indicate the actions that spirits perform.

A lecture or sermon follows the singing. Lectures deal with the belief-system of the church and instruct the congregation on laws of right living. Sometimes lectures are replaced by Bible readings with appropriate commentary on the applicability of certain passages to the congregation's daily lives.

A collection plate is then passed, and a further benediction is uttered over the love-offering collected. Such a benediction uses the same argot terms as the invocation. Up to this point the service has lasted about forty minutes; the next portion of the service, the message work, will last for about one hour, or as long as it takes the medium to answer all the billets submitted to her.

During message work the medium uses the full range of argot terms. Each medium has a style of speech of her own. Variations in style exist not only with regard to the actual argot terms used, but also with respect to the frequency and emphasis of particular terms. Following the message work a benediction is uttered, and the congregation disperses.

Two examples of message work will illustrate how the terms are actually used. The first illustration is from Reverend Cooper who was blindfolded and picked a billet sealed in an envelope from a collection of envelopes placed before her. The billet read: "Should I buy a piano and resume my music?" Reverend Cooper crumpled the billet in her hand as a way of *psychometrizing* it (*receiving* the *vibrations* from it which would indicate the nature of the question and establish the appropriate *contact* with *spirit* for an answer) and then delivered the message.[6]

> Now if you'll just speak to me as quickly as you can I'll do the very best I can to make the *contact* and I'll try to be *led* to the one that needs it most. I have in my hand an envelope and if my *vision* is correct the identification is, Roger, Roger. (Here, Reverend Cooper.) Where are you? (Right here.) You understand that right now that there are a *group* of *people* that are *invisible* to your *physical sight* but *operating* in your *consciousness* that is *bringing* a *divine urge* within you. (Yes.) Many are called and few are chosen and you are *selected,* son, to do a *great work,* and you ask here something your, a, a, *spiritual advancement* (yes) you want *spiritual guidance,* you are going to have it, here, I hear music in the distance, I hear music in the distance, somebody trying to urge you to purchase something (yes) purchase something, a wait just a little while, a little over your head, that the way you feel about it (yes) a little over your head, that a piano (yes) that a Steinway (yes) all right, little over your head, let it rest a little while without it, It'll be there for a little while. (Thank you very much.)

Another style of message work is represented in the following example. An individual submits a billet in which he asks three questions: "How much longer will I walk alone? Will sufficient income be provided by the finances which are now under due process of law? Is there a future for me in Bay City or does it lie elsewhere?" The medium responds to such a billet in the following fashion:

A. I have one that says 13 here, with you I have the vibration of a woman that's coming in very, very strong and she's trying to put

6 The following are transcript accounts of message work. Parishioner responses are placed within parentheses and punctuation is provided according to voice fluctuation.

your mind at ease to tell you that things are straightening out but I do see a very crooked path that you're going to have to go around but that before you really straighten the conditions out, it's not as easy as it seems, it's not easy because they're having to go through in and out many ways before you're able to straighten the condition out. I feel also that there is a personal connection with you and I would like you to know that maybe you feel that you are walking alone but you are not walking alone because God is always with you but I do feel that the door is going to open when there will be a friendship that exists that will make you much happier but right now I'm picking up a very upset condition with you and it's the lonesomeness and a hurt also at the same time. And they are telling me to tell you that this has been going on for a little while but I do feel that we are going to change the cycle. Somehow there's environment around you picking up because there's a little bird here who's just stirring things up, picking his features up like he wants to fly away, but he seems too tied to the ground, somehow he can't get off the ground up and this is how you've been, you've been trying to pick yourself up and change conditions around you and better yourself in certain ways and you can't seem to get ahead, but you know, he finally, it's funny how he flips his wings, and finally gets enough steam up that he does pick himself up and he goes up very slowly and then he just shoots away like an airplane would go. But it's really only a bird that I see. And this is the way that you're going to do, little by little you're going to be able to pick yourself up and change the vibration, and once it gets picked up you will go far and you will go fast, but for the time being I still see that it's going to be just a little bit of lonesomeness.

B. You're asking a question about a particular person aren't you, who is this person? Were you asking for yourself? Oh, then I was all right I think. I mean on the second one I feel it will but isn't this going to take a little while, I'm not getting what I want at the present time, it's got to take a little while before I receive this, am I correct? this is how I am picking up, it will be all right but when I am going to get it, see, this is the way I pick it up for you. You know, why don't you try it here, I think after you get your language up and the second thing is all correct and straightened up and I think you'll be much happier and you'll be able to do more for yourself. Right now you're at a standstill see what I mean, cause you're scared about your condition. No, I feel very good, like I said, I told you the bird was having an awful time, well, you're sure having an awful time on that second question, but once it does come up you will be fine, you won't have nothing to worry about, it'll be good, see, but right now you still have to work, it looks so funny to see the bird winding his wings up.

It is important to consider the format of delivery of this message. The medium picks up the billet, which is folded over several times. There is some identification on the outside of the paper; in this case it is the number 13. She reads the identification but not the content of the billet. She then gives her message as she receives it from spirit. This is Section A of the message above. Halfway through the message she opens up the billet and reads its contents and then continues to answer the questions contained in it. This is Section B of the message. The information in Section B always continues in the same terminology and imagery as Section A. No one in the audience knows who is being spoken to or what the content of the billet is. At the end the medium asks to whom the billet belongs and whether the message made any sense.

Some of the essential features of a church service relevant to this discussion are the following: First, the client can attend a Spiritualist service and virtually not utter a word during his entire stay. If a client does not have any questions on how to write a billet and does not choose to sing hymns, he can remain silent. Second, for about two hours a client has been spoken to by a variety of church personnel, each employing a certain segment of the terms in the general Spiritualist argot. A new client does not understand much of what is said to him. If he returns to the church regularly, he will learn the argot terms. Third, if any conversation takes place between a client and a medium when the latter is giving a message to the former, the conversation never includes a request by the client for the medium to clarify her terms. Mediums do not explain their argot during the church service; they use it. It is up to the client to find out on his own what terms mean. To understand the message, a client must have some command of the argot.

Mediumship Classes

The place where many Spiritualists acquire a familiarity with the church language is in the pastor's mediumship classes. Mediumship classes are known in the argot by several other terms, such as *development* classes and *unfoldment* classes. One speaks of sitting for development classes. Each of these terms has certain implications in the belief-system of the church, and the terms are not completely synonymous. For example, unfoldment implies that each person contains within himself the abilities of mediumship and sensitivity to spirit influences, while the term development emphasizes the role of the trainer over that of the trainee. Unfoldment implies the spiritual nature of man, while development connotes to the Spiritualist a certain artifice and artistry bordering on theatrics. Regardless of how a pastor prefers to name her classes, they usually have similar attributes. A pastor tries to instruct a select group of persons on how to be receptive to spirit-contact. The people that attend class are not the anonymous public that comes to services. Usually a person who has been attending church for some time approaches the pastor to ask whether she offers mediumship classes. The medium in all cases chooses her students from among the inquiring clients. When enough people have inquired and the pastor can get from eight to twelve persons, she will usually start a class. The classes meet on week nights for about two hours and may continue anywhere from a few weeks to a few months.

During class meetings an individual encounters the first instance of fluent, easygoing social conversation. People are introduced by name and engage in small talk. At the advertised hour the class begins with an invocation in the argot terms. Students are never told that they must use the argot terms for the invocation; however, they learn to imitate the pastor, which implies learning to use her terminology. In class the student does not learn a set of prescriptive rules for church verbal behavior. He learns, rather in the way a child learns his native language, the practical and customary patterns of speech required for public performance in a Spiritualist church context. After the invocation the pastor begins by telling some funny anecdotes or by singing a couple of hymns. This serves to warm the atmosphere, raise the vibrations, invite the spirit forces, or simply to relax and humor the students. Once the mood has been set, the pastor will ask if anyone has anything to report that has happened to him or her during the week. This allows each person to report either his personal tragedies or his joyful events with some comment on how these were anticipated. Such anticipation can be a sign that the individual is becoming spiritually developed, or it can serve as a sign that he received an accurate message from the pastor when he last attended the church service. In the process of this reporting, the students are taught some of the argot. For example, a student will begin by saying; "I had a dream this week. I dreamt that I was back home and there was a storm and I talked to my mother and she was so real just like she was right there." The pastor responds, "That's what we call a soul flight. We visit our loved ones and are able to communicate with them in spirit world." When the individual next recounts her dream she will say, "I had a soul flight last week, I spoke with my mother." If anyone reports an illness, he is given the term *spell* as a substitute term for either the specific name of the disease or any of its symptoms. If an individual speaks of personal anxieties, of conflicts at home or at work, he is given the term *conditions* as a substitute term. If an individual reports difficulties with roommates, landlords, or residential moves, he is given the terms *environment, home situation,* or *vibration.*

Henceforth, the student will use these terms, and the pastor will use them in return, in giving a message to the student. Once these personal accounts are related, the pastor moves on to present the substantive material to be covered in the class. Such material can be either her own teachings received by her from spirit or some published literature about a topic to be covered, such as meditation, aspects of the human body which are spiritually significant, or the various laws of life. Such material is written in the Spiritualist argot, but it has the distinction of defining contextually the terms it uses. For example, a pastor may say: "We often see spirits as colors, and different colors tell us the kind of spirit we are in contact with. Yellow means the spirit of a healer." The argot term *color* is here defined as *spirit,* and, even though spirit is an argot term itself, we are nonetheless able to see the sense in which the term color is used and its status as a synonym for the term spirit.

Following the presentation of the reading material, which is read aloud by the pastor, is a period of concentration and meditation. During this period students sit around a table with the lights turned off. After the repetition of an affirmation (a prayer which asserts the goodness of the individual and the protection he receives from spirit) students sit silently and try to see what they can see and feel what they can feel. After several minutes each person begins to report what he has *seen, heard,* or *felt.* This reporting involves using argot terms. After this period, which is variably called meditation or concentration or sitting in the silence, a benediction is offered, and class is dismissed.

The essential feature of classwork which is significant from the point of view of language is that the argot terms are presented in a rather full context. Moreover, a kind of substitute definition is given in the pastor's implicity stating that a given Spiritualist form should replace a given standard form in a given context. The pastor gives the student training in using the langauge she is not interested in operationalizing why the language is used. Her job is to train her student to know how to use the language, and not necessarily to explain to someone else why it is used. She does not probe the relative vagueness of terms or explain or factor out in explicit detail the nuances of meaning. Terms are learned and understood through usage and practical experience. The client is given an opportunity to practice using the argot in conversing with his friends and fellow students about topics of daily life. It is this further use of argot terms in social conversation with friends during church social functions which serves to enhance the socialization of an individual into church life.

Social Activities

Social activities such as dinners, bazaars, or card games are not pervasive in Spiritualist churches and are restricted in Bay City to some of the largest churches where the pastor is active in promoting either a membership or a steady clientele for church services. The example here is drawn from Reverend Cooper's Pacific Spiritualist Church. The Pacific Church sponsors activities for which tickets are sold at church services by some of the pastor's students. The work for any church social is done by the church members or the pastor's students, who are organized into small groups which meet weekly to discuss the pastor's teachings and to meditate to increase their spiritual sensitivity. The main purpose of the social event is to raise money for a particular project within the church, such as improvement of the premises or a building fund.

People who come to the socials are either regular parishioners or new people investigating the activities offered by the church. New people usually do not initiate interaction with the church staff; they wait to be approached and incorporated into a group. The church regulars associate mostly with those who are in their weekly classes. Conversation revolves around the pastor's teachings or the meanings of argot terms. There is very little conversation about personal life or daily activity. This is due in part to the lack of common bonds among many of the individuals who attend the church. The only area of commonality is the church experience, and that experience has a language to describe it, the argot. The social is an opportunity for the pastor's students to reinforce each other's use of the church argot. If one individual will discuss a church matter in standard English terms, he will be corrected and offered a substitute term from the argot. For example, one individual may complain about a parishioner who slammed the door on his way out of church while the service was still in progress, ruining the attention of the congregation. At this point another student will interrupt the speaker to simply say, "vibrations," which is the substitute term for the secular description of the church atmosphere, the drama of the message service, and so on. During social functions a church client is socialized by his peers into the use of the church argot. Those churches that have no socials usually accomplish this during classwork or in conversation before or after services. Actually, this is not a problem, because most newcomers to

Spiritualism first attend one of the larger churches, where they are initiated into the argot, and only with time discover the smaller churches, which usually do not have social events. By the time clients reach the less known churches, they are familiar with the argot.

Séances and Private Readings

The church argot is significant in two other instances, the séance and the private reading. The séance is usually offered by a medium to a select group of clients. Séances are not open to the public at large. There are various kinds of séance. First is the materialization séance, where an individual's friends, relatives, or spirit mentors materialize before him out of the ectoplasm of the medium. Second is the trumpet séance, where the same departed individuals speak to the client through the voice instrumentality of the medium. Spirits are said also to send apports, items such as jewelry or personal mementos, to the clients via the trumpet, which is a spherical object made out of tin, papier maché, or newspaper. Whichever kind of séance a person attends, one factor is paramount: either a person is addressed directly by a spirit in his or her own words and approximate voice, or the medium relates to the client what a spirit is saying to him. If a spirit speaks directly to a client, then standard English is used with an attempt to reproduce the vernacular of the place and time when the spirit lived. If, however, the medium relates information which she receives for the client, then the Spiritualist argot will be used. The distinction between the voice of the spirit and the voice of the medium is one that is made by Spiritualists. The speaker in either case is the medium; except when the voice of a spirit is heard, it is argued that the spirit is using the vocal cords of the medium. The séance is usually conducted in a darkened room, and a client only hears the voice of the medium and does not see her facial expressions or the movement of her lips.

In private readings the Spiritualist argot is only used part of the time. A private reading is a private consultation which a client secures with the church pastor or some other medium. This is regarded by most Spiritualists as the most desirable form of communication with spirits because here the medium can speak privately and therefore does not have to shield what the spirits say. Private readings are requested by clients, and pastors grant appointments mostly to those who have previously been to their churches. When an individual comes to a private reading, he usually chats with the medium for a few moments in order to warm the atmosphere. Then the medium will ask the client whether he would prefer to talk or be talked to. On some occasions the medium will ask the client to open to a section of the Bible and read. The content of the passage read will serve as a entrée for the medium to start speaking with the client. It is expected that the medium will bring forth from spirit some information which will pertain to the need, question, or worry of the client. As the information is produced, the client indicates some kind of recognition of whether the information is accurate or whether there is need for further talk by the medium in order to hit the point at issue. Once the problem has been mentioned, the medium will converse with the client about it. During the first part of the interview when the medium is receiving information from spirit, all topics are phrased in the church argot. However, when the medium converses with the client there is a shift to standard English.

As can be seen from my description of the various church activities, the Spiritualist argot is significant in the following ways: first, it is the mode of expression for any information which a medium relates from spirit; second, it serves as a social bond for a pastor's clients; third, it allows a Spiritualist church to acquire an identity vis-à-vis both orthodox churches and other Spiritualist churches; and finally, it offers a language which shields the content of the message. Shielding the content of the message is necessary for a medium if she is to avoid conflict with the law.

VI. Lexical Data and Analysis

The argot terms can be grouped into topical categories. The full lexicon consists of several hundred terms, of which I present here only an example of the kinds of terms under consideration. The topical categories for the argot terms have been defined by informants.

A. The manifestations of *spirit world:*

spirit	entities	influences
infinite intelligence	cosmic entities	invisible friends
mind	astral entities	messengers
voices	angels	spirit helpers
truth	souls	friends
love	astral forces	guides
lights	forces	loved ones
colors	angel loved ones	band
		control
		guardian
		teacher
		doctor
		American Indian
		Chinese healer

B. The place where *spirits* reside:

spirit world	astral world	ether
sphere	atmosphere	summerland
astral plane		

C. Physical features of the *spirits:*

astral body	aura	vibrations

D. *Psychic experiences* of parishioners:

astral flight	communication	soul flight
astral projection	experience	materialization
automatic writing	phenomena	

E. *Mediumistic* practices and related artifacts:

billet	communication	message work
billet reading	ectoplasm	psychic reading
clairaudience	etherialization	séance
clairvoyance	materialization	

F. Individuals who frequent Spiritualist churches:

seekers	students	travelers
spiritualists		

G. Problems that individuals bring to the church for resolution:

condition	environment	upset
cycle	vibration	

H. Styles of *mediumistic contact*:

come	have	seek
demonstrate	intuit	serve
experience	know	tell
feel	meditate	tune in
get	perceive	work
give	see	

To illustrate the analysis of the argot terms enumerated above, we may look at the category labeled "manifestations of spirit world," and see the relationships that exist between the terms. One relationship is a paradigmatic one describing how spirits manifest themselves and are thereby recognized by informants (Diagram 1).

DIAGRAM 1

Supreme Being	infinite intelligence	truth love
Individual Souls	spirit	voices colors lights
	heavenly manifestation	earthly manifestation

It is of crucial importance to Spiritualists to receive a message from *spirit*. However, it is not only the content of the message that is important, it is also the source of the message. Messages can be said to come from spirits or from infinite intelligence (God). Furthermore, in identifying the source, Spiritualists also desire to personally experience a communication from that source. The only way they can experience such communication is to recognize its form. The terms in the grid indicate the forms that such spirit manifestations assume in both the heavenly and earthly spheres.

Another relationship that exists between terms in a part-whole relationship (Diagram 2).

DIAGRAM 2

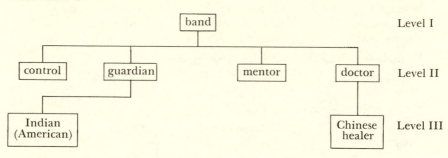

The term *band* in Level I is the most general term applied by Spiritualists to include all the spirits in whose province it is to *guide, guard,* and *protect* a parishioner. When a medium uses the term *band,* she is indicating to a parishioner that he has attracted to himself *spiritual helpers,* but that his spiritual development has not progressed sufficiently to allow him to know the particular spirits according to their specific tasks or proper names. With the parishioner's additional spiritual development or unfoldment, the medium begins to factor out for him the particular areas in his secular and religious life where individual spirits are instrumental. Therefore, in Level II we see the specialization of spirits being enumerated. A *control* directs the parishioner's psychic experiences; a *guardian* protects the individual in his daily life; a *mentor* teaches the parishioner the metaphysical laws of life; and a *doctor* guides the parishioner's development as a healer and also heals any physical or mental disturbances he may have. For those parishioners who continue to progress, the medium offers specific names of guides and identifies their ethnic backgrounds. Thus in Level III we find American Indians and Chinese healers, who specialize in guarding and healing the parishioner. Diagram 2 indicates the chronology in which parishioners are introduced to members of their bands.

A third relationship is the one organized along the dimension of time—the familiarity of a parishioner with the argot terms from his first visit to church until the time that he receives his own *guides* (Diagram 3).

Level I: *God* is the most general term applied to *spirits*. Stated another way, the occupants of spirit land are given the attributes of omnipotence, omniscience, and omnipresence which are exclusively accorded to God in orthodox churches.

DIAGRAM 3

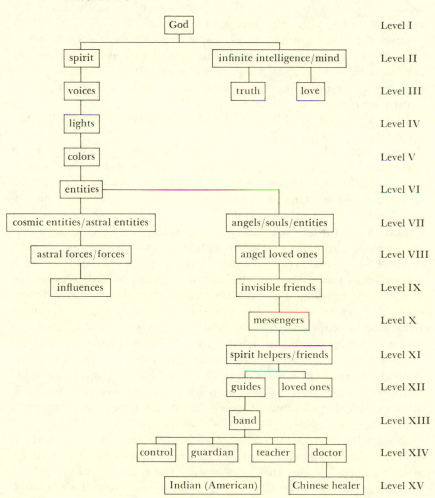

Level II: This level indicates the more specific labels for God. *Spirit* as a generic noun for all occupants of spirit land contrasts with *infinite intelligence* and *mind*, which are direct labels for God and do not include spirits.

Level III: *Truth* and *love* further specify labels for God. Both of these terms are regarded as manifestations of God on earth; truth further corresponds to the teachings of a Spiritualist church, and love, to the Golden Rule. The two terms allow the speaker to invoke both God and the essential creed of a Spiritualist church. These two labels for God are contrasted with *voices*, which are the earthly manifestations of spirit. Voices heard by a parishioner at certain times are perceived to be spirits attempting to communicate with him.

Level IV: Voice manifestations of spirit over time can become *lights,* or visible manifestations. Voices evolve into lights as the parishioner continues to develop spiritually and communicate with spirits. Hearing voices, or sounds in general, is one of the earliest kinds of psychic experience reported by parishioners.

Level V: Lights turn into *colors* with yet further spiritual development by a parishioner.

Level VI: The voices, lights, and colors are manifestations of spirit, but some individuals conceive of them as spirits in disguise, and collectively label them *entities*. Entities is the most general term to indicate the existence of a *soul* or *force* in a supra-earthly dimension, such as spirit world or astral sphere.

Level VII: Entities are differentiated into more specific categories by the mediums. They relegate entities into two contrasting categories, *cosmic entities/astral entities* and *angels/souls/entities*. Both sets of terms share the characteristic of referring to things that exist in another dimension of life; but the two contrast along a single dimension—their specific geographical or spatial location within the other dimension. *Cosmic entities/astral entities* are souls of individuals who seek to be reincarnated in a living person on this earth in order to atone for their misdeeds enacted while the entity was an earth-living individual. Such entities reside in the *astral plane.* However, *angels/souls/entities* are souls of individuals who have entered spirit land and who are able to grow and progress within spirit land and resume "a life on the other side."

Level VIII: *Astral forces/forces* are *cosmic entities* which actively seek individuals on this earth through whom they can either atone for their misdeeds or sate their vices; such forces are usually regarded as undesirable or malevolent. *Angel loved ones* are all those souls who pass on to spirit world and seek to help humans in their daily needs; such entities are desirable and helpful. Both sets of entities share the feature of being involved in human affairs, but differ in the nature of that involvement, whether good or evil from the point of view of the parishioner. In effect, an entity aiding the parishioner in his difficult is an angel loved one, and one which destroys him further is an astral force.

Level IX: *Influences* are forces that actively direct a parishioner's activity, while *invisible friends* offer guidance but allow the parishioner free will on whether to abide by their guidance. The contrast between these two terms is on the basis of explicit control over the actions of the parishioner.

Level X: *Messengers* are those invisible friends who communicate with a parishioner primarily through the instrumentality of a medium in a message service.

Level XI: *Spirit helpers/friends* are those messengers who are identified by the medium as spirits who take a particular interest in a parishioner and continuously come to his aid.

Level XII: *Guides* and *loved ones* are two sets of spirits that share the status of being spirit *helpers*, but they are contrasted by the medium along the criteria of the relationship each helper had with the parishioner while the former was on the earth plane. Loved ones are always blood or affinal relatives or close friends of the parishioner who have passed on to spirit. Guides, however, can be complete strangers who have taken an interest in the parishioner because spirit cares for the welfare of those left on the earth plane.

Level XIII: All a parishioner's guides are organized into a *band*, which is a corporate group in charge of the welfare of the parishioner. The identities of the constituent members of the band are revealed to the parishioner by the medium.

Level XIV: This level specifies the kinds of guides within the band. Each category—*control, guardian, teacher, doctor*—is distinguished by the particular task accorded it in the care of the parishioner.

Level XV: An American *Indian* is an ethnic category singled out as particularly significant for the parishioner because Indians are considered to be the most efficacious guardians. Therefore, the category *guardian* is often further specified ethnically by the term *Indian*. Because of a belief in the healing powers of the Chinese, the category *doctor* is often specified by *Chinese healer*.

The terms in this diagram are known and understood by the congregations of the three types of churches discussed in Section I. Church Type A makes use of all the terms, but Types B and C do not employ the labels for God (Levels II and III). Such terms as *infinite intelligence, mind, truth,* and *love* are regarded as unique to Type A churches, chartered by the United States Spiritualist Association.

Within each church anyone may use any of the terms if he uses them as nouns labeling referents which are believed to exist on the basis of church teachings. However, the use of these terms following such verbs as *see, feel,* and *sense* in the first-person form, active voice, is restricted to ordained ministers, students of the pastor, or parishioners recognized for their psychic sensitivity. The use of any of these terms following such verbs as *contact, get, have, communicate* is restricted to ordained mediums, who are the only ones who may explicitly contact any of the spirits during the church service.

Terms in Levels I–III are used primarily in invocations and benedictions. Levels III (voices) through VIII are most frequently used during classwork. Levels IX–XV are properly used during the message service in the church.

The configuration of the diagram is determined, in this instance, not only by the general meanings of the terms; the diagram also reflects both the notion of time from the point of view of the parishioner's involvement with a church and also the levels of stereotypes about spirits prevalent among non-Spiritualists. Any individual who comes to the church for the first time is familiar with and uses terms on Levels I and II (spirit). In order to learn and use terms on Level XV, he must have attended the church for a period of time, for the relationship that a parishioner forms with spirits in Levels III–XV is in large measure determined by the revelation of the medium to him of what that relationship is. Such revelations are offered in messages during the message service or during classwork. Both are available to a parishioner only after he has attended the church for some time.

In similar fashion, Levels I–XV also reflect the length of time a *spirit* has spent in spirit land. A spirit on Level III has only recently departed for spirit land, while a spirit on Level XV is fully developed or progressed and is able not only to manifest or make itself known to the parishioner *voices* (Level III), but can actually participate in the life of the parishioner as an *Indian* guarding spirit (Level XV).

The structure of the diagram, moving from Level I, the most abstract, to Level XV, which is the most specific, reflects the stereotypes of the community at large about Spiritualism. The individual who is least familiar with Spiritualist churches uses terms in Levels I through VI, while any individual who is somewhat familiar with the churches indicates such familiarity by using the more specific terms on Levels VII through XV.

Finally, the diagram mirrors the social structure of the church. Terms on Levels I through VI are used primarily by parishioners; however, once the service begins, the mediums resort to the more specific terms for spirits on Levels VII through XV.

Misuse of the Argot

Since most of the church work involves speaking, it is to be expected that conflict situations develop out of particular speech events. Most conflicts arise around erroneous use of the argot or by using terms of a status higher than one's own.

Erroneous use of the terms means the particular usage of an argot term by a speaker that renders his communication unintelligible or inacceptable to his listener because the speaker used a term:

(1) inappropriate *vis-à-vis* his status in the church. For example, an individual who is not an ordained *medium* used such terms as *see, feel, sense* to mean that he is in *contact* with *spirits*.

(2) more abstract in reference when a more specific term was available to him. For example, one parishioner in conversation with another parishioner refers to a pastor as a *fortune-teller* rather than a *medium*. Although *fortune-teller* includes the sense *medium*, the latter term should have been explicitly used. The usage of a more general term in lieu of a specific one is understood to be an insult.

(3) inaccurately, in a sense other than the accepted definition of a term. For example, one parishioner will relate a dream he had by saying, "Last night I *projected* myself and I saw. . . ." The term *projected* was inaccurately used. The speaker should have said, "Last night I had a *soul flight*. . . ." It is *soul flight* that is used in a sense of dream and not *project* which is "a purposeful attempt by a medium to come in contact with a particular spirit or living individual some distance away from where the medium is located."

These errors are corrected by the medium or her immediate entourage. There are never any supernatural sanctions either threatened or invoked. Dissension is secular and mundane. Part of the reason for that is that spirits are regarded as benign and beneficent, and retribution is regarded as only an earthly phenomenon. Once in spirit there is only love and harmony to be practiced.

But mediums do not need supernatural sanctions to discipline their followers. Usually, if an individual is persistent in misusing the argot the medium slowly edges him out of the church by refusing to give him a message, or by giving him very brief and recognizably inadequate counselling on his stated problem.

VII. Conclusions

In this final section we may consider the analysis of the diagrammatic presentations and the utility of this approach for the analysis of the social structure of the church. We may first draw several conclusions about the argot:

1. Since the essence of this argot is to shield the thing it labels, this argot is most elaborate for those aspects of Spiritualist culture with which Spiritualists feel uneasy. The largest number of terms is offered for the different kinds of *spirits,* the nature of *mediumistic contact,* and the sorts of problems people bring to the church.

2. The criteria for the number of terms a pradigm will have is, first, the importance of the concept or object to the functioning of the church system; second, its legal status; and third, the level of its specificity (does it have a material representation?). The largest number of terms is available for the most important and most abstract terms such as *spirits, mediums, psychic phenomena.*

3. Concepts or objects presented to the public at large are more heavily articulated—for example, the nature of a *mediumistic contact, psychometry, vision*—while concepts or objects reserved for the faithful are least elaborated—for example, *ectoplasm.*

4. Of the noun, adjective, and verb form classes, nouns are the numerous category. *Mediums* speak primarily in noun phrases to avoid giving the impression that they are the source of the information presented in the *message.* This is advantageous to the church, since most newcomers to the churches are slightly leary of mediums and suspect the veracity of their claims to mediumistic powers. If argot terms are applied to nouns, or noun phrases, the newcomer will be less suspicious, for most speakers of standard English accept the fact that their vocabulary of nouns may be limited. It is argued that newcomers to the church will be more willing to accept argot terms for nouns than for verbs. Verbs expressed in nonstandard terms, or terms used infrequently in standard English, such as *to psychometrize,* draw attention to the uniqueness of the term and therefore perhaps also to the strangeness of the practice it refers to, mediumship.

5. Some terms have an open semantic domain which is able to absorb ever changing nuances of meaning; and some terms have a closed semantic domain which is controlled by the churches. The core terms have a closed domain, while the peripheral terms are open. Verbs are frequently the core terms whose meaning is controlled. While nouns range from being core terms to peripheral ones, the peripheral ones are the most receptive to change.

6. The verbs that look superficially most like ordinary English— *see, feel, sense*—are usually the core terms. It is the opposite with nouns; nouns that are least common in standard English, like *psychometry,* are the core terms.

7. Terms like *reincarnation* that are frequently shared with other metaphysical movements get redefined most closely and thus become core terms.

8. Most of the argot is composed of standard English terms. Non-standard English terms are most evident in the noun-form class and least evident in verbs applied to the work of the *mediums*. Such verbs must remain standard in order not to be offensive to the listener or to make a potentially unreasonable experience, *spirit communication*, appear unreal or abnormal.

9. The argot is used most widely in the church service and is defined most specifically in classwork.

The argot is essentially oral and is never written. When it is written, as in classwork, the *medium* dictates her teachings, to be used by students in discussing church teachings among themselves. The fact that the argot is unwritten allows the *medium* to avoid being confronted by what she said either by her client or by the law. The purpose of the *message* is not its content, but its effect on the client.

I have pointed out that all the diagrams assume the configuration determined by the comprehensive gloss of each term. However, each particular configuration reveals additional information about the churches, of significance both ethnographically and to the argot. For example, Diagram 3 shows the concern of Spiritualists with time. The particular aspect of time relevant to Spiritualists is the length of time a parishioner participates in the church, the duration of time a student spends with a medium in classwork, and the length of time a spirit has been in spirit land for its progression. Such a concern with time is reflected in the argot. Certain terms may not be used by individuals unless they have spent a period of time within a church. Such time spent in church is measured also by the kinds of activities a parishioner has performed. This is reemphasized by the use of the argot because the most specific levels of meaning are only revealed to a parishioner after a long period of church socialization.

It is important for a Spiritualist church to have a parishioner involved with it for a long time because most churches do not have paid memberships, and so the only way they can be supported is by the continued donation of parishioners at church services or socials. Therefore, the argot is organized along the dimension of time from abstract to specific terms, with the terms most specific, and therefore satisfactory, to the parishioner being defined for him and acceptable for his use only after his lengthy involvement with a church.

The diagram may be reconstituted beyond the configuration based on general meaning. One may regroup the terms along any dimension desired, such as from the viewpoint of a speaker who occupies a particular church position and speaks in a certain portion of the service. Such diagrams can indicate explicitly the frequency with which certain terms are used within particular status positions in the church and also the changing emphasis on the components of meaning of each term according to the context of the speech event.

It is important to keep in mind that Spiritualists make up a community in only a limited sense. Most Spiritualists join a church at a time of crisis in their lives and continue to attend churches on occasions when they encounter personal difficulty. They are not acquainted with the church argot prior to their initial contact with a Spiritualist church, albeit they might know some of the argot terms as these are used in standard English senses. Most Spiritualists are aware that they are using an argot in church, especially since they step in and out of church participation according to the ebb and flow of their success in daily life.

Spiritualists prefer to keep as anonymous in church as possible. Few give their full names, and when they do, they often give nicknames or fictitious names. About 70 percent of the congregation changes from week to week, and one continuously faces a group of persons who either attend the church infrequently or are newcomers. Because of the rapid and continuous changes in the congregations the ethnographer finds that he needs some kind of index to identify the social relationships that exist between the parishioners and the mediums. Such an index is the use of language. Through observation of how an individual uses the argot the ethnographer has an opportunity to assess the relationship of that individual to the church and the pastor.

For the above reasons the methods of collecting linguistic data have to remain inductive and within natural speech contexts. Formal eliciting of specific linguistic information is virtually impossible either from infrequent attendees or from newcomers. In analyzing the material, one has to demonstrate continuously the relationships between lexical items from the point of view of a speaker or from a status position of a parishioner. Since we are not dealing with a community in a formal sense, it is almost useless to give a synthetic diagram that reflects the cultural view of the individuals involved. The only useful and accurate lexical relationships are those which are lodged in particular points of view and which therefore are indicative of the social positions of individuals within the social structure of the church.

In over a century of history in this country, Spiritualism has not become a widely supported national involvement. It has not produced large, permanent religious institutions that promise to have continuity. Rather, Spiritualism exists through small churches that last for a few years, usually the life span of their medium-pastors, and then disappear. The motif of decentralization of churches on a national basis and authoritarian structure within each church is represented in the argot of the churches. In this case, language both participates in creating the pattern as well as in reflecting it to the observer.

BIBLIOGRAPHICAL NOTE

The historical development of Spiritualism and present-day varieties of Spiritualist churches, in Bay City or elsewhere in the United States, have not been of great interest to social scientists. Although the published literature about Spiritualism is substantial, most of it has been produced and often privately published by formal organizations for psychic research or by private individuals who have either found a compatible religion in Spiritualism, become disillusioned with the claims or practices of Spiritualism, personally experienced or witnessed *psychic phenomena*, or have become self-appointed psychic researchers.

Most writings that have been done in the name of psychic research (for example, Carrington 1930; Fairfield 1875; Seybert Commission Report 1887) have focused primarily on the "scientific" claims of Spiritialism, or what is more commonly referred to by Spiritualists as phenomena. These writers have usually sought to test mediums and examine the veracity of their claims to being channels of communication with higher forces. The work of psychic research can be viewed as a recapitulation of some of the basic themes running through the belief-system of Spiritualism, such as a concern with "scientism," and an insistence upon a justification based on "scientific inquiry" for all privately-held beliefs or institutional manifestos. This literature offers little in the way of institutional or historical analysis of Spiritualist churches. Nor does it offer explicitly any insight about the use of language in dealing with metaphysical *phenomena*.

A second genre of writing has been done by those individuals who found a compatible religion in Spiritualism or were preoccupied by its "philosophical" claims (Britten 1870; A. R. Wallace 1875). This genre is interesting for its literary form which can be categorized as autobiographical declarations of faith. This literature throws light on the criteria by which people either chose or rejected Spiritualism as a religion, but offers little as background material for this study.

More relevant to the considerations of this study are the volumes dealing with the history of the Spiritualist movement or with vital statistics about its chronological progress and spread of influence (Barrows 1893; Capron 1855; Clark 1863; Carter 1920; McCabe 1920; Podmore 1910; U.S. Bureau of Census 1936; Harmann 1927). This literature is valuable as historical documentation for the origins of church organizations which are not extant today, but whose social organizations remained a model for the formation of some present-day Spiritualist churches. None of these writings deals with Bay City, and none is overly concerned with the argot spoken within the churches.

Only two volumes have been published that deal specifically with the language of Spiritualism (Blunsdon 1963 and Holmes 1942). Both volumes are dictionaries of terms used in the Spiritualist movement. The term Spiritualism is defined very broadly to include many New Thought churches which are not similar in belief, practice, or organization to the churches specifically dealt with in my study. Consequently, the corpus of terms there is much larger than the one I have been able to isolate as pertinent to Spiritualist churches, as defined in this study. The definitions given to those terms have been taken primarily from written sources and from contexts in which those lexical items have been defined explicitly and theologically. The definitions do not seem to have been gathered from an observation of their usages in verbal contexts. The significance of this is that the semantic domain of each term reflects only the officially accepted usage of the term and neglects to show its common meaning in church life, where it is in greatest use. Blunsdon's dictionary attempts to deal with terms used in Spiritualism as it is known both in England and the United States. My study is restricted to the United States and to specifically defined Spiritualist churches.

Social scientists have not been as interested in Spiritualism as the non-academic followers of the faith have. Consequently, there have been only a few historical or sociological case studies on Spiritualism. Four historical accounts deserve mention. Donovan (1954) deals with the development of Spiritualism in Britain in the second half of the nineteenth century. He sees Spiritualism as a synthesis of the concern with scientism which preoccupied the middle classes, and the utopian, other worldly visions of the wretchedly exploited urban proletariat. His study is well documented and presents a useful conceptual framework. He does not, however, deal with institutional organizations such as churches nor with church language.

A more recent account is Judah's (1967) brief but concise historical treatment of Spiritualism in the United States. Judah's account is based on field work in various Spiritualist churches throughout the country. His prime concern is to present the history of the institutional organizations of Spiritualist churches, and the philosophical themes which have become important to the movement as the result of the denominational schisms which have occurred. He does not address himself directly to any of the linguistic attributes of the church organizations described. He does, however, very appropriately bring out the analytic point that language as such is extremely important to Spiritualists (page 17, point 14). Both of these historical accounts have focused on Spiritualism diachronically over about fifty years.

The one work that most closely parallels the methods and aims of this study is George Lawton's *The Drama of Life After Death* (1932). Lawton's is a detailed and voluminous account of Spiritualist churches in New York city. His aim was to show "a complete system of belief in operation." He has succeeded in describing both the belief-system and the institutional framework in which it functions.

Although my own research follows Lawton's by forty years and is three thousand miles west of New York, I found many of the details of his ethnography equally applicable today to the Bay City churches. One of the major features of Lawton's volume is the descriptive detail that it offers to the reader and the vast documentation of only a few theoretical points. Lawton's approach has been anthropological both in his participant-observation field methods and the holistic scope of his analysis and presentation of data.

Nelson (1969) presents a current study of Spiritualism in England. He draws heavily on the historical development of Spiritualism in America in the Nineteenth century. His analysis of the social organization of Spiritualist churches in England is very applicable to the analysis of similar American churches.

Altered States of Consciousness: Processes of Religious Innovation and Social Change

In the previous section we pointed out that altered states of consciousness provide a context for certain linguistic forms. In this section three papers deal specifically with the phenomenon of altered states of consciousness and relate it to processes of social change.

Bourguignon, who has directed an extensive cross-cultural study on altered states of consciousness, points out that certain features which appear to deviate from the practices of mainline American denominations appear in significant numbers of marginal religious movements. One of these is altered states of consciousness such as trance, dissociation, and visionary experiences. Allied to these are beliefs in possession by spirits including the Holy Ghost, and possession by illness-causing demons. Trance behavior may or may not be accompanied by a belief in possession.

"Altered states of consciousness" is a cover term used to describe a wide variety of observed behavior. Bourguignon reports that a review of the data from a world sample of 488 societies showed that 87 percent of these have institutionalized forms of altered states. Even though both behaviors and beliefs show marked regional variation, in view of such a very high percentage of societies having altered states, it is quite clear that such behavior is neither psychopathological nor a figment of scholarly imagination. Societies lacking both the behaviors and the beliefs form a very small minority. A society may have trance and give it a different interpretation, or it may believe in possession, but label it as a cause of illness or some other alteration in capacity rather than in consciousness.

It is useful to make a distinction between patterned forms of altered states in relatively stable, traditional societies and those used in movements of change, often called crisis cults and revitalization movements. The vision quest of the North American Indian is an example of trance behavior in a stable society, contrasted with the trance-based revitalization movement associated with the Ghost Dance. Revitalization movements are defined by Wallace as "deliberate, organized attempts by some members of a society to construct a more satisfying culture by rapid acceptance of multiple innovations." These movements are not necessarily religious, although many are. Some revitalization movements are characterized by altered states, which may be trance or possession-trance. The definitions of crisis cult, revitalization movement, altered states of consciousness, trance, and possession-trance may form the basis for a multidimensional analysis of religious movements. Assuming the possibility of drawing a sample composed of examples of each type, it should be possible to work out the societal correlates of each type. Such a typology may help to order the vast numbers of marginal religious groups and movements that we recognize on the American scene.

Bourguignon suggests that those who utilize altered states in the context of American society, a society, which has devalued such states, are the most alienated from the total society. They are the most demanding of immediate gratification and require immediate experiential evidence of the cult's premises and promises. This creates conflict between the Protestant ethic of delayed gratification and the ethic of immediate gratification produced by altered states of consciousness.

Since our society as a whole devalues such states and penalizes them, what gains are there for people who believe in socially devalued or even penalized behavior? Trance and other altered states become a way to resanctify experience when it becomes banal and meaningless. We must look at trance as induction into new roles or repudiation of old roles. It can be seen as a regressive model that allows one to go back through one's own developmental stages; it wipes the slate clean so that you can start afresh. Altered states can affirm existing identities; they can be cathartic and give a sense of conviction and rightness not present before.

Even though the research on trance and associated altered states raises several questions, there are some generalization emerging from the hypothetical stage. And often these raise further questions. (1) Trance is used to maintain ongoing structure and to compensate an individual for not making it in the ongoing structure. It may also be used to change structure. The different functions of altered states may or may not be culturally sanctioned. It is important to determine which are, and under what circumstances. (2) Altered states and their content foster certain kinds of social structure. They allow for bypassing authority, hence individualizing membership in an organization. When information is personalized as it is through trance, it looks quite different from the way it does when only a few have access to it. (3) There may be oscillation within a particular group between these two types of trance, idiosyncratic trance which is channeled into rituals, and stereotyped trance, which is institutionalized to produce more trance. Sometimes trance may be stereotyped role playing, and sometimes it may be idiosyncratic. The quality of the state depends on the individual and the circumstance.

Trance diffuses in society with the help of technology, for example, through recordings of trance-inducing music. Trance induced via records permits greater personal variation and allows rituals to be performed privately, while trance performed in cult centers is more controlled by cult leaders. There is a wide variety of trance management, and consequently a wide variety of forms, uses, and interpretations. Rather than getting lost in the variety of forms and uses of trance, it seems appropriate to realize that trance is not an end in itself but rather a way of playing with boundaries of the self, society, and the supernatural—a field of experimentation.

The problem of altered states of consciousness is not new to anthropology. But fieldwork with them is difficult since several levels of behavior have to be observed at once: kinesic movement, linguistic behavior, and intricate performances. Fieldwork is particularly difficult when dealing with American marginal churches where the data collected in the field are in English, the same language that one is using for description and analysis. Often the very analytic terms of the anthropologist, like possession and trance, are also folk categories for the participants. This poses the doubly difficult problem of distinguishing the anthropological use of the term "trance" from the informants' use of the same term.

Bourguignon tried to address this problem by creating a typology which makes important distinctions and uses them to classify many of the disparate reports of altered states that have been made in the past. It was pointed out that between the category of trance and altered states there is a very broad continuum; however, a great many things happen in the center that are not easily placed in a given typology. This is especially true for those altered states which are neither positively nor negatively sanctioned by society.

All three papers in this section are concerned with altered states. Bourguignon discusses them in cross-cultural perspective, Goodman offers an explanatory model, and Prince relates them to the contemporary scene. What is implicit in these papers and other papers in this volume is that they all look at altered states of consciousness as endemic and characteristic of marginal religious movements. Such states are obviously more than ceremonial, or products of enthusiasm produced by drugs, alcohol, music, and so on. They can be looked on as instruments or as processes that maintain an ongoing structure, or that compensate individuals who are not making it in the ongoing larger society, or that change the structure of society.

Altered states should not be looked on as empty processes producing idiosyncratic responses with undetermined content. They should not be viewed as non-predictable. Nor, on the otherhand, are they able to transform irrevocably and permanently. Goodman postulates a model for Pentecostals which examines the role of trance behavior accompanied by glossolalia. She demonstrates how the glossolalia model works for the religious movement with its stages of onset, peak, and dissolution. She concludes that for a successful movement to develop, the society must have available to it a model of hyperarousal trance behavior and an already formulated supernatural premise. The supernatural premise is incorporated into the beliefs of the group through the experience of trance behavior, including the sharing of its peaking phase and dissolution. As a result of examining the range of beliefs and practices introduced before trance behavior and those introduced during it, Goodman considers whether culture change resulted from the religious upheavals she witnessed.

Both Goodman and Bourguignon emphasize the personal, experiential knowledge derived from an altered state as fundamental to all the groups discussed. For some groups the states are prescribed and institutionalized; in others they are idiosyncratic. But for all the groups we are considering, it is important for the follower to have an intimate contact with both the process and content of personally knowing the transcendent. This contact varies from group to group, especially as it is linked with notions of verification of mystical states. In each section of the book we have seen this variation emerge in some form.

Prince argues that in discussing current marginal movements we are really talking about movements that value ecstatic experiences. These movements are experimental and often preoccupy middle-class youth with the mystical. This is partially connected with the drug experience and with a variety of contemplative religious traditions flourishing recently. He sees these movements as rites of passage, or to choose a different image, a kind of "cocoon work." Our society, unlike the insect analogue and unlike the situation in other cultures, lacks a clear and acceptable image of the adult. These movements take in members and turn out adults. Our youth has gone from biological childhood to adulthood, and yet it seems not to be satisfied with adult roles. Some groups are not really trying to transform their members to fit the adult ways in our society; some want to change society; some want to change parental and political roles. Prince suggests that this is not only the transformation of going from child to adult but a broader attempt to find new solutions to these universally recognized, nasty problems. He ties these movements to the Transcendentalists of nineteenth-century New England who were similarly concerned with the mystical and had an interest particularly in Eastern mystical conceptions. Prince uses the term mystical to refer to a specific class of altered states of consciousness. He describes mystical states and their varieties and points out how they can range from intense esthetic experiences to the most mystical experiences of the introverted type where the individual loses awareness of the outside world and is aware of something he calls God.

Cross-Cultural Perspectives on the Religious Uses of Altered States of Consciousness

Iᴛ is the aim of this paper to consider, in a comparative and cross-cultural perspective, certain aspects shared by many of the contemporary American "marginal" religious groups and movements, but which appear to be virtually absent from the "mainline" religious institutions of modern Western society. That is, the "marginals" tend to foster religious experience of a particular intensity, a subjective verification of their religious truths through ecstatic states, which we might most generally term "altered states of consciousness." [1] Such altered states are frequently interpreted by them as possession by spirits (The Holy Ghost, demons, spirits of the dead, etc.). I wish to report in this paper on a major cross-cultural study of institutionalized forms of altered states of consciousness and of possession beliefs, and to discuss the implications of this study for an investigation of contemporary minority religions in the United States.

We may begin with a definition of terms: we must distinguish two orders of phenomena which are often confused: (1) altered states of consciousness and (2) beliefs concerning such states. These beliefs, in turn, affect the states, since the interpretations tend to pattern the behavior. It is therefore often difficult to separate the interpretation from the behavior itself. (For a discussion of this and other difficulties in culling data from the literature, see Bourguignon and Pettay 1964.) Altered states of consciousness (also variously termed "trance" or "dissociation") are a category of psychobiological phenomena, amenable to observation and other objective methods of study (Ludwig

[1] Data on altered states of consciousness presented here are derived from a larger investigation supported in whole by PHS Research Grant MH 07463 from the National Institute of Mental Health.

The literature on altered states of consciousness and on the frequently associated beliefs in possession is very broad. The reader may find helpful materials in the following selected titles: Bourguignon 1968a, 1968b, 1970, 1972, 1974; Bourguignon, ed. 1973; Bourguignon and Pettay 1964; Evans-Pritchard 1937; Prince, ed. 1968; I. M. Lewis 1966; Lhermitte 1963; Spiro 1967; Beattie and Middleton, eds. 1969; Verger 1957; Zaretsky 1967.

1968). Spirit possession, soul loss, etc., are cultural concepts, utilized, at times, to explain these phenomena. They can be discovered by interviewing informants and by studying the socio-cultural context in which the behavior so explained takes place. Such native explanations and socio-cultural contexts have provided the basis for our broad classification of altered states institutionalized, for the most part, in a sacred or religious context. Thus, we distinguish between states interpreted by the people as due to possession (termed "possession trance," or PT), and those not so interpreted (termed "trance," or T). This latter is a residual category, but for the most part it is culturally interpreted as experiences of the (or a) soul and characterized by visionary experiences.

It should be noted that this classification excludes many types of altered states of consciousness: all those states which have only minimum cultural patterning, e.g. fever delirium, and all those states which, although culturally patterned and institutionalized, occur outside a sacred context: e.g. those resulting from secular drinking or drug usage. The categories included in our study are amenable to further subdivisions. I have suggested some refinements of classification elsewhere (Bourguignon, 1968a, 1968b, 1973). However, even this first level carries with it some implications that are, I believe, worthy of consideration. I wish to stress, then, that at this level the classification concerns itself only with presence or absence in a sacred context of possession trance (PT) and/or of trance interpreted by the participants in some other ways (T). Also it deals with possession belief linked to altered states (PT) or not so linked (P). Sub-forms, such as mediumistic possession trance or possession illness are not considered here, for limitations of space. Nor are we concerned here with the manner in which the states are induced (presence or absence of drugs) or with the problem of pathology, whether this be pathology from the point of view of a particular culture or from that of a presumably supracultural science of psychiatry. Indeed, the scope of the present report is quite modest.

In five years of research, our group investigated the ethnographic literature on over 1,000 societies in all parts of the world concerning reports on altered states of consciousness and on beliefs in various forms of spirit possession. Our statistical study, however, on which some of the figures to be cited below are based, was limited to a sample of 488 societies, taken from the universe of societies represented by the *Ethnographic Atlas* (Murdock 1967).[2] The societies in our sample

---

[2] Details concerning our sampling procedure are presented in Bourguignon (1968a) and Greenbaum (1970).

are, for the most part, of the type anthropologists tend to study: traditional societies, mostly tribal in character, non-literate, non-industrial, relatively simple in political organization in comparison with modern nation-states. Yet, particularly in Asia and Sub-Saharan Africa, many traditional societies do indeed attain a considerable degree of complexity and have sizable populations, sometimes reaching into the millions. Complex national societies are under-represented in our universe, and those which are included are represented by studies of village communities of the type anthropologists conduct. On the whole, it is the peasant segment of complex societies which is represented, rather than the urban segment. While this does tend to distort some of the social and cultural realities of such societies, it provides a reasonable degree of comparability among the units of the study.

The generalizations which follow may therefore be of limited applicability to complex societies, the study of which, with respect to altered states of consciousness and beliefs concerning them, involves some special difficulties. We may briefly consider two of these complicating factors, particularly as they exist with reference to Western society: (1) The classical Graeco-Roman tradition and the Judaeo-Christian tradition both include belief in types of possession by spirits and patterned forms of mystical practices. Consequently, in these societies "possession" and "trance" are background factors; however, in modern times these have been de-emphasized by the official proponents of, in Redfield's terms, the Great Tradition. Yet these beliefs and practices have been part of an important cultural stream present to a greater or lesser extent throughout the Western world. (2) How is one to assess the strength of such practices and beliefs? For the small-scale, non-literate societies of our sample, it has sufficed for us to find a record of the existence of given practices and/or beliefs. We did not attempt or presume to weigh their importance in the total scheme of things but merely noted "presence" or apparent "absence." As we look at recent times and particularly the contemporary scene, the sheer numbers of groups and grouplets, some ephemeral and some of longer duration, are impressive, and to make such an assessment is impossible.

As noted, altered states of consciousness are widely integrated into the religious institutions of the societies we have studied. In a given society there may be one or several institutions using such states, and furthermore a society may use either trance or possession trance or both. To cite some examples virtually at random: the Azande (Evans-Pritchard 1937, 1964) utilize trance among male diviners, and possession trance in a female spirit cult. The Fon of Dahomey (Verger 1957, 1969) utilize trance in the form of deep unconsciousness to represent the death of the old personality, and possession trance in later sequences of the individual's initiation, when a spirit has, it is believed, taken over his body. The Shakers of the island of St. Vincent, in the British West Indies, experience visionary trance states during a retreat known as "mourning" and possession trance, as possession by the Holy Spirit, during prayer meetings (Henney 1973). Yet not all types of spirit possession are linked to trance: Haitian peasants experience possession trance in, or in connection with, *vodoun* rituals, but they interpret certain types of illness as possession by the spirits of the dead. Such possession, which is thought to be caused by witchcraft, is not expressed in altered states but in illness and is revealed by divination (Bourguignon 1970).

On the basis of materials as varied as these, we coded societies as having, in institutionalized form, either trance, possession trance, both, or neither. Note that this produces a typology of *societies*, not of cults or of individual religious institutions. Note also that we have attempted to deal with traditional religious *institutions*, not with religious *movements* of varying duration. As examples of movements I am considering such phenomena as the Ghost Dance among American Indians, or the various cargo cults of Melanesia. This choice is a conservative one. Revitalistic or millenial movements or crisis cults typically include at least a phase of inspired leadership, with visionary trance or possession trance experiences, sometimes restricted to the founder or prophet or, on the other hand, widespread among the membership. The very large number and great variety of such movements and cults is strikingly demonstrated in the recent work of Weston La Barre (1970, 1971). By considering movements and cults of this type we would have very notably increased the incidence of patterned states of altered consciousness in our sample and would have raised it significantly beyond that found in relatively stable societies. I shall return to the matter of religious movements below.

What, then, did we actually find? Our sample of 488 societies showed a total of 90% (437 societies) to have institutionalized one or more forms of altered states of consciousness. For the 10% which we coded as lacking such states, we must emphasize the caution: *absent insofar as we were able to determine from the ethnographic data*. It must be noted that "absence" of phenomena is rarely explicitly specified in the literature and must be inferred from contextual materials as well as from lack of report.

Our 488 sample societies represented all major regions of the world. Here we followed Murdock (1967) in dividing the world into six major ethnographic regions: Sub-Saharan Africa, Circum-Mediterranean, East Eurasia, Insular Pacific, North America, and South America. One of our most striking findings is the discovery of the existence of very great differences among these areas with reference to the phenomena we were investigating, a point which I hope to develop more fully in a moment. With respect to the distribution of altered states of consciousness, the incidence of institutionalization varies from 97% of North American (Indian and Eskimo) societies to a mere 78% of the societies in the Circum-Mediterranean area. The other areas follow in this order: Insular Pacific and East Eurasia (94% each), South America (85%), Sub-Saharan Africa (82%). There is also a broad range of variation in belief in possession by spirits, either linked to altered states of consciousness or not so linked. This type of belief is found in 74% of our total worldwide sample, ranging from a high of 88% among the societies of the Insular Pacific to a low of 52% in North America. The other areas show the following incidence of such beliefs: East Eurasia (87%), Sub-Saharan Africa (81%), Circum-Mediterranean (77%), and South America (64%).

Tables I and II present somewhat more refined breakdowns of this information. Thus, if we take a somewhat closer look at the different types of states, that is to say, trance and possession trance, as I have defined them above, we find the following: trance alone characterizes 38% of our worldwide sample, possession trance 28%, while a combination of the two is present in 24%, 10% of the societies having institutionalized neither form of the state of altered consciousness. Again, trance alone has its highest incidence in North America, with 72% of the societies being so coded. This stands in most extreme contrast to Sub-Saharan Africa, where we found only 16% of our sample societies to have trance alone. On the other hand, possession trance has its highest incidence in that area (46%), with another 20% of the societies found to have a combination of the two types of states. Again, in contrast to these figures, North America once more represents the other extreme, with only 4% of its societies having possession trance and 21% having both possession trance and trance. The other world areas fall between these extremes, with South America most closely resembling North America.

Equally drastic contrasts between world areas are to be found in respect to possession beliefs (Table II). Such beliefs are altogether absent in 48%, almost half, of our North American sample but, on the other hand, absent in only 12% of the societies of the Insular Pacific. Again, South America is a close second to North America, with 36% of its societies lacking such beliefs. It is clear that in respect to both behavior and belief, the New World is indeed a world apart.

These findings, which can be sketched here only briefly, require some interpretation. How is it that altered states of consciousness are

TABLE I. Distribution of Trance Types by World Areas (*percent*)

	Total (N = 488)	Sub-Saharan Africa	Circum-Mediterranean	East Eurasia	Insular Pacific	North America	South America
Trance	38	16	23	22	29	72	54
Possession Trance	28	46	43	38	34	4	7
Trance and Possession Trance	24	20	13	34	31	21	22
No Trance or Possession Trance	10	18	21	6	6	3	17
Total	100	100	100	100	100	100	100

TABLE II. Distribution of Possession Types by World Areas (*percent*)

	Total (N = 488)	Sub-Saharan Africa	Circum-Mediterranean	East Eurasia	Insular Pacific	North America	South America
Possession	22	15	23	16	22	27	34
Possession and Possession Trance	35	43	36	52	44	20	18
Possession Trance	16	23	20	20	22	5	12
No Possession or Possession Trance	26	19	20	13	12	48	36
Total	100	100	100	100	100	100	100

institutionalized in 90% of all the societies in the *Ethnographic Atlas* universe as indicated by our sample? How is it that, nonetheless, such a great range of variations exists between the several major ethnographic regions of the world with respect to the incidence of such institutionalization, and, even more strikingly perhaps, in the form which such institutionalizations take? Similarly, how is it that belief in spirit possession is so widely established in human societies, yet in fact considerably less so than the incidence of altered states: 74% as opposed to 90% over all? How is it, then, that almost half the peoples of North America lack such a belief?

Obviously, only adumbrations of answers to these major questions can be offered at this time. While our study can hope to shed some empirical light on the second group of questions, i.e. the reasons for the regional variations, we can only suggest some educated guesses as to the why of the high incidence of both the institutionalization of altered states of consciousness and the widespread character of possession beliefs, and to me most strikingly the greater incidence of the former over the latter. While I cannot hope to produce proof of my interpretations here, I should nonetheless like to offer some suggestions.

Altered states of consciousness are present in all human societies and undoubtedly have occurred since earliest times of human existence. They may occur in both normal and pathological forms; they are subject to modification through learning and suggestion. They represent, in other words, recurrent types of human behavior, available to be experienced by some, to be observed by others. As such, they represent raw materials for potential cultural utilization, much as is the case for dreams (see Bourguignon, 1972). As such, they are available for cultural interpretation and cultural patterning, for possible integration within an institutional, often ritual, framework, integration within a world view and a value system.

The vast majority of the societies in our sample have availed themselves of the opportunity for utilizing such raw material for cultural elaboration. What of the societies that have not done so? Aside from the fact that some may have been miscoded by us for lack of adequate information, there remain two other possibilities: societies that, in the course of their history, have never—as far as we can tell—developed this utilization, this cultural patterning of altered states of consciousness, and secondly, societies that had at some point in their history lost or rejected such ritual and religious utilization. We may go a long way toward documenting such a situation in the history of Western civilization, as has been shown by Max Weber (1930, 1963) and Erich Fromm (1941), among others. Capitalism, science, and technology are linked to rationality, and as such to a suspicion of mysticism and otherworldliness.

In any event, in both types of absence, whether from lack of development or acceptance or from rejection, we are dealing with the exceptional in human history rather than the typical if we are to define the typical by a head count of societies for which data are available. We may expect to find in the detailed examination of such cases that the development of the institutional utilization of altered states of consciousness and attendant belief systems, or the acquisition of such behavior and beliefs through the process of diffusion, is inhibited in certain cases, because these practices and beliefs are in some way contradictory to the structural requirements of the societies in question. In order to accept such practices from their neighbors, for example, some profound social and cultural rearrangements might be required in a given case. Conversely, when societies having such practices and beliefs lose them, this appears to be linked to changes that have taken place in other aspects of the social and cultural system. Perhaps this point will become clearer when I discuss, as I shall in a moment, the social structural concomitants of Trance and Possession Trance as we have discovered them in the statistical analyses of our data.

While altered states of consciousness are universal psychobiological phenomena, available to all human societies for potential cultural elaboration, possession beliefs are the result of human invention. As symbolic expressions they are, in La Barre's terms, "adaptive man-made artifacts" (1971: 27). The fact that they are so very widespread suggests that they are very ancient. The frequent linkage of such belief to trance phenomena similarly suggests that this linkage is very ancient also, particularly since both the beliefs in general and the type linked to trance states occur in all parts of the world. As La Barre (1970) has pointed out persuasively, it is likely that such practices and beliefs existed in the European Upper Paleolithic and thus have their roots in a very ancient layer of human cultural development. Furthermore, a belief in possession, as a belief in spirits, corresponds to certain basic aspects of human nature and thus, as a result of both diffusion and perhaps frequent reinvention, has come to be as widespread as it is. Yet the particular nature of the beliefs varies widely, and indeed it must vary to remain coherent with the larger world view and religious system of a society, as well as with its social structure. Spiro (1967), for example, has analyzed in detail how belief in spirits, and in particular in possessing spirits, co-exists with Buddhism in rural Burma; he has shown, indeed, not only how such co-existence is possible but in fact necessary, that is, how within the existing framework of social, cultural, and psychological facts, these two systems complement each other. Thus, the variety of contexts, into which possession beliefs are integrated, seems to me to explain the variety in the beliefs themselves, although we are only beginning to understand this in the particular case.

As indicated, the notion of possession by spirits, which is so widespread, is contingent on an even more widely accepted idea, that of spirit itself. The history of the study of religion, by anthropologists and others, is replete with attempts at accounting for the development of that concept, from Tylor's hypothesis that the concept of "spirit" constituted an answer to questions primitive man asked himself to Beattie and Middleton's proposal (1969) that the idea of spirits made problems of living amenable to the techniques used in social relations, or to the classical psychoanalytic conception rephrased by Spiro (1967) and La Barre (1970) that spirits represent projections and displacements of affective elements in the parent-child relationship.

Whatever theory or combination of theories one may wish to espouse in this respect, the problem of "possession" is one of greater specificity: possession, it seems to me, is one of a limited number of possible solutions to the problem of *communication* between humans and spirits. An abstract concept of "spirit" satisfied, I suggest, none of the needs postulated to account for the development of the concept in the first place, whether intellectual, sociological, or affective. If belief in spirits is to be of dynamic value, if it is to have, in other words, survival value, two-way communication with spirits must be established. Religious ritual and the broad variety of methods of divination (Bourguignon 1968b) address themselves to these ends. Ritual tells the spirits of human obedience, expresses human wishes, etc. Divination, through the interpretation of signs, for example, reveals the will of spirits. However, these are indirect means, requiring the skill of practitioners. In contrast to such means, visionary states and possession trance states allow more dramatic two-way contacts in a setting of, frequently, heightened emotional intensity. Visionary trance states provide communication between the visionary and the spirits he contacts. For the most part, this is a matter of private dealings, in which the society receives messages from the spirits at second hand, as it were. Possession and possession trance involve bodily manifestation of spirits, producing the presence of spirits for all to see. This presence may take the form of illness or of the dramatic enactment of possession trance. In the latter instance the actor may be unconscious and amnesic with reference to the actions of the spirit, carried out before, and for the benefit of, an audience.

The nature of the spirits that are contacted or that are impersonated varies widely. They may be animal spirits, ancestors, enemies, but rarely if ever are they high gods. The character of the spirits and of the roles they play—punitive, helpful, ambivalent, etc.—reveals much of the nature of the society, as does the role assigned to the trancer or possession trancer. The complexity of the organizational structure within which these states are utilized reveals much of the complexity of the society. Thus, we may take as the prototype of visionary trance the form that is associated with the individual vision quest of North American Indians. We may take as prototypical of possession trance the cult groups of Africa and Afro-America, in which many individuals, members but not necessarily leaders of the group, engage in this behavior. The latter organizational structures and the societies in which they eixst are, by any criteria, far more complex than the former.

Thus, while both visionary trance and possession trance represent modes of communication with spirits, the modes developed by a given society (and both may co-exist in the same society) will depend on a variety of societal and cultural variables, as well as on psychological ones. Both types are expressive of human dependence on spirit agencies, but different modalities of expression of this dependence are provided: in these modalities the importance of group participation is a significant variable.

The concept of possession, unrelated to the experience of altered states of consciousness, is, as we have seen, also widespread. It occurs both in societies where PT exists and also in societies where PT is absent. Similarly, it occurs in societies where T exists and in societies where such behavior is absent. The concept of possession by spirits provides a useful explanatory category for a variety of conditions: for illness, but also for superior skills or powers, enhanced vitality, etc. This concept, too, stresses human dependence on supernatural entities and man's potentially great affinity, or even identity, with them. As such, it expresses the idea of spirit presence and possible communication with spirits, but it does not involve the idea of impersonation or the enactment of multiple roles, as is the case in the practice of possession trance.

Possession trance, it is suggested here, involves the enactment of multiple roles by human actors. This is not true of possession which does not involve altered states of consciousness, as discussed above. Nor is this true of those trance states which are visionary in nature or are believed due to the temporary absence of the individual's soul, etc. The enactment of multiple roles, of the kind involved in possession trance, however, is more likely to exist in societies in which there is a large repertory of roles, actually or potentially. Consequently, it is more likely to exist in more highly complex and differentiated societies than in simpler ones.

We have grouped societies into those having trance, those having possession trance, and those having both forms of altered states of consciousness, as well as a relatively rare fourth category, having neither. We have called these "trance types." As noted earlier (Table I), these types are quite unevenly distributed around the world; in particular, we have noted the great difference between the New World and the Old, epitomized in the contrast between North America with 71% of its societies having trance and Sub-Saharan Africa, with only 16% in that category. On the other hand, while the latter area has 46% possession trance societies, North America has only 4% of its societies coded as such.

We also attempted to discover the relationship between the types and a series of societal characteristics, generally indicative of societal complexity.[3] Are the hypotheses stated above borne out by our empirical findings? We expect possession trance to occur significantly more frequently in more complex societies than in less complex ones. Trance not linked to possession belief and possession belief not linked to trance experience, on the other hand, are not expected to be tied to societal complexity. Thus, in addition to occurring in simpler societies, we may expect mixed types, where these appear together with possession trance.

For the purpose of this test, we drew a smaller sample of 119 societies, based on the Standard Cross Cultural Sample (Murdock and White 1969). We found five societal variables to be significantly related to possession trance, that is, the *chi* square is significant at or below the .025 level. The variables are: estimated size of population (more than 100,000); stratification; slavery (presence, or recent presence, of this institution); settlement patterns; existence of a jurisdictional hierarchy above the local level. Thus, we found that societies having possession trance are likely to be numerically larger, to be stratified into social classes, to have, or to have recently had, slavery, not to be migratory or semi-nomadic but to live in permanent locations, and to have a jurisdictional hierarchy which includes one or more levels of decision making above the local level. Societies having trance only are significantly less likely to have these features. Societies having both trance and possession trance are either intermediary between the other two types or are the most complex of the three types.

[3] These and other characteristics and their worldwide distribution are taken, in modified form, from the *Ethnographic Atlas* (Murdock 1967) and are discussed by us at length in another publication (Bourguignon and Greenbaum 1973).

Comparing societies with possession trance with those having only possession belief on the one hand and with societies having both possession belief and possession trance on the other, our findings were, on the whole, similar. With respect to the same five variables (population size, stratification, slavery, settlement patterns, and jurisdictional hierarchy above the local level), societies having both possession belief and possession trance proved to be the most complex. The first four of these variables were related to our types significantly at or below the .05 level, the last only at or below the .10 level.

We added a further, independent test of our hypothesis: Marsh (1967) coded a sample of societies with respect to an index of differentiation, devised by him. He defines differentiation in this context as "the number of structurally distinct and functionally specialized roles and collectivities in a society" (Marsh 1967: 314). We have data for our variables for 288 societies coded by Marsh. Comparing societies of index of differentiation 0–3 with those of index 4–7, with respect to the distribution of trance types, we obtain the results shown in Table III. The relationship between trance type and index of differentiation is found to be significant at or below the .001 level. As expected, possession trance is most likely to be found in societies with high index of differentiation. It is interesting to note also that societies having neither trance nor possession trance are much more likely to be among the societies with low index of differentiation.

This relationship between variables indicating societal complexity and the presence or absence of types of institutionalized altered states of consciousness and possession beliefs also contains a clue to a problem we have mentioned earlier: the uneven geographic distribution among the major world areas of the phenomena under investigation here. In another study (Bourguignon and Greenbaum 1973) we were struck by the characteristic regional profiles of each of the major world areas. Thus we note the association between, for example, a settlement

TABLE III. RELATION OF INDEX OF DIFFERENTIATION TO TRANCE TYPES ($X^2 = 17.70$, $P = .001$)

	Index of Differentiation					
	Total		*0–3*		*4–7*	
	No.	%	No.	%	No.	%
No Trance, No Possession Trance	31	11	25	12	6	7
Trance	106	37	86	43	20	23
Trance/Possession Trance	73	25	49	24	24	28
Possession Trance	78	27	42	21	36	42
TOTAL	288	100	202	100	86	100

pattern of a migratory or semi-nomadic type with trance only. Such societies predominate in North America, where 74% of the societies have such a settlement pattern and 72% have trance (see Bourguignon and Greenbaum 1973: table 18). Another example is found in the institution of slavery, the presence, or recent presence, of which is closely linked to the presence of possession trance. It is, or recently was, present in 78% of Sub-Saharan African societies (Bourguignon and Greenbaum 1973: table 20). Possession trance, we see in Table I, is found either alone or in combination with trance in 66% of African societies.

Thus, the claim is made here that the differential distribution of our phenomena is to be accounted for in part by the functional association with variables indicative of societal complexity. However, it must be recognized that cultural diffusion has undoubtedly also played a role, which must be considered in any explanation of distribution of cultural traits and complexes.

Before leaving the matter of functional associations and geographic distributions, I must add a word on the matter of slavery. It is tempting to suggest, and the suggestion has indeed been made, that possession trance is a response to cultural deprivation (Lewis 1966). As such, we may expect to find it where some groups are deprived and subjected to discriminatory treatment. However, whatever the merits of this argument with respect to the East African societies and the low status of women among them, which is the context in which this theory has been propounded, it clearly does not account for our statistical findings. There is an association between slavery and possession trance, much as there is one between settlement patterns and possession trance: both of these are variables indicating societal complexity. Nothing need be implied here regarding the psychological mechanism that leads the deprived to develop possession trance, possibly as a compensatory phenomenon. A closer look at the societies involved will show that the persons engaged in this behavior are not necessarily the slaves (or ex-slaves) but rather, as for example in the case of the Fon of Dahomey, the cult groups which support the worship of the clan ancestors and, in particular, those of the royal clan. Within the large number of societies having both possession trance and slavery we can, I am sure, develop a series of types in some of which there exists an intimate relationship between the two variables, such that the theory of deprivation is supported, while this is not the case for other types. The statistical data presented here, however, should not be construed to offer support to such a theory.

We may now consider some implications of these materials for the study of minority religions in this country. We have shown that religious institutionalization of altered states is very widespread among the societies of mankind, being present in 90% of our worldwide sample of societies. This suggests that we are dealing with an ancient as well as a widespread phenomenon. Since it exists in relatively stable societies, it cannot be explained merely in terms of social or individual psychopathology, of the type that gives rise to millenial and other types of religious movements. Correlations between types of institutionalized altered states and societal variables suggests that societal factors play an important role in the shaping of the forms which altered states assume. Thus, they are subject to cultural influences, to learning and patterning, and should not be considered as merely expressive of personal disorientation or disorganization. If they have survived in stable traditional societies, we may suggest that they are indeed adaptive for these societies, apparently providing different functions for different types of societies.

We have stressed the importance of factors of social structure in the shaping of trance types. However, we have also noted the importance of diffusion. In this connection, it is interesting that some American minority religions, notably Mormons, Shakers, and Spiritualists, have claimed Indian influence on their beliefs. Indian spirits have played a role in both of the latter. Hallowell (1967), reviewing the influence of the Indian on American culture, finds no evidence of actual borrowing of beliefs or behaviors. However, the belief in the possibility of possession by Indian spirits among the Shakers and of Indian guides among Spiritualists, appears to be a symbolic identification with the original inhabitants of this country. Interestingly, a similar belief exists in the Brazilian Umbanda cult (Pressel 1973).

We distinguish between traditional, more or less stable societies, for which we have presented our statistical findings, and those other situations, which have variously been termed "revitalization movements" (Wallace 1956, 1970) and "crisis cults" (La Barre 1970, 1971). On the assumption that such movements or cults exhibit a disproportionately high incidence of patterned altered states of consciousness, we have not included them in our sample for the most part, so that we might be able to generalize about societies in a relatively stable state, as opposed to one which might be characterized as unstable, and as such as exceptional and atypical. These cults have been described by La Barre who has recently reviewed the vast literature dealing with them as "new projective sacred systems" resulting from "culture shock and the strains of acculturation" (1971: 4). Wallace, on the other hand, has defined revitalization movements as "deliberate, organized attempts by some members of a society to construct a more satisfying culture by rapid acceptance of a pattern of multiple innovations" (1970: 188).

It may be possible and desirable to construct a typology of marginal religious movements in this country utilizing the concepts of "revitalization," "crisis cult" and "altered states of consciousness." In so doing we must note, however, that these marginal groups, whatever their origins, exist in the context of American society, with its institutional framework, its historical traditions, and its current load of acute problems. Many, but not all of the marginal groups undoubtedly concern themselves with the construction of "a more satisfying culture." There are, however, others who have such concerns, who do so in a secular, political framework and cannot be counted among our marginal religious groups. Some of those who do so within a religious context may perhaps be termed crisis cults, while others, that could be included under that latter heading do not, in fact, set out to construct a better culture but turn inward on themselves. Nor are all the minority religions "new sacred systems," although undoubtedly many are. Thus, we may begin by distinguishing established minority religions, such as the Mormons or the Pentecostals, from new groups arising in response to cultural stresses. Yet it does not appear appropriate to call these "strains of acculturation" in the traditional anthropological meaning of this term. Many of these new systems do reflect a rejection of the established forms of religion and of established ways of life in the larger society.

These newer groups might be divided into those who set out to develop a more satisfying society (revitalization movements) and those who do not explicitly do so. Furthermore, for both of these, we might distinguish between those who engage in ritualized forms of altered states of consciousness and those who do not. Among those who experience altered states of consciousness as part of their ritual, some experience possession trance and others trance, as we have defined them. Among the former are the newer pentecostal groups, appealing to middle-class dropouts, such as the so-called "Jesus Freaks," and among the latter the various drug cultists. The type of interpretation of altered states will of course be part of the overall structure of belief of the group, and this in turn, will relate to its intellectual level, its social orientation, and other factors. Also, however, the interpretation of the state may well be connected to the mode of induction. In this connection, it is interesting to recall that we have found, among American Indians, a high association between drug-induction and trance rather than possession trance (Bourguignon 1968a).

In most of these groups, apparently, altered states are sought by all participants. One might well distinguish here between those groups of which this is true and those in which only an inspired leader enters an altered state from which he brings a supernatural message, whether this state be a dream, a vision, or an inspired utterance. A distinction of this sort may help to differentiate between leader oriented and group oriented movements. Such a differentiation may have implications for the development of social action in such groups.

While, as we have seen, altered states are widely used in traditional societies, within the context of modern industrial mass society the use of such states appears to acquire a rather special significance. Here such behavior characterizes particular individuals rather than the society as a whole. And within the context of the whole society, such behavior is not approved and supported but considered deviant, pathological, suspect. I should like to suggest that those who utilize these states, then, are most alienated from the total society, most demanding of immediate gratification, requiring immediate experiential evidence of the cult's promises, a down payment, as it were, on the promised celestial rewards. The ethic of altered states, it seems, places itself at the polar opposite to the Protestant Ethic, wih its postponement of gratification, of work for the future. Obviously, such immediate gratification makes the present more liveable, whether that involves the submission to the harsh realities of the world or the difficulties of constructing a new society, or perhaps a retreat into such gratification, into "Paradise Now," as a substitute for action.

This, however, is the subject for another paper. At present, I merely wish to suggest that the use of the concepts of "revitalization," "crisis cult," and "altered states of consciousness" may help us in the development of a multifaceted typology of contemporary marginal religious movements.

Prognosis: A New Religion?

In societies under stress there is a tendency for new cults to arise. La Barre (1970, 1971) terms them crisis cults, and characterizes them as arising in the environment of acculturation, as a response to culture shock. Wallace (1956) designates them as revitalization movements and views them as conscious attempts at affecting culture change in a society. Usually, although perhaps not always, these cults incorporate a supernatural premise.[1] The questions to be examined in the following discussion are: (1) What traits would have to be present in a societal phenomenon—to put it into the most general possible terms— in order for it to become a crisis cult or a religiously oriented revitalization movement? (2) How is a new supernatural premise incorporated into a cult? (3) Does a cult produce culture change? (4) Is there a possibility for such cults to arise in our own doubtlessly distressed society?

Further on, I want to suggest an answer to these questions by formulating a descriptive model of a sample event, and by then using this model as a predictive framework. First, however, a clarification seems in order. When examining the historical and anthropological record of revitalization movements, we find that there is the large-scale, often viscous flow of the evolution of a new movement, and in addition there is usually evidence of sudden local outbursts.[2] As examples, one might

The research for this paper was begun as a part of a larger study, which was supported in whole by Public Health Research Grant MH 07463 from the National Institute of Mental Health. The project, entitled Cross-cultural Studies of Dissociational States, was under the direction of Dr. Erika Bourguignon, of the Department of Anthropology, The Ohio State University. The Dension University Research Foundation supported my field work in the form of a generous grant, and I received a Grant-in-Aid for Research from the Society of the Sigma Xi. The field work was carried out intermittently in Mexico City, in Yucatán, and in this country, beginning in 1968 and continuing today.

[1] Wallace (1966: 52) defines religion as a behavior organized into rituals, belief systems, and cult institutions, with the defining premise being that of the supernatural premise, namely that souls, supernatural beings, and supernatural forces exist.

[2] In my mind, the chief weakness of Wallace's (1966) model of revitalization movements lies in the fact that he does not make this distinction. He sees a single line of evolution leading from a steady-state oscillation of the society via personal stress, cultural distortion, trance behavior, and culture change to a new steady-state oscillation.

point to the proselyting activity of Jesus and his disciples versus the sudden episode of speaking in tongues during the first Pentecost, or the disturbing disorder in the Corinthian congregation. The Protestant reform movement and the abrupt violence of Thomas Münzer's adherents might be cited as another example, or again the widely-flung cargo cult and within its context the Vailala Madness. Even without a detailed analysis it should be clear that there is a qualitative difference between the movement and the local outburst. To be sure, the movement provides the ambient for the outburst. But the outburst has important traits of its own and may or may not affect the movement from which it sprang. It will be noted that none of these examples admits the conclusion that the local upheaval was the point of origination of the respective movement, an observation also emerging from the sample event to be discussed and incorporated in the proposed model.

The above sample event is an upheaval I had the chance to observe in its entirety in a Yucatecan Apostolic congregation. Its inception coincided with the arrival of a new minister in this small village church, in the summer of 1969. As a result of a very complex configuration of factors reported elsewhere (Goodman 1971b), this group of Mayan peasants experienced, after a gradual onset, a peak experience, followed by a period of painful disorganization and eventual dissolution of the behavior. Briefly, before the onset, there was available in the congregation the belief system of the Apostolic Church (an offshoot of the Pentecostal movement), focusing on the eventual Second Coming of Christ, a few shadowy ideas about Satan, and some minimal speaking in tongues (glossolalia) [3] by only two members. During the onset an important innovation was introduced, namely the special method which the new minister used to teach his parishioners how to go into trance and to speak in tongues. This resulted in twenty-five adults, many of them newly recruited members, engaging in the behavior by the fall of 1969 (for details, see Goodman 1972a). In the period leading up to the peak, there were visions and considerable elaboration of the ritual. During the peak, at the end of July 1970, there came other visions, tremendously prolonged trances, spontaneous acquisition of the behavior of tongue speaking by hitherto uninvolved members, and "interpretation" of the tongues. This phase was followed by a period of disorientation, with a surge of evangelizing in other villages and attempts at communal living which soon aborted. There were no regular services, only a great deal of trance behavior,

[3] For bibliographic data on glossolalia, see May (1956) and Pattison (1968a). For a bibliography on crisis cults, see La Barre (1971).

speaking in tongues, exaggerated restlessness, and criminations within the group. "Colored" property, such as dresses, shoes, radios, calendars were burned; everyone was to wear only white. Dissolution of the condition came spontaneously late in August, even before an Elder of the District Office of the Church in Villahermosa, Tabasco, arrived. He told the congregation that they had not acted on instructions from the Holy Spirit in preparation of the imminent Second Coming, but rather that Satan had been tempting them.

When the congregation was seen again by me in January 1971, the ritual and the trance behavior with tongue speaking were back at levels antedating the arrival of the minister. Satan had acquired an overwhelming reality, and the Second Coming was still expected any day.

In terms of intensity of arousal, the societal event sketched out above can be conceptualized as a wave, showing a medium onset, a rise to a peak, a descending slope, and a final dissolution. This is the same wave shape as the one detected cross-culturally also in the intonation pattern of the individual utterance of a person speaking in tongues (see Goodman 1969a and 1969b), and, even more importantly for the present discussion, in a subject's glossolalia (from Greek *glōssa* "tongue" and *lalia* "speech") over a period of time. This was demonstrated by me in a study extending over more than two years of the same Mexican and Yucatecan glossolalists. In other words, when the behavior is first learned, the sound track is usually almost entirely neurophysiologically based and similar to identical cross-cultural material. Later, the utterance becomes model oriented, reflecting the syllable inventory of the group. Although retaining this inventory of syllables, and the diagnostic intonation curve, the individual utterance continues to change in such parameters as duration, rate of utterance, intensity, and loudness. Also the overall episode, i.e. the sum of individual utterances at one occasion, shows in every way a waning of the capacity, until only vestiges of the vocalization remain. Finally, the glossolalia will in many cases become inaudible, and the behavior may be dropped altogether.[4]

What this indicates is that, contrary to expectations, an often repeated behavior, instead of becoming increasingly more anchored in memory over time, apparently fades away unaccountably. Why should this be so, one might ask?

For an answer we will have to turn once more to the individual glossolalia utterance. Observations show that subjects uttering glos-

---

[4] Occasionally, a glossolalist salvages vestiges of his utterance and incorporates them into his devotional behavior, so that this vocalization can then be called up over a long period. Even then, however, remnants of the hyperarousal persist, evidenced often by some motion, such as a twitch, shiver, etc.

solalia behave in a non-ordinary way. They show somatic symptoms of considerable excitation: flushing, exaggerated salivation, tear flow, muscle tension resulting in extreme rigidity, also shivering, shaking, twitching, to name only a few features. It is a widely held opinion (Hine 1969; Samarin 1968) that the co-occurrence of glossolalia and this hyperarousal, or trance, ecstasy, hysteria, frenzy, rage, as the state is variously termed, is merely fortuitous. However, an analysis of the data from well over a hundred services observed and recorded by me shows unequivocally that the vocalization is intimately related to the trance. In fact, the only way one can account for the cross-cultural and cross-linguistic agreement in the intonation pattern and a number of phonetic peculiarities of glossolalia utterances is to assume that the glossolalia is an artifact of the physical parameters of this trance. In other words, the vocal apparatus is no longer within the domain of the cortical speech centers, but rather expresses processes on the level of the autonomic nervous system. Apparently, both the rising to a peak or discharge and then subsequent drop or decay of the individual utterance and the "fading" of the behavior over time are expressions of some subcortical processes.

Hyperarousal is only one of many types of altered mental states. As Ludwig (1966: 69) writes, "Beneath man's thin veneer of consciousness lies a relatively uncharted realm of mental activity." Fischer (1970: 4) conceptualizes the entire range of mental states, including ordinary consciousness, along an arc, one end of which represents "the hyperaroused and ecstatic states." The altered mental state of sleep has been quite intensively researched in recent decades, as has also the meditative trance of the Eastern disciplines. But the altered mental states still represent "a relatively uncharted realm of mental activity." One insight that seems to emerge is that these states have their own, statebound, psychological correlates, such as altered memory functions and somatic perception. There is also apparently an interpretation of processes of the autonomic nervous system on the psychological level. In hyperarousal, for instance, as observations on glossolalia speakers reveal, the subject performs certain acts, such as speaking, motions, which he does not remember once the altered state dissolves. What he does remember are those perceptions which we might term as belonging to the inner space. He remembers that he was unable to control his own behavior, that there was pressure on his chest, that he felt hot; that his tongue moved of its own accord or that he was floating. Since none of these effects seemed to be emanating from his own volition, he feels that he was being manipulated, possessed by some supernatural being or entity. Thus, if he already postulated a supernatural entity before he experienced the trance, this supernatural premise will be powerfully reinforced by the trance experience.

Another psychological correlate of hyperarousal appears after the glossolalia has been uttered. At this time in many instances the trance, which as pointed out is the primary behavior, tends to linger. I have termed this state of residual dissociation a platform phase. In this platform phase the subject experiences disorientation, with retarded or altered memory functions, and a lowering of inhibitions with attendant lessening of judgmental faculties, and thus increased suggestibility.[5]

Let us keep these factors in mind then; little or no recall of observable acts, reinforcement of available supernatural premises, high degree of suggestibility. In addition, let us admit that experiences shared with a group tend to be stronger than those experienced alone. In fact, the data show that in trance this group effect is not only one of summation, but, borrowing a term from pharmacology, one of potentiation. We are then ready to attempt the formulation of a descriptive model, using the Yucatecan data and some others from the literature as an illustration.

A local upheaval involving trance behavior arises if

(a) this trance behavior is either already available as a culture trait, or supplied by an overall movement. In Yucatán, while not available as a present culture trait, it was introduced by the Pentecostal movement (Apostolic church). In New Guinea, when the local upheavals of the cargo cult occurred, considerable possession trance behavior existed aboriginally (Bourguignon 1968).

(b) the trance behavior is acquired by a relatively large part of the group simultaneously or nearly so, so that the peaking and the platform phase of the hyperarousal occur as a group experience. In Yucatán, most of the congregation learned to go into trance within three months in 1969. Considerable indirect evidence points to this simultaneous acquisition also in New Guinea (Worsley 1968).

The local upheaval is triggered by often complex local stresses. In Yucatán, there were principally two of these. There were various visions, interpreted as an attack by Satan, and others indicating the imminent Second Coming. And there was a dependency and abandonment syndrome. The latter was brought about by the new minister who first guided the congregation into the trance behavior and then

---

[5] Vivier's (1968) findings about glossolalists not being more suggestible than the conservative control group from a church not practicing glossolalia refer to subjects in the conscious state. Garrison's findings were similarly gathered from subjects in the ordinary state of consciousness.

abruptly withdrew. Mannoni (1956) points to a similar mechanism for violent local uprisings seen in Madagascar as the French colonial administration withdrew. In New Guinea, sudden and brutal culture shock may have played the same role of a triggering factor, as La Barre (1970) so cogently argues with respect to crisis cults generally.

Once initiated, the upheaval proceeds roughly in four phases from onset to dissolution.

(1) *Onset,* when the psychologically most vulnerable members of the group attempt to cope with the mounting stresses by individual responses. In Yucatán, some of these strikingly increased the duration and the frequency of their prayers, there were visions, and a deepening fear of Satan.

(2) *Gathering momentum,* where the group, unsuccessfully, tries to counter the triggering stress by adoption of innovations. In Yucatán, elaborations of the ritual were introduced, the number of services multiplied, the trance behavior of many of the members became extremely prolonged, which began obliterating the ritual structure of the services.

(3) *Peak,* a brief phase; in Yucatán it lasted only about 48 hours. Trance, as a group behavior, reaches its highest point, with many outsiders acquiring the behavior spontaneously. (In New Guinea, the "Ghost Wind" shook the people.) All ceremonial and ritual structures are obliterated, there is a burst of innovations. In Yucatán, in a service held during this peak period, there was possession trance by Satan, interpretation of glossolalia, public criminations against members for insufficient dedication, exorcism, and visions in the church—all innovations for the group.

(4) *Platform phase;* as far as the larger society is concerned, this is the most visible stage of the local upheaval, the "madness." It is characterized by a very persistent residual trance, erratically becoming more intense and then waning again in various individuals. There is a pervasive anxiety. In Yucatán, on occasion, the members of the congregation threw themselves against the door of the church and shuttered the windows to prevent Satan from entering. In Madagascar, people locked their doors against dragons that had appeared in visions. The heightened suggestibility leads to acting out many disparate suggestions, all seemingly aiming at achieving a desired utopia. In Yucatán, communal life in the church building was attempted; the church and everything in it, even the tar paper, were painted white, inadmissible (by church standards) marriages were performed. In New Guinea, people burned their property, pushed sheets of paper back and forth on a table, lifted certain sex taboos. Certain members of the group in this phase are obsessed with an inconquerable restlessness,

prompting them to wander off to other groups and communities. In Yucatán, four congregations were eventually involved in the upheaval, and the "infection" of the cargo cult spread far and wide in Melanesia.

The condition of the Yucatecan congregation after the upheaval admits the following generalizations about the post-upheaval phase:

(a) *Culture change:* None of the innovations introduced since the inception of the upheaval and its dissolution persist, with the possible exception of those concerning community organization (not, however, the communal living style) to accommodate the increased membership; traits introduced shortly before the upheaval tend to emerge weakened from the upheaval. Thus, in Yucatán, there is no longer at the present writing (nine months after the decay of the upheaval) any formal prayer for receiving the Holy Sprit, that is, for acquiring the trance behavior. This parallels the observation on the individual level of no recall of motions executed while in trance.

(b) *Trance behavior:* After reaching a peak on the group level, and dissolving at the end of the platform phase, it loses its importance for the group; in Yucatán, the congregation showed no trance behavior four months after the upheaval, and the data from New Guinea indicate a similar disappearance of this trait. Again, this recalls, on the individual level, the fading of the trance behavior over time.

(c) The *supernatural premise,* as can be expected from the psychological interpretation of the trance experience on the individual level, namely that of being manipulated by an extracorporeal principle, emerges firmly entrenched in the group. Satan is a living reality for the Yucatecan congregation today, and the expectation of the Second Coming has in no way been weakened by the fact that it did not happen in August 1970.

In summary, then, the above discussion suggests the following answers to the first three of the four questions posed in the introduction:

(1) A societal event of the nature of a local upheaval, which could conceivably strengthen or feed back into an already existing movement of culture change, would need to have available in its ambient hyperarousal trance behavior and an already formulated supernatural premise.

(2) A supernatural premise becomes incorporated into the culture of the group by the experience of acquiring the trance behavior simultaneously, and by sharing its peaking, platform phase, and dissolution.

(3) Culture change is unaffected by the upheaval.

In order to answer the fourth question about a crisis cult—here understood as a local upheaval in the sense given above under (1)—arising in our own society, I should like to analyze briefly the student disturbances we experienced at Denison University in May 1970.

Denison University is a small liberal arts college; its students come predominantly from upper-middle-class white homes. Early in 1970, one of my students, for an anthropology class on culture change (LaMoreaux 1970), examined the use of drugs on the Denison campus. She was interested among other things in the age at which marihuana was first used. Of the 2,000 questionnaires (roughly the equivalent of the enrollment) she received back 1,100. Plotting her graphs according to class rank, sex, and age when the initial marihuana experience occurred, she found that freshman women first smoked when they were 18, the sophomores at 19, the juniors at 20, and the seniors at 21. If we assume that each class is approximately one year older than the previous class, these data suggest that all initial marihuana smoking by the girls occurred late in the summer or early fall of 1969. The questionnaires from the male group showed a similar pattern with the exception of the upperclass men, who tended to be somewhat younger than the corresponding female group.

In the terms of the model suggested, the seniors, perhaps many of them as a shock response to the assassination of the Reverend Martin Luther King in April and of Senator Robert Kennedy in June 1968, acquired the drug behavior and then, as innovators, initiated it on the campus.[6] This produced the ambient of hyperarousal stipulated in the model, with a large group of students having acquired the behavior simultaneously late in 1969.

As to the external events of the Denison upheaval, it started in December 1969 with the Black Student Union presenting a list of demands to the faculty. In January, President Smith recognized the validity of these demands and the faculty and several hundred students came out in support of them. In late February, the board of trustees formulated a statement calling these endorsements hasty, and pointing out the financial problems connected with an implementation of the black demands. On other points the board seemed quite conciliatory. At the request of President Smith, a task force was formed of seven faculty members, plus one white and one black student. However, the Black Student Union refused to send a representative. The white students were also dissatisfied with the activities of this task force. At a meeting, they formed an Ad Hoc Committee, which was to "secure a more definite commitment from the trustees for a broader inclusion of the black experience in the university community." Of

[6] There is a great deal of similarity between drug induced and "naturally" induced altered states.

the subsequent events, the *Denison Alumnus* of April 1970 reported (p. 15): "Action taken by the Ad Hoc Committee included the canvassing of living units to explain the implications of an improved black program . . ., an open forum following the Chapel Service March 12, open discussions following the Alumni-in-Residence convocation Sunday, March 15, a peaceful sit-in at Doane Administration Monday, March 16, [and] visitations of students to . . . trustees. . . . Some 250 students participated in the sit-in with student marshals keeping order. At noon, a bomb scare caused the building to be evacuated and the group moved to the amphitheatre of Blair Knapp Hall."

After their return from the spring break, I asked my students to submit an account of what they thought had happened. These (about 50) papers are the basis for the following discussion.

According to these testimonies, the students experienced a local upheaval of the type discussed before. The decisive local stress was apparently the culture shock experienced by the black students, who were suddenly torn out of their home environment and brought into another culture.

I observed a Black coed giving testimony about her life as a Denison student in front of the crowd. Her name was S. She spoke of the strange food she ate and became sick from in the dining halls, and the way she sat alone in the dormitory on the weekends while the White girls whom she'd watch spend hours with their faces and hair went out to parties and dances. She poured out the travesties heaped upon her life as a Black student during this year as a freshman, one right after the other. During her testimony she became more and more animated as she stood next to her chair. Her speech accelerated and she used more and more "profanity" and "ghetto lingo." As she proceeded it became more and more difficult to pick up everything she was saying. She seldom used the word "I," but rather she used her name.

On three or four occasions her friend tried to hold on to her and guide her outside, but each time she would either ignore her or say, "No, no, I have to do this."

Toward the end she began to cry and eventually left exhausted and whimpering.[7]

The description not only details the culture shock, but also lends itself to the interpretation of showing the presence of an altered state

---

[7] This and the following quotations are lifted verbatim from student papers.

in the speaker, with its tell-tale acceleration of the speech rate and the final exhaustion.

No one seems to be able to identify exactly what the triggering incident for the upheaval might have been. Its onset also was apparently quite covert, and when the upheaval broke toward the peak, it caught the students by surprise. "The events of the week of March 16," a student wrote, "popped to the surface very quickly. I can think of no reason why the issue came to the surface so rapidly." The acceleration was indeed breathtaking, with about 250 students taking part in the sit-in, but as the student community was being swept along, there were 450 at the night meeting on Tuesday; then the crowd swelled to 600, and, on Wednesday, to 1200.

The driving toward the peak on Wednesday can be gathered from the following student statements.

> *Monday:* Enthusiasm had been aroused at the sit-in, and people were beginning to act instead of simply discussing the problem.
>
> *Monday after the bomb scare:* The amphitheater was packed. I listened for a while, and then the atmosphere seemed to become tense. One of the girls I was with wanted to leave because she was scared.

(On Monday evening, some students had forced their way into the faculty meeting, demanding to be heard.)

> *Tuesday:* The students who had been in the faculty break-in were like kids who have just been to their first circus. They were extremely keyed up about it and anxious for us to be just as excited.
>
> *Wednesday:* The meeting at Huffman dining Hall was like electricity.
>
> The meeting at Huffman had a great effect on me and my friends.

However, as in Yucatán, the peak is already charged with the signals of the dissolution into the platform phase. The same student continues:

> From here on out it is hard to remember the order in which things occurred.

The disturbed memory function is even clearer in the following statement:

> The events on Monday and Tuesday are still very clear in my mind, but for the time that elapsed from Wednesday until President Smith's speech the following Tuesday my thoughts are a collage of mass meetings, emotional speeches, personal conversations, and

questions, questions, questions, questions. I can't remember much of what specifically happened.

The trance aspect of the upheaval is especially striking in this observation:

I can remember feeling very physically involved, but not connected to anything.

On this Wednesday also, which in my mind represents the peak of this upheaval, I noticed a number of students writing graffiti around the flagpole on the walk with colored chalk. I expected slogans about the black demands, but instead the typical disorganization of the platform phase was already evident, with its lowered inhibitions:

"Peter Pan call home: Papa and Mama still love you."
"First God created idiots, then he created trustees."
"Ball your favorite chick tonight."
"Let the sun shine."
"Freedom," "Freedom," "Freedom."

The drop into the platform phase was very evident to the students:

A change occurred between Wednesday and Thursday, everything was much calmer.
The rest of the week after Smith's speech was more or less downhill.

The platform phase at Denison was very brief. At SUNY at Buffalo, acording to a faculty member from there, it lasted much longer, producing continually shifting demands and issues. By the weekend (March 21–22) all was apparently over:

By the weekend the movement had turned into a power struggle and by the 24th there was a strong sense of despair at the obvious stalemate.

It seems to me that this upheaval can very satisfactorily be analyzed on the basis of the suggested model. Its trance character is quite evident. The girl who stated that she had felt "physically involved," even reports the subsequent euphoria, so typical of hyperarousal experiences; and the "changed-life" aspect so familiar from conversion stories.

"I think the movement was unique and beautiful," she writes. "There have come out of it more changes in my life than I thought imaginable."

As in the Yucatecan case, no culture change came from the upheaval; neither did there appear any supernatural premise. Both of these results are predictable from the model: culture change is an unrelated process, and the supernatural premise must be available before the upheaval starts in order to become confirmed.

Cocoon Work: An Interpretation of the Concern of Contemporary Youth with the Mystical

My mind was a field in autumn. Naked branches were studded with black cocoons. Suddenly, one cocoon split and a butterfly with poppy-scarlet wings emerged, then another cocoon split and another, first here, then there, then everywhere, and all space was filled with the fluttering scarlet wings. (IMAGE AFTER PSILOCYBIN)

THE most striking element in the American metaphysical movement today is the preoccupation of middle-class youth with mystical experience. Mysticism is strongly linked with the use of psychedelic drugs on the one hand, and with a variety of contemplative religious traditions on the other. And, as have mystics in other times and places, today's psychedelic youth is antimaterialistic and caught up in experiments with communal styles of living. In this paper I will discuss the development of this movement and attempt to interpret it as a self-imposed *rite de passage*. To choose a different image, it is a metamorphic struggle, a kind of "cocoon work" which, unlike the insect analogue and unlike the situation in other cultures, lacks a clear and acceptable image of the adult.

WHAT IS MYSTICAL EXPERIENCE?

Mystical states are alterations of consciousness characterized by a radical change in the everyday sense of self and experience of time and space; a feeling of heightened significance attaches to the episode or its content; the mood is one of ecstasy; invariably, the subject is left dissatisfied with the adequacy of ordinary language to describe his experience (James 1961; Stace 1960: 11). These states vary greatly in mode of onset, intensity, duration, and susceptibility to recall. Some occur spontaneously (Bucke 1901; Laski 1961); others represent the culmination of a prolonged quest; still others may be the result of the use of psychedelic substances or form part of the phenomenology of a functional psychotic episode (Custance 1951; Prince and Savage 1966) or a toxic or organic brain disturbance (Ludwig 1968). Stace

255

(1960: 15) has conveniently divided these states into those in which the awareness of the environment persists—the extrovertive group—and those in which the awareness of environment is lost—the introvertive.

In extrovertive experiences the individual feels himself to have become part of surrounding nature and, in addition to the general mystical characteristics noted above, there is usually a heightened intensity of visual or auditory perception, and a quality that suggests the use of the word "religious." The experiences often light up the surroundings, so to speak, so that many years later they can be recollected complete with the setting in which they occurred. Other terms for extrovertive experiences include peak experiences, nature mysticism, or adamic experiences; the last of these suggests that during the episode the world appears as it did to Adam on the day of creation.

Introvertive experiences are more intense and for the most part occur to those who have adopted an ascetic way of life and have practiced meditation or other techniques in order to achieve them. The environment is lost and there remains in consciousness only the sense of one all-pervading aspect or, in the Judeo-Christian and Islamic traditions, the sense of two things, the self and God.

For some, these various kinds of mystical experience, including both the introvertive and extrovertive, are part of a single continuum of increasing intensity with aesthetic experiences and adamic states at one end and the high-powered introvertive experiences at the other. But others like Zaehner (1957) see a distinct difference between the adamic and monistic experiences on the one hand and the dualistic self-in-the-presence-of-God experiences on the other: according to him, only the latter are of supernatural origin. For myself, I accept the continuum view and like to think of mystical states as in some ways like a television screen: "The image on the screen is the picture of the world. The set is turned off and the picture collapses to become a point of intense light—a ball of pure meaning. With the mystical state, the perceiving ego also collapses into the globule of undifferentiated meaning and all is one. When ordinary perception returns, the globule of meaning is once again diffused over the world . . . in the transitional stages before the complete collapse of the ego and the world and the culmination in the all-is-one, there are regions of experience where the mystic finds himself interfused with the surroundings; he is part of all mankind, and of the animal world and the universe" (Prince 1968).

Mystical states, especially of the introvertive type, have of course provided inspiration for most of the world's religions. Mystical states are the origin of Shelley's "white radiance" which, transmitted through the "dome of many-coloured glass," expresses itself in the world in the multiferous imagery of the institutionalized religions.

How does the psychologist regard mystical states? Two main interpretations have been offered: (1) that mystical states represent regressions in the service of the ego (Prince and Savage 1966), and (2) they represent de-automatizations of ego functions (Deikman 1966). The regression explanation holds that mystical states occur when an individual or group is confronted with a problem which seems insoluble by habitual means. The individual's (or group leader's) ego regresses to earlier levels of adaptation in an attempt to discover an alternative solution. It is as though the ego has an elevator which can descend to several lower levels in which prior experience and earlier coping mechanisms are stored. The mystical descent is to the earliest level of experience, before the creation of the world as it were, in the primal chaos, long before self and other have become differentiated, before space and time, before language, when the only coping mechanism, the panacea for all ills and discomforts, was sucking at the breast. The mystical state is a "flash-back" of that primal experience. The mystic returns from his descent with the perennial mystical message [1]: at the root of things all is one, all is good, the universe may be trusted; salvation lies in simplification, in de-institutionalization, and above all in love.

The de-automatization hypothesis is based upon the observation that in the early stages of the learning process a good deal of attention energy is required. But with practice, the motor and perceptual patterns become automatic with attendant energy conservation. Deikman (1966) believes that through the mystic's life style of renunciation and in the process of meditation he is reinvesting attention energies in these automatic actions and returning them to awareness. The resulting relation with the world may be less efficient from a biological point of view but may permit the experience of aspects of the real world formerly ignored. The undoing of automatic structures permits a gain in sensory intensity and richness at the expense of abstract categorization and differentiation. As regards the relation between the two hypotheses, Deikman writes, "One might call the direction regressive in a developmental sense, but the actual experience (i.e. mystical experience) is probably not within the psychological scope of any child. It is a de-automatization occurring in an adult mind, and the

---

[1] Given, of course, that his primal experience was satisfactory. If it was not, the result may be psychosis rather than mystical experience (Prince and Savage 1966).

experience gains its richness from adult memories and functions now subject to a different mode of consciousness."

History of the Movement: Some Landmarks

Writing of a visit of Swami Jogut Sangooly to her father in Concord, Massachusetts, in 1858, Emerson's daughter (Rusk 1949: 397) expressed delight "to have a real live Brahmin, brought up a priest to Kreeshna etc., knowing Sanskrit and all the Vedas and able to tell father all he wanted to know." We should probably look to Emerson and the New England Transcendentalists for the early traces of the present youth movement, for the Transcendentalists, like today's youth, drew their mystical insights and formulations far more from the Eastern religions than from the Christian tradition. Emerson had a lifelong interest in the Hindu mystical tradition (though in his youth he called it Indian superstition). According to Greenland (1965) the Transcendentalists were among the first in North America to peruse translations of the *Bhagavad-Gita* and the *Vedas*. The group's interests appear to have been intellectual rather than experiential. They did not experiment with drugs; indeed, at the time of the greatest cohesion of the group between 1840 and 1850, awareness of the possible mystical effects of drugs was just beginning to dawn; Moreau brought *hashish* back from his Persian journeys and introduced it to Europe in the early 1840s (De Ropp 1957: 66; Holmstedt 1967); the pioneer American *hashish* enthusiast Fitzhugh Ludlow (De Ropp 1957: 77) did not publish his work until 1857. And, in spite of their keen interest in Indian religions, the Transcendentalists do not appear to have practiced meditation. Thoreau, and probably some of the other Transcendentalists however were subject to spontaneous adamic states (Bucke 1901: 244). Emerson wrote in his essay "The Oversoul":

> There is a difference between one and another hour of life, in their authority and subsequent effect. There is a depth in those brief moments which constrains us to ascribe more reality to them than to all other experiences. . . . In ascending to this primary and aboriginal sentiment, we have come from our remote station on the circumference instantaneously to the centre of the world, where, as in the closet of God, we see the cause and anticipate the universe, which is but a slow effect.

But Bucke (1901: 240) was skeptical. If Emerson had experienced such moments himself he would never have used such moderate and cold language!

The Transcendentalists did experiment with communal living.

Brook Farm (1841–47), which Ripley (Rusk 1949) in his founding charter felt "would prepare a society of liberal, intelligent and cultivated persons whose relations with each other would permit a more simple and wholesome life than can be led amidst the pressure of our competitive society," was not very successful.

Another important early figure was the poet-prophet of democratization and de-institutionalization, Walt Whitman (1819–1892). Several passages of his *Leaves of Grass* are probably expressions of his own intense mystical experiences (Bucke 1901: 178; James 1961). To explain the difference between Whitman's tedious early writings and the inspired *Leaves of Grass,* Braden (1967: 71) has speculated that Whitman may have used marihuana while on his visit to New Orleans in 1849!

An unusual and influential figure in the story of North American mysticism is Richard Maurice Bucke (1837–1902). A Canadian psychiatrist who was for many years the superintendent of a mental hospital in London, Ontario, Bucke was the subject of a powerful spontaneous mystical experience at the age of 35 and spent the rest of his life puzzling over its meaning (Greenland 1965). A year before he died he published his famous pioneer study of comparative mysticism, *Cosmic Consciousness.* In it he expressed his belief in the evolution of human consciousness—from simple consciousness (as possessed by animals and infants), through the self-consciousness of adults, to cosmic consciousness which he felt had been experienced by a few in the past, Buddha, Paul, Christ, and was being increasingly experienced by contemporary man. Bucke's book has been very influential. Since the publication of 500 volumes in 1901, there have been twenty-one further editions and recently the work has appeared in paperback. Bucke would not entertain the idea that chemical substances could reproduce genuine mystical states: "Just as the drinking of alcohol induces a kind of artificial and bastard joy, so the inhalation of ether and chloroform induces (sometimes) a kind of bastard and artificial cosmic consciousness."

William James published his Gifford Lectures of 1901–02 as the famous *Varieties of Religious Experience.* For the first time, James clearly separated off mystical states from other types of religious experience, clarified their defining characteristics, and illustrated them with a wealth of descriptive documents that have never been superseded. James was, moreover, willing to concede that chemical substances might produce genuine mystical states. After reading the nitrous oxide explorations of Benjamin Blood in *The Anaesthetic Revelation and the Gist of Philosophy* (1874), James himself sampled (James 1882) the gas and found that the "keynote of the experience is the tremendously exciting sense of intense metaphysical illumination." In 1896, Weir Mitchell ate a few buttons of the psychedelic cactus, peyote, and described the remarkable effects in the *British Medical Journal* (1896). Mitchell passed some buttons on to James, but they only gave him a stomach ache. "I ate one bud three days ago," he wrote to his brother, "was violently sick for twenty four hours, and had no other symptoms whatever. . . . I will take the visions on trust."

It is interesting to observe the extent to which the lives and ideas of these early American mystics intertwined. Whitman was very much influenced by reading *The Dial,* the publication of the Transcendentalists (published between 1841 and 1847). Emerson's influence was important to Whitman: "I was simmering, simmering, simmering; Emerson brought me to a boil" (Rusk 1949: 374). *Leaves of Grass* was published in the summer of 1855, and before the year was out, Thoreau, Emerson, and several other Transcendentalists had made the good gray poet's personal acquaintance. Throughout the prolonged storm of protest raised by Whitman's earthy *Leaves,* Emerson was one of the very few eminent literary figures to defend him. Bucke too admired Whitman enormously. He considered Whitman to be the most developed example of cosmic consciousness to have appeared in history! Bucke became Whitman's official biographer and, after Whitman's death, his literary executor. James made extensive quotes from the work of Emerson, Thoreau, Whitman, and Bucke in his *Varieties of Religious Experience.*

James's work marked the end of an era in American mysticism. For the next forty years, the major explorations of consciousness, particularly of drug-induced states, took place in Germany and France. Holmstedt (1967) has provided us with an excellent description of this period; suffice it here to mention Lewin (1924), Beringer (1927), and Kluver (1928), who made major contributions to our knowledge of mescaline, cocaine, kava, and other consciousness-influencing substances. An interesting and little known contribution was made by Philippe de Félice in his *Poisons sacrés, ivresses divines* (1936). He documented extensively the now familiar theme of the relationship between religious experiences and the ingestion of drugs. He proposed that the divine soma plant of the Vedic hymns may have been an important factor in the development of Yoga. Soma was brought by the Aryan invaders into India from Central Asia in about 1500 B.C. As they moved deeper into India, the plant proved increasingly difficult to find. De Félice suggests that the exercises and meditation practices may have been developed in an effort to contact the gods by a different route. In 1945, Hoffman, working on ergot alkaloids in the Sandoz laboratories in Switzerland, accidently discovered the most potent of the psychedelics, LSD.

The beginning of the new era of widespread interest in mysticism in America can probably be dated to the arrival of Aldous Huxley in California just before the second world war. Huxley had always been fascinated by the mystical, but, as he wrote of his early Oxford days, he read "Western and Eastern (mystic) writings, always with intense interest, but always with a wish to debunk them" (Clark 1968: 302). Perhaps as part of his escapist response to the horrors of the war, soon after settling in California he began to express decidedly mystical convictions. This was first evident in the novel *Time Must Have a Stop* (1944), but most clearly in the didactic *The Perennial Philosophy* (1945), which, as Huxley explains in the opening paragraph, is the metaphysic that recognizes "a divine Reality substantial to the world of things and lives and minds; the psychology that finds in the soul something similar to, or even identical with, divine Reality; the ethic that places man's final end in the knowledge of the imminent and transcendent Ground of all being—the thing is immemorial and universal."

Huxley tells us in *The Doors of Perception,* that until he used mescaline he had never experienced a state which he could call mystical or religious, but he was in fact capable of voluntarily entering a rather unusual trance-like alteration of consciousness that has been described by Milton Erikson (1965). In any case, his intellectual absorption with things mystical induced a longing for a personal experience of the Beatific Vision. It was with considerable enthusiasm then, that when Humphry Osmond [2] visited him in California in 1953 he accepted Osmond's offer to initiate him into the mysteries of mescaline (Clark 1968: 347). The result was the highly potent little book *The Doors of Perception* (1954). The title comes from William Blake: "If the doors of perception were cleansed, everything will appear to man as it is, infinite." In this book, Huxley unequivocally equated the drug-induced experience with the mystical states of the Perennial Philosophy. This doctrine, perhaps because it was so convincingly presented, or because the times were ripe, spread rapidly throughout the American intellectual world. Many were launched on their psychedelic adventures by this book.

It was the sacred mushrooms of the Aztecs—*teonanactl* or god's flesh—that launched Timothy Leary (1970) on his psychedelic career:

[2] Osmond, like Huxley, was an English *émigré* in the New World. He is one of the major intellectuals in the psychedelic movement. He in fact coined the word "psychedelic," which means "mind manifesting," to avoid the impression that the drugs were specifically related to psychoses, as was implied by the earlier designations "psychotomimetic" or "hallucinogenic."

"On a sunny afternoon in the garden of a Cuernavaca villa, I ate seven of the so-called sacred mushrooms which had been given to me by a scientist from the University of Mexico. During the next five hours, I was whirled through an experience which could be described in many extravagant metaphors but which was, above all, and without question, the deepest religious experience of my life." The story of Leary's expulsion from Harvard and his continuing jousts with the legal windmills is too well known to narrate here. More than any other, Leary has attempted to cast the movement in religious terms. Unlike the novelist Kesey's invitation to LSD as the portal to fun and games (Wolfe 1968), Leary promised enlightenment. Leary's career (up to 1966) as the high priest of the psychedelic movement is well described in *The Politics of Ecstasy* (1970).

As we have seen, exchange visits between mystics of the East and West go back at least as far as the era of the New England Transcendentalists. At first, the major North American relationships seem to have been with India. Documentation is scanty, but we have from Isherwood (1965: 318) in his biography of Ramakrishna an interesting picture of the visits of some of Ramakrishna's disciples during the 1890s. Japanese influences began even before the second world war in the writings of Daisetz Suzuki on Zen Buddhism. But these influences intensified remarkably in the postwar period due to the popular writings of another English *émigré*, Allan Watts (1957) and to such poets as Gary Snyder (1969). Zen ideas and practices form an important element in the current youth movement. Since the invasion of Tibet by China, there has been an influx of Tibetan holy men with their special type of Buddhism. There have also been exchange visits with the Sufi mystics of North Africa. A host of centers for the study and practice of Eastern religions have recently mushroomed. A 1970 directory of "Light Centers" (Mishra 1970) lists some 190 centers in the U.S.A. and Canada, and these no doubt represent only the tip of the iceberg. Two Indian groups seem particularly well organized and influential. The Hare Krishna movement founded in 1966 by Bhaktivedanta Swami Prabhupada claims ancestry from the earliest Hindu tradition of the *Bhagavad-Gita* and Krishna. It is a dualistic, devotional kind of mysticism which most Westerners would not associate with the East. It does not accept chemical ecstasies as valid: "One is frustrated . . . and perhaps takes LSD and tries to become one with the void. But this nonsense cannot bring happiness . . . it will end in LSD frustration and roaming in impersonal void concepts" (Bhaktivedanta 1970a). The group publishes a magazine, *Back to Godhead*. Perhaps even better organized is the School of Transcendental Meditation launched by Maharishi Mahesh Yogi fifteen years ago; this group has recently focused upon students and in 1966 launched the Student's International Meditation Society (Maharishi 1966). The Maharishi's is a monistic mysticism of the type we more commonly associate with Hindu belief: "Underneath the subtlest layer of all that exists in the relative field is the abstract, absolute field of pure Being, which is unmanifested and transcendental. It is neither matter nor energy. It is pure Being, the state of pure existence." Although Hindu philosophy is generally one of withdrawal, the Maharishi feels that this tendency is to be decried; it is one of the main reasons that India has remained economically backward. He feels that there is no contradiction between the mystic way and full involvement in life. On the contrary, as one of his students, Jerry Jarvis (1970), U.S. leader of the S.I.M.S., rather startlingly proclaimed, "If everyone in NASA had been meditators, we would have been on the moon years ago." Transcendental meditation requires no philosophical or religious commitment; it is simply a technique for accomplishing peace of mind, an increased ability to mobilize one's energy and to be more effective in the world. Recent neurophysiological studies (Kamiya 1969) have gone further to demystify the mystical and give surprising support to the notion that meditation really does promote serenity and can be learned quickly and painlessly.

THE CURRENT SCENE

With this background, let us now try to tie down a little more firmly the particular religious movement we are here trying to describe and interpret. Let us, for a start, give the movement a name: Neotranscendentalism. It includes the ever increasing number of people who (1) reject traditional Western acquisitive and economic values, (2) are concerned with the mystical, (3) wish to develop more direct, less role-oriented interpersonal relationships, and (4) are interested in communal and cooperative styles of living rather than isolationist, competitive patterns. As with all religious movements, there is of course a core of dedicated practitioners and a much larger number of sympathizers. A characteristic which distinguishes Neotranscendentalism from most other religious movements, however, is its lack of homogeneity and dogma. Neotranscendentalists are allergic to structure or standardization. They are young, mostly under thirty. They are clearly distinguishable from other youth movements—the activist maoists and yippies for example and the "delinquent" groups of motorcycle gangs. The Neotranscendentalists derive usually from affluent homes, are often attending universities or are university dropouts. Although their symbolism and ideas are all-pervasive, and no doubt there are pockets of practising groups in all the big North American cities, the major centers of the movement continue to be New York and southern California.

The Neotranscendentalists clearly have their parallels in the bohemians of earlier eras, most directly in such bohemian groups as those which occupied Greenwich Village during the twenties and thirties. Cowley's (1934) list of "philosophical principles" of the Villagers of the twenties has a familiar ring: the idea of self-expression— each man's purpose in life is to express himself; the idea of paganism—the body is a temple in which there is nothing unclean, a shrine to be adorned for the ritual of love; the idea of living for the moment; the idea of liberty—every law or rule that prevents self-expression should be shattered. But some principles are different; the Villagers believed "that they do things better in Europe. By expatriating ourselves and living in Paris, Capri, or the South of France we can break the Puritan shackles and become creative and free." The Neotranscendentalists, however, do not see salvation as a matter of changing locale but of changing consciousness.

Clearly, parts of the Neotranscendentalist movement were the beatniks of the 1950s and, of course, the hippies of the 1960s. The differences between these groups have been described by Gould (1971). In brief, the beat (short for beatific) scene was dominated by the novels of Kerouac, the poetry of Ginsberg, and the mysticism of Huxley. The beat was a wanderer who dropped out of life and claimed the right not to raise a family, or work, or become a status seeker; bearded, dirty, living in poverty, he lived a life of tentative personal relationships and held onto life with his fingertips. The hippie scene, launched by Kesey's celebrated trip across the U.S. in the Day-Glo bus (Wolfe 1968), saw an intensification of interest in the mystical, dominated by Leary and the Maharishi. Relationships became more important, and communes both rural and urban proliferated, particularly in California, Colorado, and New York.

INDIVIDUAL AND CULTURAL "COCOON WORK"

Van Gennep (1960) in his *Rites of Passage*, was the first to draw attention to the significance and ubiquity of the religious symbolism associated with changes of social state in primitive societies, e.g. birth, puberty, marriage, changes of occupation, death, etc. Primitive society was like a series of plateaus separated by sacred and perilous crevasses that required religious ritual for a safe crossing. Of special relevance to our present study, he analysed in detail the initiation rites at puberty. These last anywhere from a few days to several years and are generally more elaborate for men than for women. Typically, the young men are isolated in a holy place—a remote grove or a sacred hut. Removal from the secure world of women and children is usually accompanied by terror tactics, nocturnal visits by terrifying masqueraders and often by circumcision or other disfiguration. Then follows a period of limbo often associated with the symbolism of infancy; the initiate does not speak, goes around naked, crawls rather than walks, and is fed baby foods. The reintegration into the group as an adult occurs through the teaching of secret adult lore; often the initiates are shown the reality of the fearful masks used during the early stages of the initiation. The exposing of these bogeymen of their childhood is one of the central features of the ritual. The pervasive symbolism is that of the death of the old self and rebirth of the new.

Psychoanalysts have always taken an interest in these puberty rites, for they seem to confirm some of their hypotheses about the universality of the Oedipus complex. The circumcision for example was regarded as the symbolic castration of their sons by the jealous father. Bettelheim (1954), however, observed that even when these rites were not imposed by the adult world, American adolescents would often rediscover rites of passage themselves. He studied several groups which, as part of their struggle for maturation, developed their own rites, complete with real or symbolic disfigurement.

It is clear that we can derive some insight into the Neotranscendentalist movement if we regard it as a rite of passage. The crevasse between the plateaus of childhood and adulthood in America have always seemed especially wide and deep. It required Margaret Mead's voyage to Samoa in the 1920s to show that adolescence is not universally a highly turbulent life crisis. We used to regard the commencement of schizophrenia in adolescence as a distinctive part of the disease; now it is clear that the age of onset varies a good deal depending upon the stress configurations peculiar to the given culture (Murphy 1968).

Neotranscendentalism, then, can be regarded as a self-imposed rite of passage. Instead of the secret grove or sacred hut, contemporary youth remove themselves to pads in the dim hearts of our large cities, or to communes in the California hills. They may withdraw for periods of months or years. The essential task is a psychological metamorphosis—a kind of cocoon work—shucking parental authority and making ready to accept the responsibilities for a spouse and family. Brainwashing is a major feature of the task: the freeing of the initiate from his childish attitudes, beliefs, and fears. As we have seen, in primitive societies this brainwashing is accomplished through a regression induced by fear and clothed and interpreted by symbols of infancy. The initiate's ego with its childish concepts and emotional sets is reduced to a kind of primal ego-plasm by terror at the hands of masqueraders wielding circumcision knives. Then the adult identity can be imprinted like a seal in wax.

Our own youth have discovered different methods for returning to the "root." They produce regressions by psychedelic drugs or through meditation. There is an interesting parallel between the primitive youth's discovery of the reality of the bogeyman in tribal society and some of the Neotranscendentalist leader's assertions about seeing through society's games. This is a major theme in Leary's writings for example: "All behavior involves learned games. But only that rare Westerner we call 'mystic' or who has had a visionary experience of some sort sees clearly the game structure of behavior. Most of the rest of us spend our time struggling with roles and rules and goals and concepts of games which are implicit and confusedly not seen as games, trying to apply the roles and rules and rituals of one game to other games" (Leary 1964: 106).

This analysis permits us to see a little more clearly why the crevasses between society's plateaus are so often regarded as dangerous and awesome and in some sense religious. The passage from one stage of life to another presents the ego with a major problem of adaptation. The mechanisms of its current stage will no longer equip it to cope on the new level. As we have seen, under these circumstances a common ego reaction is to seek a solution by regression. Regression may result in a mystical state of some kind; or on the other hand it may result in a psychiatric disorder—even a major psychosis. Bridging the crevasse then excites both fear and religious awe.

Contemporary Western psychiatry has recently rediscovered the special significance of these developmental crises. Adolescence, marriage, childbirth, retirement, etc., are now recognized as periods in life when individuals are especially vulnerable to psychiatric disorders. Preventive methods in psychiatry are brought to bear at the time of the developmental crises.

If we are to regard the Neotranscendentalist movement as a rite of passage, we would expect that young people would continue their cocoon work for a period and that they would then emerge as adults ready to take up their positions in adult society. The following description of a participant in a beat commune seems to indicate that this may in fact occur.

We had a commune of sorts in the '50s. We rented a large old dilapidated house in the center of the city. Most of us were between about eighteen and twenty-five, and most worked during the day or went to school—we were just beatniks in the evenings and on weekends. We didn't dress differently, except that we were rather careless perhaps. Quite a few of us entered the commune after a breakup in our marriages—as if we were depressed and had to work something out. It was rather an intellectual group—there was much poetry reading and giving of papers and endless discussion. Perhaps most important were our parties—there was a great sense of the festive. They would have a theme—like a death and rebirth theme—Persephone returning from the Underworld and we would paint huge murals on the walls and make clay sculptures and there would be daffodils and dancing all night. There was a fair amount of free love, though not as much as the neighbors suspected. Of course we all read *The Doors of Perception* and many of us had psychedelic trips on mescaline and LSD.

There were perhaps fifty people who went through the commune at one time or other. Most of them have married successfully and on the whole have become highly successful people—professors of biochemistry, philosophy, English—mostly academics but a few business people—only one I know of is in a mental hospital.

The rite of passage interpretation seems applicable for the Greenwich Villagers of the twenties and thirties and even perhaps for the beatniks of the fifties. But the movement during the sixties seems more pervasive and more fundamental than during those earlier eras. The rite of passage interpretation is most applicable when considering a relatively stable society, when the culturally prescribed image of the adult is clear and acceptable for the majority of the young. The ideal is given; the problem is simply to achieve it. Such does not seem to be the case today. Youth is not satisfied with the adult models available. Let us turn to other possible explanations for the Neotranscendentalists.

Wallace's (1970: 188) concept of the revitalization movement should be considered. He has defined revitalization movements as "deliberate, organized attempts by some members of a society to construct a more satisfying culture by rapid acceptance of a pattern of multiple innovations." Wallace sees revitalization movements as a response to pervasive social disorganization. Using several Amerindian movements as a basis for his analysis, he points out that disorganization may be brought about by a variety of forces which push a given society beyond the limits of its ability to preserve equilibrium—natural disasters, epidemic diseases, warfare with defeat and colonization perhaps, and also such internal forces as "conflict among interest groups, which results in extreme disadvantage for at least one group; and, very commonly, a position of perceived subordination and inferiority with respect to an adjacent society."

He describes the various steps through which the culture passes on the road to revitalization: from its original steady state through a period of increased individual stress, with widespread anomie and disillusionment; a period of cultural distortion in which piecemeal and ineffectual individual solutions are attempted, such as alcoholism, "black market," breaches of kin or sexual mores, gambling etc.; and finally the period of revitalization. He points out that revitalization depends on the successful completion of a number of stages. First, there is the formulation of a code. An individual or group must construct a new utopian image of cultural organization. Not infrequently the new code is formulated during the course of a hallucinatory revelation or a mystical experience. The second step is the communication of the new code to a band of followers. The code is usually offered as the means of spiritual salvation for the individual and of cultural salvation for the society. Finally, as the movement gains momentum new institutions based on the code are organized, with subsequent widespread acceptance and routinization.

Can we regard Neotranscendentalism as a revitalization movement? Clearly the Neotranscendentalists are not responding to social disorganization as outlined by Wallace. If the movement has anything to do with organization, it is a response to overorganization. As Roszak (1969: 5) emphasizes, youth is revolting against the technocracy, "that social form within which an industrial society reaches the peak of its organizational integration. It is the ideal men usually have in mind when they speak of modernizing, up-dating, rationalizing, planning. Drawing upon such unquestionable imperatives as the demand for efficiency, for social security, for large-scale co-ordination of men and resources, for ever higher levels of affluence and even more impressive manifestations of collective human power, the technocracy works to knit together the anachronistic gaps and fissures of the industrial society." We may say then that Neotranscendentalism has some of the attributes of a revitalization movement in its form but is responding to an unprecedented degree of overorganization and affluence rather than to social disorganization and poverty.

Recently Turner (1969) has presented us with another model. He studied the Ndembu of East Africa for many years and became interested in their rites of passage, particularly in the boundary stages of the rites, the period of limbo during which, as we have seen, the initiate is stripped of symbols both of youth and of adulthood and resumes the role of infant. Turner became impressed with the significance of this boundary stage or *limen* for a wider social interpretation. He described the boundary stage as a period of *communitas*, which he sees as a type of egalitarian relationship typical of all groups stripped of status and property. He proceeds to show how social life generally is an oscillation between periods of *communitas* and structure:

> It is as though there are here two major "models" for human interrelatedness, juxtaposed and alternating. The first is of society as a structured differentiated and often hierarchical system of politico-legal-economic positions with many types of evaluation, separating men in terms of "more" or "less." The second which emerges recognizably in the liminal period, is of society as an unstructured or rudimentarily structured and relatively undifferentiated *communitas*, community, or even communion of equal individuals who submit together to the general authority of the ritual elders.

He characterizes these modes by the following sets of dichotomies: *communitas*/structure; absence of property/property; nakedness or uniform clothing/distinctions of clothing; minimization of sex distinctions/maximization of sex distinctions; humility/just pride of position; disregard for personal appearance/care for personal appearance; simplicity/complexity; continuous reference to mystical powers/ intermittent reference to mystical powers; and many others.

Turner makes a brief excursion into our contemporary world and draws the beat and hippie phenomena into his analysis. These he sees as clear examples of communitas and liminality on the part of the participants, who, however, "do not have the advantages of national *rites de passage*—who 'opt out' of the status-bound social order and acquire the stigmata of the lowly." He also points out that the sacred properties often associated with communitas are evident in the hippie movement in their preoccupation with the mystical.

Why does society oscillate between these states of structure and antistructure? Turner seems at a loss to answer, other than that it is a kind of balancing act to preserve equilibrium:

> Society seems to be a process rather than a thing—a dialectical process with successive phases of structure and communitas. There would seem to be—if one can use such a controversial term—a human "need" to participate in both modalities. Persons starved of one in their functional day-to-day activities seek it in ritual liminality. The structurally inferior aspire to symbolic structural superiority in ritual; the structurally superior aspire to symbolic communitas.

For Turner, then, the explanation of the Neotranscendentalist movement is that middle-class American youth, by the age of eighteen, is glutted with organization and structure. Neotranscendentalism answers the need for a period of communitas. Presumably, after the communal need is satisfied for a few years, they will happily return to the old world of structure, organization, and status.

With these various explanations in mind, I would like to put forward a somewhat rephrased interpretation of the Neotranscendentalists. American society has, in the past, neglected religious ritual in the passage from childhood to adulthood. Casualties of the crisis have been treated by psychotherapy or mental hospitalization. But in the past twenty-five years a series of unprecedented factors have appeared on the scene: the population explosion, lethal pollution levels, automation and computerization, nuclear weapons, the pill, universal education, and instant communication. These combine to render virtually irrelevant the basic values of yesterday's adult:

> What is it to be a man or a woman, a father or a mother? Educated side by side and equipped for identical roles in the same universities, how can male and female find difference and sexual identity? And the pill has radically altered the sexual game. What is the rationale for "attack" and "defense" and what now is the case for chastity?
>
> Nor are such role changes the most fundamental. Once unquestioned concepts and values require radical revision. War and peace, nationalism, pride in the large family, the virtue of work and other ideals which once gave meaning and purpose are no longer valid. In fact some have become positively malignant. We must not be taken in by words; they are no longer the solid cobblestones of our world; they have become quicksand which will no longer bear our weight. We can no longer ask, "Do you think war is ever justified?" For we are instead inadvertently asking, "Is annihilation justified?" Nor can we ask, "Ought we ever to compromise for the sake of peace?" The question has become, "What sacrifices will we make for survival?" (Prince 1968)

Many of today's youth sense that a perpetuation of the present social order is the blueprint for disaster. They must not only navigate the perilous, age-old crossing between childhood and adulthood, but they feel called upon to create almost overnight an entire new social order and world view. To the individual cocoon work is added the enormously more complicated cultural cocoon work.

Is it possible to say anything about the new society which the Neotranscendentalists have in mind? This is difficult, for they deny that they have any specific program: "My generation does not have goals. We are not goal-directed. We just want to know what is going on" (Messer 1968). Carey (1968) points out that the "new bohemians" feel part of a widespread movement which is only beginning to take shape: "At present there is little indication of where it is going. It tends to be unorganized; there is little official leadership or recognized membership. Progress toward whatever the goal seems to be is uneven. But of one thing these young people are sure: it represents an extraordinarily powerful force."

In spite of this vagueness, something can perhaps be said about the new butterfly that is emerging from its cultural cocoon. Let us consider three basic social aspects: the family, the relation between the sexes, and the problem of work. The family in primitive society consisted of a group of kin which provided a rudimentary kind of welfare system; when young, members invested their labor with an expectation that when they became old or infirm they would be cared for. The next family style was the nuclear family which was adapted to competitive industrial society. The next term in the series is a return to the extended type of family, but with the member families not necessarily kin but families sharing common interests. The function of the grouping is not economic but a remedy for the isolation of the nuclear family; the aim is enrichment of the intellectual and emotional quality of life. Related to this evolution of the family is an alteration in the relations between the sexes. Relations between the sexes in primitive societies are often I-it, with the spheres of male and female kept quite distinct and separate. Next came the era of romantic love with a possessive I-Thou relationship and often a dominant-submissive quality. The new term in the series is the I-Thou relationship without personal jealousy, the possibility of sharing mates without individual possessiveness and with group care of children and egalitarian status between the sexes. Finally, in the sphere of work the Protestant ethic is passing away and repetitive work is seen as the proper function of machines. The Neotranscendentalists believe that it is time to "live off machines rather than live like machines" (Messer 1968). One must "be" rather than "do."

But whether these implicit goals of the Neotranscendentalists will be found widely acceptable or socially viable is another question. And how far they will get with such a Herculean task, even armed with that most powerful of metamorphotic engines—the mystical state— only the future can tell.

Psychological Dimensions of Religious Innovation

In this section a variety of religious movements are examined from the perspective of culture and personality. The authors are interested in the psychological dimensions of participation in these groups and the psycho-social implications of such groups for the larger society. The specific movements discussed are: some meditation groups on the West Coast, healing cults, Pentecostals on the East and West Coasts, Satanists, Spiritists, Spiritualists, and several fundamentalist churches. They are here grouped together not to claim or demonstrate that they are ethnographically alike. Rather, the grouping serves to point out empirically the different approaches each movement takes to essentially the same goal—how to orient their members to their daily life environment—and analytically to indicate how these groups are indigenous systems of self-help, a kind of folk tradition in American religious life.

These religious groups ought not to be regarded as isolated and self-contained pockets within society. While some of them have elaborate social systems in the manner of total institutions that offer their members services and opportunities found elsewhere in society, we cannot think of them as living in a social vacuum, unrelated and without impact on the social order. Groups such as these have always existed in our society and, historically, have had points of conflict with it. They have been major competitors for controlling the life-ways of their adherents. Currently, some of the religious practices, such as trance behavior, glossolalia, and a variety of meditative and visionary techniques that make these groups unique have diffused into the larger society. It is the increased popularity of these religious practices that today draws even greater attention to the very groups that have nurtured them for so long. Increasingly the questions are asked: How do these practices diffuse into the society and even succeed in making inroads to middle America? Is that diffusion a sign of failure of our social system? Why have these religious groups not been managed so that they would not gain the popularity they presently enjoy? How is the society to absorb the current religious revival and reamalgamate the adherents of these groups into the mainstream of social and religious life?

These questions clearly speak to several issues that have been alive in the public forum and in the scholarship dealing with marginal religious movements. It has frequently been assumed that movements that subscribe to religious practices emphasizing personal and direct contact between the individual and the transcendent are deviant and should be viewed as islands of social pathology. Not only were they pathological as corporate structures within the society but they attracted individuals who were defective in their abilities to function competently in daily life. These groups have been viewed as primarily useful to the unsuccessful fringes of society and an index of social disorganization. In light of the increasing influence of these groups on contemporary America, the question is raised whether the above are accurate conceptual assessments of these groups, and whether or not the social pathology and defective individual models are useful for further research and understanding of these movements?

It is essentially to the last two questions that the authors of these papers, professional psychiatrists and anthropologists, address their work. Their basic unit of analysis is the individual and the way he orients himself to fulfill his needs within the social environment in which he lives. It is in terms of "servicing the individual" that these scholars examine the various religious groups. Not that these groups as corporate structures within the larger society are not important or interesting, but their primary significance, as stated by these scholars, lies in the services they provide through religious practices which are not available to the individual outside these groups. The belief systems and ritual practices of most of these groups emphasize that self-knowledge and a social orientation are most satisfactorily gotten from personal, direct contacts with the transcendent. Such contact is possible through a variety f meditative, intuitive, and visionary experiences. There is an emphasis on altered states of consciousness and the frequently attendant linguistic behavior of glossolalia. These groups have institutionalized within their services particular contexts for these experiences, and have elaborated specific rules for the performance of these religious practices. The questions that are posed are: How is this system of religious worship organized? What is its content? How is it viewed by participants and by the larger society?

In every society, and especially our own, there exist pockets of individuals and groups who believe in and use altered states of consciousness such as trance. Such practices serve to mediate between the individual and his immediate social environment. They are dynamic processes that allow for social change. They accomplish that by allowing the individual to experiment with new relational modes within the existing order. Rather than breaking away from society, the use of altered states of consciousness allows participants a new outlook to society and thereby a way of functioning within it. The role of these processes and the groups that are organized around them is to keep certain social and ideological premises alive and renewed through time. Although, as Goodman pointed out in her paper, altered states of consciousness as a mechanism do not guarantee social change, they nurture or guard ideas and notions that eventually can enter the social system and even become institutionalized. They are the storehouses of social antithesis to the current realities. In every historical period society attempts to manage and control the growth and development of such religious groups through legislation, the judicial process, or enforcement agencies. However, when these groups begin to attract larger and larger numbers of adherents, and when the practices which they provide spill over institutional walls and diffuse through society without any institutional support, these groups and processes are no longer manageable and are on the way to gaining a new status in the mainstream culture. There may even become a new established order which in turn will give rise to new marginal movements as areas for social and religious experimentation. It is in this sense that contemporary religious movements can be viewed from a biological metaphor as mutant forms and the raw material for the continued growth and development of religious and social life.

The papers in this section are organized to deal first in a general way with the pathology model which has been used for a long time to discuss the status of such movements in society. This is followed by a group of papers that evaluate the pathology model in terms of new data based on field research with several groups. Finally, several papers discuss the internal operations of several groups and analyze them for the methods and goals they have for serving their adherents.

Adler's paper on the antinomian personality argues that man always needs to orient himself in such a way that he is neither agent nor pawn. To the degree that an individual cannot orient himself in these terms he seeks change. The current drug and youth culture, communes, criticism of the nuclear family, enthusiasm for the occult, and the general apocalyptic ethos are viewed as expressions of gnostic and antinomian modes of adaptation to social stress and change. Such responses are seen as attempts to orient and reconstitute the self, and are viewed as attempts to resanctify experience and renew exhausted and discredited rituals. Adler's main argument is that to the degree that membership in a culture or a society is tenable and membership in it is constant, one is able to assimilate the rituals of the society in much the same way that one has an internalized and a stable sense of self. But to the degree that rituals atrophy or become banal, one has to orient the self not in any inner sense, but on external things, and at that point enthusiastic and dualistic traditions develop. He sees the current scene as a variation of fundamentally gnostic and Manichean kinds of movements, and suggests that dualistic traditions are visible today as a function of social transition and crisis. Adler's approach suggests that modes of organizing the self are a function of specific social and historical settings. Individuals and groups are subject to the same consequences. Religious movements can be the collective expression of individual existential realities, although in different dimensions and intensity. They therefore vary in social impact and consequences.

It is not enough to explain in general terms that movements of social change arise out of dissatisfaction with the system. It is also important to show the variability and the differences between movements and their respective growth. All of these have been popularly termed deviant, but it is precisely the segmentation and proliferation of movements, each attracting different adherents, that produces social change. It is the dynamics between leaders and followers that produces the change, rather than some resident feeling within the population that makes this proliferation predestined. Adler is continuously interested in what set of conditions account for the kind of leader who gets the majority of the following. He is concerned with institutional relationships and the management of people by charismatic leaders. And he suggests that often there is no disruption of the scene until a movement with a leader comes along to call attention to the failures of the social order.

In discussing the relation between a movement of social change and of the role of charismatic leader in it, Adler argues that as long as a role is socially confirmed there is a movement. When the confirmation drops, the role reverts to pathology. In both the case of a social movement and of private pathology there is a man who is a visionary, but when he is part of a social movement he has a "passport." He has a platform and a role to operate within. Deviance and private pathology are defined by the absence of confirmation of his role.

Adler's discussion of social pathologies points to the observation that society's structure seems to move within a dualistic system of good and evil, corruption and escape from corruption. He argues that there seems almost to be a calendrical basis on which certain phenomena are in trouble and out of trouble, depending on the configuration of society and the individual's relationship to it. Today's religious approach is not a new truth, it is simply another phase in the cycle of how society defines getting in and out of trouble. Many of these dualistic movements are in a sense pathological and deviant and therefore negative. But they can function as a pressure valve, and in fact they are the raw material for social change. Their basic function, given the banality of rituals and the disenchantement with the world, is to overcome profanation and resanctify experience.

Within psychology and anthropology, models of deviance have played a significant role. Torrey picks up on the theme of pathology and points out that it often does us more disservice than good. He looks at the shaman, a category not only of American Indian healers but a generic name for the religious innovator and healer, and argues that past anthropological accounts of them, derived from culture and personality studies, have focused predominately on whether these individuals are "sick." Little serious consideration has been given to them as true psychotherapists playing the same role as psychiatrists. He begins with this assumption and discusses some of the evidence for its validity. He shows that psychiatrists have much to learn from spiritualists and shamans. If they are to learn, however, they will have to look seriously at the operational aspects of curing and how the shamans conceptualize their work. Such research requires extreme care and detailed empirical work in order to give us the data base to understand the shaman's techniques and evaluate their consequences.

Evaluating groups in terms of the adequacy of the pathology model is also Garrison's objective. Garrison, an anthropologist, has examined aspects of the model in her ethnographic research in the South Bronx where she was working out of a community mental health center. She surveys the variety of religious alternatives available to Puerto Ricans in New York City in their own neighborhoods. The dominant Roman Catholic and minority Pentecostal churches are compared along with a variety of social and psychological variables developed specifically to test some of the divergent hypotheses in the literature on sectarian adaptation. The variables are based on demography, socio-economic status, migration history, family organization, patterns of social participation, and several indices of mental health. These were compared to determine: (1) what differences, if any, characterize those who choose Pentecostalism over Catholicism; and (2) what effects membership in either church has upon the individual in his everyday life. These findings are then discussed for their implications for an integrated theory of the social and psychological functions of sectarianism. Garrison concludes that Pentecostals differ very little from Catholics who come from statistically comparable subcultural situations. If it is deviant to be sectarian and to "speak in tongues," then they are deviants. But, if we demand some other criteria for the pathology model such as inadequate functioning in occupational or social roles, or emotional disturbances, we will find there is no evidence for it.

Pattison focuses on the ideological belief system of contemporary American fundamentalists from the middle class. Although adherents to fundamentalism, these people are part of the main stream of the American middle class. Their religious beliefs are at considerable variance with dominant middle-class values, producing social and psychological dissonance in the lives of fundamentalists. Therefore, it is necessary to buttress the dissonant beliefs with certain religious rituals—glossolalia and faith healing—that provide support, reaffirming the social and psychological coherence of fundamentalist beliefs and values.

Pattison shows that dissonance produced by membership in a religious subculture while holding simultaneous membership in the middle class results in specific distortions in personality development. The rituals of glossolalia and faith healing serve to reduce both cultural and psychological dissonance, thus reinforcing the very ideologies that underlay the basic dissonance. Data from rituals indicate that most members of the religious subculture are able to sustain their dissonant ideologies without ritual reinforcement. Thus only a very few members of the fundamentalist subculture actually engage in these rituals.

Lauer follows the line of argument against using pathology models by giving us a very detailed analysis of a Spiritualist healer on the West Coast. He demonstrates the kind of analysis that can be provided of the healer and his practice, and shows the relationship between psychotherapists on one hand and folk healers, psychics, and shamans on the other. Lauer argues that it is important to look at the variety of practices, beliefs, and techniques provided in a community to people in emotional distress of one kind or another.

Psychics have aided persons from all segments of American society and have had their share of success. Most psychics do not cooperate with psychiatrists, because psychiatrists usually define them as the "enemy." Little is therefore known about how mediums proselytize, teach, and advise clients. Lauer describes the teacher, students, setting, beliefs, language, messages, teacher-student roles, indoctrination, history, homework, ritual battles, and evaluation of mediums in their teaching context. He concludes that it might be useful for mental health personnel to examine the utility of folk treatment and to collaborate with such folk practitioners.

Lauer makes several suggestions that are important to consider. His essential point is that practicing psychotherapists are in a unique position as gatekeepers in our society. In a sense, they are part of a group in society that determines whether we let others benefit from folk systems of healing or discredit them. In fact, some psychotherapists acquainted with these folk systems have allowed individuals to benefit from them. The larger issue is the danger in reducing and defining all problems and all methods in terms of one model. We must recognize that there are various problems defined differently by members of a culture and they have various solutions to them. Different problems should be taken to different sources for help.

This point is implicit in several of the papers. Comparative research between religious groups and secular systems of therapy have to cope with the notion that religious groups are not direct alternatives to psychiatry. They are alternatives for those individuals who define their problems in terms and categories other than psychiatric.

Macklin examines systems of folk healing from a yet broader perspective. She examines the healing aspects of Spiritualism in the United States and Spiritism in the U.S. and in Latin America. Her research focused on rituals called "dramas of salvation." They are found in both New England Spiritualism and Mexican-American Spiritism. These dramas aim at healing the split between social and spiritual wholeness, and consequently are effective at restoring physical health to participants. She draws from Tillich's notion that "salvation" originally meant healing, including medical and spiritual healing, but adds that the final salvation must heal the "split between the temporal order in which we live and the eternal to which we belong."

Macklin traces the split between Spiritualism and Spiritism in the nineteenth century. The confrontation of science and theology produced synthesizing ideologies and in the process generated marginal religions which attempted to reconcile the conflicting sets of ideas. The persistence and renascence of Spiritualism and Spiritism in the twentieth century may be understood in part as a search for rituals and beliefs which give symbolic meaning to the collective and personal search for identity so characteristic of this century. Today Spiritualism and Spiritism each provides its adherents (Protestants in the case of Spiritualism and Catholics in the case of Spiritism) with a traditional world-taken-for-granted, while at the same time allowing for freedom of individual conviction and revelation.

The data suggest that traditional Protestant values are in fact serving the clients of Spiritualism in New England quite well: hard work, patience, delayed gratification. Spiritism functions the same way in helping isolated Mexican-Americans locate themselves in terms of family and culture. It punishes or rewards him in terms of a folk value system appropriate to rural Mexico. Both systems allow a man to orient himself; they are compasses that place him in a continuously changing world.

Moody argues that today there is a revival of black magic and Satanism in contemporary America among many sectors of the population. By membership in Satanic groups individuals make themselves the target of the community's scorn and aggression. Why then do individuals persist? They persist because the magic "works" by helping them achieve the goals they desire. He analyzes the magical rituals such as the Invocation of Lust and the Shibboleth to show how they help practicing Satanists, members of the Church of the Trapezoid, to achieve their goals.

Moody points out the kind of therapy offered by this group and examines its results. He explains the rituals of the Satanic church in terms of models taken from behavioral psychology, because he feels that much of what goes on in Satanic rituals is explained better in terms of short term behavioral change than by psychoanalytical and anthropological models. He argues that this religious group absorbs the deviants that society shuts out. These are people who sometimes have not left society or dropped out but have been shut out. In that sense the Satanists resocialize those shut out by the dominant society. Some of the groups' values are not really too distant from the culture's values. Such groups are replays of the dominant cultural value system. That was also Macklin's point.

The organization of papers in this section underlies the notion present in all the papers: we ought to move in the direction of more intensive field work studies of specific religious groups to discover how they function and operationalize their beliefs. This is a move away from the fieldwork model that looks at these groups only as examples to bolster theoretical models which may slight a group's real complexity. The focus is on understanding a particular group in its own terms and in light of new analytical questions.

Ritual, Release, and Orientation: Maintenance of the Self in the Antinomian Personality

Now again, as in recurrent times of crisis and change, the shakers and quakers renew the world—out of Babylon, by way of Bethlehem, on the way once again to the new Jerusalem. Man has a limited repertoire of characteristic responses to recurring needs. Although the metaphors used to formulate the experience may change, the behavior is similar. I am interested not so much in evaluating any specific religious or quasi-religious movement, as in making a theoretical and historical examination of the lawful relationship I think I find between such movements and their stressful social contexts. I hope to demonstrate that the data of history are more useful for personality theory and social psychology than are stimulus-response models or learning theory.

We live again in "an age of anxiety," a time of political crisis and radical restructuring of social values. The person growing up today must find a way to orient and integrate himself in the face of forces that either fragment and diffuse him or compel him to collapse in upon himself. The silent and apathetic generation of the 1950s has been replaced by the rebels of the 1960s and their psychedelic counterculture. Attempts to account for "new" life styles, both activist and dropout, are usually formulated in exclusively contemporary terms and invoke technology (McLuhan 1962) or pharmacology. But the technology and the drugs are merely foci around which behavioral forms have crystallized out of ever-present underlying social and psychological processes. Today we couch in technological metaphors the same issues formerly couched in other metaphors—in religious terms as *heresy*, for example, and in aesthetic terms as *romanticism*. Such behavioral forms, though differing in particulars within and between periods, nevertheless have a structural commonality that I have attempted to account for by use of the term *antinomian* (from Greek *anti+nomos*, law), suggesting their characteristic opposition to established values.[1]

---

[1] For discussion of the antinomian model, see papers by Adler (1966a, 1966b, 1968, 1970a, 1970b).

Antinomian social movements develop in times of transition and crisis, when traditional values come to seem inadequate as a basis for constitution of the self.[2] As a psychological mechanism, antinomian movements allow for improvisation of new roles and the institutionalization of new ways of defining the self, of modulating affect, and of establishing points of personal anchorage and orientation. There is an apocalyptic sense of the "last days." Individuals may renounce family, traditional marriage, and jobs; establish their own small communities and their own new rituals; and affirm sexual libertarianism. Radical changes in styles of dress are often accompanied by exhibitionism. Trances, visions, glossolalia, possession, and other ecstatic behavior become common, libertinism often alternates with asceticism, violence with passive resistance in challenges to the temporal power.

The Relevance of Psychohistory

Modes of sensibility and organization of self are a function of specific social and historical settings. We tend to teach history as if only the successful dominant trends ever existed. Yet just as today existentialism lives alongside systems theory and operationalism, so theosophy and mysticism flourished during the Enlightenment. And even as Columbus sought new western routes to the Indies, Beghards and Waldensians wandered through the streets of Renaissance cities. In the Anabaptist world and in the counter-culture of today (Scheuch 1968), despite dissimilarities in the dominant cultures of the two periods, one finds the same chiliastic movements against the "empire of Babylon," the same reach for a new man and the redemption of time, similar collective events and charismatic leaders, the same splintering of these movements into groups demanding conformity to the group's identity—in both periods manifestations of an inner discontent with an external exciting but too much changing world. To illustrate, it will be helpful to note similarities in the intellectual,

---

[2] The middle of the fourteenth century responded to the Black Death, a plague that seemed to be irresistible and incurable, as our time responds to radiation sickness and the threat of atomic annihilation. Church and other public institutions were discredited and values challenged in a spiritual unrest and fervor that was apocalyptic in its expectations and led to social disorder, insurrection, frenetic gaiety, and religious enthusiasm. "Assumptions which had been taken for granted for centuries were now in question, the very framework of men's reasoning seemed to be breaking up," Ziegler (1969) remarks—and, to make the issue of ecstasy, the radical autonomy of the self, and the antinomian adaptation even sharper, note that the Şūfism of Ibn 'Arabī (Corbin 1969) develops within the context of the Mongol incursions from Central Asia across Iran toward the Middle East and that the capture of Baghdad by the Mongols announced the end of a world.

social, political, and economic contexts of the two periods.

The fifteenth and sixteenth centuries saw power shift from the Catholic South to the Protestant North, from the Mediterranean basin to Holland, Switzerland, England, and the Baltic cities. In the new cities, power moved to new classes. Europe was upside down. Concepts of space changed as new continents and worlds were "discovered." Established rituals, experienced as increasingly empty, were repudiated; and primitive Christianity, private devotion, inner states of piety were opposed to the mechanical devotion of the established church. With the dissolution of a unified Christianity, secularism grew. The monasteries acted as a barrier to the demand for new kinds of production and commerce. Heretical movements developed, ranging from Luther and Calvin on the right, who sought to institutionalize new modes and to contain the chaos, to such groups as Anabaptists and witches, destroyed by inquisition and terror and driven into powerless isolation (Trevor-Roper 1968).

Born three years after Columbus's voyage to the New World, Melchior Hoffman grew up a spiritualist and a mystic. He became an itinerant evangelist and prophet who broke away from Luther to become a leader in the Radical Reformation (Williams 1962), antagonized the established clergy, and was driven from city after city as a seditionist. The year 1533 was for him the year that would see the coming of the Lord and the inauguration of the reign of saints. From his grated prison window in Strassburg he cried across the moat that "all the apocalyptic plagues had been fulfilled, save the vengeance of the seventh Angel. Babylon was falling and they were on the threshold of the new kingdom of righteousness and peace" (Bax 1903). "Redeem the time!" was the Anabaptist call. And like an echo across the centuries Bobby Seale (1970) answers "Seize the Time," and Eldridge Cleaver in justifying his arrest of Timothy Leary, the revolutionary "bust" of January 9, 1971, explains, "It makes me sad to do this. . . . I don't like being a jailer but we cannot afford to jeopardize our work toward revolution in Babylon" (Cleaver 1971).

One may also compare the hippie culture with the Dadaist and Surrealist movements that were a response to World War I. Dada too was a no-saying to the establishment. Through dreams, hallucinations, and subjection to chance, Dadaists and Surrealists sought a renewal of their experience and vision, an antidote to the increasing sterility of industrial and mercantile life.[3] The hippie movement is a large-scale,

[3] The Surrealists were precursors in their desire to explore consciousness; the Dadaists, in anti-rationalism, provocation, and the apotheosis of youth. The yippie style is the direct heir of the Dada movement (Richter 1965). Before Leary, Dada advocated "blowing your mind" and "dropping out." Its members hoped by

mass-produced, marketable version of the earlier avant-garde movement. The Surrealists, however, did not opt for the flight from thought or adopt the antirationality and anti-intellectualism of the enthusiasts of the past decade.

RITUAL AND RELEASE

The Present Situation

Today's antinomian movement repudiates rational cognition for an intuitive, visionary gnosis. Repudiating "concrete sequential thinking," a generation of university students gives credence to astrology, the *I Ching*, the folklore of extrasensory perception, flying saucers, space people. Why this retreat from rationality?

We live in a time that permits the psychotic's fanciful vision of world destruction to coincide with the actuality of atomic brinksmanship, a time in which the apocalyptic vision finds reinforcement in the sudden recognition that we do in fact live within a limited biosphere, a shallow, fragile, delicately balanced ecological system that supports the only kind of life we can have. What are we to make of the enthusiasm for organic foods and macrobiotic diets? Is it not, over and beyond the problem of contaminants, an expression of that ancient dualism that differentiates the spiritual pure from the material impure, the divine from the corrupt? (Topitsch 1966) In youth groups and communes, people seek the "real self," in a return to purity, nature, and innocence. As they gather glass, paper, and tin and return these to the cycle of nature, are they paralleling the gnostic desire to gather and return to the divine its alienated fragments?

The unresponsive, dehumanized rationality of technological and bureaucratic systems that take people into account only as expendable resources and the stuff of kill ratios leaves them with a sense of impotence and dependency. Out of such situations comes Pascal's cry about the feeble mote, flickering in a vast and indifferent universe, and the existentialist's complaint of a world bereft of meaning and of a god. The cry of the "absurd" asserts the loss of an anthropocentric cosmos and of normative myths. When expectancies are not confirmed, and old roles are discredited or ambiguous, one becomes acutely aware

---

anarchist acts of symbolic destruction to give the final coup to a dying order. Their scandals and provocations were intended to demoralize the bourgeoisie by creating disorder and emphasizing the absurdity and meaninglessness of collective values. Dada, committed only to negation, was antirational and antisystematic in principle. The Surrealists, led by Breton (1969), were not committed to disorder but were instead interested in the "irrational" unconscious aspects of experience as a source of a new, more embracing rationality.

of lack of coherence and the protean nature of existence, and one is easily persuaded of the primacy of appearance over "reality." At such times the phenomenologist speaks for the highbrow, and the less sophisticated reach for the occult, the sensate, the subjective. Sex roles are repudiated or diffused, ascetic and ecstatic exercises are cultivated, and libertine polymorphous perverse games become more widespread. Exhibitionism and pornography find a new acceptability. The ennui and insensibility accompanying stimulus hunger or satiation overreach their refractory phase in sadism and violence.

If sixteenth-century heretical groups justified the inner man and his private relation with God, they also provided him with a public framework that confirmed his identity and his membership. Likewise, in contemporary therapeutic forums, synthetic weekend communities for confession, and reports of inner or sexual, often group activity, one discerns the old Manichean ruminations: Was it real? Am I truly of the Elect? Have I found the authentic inner vision?

The new cults of sensory awareness, meditation, encounter, naked marathon therapy, public confession, and crotch eye-balling are offered as modern psychotherapies.[4] People grope and touch and hold each other as if the physical contact is necessary to reinstate their boundaries and confirm their existence and identity.

Glossolalia returns, in marginal mystic groups like Subud and in established Episcopalian churches. Like early Pentacostalists and Shakers, newer secular groups use excitement, movement, touch, and dance; when the wafer and other rituals have lost their potency, Dionysian rites and the orgy that were the initial experience of communion and community return.

Every society establishes moral holidays that structure, sanction, and institutionalize excess and release. Festivals, as Cox (1970) suggests, are socially approved occasions for the expression of feelings usually repressed or neglected. While festivals characteristically allow excess, it is always exceptional and limited. Such temporary excesses are quite different from the current practice within the drug culture of being regularly "stoned," "high," and ecstatic. In a normative system the festival intensifies time perspective; in the antinomian, emphasis

---

[4] The latest movies have obligatory group therapy scenes. A new growth industry of resorts and institutes schedule weekends of massage and "exploration of the here and now feelings," and they advertise techniques derived from "transcendental phenomenology" and promise to help people find ways to "break through" to more satisfying relationships, to be free, to make life more "exciting." They offer to improve communication at "the feeling level," "the gut level," and "the nitty gritty"—by being "primarily experiential" in "deeper" relationships that will lead to becoming more "joyful," as one finds inner awareness, euphoria, and creativity.

on immediacy diminishes perspective and continuity. The continuous and enduring self, attenuated by this loss of perspective, is to be reinstated by fervor, ecstasy, and the continuous consumption of stimuli.

Communes and Tribalism

So too, the development of communes repeats an Anabaptist pattern. There are now an estimated 1,000 rural hippie communes and at least twice that many urban communes in North America (Zablocki, in press). Many of these experiment with new forms of the extended and non-nuclear family; polygamy and polyandry, and homosexual, bisexual, or celibate communities all echo earlier antinomian groups.

These isolated young people, the cross-country hitchhikers and wandering students in search of roles, claim a tribalism that recalls a pre-World War I German youth movement, the Wandervogel. They too sought the whole man; banded together and improvised rituals; sought the vigorous life, the blood brotherhood; and set out upon the trip, the quest. Now, as then, young people seek to renew in folk culture, in folk music and crafts, the sense of the tribe. The Wandervogel found their anchorage in a pantheistic union with nature. In a deranged world, the search for meaning and purpose reinstates the first god—the tribe.

The greatest happening in the movement was a carnival-like event that reminds us of Woodstock Nation or the Berkeley People's Park parade: the Meissner Fest (Helwig 1960), a celebration on Mt. Meissner in October 1913, when the movement confronted the public as a united group and in the Meissner formulation [5] made known its desires to seek out "inner truth." Some sought a mass migration movement out of the cities or to the Orient, while others sought a "secession of all those of good will" to begin building an ideal "natural" life of farming and craft settlements.

Like contemporary mimes and guerrilla theater, play groups toured the countryside presenting both popular and mystery plays. These groups sought, as the "new theater" today does, to break out of the proscenium and to create a unity between players and audience. First the youth movement had called for "the convalescence of nature" to overcome the sickness of civilization. Later, a large part of the

---

[5] "German Youth stands at a historical turning-point. Youth, heretofore excluded from the public affairs of the nation and assigned to a passive role of learning . . . only an appendage of the older generation, is beginning to become conscious of itself. It is striving, independently of the tired customs of the older generation and of the commandments of a repugnant convention to shape its own life. . . ." Quoted in Helwig (1960).

prewar Wandervogel ultimately turned to political action, "overcoming the error of the first stage of the youth movement: individualism. . . ." Youth culture, the leaders now said, was the blabbering of sick souls; they demanded youth power. Thus the romantic symbols ultimately were transformed into soldierly rites of falling in and marching, and the prewar guitar was replaced by flute and drum (Fick 1939).

Those who turn nostalgically to the past or seek desperately to spiritualize the present move through many roles from passivity to activism. Romantics aim at conserving the old beliefs for a modern age; chiliasts affirm an ahistorical ecstasy and seek to transcend time and self in a fusion with the absolute being of nature. The flight from the city and politics to the commune may preserve the purity of the ecstatic spirit for a little while. When chiliastic ecstasy turns inward, gives up the conflict with the immediate world, and retreats to the sinless utopia of childhood, it tends to become gentle and innocuous or to lose itself in pure self-edification. But mystic and enthusiastic modes can be achieved as easily by either Black Masses or Black Shirts, as we learned in the Olympic stadium at Nuremberg.

Astrology

Each apocalyptic period also reinstates occult and astrologic preoccupations. *Newsweek* (1969) reports that astrology now has some 10 million fully committed adherents and an estimated 40 million dabblers, making this once marginal activity an epidemic. Twelve hundred of the 1,750 newspapers in the U.S. carry daily horoscopes and almost every major women's magazine runs a monthly column. The Dell Publishing Company alone releases some thirty horoscope magazines and in 1968 sold eight million copies of its purse-size edition. Beyond all the social talk about one's natal sign lies the implication that the fault is not in ourselves but in our stars, beyond our will. If one is not master of one's fate, one can at least learn to read the signs right and accommodate to the indifferent and inexorable cosmic and social process. The cosmological metaphor expresses the experienced relationship between self and society, as may the metaphoric perception of one's own body (Douglas 1970).

Astrology serves to make the cosmos anthropocentric again, even while it affirms a depersonalized and merciless transcendence. It asserts the irrationality of authority and power, abstract, anonymous, unapproachable, like any government bureaucracy to which one has to submit. The "opaque and inscrutable" face of a highly organized and institutionalized society, experienced as unresponsive, unreasonable, and absurd, is projected into the heavens. Even when the interest in astrology is admitted ironically, Adorno (1957: 2) suggests, it functions as an ideology to justify dependence, passivity, and accommodation. The individual no longer has to resolve contradictions, but can view them as dichotomies to be treated serially; he no longer has to struggle to overcome obstacles, but can surrender to the preordained and the inevitable. Astrology's anti-intellectualism also deprecates the scientific establishment and hence discredits the most potent myths of a technological society.

Two Antinomian Modes

Passivity and activity are alternate antinomian modes, sharply delineated during the recent confrontation between Eldridge Cleaver and Timothy Leary (Cleaver 1971). The ascetic and the ecstatic, retreat and attack, quietism and aggression, passive resistance and violence, control and release, discipline and pleasure, are alternative modes for meeting similar stresses and are a function of whether threat is seen as originating within the self or outside.

In a radio address from Algiers, released on tape in the U.S., Cleaver criticized Leary, repudiated "ego trips and the magic wand approach," and deplored "substituting magic words for cold calculating confrontation with reality." The same man who some time ago wrote an introduction to Jerry Rubin's *Do It* (1970) now rejected LSD as a revolutionary instrument, demanded that the white counter-culture be critically reassessed, and spoke of Rubin, Abbie Hoffman, Allen Ginsberg, and Stew Albert as "that silly psychedelic movement" (Cleaver 1971). (Even this confrontation between the ascetic and the ecstatic parties repeats history. Several years ago the Haight-Ashbury Diggers abandoned the street scene for communes. They felt that the street had become corrupted, commercialized, and co-opted by the business world. The twentieth-century Diggers denounced the commercialization of rock and acid rock and called for new forms and a new ethic as they retreated to the countryside.[6])

Cleaver's view has received support from another significant and influential quarter. Herbert Marcuse, one of the most consistent mentors of the counter-culture, said in an address at the University of California, Berkeley, "The period of beautiful spontaneity of hippie

---

[6] Cox (1970) speaks of this when he says: ". . . to frolic and gambol in what *is* can produce as its extreme a lack of any interest in hoping, creating, or changing. To express it in the language of theology, a needed emphasis on *incarnation*, the presence of the spirit in the flesh can, if overdone, lead to a kind of presentism, a total absorption of interest in the here and now. This presentism can in turn slip over into a supine acceptance of the world as it is and the consequent disappearance of fantasy, hope, revolt, or vision. . . . It looks forward to nothing and risks satiation and boredom!"

rock and shock is over. . . . The period is over because the Establishment has become immune against shock, against ego trips styled as political action" (Marcuse 1971).

Mannheim (1936) remarks that chiliasm has always accompanied revolutionary outbursts, and when this spirit deserts the revolutionary movement there remains behind a despiritualized mass frenzy and fury. For chiliasm, revolution is a value in itself, the only creative principle of the immediate present rather than an unavoidable means to a rational end. Another instance of such a view is to be found in the acts of the Weathermen, which has led to the repudiation of violence by Bernardine Dohrn (1970),[7] and in the assertion of the New York Panther deserters, who said in their letter to Weathermen, "Revolution is in the final analysis . . . ARMED STRUGGLE . . . revolution is VIOLENCE . . . revolution is WAR . . . revolution is BLOODSHED" (emphasis in the original, *East Village Other* 1971).

REORIENTATION

The Present Situation Again

The moon walk confronts man again with his potential and his helplessness, with his awe and his dislocation, with the banality of exhausted forms and the need to renew experience and make it again sacred. The organization man, instructed by the company how his wife is expected to behave, finds in the bureaucratization of industry and government rigidities comparable to ossified ecclesiastic and monastic institutions. This leads again to an emphasis on faith and works; the validity of "objective" standards is challenged; "mere" value judgments are suspect as all are urged to "do your own thing."

In an automated world focused on consumption more than on production, latter-day Luddites become wreckers by refusing to consume the products of the machine or by creating new modes of consumption. The establishment is mocked, confronted by passive resistance or by violent guerrilla movements. As in the sixteenth-century cities of Amsterdam and Munster, and as in the towns of Old and New England, naked people wander the streets. Multiple and group marriage and extended families reappear.

---

[7] Dohrn invokes the Yaqui way of knowledge and affirms the validity of the drug experience, failing to note that Castenada (1968) fled in panic. She fails to recognize that one never consumes a drug without at the same time ingesting a total culture complex that establishes, sanctions, and limits. The ritualization of Don Juan's behavior is in sharp contrast with the unstructured stoned, mind-blown users who consume pharmacologic agents outside the patterned cultural system that structures its use.

In the same way that Kautsky (1897) noted that Anabaptist institutions prepared for new developments in socialization,[8] so Marcuse suggests that the new life styles and the attack on the nuclear family may serve to create the brave new world of conformity and consensus. Extrafamiliar authority supersedes that of the nuclear family. "Loosening sexual authority," he writes, "makes it possible to overcome the oedipus complex . . . the effect of this is to strengthen rather than to weaken the omnipotence of domination . . . the more models and examples are taken from outside (the family) the more unified and uninterrupted become the 'socialization'" (Marcuse 1970: 14). Synanon, too, seeks to build the New Jerusalem, sets up Manichean castes of the novitiates and the elect, and even within its ascetic mode discourages the nuclear family, encouraging ties to the total community.

The publicly shared confessionals of the Synanon game, shared income, public communal eating, and often group marriage all repeat Anabaptist forms. As Kautsky saw wholesale and manufacturing techniques developed in the earlier institutions, we are now seeing in both the Synanon and commune cultures not only ways of dealing with shared rent and expenses but ways of creating the new uniform packaging of the consumer society, and the New Man who will live in it.

Alienation

Whenever mobility is blocked and roles are ambiguous or discredited, when one needs to avoid fear, threat, and loss of membership, the experience of time changes. The past is repudiated or one turns to it as a lost golden age. Under such conditions immediacy becomes an imperative style. Yet it is always and forever Now, and past and future are contemporary events of memory and anticipation. But it is Now only if one knows how to move in and take title; instead, the depressed sulk in the basement of memory and the obsessional run to the outer margins of anticipation while the house remains vacant and unpossessed. To be alienated is to be alienated from duration, from one's own body, and from the Other.

The cry of alienation is embedded in a dualistic view that splits subject and object and sets the self against the other, God against

---

[8] Kautsky (1897) suggests that communal housekeeping—of both the monasteries and the Beghard houses—always encouraged the tendency toward the establishment of industries and farms on a large scale and served to overcome technological problems. "If about twenty weavers shared a common household they always bought the raw material in common, and manufactured it together in one place. . . . Both of these flourished as associations for work in an age when, socially and technically, the conditions of wholesale business were not in existence."

world, man against nature, the individual against society. Trapped in the names and categories of a language whose structure creates for us a dualistic subject-predicate "reality," we are deluded by the nouns we name into shadow boxing inside Plato's cave.

Consciousness, reality, and time are interrelated, as Ricoeur (1970) has said, and the dualistic formulations we construe are a function of our derangement.[9] Such formulations are precisely the expression of a loss of a sense of community, of an extrusion from one's field so that one has to grope for "authenticity" and reach for ways to be real. When there is an interpenetration of value and fact, when norms are accepted as in "the nature of things," as "reality," such a fragmentation does not take place. Where a relative stability of facts, things, and values exists, one lives with title and membership in a community, part of a shared public that sustains one so that it is even possible to lapse from self-involvement. The awareness of self usually returns like a nagging toothache only in moments of stress, ennui, and disequilibrium. It is only when the "looking glass self" (Cooley 1902), the image reflected by the public mirror (Lacan 1968), blurs and becomes diffused that immediacy, sensibility, and consciousness in its ongoing flux become imperative.

The Phenomenal Self and the Field

Man is neither agent nor pawn. Given a relatively stable surrounding world, he is able (in interaction with his field) to overcome his primary narcissism, symptoms of which are ego inflation and feelings of fusion with the universe. Things identified as the spiritual and the sacred are usually those in which the self is involved—in which there is an emotional self-investment, in which collective experience is a meaningful rather than a mechanical activity, in which values and meanings are shared within a community. A person constructs the image of himself from feelings and impulses that originate internally and from stimuli arriving from the outside world. From this interaction emerge the reliable boundaries of the self and differentiation of subject and object. Cognitive growth demands precisely this differentiation—of inner and outer, of mechanisms of release and of control. Ideally, a balance between these is achieved.

But if in childhood this balance is disrupted, sequential development is disorganized and a disordered awareness of the body and its

[9] Buber (1958) has described this ruptured state: "Institutions are 'outside' where all sorts of aims are pursued. Where a man works, negotiates, bears influence, undertakes, concurs, organizes, conducts business, officiates. . . . Feelings are 'within' where life is lived and man recovers from institutions."

functions leads to such clinically identifiable problems as obesity, alcoholism, drug abuse, and anorexia. When the external world fails to respond, or responds in contradictory or inappropriate ways, the individual loses the sense of ownership of his body and experiences a loss of control of its functions. In mysticism, drug experiences, and clinical syndromes alike we find reports of similar somatic distortions.

Within a stable situation the self achieves constancy as it differentiates itself from the not-self. If ambiguity replaces constancy, if the not-self acts as a barrier rather than as a reflector and reinforcer, the individual retreats or seeks fusion with the threatening object. In pain he can precipitate consciousness and awareness of self; in rapture, a swoon into the Other. Figure and ground dissolve and resolve. His procedures may be ascetic or ecstatic; the issue is the orientation, whether it be outward or inward, field-dependent or independent.

As we view the historical recurrence of antinomian strategies, it appears evident that beside organismic and familial developmental factors, such social parameters as customs, norms, and rituals also operate to reinforce and sustain the experience of the self, its roles, and its construed identity.

The stable self incorporates the norms and symbols of the surrounding world and elaborates rituals which serve for man the same function that hereditary instinctive behavior serves for other animals. These rituals provide the regularity for binding and discharging affect; they orient the person and transmit tradition from generation to generation. When rituals and symbols become atrophied and emptied of meaning, when the self-other axis breaks, one either repudiates or loses contact with the Other. A frequent consequence is that God is perceived not as the Other but as the Self.[10] The elect see themselves as God coming into consciousness. The greater the isolation of this elect, the more they see themselves as chosen. Subject and object fuse into subject, and, as we have had occasion to note in a recent murder, the immanent god stalks the world.

The concept of the self is still marginal in psychology and social psychology. There lingers about it the taint of the "soul" and of the

---

[10] Aberle (1966: 6–9) remarks that drugs are ingested to give a feeling of personal significance to external and internal stimuli. One reaches, not for the vision, but for the meaning and significance of the vision in an effort to create and replace the lost continuity and time perspective. In an emptied world one seeks to re-establish the sacred and to re-ritualize experience. Aberle says, "Peyote is relevant. When a person eats peyote, something external to him proves able to affect his thinking, his feelings, his perception and his behavior and to do so without his own volition." It is also noteworthy that the experience is a group experience in a group setting.

interior homunculus as helmsman. G. H. Mead (1934) struggled with the differentiation between self as subject, the "I," and self as object, the "Me." He spoke of the I that reacts to the Me but tended to over-emphasize the social context and minimize and neglect the role of the subjective aspect of the self. He said, "When the self does appear it always involves an experience of another; there would be no experience of the self simply by itself."

Sarbin (1952: 11–21), in a formulation in which I was pleased to share, attempted to expand and differentiate Mead's construct. He defined the self as a cognitive structure that functioned as an object for the individual, was learned, and grew through specific developmental phases in a process of individuation or regression or both. But this formulation, too, neglects the functions and role of the internal and subjective self.

Allport (1955) has attempted a convergence between the socius, or object self described by Mead, and the proprium, or perceived self (the subjective I). He differentiated the I and the Me as the polarities of individualism and tribalism.[11]

The self is suspended between these two poles, and loss of either the inner or the outer anchorage forces the individual into restitutive behavior. We are familiar with the alternatives of the inner-directed man or the outer-directed man as styles of adaptation and accommodation. Either style can be at home in the universe, as long as there is effective commerce between the self and the Other.

When in times of crisis and transition the reciprocal modes break down, the self no longer exists as congruent figure in an expected, intended, and acknowledged ground. Then sources of information to sustain the Me are inadequate, and the individual is forced back upon the I. Rational cognitive modes based on vision and objectification are displaced by haptic and subjective intuitive styles. Gnostic and antinomian values and techniques return. Hyperactivity and dropping out are attempts to reorient and stabilize the threatened self. In the struggle between man's "nature" and his need for order, between release and control, issues of man *vs.* social order, good *vs.* evil, and God *vs.* Satan historically recur.

Allport's formulation implies more than the attempt to account for the role of sensation, perception, memory, and symbolization, and the ways in which these interact with the social in constituting the self. Beyond the acknowledgement of becoming as an ongoing process,

11 He maintains, "If the demand for autonomy were not a major force, we could not explain the prominence of negativistic behavior in childhood. . . . All his life long, this being will attempt to reconcile these two modes of becoming, the tribal and the personal."

there linger rumors in this formulation if ancient polemics between theology and philosophy. The Neoplatonists and the theologians struggled to separate intelligence from the individual, intending corporeal being. The Neoplatonists saw intelligence invested within the body as "little trapped particles of the divine godhead," parts of an eternal, absolute transcending Intelligence independent of separate people.

Self-actualization, a rallying slogan of the past decade, not only echoes *das Heilige Werden,* the holy becoming of the German Wander-vogel, but resonates with the old gnostic conceptualizations of the Holy Spirit. In that view the angel needs the response of a soul if his being is to become what it has to be. Self-actualization refers to I, my perfect nature, rather than to Me. In comments like "I don't know what's gotten into me," or "I am not being faithful to my true self," there is the long shadow of the gnostic Angel Gabriel, the Holy Spirit of the individual reaching for the lost collective Other. It is an expression of the individual's alienation.[12]

The dichotomy of the self as subject and object, as agent and agency, is enmeshed in parochial, ideological, and theoretical issues. As long as one is not tied to ideological commitments to a model, or to the notion that models are real rather than merely nominal categories, the principle of complementarity can resolve what appear to be contradictory issues.[13]

If we can transcend the limits of our language which incapacitates us in nouns and permit ourselves instead to construe the self as gerund, as process rather than as reified category, we may be able to escape from the dualistic formulation of man as agent or agency. Then we could see the issue not as self or ego, but as a selving and coping, which in particular settings establish the locus of control within or without.

The psychoanalytic investigators (Jacobson 1964; Kohut 1966: 243–

---

[12] In the Sūfī view, "the nostalgia of the divine names crying out for the beings who would will them" (Corbin 1969). In this context self-actualization is to be understood as the manifestation of particular *roles.*

[13] Kohler (1947: 26–175) ". . . organization concerns the whole field, which means the self is included. In other words I maintain that certain general principles of function apply as much to the self as to objects in a more common sense." Schafer (1968) as a psychoanalyst also struggles with this subject-object formulation. "Although it may come about ultimately that the propositions cast in terms of the self will replace those cast in terms of id, ego, and superego, it becomes a source of confusion to try to have it both ways at once. Working with two types of systemic formulations at once circumvents certain theoretical problems, but it does not resolve them. Propositions cast in terms of self have the advantage of greater plasticity, greater closeness to subjective experience and easier accommodation of the principle of multiple function."

272; Lichtenstein 1964: 49–56; Levin 1959; Modell 1968; Spiegel 1959: 82–106) have traced the child's interior development from an autistic state with its failure to differentiate subject and object to that of the autonomous and individuated person. They have traced those narcissistic alternations of gratification in which the person invests feeling in objects or representations of the self. These alternations have been noted in fugue states and in the experiences of depersonalization. As Spiegel (1959) remarks, "When in traveling objects that are constantly part of the self are no longer available as a frame of reference, then alternations in self feeling may occur."

There are always pockets of disorder in any society, but these are usually contained and marginal. One may always find isolated cults of astrologers, witches' covens, spiritualist circles, ascetic bands, and libertine clubs, but sometimes these isolated circles lose their marginality, break out of their deviant stigmata, and become popular and epidemic. Once more a challenged establishment confronts the old heresies and enthusiasms.

Every society elects its deviants and defines its pathology. But in times of crisis and change the pathologic may find a social platform and a public role that validates its nay-saying. In new roles, deviants thus achieve prominence and are confirmed in modes of behavior that otherwise might be stigmatized as sickness. Petrus Borel was the leader of the Bouzingo—or a solitary, isolated paranoid (Starkie 1954); the leader of the Taiping rebellion (Thrupp 1970) was a seer—or a patient; today's guru was once the forlorn man in the back ward of the state hospital. Bax (1903) remarks that in the revolt against a moribund feudalism in the early sixteenth century one also found "the flotsam and jetsam cast forth by decay—as in all movements whose seed ground is a dying economy"; yet of this population cast adrift from its social and economic moorings, he says that most of those who flocked to the city of Munster in 1534 "were more honest and nobler than the unscrupulous ruffians of the moribund feudalism with whom they were at war."

In the first days of our history, shortly after the landing on Plymouth Rock, naked Quakers ran down the streets to the dismay of the good citizens of Massachusetts. The Antinomian Controversy (Hall 1968) is well documented in the New England of 1636–38, and Emerson said of Thoreau, "Henry could have been a leader of men. Instead he became the leader of the huckleberrying party." Brook Farms, Shakers, Movers, Utopian colonists have been before and again return.

Sectarianism and Psychosocial Adjustment: A Controlled Comparison of Puerto Rican Pentecostals and Catholics

I<small>N</small> the light of cross-cultural research on ideological movements and new data from major church and sect members drawn from the Puerto Rican population of a low-income neighborhood in New York City, it is possible to reevaluate and integrate some of the conflicting and often untested hypotheses on the psychosocial characteristics and adjustment of members of sectarian religious groups.[1]

There have been many studies of sectarian groups, among which Pentecostals are usually considered.[2] These studies have, in general, taken one of two approaches reaching related conclusions. The first approach is based on qualitative analysis of the belief system and behavior of the minority religious group, implicitly or explicitly compared with the characteristics of the dominant churches or larger society. Inferences are then drawn from the collective verbalizations or ecstatic behavior of the group, together with its minority status, regarding the characteristics of individuals who might be attracted to the minority religion and the functions of sectarian membership for such individuals. These studies usually conclude that the minority religious group attracts members who are economically, socially, and/or psychologically deficient. It is then argued that sect membership helps the individual to cope with this disadvantage by either (1) providing a *modus vivendi* apart from that of the larger society within which he can function more comfortably, or (2) altering the distinguishing characteristics so that he can function more adequately, e.g. the sectarian is socialized in dominant values (Johnson 1963). Such

---

[1] This research was supported under Public Health Service grant MH–02308 from the National Institute of Mental Health to Lincoln Hospital Mental Health Services, a division of Albert Einstein College of Medicine, Bronx, New York. Also, I have received kind assistance from Yale University, Department of Psychiatry, in providing time and computer facilities for analysis and write-up.

[2] For accounts of the Pentecostal Movement, see Kelsey 1964; Nichol 1966; Sherrill 1964; Stagg, Hinson, and Oates 1967. For accounts of pentecostal beliefs and practices written by Pentecostals, see Conn 1955; McPherson 1946; Wilkerson 1963.

inferences are often confused by social class and subcultural differences between the sectarian subjects and the investigators from the dominant culture and have rarely been subjected to systematic measurement or statistical test. The second major approach consists of systematically comparing the characteristics of members of minority church groups with major church members or with national norms on quantitative standardized measures. Such studies reveal that sectarian group members are on the average of lower socioeconomic status and differ from major church members in some characteristics, e.g. higher F-scale scores (see Pattison, this volume), many of which are also found more frequently in most lower socioeconomic groups. Without controls for subcultural and socioeconomic variables, it is impossible from these studies to know which characteristics actually distinguish sectarians and which merely reflect class differences. In contrast to the inferences drawn from qualitative studies, in those few studies where controlled comparisons have been made of the social and psychological characteristics of sectarians and major church members drawn from the same ethnic and socioeconomic background (Hine 1969), only minor psychological differences have been evidenced, and not greatly increased rates of social and psychological ills.

LaBarre (1971), in a recent review of the cross-cultural literature on new ideological movements, has argued that such movements are the result of multiple part-causes and represent an "adaptive technique" of "mutations in culture" occurring under a variety of circumstances, historical, environmental, cultural, biological, and psychological. While arguing that no particularistic explanation, including psychological explanations, will suffice, he suggests that the starting point for an understanding of the phenomena is to be found in the human predicament wherein an individual or group of individuals, disillusioned with the accepted model of the world, invent or adopt a new one. / Wallace (1956: 265), before him, delineated stages of a common process of reintegration of the individual and the society in what he called "revitalization movements," or "a deliberate, organized, conscious effort by members of a society to construct a more satisfying culture." Data from the present study suggest that membership in the sect also represents an adaptive strategy for individuals under a variety of circumstances and that it is the circumstances surrounding entrance into the sect and the conscious choice of sect membership over other alternatives, rather than any enduring social or personal deficits, which distinguish them from the majority population from which they are drawn.

In the following pages the variety of religious alternatives available to the Puerto Rican in New York City are reviewed in broad perspective. Members of the dominant Roman Catholic and minority Pentecostal churches are then compared on a variety of social and psychological variables developed specifically to test or re-test some of the divergent hypotheses in the literature on sectarian adaptation. Specifically, demographic characteristics, socioeconomic variables, migration history, family organization, patterns of social participation, and several indices of mental health are compared to determine: (1) what differences, if any, characterize those who choose the minority religious group over the major denomination, and (2) what effects membership in the sect has upon the individual in his everyday life. The implications for an integrated theory of the social and psychological functions of sectarianism are then discussed.

The research reported was conducted in several overlapping stages from 1966 to 1969 in a slum area of the South Bronx, consisting of ten census tracts with a total population of approximately 100,000, 55% of which is Puerto Rican. First, services in each of the 87 religious organizations of the area, 57 of which serve the Puerto Rican population,[3] were attended on one or more occasions by the investigator and two research assistants.[4] Systematic observations were made of attendance, ritual, themes of sermons and testimonials, and spontaneous expressions of beliefs and attitudes. The pastors of each group were interviewed following a standardized but open-ended interview schedule dealing with organization, affiliation, membership, programs, religious beliefs, pastoral counselling roles, and attitudes toward social and mental health problems and programs. Second, two area surveys were made of 1% probability samples of the households of the area to obtain information on the distribution of religious affiliations, frequency of church attendance, and related demographic and social variables among a representative sample of the population (N=398). Third, a brief interview covering basic demographic and social variables and the Cornell Medical Index (CMI)[5] were admin-

---

[3] Hereinafter when I mention numbers in samples, characteristics of the population, or numbers of churches, I am referring, unless otherwise specified, only to the Puerto Ricans in the samples, or in the population, or to the Puerto Rican churches only.

[4] My thanks to Garrett Green, Ph.D. and Raphael Ruiz, B.D., then of Union Theological Seminary, for their invaluable assistance in observing, recording, and interviewing during this phase of the research. Thanks also to Susan Deutsch, Ruth Dominguez, Theodora Garris, and others who helped with the survey interviewing.

[5] The Cornell Medical Index (CMI) is a health questionnaire containing 195 "yes-no" items organized in sub-scales covering symptoms in eight organ systems (eyes and ears, respiratory, cardiovascular, digestive, musculoskeletal, skin, nervous system, urogenital), three areas of general medical concern (fatigue, general health, miscellaneous diseases), one on habits (drinking, smoking, sleep, etc.) and six categories of mood and feeling state (inadequacy, depression, anxiety, sensitivity,

istered to the total congregations of two Pentecostal churches and to one person in every fourth household on a nearby block. These samples included 80 Pentecostals (27 males and 53 females) and 62 Roman Catholics (16 males and 46 females). Finally, an extensive interview and the CMI were administered to (1) a Pentecostal sample drawn randomly from the membership lists of three Pentecostal churches (11 males, 17 females), (2) a random sample of the population, from which a Roman Catholic control group has been sub-sampled (10 males, 22 females), and (3) a consecutive sample of new admissions to an outpatient mental health clinic serving the same population (21 males, 35 females). Data from Puerto Rican Catholics and Pentecostals in all samples have been combined for analysis on those variables which are comparable in all studies. All comparisons of the Pentecostal and Catholic samples have been controlled for sex, age, and frequency of church attendance. However, due to the limitations of numbers and the complexity of the data, results of comparisons are reported only for the total samples, unless the results differed in the controlled tests.

RELIGIOUS ALTERNATIVES AMONG PUERTO RICANS IN NEW YORK

Puerto Rico is historically a Roman Catholic country and the great majority (74%) of the Puerto Ricans in the study area are practicing Catholics (Table 1). Protestantism was represented in Puerto Rico prior to the annexation to the United States in 1898 by only a few Episcopalian churches serving the needs of English settlers and a few dissenting religious movements (LaRuffa 1971: 84). Soon, thereafter, Presbyterian, Congregationalist, Methodist, and Baptist missions were established in different parts of the island to be followed by diverse Protestant denominational and sectarian groups. The Pentecostal movement, introduced into Puerto Rico in approximately 1916, has had the greatest success there. Today the various Pentecostal organizations claim the largest proportion of churches and the greatest membership of all Protestant denominations both in Puerto Rico (LaRuffa 1971: 84) and in New York, where they have a greater total membership than all other Protestant denominations combined (Protestant Council of Churches 1960; Table 1). Thirty-eight of the 57 Spanish-speaking churches in the study area are Pentecostal groups. The two largest churches are Roman Catholic. Six are affiliated with major Protestant denominations (Protestant Episcopal Church in America,

anger, tension). It is designed for standardized scoring of levels of emotional disturbance on a four-point scale from not significant to severe, using total number of "yes" responses and critical scoring levels (Brodman, et al. 1949).

TABLE 1. Distribution of Religious Affiliations of the
Puerto Rican Population

	N Males	Percent Males	Females N	Females Percent	Total N	Total Percent
Religious Affiliation						
Roman Catholic	87	69.6	218	75.5	305	73.7
Major Protestant	7	5.6	9	3.1	16	3.8
Pentecostal	10	8.0	18	6.2	28	6.8
Other Sectarian	4	3.2	13	4.5	17	4.1
None *	17	13.6	31	10.7	48	11.6
	125	100.0	289	100.0	414	100.0

* Individuals were asked to report their religious affiliation only after they had responded positively to the question "Do you attend church?" Therefore, the non-affiliated in this breakdown includes individuals who might have reported a religious preference had the more usual question, "What is your religion?", been asked.

United Presbyterian Church in the U.S.A., United Church of Christ, and The American Baptist Convention). There are, in addition, three miscellaneous sectarian groups (Seventh Day Adventists, Jehovah's Witnesses, and an unaffiliated congregation calling itself "United Church"), and a number of Spiritist centers, described elsewhere (Garrison 1972).

Table 1 shows the distribution of religious affiliations of the Puerto Rican population of the study area. The data given in Table 1 indicate that approximately 7% of the Puerto Rican population is affiliated with Pentecostal churches, another 4% each with major Protestant denominations and with other sectarian groups. This must be taken as a very rough approximation and, most likely, an under-representation of the true proportions of Protestants, generally, and Pentecostals, specifically, because of the difficulties of identifying these affiliations in survey research.[6]

Pentecostalism among the Puerto Ricans represents the statistically dominant Protestant denomination, rather than a sectarian minority dissent against the major Protestant denominations of the mainland.

[6] In the area surveys, where interviewers were unfamiliar with Pentecostalism, results showed 4.8% and 7.7% of the population affiliated with Pentecostalism. In the block survey and in the intensive sample, where interviewers were familiar with Pentecostalism, results obtained indicated 15% and 21% Pentecostal, respectively. There were very few refusals in any of these samples and the higher percentages cannot be explained as a higher Pentecostal response rate to sympathetic interviewers. We suspect a tendency on the part of some of the less conscientious interviewers to assume Roman Catholic affiliations for Puerto Rican interviewees. Our best conservative guess is that approximately 12% of the New York Puerto Rican population is now affiliated with Pentecostalism.

It is, nonetheless, a minority dissenting religious group vis-à-vis the dominant Roman Catholic Church. This may or may not influence the character of Pentecostalism and its adherents among Puerto Ricans, but it is a difference which should be kept in mind in generalizing from Puerto Rican Pentecostals to other Pentecostals or in considering the sectarian adaptation more generally.

A brief overview of the organization and range of services offered by the variety of churches in the study area provides some idea of the appeal of Pentecostalism. The two Catholic parishes provide in both Spanish and English the usual range of Catholic religious services (masses, confessions, baptisms, devotions, religious instruction), church societies (Holy Names, Mothers' Club, League of the Sacred Heart, Daughters of Mary, etc.), Catholic Charities (family counselling, child guidance, aid to unwed mothers, etc.), and youth recreational programs. They each sponsor a parochial school and a number of secular programs designed to meet the needs of the low-income population. These programs include adult education with particular emphasis upon English language instruction, Headstart, "Summer in the City" block recreation programs, karate and judo classes, Alcoholics Anonymous groups, and many more. Religious services in the Catholic churches, although now in the vernacular, are relatively formal and liturgical. The "community" of members consists of all baptized Catholics living in the parish. However, the active membership (those who regularly attend masses on Sundays) was estimated at 6,000 and 8,000, with an additional 4,000 to 6,000 who attend "once in a while." Only a small proportion of the membership belongs to any of the religious societies or participates in the secular activities of the church. Approximately 65 to 75 percent of the active membership in each church is Spanish-speaking, but the total membership reflects the ethnic diversity and general socioeconomic level of the neighborhood as a whole. The only racially and ethnically integrated churches of the study area are the two Catholic churches, the Episcopalian church and the Jehovah's Witnesses.

The major Protestant churches among the Puerto Ricans take the form of the "historical church" (Kincheloe 1928), emphasizing the Sunday Service, Sunday School classes, social activities of the church societies, and one mid-week service. They are relatively inactive in secular activities. Membership in these churches ranges from 90 to 420 members and the membership has higher average values on all socioeconomic indices than the general population.

"Pentecostal" refers only to the recognition of the "Baptism of the

Holy Spirit" or the "gift of speaking in tongues" [7] and the central place of this gift in worship. The churches which are here classified as Pentecostal are known by almost as many names as there are churches and the members refer to themselves interchangeably as *Pentecostales, Protestantes, Evangelicos,* or just *Cristianos.* While they are remarkably homogenous in beliefs and practices and are all united by a complexity of formal and informal ties, they do not constitute a single denomination in any doctrinal or organizational sense, other than the sense of identity among all those who emphasize this gift in their worship. Fifteen, or 39%, of the 38 groups are affiliated with large Pentecostal councils, such as Assemblies of God, The Church of God (Cleveland, Tennessee), or, the exclusively Puerto Rican, Assembly of Christian Churches. Another 7, or 18%, are affiliated with small councils of three to thirty member churches. Sixteen, or 42%, are totally independent of any formal council affiliation. Regardless of council affiliations, they are all united by cross-cutting associations of church societies, common participation in such organizations as the Full Gospel Business Men's Fellowship, the New York Bible Society, a limited number of Bible Institutes where all of the ministers and many of the laity receive training, a local ministerial association, mass evangelistic campaigns with travelling evangelists, Pentecostal sponsored social programs (Teen Challenge and two locally sponsored programs for the rehabilitation of "drug addicts, prostitutes, and other outcasts of society"). Beyond these formal organizational ties, there are the informal relationships of "mother" and "daughter" or "sister" churches, reciprocal visiting patterns among churches, and reciprocal services, such as use of the baptismal fount, buses, or other facilities of the largest church by smaller churches all over the City and the contributions of the smaller churches to the social programs of the

---

[7] Belief in the "Baptism of the Holy Spirit" and the "gift of speaking in unknown tongues" is based primarily upon an account in Acts 1 and 2. Jesus had charged his disciples:

> . . . not to depart from Jerusalem, but to wait for the promise of the Father . . . for John baptized with water, but before many days you should be baptized with the Holy Spirit [Acts 1:4–5]. . . . When the day of Pentecost had come, they were all together in one place, And suddenly a sound came from heaven like the rush of a mighty wind, and it filled all the house where they were sitting. And there appeared to them tongues as of fire, distributed and resting on each of them. And they were filled with the Holy Spirit and began to speak in other tongues, as the Spirit gave them utterance [Acts 2:2–4].

The phenomenon objectively observed consists of the utterance of an unintelligible vocalization patterned similarly to normal speech but of no known language, usually called glossalalia (see Goodman 1969, and this volume). It is also believed that the Spirit can cause utterance in known languages which the speaker has never learned, but this is rare and almost undocumented.

larger ones. Above all, there is a sense of identification with a much larger and nebulous entity sometimes called "the Pentecostal Faith." In general, although they are Biblical literalists, perfectionists, and revivalistic in the Wesleyan, then Holiness, traditions, they are relatively unconcerned with issues of doctrine or correct interpretation of the Bible. There are only two schisms among them.[8] This contrasts strongly with the other 15 non-Puerto Rican "Pentecostal" churches of the area, in which the 15 congregations are divided among at least 12 doctrinal schisms. In this respect the Puerto Rican Pentecostals are less "sectarian" than many other Pentecostal groups. They are all firm believers in the blessings of salvation and sanctification, through which the individual is freed of sin and his life is completely changed, but they are relatively unconcerned about whether these are discrete or simultaneous events. Speaking in tongues is the evidence for all the blessings, but one can be saved and sanctified without receiving this gift. They vary somewhat in their emphasis on the Second Coming, but in general they are only mildly pre-millenarian in comparison with other groups such as the Seventh Day Adventists.

Activities in the Pentecostal churches are predominantly religious with few organized social or secular programs. Exceptions include the social programs mentioned above and extensive activities of the ministers as individuals in providing material, as well as spiritual, assistance to individuals in times of need. Services are usually held six, and sometimes seven, nights a week and Sunday morning. The major service is the Sunday evening Evangelistic Service. Week-night services are prayer meetings in the church or in homes, visits to other churches, or worship services conducted by the societies of the church. The belief system emphasizes a lay ministry and services are informal and have a high degree of spontaneous lay participation as "the Spirit moves them." Membership ranges from one with a membership of 700 families to one with a membership of 7 individuals. The mean number of members, not including the largest church, is 37. The membership of each church is divided into sex and age graded societies to the extent that the size of the congregation will permit such subdivision. Most of them have societies for children, young people, men, and women. Some have the young people's society divided by sex and others have separate societies for young adults (ages 20–35). A few have missionary societies which visit homes of the troubled upon request. All members belong to one of the societies. The typical "good

[8] One point of doctrinal dispute is related to the interpretation of the Trinity, with a minority of one church baptizing in the name of "Jesus Only," the epithet by which the other groups distinguish it. The other is related to the interpretation of the Sabbath, with two groups celebrating the Sabbath on Saturday.

member" attends church two to four times a week. Ninety percent of those interviewed reported that they attend at least once a week; 81% said they attend more than once a week. The "community" of the Pentecostal church consists of a small intimate group of congregants and a much wider unbounded network of Pentecostal associates.

SEX AND AGE DISTRIBUTION OF THE CATHOLIC AND PENTECOSTAL MEMBERSHIP

The active membership and regular attendance in all of the churches of the area are approximately two-thirds female and one-third male by pastors' reports and observations. In this respect the Catholic and Pentecostal churches do not differ from each other or from other formal voluntary associations among the Puerto Ricans, whether religious, civic or social, where a similar sex-ratio was observed.

The age distribution of the practicing Catholic population (those who attend church at least once a year) differs little from the age distribution of the general Puerto Rican population as reported in the 1960 Census, with the exception that there is a slight non-significant over-representation of 25–34 years-olds in the Catholic sample. On the other hand, the age distribution of the membership in most of the Pentecostal churches as reported by the ministers and that of the Pentecostal samples studied, forms a bimodal curve, with one peak in the years 15–19, a sharp drop thereafter, and another peak beginning with the 35–39 year-old category. Approximately 25% of the total membership reported by the 38 ministers fell in the 16–24 year-old age group, another 25% fell between the ages of 25 and 39, and approximately 50% fell in the over-40 age categories. Table 2 shows graphs of the age distribution of the Catholic and Pentecostal samples superimposed on a histogram of the Puerto Rican population reported in the 1960 U.S. Census.

The discontinuity in age distribution of the Pentecostal membership suggests that there must be discontinuity in individual membership. The young people in the churches, or at least a large proportion of them, apparently leave the church as they become young adults. The older group must then be either returned members or new converts. Examination of the distribution of age by age at conversion (Table 3) of the Pentecostal intensive sample sheds some light on this. The five 16–24 year-olds in this sample are all second generation in the faith, whereas there are only three second generation Pentecostals in the much broader span of years over 24. Given that Pentecostalism itself is only a little over 50 years old among Puerto Ricans, it is surprising to find three second generation Pentecostals over 40 years

TABLE 2. AGE DISTRIBUTION OF CATHOLIC AND PENTECOSTAL SAMPLES COMPARED WITH TOTAL PUERTO RICAN POPULATION AS REPORTED IN U.S. CENSUS, 1960

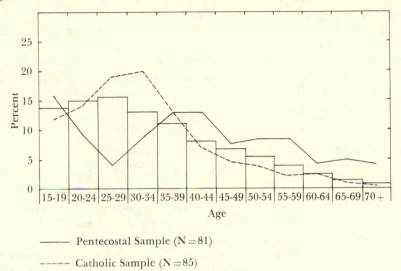

——— Pentecostal Sample (N=81)

----- Catholic Sample (N=85)

old in this small sample. The absence of second generation Pentecostals in the age group 25–40 does suggest further, however, that a good proportion of the second generation leave the church on achieving adulthood. Concern over this was also expressed by several of the ministers during interviews. One, for example, had organized an affiliation of the Young People's Societies of seven small churches "so that they can find good Christian husbands or wives and they don't have to go out of the church." One of the five 16–24 year olds also said he was planning "to start life anew as a Catholic upon marriage" to his Catholic girlfriend. When we look at age at conversion alone, however (Table 3), it appears that there is a continuous

TABLE 3. AGE BY AGE AT CONVERSION (PENTECOSTAL INTENSIVE SAMPLE ONLY)

Age	Second Generation in Pentecostalism	Converts			
		Age at Conversion			
		16-24	25-40	41 & Over	Total
16-24	5	—	—	—	5
25-40	0	5	3	—	8
41 & Over	3	2	6	5	16
	8	7	9	5	29

distribution across the age groups with, in fact, the greatest number of conversions in the age group 25–40, which includes the most under-represented categories in the church population. There is also a considerable number of conversions in the 16–24 age range. This suggests that there is a constant recruitment from all age groups and also a constant falling away of members recruited at all ages so that the larger proportion of older persons in the Pentecostal congregations is explained not by a disproportionate recruitment from the older age groups, but by continuation of membership in the church by individuals recruited at all ages.

Socioeconomic Status, Mobility, and Aspirations

Most writers (Boisen 1939, 1955; Kaplan 1965; Lanternari 1963; Pope 1942; Wood 1965; and others) have emphasized the low socio-economic status of sectarians and the special needs of the lower class which must be served by these religions. Other writers (Gerlach and Hine 1966) have insisted on recognition of the fact that there are some sects which have drawn their membership primarily from the middle class and that even the so-called lower-class religious movements, like Pentecostalism, have their middle-class adherents. Regardless of the exceptions, the majority of Pentecostals are drawn from the lower and lower-middle socioeconomic strata. The appeal to the economically disadvantaged, however, cannot alone explain the attraction of sectarian religion, since sectarians are a minority even within the lower socioeconomic strata.

The more important question is whether sectarian membership serves to perpetuate and reinforce lower class status or whether it provides alternatives for the member which facilitate upward mobility. Sectarian verbalizations such as "We separate ourselves from the things of the world," and "The poor shall be rewarded in Heaven," have led Yinger (1957, 1963), Kaplan (1965), and others to the conclusion that sectarians do not attempt to compete socioeconomically in this life but accept a subordinate status and await rewards in an afterlife. Others, such as Boisen (1939, 1955) and particularly Johnson (1963), have argued that sectarian membership serves to alleviate the stresses of lower socioeconomic status, to socialize members in the dominant values of the society (particularly the frugality, saving, discipline, and aspirations associated with the "Protestant Ethic") and, thereby, to pave the way for upward socioeconomic mobility.

It was our impression throughout the fieldwork that the Pentecostal people were more frugal, more industrious, and possibly more social striving and upwardly mobile than the general population. These impressions, based largely upon observations of the ministers and the young people in the church, and on testimonials heard during services, have been supported only in part by the statistical data collected. Puerto Rican Pentecostals locate employment and housing by word of mouth through the Pentecostal grapevine, employment opportunities are announced from the lectern during services, and testimonials to God's help in finding employment, promotions, procurement of a house or automobile and other socioeconomic gains are regularly heard in the Pentecostal services. A content analysis of the testimonals recorded during attendance at the 38 churches revealed that testimonials of this type are second in frequency only to testimonials for healing. Testimonials to the change in life brought about by conversion often contain socioeconomic elements as well as social and spiritual factors. Six of the 17 complete conversion stories collected placed special emphasis upon changes brought about in their economic situation. The Puerto Rican Pentecostals also carry identification cards showing that they are members of the church. These they say help them to get jobs or secure credit "because people know that Christians are reliable and good workers." Clearly, not all of the "material" things of this life are disparaged by the Pentecostals.

Based on the literature and these impressions, we hypothesized that: (1) the Pentecostal groups draw their membership in large part from the lowest socioeconomic stratum and from those in acute economic distress; (2) membership in the sect serves to facilitate social striving through changes in value orientation and through the expanded resources available to the individual through the Pentecostal network; and (3) members tend to leave the church as their socioeconomic conditions improve. These hypotheses cannot be fully tested without longitudinal studies or, at least, cross-sectional studies of Pentecostals before and after conversion and after separation from the church. The present study provides only a partial test and suggestions for further research.

The Pentecostal and Catholic samples were compared on education, occupation, family income, change in earnings over the past three years, and employment histories coded in several ways to reflect economic stability or instability and upward or downward mobility. No significant differences were found between the two groups on any socioeconomic status or mobility variable. Both groups, men and women, had a mean number of years of schooling completed in the 7 to 8 year range. There are no differences in the proportions unemployed, receiving welfare or other benefits, or in different status occupations. The majority of both samples, both sexes, are employed in the unskilled, semi-skilled, or skilled labor occupations. The highest status occupations represented in either group were, for the males, proprietor of a small business, and for the females, clerical work. Distributions of total family income for the two groups are nearly identical with the median falling in the $80–95 per week category. All but a few individuals (9) from both groups had been constantly employed throughout their employment histories in one or more jobs all on the same level in the Hollingshead (1957) occupational ranking scale. The evidence is overwhelming that the Pentecostals are not drawn exclusively from the lowest socioeconomic stratum of this generally disadvantaged community, or, if so, the sect does not serve to perpetuate that status. The Pentecostal group does not show any greater contemporary or chronic economic distress than their Catholic counterparts.

Closer examination of the occupational histories of the males interviewed in depth reveals that three of the eleven Pentecostals but none of the Catholics had at some time established a business of his own which had subsequently failed. At least one converted to Pentecostalism explicitly during the aftermath of this economic crisis. Among the 14 female Pentecostal converts interviewed in depth, the family economic histories of six showed downward mobility or financial ups and downs. There is some evidence, therefore, that the appeal of Pentecostalism among economically disadvantaged Puerto Ricans is to be found more among those who are upwardly aspirant but have suffered sharp reverses or economic crises, as suggested by Boisen (1955), than among those suffering chronic economic hardship as was the case with the Free Will Baptists studied by Kaplan (1965).

To test for changes in economic conditions over time in the sect, the small number of Pentecostal converts in the intensive sample was divided on years in the church (0–10 and 11 or more) and compared. Table 4 shows a comparison of occupations of short and long-term

TABLE 4. OCCUPATIONAL STATUS BY YEARS IN THE CHURCH (CONVERTS ONLY)

	Years in the Church		
Occupation	*0–10*	*11 or More*	*Total*
Small proprietor, clerical or sales	–	3	3
Skilled manual	–	1	1
Semi-skilled	–	4	4
Unskilled	2	2	4
Unemployed or on welfare	3	–	3
Housewife, student, retired, or disabled	2	4	6
	7	14	21

TABLE 5. SOCIOECONOMIC MOBILITY BY YEARS IN THE CHURCH (CONVERTS ONLY)

Family Employment or Economic History Shows:	Years in the Church 0–10	11 or More	Total
Upward mobility	–	4	4
Stability	2	6	8
Downward mobility	1	1	2
Ups and downs	4	3	7
	7	14	21

members. The differences have not been tested for statistical significance with this small number and the arbitrary division of ten years more or less, but a notable trend toward higher occupational status and upward mobility among the long-term members is evidenced. All of those in the higher ranking occupations are long-term members, while all of the short-term members are unemployed or are employed in unskilled occupations. Similarly, all of the upwardly mobile in the sample are long-term members and the majority of recent converts have economic histories which show reverses and recoveries (Table 5).

Socioeconomic status and achieved mobility are exacting measures of socioeconomic striving. Therefore, a socioeconomic mobility scale was developed from a number of items included in the interview schedule to reflect not only socioeconomic gains but aspirations as well.[9] The results of comparison of the individual indices and the scale score between the Pentecostals and Catholics by sex shows no differences whatsoever between the Pentecostal and Catholic men, but significant differences between women of the two samples. The Catholic women scored consistently higher than the Pentecostal women on all items,

---

[9] Indices included in the socioeconomic mobility and aspirations scale were: (1a) *Economic mobility*. (For all respondence except unemployed, married females:) Respondent's job history shows upward mobility either in terms of Hollingshead's occupational ranking scale or salary increase. (1b) Economic mobility of spouse. (For unemployed, married females only:) Husband's job history shows upward mobility as defined in 1a. (2) *Job aspirations*. Respondent wants a "better" job, or if unemployed, wants to return to work. (3) *Incentive*. Respondent is doing something at the present time to get a "better job," or, if unemployed, to get a job. (4) *Aspirations for children*. Aspirations for children include "good job," "profession," "money," "good education." (5) *Residential aspirations*. Respondent wants to move to a "better neighborhood" or one that is known to have higher socioeconomic status. (6) *Educational improvement*. Respondent has returned to school to complete regular school, learn English or a vocation since originally leaving school. Each index was scored No = 0 or Yes = 1. All indices on this scale are strongly and significantly correlated with the total scale score (.388 to .613), with exception of 1a (Economic mobility) and 5 (Residential aspirations), which are less strongly correlated (.340 and .245, respectively).

these differences being statistically significant at the .05 level for economic mobility of the spouse and for the total scale score.

It would appear from this evidence that, while Pentecostal males are as mobile and upwardly aspirant as their Catholic counterparts, they have had more setbacks, and that the females, who are dependent upon the economic stability and success of their husbands for their own economic security, are not. Husbands of Pentecostal women interviewed who were not also active members of the church were overwhelmingly (90%) rated either nonmobile or downwardly mobile. For females with children, dependent upon nonmobile husbands, Pentecostalism may serve to devalue the present life, teach forbearance, and offer rewards projected into an afterlife, as has been suggested for sectarians more generally. It does not appear, however, to be the case generally for males or for females where both spouses are active members of the church.

Facility in English, another variable related to socioeconomic status and aspirations among the Puerto Ricans, reflects a similar sex and age difference. There were no differences between the Pentecostal and Catholic males in facility in English and a considerably larger proportion of the Pentecostals of both sexes under 30 (67%) had an adequate or better command of English than the Catholics of the same age group (46%). Among the females over 30, however, a significantly smaller proportion of the Pentecostals had an adequate command of English.

If the first two hypotheses proposed above were true, i.e. if the sect draws the very disadvantaged or acutely distressed and their circumstances improve over time in the church, differences between short- and long-term members would average out any initial differences between the Pentecostal convert population and the population from which they were drawn. This is consistent with the evidence. We have found at least a strong suggestion of differing socioeconomic conditions among short- and long-term members, but no differences whatsoever in the current conditions of the Pentecostals and Catholics. Likewise, if the third hypothesis is true (that members leave the church as their socioeconomic circumstances improve), then differences between Pentecostals who stay in the church and those who leave the church would average out differences which might otherwise be found between short- and long-term members. In other words, the evidence for change in the socioeconomic conditions of Pentecostals after conversion might be much stronger if we had longitudinal measures of the experience of individuals, including those who had left the church. We have no way of testing the third hypothesis with the present data. The data are consistent with the hypotheses, but they remain neither proven nor disproven. What has been shown quite conclusively, however, is that there are no great differences between active Pentecostals and Catholics drawn from the same low-income neighborhood on socio-economic variables. The Puerto Rican Pentecostals are *not* the most deprived segment of this generally disadvantaged population. While chronic, irrevocable economic hardship may characterize a few of the members, particularly women, as a group they show no greater chronic economic disadvantage than Catholics in the same community. The explanation for their having chosen the minority religion must, therefore, be sought in economic crisis, in socioeconomic striving, or in other factors.

MIGRATION AND CHURCH PARTICIPATION

Several studies (Holt 1940; Curry 1968; Willems 1967) have shown a relationship between migration from rural to urban areas and sectarian membership. In a study of some of the same churches included in this study, Poblete and O'Dea (1960) hypothesized that the formation of sects among Puerto Rican migrants in New York is a response to anomie resulting from migration and, further, that the sect represents a search for a way out of that condition and is therefore an attempt to redevelop the community in the new urban situation. Poblete and O'Dea made no attempt to measure variables of migration or "anomie" among Pentecostals and non-Pentecostals. Instead they supported their hypothesis with the observed presence of three conditions in the sects which constitute sociological criteria of "community," i.e. "we-feeling," "role feeling," and "feelings of dependency."

This is a logical hypothesis with considerable support in the literature and in the reports of ministers. Orientation of the newcomer to the city was the third ranking problem area in the pastoral counselling role as reported by the 38 ministers. Only domestic conflicts and destitution, of 13 problem areas, were allocated more time. They spoke often of meeting new arrivals at the airport, helping them locate housing and employment, and generally orienting them to the city and its essential services.

This hypothesis was supported in an exploratory analysis of the data from the block sample. It was found that among those who had migrated to the city as adults and had been in the city less than 10 years (N = 14) 50% were sectarian, whereas only 13% of those who had been in the city more than 10 years (N = 15) were sectarian. This difference is statistically significant at the .01 level despite the small numbers and leads to the conclusion that sectarianism does, in fact, flourish among the recent migrant population, but that these recent migrants do not remain in the church into the second decade after migration.

As a further test of this hypothesis we put forth the following proposition: if sectarianism is a response to the disorganization incumbent upon migration, recent migrants will be disproportionately represented in the Pentecostal churches. Comparison of the Catholic and Pentecostal samples, however, did not reflect any disproportionate representation of recent migrants in the Pentecostal group. This Pentecostal sample shows a fairly even distribution over years in New York and does not differ from the Catholic sample in this regard. Analysis of years in New York at the time of conversion also failed to reveal a relationship between recent migration and conversion. Of the 29 individuals interviewed intensively, 8 were second generation in the faith, 6 converted to Pentecostalism while in Puerto Rico (all in rural rather than urban areas), and of the 15 who converted in New York, only three converted before they had been in the city 10 years. This sample, drawn as it is from the congregations of churches rather than from the general population as with the block sample, represents disproportionately the continuing membership of the church and under-represents the transient membership of the Pentecostal churches. Therefore, if the evidence from both samples is accurate, Pentecostalism does serve recent migrants disproportionately, but those who convert as recent migrants are only proportionately represented among those who become permanent members of the church. This is consistent with the evidence from the block sample that Pentecostals were under-represented among those who had been in the city more than 10 years compared with the more recent migrants.

Examination of frequency of church attendance in the Catholic sample, however, provides evidence refuting the idea that support of the recent migrant is a function specific to the sect and not one more generally shared by the churches, whether denominational or sectarian. Catholics in the city less than 10 years show a significantly greater rate of church attendance than those who have been in the city more than 10 years. It is probable that the functions for recent migrants of church participation observed by the above writers for sectarian groups are functions of churches more generally and they cannot be evoked to explain the choice of one religious group over another.

FAMILY AND SOCIAL DISORGANIZATION

Poblete and O'Dea (1960) did not attribute the growth of sects directly to migration, but to the conditions of disruption, isolation and *anomie* which follow upon migration. Sectarians generally have been seen in the literature of the sociology of religion as "alienated, isolated, withdrawn" and even "hostile to the larger society" (Yinger 1957). Wood (1965) asserted that Pentecostal people typically live in conditions of deprivation or disruption, noting among other things, an excessive number of broken homes among the small congregation of his rural Church of God, but he did not report the comparable rate among his control group. There are a number of concrete measurable conditions of life which should differ between Pentecostals and Catholics of the same socioeconomic level if these assertions are, in fact, accurate. First, there is family disorganization. Secondly, there is "isolation" or disruption of interpersonal relationships with others as well as the family. Finally, there is disengagement from the institutions of the larger society. We will consider each of these factors in turn.

Family Organization

The ideal Puerto Rican family, as described by Padilla (1958: 101),

. . . consists of a father, a mother, and their unmarried children who all live together in the same household. This is the basic unit, the immediate or nuclear family. The father is supposed to impart respect to the children and to provide for the family; the mother, to care for the children and her husband and to maintain the standards of respect and good behavior set up by the father. Ideally, their home will be near those of close relatives, members of the "great family," including uncles, aunts, sisters, married children, grandchildren, and so on, and they will get along well with each other. All these relatives are supposed to help one another and to share in many common activities as members of the extended family.

Comparison of the Pentecostal and Catholic samples on marital status characteristics and household composition (Table 6) reveals greater contemporary disorganization of the nuclear family among the Catholics. A significantly greater proportion of the Catholics (26.2%) than the Pentecostals (5.4%) were separated, widowed, or divorced. Broken homes (truncated families) among the Catholics exceed the Pentecostals by 22% and fewer Catholics live in either nuclear or extended family households.

Examination of marital histories, however, indicates no differences in the two samples on indices of marital stability in the past. Approximately 75% of the females and 60% of the males in both samples were living with the spouse of their first marriage. There are no significant differences in the two samples for either sex on the number of previous

TABLE 6. HOUSEHOLD COMPOSITION (BLOCK AND INTENSIVE SAMPLES)

	Pentecostals		Catholics		Total	
	N	Percent	N	Percent	N	Percent
Household Composition						
Nuclear family (husband, wife, and own or other minor children only)	20	57.1	39	48.7	59	51.3
Truncated family (an incomplete nuclear family consisting of one parent and children)	2	5.7	22	27.5	24	20.9
Extended family (more than one nuclear family or parts of several related nuclear families)	10	28.6	14	17.5	24	20.9
Non-family arrangements (boarders, roommates, single individual households)	3	8.6	5	6.2	8	7.0
	35	100.0	80	100.0	115	100.0

$X^2 = 7.490$, 3 d.f., significant at the .058 level.

legal or consensual unions. This suggests that Pentecostals are drawn from the same population as the Catholics with respect to nuclear family organization but that Pentecostalism promotes stability of the nuclear family. This finding supports the impression of Hine (1969: 216) that "when both husband and wife participate actively in the 'tongues movement' family life tends to be more than normally well-integrated." The possibility must, however, be considered that dissolution of the nuclear family bond after conversion might lead to expulsion or voluntary withdrawal from the sect leaving a spuriously low representation of disorganized nuclear families in the core membership.

Comparison of extended family ties beyond the household indicates that the Pentecostal extended family is less inclusive and less extensive than the Catholic, but no less intense in its frequency of interaction, and that the paternal authority structure may be more intact among the Pentecostals. The majority of both samples (78% of the Catholics and 66% of the Pentecostals) had relatives living in other households in the Bronx with whom they were in regular contact. The Pentecostals, however, named fewer relatives living in the Bronx, in New York more generally, or in Puerto Rico. They were in frequent contact (once a month or more) with far fewer siblings and fewer relatives in general (mean 3.1 compared with 8.9 for the Catholics). They are more likely to have relatives with whom they maintain no contact. Only 7.4% of the Pentecostals, compared with 28.1% of the Catholics, live in extended family groups such as Padilla described as the "great family." Nonetheless, the average total frequency of seeing relatives and the mean frequency of seeing those relatives with whom contact was maintained is equal to that of the Catholics. The Pentecostal adult males and females interviewed had significantly more frequent contact with their fathers than their Catholic counterparts.

This difference in the extent, if not the intensity, of family ties between the Pentecostals and Catholics suggests several possibilities: (1) Pentecostals are drawn from a population in which extended family ties have been weakened, (2) affiliation with Pentecostalism in a family which has traditionally been Catholic weakens family ties, or (3) since the *ambience* in the Pentecostal church is that of the extended family—members call each other "brother" and "sister" and the congregation concerns itself with the total life and welfare of the individual—it may represent a functional alternative and substitute for extended family ties, which therefore fall into disuse with sect participation. Further research is required to test these alternative hypotheses, but it is probable that all three factors operate.

The hypothesis that there is greater family disorganization among Pentecostals is not supported by the South Bronx data; differences found suggest, to the contrary, that Pentecostals have a lower rate of nuclear family disorganization, stronger patrilineal ties, and a tight-knit, although restricted, extended family structure.

Interpersonal Relations

Wood (1965) found "feelings of insecurity in interpersonal relations" to be the predominant characteristic distinguishing the Southern Pentecostals studied from the Baptist control group on Rorschach responses. He hypothesized, in part, that: (1) Pentecostal people have an uncommon degree of uncertainty concerning interpersonal relationships; (2) they have an emotional organization which makes possible the establishing of positive and satisfying interpersonal relations and a strong drive to feel close fellowship with others, but they are uncertain that these interpersonal involvements will be satisfactory; (3) they are attracted to Pentecostalism because it provides a secure and satisfying social environment with close, positive interpersonal relationships; and (4) Pentecostalism provides patterns of behavior leading to personality integration, interpersonal relatedness, and certainty. Plog, in an unpublished study cited by Hine (1969), using the California Personality Inventory, also found that Pentecostals were weak in interpersonal relationships but that most reported improvement in their ability to get along with others after the tongues experience.

Observations, experience in interviewing, and the data from this study lend further support to the findings of the Wood and Plog studies. Pentecostal subjects often responded when asked directly about their friends that they had "no friends except Jesus Christ" or "only the brothers and sisters of the church." However, when we proceeded to ask them, for example, about neighbors or coworkers that they "knew well" or "knew well enough to visit with in their homes or to do things together," [10] they reported as many and as intense affective relationships as did subjects in the Catholic sample. The Pentecostals had as many friends in all categories as did the Catholics and, in addition, a much larger number of friends known through the church. The same phenomenon occurred when we inquired about who they might tell their troubles to or about helping relationships. They would say that they took their troubles to Jesus or that Jesus was the only one they could count on for help, but the actual number of people they named as being in a relationship of confidence or in either a reciprocal or unilateral helping relationship with them was equal to or actually exceeded the numbers named by the Catholics.

One outstanding difference did appear between the two samples in the nature of friendship relationships. All of the Catholic males and 82% of the Catholic females participated in an informal group of friends of the same sex who meet on the street, in local establishments or in each other's homes for conversation or games. None of the Pentecostals, male or female, participated in such a group. Several of the males mentioned, as part of the change which had been brought about by conversion, their leaving one of these groups of associates from the street. This is probably a difference which results from membership in the intimate sectarian religious group, rather than from any deficit in the interpersonal relations of the Pentecostals prior to conversion.

Participation in the Institutions of the Larger Society

In order to test the assumption, which has never been subjected to systematic measurement or statistical test, that sectarians withdraw from participation in the institutions of the larger society, the two

---

[10] In the intensive interviews an attempt was made to elicit information on every habitual interaction pattern of the subject. Inquiry was made specifically into neighboring, friendships with coworkers, fellow hometowners, church friends, recreational interest friends, other friends and acquaintances, and informal groups. Two measures of intensity of the relationship were used. With neighbors, coworkers, church friends, and other individuals where there was a basis for contact other than the relationship between the two individuals, respondents were asked to identify those individuals that they "knew well enough to visit with them in their homes or to do things together outside" of the primary place of contact. All other relationships were coded as to the frequency of contact on a nine-point scale from $0 =$ never to $8 =$ once a day or more.

samples were compared on voluntary associational memberships, leisure time activities, use of medical facilities, attitudes toward education, and attitudes toward social and political action.

Lack of membership in unions and other formal voluntary associations is attributed to low-income populations generally (Lewis 1965 and others). In this study there were no significant differences in the rate of union membership in the two samples. Approximately 50% of the males and 20% of the females in each sample belonged to unions. However, only 9% of the male Pentecostals, compared with 30% of the male Catholics, and 11% of the female Pentecostals, compared with 23% of the Catholic females, belonged to any other civic, social, or political association. The secular associations to which the minority of the Catholics belong are hometown clubs, lodges, domino or other recreational clubs limited to males, and, very rarely, a political club. Apart from the dancing, drinking, and games of dominoes and cards, the church provides the same range of services and activities offered by the secular associations represented, e.g. a place to go any night of the week, people to socialize with, inexpensive recreation for the whole family in the form of excursions to the country or beach, mass evangelistic campaigns, visits to other churches, emergency aid in time of need, either financial or other, and advice and direction in political matters, as we will see below. The sectarian churches and the social clubs may well be functional equivalents. The Catholic churches also provide many social and recreational activities, but these are not confined to a small, intimate, and relatively continuous group as in the clubs and the Pentecostal churches. Both groups are actually very limited in their voluntary association memberships.

Similarly, both groups are very limited in the range of their recreational and leisure interests. For both, watching television is the major leisure activity. A significantly greater proportion of Catholics, however, had leisure interests outside of the home or church. These interests included, for the males, sports (particularly baseball), games (usually dominoes), and for both sexes, music, dancing, movies, visiting, and "just talking." With exception of the last two, these are all activities proscribed or largely disapproved by the Pentecostals. For the Pentecostals, Bible study was a frequent leisure activity, and church activities have replaced most of the other recreational pursuits.

The Pentecostal emphasis upon faith healing has led to the assumption that Pentecostals are antagonistic to medical institutions. Pentecostals continually give thanks to God for "being able to get up this morning," for "being able to be in the church today," and, first and foremost, for cure or correction of any difficulty. There is substantial evidence from the present study, however, that this attribution to God of the source of the cure does not constitute an impediment to seeking medical help when needed and the Pentecostals do not differ from the Catholics in their actual use of medical facilities. The vast majority of the ministers interviewed assured us that they seek medical help, that "God heals through the doctor." There are no differences between the Pentecostal and Catholic samples in (1) the number of complaints on the CMI for which medical attention had not been sought, (2) the average length of time since the last visit to a doctor, or (3) the total number of medical visits in the preceding two years.

Some Pentecostal groups have expressed very negative attitudes toward education. All of the ministers in this study responded positively to the question "Do you encourage your members to get all the education they can?" Similarly, all of the members interviewed responded that they would want their child to finish school when asked: "If your child were offered a well-paying job before he had completed school, would you want him to take it or to finish his education?" The Puerto Rican Pentecostals clearly do not share the earlier sectarian hostility to education.

To test attitudes toward social and political action, a 20-item social activism scale related specifically to concrete conditions and programs of this neighborhood was developed for use in the intensive study.[11] There were no significant differences between the Pentecostals and the Catholics on the total scale score or on any item with exception of the three which used the words "strike" and "demonstration," on which the Pentecostals scored significantly lower. More Pentecostals than Catholics reported that they were registered to vote. They were consistently more positive about community workers, and the great

[11] The social activism scale contains items covering: (1) attitudes toward the community workers of the Poverty and Model Cities programs (whether they are needed, whether they would be used by the respondent, whether such a community worker should come to the church or maintain an office in the church); (2) voting (in local elections, in national elections, whether the person is registered); (3) working for a political candidate; (4) community meetings (attending one, or holding one in the church); (5) writing letters or signing petitions to officials, circulating a petition in the church; (6) tenants' councils (are they a good thing, would they join one); (7) rent strikes (are they ever justified, would they participate in one); (8) opinions about public housing and action proposed by some groups (more public housing wanted, would they participate in a demonstration on an issue of concern to them around housing, should the church be involved, what can be done to improve housing conditions in the neighborhood). These items were scored 0 = No for opposition or for no opinion where it was an opinion that was asked for, 1 = qualified for equivocal responses, 2 = Yes for the positive social activist response. Another question in the same series, but not included in the score, was "Do you ask your pastor for advice about what to do about community matters?"

majority would even circulate a petition in the church for redress of some secular ill. The Pentecostal women without exception, and many of the men, said they ask their minister for advice about what to do in community matters. The Pentecostals appear to be as active in working for social change in their community as the majority of their Catholic counterparts, with the exception that they do not approve of or participate in the more radical forms of political or social action, such as demonstrations or rent strikes.

The 38 ministers were also questioned at length regarding their pastoral counseling role, their use of social and welfare agencies, and the possibility of their collaboration with a neighborhood service center in the possible development of jointly sponsored social action programs. Thirty of the 38 ministers reported that they make referrals to various social agencies. Only five expressed no interest in cooperation in the development of new programs or expressed the opinion that the "spiritual" and the "material" should be kept separate. Nineteen made specific suggestions as to the types of programs they would like to undertake. The majority of the suggested programs involved action to improve facilities for children (play areas, recreation programs, etc.), prevention of juvenile delinquency (including drug abuse), public education regarding services available, or problems of inter-group communication.

There is little evidence from these comparisons of greater disengagement from the larger society among the Pentecostals than among the Catholics in this low-income population, with the minor exceptions of participation in secular voluntary associations and leisure time activities.

Yinger (1957) proposed a typology of sects based on their orientations to the larger society as (1) accepting, (2) aggressive, or (3) avoiding. He classified Pentecostal sects as "avoiding," describing this orientation as follows:

If one cannot accept society . . . or have hope of reforming it . . . , one can devalue the significance of this life, project one's hopes into the supernatural world, and meanwhile reduce one's problems by forming into a communion of like-minded fellows. . . . This is the most common sectarian protest. . . . It faces the hard facts of life for the lower classes. . . . (Yinger 1957: 152)

This does not do justice to the complexity of thinking of the Puerto Rican Pentecostals, and possibly not to that of other Pentecostal groups where the behavior behind the verbalizations has not been studied. Given the alternatives available to a member of the middle class, the sectarian adjustment might be "avoiding." Given the prevailing conditions in the Puerto Rican slum and the available alternatives, Pentecostalism appears to provide a means of access to the resources of the larger society as well as providing, through its own informal channels, the pooled resources of the Pentecostal network. It may provide greater opportunities for the member than those available to the general population from more fragmented and less personal sources. It was noted above that despite verbalizations which appear to disparage this worldly "material" goals, the Puerto Rican Pentecostals do not disparage economic gains. Similarly, verbalizations about the evils of this world and the imminence of the "Second Coming" do not mean that they have given up all hope of improving conditions in this life for themselves or their children, or that they renounce all secular action to accomplish worldly goals. They do not, in fact, "devalue the significance of this life." They are very concerned about the conditions of this life, particularly the evils and temptations that lead people from the way of Christ and threaten their salvation. They have also not given up hope of reforming society, or a part of it. They believe in radical individual change through conversion to Christ and gradual social change through the conversion of many individuals, but they do not believe in radical secular methods to bring about social change. Their purpose in recruiting converts is not simply a matter of wanting to save individual souls, but it is also an attempt to reform society. Unlike the Pentecostals studied by Gerlach (this volume), the Puerto Rican Pentecostals studied do search out the most marginal members of society for conversion, particularly those that concern them most—those that threaten their children—the addicts on the street.

When Pentecostals say that they "separate themselves from the world," they will also paraphrase this immediately to something like: "We don't drink, smoke, gamble, play around with women, or waste our time and money in idle pursuits like movies." Several of the more sophisticated Pentecostal ministers said, and we suggest, that what the Pentecostals mean is that they separate themselves from the vices and costly leisure pursuits characteristic of the lower-class slum to reallocate their resources to their self-improvement both materially and spiritually. The "world" from which they are separating themselves is the vice and disorder prevalent in the slum community from which they are drawn, not the larger society and its institutions.

Finally, returning to the larger hypothesis that sectarianism has a particular appeal for individuals living under conditions of social disorganization or anomie, we have found no evidence for greater disorganization among the Pentecostals than among the Catholics. In fact, Pentecostalism appears to promote social cohesion in the family and in the social circle, and to provide a means of integrating the individual in the larger society at the same time permitting him to reject the disorder in his environment. It would provide a relatively clear set of values and norms of behavior for the anomic and a "community" for the isolated or alienated. It is probable that it does have a particular appeal for those who perceive a need for the greater structure and order which the sect provides or for those to whom a well-structured system of beliefs and behavior is particularly compatible. However, since there is no greater disorganization among those who choose the sect than among those who do not in this population, it must be considered an active seeking after something more than the individual has available through other alternatives and not a resort for those who lack something common to others in the same population.

MENTAL HEALTH

LaBarre (1962) and others have suggested that the members and leaders of the more extreme sectarian groups show severe psychopathology, and that the religious subculture itself may be psychopathological. The popular pejorative "Holy Roller" suggests that the lay majority also believes there is "something wrong" with those who experience involuntary motor behavior in religious ecstasy. Kaplan (1965) considered the sentiments of the Free Will Baptists in Appalachia "more interfering than facilitating of postulated essential goals," although they "provide several adaptive retreat devices which may be quite functional in inhibiting even more severe social and psychological disintegration." Ribeiro (1962) found Brazilian Pentecostals to be naïve and poorly educated, but of sound mental health on psychiatric examination. Wood (1965) found them to lack an adequately structured value-attitude system and to be uncertain in their interpersonal relations but within the normal range of variation on Rorschach protocols. Hine (1969), reviewing the literature on pathology in tongues speakers, concluded that the explanation of glossolalia as pathology must be discarded and suggested, instead, that it be considered as one component in the generation of commitment to behavior and attitude changes associated with the movement. Wallace (1966) and others have suggested that sectarian membership constitutes a therapeutic process leading to "mazeway" reintegration and improved functioning. Frank (1961), Prince (1969), and others have attributed therapeutic effects to the conversion experience. The Pentecostals studied in depth all testify to a great change in their lives brought about by their acceptance of Christ. The majority talk of crises and miseries in their lives prior to salvation and describe a "calm," "contentment," "happiness," and a "new way of seeing the world" which followed upon this conversion. Twelve of seventeen conversion stories emphasize these psychological changes. Thus, the theories, hypotheses, and opinions regarding the mental health of sectarians range from most ill, through normal, to most healthy.

The data of this study do not permit test of what psychological change may occur in the Pentecostal after conversion, but we do have three measures of the relative mental health status of Pentecostals and the Catholic population from which they are drawn. The Pentecostals appear as healthy or healthier on all measures. First, on psychiatric histories collected, 13% of the Pentecostals (N=76), compared with 17.5% of the Catholics (N=80), reported previous psychiatric treatment or a "nervous breakdown." This difference is not statistically significant. Second, the proportion of Pentecostals in the Puerto Rican patient population of the mental health clinic serving this same neighborhood (11.1%) is proportional to or under-represents that found in the general population by the same interviewers (see footnote 6). The last measure is the Cornell Medical Index (CMI).[12] Table 7 shows CMI scores for the Catholic and

[12] There are many difficulties with the CMI, or with any instrument developed to measure variables of mental health for lay administration in survey research. There are particular problems with instruments which, like the CMI, rely upon psychophysiological complaints as the measure of emotional disturbance for use with certain populations, including the Puerto Ricans, where scores on such items are consistently higher than for the norming populations. The validity of this instrument as a measure of emotional disturbance for this population, as well as the norms and critical scoring levels, is therefore in doubt. A great deal of effort has, therefore, gone into testing the validity of this instrument for use with this population for purposes of this study. In one test, a random sample of the population was compared with a sample of mental health clinic patients on CMI scores. There are significant differences between the two populations on total scale score and a number of sub-scales. The CMI does, therefore, discriminate between a psychiatric patient population and a random sample. We have concluded from this that it is an adequate instrument for measuring differential levels of emotional disturbance between subgroups within the Puerto Rican population. In another test, however, CMI scores of clinic patients of each psychological sub-scale and total scale were compared with therapists' ratings of (1) symptom manifestation in each of the areas purportedly measured by the CMI, (2) over-all level of emotional disturbance, and (3) over-all degree of impairment of function. The intercorrelations of CMI scores and the therapists' ratings as criterion measures were totally unsatisfactory. In this situation, where therapists largely of the majority culture were evaluating individuals from a minority subculture, the validity of the therapists' ratings are as suspect as the CMI scores. However, with this evidence we cannot at this time consider the CMI an adequate instrument for detecting clinical cases or for making diagnostic assessments of individuals or groups from this subculture.

TABLE 7. CMI Subscale and Total Scores Compared on Three Population Samples by Sex

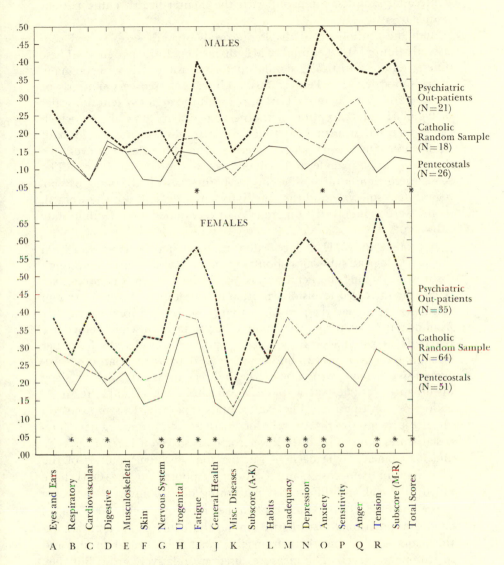

(Scores are expressed as the mean number of yes responses per item on the scale or subscale, i.e. $\frac{\Sigma X/N}{N_1}$ where $N_1 =$ Number of items per scale)

* Differences between clinic patients and others significant at .05 level or better on a T-test.

° Differences between Catholic and Pentecostal samples significant at .05 level or better on a T-test.

Pentecostal samples, compared with the mental health clinic patient sample by sex.

Both the Catholics and the Pentecostals of both sexes scored consistently lower on the total CMI than the clinic patients. These differences are statistically significant for the total scale and for many of the sub-scales. The Pentecostals, both sexes, scored very similarly or only slightly lower than the Catholics on all the organ system sub-scales of the CMI with exception of the nervous system sub-scale, on which the Pentecostal women scored significantly lower at the .01 level of confidence. On the mood and feeling state sub-scales, however, the Pentecostals, both male and female, scored consistently lower. The scores were significantly different for both sexes on the total psychological item sub-scale and the sensitivity sub-scale, and, for the women, scores were significantly different on every mood and feeling state sub-scale.

If we take the CMI at face value, the consistently lower scores on the psychological sub-scales should reflect a lower rate of emotional disturbance among the Pentecostals, particularly when it is not accompanied by increased levels of symptom expression on the organ system sub-scales. However, the possibility that these lower scores result either from denial (cf. Pattison, this volume), or from a conscious reluctance to admit to psychological symptoms must be considered. In either event, one might expect to find evidence of depression or an obsessive-compulsive defense structure in the indirect measures, such as sleep disturbance, fatigue, vague pains, headaches, lack of appetite, over-eating, or constipation. The Pentecostals report fewer symptoms on all of the items specifically relating to these conditions. The Pentecostal scores are significantly lower for both sexes on lack of appetite and for women on headaches. Further item by item analysis of the variations in Pentecostal and Catholic responses on the CMI have failed to reveal any differential patterning of responses.

We have found no evidence of higher rates of psychiatric disorder or greater emotional disturbance among the Pentecostals than among the major church members from the same sub-cultural group and socioeconomic level. The measures used are relatively gross, but they are adequate to rule out a high rate of severe pathology above and beyond that prevalent in the general population. It is possible that more refined measures might have revealed more subtle psychological differences between the two groups. However, these results are consistent with those of three unpublished studies reviewed by Hine (1969) in which tongue-speakers were compared with control groups on sophisticated personality inventories. These studies also showed the religious minority groups to be well within the range of normal, in some ways better adjusted than the control sample, and to differ from the control samples only on a few sub-scales, the significance of which is difficult to interpret with present knowledge. The data of this study do suggest that rates of emotional disturbance, or at least levels of felt distress, may be lower among the Pentecostals. Combined with the evidence from conversion stories and the theoretical psychotherapeutic value of the conversion experience, it is suggested that the lower rate of symptom expression results from sectarian membership, rather than discriminating those who are attracted to the sect, but this remains to be tested.

SUMMARY AND DISCUSSION

The salient conclusion from the above comparisons is that the Pentecostal people studied differ very little from the major church members of the same subcultural and socioeconomic situation in characteristics other than those specifically related to the religious life. If it is deviant to be sectarian and to "speak in tongues," then they are deviants. But, if we demand some other criteria such as inadequate functioning in occupational or social roles, or emotional disturbance, we have found no evidence for it. The Puerto Rican Pentecostals are not drawn disproportionately from any specific age group, from the lowest socioeconomic stratum, from the most recent migrant population, or from among those whose family and other interpersonal relations show disorganization. They are no less, and possibly more, socioeconomically mobile as a group and are as involved in the life of the community as the Catholics from the same environment. They show no greater, and possibly lesser, rates of psychiatric disturbance.

Small differences found in these comparisons and in examination of age distributions and characteristics of sub-segments of the Pentecostal sample suggest, however, that possibly Pentecostalism serves individuals in times of acute distress in a number of different areas: economic crisis, migration, extended family disorganization, and, possibly, developmental crises of youth and middle age. The discontinuous age distribution of Pentecostal congregations, together with a continuous distribution of age at conversion, suggests that the church serves many individuals for varying periods of time who do not become part of the continuing core membership of the church. There is some evidence that these include disproportionately recent migrants and those who convert during the young adult years. Perhaps for these individuals sect membership serves to alleviate acute distress, after which the individual leaves the church. Others may leave because they do not find the resolution they seek through sect membership. The evidence suggests, while it does not prove, that for those who remain in the church socioeconomic conditions are improved, nuclear family relations are stabilized, and felt distress is reduced. There is also some evidence that the church may serve to support and sustain some individuals, e.g. wives of downwardly mobile males, who are powerless to alter the conditions of their distress.

It would appear that individual sectarian membership, like the emergence of the new religious movements themselves, has multiple explanations, probably reflecting the multiple part-causes of the rise and success or failure of the movement itself (cf. LaBarre 1971). We have found some evidence for many of the hypotheses examined for at least a segment of the sect membership. Chronic and acute economic distress appears to play a part in the conversion of some individuals, migration may play a part for others, disturbed interpersonal relations, insecurity in interpersonal relations, or a perceived need for structure may explain the appeal for still others, but in no event does any single characteristic distinguish the Pentecostal people as a group from the Catholics of the same neighborhood. Future research should distinguish between the core membership and the transient membership of sectarian groups and discriminate the functions for each. It should also discriminate the predisposing factors and functions for different segments of the congregations, e.g. males or females alone or in couples, the second generation sectarian reaffirming his membership, the young convert, the middle-aged convert, those in the child-rearing phase of the life cycle who appear to be under-represented in the Pentecostal membership, etc. Above all, longitudinal studies are needed if we are going to discriminate those traits which mark the sectarian prior to conversion and those which may result from sectarian membership.

One thing does distinguish the Pentecostal converts as a group from the predominantly Catholic population from which they are drawn. This is the conscious choice of the minority religious affiliation. If this choice is to be understood, there must be more examination of the specific circumstances under which the choice is made, the alternatives, both sacred and secular, available to the individual making the choice and the advantages and disadvantages accruing to each. This choice must be considered from the point of view of the alternatives available to the individual making the choice, and not from the point of view of the range of alternatives available within the larger society.

In conclusion, I would suggest that in future research on the characteristics of sectarians or the functions of sectarianism for the individual, the view be taken, following Wallace (1956) and others on ideological movements cross-culturally, that individual sectarian membership, like the sect itself, is: *a deliberate, organized, conscious effort to construct (or adopt) a more satisfying culture (or life style, or symbol system)*. Or, following LaBarre (1971), it might be viewed as: *an adaptive technique of cultural permutation*. Explanations might then be sought in the circumstances leading to conversion, the impact upon the life of the individual convert of the alternative choice, and the processes by which this occurs. The functions and dysfunctions of the sect could then be assessed. This dynamic approach should replace the static comparisons of beliefs and behavior or characteristics of membership, as outlined in the first pages of this paper and as employed in this study. This view would make studies of the sectarian adaptation in American society comparable cross-culturally with those of ideological movements, both secular and religious, and would lend a broader perspective which is badly needed in studies of American minority religious groups.

Spiritualists and Shamans as Psychotherapists: An Account of Original Anthropological Sin

Pᴀsᴛ anthropological accounts of spiritualists and shamans have focused predominantly on the relation of culture and personality, specifically on whether these individuals are "sick." Little serious consideration has been given to them as true psychotherapists playing the same role as psychiatrists play.

This paper begins with this assumption and discusses some of the evidence for its validity. It will be shown that psychiatrists have much to learn from spiritualists and shamans about psychotherapy. If they are to learn, however, anthropologists will have to focus on spiritualists and shamans in ways other than they traditionally have. Specific suggestions are given regarding appropriate areas for this focus.

The roads of religion, anthropology, and psychiatry meet at a junction, and in the middle of the junction stands the healer. If you approach the junction on the three different roads, you will see different aspects of this individual—the spiritualist, the shaman, and the psychotherapist. But when you get close, you see that they are just different ways of viewing the same man.

The serious study of the healer in his different forms has been sadly neglected. Travelers on each of the three roads have gone their separate way to the detriment of all. Spiritualists, shamans, and psychotherapists are essentially the same person, and any one of them may be defined in terms shared by the other two.

Now travelers on the roads of religion and psychiatry are expected to be narrow in their view. But not so the anthropologists. Like accountants who are supposed to always balance their own checkbooks, anthropologists are supposed to always see individuals without a cultural bias. When they fail to do this, they are guilty of Original Anthropological Sin.

Alas, anthropologists turn out to be only human. In categorizing spiritualists and shamans as "sick," they have erred often and erred widely. This paper will describe the origins of this error and then

Note: The opinions set forth in this paper do not represent the official policy of the National Institute of Mental Health or of the Public Health Service.

show its effects. The error has helped produce a myth among psychiatrists and psychologists that spiritualists and shamans may be safely ignored or, even worse, glibly written off as "just crackpots." In fact, spiritualists and shamans do the same thing as psychiatrists and psychologists do, using the same techniques, and getting about the same results.

The Origin of the Error

The widespread myth that spiritualists and shamans are "sick" reaches back into the eighteenth- and nineteenth-century European exploration of Africa. The world was simpler then, and the new cultures were rapidly assigned their proper status in The Order of Things. We were white, they were black. We were civilized, they were primitive. We were Christian, they were pagan. We used science, they used magic. We had doctors, they had witchdoctors. And spiritualists and shamans are, in the popular myth, direct offspring of witchdoctors. This simplistic reductionism is still remarkably prevalent in our thinking about other cultures. It affords an easy rationale for assigning spiritualists and shamans to the realm of the irrelevant.

In anthropological literature this error originated with Bogoras' study of the Siberian Chukchi early in this century. He contended that their shamans were "as a rule extremely excitable, almost hysterical, and not a few of them were half crazy" (Bogoras 1907). Anthropologists A. L. Kroeber, George Devereux, and Ralph Linton have all perpetuated this myth, and being prolific writers they have succeeded in establishing it as a fact which was until recently unchallenged. Kroeber, for instance, even contended that one of the differentiating points of "primitive" from "developed" societies is that the former rewards its psychotics with a socially sanctioned role as a healer (Kroeber 1952). Such thinking slowly became a canard in anthropology, and was incorporated uncritically into courses on culture and personality as fact.

The reasons are many for this error by anthropologists. One of the most important, and most difficult to assess, is the fact that many of these well-known anthropologists were profoundly influenced by psychoanalysis. In some cases (e.g. Devereux) they had undergone an analysis themselves; in other cases they worked closely with analysts. Linton's work with Kardiner and Sapir's work with Sullivan are examples of this. I believe that this experience with psychoanalysis deprived them of their objectivity in viewing therapists in other cultures. After all, if your analysis is successful, how can you see your analyst as analogous to those strange people in other cultures who are chanting and shaking a rattle?

Another commonly cited fact used to support the spiritualists-and-shamans-are-sick thesis is the selection of transvestites as therapists in some cultures. This was a well-known (and widely commented upon) arrangement among the Plains Indians where such individuals were called *berdaches*. For anthropologists like Kroeber this "proved" that therapists in other cultures are disturbed (Kroeber 1952). The fact is that *berdaches* certainly did exist, but this arrangement is a rare one. It is found in a few other cultures in the world but not nearly as often as Western anthropological preoccupation with it would lead one to believe. Most therapists in other cultures are as heterosexual as most therapists in our own culture.

Still another source of the error is the inability of anthropologists to see healing activity as culturally variable. Spirit possession is a good example of this. A shaman or spiritualist who becomes possessed and throws himself around in a frenzy of activity makes the anthropological observer uneasy. Such behavior is labeled as "hysterical" in our culture and when excessive is considered deviant. In other cultures, however, it may be considered not only normal but desirable for a healer to do these things. It was just this kind of behavior that led Bogoras to the conclusion that the Siberian shamans must be crazy.

Finally, anthropological observers have often erred in labeling shamans and spiritualists as sick by studying only a single individual. L. B. Boyer, a psychoanalyst who studied Apache Indian shamans, provides a classic example of this. His early work was based upon work on a single shaman, whom he concluded was a disturbed individual:

> He was shown to suffer from a personality disorder, with impulsive and hysterical traits, and to have characteristics of the imposter. His principle fixations were oral and phallic. There were suggestions he lacked clear masculine identity and suffered from problems resulting from latent homosexuality. (Boyer 1961a)

From this he generalized that all Apache shamans were disturbed (Boyer 1961b).

Three years and eleven shamans later Boyer completely reversed himself. After further studies he concluded that the "Apache shamans have not been psychological deviants at any period of their lives" (Boyer 1964). In fact he says that they are *healthier* than the average member of their society (Boyer et al. 1964).

Boyer's observations are instructive. If you look at only one therapist in any culture you may find a deviant. There are abundant accounts of single therapists in other cultures who are psychopathic, manic, emotionally unstable, psychotic, or frauds. It is no more valid, however, to generalize from these single therapists in other cultures than it is to generalize from a single therapist in our culture.

Spiritualists and Shamans as Healthy

Up to this point, I have reproved anthropologists for ethnocentrism in their descriptions of spiritualists and shamans without having shown that such descriptions are wrong. Increasing anthropological evidence in the past few years shows this indeed to be the case. In fact many observers note that, as a group, the spiritualists and shamans appear to be among the least disturbed members of the society. Typical is the judgment of anthropologist Jane Murphy on Eskimo shamans:

> The well-known shamans were, if anything, exceptionally healthy in this sense . . . to become a successful healer he often had to display an exceptional ability in emotional control and in taking responsibility. . . . The full-fledged shaman who is capable of dealing with the crises of illness and death and of offering psychological support to the groups of individuals taken into his spiritual custody displays qualities that can hardly be separated from those of leadership, responsibility, and power. (Murphy 1964)

Unusual intelligence and memory are frequently ascribed to these therapists. For instance, a Navaho medicine man must learn a volume of details for a curing ceremony that has been compared to memorizing a Wagnerian opera, including "orchestral score, every vocal part, all details of the settings, stage business, and each requirement of the costume" (Kluckhohn 1952). And a Yakut Indian shaman must have a professional vocabulary of 12,000 words compared to the usual Yakut vocabulary of 4,000 words (Eliade 1964). Other commonly mentioned attributes are "mature, poised, and serious in personality" (Opler 1959), and "unusual decency, upright character, judgment, and responsibility" (Murdock 1965). An observer of Yakut Indian shamans sums up best of all the qualities that make a good therapist in that culture, and probably in many cultures: "One must feel an inner force in him that does not offend yet is conscious of its power" (Eliade 1964).

Many other testimonials could be proffered to support the thesis that most therapists in other cultures are unusually stable and mature individuals. They cover a wide area from African witchdoctors (Jilek 1967) to Australian medicine men ("altruistic and intelligent men": Cawte 1964) to American Indian shamans and medicine men (Handelman 1967). After an extensive survey of the character of this last group, one field worker concluded: "quackery and charlatanism are no more prevalent in primitive than in civilized society" (Maddox 1923).

To make a generalization about the mental health of therapists an observer must study several of them and must also know what kinds of behavior is considered normal in that culture. The best study to date which meets these criteria is a study by Dr. Yuji Sasaki, a Japanese psychiatrist, of 56 Japanese shamans. He found that 38 of the shamans were without evidence of personality deviation, 10 had some degree of neurosis, 6 were psychotic, and 2 had organic brain disease (Sasaki 1969). Unfortunately there is no data on Western therapists against which to compare these figures.

My own experience with spiritualists and shamans in other cultures corroborates the impression that they are usually mature, stable individuals. A Zar priest whom I studied in Ethiopia, the best known indigenous therapist in that country, was regarded by his community as a leader in both a spiritual and a political sense. Furthermore, it was known that he had fought against the invading Italians in World War II with distinction, and he had become a major landowner by wisely investing the earnings from his healing enterprise.

Similarly an Iban *Manang* with whom I spent time in Borneo was widely regarded as one of the most stable and sensible men in his area as well as being an excellent therapist. Overall, my subjective impression of therapists I have known in other cultures and subcultures is that, as a group, they are no "sicker" than psychiatrists and psychologists whom I have known.

The Price of Original Anthropological Sin

One may well ask, at this point, so what? What if spiritualists and shamans *have* been labeled as "sick" by mistake? What difference does it make?

From the point of view of Western psychotherapists who are trying to learn more about themselves it makes all the difference in the world. The labeling of someone as "sick" (implicitly mentally sick) is pejorative. It is a means of relegating such individuals to the realm of irrelevance. Since spiritualists and shamans are "sick," they are not like us, and we can safely ignore them. Anything they do that happens to resemble things we do can just be called coincidence, and does not bear closer scrutiny. Up until recently this thinking has been the state of affairs.

It has become increasingly clear in recent years, however, that spiritualists and shamans are neither "sick" nor different in kind from psychiatrists and psychologists. All of them do psychotherapy—that is, they help people who have problems in living and "mental diseases." And insofar as the common elements underlying the activities of spiritualists, shamans, psychiatrists, and psychologists have been ignored, to that extent the study of psychotherapy has been retarded. Thus the wages of Original Anthropological Sin have been paid by those who would do research in psychotherapy.

Let me illustrate what I mean by common elements underlying psychotherapy. These elements appear to be operant in all cultures, and so would be suitable foci for anthropologists when they observe therapists in other cultures.

1. *A shared world-view:* Recent studies in cognitive anthropology have confirmed what was long suspected: different people divide up the world differently. Simultaneously clinical psychiatrists and psychologists have been discovering that their attempts to do psychotherapy with patients from different cultures or subcultures are often futile. The reason is that a certain degree of shared world-view is necessary for successful psychotherapy to occur. It is not just a language barrier that makes cross-cultural psychotherapy difficult; it is a cognitive barrier.

2. *Personal qualities of the therapist:* The recent outpouring of research on personality characteristics of therapists has raised some interesting and important questions about psychotherapy. The research, much of it inspired by the theories and early work of Carl Rogers, indicates that certain personality traits are therapeutic and others are not. A psychotherapist who has these traits will therefore be effective, whereas one who does not will be ineffective. Presumably this is true for spiritualists and shamans as well as for psychiatrists and psychologists, though the specifically desirable personality characteristics may vary from culture to culture.

3. *Patient expectations:* Although the power of patient expectations have long been known in anthropological lore under the designation of "voodoo death," not enough attention has been given them as important factors in the psychotherapeutic situation. There is now abundant evidence indicating that people who expect to get well are more likely to do so than those who do not expect to. Spiritualists, shamans, psychiatrists, and psychologists all raise (or lower) their patients' expectations by the exterior and furnishings of their office, their accessory paraphernalia (e.g. rattle, special mask, religious objects, couch), their training, and their reputations generally.

4. *Techniques of therapy:* Psychotherapists all over the world use the same spectrum of techniques for therapy. In a recent survey I was able to find examples of every known Western psychotherapeutic technique in other cultures. Even a technique like shock therapy, "discovered" in the 1930s, was used in the form of electric eels up to 4,000 years ago by the Egyptians (Kellaway 1946; Cerletti 1950). Though

all known techniques are widespread, some are favored much more by particular cultures.

How Anthropologists Can Contribute More to Psychiatry

As more is becoming known about psychotherapy there is a great need for more data from other cultures. Anthropologists are in a position to supply such data. In order to do so, however, they must enter the psychotherapists' dwelling in the other culture with their eyes open, not wearing glasses tinged with Freud or any other Western system of thought. An observer who has his mind encased in Truth will be unable to free it up to see the many smaller truths before him.

It may be argued that this should be the job of a psychiatrist, not an anthropologist. Unfortunately psychiatrists have had little training in objective cross-cultural observations. And in addition to being an unsuspecting prisoner of their own cultural system generally, they are usually committed to a particular Western therapeutic system which they regard as Truth. Thus it is unlikely that psychiatrists will contribute heavily to cross-cultural observations of psychotherapists in the near future, though isolated exceptions, such as psychiatrist Raymond Prince's brilliant observations of Nigerian *babalawos,* will occur (Prince 1962, 1964).

From the point of view of research on psychotherapy an anthropologist could be most helpful if he asks himself the following questions during his observations:

1. Do the therapist and patient come from the same culture? The same class? How successful has this therapist been when he has seen patients from another subculture? What kinds of patients does the therapist consider himself to be most effective with?

2. How would I describe this therapist's personality? How do others in his culture describe him? Are these personality characteristics valued in that culture? What other kinds of people in that culture share these characteristics?

3. What does the therapist do to raise patient expectations? What is their perception of the building where he sees his patients? How far do they come to see him? What paraphernalia does he use during the course of treatment? What kind of a training does he have? Does he advertise in any way? What is his reputation? What kinds of things does he do to increase his reputation?

4. What techniques of therapy does he use? Does he take a history? Does he use drugs? Shocks of various kinds? Massage or hot baths? Conditioning techniques like relaxation exercises? Confession or abreaction? Suggestion? Hypnotic techniques? Dream interpretation?

Group therapies? Role playing or possession? Environmental manipulation or social reintegration? Is the family involved in the therapy? Is hospitalization used?

5. What are the goals of therapy? Is he trying to remove a symptom? Change an attitude? Alter behavior? Produce insight in the patient? Improve the patient's interpersonal relationships? Improve his social utility to the group? Educate the patient to be able to cope with future situations?

This is indeed a big order, but it is what is needed. If such questions are asked in the course of observing spiritualists and shamans, then anthropologists will make a major contribution to research in psychotherapy. Furthermore they will help psychiatrists and psychologists to see spiritualists and shamans not as people who are "sick" and different from themselves, but rather as colleagues who are related under their respective therapeutic masks.

A Medium for Mental Health

For many years, psychics have aided persons from most if not all segments of American society: serving millionnaires and paupers, urbanites and farmers, WASPs and minority group members. Their teaching and counseling efforts with many types of followers have been described (Steiner 1945; Williams 1946; Ford and Bro 1958; Montgomery 1965; Stearn 1967; Gauld 1968; Pike 1968; Steiger 1968).

However, scant attention has been given to their work with one interesting and important group of people—psychotherapists. Such persons might be expected to be competitors and enemies, rather than clients. Little is known about how mediums proselytize, teach, and advise them, and why *rapprochements* occur.

Recently in a large city on the Pacific coast, a psychic captured the interest of six psychotherapists. First, he provided mediumship training, then group therapy. From my experience as participant observer, I will describe the special backgrounds of followers and leader, summarize the group activities, and evaluate the counseling. All names have been changed, and identities have been disguised.

The Teacher

Dave Johnson, the teacher, was a high school graduate and a successful self-employed merchant. A short, handsome man of 45, he dressed in expensive, fashionable clothes and radiated power and certainty.

He had been trained in the occult by Spiritualist ministers, then became dissatisfied with their "ritualism" and left them to develop his own skills. At first his hobby, mediumship in time became cause, crusade, and business. Fired with his metaphysical beliefs and experi-

Note: Field work was carried out in 1970 under the auspices of the Langley Porter Community Mental Health Training Program, and the assistance of Dr. M. R. Harris and Dr. Joan Ablon is gratefully acknowledged. I also appreciate the useful suggestions of Drs. Fred Depp, Fred Ilfeld, Henry Lederer, Dee Lloyd, Milton Shore, and Fuller Torrey, and of many other staff members of the Langley Porter Institute and National Institute of Mental Health. Finally, I would like to thank Dave Johnson and my colleagues in his group for their help and cooperation.

This report does not necessarily reflect the opinion, official policy, or position of the Langley Porter Institute, National Institute of Mental Health, Health Services and Mental Health Administration, or Department of Health, Education and Welfare.

ences, aware of chances to make money, and skillful at selling his ideas and products, Dave combined righteousness and pragmatism to become an aggressive, effective proselytizer. He gave instructions in mediumship and advice for personal problems with zeal that was both missionary and mercenary.

Backing him with knowledge, skill, and prestige was his spirit guide, Dr. Wagner, a deceased, European-trained psychiatrist who had been well known locally as strong-minded and competent. Dr. Wagner had been during his lifetime a personal friend of Dave's and a persistent scoffer at psychic phenomena.

After dying at the age of 77, he "contacted" Dave by spiritual means and repented his earlier skepticism. He offered to help counsel clients and educate students, particularly former colleagues in the mental health field. Overjoyed at hearing from this old friend, and enthusiastically accepting his aid, Dave was emboldened not only to call himself a "psychic therapist" but to offer mediumship training to psychotherapists.

A recruitment opportunity came when Dave was invited to discuss his methods at an ongoing seminar of a local psychotherapy society. Despite receiving many hostile comments, he enticed several persons in the audience to join a proposed class in elementary mediumship, and they in turn interested some friends. When the class started a few months later, all of the entering students had heard about it either directly or indirectly from that one seminar.

The Students

Most of the students were well known locally and were respected as competent psychotherapists by their professional colleagues. In this sense, they were not marginal as has been the case with some other proselytes to metaphysical cults (Lofland 1966).

Bill and I were psychiatrists in our thirties; Alfred, 40, Brenda, 35, and Ann, 50, were psychiatric social workers with masters degrees; and Mary, 45, was a Ph.D. psychologist. By our willingness to pay $100 tuition and to commit more than 30 hours to class, all of us showed a high level of motivation.

Mine stemmed from wondering whether psychics might provide useful counseling for emotional disturbances. This concern with psychics as mental health resources was stimulated and strengthened by the work of many others (Frank 1961; Rogler and Hollingshead 1961; Kiev 1964; Bolman 1968; Lubchansky et al. 1970; Purdy et al. 1970).

Dave professed sympathy with my professional orientation, but nevertheless hoped to persuade me of the ultimate reality of his mediumship, and to convert me to his views. However, I was basically unconcerned with the truth of his belief system. I wasn't a parapsychologist or occultist out to prove or refute it, accept or reject it. Rather, I was a clinician with some field work experience (Ilfeld and Lauer 1964) who wanted to learn about mediumship as a folk healing technique.

In contrast, my fellow students were earnest, eager mystics, seeking spiritual development and "self unfoldment." Impressed by Dave's psychic skills and receptive to his ideas, they entered class either believing or wanting to believe in mediumship.

Some were veteran searchers; others, stimulated by occultism in popular culture, had just begun a metaphysical quest; but all felt that their efforts were praiseworthy. Considering themselves awakened and aware, they felt ennobled and aggrandized. Dave supported their views with flattery, saying that they were serious students, pilgrims in search of enlightenment, not mere curiosity seekers.

Ironically, Alfred, a social worker, used his lofty spiritual pursuit for the mundane purpose of "scoring" at cocktail parties. His knowledge of the occult was bait to snare attractive women.

My classmates seemed able to link mysticism to their mental health beliefs and thus to avoid internal conflict or cognitive dissonance (Festinger 1957). Bill, a psychiatrist, smugly pointed out that Sigmund Freud himself had said, "If I had my life to live over again, I should devote myself to psychical research rather than psychoanalysis (Jones 1957: III, 392). Brenda and Ann, psychiatric social workers, recalled using techniques similar to mediumistic counseling. They had asked clients to enact conversations with their deceased parents so as to expose and resolve buried conflicts. All students were capable of going beyond traditional or parochial concepts to new ideas and methods. They were flexible, eclectic therapists, not bound to any psychiatric orthodoxy.

The Setting

This unconventional class met in a conventional locale—an inconspicuous suite on the second floor of a downtown office building, across the hall from a busy medical clinic. Behind Dave's unmarked door was a deep-carpeted, wood-paneled waiting room containing comfortable, tasteful furniture. On a table was a vase of fresh flowers and books on healing and mediumship (e.g. Worral and Worral 1965). An adjoining room, used for treating individual clients, contained a filing cabinet and a large desk. The wall held a painting which Dave found symbolic of his counseling: a thin beam of sunlight illuminating a ship tossed on wind swept seas. All in all, the setting was remarkably similar to the students' own professional offices.

Dave mentioned that Mr. Reilly, the previous occupant of the office, had committed suicide, but promised this would not impair our work. Mr. Reilly was reported at peace in the spirit world and happy over the way his former quarters were being used.

The class met in Dave's waiting room for 10 consecutive Monday mornings. Formal sessions lasted about three hours, following which many people rehashed events at lunch in a nearby restaurant.

The Beliefs

Dave introduced us to his idiom and ideas as a sage passing down wisdom, not as a peer in a symmetric relationship. His beliefs, which owed much to Spiritualism (Boddington 1947; Judah 1967; Nelson 1969) were intricate and complicated, and thus difficult to describe both accurately and briefly. Denying a need for belief, Dave said that he presented basic facts. He stressed that belief implied faith, whereas his "knowledge" had been empirically and scientifically verified.

He said that human beings obviously embody or include spirits and that psychology, religion, and everyday speech implicitly accept this fact in such terms as mind, consciousness, ego, and soul. Spirits temporarily leave living bodies in a phenomenon called "astral projection," but after death they separate permanently and move into a non-physical or "etheric" realm. As disincarnate entities they are nonetheless capable of influencing human beings. Some spirits frighten or harm people and need to be guarded against, but most spirits are benevolent and can be welcomed. They can provide valuable information and advice because of their ability to perceive events in the physical world and to tap the knowledge of deceased experts.

Spirits communicate through mediums. In spite of emphasizing mediums' passivity in receiving and relaying messages, Dave recommended that they be actively helpful and supply only constructive messages. Dave himself held back a person's date of death if it appeared immutable, believing that this information could prove needlessly upsetting. He often staged the presentation of messages with dramatic flourishes for maximum therapeutic effect. Considering everyone capable of mediumship, Dave sought to release or unblock this latent skill. He also considered telepathy to be universal, but either ignored or derogated this particular paranormal power—probably because it could be used to explain much of his mediumship, thus making his spiritualistic beliefs superfluous.

The Language

To explain and buttress his concepts, Dave used figurative language liberally. For example, he elaborately described a beautiful redwood, with thick trunk and magnificent branches, which was firmly anchored by sturdy roots in a lush valley. In contrast, a small, scraggly elm, bent by the wind, barely clung to life on a harsh, desolate hillside. The moral: trees aren't responsible for being what they are and neither are people, particularly insofar as they have difficulties loving and being loved.

Although persons may have such difficulties because of poor rearing, the fault doesn't lie with parents either. Parental inadequacies are due to the preceding generation, and so on in a causal chain of innocent injury. To stop further promulgation and secure emotional peace, an individual must first realize that he is as blameless as a deformed tree, then understand, forgive, and love his parents.

This tree imagery had popular and professional echoes. Alexander Pope (1931: 159) had made the oft-quoted remark, "Just as the twig is bent the tree's inclined." The tree of life and the family tree are common allusions. Jung (1961: 67) called trees "the direct embodiment of the incomprehensible meanings of life." Clinical psychologists (Hammer 1958; Buck and Hammer 1969) sometimes ask clients to draw a tree so as to reveal their self image. Frazer (1922) pointed out the pervasiveness of tree symbolism in mythology and religion.

Going beyond traditional imagery, Dave often expressed himself in a special language used by occultists, and devoted much class time to teaching this argot. He furnished a new vocabulary and gave supplemental definitions to standard English words.

For example, problems in communicating with spirits he generally attributed to "low vibrations"—a catchall term which covered a variety of inhibiting factors, including the tenseness or skepticism of a séance member. Specific action was considered necessary to remove the inhibition and to raise the rate of vibrations.

Some of Dave's terms with particularly subtle, arcane, or controversial meanings were learned and digested with difficulty. Combining an attitude of semantic superiority with one of benevolent flexibility, he carefully explained such terms, trying to reconcile them with students' prior usages and ideas.

Mary, a social worker slow to accept Dave's language, thought spirits meant spooks or ghosts and doubted their existence. Reassuringly, Dave agreed that spirits did not exist in any Halloween sense, but rather as the intrinsic nature of a person. He convinced her to accept spirits as "essences."

Dave often said that "the child" within emotionally disturbed people needed to be killed. No! cried most of the students, unwilling to kill anything, let alone this part of self which they wanted to preserve and cherish. Eventually they and Dave discovered that their disagreement was largely semantic. To the students, "the child" implied such desired qualities as creativity, imagination, and exhuberance, while to Dave it implied such undesired qualities as petulance and spitefulness. Subsequently, Dave explicitly specified "the angry child" and spoke of putting it to rest rather than to death.

Quick witted and verbally facile, Dave frequently used occultist words in jokes and puns. He invited his students to do the same, and even to compete with him at it.

The Messages

As preparation for receiving mediumistic messages, Dave provided the following instructions:

> Imagine yourself inside an impregnable concrete-enclosed fortress accompanied by your guide, the spirit who looks after you. Has everyone done this? Good! Your sanctuary has a single entrance— a long tunnel with heavy steel gates every few feet. There is just one key to the gates. Is everyone with me? Give the key to your spirit guide. He will permit only benevolent influences to come inside and will defend you from demons. Protected by this procedure you will avoid the difficulties that sometimes have plagued other mediums.

> Now, picture the bedroom in your home . . . then a loved person entering and saying a characteristic phrase. O.K., hold that scene. This is like switching on channel 2 and watching a television program. Erase all such self-generated pictures from your head. Turn the television dial to channel 7 where no local station transmits anything. Keep your mind clear and open, and wait patiently for psychic communication. Ask your spirit guide to screen out symbols because they are difficult to interpret.

Using this technique, students practiced picking up information about each others' childhoods. They reported seeing, hearing, and feeling family members, pets, toys, and houses—at first in a tentative, fragmented manner, then later with increasing confidence and coherence. They also progressed to attempting such other occult activities as detecting a drawing on a folded piece of paper or billet, predicting future events, diagnosing illnesses, and describing spirit guides.

Dave often told students to practice certain of these activities outside of class. In addition, a standing assignment was to note any intuitions, premonitions, dreams, or other events during the week that might have mediumistic import. The beginning of each class session was devoted to evaluating this homework.

Ann, a social worker gifted with subtle charisma, quickly earned the role of star pupil and the right to high praise and recognition. In contrast, Mary was sometimes blamed for hindering class progress by lowering the vibrations. Her low status stemmed from her distraught appearance, erratic attunement to Dave's doctrines, and strange psychic readings. Once, Dave even told her directly that she was mistakenly reading herself not someone else. Such an error is analogous to psychotherapists' attributing their own desires and attitudes to patients—that is, counter-transference (Cohen 1952; Greenson 1967). Despite Mary's difficulties, she, like everyone else in the class, was considered to have unquestioned psychic sensitivity and skill.

All students' occult pronouncements were assumed correct until disproved; there was limited motivation to search out disconfirming evidence since inaccuracies provoked disappointment and discomfort. Still, occasional readings would be incontrovertibly wrong: these were often ignored, and instead successes would be recalled or anticipated. As mediums, we sought confirmation and validation for our work. As subjects, we learned to be suggestible and covertly cooperative, to substantiate each others' messages while appearing to be objective and critical.

Inspired by successful messages in class, the students tried to teach psychic science to their friends and peers, and persisted despite some hostile rebuffs. For example, one psychiatrist told Bill that anyone believing in mediumship must be deranged. He attributed Bill's convictions to the death of his psychoanalyst and a wish to regain contact.

The Teacher as Student

Although maintaining a stance of spiritual preeminence throughout most of the course, Dave sometimes turned to his students for encouragement and for psychiatric information. When tired, discouraged, and frustrated, he might seek consolation and appreciate students' solicitously telling him to work fewer hours and to rest more. When perplexed about matters bearing upon psychotherapy, he might seek expert opinions. This could involve definitions, diagnostic categories, treatment methods, and clinical problems, but very frequently it concerned such intricacies of running a private practice as the decoration of an office, the keeping of records, the billing of clients, the scheduling of work, and the ways of handling persons who failed to keep appointments.

The New Contract

By the closing class sessions, students felt trusting and intimate with one another. They had revealed many personal problems and acted as mutual confidants. Furthermore, students had developed a strong investment in Dave and his metaphysical system. They desired more training and more contact with their guru. To illustrate, Bill repeatedly asked Dave to sponsor a salon like the one Freud had formed for his psychoanalytic followers.

In this context, Dave suggested continued group work and offered free "psychic therapy"—previously available only to paying clients seen individually in private practice. His stated motivation was the wish to improve his skills by developing group techniques. Although considered guinea pigs in an experiment, we were promised rewards: the solving of deep-seated problems and the acquisition of more effective ways to aid patients. We readily accepted his proposal. Brenda, in her enthusiasm, thought we should pay him, but she was outvoted by the others.

The Last Class

Dave began the last day of class with a special exercise. After arranging the furniture for proper vibrations and turning off the lights, he held a burning candle underneath his face and told us to expect an interesting, perhaps puzzling, spiritual manifestation—to see his face melt like wax, then flow and change into a new shape. Eagerly obedient, we watched and waited through a minute of eerie, tense silence. No one saw the phenomenon. Undaunted, Dave readjusted the candle nearer his face, and almost singed his chin. A few minutes later, only Mary and Alfred, who had lagged in some other class activities, denied seeing anything. But when Dave turned to face them more directly, they reported success. Class members saw an astonishing array of personages, including an Indian sage, a Mongolian priest, a Chinese scholar, and an Italian bishop. As most of these people were described, Dave nodded his head in pleased recognition.

Turning the lights back on, Dave asked us to read him psychically, then give our final opinion of the class. Everyone claimed to tune in on Dave's spirit guide, Dr. Wagner—but the descriptions varied greatly. For example, Brenda saw a tall, imposing man with an authoritarian air, while Bill reported a short man, warm, friendly and empathic. Dave resolved the discrepancy by telling some people that they were accurately reading other spirits than Dr. Wagner.

Regarding the class, nearly everyone told Dave to be less pushy and aggressive. Dave countered that he was picked for this work largely because of his strong, forceful salesmanship—perhaps repellent to some people, but attractive to many others.

To the accompaniment of popping flashbulbs, class ended with a graduation ceremony. For each student, Dave called his name, gave a kiss of congratulations, brought a benevolent and encouraging message from the spirit world, and presented a diploma emblazoned with a B.S. degree, for bachelor of spooks, from the Johnson School of Psychic Development.

Psychic was inadvertently spelled physic on the diploma—an apt misspelling which the graduates, sensitized to puns, noticed. They joked about physic meaning the science of physics or medicine, just where David would place his discipline, and about it meaning a cathartic, thus appropriate to Dave's task of unblocking natural processes.

After graduation we met for another 10 weeks at the same hour and place as clients in therapy.

The Indoctrination

Dave began treatment by furnishing some basic information about his methods and theories—a procedure some psychotherapists recommend (Goldstein et al. 1966). There were few surprises in what Dave called an indoctrination. Much of the material had been presented earlier in the mediumship class. With a long monologue, Dave oriented us to his views on therapy, and defined in broad outlines the nature of his work.

Many emotional problems involve the inability to give and receive love, and stem from poor upbringings and childhood neuroses. Parents, with their own difficulties in loving, warp children in various ways. What went wrong is usually blocked from a person's awareness, although sometimes partially revealed in dreams. Through my mediumship, breakthroughs invariably occur and persons learn why they are what they are.

In addition to the ever-present problem with loving, some of my clients think that they are hallucinating and therefore crazy. An error! They actually are perceiving "something." Spiritually sensitive, they should be proud and pleased to receive mediumistic communications, and can learn to control and properly use this ability. They should open the channels only under proper circumstances such as in séances, and close them during everyday activity.

Following the presentation of therapeutic principles, Dave described some dramatic case histories in which people were said to be profoundly grateful for his mediumistic aid.

For example: Gloria, a black maid who cleaned Dave's office, was frequently beaten in fights with her husband. Although she rarely spoke of the problem, through clairvoyance Dave told her the causes. Because of her resemblance to her dead mother, her father was aloof, cold, and abusive. Gloria both sought love from him and revenge upon him—conflicting desires which in time were directed to all men, and led to a stance of provocative spitefulness. Her husband was exquisitely sensitive to such treatment, and felt inadequate and inferior because of specific deprivations in his own background.

Reportedly awed by a wealth of accurate details, Gloria agreed to Dave's overall analysis of her situation. He gently suggested that she give love unconditionally to her father, not seek it, and that she pamper her husband, not irritate him. A few weeks later, she joyfully reported that this advice worked wonders.

In closing his introductory lecture, Dave guaranteed that nothing which occurred in the room would be revealed outside, but with one possible exception. Case histories might be used to illustrate his techniques, and if so, client identities would be disguised. Group members seemed satisfied with this policy, even Bill who had first raised the issue of confidentiality several weeks earlier.

Then to complete the indoctrination, Dave asked us to enter our "sanctuaries" with our spirit guides. We were to make ourselves comfortable and secure, then visualize two trees: one thriving in a favorable locale, the other suffering in a hostile one. After embellishing this familiar imagery, he pointedly asked whether either tree was responsible for being what it was—and subtly dared us to say yes.

Mary accepted the challenge and gravely said that the successful tree had responsibility for its condition. With a flurry of words and gestures, Dave strongly disagreed, saying that it was inconsistent for only one of the trees to be responsible. As a result Mary retracted her statement. Then Ann halfheartedly developed a tangled argument that both trees were to blame, but withdrew it in the face of Dave's fervent rebuttal.

Dave went on to say that although trees, like people, are not responsible for the way they turn out, improvements are nonetheless possible. "Psychic therapy" stimulates healthy growth by acting like fertilizer, water, and rich soil. Bill opined that this was biologically unsound and suggested transplanting instead. But Ann, a home gardener, defended the idea and the group agreed with her.

The History

In subsequent sessions, Dave delineated our childhood stresses and focused upon why our parents had deprived us of love. Although aggressive in manner, he nonetheless projected warmth, concern, and optimism—qualities that seem important in psychotherapy (Truax and Carkhuff 1967; Yalom 1970).

For his work with Alfred, he began by asking, "Is mother small?" "Yes," said Alfred who was but 5'9" and slender. Satisfied with being tuned into mother, Dave continued that she was very quiet and that Alfred was her only child. Alfred nodded his head. Then Dave described Alfred's first day in school, but Alfred denied any recollection of the event and furthermore seemed skeptical of Dave's description. Several minutes later, Alfred volunteered about wanting to stay home rather than attending school. Smiling, Dave attributed this reluctance to mother's lack of affection and Alfred's consequent insecurity regarding her love. Alfred was disbelieving, but Dave was adamant in his interpretation. He demanded to know how and when mother showed in a physical way that she loved Alfred. To demonstrate what he meant, he gave Alfred a hug. Alfred hung his head in silence.

Dave continued that Alfred was very good in mathematics. Dramatically pausing and batting his eyes, Dave said he could see Alfred's bringing home a picture for mother, but then destroying it. Alfred was puzzled. Dave asked, "Were you ashamed of such a painting? Were you a poor painter?" "Yes," admitted Alfred.

"Aha," said Dave, "That explains it then. Wait, another message is coming through. Mother didn't appreciate your accomplishments in school. She expected excellent work but took little notice when this occurred." Next, Dave asked what negative things mother had done. Alfred told about her reluctance to let him sit away from her on the bus, or to let him ride his bicycle into outlying areas of the neighborhood. Dave concluded that Alfred had fought against being smothered in childhood, and was still inclined to be rebellious.

Dave claimed that histories like Alfred's were psychically derived, but he offered little confirming evidence. He said his clairvoyant skills had been demonstrated sufficiently. Guided by some conspicuous biases, he generalized, extrapolated information from obvious cues, and enlarged upon matters that clients had mentioned earlier. The results were sometimes quite unacceptable.

For example, Mary in a wistful aside mentioned that her stepmother's house was not kept up properly. Very shortly, Dave said that stepmother was sloppy, and her untidiness made Mary feel abandoned. Angrily, Mary sputtered that stepmother was neat, conscientious, and industrious. Overwhelmed by the chores involved in taking care of a large house, and with no help, stepmother was physically unable to do all the required cleaning. Dave retorted, "if you really want to do something, you can always do it." Then he dropped the issue.

Usually Dave would insist tenaciously about his accuracy. A juggernaut in smashing resistance, he was fond of saying, "When I see something (clairvoyantly), I see it! I don't back down!" He was autocratic and emphatic. Rather than taking a client's history he gave it.

In addition he often supplied platitudes, which were very meaningful to him and centered upon love:

What the world needs now is love, sweet love.

You have to have received love before you can give it. Your cup must have runneth over with demonstrative affection. After school, your parents must have taken you in their arms, hugged you, said I love you and given you a cookie.

You have to love your parents, for you come from their loins and are flesh of their flesh.

When this was labeled preaching by some clients, Dave responded tangentially that his exhortations were useful and helpful for real life problems.

Dave explored an individual history for approximately one hour and during this period disregarded the other group members. Encouraged to listen quietly and to learn, told not to interfere, they were permitted to rest or to talk to "spirits." Some retreated inwardly and ignored events in the room; others even slept. Once Ann reported that she took an "astral trip" with her dead parents and settled many issues. Jubilantly she hugged everyone present.

Displays of emotion pleased Dave, since he generally interpreted strong feeling as evidence of progress. He particularly encouraged us to express all angers, resentments, and hatreds towards our parents, and suggested doing so by entering our "sanctuaries" and conversing spiritually with them. When we had difficulties "discharging venom," he acted as a dialogue coach, and sometimes even assumed a spoken role. These talks were reminiscent of gestalt therapy (Perls 1969; Perls et al. 1951) and guided affective imagery (Leuner 1969).

Eventually satisfied that all negative feelings were released, he supervised further discussions for us to gain other needed insights. These spiritual conversations involved parents, relatives, friends and spirit guides, as well as the spirits of ourselves at various younger ages.

The Homework

Each week Dave made assignments which were to be completed and mailed to him before the next meeting. Generally he asked us to describe events in the session. We relied upon memory because note-taking was considered disruptive and consequently prohibited. In addition he often asked us to enter into conversations with spirits on our own and to record them.

Dave would ask us to read our homework to the group. Listening carefully, he was alert for conflicts and defenses. Along with using the assignments as projective tests he also used them as didactic tools. His success in instilling insight could be judged, and erroneous conceptions could be detected and corrected. Our very words and concerns were used as springboards to develop further important items. Similar therapeutic uses of written material have been described in the psychiatric literature (Pearson 1965; Lauer and Goldfield 1970).

Group members were asked to retain duplicate copies of all homework, so that in any future emotional disturbance, they could re-examine the assignments and relive the therapy. Dave relayed several testimonials from clients for the efficacy of such recall.

Some members at times resisted homework. It reminded Bill, for example, of school which he detested. Dave lightly scolded us when the work wasn't done, and his restraint may have derived from fear of losing high status converts. Nevertheless under his gentle prodding, most persons did the work each week.

The Ritual Battles

Throughout most of therapy, Dave was bluntly authoritative, more so than he had been in the mediumship class. A dogged huckster, he pushed his ideas loudly and forcefully, and when criticized asserted that he was simply echoing his spirit guide's style. While expressing a willingness to experiment, generally he acted omniscient. He discouraged our suggestions by insisting that for heuristic purposes we discard our professional roles and adopt his thinking.

On one level he wanted agreement. Yet by expecting it to come reluctantly, he subtly provoked resistance. He assumed that we could not have discovered his concepts independently, and that we must have been unenlightened and mistaken. Consequently, we were to confess our ideological differences with him—then correct our errors and repent our sins. In short, he said challenge me, but be sure to lose.

The result was a series of mock struggles between Dave and each individual client. Dave would act determined and seek to win by force of will. Occasionally he would describe the perils of continued disagreement: "You will continue your wretched, miserable existence, never escaping your guilts and conflicts nor becoming a warm human being." Other times he would enlist his spirit guide, Dr. Wagner, whose authority the clients had already accepted. Once Dr. Wagner supplied this transference interpretation as a psychiatric dénouement. "Alfred stop this arguing. Dave is not your father, and don't act as if he were."

Continually, Dave overwhelmed his clients and emerged triumphant. However, some of them missed or came late to group meetings, and in this way may have retaliated.

The Finale

Repeatedly, Dave tantalized us with a "carrot." The final phase of therapy would have great impact and value: we would learn who and what we were, cut the "umbilical cord" with our parents, and put on an "armor of love." Truly, a miracle! Yet we must remain in some suspense since the precise staging could not be revealed prematurely.

To ready us for the breakthrough, Dave had worked from the first session towards one general target. We had to accept, like catechisms, certain basic principles, and understand their relevance to our lives.

I have difficulty loving and being loved.

It is not my fault.

It is due to my parents who were unable to give and receive love themselves.

It is not their fault, but due to their parents, and so on for proceeding generations.

Dave was disappointed that it took such a long time to ready us. The work was not quite completed after eight weeks, yet the group was about to dissolve due to vacations and moves out of the area. The culmination had to occur then if it was to take place at all. Dave decided we were sufficiently prepared to resolve our "root" difficulties, but that certain secondary problems or "leaves on our trees" might remain and need attention later.

Placing us in a circle with chairs facing outwards towards the walls, he asked us to avoid looking at one another so as to prevent disruptive "cross vibrations." Off went the lights, and in a commanding voice he told how we would soon find peace and happiness.

We were to ensconce ourselves in our individual "sanctuaries," invite Dave, Dr. Wagner, and our spirit guide inside, then tune in on the spirit of ourselves at the youngest age reachable. The next assignment was to slowly and carefully regress this spirit (which typically was about three years old) to the time of birth, age him to puberty, then regress him back to birth. With this accomplished, we were to progress the spirits forward in five-year jumps to the present. Mary's spirit was mired at age 15, but with effort she managed to move "her" along. When all had matured their child-spirits to adulthood, Dave told us to blend and merge them with ourselves, thus putting to rest what had been a hurt, frightened, irritable child.

Afterwards, we were to convey our love to the spirits of our parents. Filled with forgiveness, acceptance, and understanding, we were to be compassionate for our parents' sad, bleak, loveless lives, and for the circumstances which limited them and produced pain. If they were alive, we were to visit them as soon as possible and express our feelings.

Dave then read two long letters from people who had completed "psychic therapy," and were now leading fuller, richer lives. After these paeans, he requested we end by meditating, and then leave one by one without further talk.

The group found this finale powerful and moving, and in looking back believed that Dave's treatment had been helpful. Mary claimed to empathize more and avoid stereotyped games, while Bill was grateful for new insights about his family. For me, the main personal value was a heightened awareness of certain childhood problems.

Group members appropriated "psychic therapy" techniques into their own professional practices and referred clients to Dave. Nevertheless, they also considered his therapy to be just one of several effective treatment approaches, and thus not the sole answer for everyone's personal difficulties.

Dave, too, considered the sessions successful in meeting his needs. Despite his rebuffs of our teaching attempts, he thanked us for enabling him to learn new and useful matters. He avoided specifying just what was learned, although he alluded several times to an increased awareness of how long therapy can take. In the future, he hoped to accelerate treatment by correcting his client's descriptions of their parents, rather than furnishing the entire account himself.

Although unacknowledged by him, certain other benefits of the group were evident. He gained experience in dealing with psychologically sophisticated clients, built a channel to local mental health professionals so as to spread his ideas and secure referrals, and enhanced his standing with clients by his work as a therapist's therapist.

Evaluation

"Psychic therapy," although different from standard psychotherapy, utilized many commonly-accepted clinical principles. Dave Johnson believed that childhood conflicts impaired interpersonal relationships and caused psychosomatic symptoms. Working with individuals or groups, he projected confidence, hope, warmth, and trust. He maintained confidentiality, but reserved the right to disseminate case reports with disguised clients' identities. Using interpretations, suggestions, active imagery, writing, and role playing, pointing out traumas, resistances, defenses, conflicts, and transferences, he unraveled histories and fostered insights, thus influencing attitudes and behaviors. Because of this face validity, "psychic therapy" should have worked— and it did. Group members, who were trained psychotherapists, considered it effective in producing constructive psychological changes within them. In short, "psychic therapy" appeared to be potent on the basis of both psychiatric theory and clients' satisfaction.

A similar case could be made for the effectiveness of other types of mediumistic counseling in aiding emotionally disturbed people. Such folk methods are becoming popular as part of the current renaissance of occultism (Krippner and Fersh 1970; Roszak 1969; Truzzi in press). This effectiveness and popularity has relevance to some critical mental health problems. Mental illness is rampant and orthodox treatment is often unavailable or unsuitable (Joint Commission 1961; Srole et al. 1962; Leighton et al. 1963). New methods of intervention and additional sources of manpower are needed.

Under the rubric of "community mental health" (Bellak 1964; Goldston 1965; Dumont 1968; Adelson 1970), professionals are now trying to strengthen indigenous resources. They assist various personnel who supply reassurance, companionship, encouragement, guidance, training, protection, and other services with mental health impact. In this regard, they already have worked with teachers, clergymen, policemen, radio broadcasters, bartenders, and public defenders. Psychics, despite their possibly alien beliefs and values, also might be regarded as community assets, and consequently would warrant attention. Mental health personnel could learn about mediums and consider developing appropriate ways of utilizing them. Professionals might find it worthwhile to discuss problems and trade ideas with psychics, or to enter with them relationships of consultation, teaching, supervision, or therapy. A number of mediums seem amenable to overtures from the mental health establishment and some, like Dave Johnson, have even initiated contacts on their own. Collaboration could bring mutual advantages in terms of sharing information and exchanging sanctions and referrals. In return for support and advice, mediums could provide the community mental health effort with added manpower; rapid, inexpensive intervention techniques; and access to previously unreached people. Visits of mediums to hospitalized patients could be legitimatized instead of as at present having them occur covertly.

Hindering this proposed alliance are several factors. Some professionals worry that they might overwhelm mediums with superior methods. The psychics would feel inadequate and their clients would lose faith. Other professionals accept negative stereotypes of occultists, viewing them as weird and repugnant (Loyd and Irwin 1970). They claim that psychics purvey magic, deny reality, support spiritual delusion, defraud through tricks and deceptions, and reduce stress which could lead to a better adaptation. They denounce mediums for their egregious conduct in promoting pathology. Partly to retaliate, some mediums claim that mental health practices are foolish, even dangerous; that people need to develop and progress spiritually, not be labeled sick and crazy; and that professional practitioners are insensitive and incompetent.

Obviously, obstacles to collaboration are formidable, yet possibly they can be surmounted. Psychic-psychiatric alliances may be quite useful, and attempts should be made to develop and assess them.

Summary

This report described the mediumship training and "psychic therapy" given to a group of psychotherapists. Dave Johnson, the medium-leader, gained money, sanctions, and information from the group, but his stated purpose in organizing it was to obey his psychiatrist spirit-guide. The pupils, myself excepted, previously had developed metaphysical interests on their own and were ripe for Dave's training. Dave explained his doctrine, language, and technique for "picking up" spiritual messages. The pupils discussed his concepts, used his vocabulary and practiced his methods, gaining facility in mediumship and becoming his partisans. A gracious guru, he sometimes permitted role reversal and asked students to teach him. Classwork ended in a clearly-marked way with a formal graduation ceremony, following which the group reformed and centered on therapy. Through mediumship, Dave pointed out to individuals the ways in which parents had hurt them. Following his guidance, the group members responded first with anger, then with forgiveness—and finally accepted their parents as blameless.

Just as Dave's therapy appeared helpful, so too may other types of mediumistic counseling. Mental health personnel should examine the utility of such folk treatments and consider professional collaboration with psychics.

Magical Therapy:
An Anthropological Investigation
of Contemporary Satanism

There is a revival of Black Magic and Satanism in the West at the present time. Many well-educated individuals are practicing the Black Arts. In so doing they make themselves the target of the community's scorn and aggression. Why do they persist? They persist because their magic "works" by helping them to achieve the goals they desire. This paper attempts to indicate how magical rituals such as the Invocation of Lust and the Shibboleth Ritual help practicing Satanists, members of the Church of the Trapezoid, to accomplish their desires.

THE crashing music stops and in the sudden silence the air seems to throb and pulse. Then a candle flickers into life, and then another, and another. In their flickering light dark and shadowy figures can be seen, their shadows dancing grotesquely on the wall of the ritual chamber. From above, the Goat God gazes down upon the motionless tableau. Then a black-robed figure steps forward to the stone altar beneath the Baphomet and, as the gong is struck, lifts the gleaming sword high above the naked and motionless body of the young girl stretched supine upon the altar before him . . .

Africa? Medieval Europe? No! The time is the present and the setting is the First Church of the Trapezoid, the Church of Satan, San Francisco, California. The members of the congregation, many of them by day respected and ostensibly respectable citizens, are members of a group of witches and magicians practicing the Black Arts of witchcraft and magic. They are part of a contemporary rebirth of black and white magic in the modern and urban environment that is sweeping the Western world, a rebirth that is part of a growing interest in the occult and is seen in the growing number of cults or religions devoted to the "mystic arts." [1] Who are these people? Why do they

---

[1] It is not my intention to argue the question of whether or not the Satanic Church is indeed a religion as measured by some set of "universal" objective criteria. My definition of "religion" is a simple one which follows that developed by Wallace (1966: 107): "Religion is a set of rituals rationalized by myth, which

risk exposure, ridicule, even social sanction to practice the ancient art of Black Magic? Why do they become Satanists? It was in order to seek an answer to this and related questions that I joined the First Church of Satan. For two years I was an active member of the group, a participant-observer in the anthropological sense of the term, taking part in all aspects of the religion. Although the answer to my original question proved deceptively simple—people become black magicians because magic "works," it accomplishes many of the ends which the Satanists desire—an answer to the next obvious question, *how* magic "works," proved to be less obvious, and it is that topic which is the subject of this paper.

Anthropological, historical, and theological scholarship is filled with learned and semi-learned articles on the phenomenon of witchcraft. The mysterious power of magic has a fascination even for the staid and rational scholars of the West, and indeed it should have, for magic and evil are ubiquitous parts of the total "world view" of virtually every culture investigated to date.[2] Whether investigators acknowledge the existence of actual confessed witches (Crawford 1967) or not (Evans-Pritchard 1937), no study of any culture, including those of the West, would be complete without a description of beliefs about witches and witchcraft.

In 1967 I became aware of a new group of practicing witches and became fascinated by the possibility of investigating the Church of the Trapezoid and its members. Almost without exception anthropologists working in non-Western cultures have analyzed witchcraft as either

---

mobilizes supernatural powers for the purpose of achieving or preventing transformations of state in man and nature."

A more complex problem is distinguishing the witches and the Satanists. The two terms are not mutually exclusive. Simply put, witches may have power even without making a pact with the Devil. Devil worship is a product of the Judeo-Christian tradition. Indeed, it is ironical that a good part of the Satanic practice used today may be the product of the overactive imagination of overzealous inquisitors rather than duplications of the "real" activities of the Devil worshipers of the time.

Most material on non-Western witchcraft has no mention of the Devil or Satan. Any mention of witchcraft in the West indicates that it was the learned opinion of the time that witches' power comes from a pact with Satan, "the Opposition." This is the structure of the institution today. For further information on Satanism and demonology, see the following works: Cristiani 1962; Crow 1970; Dodson 1969; Gardner 1959, 1954; Hansen 1969; Holzer 1969; Huebner 1969; King 1970; LaVey 1969; Leek 1970; Lyons 1970a; Maple 162; Martello 1969; Marwick 1970; Parrinder 1963; Paulsen 1970; Rhodes 1954; Roberts 1971; Robson 1969; Schurmacher 1970; Seth 1968; Valiente 1962; or C. H. Wallace 1967; and for special information on the Salem Witch trials, Burr 1914; Fox 1968; and Starkey 1961.

[2] The world view of every culture which I personally have investigated distinguishes between good and evil, the presence of evil frequently being given as the reason for or cause of misfortune.

behavior based on ignorance or lack of scientific knowledge (e.g. Parrinder 1963), as a social institution functioning to control deviant behavior (deviants could be accused of witchcraft and punished), or as an institutionalized outlet for the culture's forbidden aggressions. Virtually no one has viewed the institution from the point of view of the witches except to cite the culture's "folk" explanation for the abnormal and deviant behavior of the witches. Few modern writers apparently have actually encountered witches, a fact that has not prevented most of them from making ethnocentrically biased observations concerning the personality characteristics of the witch (see Caro Baroja 1964). Even those who have encountered self-confessed witches have been more interested in the social and psychological functions of the act of confession than in the functions of the practice of witchcraft itself. The modern view seems to be that there are no such things as witches except in the imagination of the members of a culture. The historical literature contains many references to witch crazes and even to confessions of witchcraft throughout European history, and though the validity of many of the statements is questionable due to the methods by which the statements were obtained—torture of various and sundry kinds—and the obvious biases of the investigators (Sprenger and Institoris 1948; Summers 1926; Robbins 1959), it is clear that Black Magic and Satanism are not new phenomena, even in the West. The lack of scientific interest in the topic is therefore astounding.

Although it is not my intention to deal specifically with the sociology of witchcraft, an examination of witchcraft beliefs in various cultures reveals several common characteristics uniting those *accused* of witchcraft. Witchcraft is usually suspected of those who are envious, resentful, or powerless. It is expected from people who are not full members of the community, whose position within the culture and society is not well defined and whose behavior is therefore somewhat unpredictable (these people are usually low on the scale of social status). Moreover, witchcraft in non-Western cultures does not operate at a distance but is expected in face-to-face relationships. The accusation of witchcraft may be made against mothers' brothers in a matrilineal society (Nadel 1952), co-wives or brothers in another type of social system (Lienhardt 1951), or even non-related individuals in a small community (Kluckhohn 1967), but all accusations come in relationships which are unavoidable but which tend to produce socially forbidden hostility (Lienhardt 1951). Accusations come in situations in which the relative status of the two persons is not rigidly defined, where expectations are not fixed, in the "cracks and crevices of the social system," as Mary Douglas puts it (1967). The accusation of witchcraft is an expression of fear: fear of the resentment and envy of those people who are in subordinate positions without legitimate means of either modifying their position or expressing the hostility which the accuser knows they must feel. The suspected witch is believed to be the frustrated, powerless one—be she a wife from outside the husband's community or merely an asocial or marginal person like the traditional crone of Western witch beliefs, old, ugly, widowed or never married, and envious.

This characterization of persons accused of witchcraft in other cultures is a surprisingly accurate depiction of many if not all of the Satanists I encountered. They too turn to witchcraft out of envy and frustration. They desire successes denied them—money, fame, recognition, power—and with all legitimate avenues apparently blocked, with no apparent means by which legitimate effort will bring reward, they turn to Satanism and witchcraft. In some cases the resentment is that of a frustrated, hostile, but powerless figure who lacks legitimate means of striking back at supposed aggressors: the subordinate striking back at his boss by the only available means. The practice of witchcraft appears, in fact, to spring from the very sources which produce accusations of witchcraft: unfulfilled desire, frustration, envy, and need for "power."

It is easy to bring the accusation of witchcraft, to accuse others of hostility and anger, to accept the "boundless possibilities of sheer human malevolence . . . because we all know the depth of our own hearts" (Mair 1969: 13). Most of us know personally the anger of resentment and frustration, have said in our own hearts, "I wish he was dead," and have refused to accept our own inadequacy as a reason for the greater success of our rivals. It is easy to project this feeling into others and not unreasonable to expect them to have similar feelings.

The next obvious question is: Why do some turn to the Church of Satan, to Black Magic and the Occult? In answering this question, I will attempt to depict some of the characteristics of the individual who turns to magic. This depiction is a model, a type case, and certainly does not provide a list of characteristics which would allow one to predict just who becomes a Satanist and who does not. There are types of individuals who are more likely to become Satanists than others, but certainly the circumstances of various life crises—does the individual come into contact with some form of magic at a crucial time and so on—has an effect.

Upon becoming acquainted with the Satanists [3] I began searching

[3] Data was collected during a two-year period of participant observation. I would like to emphasize that the San Francisco Satanists are one group among many and that the forms of Satanism and witchcraft are many. I would also like to point out that the period of investigation was during the early stages of the

for some traditional sociological pigeonhole into which I could put them. It wasn't easy to find. Famous and obscure, wealthy and poor, "successes" and "failures," upper to lower class, young and old, right-wing to left-wing political opinions—all were represented in the early Church membership, along with a baker's dozen or more assorted psychological "syndromes" ranging from transvestism to sado-masochism. A single factor seemed to typify all of them: all were deviant or abnormal in some aspect of their social behavior. Although they usually were behaviorally "normal" in most social contexts, in some areas each exhibited maladaptive or abnormal responses.[4]

By abnormal behavior I mean simply that they engaged in some behavior which was disturbing to other members, especially important members, of their society, behavior which deviated from established cultural norms. It is the position of the behavioral therapist that abnormal behavior is no different from "normal" behavior in its development or maintenance; it is simply socially incorrect (Ullman and Krasner 1969: 92–105). The abnormal person, behaviorally, is deficient in either his ability to perceive or receive social stimuli, or in the skills necessary to make the appropriate response. If he lacks these skills and responds in an "abnormal" or unpredictable fashion he is labeled abnormal by other members of society. Abnormal behavior is frequently no more than culturally unanticipated or unexpected behavior. The deviant's behavior is not so much disturbed as disturbing, for the person who does not play according to the rules casts doubt on the validity of the game and causes anxiety in the minds of others who do play according to the rules.

Other members of the social network frequently respond by excluding the deviant from social interaction and, by labeling him abnormal, creating at least a partial set of expectations for his behavior: the "crazy" role. In so doing they deny the "deviant" member of the system the accurate feedback necessary for him to evaluate his behavior. Thus deviants are placed in socially and often geographically marginal positions, denied interaction which will allow them to adapt their behavior via feedback, and forced to interact only with other marginal or abnormal individuals who reinforce abnormal responses. The deviant

---

Church of the Trapezoid's growth. A visit this year indicates changes in the composition of the membership and in the structure of the Church. Over the past three years, as the Church of Satan has become more institutionalized and less marginal, criteria for membership has been stiffened, and the process of advancement formalized.

4 "Normal" and "abnormal" are, in my opinion, relative terms. Not only are they culturally relative, but relative to social context. In some cases abnormal may mean that the individual exhibits "correct" responses, e.g. sexuality, in socially "incorrect" settings.

becomes locked into a vicious cycle with improper behavior leading to negative responses from others which increases anxiety or expectations of failure, which further inhibits behavior, which leads to more failure, which leads to more negative social response, and so on. The result can be generalization of an avoidance response, a desire to avoid negative responses from others as the result of aversive conditioning, which becomes extended to all social interactions. Such is the case among the pre-Satanists—individuals who will eventually become Satanists. Although a man may be successful in business, for example, the negative responses which he gets as a homosexual may influence his interactions generally. Failure due to inability to respond correctly in social situations results in a generalized feeling of inadequacy and negative self-evaluation, especially if he accepts the label of deviant placed upon him.

Lack of knowledge of the rules of the social game and the lack of success which springs from social ineptitude bring a general feeling of lack of power, of inability to achieve one's goals or to make the outcome favorable to oneself—simply put, inability to make the system respond.

The roots of abnormality among the pre-Satanists are not difficult to find. A great many of the Satanists whom I interviewed reported childhoods marred by strife: they spoke of broken homes, drunken parents, aggressive and hostile siblings, and so on. While it is not necessary to trace childhood causes—knowing that the pre-Satanist's behavior is abnormal is sufficient for analysis—this report indicates that the people who socialized the pre-Satanists were themselves frequently less than adequate social actors. It is not likely that socially inept agents could teach their children completely appropriate responses. It is, in fact, likely that the discriminations, generalizations, and responses taught were themselves abnormal and likely to bring negative or aversive consequences in social interaction, or, in some cases, were responses appropriate only in a specific social context and abnormal in other contexts.

Furthermore, social rules are constantly changing and, especially in our pluralistic culture, conflict between sets of rules is highly likely. The complex and diverse sets of rules, both overt and covert, which govern our behavior make it almost impossible to avoid some transgressions (see Wallenstein and Wylie 1947). Gluckman (1965) and others point out that the number of witchcraft accusations in a social group rises in times of culture change, such as when rural Africans move into an urban environment. It is at times such as these that the rules change and expectations are weak.

In summary, the various individuals who are members of the Satanic cult exhibit behaviors which are at variance with cultural norms. They suffer aversive consequences as a result of this behavior: rejection, social failure, punishment, etc., and learn to perceive themselves as inadequate and powerless, unable to accomplish what they desire.

There are several ways in which they can alleviate the fear and anxiety that they feel in such a situation. Some "pre-Satanists" (the term I will use to designate Satanists before they join the Church) go to acknowledged socialization agents for help: to the Judeo-Christian religious practitioners, or to psychotherapists. Usually these attempts at behavior modification fail for one of several reasons. In both cases the pre-Satanist is asked by the practitioner to admit his inadequacy or abnormality, and although he may want help in learning the accepted social mores, the pre-Satanist usually balks at admitting that the source of his difficulty lies within himself. Moreover, in the case of the religious specialist, success is usually of a spiritual nature, while the Satanist is concerned with immediate results in the mundane world.

The pre-Satanists report that the psychotherapist usually spends a great deal of time attempting to get the individual to redefine his problems in terms with which the therapist can deal, terms familiar to the therapist but not meaningful to the pre-Satanist. The deviants' unwillingness to do this means that they do not do anything which the therapist perceives as warranting reinforcement, and their behavior soon becomes aversive to the frustrated therapist and his to them (Rickels and Anderson 1967).

And so the potential Satanist, anxious and socially inept, exhibiting behaviors and having feelings (so they say) which are forbidden and which cause them to doubt their own worth, are kept at the margins of society, denied feedback other than negative responses (Moody 1971). Poorly socialized, unaware of the "chains of causality" which bring results in social action, the pre-Satanists have no explanation for the successes of one person and the failures of others. The pre-Satanist too wants the rewards, the monetary successes and sexual conquests, that are the symbol of social adequacy in our culture. Unaware of the covert rules by which others operate, the type of implicit understanding which aids one in successful social interaction, the Satanist can see no good reason for the inordinate success of one man as opposed to another, just as they can, even more to the point, see no good reason for their own failure.

And yet they have a sense of there being something moving and influencing both themselves and the world around them. It is difficult to accept a chaotic world. A world in which there are no expectations, in which all is unpredictable, is an anxiety-provoking world. And so they strain to structure the world and to make it systematic and consistent. They attempt to give a name to the unnamed forces which they feel moving and influencing them, the forces of sorcery, perhaps, or conscience; and they attempt to find an explanation for misfortune.

Frequently this attempt leads to magic. The step from our "rational" and "scientific" world to the world of magic is not a difficult one. Our Western world view is shot through with magical thinking. The Judeo-Christian notion of the world of Good has as its necessary complement the world of Evil; God is opposed by the Devil, the forces of white light and spirit are opposed by the legions of darkness and earthiness. It may be that this bipolar division of the categories of understanding is innate in man, but it is certainly true that the division is part of the Western tradition. To be a good Christian, one must believe, of necessity, in Evil and the Devil. Satan was, and is frequently used, as witchcraft is used in all societies, as an explanation for the otherwise inexplainable evils and misfortunes that befall man.

Given this world view, the pre-Satanist frequently takes his first step into the world of magic in an effort to make the world in which he lives predictable and therefore less anxiety-provoking. Astrology, card-reading, the tarot, crystal-gazing, and other forms of divination are an accepted part of even our sophisticated urban environment. It is possible to gain a sense of partial control over one's fate by reading daily horoscopes or divining the course of the cosmos. The concept of inexorable fate influencing man's future is appealing to many of the pre-Satanists. They are people troubled by a lack of self-esteem, by failure and doubt. And how much better it is for such a person to know that one's failure is not caused by personal shortcomings alone, but is also a function of great and mysterious powers, the power of evil, for example, before which *all* are relatively helpless. Fate or Satan serve as a reasonable explanation for the differential success.

For some individuals, this level of magical involvement is sufficient to reassure them and reduce their anxiety, and they may stop here and not move beyond. For others, the "seekers," in Catton's terminology (Catton 1968), astrology does not fill the bill. Although it may improve one's feeling that the world is predictable if one knows the rules of prediction, astrology does not guarantee success and may not improve one's success in social interaction appreciably. The pre-Satanist usually believes that further investigation is called for and more powerful means of control of one's fate necessary. Having been introduced to the notion of esoteric science through astrology, it is not a difficult step to the notion of a magic more amenable to individual control. Those who eventually become Satanists usually have begun with astrology but have come into contact with other types of magic in the magical subculture of the urban center (the "candle shops" and magic stores which sell occult supplies). Others have come to magic via the medium of magazines dealing with the occult. Astrology magazines frequently contain advertisements for occult groups which promise one the secrets of success, of magical control and power. The Rosicrucians come to mind, or the Keepers of the Golden Key. They promise the seeker the key to that success that he has always wanted but which has eluded him, the secrets of the ages which he has perhaps felt accounted for the success of others but which he himself has never learned.[5]

I am not sure why other occult groups fail the pre-Satanist. I believe that perhaps the lack of practical application, the lack of demonstrable effect of the teachings of many of these groups, the constant demands for money, serve to disillusion the pre-Satanists who have tried one or more of these organizations. In some cases he has actually attended meetings or lectures given by groups interested in such occult subjects as flying saucers, etc. (Catton 1968). In so doing, he moves into an occult subculture that operates in most major urban areas. The meeting places of the subculture vary from the lecture hall to the magic store where the implements for magical working may be purchased. Whatever the other results of this experience, the pre-Satanist has been brought into contact with people whose world view includes the possibility of forces and powers unknown to the ordinary man. It is usually in this context that the pre-Satanist first discovers the existence of Black Magic and, eventually, hears of Anton LaVey and the First Church of the Trapezoid.

Such an individual is the model convert. He is, in Toch's terms, "a disillusioned person, and disillusionment is a slow, surreptitious type of change. . . . It represents a cumulative record of the costs of adaptation. Whether it dies in its suppressed state or becomes publicized in awareness depends on the number and import of disillusioning experiences that are encountered . . . a person will tend to become disillusioned if he becomes actively involved in life situations for which he has been ill-prepared by socialization" (Toch 1965: 128). The pre-Satanist is such a person—marginal, unsuccessful, faced by experiences of which he has no knowledge and for which he has no

[5] These groups—the Rosicrucians, the Keepers of the Golden Key, and others—promise literally that all the ills which plague the anxiety-ridden sociopath, sickness, failure, impotence, and so on, will be eliminated once the "Secrets of the Ages," the "esoteric knowledge of the ancient masters" is acquired. For the potential Satanist, convinced that there must be some key to his failure and other's success, this is an obvious answer.

precedent. He has been receiving negative responses from the social system and now wishes to begin "reduction of ties to a prior evaluative system and of aversive consequences for deviation from it" (Ullman and Krassner 1969: 206): Having consciously or implicitly identified the source of his problems as the evaluative system, an essentially Judeo-Christian system of his culture, the pre-Satanist wishes to reduce the anxiety caused him by behavior at variance with his culture and his beliefs. In reducing this cognitive dissonance (Festinger 1957), "if one's labeling of proper behavior and one's own behavior do not match, the procedure requiring the least effort is to alter one's concepts of proper behavior" (Ullman and Krassner 1969: 208). This is precisely what the Satanist does during his initial period of membership in the Church of the Trapezoid.

He is already at odds with the values of the larger society, and by changing that evaluation for the evaluation of a more highly esteemed but select group he can change his perception of himself and his world. And so he comes to witchcraft and, tautological though such an explanation may be, for the believer, Black Magic provides a solution. It solves the problem of the fragmented self, of guilt, of inadequacy, of anxiety, of lack of success, and it solves them "magically."

With few other options open to him, faced with the problems of fragmentation of self, social ineptitude, and a lack of any explanation for his failure and the success of others, the pre-Satanist turns from astrology and card-reading—"magic in sports clothes" as the High Priest Anton LaVey would say—to serious practice of magic. He has, from the behavioral point of view, two basic problems which he must solve: a high level of anxiety (the product of an unpredictable environment and the expectation of failure in social interaction); and some maladaptive behavioral characteristics which, based upon an incomplete or erroneous perception of the social situation coupled with an abnormal set of conditioned responses, lead to negative responses from those around him.

The would-be Satanist expresses his problem in terms of lack of power. His anxiety must be lowered, his maladaptive responses extinguished, and appropriate responses conditioned. This is all accomplished primarily through the ritual of the Satanic Church, and Black Magic rituals. I would like to devote the remainder of this paper to a discussion of the function and effect of various Satanic rituals on the Satanist himself.

The would-be Satanist asks, "Is there a secret to success?" Anton LaVey, High Priest and sorcerer, responds, "Of course, magic." The pre-Satanist asks, "Will you teach me?" LaVey replies, "If you are worthy." When after a series of tests and interviews the pre-Satanist is asked to become a member of the elite Inner Circle, his low opinion of himself is already slightly altered and, with social support of his new friends, his anxiety begins to diminish.

The Satanic novice, already disillusioned, has a concerted effort made to make him change the very basis of his value system. In addition to teaching the novice Satanist magic, his fellow witches and magicians teach him that he is "evil," but the definition of evil is changed. In some cases the new Satanist has harbored a nagging belief that he is evil—his deviant behavior is usually at odds with some aspect of the Judeo-Christian tradition in which most of us were raised—but his fears are at last out in the open. He is actively encouraged to speak of his evil (deviant) thoughts and deeds and lauded instead of reviled for them. It is a tenet of the Satanic theology that evil is relative to the time and place in which the deed is done—a sentiment which sounds very Boasian to an anthropologist—and only when one feels guilty about doing something is he really "doing wrong." The Satanists persuade their adherents that the Judeo-Christian value system was a trick perpetrated on our forefathers. It is the position of the Satanic church that the "white light magicians" (Christians) made sins of natural human impulses in order to be sure that people would transgress. They then, by making salvation dependent on belief in Christianity, "hooked" the population and made them dependent on the Christian church for freedom from fear. The Satanists, by contrast, persuade their new members to revel in their own humanity, to give free reign to their natural impulses and indulge their appetites without fear or guilt. Members are constantly reminded that man is the human *animal,* and members are encouraged to throw off the shackles of Christianity and rediscover the joy of living. "Evil" is redefined as human, free, unafraid, and joyful.

It is interesting to note in passing that the image which the Satanists adopt is virtually identical to the symbolic image of the witch in many cultures. The witch in all cultures is the symbolic antithesis of the well-socialized "good" member of society: free where the "normal" person is controlled, unreservedly sexual or aggressive where the good member of society obeys rules, animalistic where the ordinary member is spiritual. Witches are depicted as ugly, abnormal physically, and depraved; given to performing the most horrendous of acts, they are aggressive with absolutely no possible reason (witches kill innocent and helpless newborn infants and eat them). They are, in short, more animal-like and less social. It is an almost universal belief that witches can converse with animals, implying that they are closer to the animal world. In many parts of the world the witch is believed to have the power to actually turn himself into an animal, a clear indication of the animalistic aspect of the witch's nature. In the Western tradition, the Devil clearly stands midway between the completely animal (or physical) and the completely human (or spiritual). He has a mixture of animal and human parts: he is hermaphroditic with a man's torso but a woman's breasts, with human arms but animal legs. He is the very symbol of confusion between the animal and the spiritual. In some African tribes witches are believed actually to be reversed or inverted humans, going about on their hands upside down.

The Satanists accept most of this image, but change the associated semantic evaluation of "evil" from bad to, at the very least, natural. They deliberately set out to be the antithesis of Christianity, preaching indulgence rather than abstinence, strength rather than meekness, worldly rather than other-worldly orientation. They preach power rather than weakness and depict the image of the crucified Christ as "pallid incompetence nailed to a tree." The new member is likely to find himself praised and rewarded for the very thoughts and behaviors which brought him pain and scorn in the larger community. In Wallace's words, what has been initiated is a "ritual of salvation" in which the "desperate quest for an experience that knits together the raveled aspects of an identity into a new coherent synthesis" (Wallace 1966: 207) has temporarily ended, the individual's disorder partially molded into a more socially understandable if not generally acceptable pattern. This aspect of the Satanist's indoctrination obviously has characteristics of a religious "revitalization" movement in the truest sense, for it brings "organization into a rich but disorderly field by eliminating some of the materials (thus reducing the cultural repertoire to more manageable size) and combining what is left into a more orderly structure" (Wallace 1966: 211). For the new Satanist, the lack of predictability in social interaction has been reduced by removing certain elements and organizing the others into a more coherent and simpler whole. In a confused world of shifting values, often in an anomic urban world, such extraneous things as the "Golden Rule" and the "Seven Deadly Sins" have been eliminated and replaced with a pragmatic belief in man's basic animal nature. In the world of My Lai and Dallas, of massive retaliation and graft scandals, it is not difficult to argue that the Satanist's position is more realistic and that expectations based on their view of man as being self-aggrandizing and greedy are more likely to be accurate.

If the Satanist is brought to accept, even relish, his shortcomings, and believe in his own worth, if his guilt and anxiety are diminished, he is already on the way to more effective action, to a more successful social adaptation.

The Black Mass and Other Blasphemies

For many individuals, as you might expect, the transition from Christian to Satanist is not as easy as I have pictured it. The ingrained and conditioned responses of a lifetime are not so easily altered. Many would-be Satanists, like that personification of evil the Hollywood vampire, still cower in guilt and fear before the charismatic power of the symbols of Christianity. Though they may want to be "evil," the conditioned fear or awe response ingrained by twenty years of conditioning does not extinguish easily. Guilt may still inhibit their behavior, anxiety prevent them from giving up an old and fear-conditioned response and, facing a new reality, developing a new behavioral adaptation.

It is for people such as these that the Black Mass is intended. Not only is it a symbolic expression of the opposition of the Satanists to the superstitions and rituals of Christianity, but it also has a more direct function. It is a blasphemy.

Behavioral therapists [6] tell us that there are several ways to modify an anxious or fearful response to a given stimulus. The anxiety response must be replaced by another response antithetical to fear or anxiety. The purpose of a blasphemy is to bring about a change in the Satanists' responses.[7] Any institution can be blasphemed, but the most frequent and popular target among the Satanists is Judeo-Christian symbols. The traditional Black Mass parodies the Christian Mass using urine for communion wine, a beet rubbed in vaginal fluid for the wafer and so on. The cross is hung upside down, and in some cults was and is used for other bizarre purposes of a sexual nature. A naked female was and is the altar, and in some instances the mass itself is ridiculed, the "Lord's Prayer" is recited backward, obscene phrases chanted in Latin, and so on.

Like the rat who is trained to expect food for bar-pressing when a light goes on, the Satanist has often been trained to feel guilty or awed in the presence of the Cross, or a priest, or even a nun. But like

---

[6] There is some controversy over the efficacy of treating "symptoms" of the "deeper problem." Can one change more "basic" attitudes by modifying surface behavior is a question asked. The work of Bem (1967) and Bandura, Blanchard, and Ritter (1969) indicates that attitude change, regardless of the original cause of maladaptive responses, can and does *follow* modification of the maladaptive behavior rather than precede it.

[7] As Wallace (1966: 106–107) points out, "all ritual is directed toward the problem of transformations of state in human beings or nature." Sometimes the purpose is to insure rapid transformation, sometimes to prevent it. The Satanists are more explicit about the ritual effects desired than any other religion I have encountered. In some cases they describe the effects in terms of magic, at other times their explanation is very sociological.

the rat when his response is no longer rewarded, the Satanists' guilt reaction often disappears when their fear response is no longer rewarded but in fact ridiculed by other Satanists (an aversive stimulus). The absence of lightning bolts from above or other aversive stimuli following a blasphemy weakens the conditioned response of fear. But as Ullman and Krassner put it, "the therapist who removes a particular behavior without helping to replace it with some more adjustive response to the situation in which the former behavior was emitted is doing only half his professional job" (1969: 253).

In addition, a response antithetical to fear or anxiety must be and is conditioned to the old stimulus. The new response may vary. Some responses antithetical to anxiety are anger, disgust, or laughter. If one is made to consume the "bread and wine" mentioned previously (urine and vaginal fluid), the Christian ritual and its symbols will eventually become associated with or evoke a "disgust" response rather than "fear." In some rituals, aggression, another antithetical response, against the symbols is encouraged, breaking them, urinating on them, and yet another non-anxiety response is conditioned.

One of the most effective tactics is the use of laughter. Some blasphemies are grotesque burlesques or parodies of religious rituals and evoke laughter. Eventually the formerly anxiety-provoking stimuli bring disgust, anger, or laughter, but not fear.

As a result of religious rituals within the Inner Circle, the new Satanist is now going through a "personality" transformation, a modification of many formerly maladaptive anxiety-producing behaviors. He is becoming less anxious (the world is more predictable) and more sure of himself (he is learning to do magic). But this in itself would not be enough to insure continuing interest in the Church. LaVey has promised success and help via magic; and now he must and does make good his promise.

AN EXAMPLE: THE INVOCATION OF LUST AND SYSTEMATIC DESENSITIZATION

An individual named Billy G., who became a member of the Satanic Church shortly after my initiation, is an almost classic illustration of the efficacy of "magic." The son of Fundamentalist Baptist missionaries, Billy G. had been raised in the Billy Graham tradition. He had been taught that most impulses which he had were "the Devil tempting him." By the time Billy G. was 18 and had moved away from what he termed the "up-tight" atmosphere of his home, he found that the Devil was after him a good deal of the time. He was being constantly beset by impulses which were, by his family's definition, "evil." Especially in his heterosexual interactions he was extremely anxious. He had been taught that any "lustful" thoughts about a female were wrong and sinful, and as a result he had great difficulty interacting with females. This problem had become so serious by the time he became a member of the Satanic Church that he could not stay in the presence of a young woman without showing symptoms of severe anxiety—sweating, alternate flushing or paling, and so on.

After joining the Satanic Church he began to relax a bit as his conception of what was "right" and "wrong" were altered, and along with them his perception of himself. Generally a little less anxious and guilty, Billy G. was still anxious about females and lacking in general social ability in heterosexual situations. He still had not been taught the "magical" power to attract and win females. To accomplish this he was instructed in both Greater and Lesser Magic, and I will use his case to illustrate a few additional facets of magical therapy.

It is worth noting that the explanations just given and those to be given do not rely on psychoanalytic theory, as do so many discussions of religion and magic. It is not necessary to postulate or even hypothesize about childhood traumas or deep-seated neuroses in order to explain the process of magical therapy. It may be true that many of the members of the Church have, by our culture's standards, neuroses—transvestism, for example, probably is a surface manifestation of "deeper" problems—but it is not necessary to deal with the problem on the deeper level in order to change the behavior. The associated problem is less one of psychopathology than sociopathology. The source of difficulty for the marginal or deviant man is not his inner thought so much as it is his external behavior based on those thoughts. Many of us have deviant thoughts from time to time, a situation which does not disturb our social relationships until those thoughts are expressed in action. It is my contention that changing behavior is all that is necessary for one to be adjudged "normal" by society. If society reacts favorably to one's behavior, then in most cases one's anxiety diminishes and one's rate of behavioral or social success increases. Change in behavior may require a change in values or meaning such as the reconditioning of responses to charismatic objects just described, but it is difficult and perhaps unnecessary to demonstrate changes in the "deeper" structure of the personality in order to show adaptation and even adjustment.

In Billy G.'s case his resocialization was begun the moment he stepped into the Inner Circle. Different behaviors and perceptions were reinforced; he was lauded for being natural and spontaneous. He was told that his sexual desires were commendable illustrations of a strong-willed person struggling against the trammels of a Christian-dominated culture. He was soon better able to accept his desires as part of himself, not something ego-alien sent by the devil to torment him.

He was still faced with two additional problems, however: a high level of anxiety about heterosexual interaction and a lack of knowledge of approved social technique. Because of his socialization, he had been taught to fear women as sources of danger, especially if they were viewed as possible sexual partners. Subsequently his inept and fumbling attempts at any type of heterosexual contact, met by rejection, increased his anxiety. As is frequently the case in our society with its preoccupation with masculinity, his sexual inadequacies came to symbolize for Billy G. a more general social impotence and inadequacy, which caused him great anxiety. He was so anxious that his behavior was impaired, which raised his anxiety, and so on. He exhibited symptoms of an anxiety reaction in the presence of females and could not sustain an encounter with one.

The atmosphere of the Church, relaxed and amoral, began to effect a change in his attitude. Casual conversations about sex allowed him to voice his fears and attitudes without fear of ridicule or recrimination. But it was the general ritual itself which began to actually reduce his specific anxieties. Each ritual is performed before the "altar of flesh," the naked body of some young and usually attractive young witch (different witches play this role each week). For Billy G. the initial weeks he spent watching the ritual acted to systematically desensitize him to the anxiety-producing stimulus, the young woman's body.

Systematic desensitization (Haugen, Dixon, and Dickel 1958; Wolpe 1954, 1958) is the name of a general technique of behavioral therapy designed to take a previously anxiety-producing stimulus and condition a new response to it. In clinical practice, if a person is fearful of dogs he is asked to construct a hierarchy of ever more anxiety-producing situations involving dogs. He is then taught a response which is antithetical to anxiety, usually complete relaxation. When he is relaxed he is asked to imagine the least anxiety-provoking of the various scenarios involving dogs—looking at a dog through a telescope, for example. He repeats this procedure, relaxing each time the scene makes him tense or anxious, until he can imagine the scene without anxiety. He then proceeds to the next most anxiety-provoking image and repeats the process. If he tenses, he attempts to relax once again and goes back to the previously desensitized situation. This is kept up until he can imagine all the scenes involving dogs without fear. He is now desensitized. He has conditioned a new response, relaxation, to a previously fear-producing stimulus. The surprising fact is that his reaction to real dogs is usually discovered to have altered at the same time. The subject is able to generalize his new response to the extratherapeutic situation (Rackman 1966).

Billy G.'s initial period in the Church of the Trapezoid may be viewed as systematic desensitization. If we consider his problem as being strong fear or anxiety in response to women, his progress can be viewed as follows: initially he comes into contact with others who are friendly and accepting and who, by example, encourage him to voice his fears. They persuade him that he is not different or detestable. He begins to relax and modify his defensive posture. When at last he is invited to view the ritual it is a further symbol of acceptance and warmth, of belonging. In the darkness of the ritual chamber he is surrounded by friends, and he eventually relaxes. But when the candles are lighted he is face-to-face with the ultimate anxiety-producing stimulus, the body of an "evil" female. Although his initial reaction may be one of fear or anxiety, this soon begins to change (he is after all in an atmosphere conducive to relaxation). The witch on the altar makes no demands on him and does not move about; she just lies quietly. He sits in the darkness, his reactions masked, surrounded by friends—secure and safe from the negative consequences of his behavior. Eventually he relaxes. In the case of Billy G., I watched him, over a period of months, move forward through the rows of seats, coming closer and closer to the altar. Like the man envisioning ever more anxiety-provoking scenarios, he sometimes paused for several weeks before feeling confident enough to move forward again. Eventually he moved very close and even began assisting the young witch on and off the stone altar. Meanwhile he had begun talking to the female members of the Church, and eventually signs of anxiety diminished and then vanished. At this point he was instructed in both Greater and Lesser Magic concerning the Invocation of Lust and other phenomena associated with heterosexuality.

Greater and Lesser Magic are relatively easy to distinguish. Greater Magic is ritual magic in which the purposes of the ritual are usually specific, the structure of the ritual formalized (usually it takes place in a special ritual setting at a special time and so on), and the magical rationale for the success or failure of the ritual codified. Lesser Magic is a type of magic used to bring the results one wants in *daily* interactions with others in the *workaday* world. It is a specification, in **magical terms, of rules of social interaction which resemble the work of Erving Goffman.**

I stated previously that the Satanists were, prior to becoming members of the Church, poorly socialized individuals who were unaware of the subtle and often unwritten rules governing successful social interaction in various situations. It was for this reason that the successes and accomplishments of others around them often appeared "magical." The intermediary and implicit steps in the progress of a social interaction often were beyond their ken. For the pre-Satanist, social exchange frequently looked magical, progressing from stage A to result Z without apparently, as far as the Satanists were concerned, passing from B to Y (if, indeed, they were aware of the existence of B or Y). Nowhere is this fact more obvious than in the necessity the Satanists feel for training their members in the subtle (and sometimes not so subtle) aspects of social interaction. As "Lesser Magic," the type · of magical knowledge taught may range from how to flatter a girl to how to dress and groom oneself in order to be attractive to others. It is true in fact that a knowledge of these social mores does improve one's chances of success in the everyday world. Couching these rules in magical terminology merely underlines their importance and makes them more acceptable to the magician and the witch. If the desired goals—a date with a girl or more success in business—do follow lessons in Lesser and Greater Magic, the Satanist, not unreasonably, attributes his success to his new magical awareness. He was unsuccessful; then he learned magic, and now he is successful. Ergo, the Satanist reasons, magic caused my success. To the other members of society it makes no difference what the motivation for socially appropriate behavior is; so long as the manifest behavior is culturally correct, the social response of others to the Satanist is positive.

In the case of Billy G., the Greater Magic he learned initially took the form of Love Magic. He was instructed in the art of preparing a love amulet and conjuring lust in his love object. Preparing a love amulet is a rather difficult and time-consuming thing to do. Exotic or rare ingredients must be gathered and ritually combined accordingly in a special setting. If one views this activity from the point of view of a behavioral therapist, it is easy to see why such activity would have the beneficial effects ascribed to it. Obviously the individual's confidence is being built up (or, if you prefer, his anxiety lessened). His fellow magicians swear to the efficacy of the amulet he is constructing and, since the magic of the group has already begun to work, making him feel better and more confident, he tends to believe them (perhaps because he wants to believe them). In addition, however, the process of desensitization is continuing. It is one thing to stand in a group of Satanists and converse with a young woman, quite another to consider sexual interaction with her. Frequently, as noted, sexual failure has come to symbolize the general inadequacy and lack of power one feels. The process of gathering the ingredients for the amulet and the actual preparation of the amulet, usually after long discussions with one's fellow magicians, allows one to consider sexual interaction, the obvious goal in creating the amulet, in non-anxiety provoking situations. Riding on a street car, sitting in one's room reading old magic texts, or talking with fellow Satanists in a casual setting is not anxiety-provoking. The Satanist, just as Billy G. did, gradually develops the ability to consider a formerly anxiety-provoking subject with some aplomb. This is a continuation of the process of desensitization.

But even this is not enough. Eventually, when the amulet is prepared, the act of seduction or heterosexual intercourse of some kind must be attempted. With his inappropriate behavior patterns, his strange or poorly developed social techniques, Billy G. would fail if he were turned loose at this point. He is not. First the theory of love magic is explained to him. He is taught that every individual gives off "vibrations" of one kind or another. To be successful as a lover you must transform yourself into a love magnet by focusing and concentrating these emanations. You must make yourself attractive to others, a "magnetic personality." To do this you must learn some more of the Lesser Magic. The Satanists, both male and female, are taught good grooming, social graces, how to indicate interest to another, and many other social techniques which many of us take for granted. They are taught to emphasize and capitalize on some characteristic of theirs that is appealing to others. Males and females both are taught how to give off an aura of mystery, or of power, or even of helplessness if that is the technique best suited to their particular personality. They are told that it is ridiculous for an individual who is short of stature and slight of build to attempt to use the powerful image. Rather they are taught that they must develop what they really are to its fullest. A slight individual, and Billy G. was such a person, is told that he might be more successful if he adopted an "apple-cheeked, clean-cut, youthful image" that would appeal to the maternal instinct in women. This type of training not only increases the Satanist's knowledge of appropriate behavior, but gives him a relatively accurate picture of himself through the eyes of the "significant others" in his life. He develops a more realistic perception of himself and of his own capabilities, learning to magnify his strong points and de-emphasize his weaknesses.

He then begins to work his love magic in earnest. He utilizes his confidence-giving amulet, and with the aid, support, and encouragement of the rest of the congregation performs an Invocation of Lust at one of the weekly meetings. The form of weekly ritual is such that there is a basic or core ritual which can be modified for a variety of special purposes. Just as the Catholic Mass can serve as the basic vehicle for communion or baptism, the Satanic ritual can serve as the medium for an Invocation of Lust, or an Invocation of Destruction, or several other ritual purposes.

Without going into the details of the love magic—it involves the use of certain ritual objects, the preparation of certain types of candles, parchments, and so on—the ritual process in the conjuration of lust can be typified as encouraging the individual to give voice in a direct and graphic way to the desires that are moving him. For perhaps the first time, Billy G. was given support and encouraged to give vent to his secret wishes and dreams, but still in a safe ritual context (the progress of the action and the reaction of others is stereotyped and therefore predictable).

In order to avoid initial failure, the Satanist is told that there are others in the world who are powerful love magnets in their own right, and he is advised against choosing as his initial target a powerful person widely recognized as a sex figure. He would be unwise to choose Brigitte Bardot as his first choice, for example, for she might not only fail to respond to his yet undeveloped and comparatively feeble powers, but might also overwhelm his power with her own magnetic strength and leave him weaker than before (one does not attack an obviously magical and powerful figure such as Brigitte Bardot). Instead the Satanist is encouraged to build up his power gradually, to start with someone close at hand, someone within the group, for example. There were several girls in the group to whom Billy G. was attracted and he chose one of them as the subject of his first magical working.

Although he did not name her specifically in the ritual, it was not difficult to tell which female was the target of his magic. His success, once he began his magic, was virtually assured for several reasons. First, to be chosen was very flattering to the girl and indicated that her magic was working and making her powerful and attractive. One of the main measures of the power of a witch is believed to be the power to enthrall, the ability to exercise the "command to look." Second, once the girl is aware that she is the desired person, to deny the efficacy of Billy G.'s magic would be to deny the efficacy of the system of magic from which she herself is gaining her own sense of adequacy and power. She usually surrenders, but not without a bit of further resocialization. If Billy G. were to attempt just to drag her off to his apartment at this point, he would be rebuffed with the explanation that while his manipulative or Greater Magic was working, he needed to polish his Lesser Magic a little. The young witch in question usually helps him do this, explaining the Lesser Magic practices required to attract a girl and make her amenable to suggestion. She describes the proper technique for getting a date, what to do on a date, when to get more serious, and eventually even instructs him in seduction and love-making techniques, all as aspects of the Lesser Magic. Eventually, when he has performed all of the necessary behavioral steps, she allows herself to be seduced, a type of positive response or reward which is likely to condition Billy G.'s social behavior rather quickly, as any behavioral psychologist could tell you. His success is a validation of the magical power of the Church, its teachings, and of the amulet for Billy G. and he tends to listen with a great deal more attention and less scepticism to the next explanation of Lesser Magic techniques. If he now attempts another conquest—and Billy G., flushed with success, did—it is usually another witch whom he chooses as his subject, and he goes through the socialization process again at the hands of a different girl who has slightly different tastes and behavioral predilictions. After several such encounters, he is ready to attempt a conquest outside of the safe confines of the Satanic group. Confident, poised, and socialized in a number of different behavioral techniques, Billy G., like most Satanists, was successful. If he is not, he can now say with some assurance that it is not because he himself is unattractive but because he did not perform the magic correctly. This is a rather realistic assessment of the situation if "social graces" is substituted for "Lesser Magic." He discusses any failure with the other members of the group and solicits opinions about why the magic failed. He now has the source of feedback so necessary to the socialization process.

There is a "halo effect" in the process of interaction and behavioral modification. While he is learning seduction techniques, the Satanist is also learning a number of other generally valuable lessons about social expectations. His general level of adaptation to the demands of society becomes better. He grows more confident and socially adept and the general quality of his relationship with others improves. He has moved from anxiety and ineptitude to confidence and expertise, and in his eyes his success is attributed to magic. Perhaps by framing the resocialization process in terms of the subject's world view, even a magical world view, the socializing agents made the behavioral modifications easier for the individual to accept. They were certainly made more understandable.

THE CONJURATION OF DESTRUCTION: ASSERTIVE RESPONSES AND THERAPY

Witches are believed to be aggressive and destructive. In part this is true. One of the common problems besetting many of the Satanists prior to their becoming members of the Church was, as previously mentioned, a pervasive sense of powerlessness, of victimization or manipulation by other individuals or uncontrollable forces. Frustrated and hostile because of this and because of his own inability to realize his desired goals or satisfy his needs, the Satanist is frequently a very aggressive individual who, because of the particular mores of our culture, feels very guilty about his forbidden and unacceptable hostilities. Often his perception of the aggressiveness and hostility of the natural and social environment around him is caused by his projection of his own unacceptable, hostile impulses into other individuals or even into inanimate objects.

Satanic theology encourages rather than discourages the Satanist's aggressiveness, but teaches him to be discriminating about the targets of his aggression. Only deserving victims are to be the targets of aggressive magic, only people against whom one has a right to feel hostile. This tendency is congruent with the image of the medieval witch. Rarely does one find an accusation of witchcraft against some marginal individual in medieval society without the victim being able to hypothesize some cause for the witch's anger: a request for a drink of water refused, a demand for help ignored, etc. The modern witch also directs his aggression against those individuals who have behaved badly toward him or her. Frequently these are people against whom the witch or magician would be powerless were it not for magic, people against whom there is no legitimate means of retaliation within the social code of the given culture and society (see McFarlane 1967). An individual's boss, a person's business acquaintance, anyone can be perceived as a deserving victim. Most curses that I witnessed were directed at some person against whom the curser had what he considered a legitimate grievance. A boss might have been unfair, or a business acquaintance cheated him in a way for which the boss was not legally liable. It is against these individuals that the Satanist is encouraged to react with magical aggression. "Be a lion in the path," the Satanic Bible urges, and "if a person smite you on your left cheek smash him on his right cheek" (LaVey 1969).

Such ritual aggression has a number of functions. First, and least obvious, it continues the process of resocialization. When an individual wants the group's help in cursing an enemy, he must persuade the group that his grievance is just. Although it is not common, I have on occasion heard a group of Satanists chastise another for bringing a problem to the group that he could and should have handled himself if he were indeed a powerful magician as he claimed. I have heard an individual's version of the situation challenged and, in the course of the discussion, alternative interpretations of the action of the transgressor put forth. This is a form of "taking the role of the

other," and for the poorly socialized Satanist the additional perspectives of his fellows may suggest interpretations of the event that
he himself had not considered but which now become part of his
experience. Although virtually all of the Satanists have some "blind
spots" in their social make-up when they come to the group, the blind
spots of all the Satanists do not usually overlap and as a result there
is always someone who has an alternative view or interpretation of
the situation.

Second, in a situation in which the fledgling Satanist may still feel
anxious or inept, may feel used and manipulated, the use of ritual
aggression provides a means of restructuring his response to the situation. You will recall that one of the effective techniques for eliminating the paralyzing anxiety response was to condition an antithetical
response, a response which an individual could not maintain while
simultaneously remaining anxious, to the same stimulus that previously
had caused the anxiety reaction. We have discussed the use of relaxation, laughter, disgust, and a number of other hypothetically antithetical responses; anger is another effective alternative to anxiety
(Wolpe 1958). If an individual has been conditioned to expect failure
and negative responses from others because of that failure, he sometimes, and in the case of the Satanist frequently, develops a general
anxiety about social interaction that is cued by almost any individual
whom he perceives as being more adept or powerful than he. This
anxiety can cripple and inhibit such a person's activity in many areas,
sometimes becoming a generalized fear of social interaction. It is in
this situation that the cursing or aggressive response is most effective.
It has been demonstrated that if one can develop an assertive or
aggressive response to a formerly anxiety-provoking symbol, the level
of anxiety evoked by that symbol diminishes and eventually disappears. Small children may be taught by a behavioral therapist to
yell threats at a noisy and frightening fire engine. "Get out of here
you fire engine or I'll punch you in the nose," one three-year-old girl
was taught to yell upon hearing fire sirens, and with that her anxiety
reaction to the fire engine disappeared. For the Satanist, this aggressive response is turned on the people who are causing him difficulty
and whom he cannot attack in any other way. "Rend his gaggling
tongue and close his throat . . . pierce his lungs with the stings of
scorpions," reads the Invocation of Destruction in the Satanic Bible,
and some members write their own more personal curses.

Not only is the Satanist's anxiety reaction to the person in question
diminished or eliminated by ritual cursing, but the aggressive response
which might impair or destroy a necessary social relationship is kept
within the confines of the ritual chamber and seldom allowed expres-

sion in direct face-to-face contact with the feared person. The Satanist, having learned to be assertive toward certain persons, can face them without fear.

The Satanist who has cursed a person then waits patiently for the inevitable destruction to descend on his victim. The curse is not usually designed to cause death—I observed only one death rune case during the two years that I was active in the Inner Circle—and eventually, when in the course of daily living the "victim" has some bad luck or misfortune, the Satanist chortles with satisfaction and murmurs, "Got him!"

The casting of a death rune is a more serious matter and is not taken lightly. Although the cause of the victim's death is purportedly magic, science explains voodoo death, as it is called (Cannon 1942; Wallace 1966: 178), in terms of the General Adaptation Syndrome in which anxiety is *created* instead of being eliminated and pressure is kept on the victim so that he cannot return to a state of physiological equilibrium. The physiological changes which accompany an anxiety reaction, endocrine changes in response to stress, eventually cause the victim to die of shock. In the one case I observed in which a death rune was cast, the victim, a former member of the group, was, after many warnings, cursed. Though he became quite ill with ulcers and left San Francisco, he was still alive when I last heard of him.

SHIBBOLETH

There is a special ritual called the Shibboleth ritual which is especially enlightening concerning the means by which resocialization takes place. In the Shibboleth ritual each Satanist comes to the meeting place dressed in the guise of the person or type of person whom he least understands or who causes him the most difficulty in life. During the course of the evening the Satanist is required to act like, think like, talk like, and in fact "be" that individual. At the end of the evening the hated individual is ritually killed and the Satanist is brought back to life in his own identity. During the course of the evening, however, he gets a great deal of feedback from others concerning his performance. In response to my performance of the "right-wing extremist" role, for example, I had the benefit of the opinion not just of run-of-the-mill Satanists, but was also criticized by some genuine right-wing extremists who were members of the group at that time. In this sense I was able to develop a much better knowledge of the expectations of the group of people whom I least understood and, in fact, subsequently interacted with the right-wing group much more successfully because of the experience. This is "taking the role of the other" in its purest form. Developing a knowledge of social expectations does enhance one's ability to interact in some form of an equivalence structure with previously misunderstood people. This is resocialization. In the context of the Satanic Church, the rationale for this ritual was that a better knowledge of others would enhance the Satanist's ability to manipulate them with Lesser Magic. Whatever the reason, the Satanists who took part in this ritual were more adept social actors because of it. Again they assumed magical reasons for their new success but, regardless of the reason, the results of this role-playing were the same: more successful adaptation (Wolpe 1954, 1958; Wolpe and Lazarus 1966; Kelly 1955).

IDEOLOGICAL RITUALS

There are a number of rituals which serve as ideological rituals. They serve to enunciate the position of the Satanists and teach the new Satanists, either directly or indirectly, the ethos and eidos of the subculture in which they now operate. These are rituals in which the animal nature of man, the similarity between his behavior and that of the animals, is demonstrated by delibrants dressed as men with animal heads who perform animalistically in the ritual, gradually shifting back and forth from human to animal.

The Black Mass can also be seen as an ideological ritual. The Satanists clearly recognize that the very name "Satanists" puts them in opposition to the accepted religions of the larger society and they express this position in the Black Mass in which the Christian practices and symbols are inverted and the ritual literally "turned upside down." The ritual becomes a ritual *of* the flesh rather than a ritual *de-emphasizing* the flesh and emphasizing the spirit, as is the case in Christianity.

MAGIC TRANSFORMATION

Finally, for the purpose of understanding the social effects of Satanic or magical therapy, there is the ritual of magical transformation. Most of us are familiar with the Bela Lugosi vampire who transforms himself into a bat and flies through the night to turn himself, when necessary, back into human form. The legends and myths from other cultures concerning witches are almost unanimous in their assertion that witches either associate with animals or can turn themselves into animals (Parrinder 1963: 145–147). From the Satanic point of view this is a misunderstanding of the concept of magical transformation. The Satanists are well aware of the fate that befalls deviants and they are equally well aware, from bitter experience in many cases, that the fear of witches is not a thing of the past but still exists, bringing punishment and pain to the unwary witch. It is for this reason that they teach the members of the Church the art of magical transformation.

The member is taught that those fearful of his great power will attempt to destroy him if possible just as some of his predecessors were destroyed. He is taught that though he may be a powerful magician, he must use his magic not only to protect himself but to take advantage of the stupid and insensitive non-magicians of the world. It would be unwise, he is told, even though he knows he is a powerful magician or witch, to flaunt that fact in the faces of the fearful. Instead it is smarter and better magic to turn their fear and your power to your own advantage. For that reason, each day the magician magically transforms himself from Paimon the Powerful to Homer Smith, bank teller, and from 9 to 5 acts the part of Homer Smith. Inside he may be laughing at the inability of those around him to see through his disguise and reveling in the way he is using his magic to fool them and make them do his bidding. He takes delight in his raise at the bank, for he knows that it was his ability to practice the Lesser Magic of social manipulation that made it possible, and his magical transformation that enabled him to disguise his real purposes and his real identity. In the evening, safe in his room or secure in the ritual chamber, he can revert to his "true" self and become the powerful and vaunted magician that he knows he really is.

In the eyes of the larger society this former "deviant" may be thought to have undergone a pleasing and unexpected personality modification. Others, after all, do not know the motivations "behind" his changed behavior. They might become concerned if he expressed his motivations, but as he does not, for good magical reasons, the other members of his behavioral environment must and can base their judgment of him on his overt actions and his expressed motivations only.

The benefits of Satanism and Black Magic to the witch or magician are obvious: he need be less anxious or fearful, he is more able socially, and he is actually more successful in many spheres of activity due to his enhanced ability to interact with others. He now has, after all, a better knowledge of the expectations of the rest of the society, a better awareness of the rules of the cultural or social game. He has been taught to curb his maladaptive behavior and exhibit "proper" behavior in response to certain cues. If he attributes this new-found power and success to magic rather than to the insights of sociology, anthropology, or psychology, it is because such an interpretation is more in accordance with his world view and the categories of understanding which he uses to give structure and meaning to his world.

In fact, it is sometimes difficult to argue against his interpetation.

If psychology explains personal interaction in terms of hypothesized "forces" at work, forces which are known and measured only through the perception of their effects, then how is that different, the Satanist asks, from magic? Satanists say, with some justification, "When magic becomes scientific fact we refer to it as medicine or astronomy" (LaVey 1969).

The benefits to society are equally numerous. Not only are all of the previous cultural functions of witchcraft still in effect—witches are still the focus of a community's aggression, still used to symbolize the anti-social and anti-cultural, still cited as an explanation of the evil and misfortune in the world—but there are, in the case of the contemporary Satanists at least, a number of other benefits as well.

The use of magical therapy helps to resocialize deviants and bring their behavior, for whatever reasons, closer to the cultural and social norms necessary to ensure the continued "smooth" running of the society. The Satanists are clearly better citizens after their magical therapy than before, if one is speaking in terms of social cohesion and equilibrium.

In addition, deviant behavior not modified is confined to a specific social context, a special time and place, and not allowed to spread into the wider social environment. The Satanists preach indulgence of all desires, but the indulgences they enjoy are confined to the Satanic context and are never forced on unwilling victims. The socially dysfunctional nature of some of the modes of gratification is kept from spreading and influencing the wider social environment.

SUMMARY

Why is witchcraft on the rise today? A resurgence of interest in Black Magic is today being reported not only in most of the Western world but in many other culture areas as well. I would like to speculate that perhaps the rise of witchcraft belief is an attempt by various people to regain a sense of control over their environment and their lives.

This seems to be a time when many of the gods of the Western world, like the old traditional gods of the urbanizing African, are being challenged. God is dead, but that means not just the Judeo-Christian god but also the gods of progress, science, and technology. We put our faith in "him," but now the god of progress is discovered to be a two-faced Janus about to extract a terrible price for our progress and comfort; the god of science has failed us and has not created the paradise we were led to expect, free from disease and ignorance and death. Instead he threatens us with destruction with either the apocalypse of atomic conflagration or a slow death by chemical pollution. The god of technology reveals his "true" face and our streams die, our lakes atrophy, and the very air is turned into a subtle poison. Like the Ashanti or the Bete, many people in the Western world today feel themselves "surrounded by undefinable dangers that their fathers never knew" (Paulme 1962). In such time the people look to new gods or try to refurbish the old ones. They need a method of making what is happening understandable, of coping with the contradictions in daily life and organizing them into a new meaning.

Now that external sources of truth, the experts and scientists, have failed us, many persons have begun to look within themselves for their source of wisdom and security. Some have begun to reassert the necessity of finding personal solutions. In a certain sense witchcraft is a product of these needs. If the world of the Satanist is a criterion, the Satanist is training himself to be assertive and powerful *as an individual*. Although he draws a sense of security from his association with powerful forces, he is finding inner sources of strength. He is casting off the need for powerful gods to protect and care for him, insisting that he is strong enough to care for himself. He commands the gods and does not beseech them. He is turning from an ethereal and other-worldly orientation to a somewhat more realistic assessment and concern with the mundane and real world.

Perhaps it is for this reason that marginal religions such as the Church of the Trapezoid should be encouraged. They appear in many cases to be revitalizations that spring, in response to a changing world, more directly from the needs of the individuals who comprise their membership.

Perhaps what is needed is greater tolerance for a multiplicity of alternative solutions from which various individuals may select the one most applicable to their particular needs. Perhaps we need more religions in which speaking in tongues is not a sign of abnormality, or in which "honest" aggression is accepted and recognized as a realistic response to some situations.

As the pace of change increases and the rules that have governed our social and cultural system seem more and more transitory, we will need other means of giving meaning to our environment, of bringing cosmos from chaos and making life predictable and understandable. The more flexible nature of marginal religions provides one answer. Whatever increases the individual's ability to adjust and adapt to the world in which he lives may be, perhaps must be, the criterion we ultimately use to evaluate new and initially marginal institutions in our society.

Belief, Ritual, and Healing:
New England Spiritualism and Mexican-American Spiritism Compared

INTRODUCTION

Health and illness have always been significant concerns of religious systems, the shaman emerging as the first professional in human history. This paper is an examination of healing in two metaphysical religious movements, Spiritualism (North American and English) and Spiritism (Continental and Latin American).

Theologian Paul Tillich tells us that the word "salvation" originally meant healing,[1] including medical healing and psychotherapy, but adds that the final salvation must heal the "split between the temporal order in which we live and the eternal to which we belong" (Siirala 1964: vi).

In this paper, I shall argue that ritual "dramas of salvation" are to be found in both New England Spiritualism and Mexican-American Spiritism and suggest that these dramas do heal just that split, restoring personal, social and spiritual wholeness—and consequently physical health—to participants.

The nineteenth-century origins of Spiritualism/Spiritism reflect the sources of the split. The religious "world-taken-for-granted," with its belief in the powers of supernatural agencies, was being threatened by rationalism and science—and "belief in science swiftly became the faith of scientism" (Matson 1966: 5). An age of "isms," the search for a grand syncretic ideology generated marginal religions which attempted reconciliation among competing ideas. Participants hoped to enjoy the

[1] "Healing is one of the most conspicuous features of religion in the past decade, while . . . more material, both in articles and books, was published [on this topic] in any month in 1949 than in the last 50 years of the last century and the 25 of the present" (Gernster 1960: 110). H. H. Bro concurs: "Interest in healing through some form of prayer activity appears to be growing, both in those churches which allow intense emotion in worship and suspend a certain amount of learned doubt, and in the traditional churches of the religious establishment in both the U. S. and Europe" (1970: 252); while J. Stillson Judah asserts that "all these [metaphysical] movements make healing through the mind or spirit a part of their mission" (1967: 18).

best of both worlds. As Nelson (1969: 15) remarks, Spiritualism in the nineteenth century was a ". . . half-way house for those who could neither accept unsubstantiated religious doctrines on the nature of the after life or the claims of materialists that man was a purely material being." Curing of the sick offered proof of the medium's authority as well as "scientific" evidence of communication with the spirit world.

The advent of truly modern medicine and improved medical technology after 1870, along with increasing secularization in Western society, resulted in an inordinate faith in the omnipotence of science, and a *fin de siècle* decline of Spiritualism and Spiritism. Scientism won temporarily and the dominant ideology favored a mechanistic view of health, illness and the human body.

It is suggested, then, that the persistence and renascence of Spiritualism and Spiritism in the twentieth century may be understood in part as a rejection of such scientism and "infallible" medicine (which none the less often fails). Furthermore, each of these religions proffers rituals and beliefs which give symbolic meaning to the collective and personal search for identity so characteristic of this century. Today each provides its adherents with a traditional world-taken-for-granted (Protestantism in the case of Spiritualism, and folk Catholicism in the case of Spiritism), while at the same time allowing for freedom of individual conviction and revelation. Both social and individual needs are met.

The Spiritualist church I shall discuss here calls its system "a religion, a philosophy, and a science," while the ritual, music, and values are Protestant (and therefore conforms closely to Nelson's "Christian Spiritualists" [1969] and Zaretsky's Type A Churches [1970 and this volume]). The Mexican-American Spiritism I shall discuss is firmly rooted in folk Catholicism. Upon these traditional infrastructures, however, the individual's freedom to build a symbolic universe at once locates him personally in a social order, while it also allows him to transcend the "terror of history" (Eliade 1959: 150). The person is made whole; the split is healed.

Although the actors, *modi operandi,* and content of the dramas of salvation vary in detail, the two movements share common intellectual origins and a common ritual structure. The relationships among the *dramatis personae* are structured similarly, also. A comparison of the two, then, is illuminating. The characters of the dramas can be limned. The *medium* or *materia* embodies special shamanistic abilities which permit him to communicate with and utilize the power of the *spirit world*. The *client,* beset with health and personal problems, participates in the same "assumptive system" (Frank 1961: *passim*) as does the medium. He—the client—is the beneficiary of the goodness of the dieties, the spirits, and their instrument, the medium, *if* he reciprocates behaviorally and faithfully.

In order to understand either the structure of the healing rituals or the ideological content of the belief systems under consideration, it is necessary (1) to examine briefly their intellectual origins in the nineteenth century; (2) to describe and analyze the rituals found in present-day Spiritualism and Spiritism.

SPIRITUALISM/SPIRITISM: INTELLECTUAL HISTORY BRIEFLY TOLD

Most of the ideological elements which were to become incorporated into nineteenth-century Spiritualism had long been present in Europe. In fact, Podmore's admirably detailed two-volume study (1902) of Spiritualism demonstrates clearly that all of the manifestations of "modern" Spiritualism—spirit rappings, communications, and possession; trance states and vision; materializations and table turnings; clairvoyance and clairaudience, etc.—were widely known on both sides of the Atlantic well before March 31, 1848, when the now-famous Fox sisters communicated with the rapping spirits occupying their home in Hydesville, New York.

Belief in the existence and manifestation of spirits is old and nearly universal. A. Conan Doyle initiates his discussion of "spiritualism" with the observation that there is no time in recorded history when one could not find traces of preternatural interference and a tardy recognition of them (1926: 11) by man.

The Middle Ages saw much spirit possession within Christianity. But in the sixteenth century, one sees the beginnings of a rationalistic approach to metaphysics. Paracelsus incorporated and elaborated astrological theories into a system of philosophy, believing that the human body was endowed with a double magnetism. Podmore comments that mysticism of the seventeenth and eighteenth centuries depends mainly upon Paracelsus' ideas that there was: radiation from all things but especially solar bodies, magnets, and the human body; that a force directed by the indwelling spirit would act on all things; and that there was perpetual contact between reciprocal forces (1902: 1, 4).

Other influences may be seen. The seventeenth-century Shakers—descendants of the radical French Calvinist sect known as the Camisards and of the English Quakers—were already millenial, apocalyptic, and anti-clerical. Persecuted in England, the group came to New England in 1774, and was led by a clairvoyant, "Mother" Ann Lee. Although these early "Shaking Quakers" had no clearly formulated

doctrine, most of the above-mentioned elements of later Spiritualism/
Spiritism are clearly presaged amongst them by the 1830s.[2]

Of particular importance to our understanding of present-day beliefs
was the nineteenth-century emphasis on guidance by "gifts" of continuous revelation, and the notion of perfectibility of man and society.
This last principle stated that man progresses toward perfection
through strict rectitude of thoughts and deeds, first in his mundane
existence, and then eternally in heavenly spheres (Andrews 1963: 97).
And spiritual perfection usually implied an accompanying physical
perfection.

Mediumship was epitomized by Ann Lee, who communicated mostly
with Jesus. She was regarded by the Shakers as His special Instrument. " 'It is not I that speak,' she told her followers, 'it is Christ who
dwells in me. . . . I converse with Christ!' " (Andrews 1963: 11).
"Mother Ann's" group might be viewed as immediate forerunners
of modern Spiritualism, and certain "instruments" of the Shakers
actually *had* prophesied that manifestations soon would appear.
Although they were not surprised by the 1848 rappings, then, the
"mechanics of modern spiritualism—the automatic writings, table
liftings, knockings, and ectoplasmic materializations"—did not appeal
to them.

Secularization, beginning among the social and intellectual elites
at the end of the seventeenth century, progressed rapidly during the
eighteenth and nineteenth centuries. The eighteenth-century deist
or materialist became the non-believer, the Marxist, anarchist, or
positivist in the nineteenth and twentieth centuries. Such secularization filtered down to the masses only in the nineteenth century, which
experienced a mushrooming of ephemeral cults and sects.[3] Spiritualism
and Spiritism, as occultic non-Christian philosophies, also followed this
pattern. It is in the twentieth century that the masses have modified
pragmatic aspects of these syncretic ideologies to fit contemporary
needs.

Of particular interest to understanding present-day curing rituals,
however, are other immediate precursors of Spiritualism and Spiritism.
One can see the direct influence of Mesmer and other eighteenth- and
nineteenth-century animal magnetists, who presented the first grand

[2] Spirits of Indians, Eskimos, Negroes, Chinese, Abyssinians, and Hottentots
entered into the bodies of the Shakers and "once possessed by the spirits, the
visionists acted in a manner characteristic of the race" (Andrews 1963: 6).

[3] Cross has carefully analyzed the social, economic, and political conditions in
western New York state (between 1800 and 1850) which produced in this area, in
microcosm, nearly every religious excess which arose in the United States before
the Civil War. "Few of the enthusiasms or eccentricities of this generation failed
to find exponents here" (Cross 1950: 3).

system of treating disease which did not claim religious authority. Mesmer's method of curing a multitude of ills (including dropsy, paralysis, gout, scurvy, etc.) "consists in the application of a *fluid* or agent that M. Mesmer directs" (Darnton 1970: 6). He also used a tub filled with magnetized iron filings and bottles of mesmerized water which "stored the *fluid* and transmitted it through moveable iron rods, which the patients applied to their sick areas" (Darnton 1970: 8). *"Harmony"* was emphasized by the mesmerists as an important aspect of curing by which they meant the physical and moral accord of man and the laws of nature. "Health in the broadest sense of the word was their supreme value" (Darnton 1970: 6). Some of his patients fell into deep sleeps, "some of which provided communication with dead or distant spirits, who sent messages by way of the *fluid*" (Darnton 1970: 8).

The 1967 edition of the *Spiritualist Manual* says that results of spiritual healing are produced by spiritual influences *"infusing* curative, stimulating and *vitalizing fluids* and energy into the diseased parts of the patient's body", and adds that "Healthful and *harmonious* thoughts . . . rouse the vitality . . . bringing order out of chaos, and tend to cure body and mind" (National Spiritualist Association 1967: 51; italics mine).

Add to this potpourri the magnetically induced trances of one Andrew Jackson Davis, an American who has been called the first medium to claim divine inspiration. He claimed that Galen (the second-century physician) and Swedenborg (the seventeenth-century Swedish seer) came to him while he was in trance and revealed secrets of healing to him. He became a highly successful medical clairvoyant and published his first book (including careful accounts of his early visions) in 1847, just one year before the Fox family rappings. Although he is not much read today, his ideas had much influence on early Spiritualist philosophy.

By 1850, "modern" American *Spiritualism* was spreading rapidly into all parts of the United States, England, the Continent, and Latin America, as well. A correspondent of the redoubtable Emma Hardinge reported that he had convened a "circle" at his residence in Guatemala City as early as 1853 (Hardinge 1970: 465). By 1854, Spiritualism had appeared in Cuba and had gained a good foothold even in that "devoted and conservative" Catholic land (Hardinge 1970: 467). By 1865, Spiritualistic circles appeared in Caracas (Venezuela) in which the president, high government officials and "every influential family in Caracas" participated. Significantly, the correspondent there reported that "we are continually surrounded with spirits of the highest order", and predicted that the time was approaching when all sectarian feuds would cease and all mankind would be united in one universal and spiritual church (Hardinge 1970: 472).

The literature on the subject of Spiritualism is staggering and the number of authors attempting to codify and promulgate the "new" faith large. However, the works of Frenchman Leon Denizarth Hippolyte Rivail (born October 4, 1804, in Lyons; died March 31, 1869) are primarily responsible for the form of *Spiritism* adopted almost universally on the Continent, as well as in Latin American countries, and therefore of most interest here. Rivail published seven books on Spiritism under the *nom de plume* of Allan Kardec, an old Breton name in his mother's family. This pseudonym allegedly was used at the insistence of the spirits who dictated the works through mediums.[4] Rivail, born into "an old family of Boury-en-Bresse, that had been for many generations honourably distinguished in the magistry and at the bar,"[5] was educated at the Institution of Pestalozzi in Yverdun, Switzerland, and returned to France at age twenty. The young Rivail then went to Paris and set about translating various books "for youth" into German, and giving gratuitous lectures on chemistry, physics, comparative anatomy, and astronomy. Of particular significance for his later influence on the course and development of Spiritism, was his participation in "several learned societies" such as the Phrenological Society of Paris and the Society of Magnetism. He investigated somnambulism, trance, clairvoyance, and other mesmeric phenomena (Blackwell 1875: 10). As we have seen, all of these interests of Rivail-Kardec's had already been introduced into the United States, and were the forerunners of Spiritualism as well as Spiritism. Further, an explicit point is made of Rivail-Kardec's "*constant endeavor to be useful to his fellow men* [my emphasis]" (1875: 12).

By 1850, when the table turning and spirit rappings of Hydesville were attracting attention in England and on the Continent, Rivail, not surprisingly, decided to investigate the relationship between the visible and invisible worlds. Much of his information came from

---

[4] " 'To the book in which you will embody our instructions,' continued the communicating intelligences, 'You will give, as being our work rather than yours, the title of *Le Livre de Esprits (The Spirits' Book);* and you will publish it, not under your own name, but under the pseudonym of Allan Kardec. Keep your own name of Rivail for your own books already published' " (Blackwell 1875: 13–14).

[5] Miss Blackwell, one of the few English adherents of Kardec, prepared an eulogizing preface which has been used frequently—almost verbatim—in simplified paperbacked versions of Kardec's teachings which appear today in bookstalls all over Latin America (1875: 9). Miss Blackwell evidently was attempting to establish that Rivail not only came from a socially prominent family and was well-educated formally, but that he also was a dispassionate, *scientifically*, experimentally, and practically oriented rationalist.

séances with two "frivolous" young girls known to be mediums. Sessions took on a "grave and serious character" when Rivail-Kardec was present and the spirits spoke to him of an "important religious mission."

The Hydesville phenomena were being referred to as Spiritualism. Rivail-Kardec objected that this word already had wide currency and was a general term which could be applied to anyone "who believes that there is in him something more than matter," but not necessarily belief in spirits; *e.g.,* anyone opposed to *materialism* then, could be called a spiritualist. Consequently, he proposed that a specific term be applied to the phenomena under consideration in order to eliminate semantic confusion. For this purpose, he introduced *Spiritism* (Fr., *spiritisme;* Sp., *espiritismo).* These definitions of "Spiritualism" and "Spiritism" continue to appear in the anthropological literature (adding confusion to an already complex subject), but are not the distinctions which are relevant to present-day practitioners.[6] One finds the terms Spiritualism and Spiritism used etically, and as if they referred to distinctive aspects of phenomenal reality (Kelly 1965; C. Madsen 1966; W. Madsen 1964, 1967). Spiritualists formally distinguish themselves from Spiritists by stating that their set of beliefs is a religion, while Spiritism deals with the occult (National Spiritualist Association 1967: 59). But the terms do not have agreed upon meanings for Mexican and Mexican-American informants. When one examines the classificatory system of the folk, one finds that Kardecists do call themselves "spiritists," think of their system as non-Christian, a philosophy and a science, but compatible with all religions. Other groups,[7] who consider Kardec to have laid the groundwork only and think the system of the twentieth-century Argentinian Joaquin Trincado is more "scientific" and "rational," claim that *they* are the Spiritists. The Trincadists are usually of higher social status in their communities than the Kardecists, and patronizingly relegate the latter to the status of Spiritualists because they (Kardecists) supposedly are all involved with "mystification, religion, and supernaturalism." Still other groups in Mexico and the United States, who use the same healing techniques, vocabularies, and who also share many of the Spiritualistic/Spiritistic ideas, claim to be good Roman Catholics. They assert that they would have no truck with such paganism and black magic as do Spiritualists and Spiritists.

[6] I have attempted to cope with this confusion in more detail elsewhere (Macklin 1974).

[7] To be found in most South American countries, Mexico, Puerto Rico, Texas, and New York City.

Viewed analytically, the major difference between Rivail-Kardec's Continental Spiritism and American-English Spiritualism is the idea of multiple incarnations. The Spiritualists officially hold that the soul is incarnated only once, while Spiritists (both Kardecists and Trincadists) believe that the process is repeated again and again. But several American Spiritualists have told me that they feel that this belief should be up to the individual believer, and that they have had experiences which lead them to believe in the reincarnation of spirits.

The rejection of the idea of reincarnation by the English and Americans [8] is used by Thurston, Podmore, and Doyle to explain why Kardec's system never was accepted in these countries. It seems much more likely that the differences in their social, political, and economic histories account for this rejection: the English and Americans did not need the romantic, idealistically based, nationalistic ideology which Rivail-Kardec synthesized. The U.S. was already the "oldest country in the world," as Gertrude Stein has put it, and both the English and Americans were energetically and successfully pursuing material interests. Scientism provided them with a much more promising assumptive system and they promptly applied the techniques of science to the data of Spiritualism.

As Kardec, Rivail's *The Spirits' Book* set forth the *doctrine* of Spiritism in 1853 (Sidgwick 1887: 404) but was revised and republished in 1857. This volume has gone through more than fifty-two editions, and with it he provided not only a "textbook" but also a press organ, *La Revue Spirite*, "which secured a practical monopoly in the field of such discussions" (Thurston 1933: 109).

Taken together, Rivail-Kardec's books include nearly all of the concepts and phenomena of "modern," post-1848 Spiritualism, as they already had been adumbrated in the United States and England. As Father Thurston points out, the leading early Spiritualists had tended to accept Swedenborgian philosophical views, but the majority of those attracted to Spiritualism in the U.S. and England were interested only in the physical phenomena and "the supposed communications from their departed friends" (Thurston 1933: 109).[9] He adds that a

[8] Podmore comments that Kardec's "books sold by the tens of thousands and were translated into nearly every European language" (1902: 161). As Professor Judah pointed out to me, the widespread enthusiasm in America for the books of Andrew Jackson Davis acted as a further deterrent to the acceptance of the doctrine of reincarnation. As has been mentioned, Davis—trance medium, clairvoyant, and curer—was an influential precursor of Spiritualism, and rejected Kardecianism.

[9] Englishman Podmore's study, thorough as it is, emphasizes physical *phenomena* and spirit *techniques* somewhat at the expense of the religio-philosophical aspects of the movement. This results in a rather cursory dismissal of Kardec's doctrines, on the one hand, and detailed examination of spirit manifestations and "problems of mediumship" on the other (1902).

formulated *system* of spirit teaching such as there was regarding this world and the next was "by no means enthusiastically received [in the U.S.]." However, the system of ideas organized by Rivail-Kardec into a moral, social, and political philosophy hit France and the Continent when the time was ripe for new prophets and grand syntheses. Therefore, I shall discuss the system of ideas found in Spiritualism and Spiritism by focussing on Kardec's synthesis.

Although Rivail-Kardec's informing spirits were supposed to have come from all the ages of man's past and embody the wisdom of human history, it is clear that they were actually trapped by the conventional wisdom of their own (or Rivail-Kardec's?) intellectual *Zeitgeist*. (The messages dictated to Rivail-Kardec show, alas, that his earnest, humorless, assisting spirits were as "unimaginative" as he reputedly was [Blackwell 1875: 16].)

Although occultic, non-Christian and anti-Catholic, the major points of the doctrine which the spirits transmitted to Rivail-Kardec are based on traditional Christianity. God is seen as eternal, immutable, all-powerful, just and good, while the moral teachings of the higher spirits may be summed up in the golden rule (Kardec, 1875: 24).

The Rivail-Kardecian spirits also are clearly late eighteenth- early nineteenth-century Romantic idealists in emphasizing the primacy of the spiritual over the material. Dualistic in nature though man is, we are told, "the corporeal world is only secondary; it might cease to exist, or never have existed, without changing the essentiality of the spirit world" (Kardec 1875: xix).

Nor did his spiritual informants escape the progressionism inherited from the Enlightenment: "A spirit's successive corporeal existences are always progressive, and never retrograde; but the rapidity of our progression depends on the efforts we make to arrive at perfection" (Kardec 1875: xvi). Here, then, is emphasis not only on progressionism, and in the perfectibility of man, but also that human effort is necessary and will be rewarded. Progressivist doctrine—and Spiritism—are both man centered, and later served to rescuc *homo sapiens* from the Darwinian demotion he was about to suffer. The human species gained moral and intellectual superiority because it was God-chosen for the incarnation of spirits.

Further, democratic principles born of the American and French revolutions and fostered by those of 1830 and 1848 in Central and Western Europe are to be found here. *Equality* of spirits is stressed, one's previous station in "this lower life" giving him no supremacy in the higher side of life. Such egalitarianism plays a large role in the promulgation of today's Spiritualism/Spiritism. One sees traditional Christianity's other-worldly emphasis, a spirit world where all God's "chillun got shoes" in spite of the inequalities of the here and now. The spirits were anti-clerical and non-Christian in that they asserted that there was no unpardonable sin (which disposed of the Fall and Catholicism's original sin). There are many other ideas in Spiritualism/ Spiritism which one could analyze—anti-materialism, the utilitarian notion that it is man's "nature" to be happy, a positivistic faith that human progress lies in the practical application of the laws of justice, love, and charity founded on the certainty of the future and humanitarian nationalism ("all of the nations will be sisters")—and all are familiar to any student of nineteenth-century intellectual history.

The conception of Rivail-Kardecian Spiritism is, then, typical to the point of being pedestrian: linear, pre-Darwinian, and eighteenth century in its emphasis on equality, optimism, and utopianism. Spiritism enjoyed a further advantage as far as its propagation went: a sufficient number of the intellectual and social elite embraced it (or a similar set of ideas) to lend it an aura of respectability. In addition, Rivail-Kardec's books were being published in French, the international language of the educated. France was the Mecca of the European and Latin American intelligentsia. The movement's ideas already were current in the works of such social reformers as St. Simon and Auguste Comte, as well as the Italian revolutionist Joseph Mazzini (Charlton 1963).

One can begin to see why Spiritism as an ideological system caught on, on the Continent: it was an age of revolt and the impact of political and social revolutions was being felt. There was already a questioning of religious values, and a decline in religious belief. The church still was powerful, and hostile to liberal and republican thinking. Anti-clericalism was rampant then—as it still is—not only in France but also in much of Latin America.[10]

Spiritualism and Spiritism, eclectic in the utmost, extended the apparently scientific, rational, and logical to include the spiritual and intuitive. However, Spiritualism failed completely to develop a "coherent and comprehensive doctrine. The only common belief to be found among Spiritualists was the belief in communication with the spirits of the dead. . . . Beliefs ranged from extremely orthodox Christian, to Unitarian and Universalist, while many spiritualists were non-Christian. . . . [However] some Christian Spiritualist churches were formed" (Nelson 1969: 84). Most of those interested were busily applying the techniques of science itself to the phenomena of Spiritual-

---

[10] Muller observes that anti-clericalism typically has been most bitter in Catholic countries. Anti-clericalism should not then be interpreted as *prima facie* evidence of Protestant influence (Muller 1963: 14).

ism, attempting to photograph ectoplasmic materializations, looking into alleged hauntings, and investigating apparitions (see Murphy and Ballou 1960).

Continental Kardecian Spiritism did develop a coherent doctrine but was soon as varied as Spiritualism. Introduced to Latin America as an occultic, egalitarian, and potentially revolutionary ideology (which intrigued the intellectual and social elites), Spiritism had to contend with a viable system of folk Catholicism [11] when it filtered to the urban lower classes and the peasantry. These latter groups borrowed those pragmatic aspects of the system which were useful in solving daily problems of life, illness, and death. These they transmitted in the oral tradition as well as in family and neighborhood curing and cultic rituals. The resultant variability boggles the mind of the investigator.

We have seen that Spiritualism and Spiritism originated in a concern with health, illness, and healing, and from attempts of the science of the era (mesmerism and phrenology) to eradicate disease. But to diagnose an illness, a healer must make assumptions about the nature of man, his relationship to other men and to the universe. Mid-nineteenth-century codifiers attempted to synthesize the social, political, religious, and scientific ideas of the century, but failed to provide a system which could compete successfully with scientism and the mechanistic view of man. In particular, they could not compete with the empirical successes of medical science.

Having failed, both Spiritualism and Spiritism subsequently became syncretized with the beliefs and rituals of established religions. Belated recognition has come (Hollingshead and Duff 1968) that the assumptions of medical science are inadequate, that one cannot heal successfully if one's definition of man reduces him to nothing more than a machine which can be adjusted. Spiritualism and Spiritism persist in the twentieth century—in an increasingly anti-rationalistic, anti-mechanistic milieu—by treating the whole man.

The data to follow are drawn from a New England Christian Spiritualist Church, and a cult-like [12] group which considers itself

---

[11] An amalgam of pre-Columbian and sixteenth- and seventeenth-century Iberian peninsula beliefs and practices.

[12] I do not propose to present a new definition of cult, but shall refer to Spiritism and Spiritualism as "cult-like" in that they are "loosely structured movements having minimal organization; composed of individuals who have had or seek personal mystical, psychic, or ecstatic experiences; concerned mainly with the problems of individuals," and (less true for these groups than for other cult groups) "they make a fundamental break with the religious tradition of the society in which they arise" (Nelson 1969: 156).

to be Spiritist and Catholic, focussed around a Mexican-American curing medium living in the Mid-West.

SPIRITISM: CHICANOS [13] AND CURING

The Mexican-American cult in a small Indiana town centers around a curing medium (*materia* and *curandera* [14]). The description which follows varies only in detail from innumerable others which I have observed in Texas,[15] Mexico, and California, and is intended, therefore, to have generic implications. Mrs. A. enjoyed a very successful career as a healer long before she realized that she had a spirit assistant. Both Kardecian Spiritists and American Spiritualists recognize that there are certain mediums who possess the gift of spiritual healing, themselves, whereas in other cases the medium is under the "control" of a "spirit of intelligence and the consciousness of the medium is, for the time being, dethroned"; *i.e.,* in trance (National Spiritualist Association 1967: 50; Kardec 1963: 212). So while Mrs. A. had *el don* (the gift) for curing others, she herself fell ill, as a young married woman, and members of her family began to take her from one Spiritist *centro* (center, or temple) to another for treatment. [Her own mother had been a well-known curer in Mexico where she had grown up, but she was living in Texas near the Mexican border at the time of her daughter's illness.] After several months of unsuccessful treatment in

[13] I shall use *chicano* and Mexican-American interchangeably throughout this paper. *Chicano* is said to have derived from *mexicano,* and was used among Americans of Mexican descent as a self reference in order to distinguish themselves from Mexican nationals and from *Anglos,* a category which included everyone *not* of Mexican descent. With the growth of "Brown Power" in the middle and late 1960s, the national news media took up the term chicano in an attempt, one supposes, to find a neutral term to refer to this group; and already (1970–71) many chicanos look askance at the term, claiming that it is pejorative, even in its etymology.

[14] I shall use the Spanish word *materia* to distinguish the Mexican-American medium from the New England medium, although the word medium is used widely in Latin American countries.

The *curandero/a* in Mexican culture is a healer or curer. He (or she) has, in many cases, not only a specialist's knowledge of herbs and appropriate prayers for healing, but in many cases has the gift (*el don*), a special, divinely bestowed power for curing. Techniques are well known from the literature: Adams and Rubel 1967, Clark 1959, Crawford 1961, Gillin 1948, Madsen 1955, Rubel 1960, 1966, Saunders 1954. Most Mexican and Mexican-American women (including those now permanently residing in Middle Western cities such as Chicago, Detroit, Ft. Wayne, and Toledo) know some of these cures. They raise the necessary herbs, purchase them in the Mexican food shops, or have them sent up from "home" in Mexico and Texas, *ruda, yerba buena,* and *manzanilla* being among the most common.

[15] Cf. Arthur J. Rubel's illuminating discussion of "illness behavior and attitudes" among Mexican-Americans (1966: 155–200).

the *centros,* a *materia* diagnosed her ailment as no ordinary affliction: "You are possessed by a spirit," she announced, although she was unable to identify which spirit it was. Soon Mrs. A. herself fell into trance, and the spirit identified himself, speaking through her, his selected vessel. He said he was El Niño Fidencio,[16] a famous Mexican *curandero* who had disincarnated in 1938. She realized in retrospect that he had been assisting her in her curing for quite some time, but that she had not recognized it. Once she acknowledged his help and began to devote herself to the service of his spirit, she had access to a much greater range of diagnoses, and more diversified techniques and prescriptions. Her clientele increased considerably. Although she has the "gift" and she simply "knows" what to do (which she feels is superior to having to study in order to be able to follow El Niño's way), she acknowledged that one can study to develop one's ability. She would fall into the category which the Spiritualists define as healing "by the spiritual influences illuminating the brain of the healing medium and thereby intensifying the perception of the medium so that the cause, nature, and seat of the disease in the patient become known to the medium." Most of the chicano *materias* are able to perform absent healing as well, of which the *Spiritualist Manual* also speaks (National Spiritualist Association 1967: 51). Mrs. A. has not studied the works of Kardec directly, although she refers to him as the great Maestro (teacher) and uses many of the prayers for invoking spirits which are included in his *Coleccion de Oraciones Escogidas (Collection of Selected Prayers),* which displays a Christ-like figure on the cover. Kardec's framed picture hangs on the wall of her curing *centro,* which she feels makes her work legitimate to both clients and secular authorities.

One may become a *materia* as a result of having a dream or vision which signifies that one has been singled out to become a curer. But the pattern seen in Mrs. A's case is very common: the *materia*-to-be is ill and is taken from one Spiritist *centro* to another for treatment, without success. Finally, the source of the problem is recognized by an already-validated and practicing *materia*: this client is unique, a sensitive who also can communicate with the spirit world. In fact, such a period of illness serves as a very valuable apprenticeship. Had the chosen one known nothing of diagnosing, healing techniques, or Allan Kardec, he could not emerge from such a ritual curing cycle uninitiated. He had been secluded, treated, and then selected, educated, and launched during his epoch of suffering.

16 A detailed account of "folk saint" Fidencio's life, influence, and the *curanderismo* complex has been published earlier (Macklin 1967).

From May—when the migrant workers begin to come into Indiana, Ohio, and Michigan to harvest the crops—until the first heavy frost terminates harvest activities, Mrs. A. holds regular sessions on Saturdays and Sundays, and is available on other days to handle crises. From about one in the afternoon until every supplicant has been heard and treated—which may be well after midnight—she works: "El Niño's way is very hard; it demands much sacrifice, but I can not do otherwise."

Mrs. A. works in the low, whitewashed, cinderblock *templo* (or *centro*) attached to her modest home, located in an area of small run-down houses, most of whose yards have been converted into final resting places for junk automobiles. The building now has an ample graveled parking lot, and toilets have been put in to accommodate those who come to consult her. Prior to the service itself, she feeds many of those who come: *tortillas, frijoles, taquitos,* and coffee. Many who come bring food as offerings to El Niño Fidencio, most of which she redistributes to her weekend guests.

While the clients wait for the session to begin, they talk of El Niño Fidencio. Often they have come by to give thanks to him for having given them safe conduct on their trips from Florida, Texas, or Mexico; sometimes it is to thank him for having come in a time of need to save a sick child or husband, and they want to leave a *retablo* (painting depicting the miracle performed by Fidencio or other spirits). Even as did the ancient Greeks and Romans offer thanks to their gods (Foster 1960), the grateful also may leave ex-votos in the form of tiny legs, arms, the entire human body, or even an animal on the altar to commemorate the healing Fidencio effected for them. Myths about El Niño's prowess are recounted. One man relates repeatedly that he can come from Ohio, a distance of 125 miles and return, while using very little gasoline in his pick-up truck: "I use that truck all the time, and I know how much gas it needs. But when I come here, I can make the round trip, and use almost none at all. It is El Niño's influence." (Translated from Spanish.) Another tells of how he came to her *"en persona"* (in person, not in a vision) when her baby was dying, and immediately the fever left the child who recovered rapidly. Others recount how he can perform "invisible" operations, and therefore make it unnecessary to go to a doctor "with a title"; how his soul could leave his body during his life (as could those of Swedenborg and Andrew Jackson Davis) and go to the assistance of those who were far away; how he could heal the blind, the cancerous, and the leprous. All marvel at his ability to divine and overcome the evil effects of witchcraft.

For those who are there for the first time, the stories tend to allay initial skepticism. Those recounting the stories now have reinforced their own faith by repetition, and have enlarged their repetoire of myths. They have now evidence of Fidencio's concern for them and *la raza* (people of Mexican descent).

As one approaches the *templo*, a plaster statue of Our Lady of Guadalupe welcomes him, and identifies this place as offering help for Mexicans: here they know who they are, and she, the patroness, the Queen of Mexico (of whom most Anglo-Americans have never heard), will help them. Inside, the walls of the *templo* are decorated with laboriously handwritten and framed testimonies of Fidencio's effectiveness often accompanied with graphic "before-and-after" photographs. The testimonies follow a pattern in which the power hierarchy is clear: the grateful cured one gives thanks first to God Almighty, the Holy Ghost, El Santo Niñito Fidencio, and then to the *materia* (*curandera*) for having lent her *caja* (body) to the cause. The illness—from which the patient always has suffered long, and which expert physicians and other persons who cure could not treat—is named: "paralysis," or "some sharp pains in all of my body." These statements often conclude that now there is peace and tranquility in the home, and the testifier always will be grateful, and in his heart a follower of Fidencio.

At the front of the room is a richly decorated altar. Many of the familiar deities are represented but particularly those who are well known for their curing miracles: the Virgin of Guadalupe (*la virgen morena*, the dark virgin) with whom Mexican-Americans can readily identify, in a white Yankee world; the Virgin of San Juan de los Lagos whose miraculous cures are known to Mexicans and Mexican-Americans alike; and La Purissima, yet another virgin who has worked healing miracles when no physician was available, is there. Flowers and fruit, offerings to all of them, also adorn the altar. Jesus is on one side, behind candles which one may light. Among other gifts which have been presented to fulfill the clients' side of the "dyadic contract" (Foster 1967: 212 ff),[17] four rearing china horses, each two feet high, command one's attention. But dominating the altar are photographs of El Niño Fidencio himself, appearing in various poses and costumes. All are impressive. One shows him dressed in a white riding habit, a crop in one hand, representing the "masculine principle," as one of his followers says. Another shows him in profile, the photograph dramatically lighted from below. Yet another shows him reinacting the passion of Christ, carrying a cross as he proceeds pain-

---

[17] Foster's model is especially applicable here. *Pairs* of contractants are involved, not groups.

fully on his knees. (Then one learns that he always took the role of Jesus in the Holy Week dramas which he and his twelve disciples presented for his patients during every Lenten season from the late 1920s until his death in 1938). One revered photograph shows him lying in state, ensconced in his casket and clad in a sequined gown. The photograph which is most favored, however, shows an androgynous Fidencio, dressed in a long flowing gown (*bata*), covered by a blue cape like that of Our Lady of Guadalupe, and further identifiable by the rays of light which illuminate his head (of all the Spanish and Mexican virgins, only Guadalupe has these rays about her). Like her, he stands on a crescent moon base above a solitary Cherub's head. In this composite photograph, Fidencio also has his right hand raised in priestly benediction, while his left hand assumes the position portrayed by the image, Sacred Heart of Jesus. Labelled "El Niño Guadalupano," the photograph presents him as the embodiment of a unique trinity: the Christ figure, the highly revered Virgin of Guadalupe, and "Saint" Fidencio himself (*El Santo Niño*), "who is really close to you and really cares what happens to you."

Those seeking help come to the door of the *templo* and remove their shoes. After crossing themselves with holy water provided at the door, they proceed to the altar on their knees. Instructions are provided on how to behave: a hectographed, framed statement urges that women should not enter wearing hair curlers, one should not chew chicle, whisper to one's friends, or pay attention to what is going on between *la materia* and others. One is enjoined further to concentrate on invoking the spirit of El Santo Niño and otherwise purify the mind by thinking holy thoughts. (These regulations are typed in phonetic and ungrammatical Spanish, and have been translated into even less adequate English for those educated in U.S. schools and who never have learned to read Spanish.) A crudely printed sign on the wall announces that "missionaries" should attend mass before coming to the *templo*, if possible.

Finally Mrs. A. comes to the door, crosses herself with the holy water, and falls to her knees as does the collectivity. She proceeds to the altar, singing lustily in unison with the audience, *alabanzas* (hymns) praising El Niño Fidencio and God. Sometimes Fidencio is referred to in the hymns as the son of Joseph and Mary, and at other times as the son of God, or the Niño Guadalupano. Clearly, he is seen by some as a reincarnation of Jesus.

Me boy [sic] con mucho dolor en este penoso dia, adios, Niñito Fidencio, Hijo de Jose y Maria.	I go with much grief on this painful day, Niñito Fidencio, Son of Joseph and Mary.

"Gentle" Fidencio also is sought as a *padrino* (god father), a fictive kin position which remains very important in Latin American countries. Appeals are made to Our Lady of Guadalupe also, and she is clearly identified with Mexican nationalism:

Levanta tu bandera	Raise your flag
O Patria Mexicana	O Mexican motherland
Diciendo que viva	Saying that Maria
Maria Guadalupana.	Guadalupe lives.

Much of the oral tradition about Fidencio is transmitted in these songs because they deal with specific events which occurred during his life of curing in Northern Mexico (Espinazo, Nuevo León). Consequently, those who never had the opportunity to visit his tomb during the twice-annual fiestas none the less know what it is like there and of the events which occurred about forty years ago.

Adios, Doctor de Doctores	Goodbye, Doctor of Doctors
Te llevo en mi corazon	I carry you in my heart
Adios, arbolito lindo	Goodbye, beautiful little tree
Adios, hasta otra ocacion [sic].	Goodbye, until another time.

God reportedly conferred his divine election on Fidencio with the phrase, "You will be the Doctor of Doctors," near a small pirúl tree, now one of the most revered spots in Espinazo (its leaf often is used in the curing practices themselves). Yet other hymns make explicit the dyadic contract between Fidencio and the supplicant:

A pagar una promesa	To pay a promise
de mi tierra he venido.	From my land I have come.
Y admirar tu gran belleza	And to admire your great beauty
Santo Niño aparecido.	Appeared Sainted Niño.

His ability to cure hopeless cases is affirmed as mention is made of the "blind, the lame, and the demented." Illness is identified in song as the result of ingratitude and sin:

Meresco [sic] ser castigado	I deserve to be punished
por lo ingrato que yo he sido.	For having been ungrateful.
Ser mi patron y abogado	Be my patron and mediator
Santo Niño aparecido.	Appeared Sainted Niño.

Mrs. A.'s clients consider her to be an integral part of the Catholic institutionalized religious structure. But in part her effectiveness results from "sessions coterminous with the values, beliefs, aspirations, and problems of the participants: no discontinuity in social contacts is required of participation. Little social distance separates the afflicted person from the 'expert' " (Rogler and Hollingshead 1961: 21). Mrs. A. is egalitarian as were Kardec and Fidencio: they preferred the humble to the mighty.

She lacks one advantage that many such practitioners have; she does not operate in a small, reasonably well-integrated community where she can be apprised of all of the local gossip, and thus base her diagnoses on real knowledge of actual social relationships. Her clients come from widely dispersed areas such as Illinois, Indiana, Ohio, Michigan, and even Texas and Mexico. Therefore, she must use her general knowledge of the culture diagnostically. She probes in the area of Mexican-American values, and commonly shared problems.[18]

Mrs. A. functions therapeutically, as such practitioners often have been reported to do. Specifically, Mexican-Americans are having group problems of identity, and this is not surprising.[19] Although most of them are citizens of the United States, they distinguish people *not* of Mexican descent from themselves with the appellatives, "white" or "American." The Mexican nationals among the group never let the Mexican-Americans forget that they are not "really" Mexicans, and the majority white American group never lets them forget that they are not "really" Americans. Mrs. A. herself can speak almost no English, and her use of Spanish gives her clients a further sense of identity: "We are a group apart. We are Mexican." This serves to reinforce the present quasi-caste structure of intergroup relations and, therefore, functions to inhibit acculturation.

Mrs. A. uses her knowledge of the structure to function on the level of personal identity as well. The majority of cases which are brought to her for treatment manifest psychomatic symptoms, e.g. fatigue, vague aches and pains, skin rashes, nervousness. She handles some of these cases privately by drawing the client into the middle of the room while her assistants encourage loud group singing which not only drowns out the conversation between *la materia* and client, but also indicates that *all* present affirm the efficacy of her power and that of Niño Fidencio. At such times, the situation offers the comfort of

[18] One married client indicated to Mrs. A. that her (client's) husband "had a problem" but that he would not come for treatment. The client was astounded by *la materia's* perspicacity when she inferred that men frequently had problems with "other and evil women." The client was totally unaware of how much hostility and ambivalence she had communicated, kinesically, when discussing her husband's "problem."

[19] In fact, problems of identity may well be part of the "cultural baggage" which Mexican-Americans brought with them, if I interpret correctly comments by perceptive Mexican observers themselves, such as Octavio Paz (1961) and Samuel Ramos (1938). The alien environment certainly does not ameliorate these problems. As Orozco (1962: 104) so graphically puts it: "Like victims of amnesia, we haven't found out who we are."

repetitive ritual and the solidarity of the "church," in Durkheimian terms. In this role, the *materia* is largely supportive and shows a full grasp of the concept of projection (Gluckmann 1955: 90). She may indicate that one has been bewitched by envious neighbors for having been too successful, but that she will remove this; she may admit that, true, one's job is very difficult, but encourages him that he is talented enough to cope. Or she may reassure a client that she really is a good wife and mother, and not to let her in-laws get her down.

She handles cases publicly which support and reinforce faith in her own power. On one occasion, she had advised a Mexican national not to make a proposed trip to Mexico; he ignored her advice, and having lost all of his identification papers just this side of the border on the return trip, had come again to her for help in locating them. She stopped all singing, pointed an accusing forefinger at him from a distance of five feet, and said clearly for all to hear: *"Decisión de hombre* (a man's decision)! You went against my advice! Of course, something like this would happen!" She condescended to help him, anyway.

Mrs. A. also handles many cases publicly where basic Mexican-American values are involved: e.g., she chided one working woman whose child was suffering from *espanto* (fright) following a fall into a pond, that she had not been a good mother and that a woman's place was in the home with her children. "Although *la materia* had never met that woman before, she must have been right, for the woman began to cry," asserted a witness. Another woman's illness, Mrs. A. said, resulted from violating the *cuarenta dias* (the forty-day period before and after the birth of a child during which the mother is restricted by many taboos). In this way, Mrs. A. inhibits intergroup "validation of acculturation" (Broom and Kitsuse 1955) because she nearly always interprets illness in terms of deviation from approved Mexican-American behavior.

Partly as a result of these techniques, a mythology has grown up around Mrs. A., drawing ever more clients and tending to silence the skeptical. Everyone "knows" of a case in which some scoffer has been punished, usually with a physical affliction—facial twitches, severe skin rashes, and the like—for doubting her power. So great is her reputation that many chicanos bring relatives from Texas and Mexico to consult her.

To have the gift (*el don*) to heal and communicate with the spirits is generally considered to be superior, qualitatively, than to have to study for it, but it is conceded that one who is sincere and does study, could become more receptive spiritually and also work with the spirits for the "good of humanity." Although an already established *materia* recognizes and validates the signs of divine election in another, there is much competition among them. Mrs. A. now is assisted by two or three others who, she privately says, are not leading good lives and are not following El Niño's demanding way, or else they are in this work for personal gain rather than to serve. She will allow, however, that they have *some* "light."

The session ends when all have been attended, sometimes as late as 1:00 or 2:00 A.M. The spirit leaves, *la materia* shudders, and her own soul returns to her exhausted body.

While such practitioners know little of the formal Kardecian system (some even reject the notion that he has anything to say to them), they talk in terms of the same images and powers which he used: one hears of the "telephonic lines of the Divine Science of God," saying that El Santo Niñito Fidencio transmitted what the "orders" are. The figure of the "message system" being like a telephone network is used frequently by the Mexican-American Spiritists. Mrs. A. frequently refers to this or that *materia* as being "clairvoyant, clairaudient, or mental."

Even when the folk-Catholic follower of Fidencio insists that he communicates only with Fidencio, he is likely to add that other spirits do come down occasionally when he is invoking Fidencio. No other spirit can come down to the *materia* without the permission of Fidencio, though, a notion which is very close to that of the Spiritualist who has spirit "protectors" and spirit "guides."

We see, then, that Mexican-American Spiritism is based on the world-taken-for-granted of folk Catholicism. At the disposal of the *materia* is the power of God, the hierarchy of saints, virgins and their powers, Jesus, as well as the power and concern of Fidencio. All this is reinforced by Mrs. A., who has power from her own gift as well. There is concrete evidence in the testimonies of others that this power has been effective. Additionally, one has all of the benefit of assistance for one's *particular* personal trouble, one's specific problems, for a particular illness, and a blessing for a particular trip or undertaking.

Fidencio, the mythical hero, transcends time and space, to come down into the *materia* to help an individual client confront his particular historical reality.

Spiritualism: New England

Even as it was difficult to describe a "typical" Spiritist curing session, it is hardly safe to generalize about services held in a Spiritualist temple in New England. However, the procedure is almost identical to those described by Nelson (1969) and Zaretsky (1970). What I shall attempt to do here is to describe the structure of a service with the intention of showing how it locates the individual socially and specifically, while at the same time presenting him with a ritual and belief system which he can take for granted.

Here, too, people may congregate before the Sunday service begins, and although the congregation's composition varies from week to week, there is an at-homeness with one another, and strangers will talk with each other, exchanging experiences about psychic phenomena much as the chicanos sit about discussing Fidencio's visitations: I asked one couple new to me if they came often, and the husband responded (with a wondering tone of voice), "No, this is the first time in several years, but something just told us we should come here today. We've driven over from ——— (a town about sixty miles away). Spirit just urged us to come." Another reported that he had been born into the Spiritualist religion as his mother was a Spiritualist and very "mediumistic." Yet another member of the group, who had not attended for some time but is considered to be a very "spiritual" person, related one of her recent psychic experiences: she had anticipated through dreams the deaths of De Gaulle, Nasser, King Peter of Yugoslavia, and the Canadian La Porte. She also reported a premonition about the death of actor Ed Begley.

At the appointed hour of three, the service begins with the entrance of the president of the Temple, the secretary (who also doubles as organist in this case) and the medium(s). Here there is no medium-in-residence, the service being managed by a different medium each Sunday. A rousing hymn, with positive beat and major key, opens the service. Even as the Mexican-American Spiritist curing session was accompanied throughout with familiar Catholic hymns and chants, these Spiritualist sessions in New England feature hymns with a Baptist beat and lyrics which convey the prevailing system of Spiritualist values. Again, a collection of individuals is beginning to move toward "liminality," to become a group comprised of the visible and the invisible. Let us consider "Communion with the Dead" from the *Spiritualist Hymnal* (National Spiritualist Association n.d.: 130; my emphasis):

> How *pure at heart* and *sound in head* . . .
> Should be the man whose tho't would hold
> An hour's communion with the dead.
> In vain shalt thou, or any call
> The spirits from their golden day.
> Except, like them, thou too canst say,
> My *spirit is at peace* with all.

Evidently, one must be moral, scientific, and at peace to communicate with spirits, who are leading a halcyonic existence. Many hymns illustrate the spirits' power to dispel spiritual benightedness and death. "Message from the Spirit Hand" announces that "some morn the spirit friends will rap," and "doubt" will be no more (*Hymnal*, 58). The lyrics are uniformly optimistic, reassuring the individual that he *can* transcend the here and now, and death, with spirit help, e.g., "Isn't it Wonderful" (*Hymnal*, 132):

> Isn't is wonderful what Spirit can do?
> Oh, isn't it wonderful so perfect and true . . .
> Eternal victories laying over all [sic]
> Deepen spirit messages when the spirits call.
> Greeting and heralding all of mortal clay,
> Singing of eternity in a joyous lay.[20]

The *Spiritualist Manual* asserts that "Thought is the basis of all action. . . . Every thought we think has its effect on every cell of the human body, either for health or disease" (103). Hymns express this same concept, also. The dyadic contract between those on the material side of life and those on the higher side is clearly adumbrated in the song, "Spirit Takes Care of Me," where we learn that spirit takes care of me *if* I pray, and *if* I am thankful. Womb to tomb security is offered, as one learns that angels have been near "since birth."

Even as the chicanos asked the spirits to come down and prepare themselves for the visit, the New England medium is likely to enjoin his congregation to ask for spirits to come during the invocation:

> I am going to use a prayer that was given to me by a friend, who had it given to her by a spirit, and is very beautiful. But before I do, before I read it, I want each and every one of you, as is my usual custom, to sit in a little silence for a moment, and ask your spirit loved ones to come and visit with you this afternoon. You know they like to be invited especially, just the same as you and I do from day to day by our friends and loved ones here.

The spirits exhibit the very "human" quality of being a bit touchy unless they receive a special invitation to visit. The spirits being invoked clearly are not regarded as being as awesome as those which come to assist in Mrs. A.'s curing rituals, and evidently are less god-like, at this point in their careers, at any rate. Children are welcomed in the Spiritualist Temple and messages are given to them, but as they know much less about those loved ones who have "crossed

---

[20] Middle English signification.

over" to the spirit world, most mediums say that it is very difficult to read for them. In this temple, many mediums will terminate the invocation with the Lord's Prayer; this is followed by another hymn, and then the Declaration of Principles which the congregation, officers of the temple, and medium affirm in unison. The Healing Service is a standard part of every session and is read in unison (*Hymnal*, end leaf):

I ask the Great Unseen Healing Force
   To Remove All Obstructions
   From My Mind and Body
And to Restore Me to Perfect Health
I ask This in All Sincerity and Honesty
   And I Will Do My Part.

I ask This Great Unseen Healing Force
   To Help Both Present and Absent Ones
   Who are in Need of Help
And to Restore Them to Perfect Health
   I Put My Trust
In the Love and Power of God.

During the prayer, one concentrates on those who are ill and needing help. There may be separate services in which the medium, if he or she is especially gifted in healing, brings healing "vibrations" to the congregation. Yet another hymn follows, dispelling gloom, or declaring death to be shorn of power. Finally comes the medium's sermon which embodies the Spiritualist value system, the wholeness of man, God, and spirit. This is in contrast with Mexican-American Spiritism where the value system is communicated through the healing relationship between *la materia* and the client, or in public diagnoses.

During the last hymn, the medium usually has been concentrating, breathing deeply, preparing himself (or herself) for receiving the spirits. He (or she) then presents the scriptural reading and the lecture, the two usually having related themes. Most of the mediums in this temple do not go into trance (by their own definition) for the "lecture," but consider it to be "inspired" by their spirit teachers and guides. It is a dangerous time for the medium, for he is tied—invisibly but powerfully—to the client. Should someone pass between them, physically, the "spirit cord" connecting them may "snap" back into the medium and injure him, sometimes seriously.

The spirit guides are expected to prevent the coming of mischievious and misleading spirits. Although most of the mediums in this study are not principally healing mediums, *all* included many references to perfect health and how to achieve it in their presentations. Influences of nineteenth century "mental healing" permeate the lectures (italics mine):

> Psychology teaches us that the subconscious phase of mind continues to work while we are asleep so think health, happiness, and success so that the subconscious may have constructive thoughts upon which to work during our sleeping hours. . . . Cease to blame fate, environment, and every known cause but yourself for your mistakes in life. We now are becoming aware of the existence of an unseen world within each and everyone of us. This inner . . . world is a world of causes. These causes are set into motion with our thoughts and our thoughts are governed or controlled by our own will power. The kind of thoughts we permit to dominate our invisible world determines the status of our visible world. By realizing and overcoming the errors of yesterday, we create a new world of tomorrow. . . . *You are the master of your fate.*

The individual is told that his parlous state is of his own making, and he also is shown to be the architect of his own destiny. However, he is to be assisted out of the maelstrom—as are the followers of Fidencio—by beings more powerful than he, and very much concerned with his personal well-being, and presently in the same community as he.

Sessions of both the Spiritists and Spiritualists then bring helpful spirits eager to attend to individual wants. As historian Donald Warren (1968: 399) points out, spirit intercedance "may serve to soften the harshness of 'All is forseen but free will is granted,' the famous paradox which Akiba ben Joseph uttered two millenia ago and to which Kardecism implicitly adheres," as does North American Spiritualism. Not only are these helpful, attentive spirits, but most are friends, acquaintances, or kin. Since spirits can atone for sins committed on the earth "plane," they frequently apologize for improper conduct toward those left behind, which presumably reestablishes some kind of equanimity and good feeling in the listening client (although one youngish widow on hearing her husband's spirit apologize, retorted heatedly, "He sure ought to!"). Sometimes the precise identification of the spirit eludes the medium. The recipient of the message often will identify the spirit (and mediums chide audiences which do not assist them), and occasionally the medium will address one of the unseen minions which crowd around him: "Why don't you tell them who you are?"

Although it hardly constitutes a trend, female spirits outnumbered male spirits four to three during the sessions analyzed here. Of those who are identified as kin (by either the audience or the mediums), females outnumber the males two to one. For example, "Could I bring a mother to you?" or, "I'm coming in touch with this elderly lady; I feel very motherly with her, like I would be bringing a mother to you from spirit." All kin regardless of sex, bring love, are very concerned and supportive ("I stand in back of you, firm and tall"), while the women kinfolk are particularly nurturent ("She thought you were pretty special," and "I'm with you a great deal"; "We'll help you with that condition"; "She brings you a great deal of love"). All the spirits are happy in their new plane, but their happiness is affected by that of their kin on earth: "A man is speaking, and he says that I should tell you, 'I'm her brother; I want her to know that I'm happy, but I'm unhappy when she is; I'm helping her.'" The heavy emphasis on personal responsibility—traditionally Protestant—could be quite onerous, were one not also provided with a patterned way out to escape it from time to time. Sometimes, a medium may point out, the spirits are responsible: "There are earth bound spirits which do not want to progress and they can affect you negatively. I don't know why. I do feel lonely with you, much as I don't want to. Do you feel lonely sometimes?" The client, an elderly woman, acknowledged that she did. The medium continued: "I would say, I would go and visit. There is a lonely spirit attracted to you, and you don't want to get too lonely, do you understand? Because you've done so much to make it nice for everyone." So while spirits can help, they also can afflict with their all-too-human frailties. The client achieves balance between having to take some responsibility for his problems and being able to blame meddling, low, and undeveloped spirits.

Even as the singing provided privacy for the chicano consulting the *materia*, privacy for the client is provided in the Spiritualist temple by the vagueness of the messages, as Zaretsky (1970) has pointed out. Often a medium will say: "I don't understand what I'm saying. It's *your* message, but that's the way I get it." This encourages the individual receiving the message to build his own interpretation; he can project his *own* social reality onto the message, and so tailor the mediumistic vision to his personal situation:

> I just feel that, well, if you haven't seen in reality, you've seen in a picture how, if you have a basket of yarn, how a little kitten got into it, what a nice confused mess it is. It is not all ruined but there are entanglements that are very hard to sort of untangle. So conditions around you are a little bit like this?

This description of "conditions" was electrifying to the recipient of the message, who later commented on the medium's prescience. Encouragement also was here for one could hope to untangle what now appeared to be only the result of a "mischievous vibration, a sort of kitten's play, rather than really an . . . anger vibration. We can accept it with a different attitude, can we not?"

Most of the health advice comes interspersed throughout the message session, often on a very practical level: "You should watch your eating habits and drink lots of water." Or, "You should eat more green vegetables," asking also whether the client liked a lot of meat. When he agreed, this was translated into evidence of the medium's clairvoyance, even as a subsequent question elicited the response that *that* client did not like water. Medium, triumphantly, "I didn't think so. You must drink more water because your system is very dry." She then called a spirit doctor to work for yet another woman who was suffering from sinus trouble.

Again, one is not left to fight the battle alone:

Spiritualism has the advantage over other forms of healing because through spirit communication, by means of mediumship, the healers are able to contact the spirit doctors and from their advanced state of progression they are able to advise and instruct the healer as to causes and treatments. All methods of healing are **guided by spirit forces. But Spiritualism alone is conscious of that guidance and is able to use it to greater advantage.**

And all is explained according to the working of natural law. Mesmerism lives on:

There is no special mystery or miracle about the laying on of hands when one learns to understand nature's processes. When the recuperative forces are aroused, and negative thinking has been overcome, nature then proceeds to send an increased nerve current to the affected parts. This work is done along subconscious lines over the great nerve centers and the sympathetic nervous system. This current is like a current of electricity being sent to the parts from a great dynamo, *the brain.* This electrical vital force vitalizes the diseased organ and also sends an increased circulation of blood to it.

Negative emotional states are important causes of illness:

Many healers refuse to treat a patient until they've had a personal interview with them. If they find that patient is holding within themselves a thought of hatred or jealousy toward another person, the healer usually tells them that they must first cleanse his own mind of negative thoughts before the healer is able to treat him with any degree of success. Because this causes a destructive thought vibration that can tear down the physical body as fast as the healing forces can build it up.

Some mediums communicate an avowedly anti-medical bias:

When people die, it's their time, regardless of what the doctors do, regardless of what plans are. . . . Science sets them [facilities] up thinking of the lives they save, heart transplants and others. They go, don't they, just the same. . . . I have prayed and the Bible says there's no such thing . . . because if God had wanted man to have another man's heart, that would have been long ago, not now, the last days. I have a spirit doctor teacher who tells me there's no such a thing. That it's sciences: they went a-whoring with their inventions.

Of no small interest is the frequency with which the spirits of Red Indians appear, as medical practitioners as well as guides. A. I. Hallowell, reflecting on the "backwash of the frontier," mentions that popular confidence in Indian medicine remained strong during the nineteenth century. He goes on to emphasize the role of the Indian in American religion: "In Spiritualism, the United Society of Believers (Shakers), and the Church of Latter-day Saints (Mormons), the American Indians had a special significance for the founders or adherents" (Hallowell 1967: 331). He adds:

The names of more than a dozen mediums, men and women and their Indian controls, appear in the *Encyclopaedia of Psychic Science*. Such historic figures as Red Jacket, Black Hawk, and Tecumseh are on the list, as well as spirits with such names as White Feather, Bright Eyes, and Moonstone. What is particularly significant is that these Indian spirits were thought to be beneficient in their influence, especially because of their healing powers, although they often manifested themselves at séances in a somewhat rambunctious manner. As time went on and spirit photography was introduced, some of these spirits appeared in native costume in the photographs. (1967: 332)

This interest of the Spiritualists in Indians can be documented amply in 1971. A thirty-year-old male adherent has as a rather constant companion the Indian guide White Feather. He reports that he had felt compelled to carry a white feather somewhere on his person long before White Feather was identified by a medium as his guide. He can "feel" the comforting presence of White Feather, and always says to him when he appears: "Hi there! Glad you're back." Others with psychic abilities have told me of "seeing" an Indian or a group of them from time to time, and they are dressed in "full regalia" (i.e. a Plains Indian war bonnet) when they appear, even as they were in the days of spirit photography in the last century.

One the leading mediums of Spiritualist Camp Chesterfield in Indiana has an Indian, Silver Bell, as her guide. A Spiritualist camp in Pennsylvania is called Silver Bell. Not one of the sessions being analyzed here passed without some appearance of an Indian spirit, and all such spirits were regarded as benevolent.[21] Indian spirits are regarded as closer to "natural forces," not so "spoiled" by civilization, and very "spiritual." One can only speculate that this may be expressing a weariness with the struggle against things technological—or that it is a statement of the devastating effects of civilization on the "natural" man.

Usually each individual in the Spiritualist meeting has received a message. The spirit(s) then leave, and individual mediums react variously. One may plead softly, "Spirit, release your instrument," while from another, the spirit departs while his earthly vessel shudders a few times, or experiences a twitching of the head. Other mediums sigh audibly, blink their eyes a few times, and retreat spent, to meditate for a few minutes in the chair near the podium.

Individuals in the audience have been drawn for various reasons, but the majority has experienced some event which he or she considers to be psychic. The medium often (perhaps three or four times per session) identifies individuals in the audience as having much psychic ability, and occasionally predicts that a given individual will himself become a medium. The individual hearing this then sees himself not only as one receiving power from the higher side of life, but as also possessing special powers which can be developed:

> Now this may surprise you. If you've got the time to study, study Spiritualism. Study it. Because within two years, I'm told you're supposed to be up here [pats the podium] where I am . . . in two years! People can help you, they can tell you how to study. [The girl receiving the message did attend spiritual development classes.]

There is to be found the same type of competition among Spiritualistic mediums as was noted among the Spiritists. A medium in the audience approached a participant after one session to report, in gently reproving tones: "I saw many more deceased around you than

---

[21] Indian spirits also appear to the *mestizo* Mexican *materias*, usually identified as nothing more than *un Indito*, and usually regarded as vigorous, sometimes uncultured, but especially powerful.

Reverend E. mentioned. There were so many, I don't see how he could have overlooked them."

Even as the Kardecian philosophical system was seen to be of little concern to those participating in Mexican-American Spiritist sessions today (although they utilize the pragmatic aspects such as special prayers for invoking the spirits, techniques of extending curative vibrations, etc.), so to the majority who come to the Spiritualists' sessions the philosophical and religious aspects of the system are not a primary concern. The mediums recognize this. Said one as he finished his brief lecture:

> My friends, I hope that I am instrumental in helping you to be more aware of the reason we are in church. We are here to communicate with our loved ones primarily, in a spiritual church, but we are also here to commune with our Heavenly Father. If we watch our health, if we take care of our physical and spiritual lives by our attitudes toward them, we will be living in accord with nature and with nature's God.

The community of God, nature, the invisible and the visible which has been joined for a time by the abilities of the medium now dissolves. Atomistic again, each returns to the secular social structure from which he emerged, but better able to cope with it for having been out.

ANALYSIS

Luckmann (1967: 102) has pointed out that the "sacred cosmos of modern industrial societies no longer represents one obligatory hierarchy and that it is not articulated as a consistent thematic whole." I have tried to suggest here that New England Spiritualism (based on traditional American Protestant values) and Spiritism (based on Mexican folk Catholicism) have succeeded in providing a consistent thematic whole for their adherents which heals the split between temporal order and the eternal.[22] In both, a familiar set of religious representations are offered to the "consumers," most of whom have shopped around a bit before coming into these groups. Neither has a large formal membership at this time, and few of those attend sessions regu-

---

[22] "In Brazil and Chile divine healing constitutes one of the secrets of Pentecostal advance. Several historical churches realize this, and concern was voiced in 1963 by the Pan-African Congress of Christian Churches: 'Healing,' they said, 'is becoming one of our grave issues. We have seen that healing in Independent (mostly Pentecostal) churches stresses the reality of the spiritual world, the basic unity of man, and the profound interrelation of religion and healing in a way which has met the previously unsatisfied needs of many African Christians.'" (Damboriena 1969: 124).

larly (not more than two or three). In both we find a hierarchy of familiar deities and supernaturals presented to the client ("You can thank God, and the spirit, and the control"; or "*Primero Dios, después El Niño Guadalupano [Fidencio], y después la materia*") , along with the spirits of friends and kinfolk (with Jesus representing the ideal type medium) who help him to cope with his quotidian troubles. At the same time, the "help" is sufficiently vague that one is not inhibited in his search for self-realization and self-expression.

Spiritualism is optimistic ("God did not make us evil; He made us good in his sight"; "I like this vibration which comes to you"; "We find that things are going to be much nicer in the coming year than they have been in the past"; "And the spirits say, but remember, son, our **disappointments are appointments that we have with God.**"). **Death has been conquered; we merely change our way of life and that is a happy way.** Both Spiritualism and Spiritism—from the point of view of the client—can be considered to present and reinforce a "world-taken-for-granted" with which he was familiar when he came to the temples, searching.

Both Spiritualists and Spiritists see clearly the dyadic contract which is demanded. Clients have responsibility and obligation to the supernatural world, and they offer faith, ex-votives, *milagros, retablos, promesas,* or a "happy" attitude, patience, love, and prayer to those wiser, more powerful and helpful beings. ("The spirits are happy, they want you to be happy, wear happy colors"; "Grief is not of the Lord, grief is the Adversary . . . because if you love the Lord, the Lord doesn't bring you grief.")

In both groups, manifest dream content is interpreted as meaningful and considered a means of communication with the supernatural world, to receive guidance and prophecies. Dreams also figure importantly in announcing and validating the divine election of mediums and *materias*.

Both groups know that they are opposed by, and outside, the established systems of religious belief. (Medium [to client]: "People say, 'Oh, I don't want to tell people I'm a Spiritualist.' I say, 'Why not?' 'Because people will laugh.' I said, 'How many laughed at Jesus Christ when he was a preacher? There were a lot of them that laughed at him.' " *Materia* [to anthropologist]: "Maybe if you write something about me they'll know I'm not a *bruja* [witch]. A lot of people think that I'm practicing *brujería* [witchcraft], and many people in this town don't believe in Fidencio, but it says in the Bible that Jesus was mocked, too.")

The structure of the ritual drama is the same for both groups. The medium/*materia* prepares those in the audience to separate themselves from the secular world (the hymns with unique lyrics; the insistence on physical relaxation, and concentration on the spirits and on healing; the invocation of the spirits; the medium's lecture and the *materia's* "sermonettes"). The individual messages and "healing" provides the client with a self-transcending mythic experience in which the temporal and the eternal are joined. (Fidencio is one with Jesus and Guadalupe, the *materia* united with Fidencio and client. Medium, clients, and spirits occupy one time and space.) In both persuasions the client is treated as a significant individual, worthy of the special and unique attention of the caring powers:

> Do not try to be someone else—Don't be an ape! Cultivate your individuality; you can express yourself better than you can imitate someone else. There is only one You—let that shine forth in all the resplendent selfhood which the real You possesses. It will be infinitely easier than trying to be someone else. (National Spiritualist Association 1967: 142)

Mediums and *materias* alike may be "called" in various ways: one may be born with the gift or it may come through dreams, visions, or visitations of the supernatural, nearly always recognized, interpreted, and validated by other members of the "elect." Both are vessels, instruments of the supernaturals, but many also have power of their own. Both must live "good" lives ("There must be a way of life that is correct"). Both run sessions "coterminous" with the values and socio-economic status of their clients (the folksiness of the jokes of the mediums, and the "hip" talk of a Black medium, employed only when she addressed Blacks in the audience; the *materia's* use of Spanish with the Chicanos.) In both persuasions there are mediums with varied talents, but commonly the spirits take possession and speak through their instruments.

Illness is identified and diagnosed—and therefore is manageable. It may be caused by possession by an evil spirit, a lonely spirit hanging around, or negative psychological states. ("You must not hate; gossip is bad; there are those who are envious.") Social ties are reestablished with family and kin in the here and now. Spirits also are repentant; guilt may be expiated on both sides of that dyadic contract. Transcendence of death has been provided by means of a returning hero (Fidencio), or by a "scientifically proven" redefinition of death as merely a change in status.

The mediums, then, build on a vague, undogmatic, constantly revealed and developing doctrine, the pragmatic aspects of which have been and are being transmitted by means of the oral tradition. Adherents are provided with a perception of phenomenal reality which differs from that held by the orthodox Protestant or Catholic.

One's own personal revelations and spiritual development are not only acceptable, but encouraged. This is part of the problem of developing a coherent and comprehensive doctrine. The ability of the individual to develop power, to receive help, the openendedness, and the individualism keeps a body of doctrine from growing. The spirits, it would appear, are as individualistic in their beliefs as those on the earth plane, and teach varying doctrines to different individuals and groups. Competing "messages" often are presented to validate rival positions. So it is that the strength given the individual, the private vision given him by his communicating spirits comes at the cost of building doctrine and group—even as was the case in the nineteenth century.

The role of the mediums or *materias* is critical in helping the individual to create a meaningful personal identity. The mediums enter into a dangerous relationship with the spiritual world, one in which the benevolent spirits must protect and help them. Although emotionally and physically demanding, the medium's role provides that individualized private contact during which those spirits who care about one are reached ("they're in the family tie"). Because of their special powers, the mediums are responsible for taking the entire congregation for a time, into a liminal world (Turner 1969) where secular and sacred time are joined. The hymns, the prayers, the chants, and the supplications all help the transition to occur for the group. Once there, with the spirits crowding about, in the self-same space occupied by those on this earth plane, the medium/*materia* proceeds to escort each individual further into liminality for the personal attention he desires.

The messages and revelations which serve to create a personal identity and locate the individual socially and psychologically lead to competition among those developing spiritually. This is especially true among those most developed, the mediums and *materias*. Gossip, condescension, and jealousy typically are found within a group of adherents and among groups. Such competition, inherent in the tenets of each belief system, leads to fission and the formation of splinter groups (even as Joan Koss [in press] found fission to be the case among Puerto Rican Spiritists in Philadelphia). Partly for these reasons, neither Spiritualism nor Spiritism is likely to be transformed into social or political movements. This has been dealt with elsewhere (Macklin and Crumrine 1973).

The individual also finds help apart from the temple sessions. The supernaturals are not left in the church edifice. One may have a home altar dedicated to El Niño Fidencio. The sainted Niño may come at night in your own home to perform an invisible operation or cure your sick child. One may find that his spirit guide comes at unexpected moments to keep him company. ("Hi, White Feather, I'm glad you're back.")

There seems to be one significant difference between the Spiritualism and Spiritism as they function today, and that is to be found in the "worlds-taken-for-granted" underlying each. Those values promulgated by the New England *Spiritualist* medium prepare *his* client for upward mobility in a traditional American way. *Perfectionism* is stressed. One is told which plane in the spirit world he is going to inhabit; that it is going to be according to the life and the good you have done in the material world. And if you are in a lower plane, then you have got to progress and earn your way up to the higher planes. Personal *responsibility* is stressed:

> You took a step back, didn't you? Oh yes you did, because I'm told that you did . . . and you'll find that it will be satisfying to you, but you've got to buckle down yourself again. You understand?
> The spirit says *you* are the key to the situation. Now it is up to you whether or not you keep the door locked.

Delayed gratification also is stressed:

> I want to say, time will tell. Time will tell, and time will reveal things to you that you don't realize at the present time. . . . Now I don't know why they say that, but that's the way it is given. And they say, patience, my child, patience. But you certainly will progress on, to another level, as they express it. . . But I am told it will be a little time yet.

All are enjoined to work hard, but especially those appearing to be of school age are admonished that we must crawl before we walk. This is what McLoughlin (1967: 64) has referred to as the "third force" in Christendom, the "pietistic spirit of American culture itself." Being pietists, Americans believe that God has yet "further light" to shed to them as well as to the rest of the world. This faith in the *search* for truth, this belief that happiness must be pursued constantly—epitomized in Spiritualist philosophy—still is the dynamic religious force in America as a civilization.

Comparatively, folk-Catholic Spiritists emerge as more dependent on the powers of the supernatural world, hoping for a satisfactory outcome—*si Dios quiere* (if God wants it). Chicanos constitute a group which has strong structural ties with, and geographical proximity to, other people of Mexican descent in Texas and Mexico. This advantage has been enjoyed by few other immigrant groups in this country: the Puerto Ricans and French Canadians are exceptions with which there are some interesting comparisons and contrasts. Illness, childbirth, and other crises are times when they, like Lewis's Tepoztecans (1951), want to go "home," and often do. They came to Indiana, Ohio, and Michigan bound in *gemeinschaftlich* social relations, and have not had to participate—except economically—in social relations apart from extended and ritual kin. Because of Mrs. A's. renown, many bring ailing relatives to the Middle West, which entails visits of from one to many months with all that this means by way of cultural and social reinforcement. Others, drawn by the reputations of similar *materias* in Texas and Mexico return to kith and kin for help during such crises.

Basic orientations regarding the nature of the universe are slow to change. Here such *cultural* orientations about health and illness, appropriate to a *gemeinschaftlich* society contribute to and reinforce strong *structural* ties, which are (with few exceptions) also *gemeinschaftlich;* or perhaps more elegantly put (see Geertz 1957): the *materia* functions to help keep integration in the "causal-functional" dimension continuous with the form of integration existing in the "logico-meaningful" dimension.

SUMMARY AND CONCLUSIONS

I have attempted to show that Spiritualism and Spiritism originated as one kind of response to the stresses engendered by the nineteenth-century science/religion, materialistic/vitalistic ideological conflict. Both failed to develop organizations, rituals, or doctrines which might have permitted them to persist into the present century as viable religious or philosophical *systems*. Rather, the pragmatic "scientific" experimental aspects of Spiritualism persisted in the United States and Great Britain, while Allan Kardec—with Gallic love of system—put together an occultic philosophy which swept the Continent. Both forms reached parts of Latin America in the early 1850s, but the Kardecian system seems to have diffused throughout this vast area very effectively,[24] filtering from social elites to rural peasantry. Again, the system was lost while the pragmatic details of managing the supernatural world were adopted.

The twentieth century's sacred world-taken-for-granted, scientism, is crumbling. Even that area regarded as the most "scientific" of the scientific—medicine—now is being questioned, the "shamans" themselves announcing in *McCall's Magazine* that they sometimes are

[23] Donald Warren avers that Spiritism is the coming religion of Brazil (1968).

fallible (Beeson 1968: 226). Another recently has "told all," gleefully revealing the inside slights and slips of hand which go into "the making of a surgeon" (Nolen 1970)—a betrayal so unprofessional as to have been unthinkable to Lévi-Strauss's shaman, Quesalid (1967).

The individual is divested of the "myth that this is a mythless" age. But Spiritualism, now resting on the old Protestant pietist values, and Spiritism, thoroughly integrated with folk Catholicism, have persisted. Neither is developing its own organization, ritual or doctrine, but both function to help the bereft twentieth-century individual construct a meaningful personal identity on known infrastructures, and so enjoy health.

The data suggest that on the one hand, those Protestant values (which sound so out of date in an era of the anti-rational, anti-work, "now"-oriented, counterculture which desires and expects "instant" results) are, in fact, serving Spiritualism's clients very well. If Berger and Berger (1971) are right, technology is here to stay, and the U.S. is going to continue to need disciplined technically educated young. Those hearing the spirits admonish them to be patient, to work hard, to delay gratification, to get an education, to be optimistic *and* make effort could become the technocrats of tomorrow. The "bluing of America" will probably occur, "Consciousness III" notwithstanding.

On the other hand, while Spiritism functions positively in precisely the same ways to help the isolated chicano locate himself in family, kin, and *la raza,* it punishes or rewards him in terms of a folk value system appropriate to rural Mexico. By healing the split between the temporal and eternal order, Spiritism serves to inhibit individual behavioral changes.

Whatever their differences, mediums, *materias,* and clients alike would probably agree with poet Octavio Paz (1961: 211) that the dramas of salvation in which they participate repeatedly—like myths and fiestas—"permit man to emerge from his solitude, become one with creation" and find grace.

Ideological Support for the Marginal Middle Class: Faith Healing and Glossolalia

THIS paper focuses on the ideological belief system of contemporary American fundamentalistic religion, as practiced by predominantly white middle-class Americans. Although adherents to fundamentalism are part of the mainstream of the American middle class, their religious belief systems are at considerable variance with dominant middle-class values. This paper will illustrate how the disparity between fundamentalistic values and dominant middle-class values produces major social and psychological dissonance in the lives of fundamentalists. Therefore, it is necessary, it will be argued, to buttress the dissonant fundamentalistic beliefs with certain religious rituals—glossolalia and faith healing—that provide ideological support, reaffirming the social and psychological coherence of fundamentalistic beliefs and values in the face of dissonant American values that challenge the religious belief system.

POPULATION

The religious subculture under consideration is popularly termed fundamentalism. In part this is merely an extension of traditional American Protestantism. In this sense fundamentalism cannot be considered a marginal religious movement in America. However, it should be recalled that since at least 1875 there have been a series of schismatic splits off the mainstream protestant denominations. As a consequence a considerable fundamentalistic influence can still be found to a varying degree in each major protestant denomination. But the major fundamentalistic movement is seen in various splinter groups such as Orthodox Presbyterians, the Free Methodists, the Conservative Baptists, etc. Of great interest is the fact that membership in these groups consists of solid white middle-class Americans, who nevertheless perceive of themselves, and interact socially, as a group marginal to, and alienated from, their own middle-class society.

This marginal middle-class white religious subculture must be dif-

418

ferentiated from the fundamentalism of the marginal poverty and working class subculture, as typified in the traditional pentecostal sects. As will be illustrated, the middle class fundamentalists have become marginal because the society is moving *away* from them. Whereas the lower class fundamentalists share the same religious ideologies, but are moving *toward* the dominant middle class.

IDEOLOGY AND PERSONALITY: THEORETICAL ISSUES

It is taken for granted that cultural forces influence secondary and tertiary manifestations of neurotic process; but the question is do they effect the basic dichotomy between conscious and unconscious activity. (Kubie 1950)

Cultural phenomena do not belong to the outer husks of personality structure, but are found right down through to the heart and core of the ego organization itself. (Murphy 1965)

The question posed by Kubie in 1950 and answered by Murphy in 1965 reflects a growing interest in the effects of values in shaping not only behavior, but also the intrapsychic components of behavior. Neither classic psychoanalytic theory which emphasized instinctual conflicts, nor classic behavioristic psychology which emphasized mechanistic datum, provided effective conceptual tools. However, the advent of ego psychology has provided means for understanding the role of the cognitive and conceptual frameworks of culture as they affect the structure and function of personality.

COGNITION AND THE ROLE OF VALUES

It is well-established that personality variables, particularly affective states, are involved in perceptual-cognitive process and indeed may significantly distort these processes even to the point of misinterpreting one's entire community (e.g. Cameron's paranoid pseudo-community; (Cameron 1951, 1959).

This is also evidence for the reverse, namely, that socio-cultural factors influence one's perceptual-cognitive apparatus (Triandis 1964; Bernstein 1958). J. McV. Hunt (1965) summarized the evidence "to indicate that cognitive experience—or more precisely, the organism's informational interaction with the environment—can be as important for psychological development as emotions based on the fate of the instincts, and perhaps it is typically more important." He adds that although intellectual characteristics have been thought to be more nearly fixed in genotype than emotional characteristics, it now appears that intellectual characteristics may be more subject to substantial effects of environmental encounters.

The Sapir-Whorf hypothesis on specific cultural "views-of-the-world" implies that general abstract cultural concepts may shape specific personality structures (Whorf 1956). This idea has been followed in the work on national character and modal personality (Inkeles and Levinson 1954). The problem with this approach, however, has been the difficulty in distinguishing among (1) a personality structure which is merely characteristic of a culture (modal personality), (2) personality characteristics found in each member of a culture (national character), and (3) general cultural influences on the development of personality which modify the formation of individual personalities.

It is toward the third alternative which recent research leads. From a solely psychological viewpoint Harvey, Hunt, and Schroeder (1961) present experimental data which suggest that conceptual systems directly influence personality and psychopathology. And from a socio-economic viewpoint Hagen (1962) has shown that social conflict may evoke sequential *generations* of specific personality types.

More specifically, Kluckhohn and Strodtbeck (1961) have proposed a limited number of basic human problems for which all people at all times and in all places must find some solution. They propose five basic orientations for each of which there are three types of solutions (see Table I). The particular constellation of solutions a culture employs, its "value orientation profile," can be expected to play a determinative role in the personality development of that culture's members. I shall use this profile in this analysis.

TABLE I

Orientation	*Postulated Range of Variations*		
Human Nature	Evil	Neutral	**Good**
Man-Nature	Subjugation to Nature	Harmony with Nature	**Mastery over Nature**
Time	Past	Present	**Future**
Activity	Being	Being-in–Becoming	**Doing**
Relational	Lineality	Collaterality	**Individuality**

THE ROLE OF CULTURAL VALUES IN THE EGO

Although couched in various terms, there is a growing consensus that personality development reflects not only psychodynamic needs but also value needs. Such needs to "make sense out of the world" have been termed the "quasi-needs" of the ego (von Bertalanffy 1958), the will to meaning (Frankl 1962), ego efficacy (R. W. White 1963), cognitive coherence (Festinger 1957). Now according to Hartmann's formulation of ego development, there is an initial undifferentiated id-ego matrix from which emerges aspects of ego function separated from instinctual drive processes; and these autonomous ego activities are involved in the process of developing a coherent effective adaptation to the external world (Hartmann 1964; Rapaport 1958).

These autonomous ego functions assume the function of "ego drives" in contradistinction to "instinctual drives." These ego drives are dependent upon the beliefs and values of the culture, and these drives become important if indeed not the overriding determinant of behavior. Thus it can be seen that belief systems are the data that the ego uses to organize individual behavior. The lack of such cultural value data results in the failure to develop an effective coherent ego structure; or the cultural value system may result in significant distortions in the formation of ego structure. Belief systems, whether they be religious or otherwise, then, are both necessary and influential in the development of personality (Parsons and Shils, eds. 1954).

Religious Subculture as a Source of Values

Religion has been viewed at times as a sort of socio-cultural epiphenomenon which really did not affect the matrix of social interaction or personality development. Contrary to this view is research, such as the 1961 Detroit study, which demonstrated that religion profoundly influenced politics, vocations, economics, and social relations (Lenski 1961). Furthermore, the study surprisingly revealed the pervasive presence and influence of religious subculture units which functioned as "small societies" within the larger culture.

These religious subcultures provide an important area of study because they are (1) functionally isolated, (2) their belief systems are well-defined and strongly held, and (3) their beliefs and practices are at variance with the culture at large. As Dollard and Miller (1950) point out, formal religious affiliation is not important in personality dynamics, but strongly held beliefs are; and these beliefs provide an extreme example of the relative importance of ideology and belief in shaping personality.

The fundamentalist subculture under discussion is not just a subculture, however, but rather what Yinger (1960) calls a "contraculture." That is, the normative systems of the group contain a pervasive theme of conflict with the values of the total society; personality variables are directly involved in the development and maintenance of group values; and the cultural norms can only be understood in reference to the relationship of the group to the surrounding dominant culture.

The "value orientation profile" for the fundamentalist has received extended discussion in the literature on Max Weber's thesis that the protestant ethic promoted the development of capitalism (Bendix 1960). Although this profile can be readily deduced from the extant literature, I conducted several preliminary surveys of fundamentalist populations, using the Kluckhohn rating scales, and obtained strong verification of the general profile used here. (For the purposes of this discussion, I have deliberately chosen not to focus on the technical permutations of this profile.)

The fundamentalist value profile then is:

1. Man's basic nature is *evil*.
2. Man is to *subjugate the world*.
3. Time orientation is *futuristic*.
4. The valued personality is oriented to *action*.
5. Interpersonal relationships are *individualistic*.

THE FUNDAMENTALIST PERSONALITY

My descriptions of general personality traits are drawn from both social observations and clinical data. My own observations are based on participant observation, from student groups, student and faculty contacts at fundamentalist colleges and seminaries, from psychiatric consultation to church groups, and the psychiatric evaluation and therapy of lay and clerical members. In addition, I have had the advantage of extensive case discussions with mental health professionals working with fundamentalist constituency.

In general, the fundamentalist typically manifests the following traits: (1) a marked degree of covert hostility although overtly passive, (2) a pervasive masochism, (3) frequent use of paranoid mechanisms, (4) frequent psychosomatic symptoms, (5) a depressive tenor, and (6) conflicts over sexual identity. For example, a prominent fundamentalist theologian made the following *self-description:* pugnacious, censorious, negativistic, hypocritical, individualistic, and self-seeking (Grounds 1961).

Corroborative of these conclusions is empirical data. Devout religious patients seen in psychoanalysis are described as extremely permissive, with deep feelings of dependence and passivity, crippling self-doubt, strong feelings of guilt, and a pervasive reactive hostility (Lorand 1962; Mann 1964). Identifications with God or Jesus are attended by excessive narcissism, feelings of superiority and omnipotence, but with reactive masochism and self-depreciation (Bowers 1963; Evans 1943; Jones 1951; Lubin 1959; Maloney 1954). Social relations are marked by aloofness and restricted social interaction which at times are interpreted as being schizoid (Bronner 1964; McCarthy 1942). Sexual identity is often immature resulting in hysterical character formation among women and various degrees of homosexual conflict among men. Thomas (1962) even goes so far as to state that sexual conflict is a leading neurotic manifestation among European fundamentalists, which he calls "ecclessiogenic neurosis."

Freud's classic interpretation of religion as an obsessive-compulsive neurotic defense is partially substantiated by clinical observation of the scrupulosity syndrome, and a high incidence of obsessive-compulsive disorders among ministers (Christenson 1963; Weisner and Riffel 1960). However, as Walters (1964) notes, such instances of psychopathology do not necessarily represent cause and effect or the natural course of religious influences. Nor does Freud's simple reductionistic formula adequately deal with the complexity of the data at a psychological, sociological, or philosophical level. Draper et al. (1965) conclude that there are a "variety of developmental, structural, and psychodynamic potentials that religious ideation . . . manifests."

Religious activities may precipitate psychotic reactions, although such activities may just as well provide security, integration, and generally valuable adaptive mechanisms. Taken as a whole there are few significant differences between Protestant, Catholic, and Jewish rates of psychosis or hospital admissions. But when religious subgroups are examined, some important differences do show up. Specific groups with deviant social status, such as fundamentalists, show more extreme aggressive and withdrawal behavior during psychosis (Kleiner et al. 1962). And specific religious ideas can color or play a decisive role in the development of paranoid and delusional systems (Lowe 1954, 1955; Rokeach 1964).

A high incidence of depressive syndromes is found. Indirect evidence is reflected in the study by Eaton and Weil (1955) of the North American Hutterites with a reversal of the usual psychosis patterns, for the Hutterites had virtually no schizophrenia but an extremely high incidence of manic-depressive illness. Although Murphy et al. (1964) found depression rates fairly similar worldwide, in the strongly Christian countries there were high rates of guilt feelings and self-condemnation in addition to the primary depressive symptoms. Kelly (1961) found a high rate of depression among Catholic nuns characterized by intense self-accusation; and hospitals serving the Reformed denominations which stress the depravity of man have more depressive admissions than schizophrenic (Jansma 1962). Bateman and Jensen (1958) found that fundamentalist students exhibited strong intropunitive attitudes, denied anger provoking situations, and used primitive defense mechanisms to handle hostility.

Fundamentalists scored high on authoritarianism as demonstrated in many studies based on *The Authoritarian Personality* (Adorno et al. 1950). However, Rokeach (1960) has demonstrated that in large part this is a function of *attitudinal dogmatism* rather than the *content* of "right wing" beliefs—the same authoritarianism showing up among dogmatists of "left wing" belief. However, there are a cluster of traits derived from the psychological testing of college and seminary students that are found in association with authoritarianism and fundamentalism: a dependent-submissive attitude, hostile ethnocentrism, poor social skills, constricted and rigid cognitive and perceptual functioning on projective and intelligence tests, lower scholastic achievement, lack of creative responsivity with conventional routine aesthetic attitudes, low self-esteem, a high rate of general nervousness and psychosomatic symptoms, and generally poorer overall adjustment and achievement in comparison with students in matched groups (Bowers et al. 1958; Brown and Lowe 1951; Christensen 1961; K. C. Garrison 1962; Gregory 1957; Hanawalt 1963; B. Johnson 1962; Kimber 1947; Mayer and Sharp 1962; Martin and Nichols 1962; Pattison 1969; Pearl 1954; Photiadis and Johnson 1963; Ranck 1961; Rosenberg and Zimet 1957; Salisbury 1956; Stern 1954; Stewart and Hoult 1960).

Yet these characteristics may in part reflect the social psychology of minority subgroups rather than just the doctrines of fundamentalism. For example, Rorschach protocols of orthodox Jewish students are described as: constricted, defensive, rigid, lacking spontaneity, and lacking sensitivity or adaptability in social contexts (Siegman 1956). Roger Brown (1965) makes a telling criticism of current assumptions about authoritarianism which imply that all authoritarian traits are per se undesirable, passing social judgment instead of making social observation. For example, Dreger (1952) found that conservative seminary students adjusted better because of their firmly held beliefs, while the liberal students often had severe conflicts during the search for a meaningful identity. Similarly, Grinker (1962) found that YMCA college students presented no psychopathology and experienced no conflicts or symptoms, but were rather drab, uncreative, and conventional mediocre achievers. Thus personality attributes must be interpreted in terms of the social milieu.

In sum, the present data consistently describes the fundamentalist as one who has a basic passive-dependent attitude with omnipotent narcissistic feelings on the one hand; while, on the other hand, there are deep feelings of guilt, inadequacy, inferiority, and self-rejection, resulting in a depressive tenor and a masochistic mien. There is a lack of social adaptability with a tendency towards aloof schizoid types of social relations, with a defensive, hostile ethnocentrism. There is a lack of spontaneity and creativity with constriction of cognitive and perceptual functions reflected not only in dogmatic attitudes, but also in actual lowered achievement and aesthetic inhibition.

IDEOLOGY AND PERSONALITY: CLINICAL ISSUES

In this section each of the five value orientations will be examined to demonstrate how this ideology influences the development of specific personality traits presented in the prior section.

1. Man's Basic Nature is Evil

A. *The Genesis of Basic Hostility*. According to the doctrine of original sin, man is born in a state of depravity. The early American Calvinist preachers taught that a baby was born an accursed and evil creature. And infant behavior is still commonly cited as an example of man's innate sinful nature (H. S. Smith 1955). For example, if a baby cries at night he is being selfish and greedy. If a two-year-old does not obey he is manifesting sinful self-assertion, pride, and rebellion. Child-rearing is an exercise in bringing the evil impulses of the child under holy control by the parent as God's representative.

These suspicions of emotion are at least as old as Plato, who saw reason and emotion as antithetical forces. This Platonic philosophy can be traced through the teachings of Augustine, Aquinas, and Calvin. According to Calvin, human emotions were manifestations of man's sinful desire, whereas conscious willful rationality reflected the regenerated portion of man's personality that would keep sinful emotion under control. This view of man identifies original sin with basic instincts, deprecates emotion, and exalts rationalism.

This view condemns all aggressive behavior by interpreting all aggression as hostility. It fails to appreciate the destructive result of aggression as a by-product of action rather than the purpose of action. This difference is illustrated by Lauretta Bender's (1953) description of the exploratory striving behavior of small children during which they may damage objects in their environment. Spitz (1953) found that infants who showed depressive withdrawal from their environment when separated from their mothers would so vigorously recathect their world when returned to their mothers that the infants literally tore things up enjoying themselves. The interpretation of behavior is the key, for as Engel (1962) notes, "initially the element of destruction not only is purely incidental but also has no reality for the infant or small child, only for the observer."

This interpretation of the child's behavior as evil is important in the genesis of hostility in children. Adelaide Johnson (1951) found that if a mother *interprets* her child's actions as hostile, she will respond with hostility. The child identifies with the hostile mother and develops a hostile self-image. This dynamic, she suggests, is one of the primary mechanisms producing basic hostility. Empirical studies of authoritarian ethnocentric children bear this out, revealing that their parents use harsh, punitive, rigid forms of discipline (Lyle and Levitt 1955). Further, fundamentalist ministers favor punitive retaliatory means of handling social problems in contrast to methods of reconciliation (Alberts 1963).

Here, then, the early experience of the child is with a hostile parental model which forms not only a harsh superego in the child but also provides a hostile image for the child's own ego self-image. Hence the ground is laid for a basically hostile person.

B. *The Inhibition of Ego Maturation and Mediation.* Another consequence of viewing all aggressive expressions of self as hostile is the inhibition of ego maturation. Spitz (1953) has emphasized the necessary role of hostility in early childhood for the development of sound object relations. The child must actually put his hostile responses into use before he can develop appropriate modifications. Suitable modifications will ensue as the ego matures if the adult helps the child modify his harmless hostility. If all expressions of hostility are suppressed, the child will likely not develop ego mechanisms for controlling and expressing hostile feelings, nor have any means of measuring the effects of hostility. This leaves the self prey to magical and omnipotent phantasies about one's destructive potential on the one hand, and prey to fears and anxiety about one's ability to protect and defend oneself on the other hand (A. Freud 1949).

For the fundamentalist, not only are expressions of hostility proscribed but all sublimated forms of aggression are prohibited. Hence there is no acceptable mechanism for mediating aggressive drives in an ego-syntonic fashion. For example, all competition is proscribed. Children are not allowed to fight or display either verbal or physical aggression. Games of war and violence are discouraged. Children might play cowboys and Indians, but they must not shoot each other— only harmless buffalo. This also applies to athletic competition. An editor reviewed a missionary's biography as confusing for he could not understand how this young missionary could wrestle on a college team and still be a loving person with missionary zeal. At another college, all team sports were forbidden because it was unchristian to "fight" each other on the basketball floor. Besides, someone might get angry! In other words, there can be no aggression, no competition, really no interaction with others if one is to consider interpersonal relations as reflections of aggressive cathexis of a person-object. Indeed this fits with the clinical observation of difficult social relations, schizoid and aloof attitudes, and the lack of social adaptiveness among fundamentalists.

If ego mechanisms for handling aggressive impulses are undeveloped, then all ego behavior remains tied to instinctual drive demands—no parts of the ego become independent of instinctual conflict. Hence a sort of all-or-none situation obtains. Either there is total expression of affect involving the whole organism or there is none at all. There is neither ego perception of gradations of expressions nor ego mechanisms for mediating gradations of expression.

For example, the Sermon on the Mount is taken to teach that the thought *is* the same as the act: lust *is* adultery, anger *is* killing. There is no perception of the difference between thought and act, or degree of action. So if young people hold hands, their "passion may sweep them away." One college girl sought therapy because she felt so guilty about dating boys and holding hands. She stated her problem: "Since holding hands means affection, it's just the same as intercourse!" Or if one ever got angry, "you might go berserk"; or if you take one drink, "you may end up an alcoholic." In this latter instance it is noteworthy that the incidence of alcoholism is much higher among those who were reared in churches teaching a phobic abstinence policy than among those reared in churches teaching moderate drinking.

Of course, if feeling states are unacceptable yet unavoidable, the ego must develop some type of mechanism to deal with feelings, impulses, and reactions. In the normal course of events the ego develops "affect signals," that is, the conscious ego appreciation of feeling states without having to deal with the entire intensity of feeling or to allow the feeling to become action (Rapaport, 1952). However, if the apperception of sexual or hostile feelings in the ego are not acceptable, if even thoughts must not be allowed, then the ego is deprived of its most useful mature mechanisms for assessing and reacting to reality. Consequently, the only recourse left to the ego is the use of neurotic defense mechanisms, as will be outlined now.

C. *Obsessive-Compulsive Defense.* A major defense is obsessive-compulsive, and it begins with suppression, as suggested in a well-known Catholic psychiatric text: "[The psychiatrist] says no close relationship exists without hostility . . . and release of hostile feelings is therapeutic . . . they look askance at religious suppression of hostility . . . [but we argue] they are wrong, we should just not suppress hostility but positive attempts to resolve it by opposite virtues of humility, etc. [should be made]" (Vanderveldt and Odenwald 1957). Note how this appeals to passivity, denial, and the neurotic mechanisms of undoing. This undoing defense and the reaction formation defense lead to compulsive "do gooder" attitudes where one is pervasively "nice" in situations which are realistically provocative of fear, anger, or hostility. A corollary is the "Pollyana" attitude—one cannot admit that there is anything wrong in the world.

In addition to conscious evil thoughts, God can read one's unconscious thoughts. So further guilt and anxiety are engendered, and the confession of known guilt does not alleviate the fear of unknown guilt. This leads to the obsessive-compulsive scrupulosity syndrome— continuing fear of the unknown sin (Weisner and Riffel 1960).

If the ego has few devices for handling feeling states, then it must defend against the expression of any affect lest it lead to the capitulation of the entire unstable system of obsessional defense mechanisms. And again since the ego has not developed mature separate aspects of ego functioning, all ego behavior is prey to conflict, and all ego action must be carefully controlled and regulated lest some irrelevant action "give one away." Thus behavior is rigidly controlled; "cleanliness is next to godliness," "let all be done decently and in order" are spiritualizations of anal control patterns which Evans (1943) sums up as "sphincter morality": "morality is a matter of discipline . . . self-control is a mark of piety. Dirty and filthy are adjectives to describe sin . . . nocturnal emissions are signs of internal pollution." To challenge any point of morality rocks the whole balance of defenses. For example, a lady was offended at a breach of table etiquette and as a result launched into an angry tirade about such ungodly behavior.

Hostility toward others stems from both jealousy of others doing what you dare not do and fear lest their behavior lead you to violate your own code. This leads to attempts to dominate and control others' behavior as a buttress to your own system. For example, the alcoholic in Alcoholics Anonymous may conduct twelfth-step rescue work to save himself vicariously in the other, and prevent the other from doing what he dare not do himself (Thorner 1953). In the same fashion, a group of young people in California combed the streets each day to convert people to Christianity and "save" them. If you did not save someone each day, your soul was in jeopardy. This group might have been called "soul savers anonymous."

In sum, then, this outlines a sequence of obsessive-compulsive defenses used by the ego because the culture does not encourage the development of more mature ego mechanisms. An important social consequence is the hostile compulsive need to control and dominate other people to maintain self-control.

D. *Intellectual Defenses*. Another major defense is intellectualization. As modern science began to require major revisions in theological thinking, a schism developed when theological thinking among fundamentalists not only failed to keep pace but actually returned to theological concepts of a century or more ago (Dillenberger 1960). These theological ideas then became the a priori by which to measure all other ideas. This reached extremes such as attempts to find scriptural justifications for just about every new technological advance that came along. For example, blood transfusions, radios, TV, space ships, have been said to be described in some ambiguous Old Testament scripture. This then allows the fundamentalist to accept such advances as the predestined will of God.

Actually, this presents a more basic problem, for as scientific and theological thought drifted apart the fundamentalists separated themselves from the culture at large, declaring that all usual cultural interests were irrelevant and the only worthy activities were those having immediate practical spiritual value. Hence all intellectual activity became bound in the need to justify its very existence. One had to justify thinking—and indeed there is a strong current of anti-intellectualism in contemporary America.

The practical result is that all intellectual activities are organized around a cause—justification of the faith—defensive and hostile. Thus instead of autonomous thought spheres, ego intellectual activity became "aggressivised," that is, imbued with instinctual energy and therefore caught in all the vagaries of affect and instinct discussed before. As a consequence, intellectual activities became merely a more sophisticated level of anxiety, conflict, and hostile response.

For example, two men recently published a scholarly account of the Genesis Flood in which they attempted to refute the whole structure of contemporary geological theory because they felt that the Bible would be proven untrue otherwise (Morris and Whitcomb 1961). This book is an immense intellectual enterprise which serves only to maintain the defensive ego system. It is easy to see why fundamentalists are found to have rigid cognitive and perceptual ego structures and why creativity is lacking in their intellectual work. There is an intolerance for ambiguity—that would create insecurity and anxiety. One theologian complained of a journal article "the choice is left up to the reader. It produces uncertainty and bewilderment in both laymen and clergy." Another example of conflictual binding of intellectual process results from the definition of salvation as assent to certain specific biblical interpretations. For example, if the church teaches that evolution is evil, then one cannot be saved and believe in evolution. As one student told me, "If I even thought about evolution, I'd be endangering my soul."

It is also understandable why fundamentalist colleges remain almost totally utilitarian in their orientation: they can find easy spiritual justification for their learning, and by remaining practical they avoid direct confrontation of theoretical and philosophical problems. Thus one can find curricula for school teachers, medicine, nursing, social work, or church music. But you will look hard to find offerings in sociology, humanities, or creative arts (Witmer 1962).

One might anticipate that ego energies might find expression in various aesthetic activities, but here one runs into the problem of self-satisfaction and self-expression being interpreted as bodily (self) and hence bad. For example, to be a church musician is serving God, but to be a concert musician is serving self. Any degree of narcissistic gratification is interpreted as "yielding to the flesh," sinful because it is part of sinful self—depraved man. One is not supposed to waste time painting pictures which do not mean anything, or reading novels which are just made up anyhow. In this vein, an English professor defended the non-sinfulness of reading and writing novels, which he justified on the basis that novels were a moral exercise in portraying man's spiritual degradation. Here again the narcissistic pleasure was denied.

In sum, intellectualizing defenses prove unsatisfactory because academic studies lead directly to areas of conflict which must be defended against, imbuing intellectual activity with hostile impulses. Vocations are restricted and their scope limited, while aesthetic sublimations are rejected or lead to guilt if indulged. Inhibition is perhaps the best overall word to describe both the ego and its intellectual activities. This correlates with Holzman's (1963) experimental work on repression and cognitive style. He found that the ego that characteristically represses treats all data in a reductionistic concrete style just as described above.

E. *Distortions of Ego Identity.* The definition of self as bad and the rejection of necessary ego narcissism also has implications for the development of ego identity. Because self-gratification is defined as sinful self-love or self-pride, the ego is robbed of its necessary store of ego narcissism, or simply self-respect. Yet the ego must be invested with a certain degree of energy to merely sustain itself (Colby 1955). Lack of self-involvement and self-respect can most readily be seen in extreme psychotic states of decathexis of the body leading to starvation, mutilation, or catatonic immobility. Other forms of loss of ego narcissism are found in depersonalization syndromes.

Since the self is sinful, one is taught to repudiate self. For example, if a minister preaches a notable sermon, he must properly reject any praise and state that the sermonic success was due to God. On the other hand, if the sermon was a flop, he cannot similarly blame God but only himself. Success in business is not the result of one's labors but the reflection of God's blessing. But to constantly reject one's achievements can hardly be expected to nurture feelings of fulfillment and satisfaction. Likewise, failure reflects God's condemnation and must reflect upon some hidden sin. On the one hand, the fundamentalist is urged to be perfect; indeed the holiness idea is that one can become sinless and holy. Yet, on the other hand, he is taught that his life counts for nothing and that what he achieves is worthless anyway. It is easy to see how self-esteem and a vulnerability to depression can result (Hollender 1965).

The development of self-identity is also distorted by disciplinary tactics. The child is not presented with punishment or reward from parents but from God. It is not mother who is displeased if you don't brush your teeth—it is Jesus. It is not father who is angry if you do not obey—it is Jesus. Positive sanctions are treated likewise. The child may be taught that mother and father love the child, but Christ's love is superior and more to be desired than parental love.

By relegating positive and negative sanctions to an invisible diety the child cannot test out the realities of those sanctions and is left prey to magical concepts of interpersonal relations. It fosters harsh rigid superegos because negative sanctions cannot be modified by actual experience. And it fosters insuperable ego ideals which cannot ever be attained because they are penultimate. Consequently, the child is more prone to both guilt and shame and less able to handle them because relationships with an invisible God cannot be tested and the displacement to people are subject to the distortions of primitive phantasy. Psychotherapists find that fundamentalists often have very diffuse pre-object identifications with God, reflected in phantasies of a symbiotic nature characteristic of the early undifferentiated child-mother relationship (Lampl-de-Groot 1962; Nunn 1964). It is relevant to note that Frieda Fromm-Reichman (1949) found that manic-depressive parents were reared by multiple parents without early concrete persons with whom to relate. The absent parent-God appears to play a similar role among fundamentalists and may indicate another factor in the high incidence of depressions and manic-depressive syndromes reported among fundamentalists.

If self is to be denied, and parents are discouraged as objects for identification, then identity must be sought somewhere. And indeed identification is made with Christ. The ideal protype would be the person who has no individual identity at all, whose existence was total identification in Christ, a vicarious living of one's life in the projected deity. Such cases of psychotic identification have been clearly described by Fodor (1958). The problem is similar to that of any child during the oedipal phase of identification. There is the desire to assume the parent's role, and there is guilty fear about assuming that role, along with the fear of inferiority in ever being able to measure up to the adult parent. What we observe then is a process of guilty omnipotence. Thus the minister who asserts that he is God's representative may not feel bound by normal social conventions and may feel quite at liberty to borrow from the church treasury or disregard constitutional procedure in the church. It is not uncommon to find a charismatic leader being sued for sexual, financial, or legal breaches which he feels are his due right as a superior being. Yet, on the other hand, there may be crippling feelings of inferiority about ever living up to the lofty ideal, hence a pervasive sense of inadequacy and despair over even trying.

Another result of identification with Christ is an ambiguous sexual identity. It is not uncommon to find men conflicted by homosexual phantasies about Christ, just as women report overt heterosexual phantasies which indeed are ritualized in certain sacred orders where the woman becomes the bride of Christ (Nunberg 1938). These sexual conflicts are often accentuated by a denial of the enjoyment of sexual activity, even within marriage. For example, a recent survey of an American denomination revealed that 3% of its physicians believed that sexual intercourse in marriage was basically sinful! (Pattison 1963). Klaus Thomas (1962) has described many case vignettes of fundamentalist ministers who could not engage in guilt-free marriage relationships, only to later develop overt homosexual conflicts, while their wives were either frigid hypochondriacs or unwitting partners to unconsummated affairs.

F. *The Demeaned Ego in Interpersonal Functions.* A final consequence of the evil self-image is found in interpersonal relations. A despised evil self immediately places one in an inferior position with others. The obvious defense is to project this evil image onto others. Then the fundamentalist can be a good saved person while the sinner is the despised lowly person the fundamentalist once was. The hostility toward self is also projected so that all others are seen as hostile and attacking people eager to persecute the hapless fundamentalist. Here lie the roots of paranoid attitudes so often seen.

More often the fundamentalist is ignored instead of attacked, and this too may be a demeaning blow to his already low self-esteem. At any rate, the admonition to love others is difficult to follow when there is no love for self. What follows then is a pseudo-love and concern. This is concretely demonstrated in the frequent arguments among missionaries about whether they can "really love" natives who are so unlovable. Frequently missionary work is an expression of angry self-exhortation instead of an altruistic labor of love. This is substantiated by empirical studies which reveal that fundamentalists do *not* score high on scales of humanitarianism or social concern (Kirkpatrick 1949; Weima 1965). Such studies indicated that there is little concern for the other person as such, and often the other person is despised. Instead there is preoccupation for the soul of the person in order to affirm one's own identity.

Likewise, despite the claim to superior moral behavior, fundamentalist college students have been shown to actually behave about the same as agnostic and atheistic peers in actual situations of moral decision, the only difference being the fundamentalists also maintained ascetic norms of behavior (Middleton and Putney 1962). The ascetic norms appear to be a means of maintaining an identity and affirming a superiority in the face of the fact that the fundamentalist covertly follows the norms of the society he rejects.

Moral behavior for the fundamentalist, then, is another ego defensive maneuver. In a cross-cultural study of model conscience Monica Holmes (1960) reported that, for the fundamentalist, morality was a hostile demand rather than a positive affirmation. In ego terms, Beres (1963) comments that this type of morality is compiled with but not introjected into the personality and made part of one's identity. I have termed this "superego morality" in contradistinction to "ego morality," which is morality resulting from the affirmation of one's identity and willful commitments (Pattison 1968).

A consequence of this superego morality for the fundamentalist is that, like members of other minority groups, he does not identify with the secular authority of knowledge or the secular authority of law. Indeed, the fundamentalist may condone deviant behavior because society is evil and its standards false. This mechanism is a balm to the ego, allowing the individual to maintain self-respect and deny dependence on the dominant secular society. A good example are the Amish, who are allowed to flout many of our social conventions and laws, yet the very existence of their colonies is dependent on the tolerance and support of the society at large. For the person, this deviant cultural attitude augments the development of a superego which is not constrained by reality but is allowed to ignore reality.

This of course plays into the problem of omnipotence and diffuse primary identification already described.

Against this background of a self unacceptable to oneself and unaccepted by others, the moral masochist character is developed. Frustration and anger are defended against by passivity and the denial of any personal needs (Brenman 1954). But since the needs are there nonetheless, they are projected onto others and then one can give endlessly to others in a vicarious self-gratification. This leads to the hostile demand that others accept one's gratuitous gifts. Charity, self-sacrifice, love offerings, etc. are guises to cope with anger over not being able to get what one needs, and neurotically trying to give to oneself via others. It is no accident that the saint of the church often turns out to be the masochistic wife of an alcoholic who is the scourge of this church.

G. *Summary of Man as Evil.* The effects of the orientation toward man as evil may be briefly reviewed. Because the infant is seen as bad, his behavior is interpreted as hostile. The mother may then treat the child in hostile fashion, as well as present a hostile image for identity formation. The interpretation of all aggressiveness as hostility and the rejection of all overt expressions of aggression, much less hostility, inhibit ego maturation. Further, the culture does not provide mechanisms for the development or utilization of sublimating or mediating mechanisms in the ego. The use of obsessive-compulsive or intellectualizing mechanisms of defense against basic hostile impulses are undercut by the culture. Ego identity revolves around identification with God, which leads to an ambiguous uncertain identity of guilty omnipotence. Sexual identity is confused and immature. Relationships with others are based on the perception of self as inferior which is defended against by an attitude of superiority and hostile omnipotence. Moral masochism becomes a character trait of vicarious sacrifice for others to obtain the necessary narcissistic supplies for the ego that must be overtly denied.

2. *Man is to Subjugate the World*

In the Protestant Ethic the world was given to man to conquer and control. This was felicitous for an expanding world for it fostered economic and geographic exploitation. It also was a motif undergirding the development of modern science (Merton 1957; Thorner 1952). But this orientation to conquer and subjugate which was culturally syntonic for centuries eventually ran into trouble by 1900 when geographic and entrepreneurial frontiers began to close and science began to call into question many theological explanations of the universe. The loss of the material world to conquer, and without a scientific world available for conquest, resulted in a defensive reaction, and fundamentalism came into being in the twentieth century as an attempt to recapture society and return it to a bygone era (Furniss 1954; Roy 1953).

For example, in economics the fundamentalists defend a laissez-faire capitalism; in politics they support the right wing extremists who in paranoid fashion accuse the most eminent American leaders of being communist; and in social welfare they suspect and repudiate corporate social mechanisms for coping with the social problems of a complex urban society. These attitudes are reactionary—that is, an attempt to return to prior cultural solutions; and that should be distinguished from conservatism, which is an attempt to deal with the future. The fundamentalists repudiate cultural change and view themselves as isolated and independent, which indeed they are.

The fundamentalists form a functional discrete subculture and remain marginal members of society. For them an ideal society exists for the members, a "sacred society" experienced through church-related interests and activities. Existence and experience in the culture at large are viewed as an inescapable evil. For example, a new multi-million-dollar church was built with its own basketball court, snack bar, swimming pool, bowling alley, and social director. This was to ensure that the church youth had their recreation in a safe place protected from a malicious evil world. There is suspicion of the behavior of the world and fear of its temptation, while there is jealousy and envy of those who participate in the activities of the world, which is interpreted as proof of the alluring destructiveness of the world's enticements.

The extent to which personal identity is bound up in this subcultural identification is well illustrated by an article in a sophisticated college religious magazine. Titled "Bible City," it cleverly satirized this isolationist subculture ethic. Many students wrote letters to the editor either criticizing or applauding the idea of a "Bible City," but interestingly neither group grasped the satire! Just as pertinent is the fact that at the same time other church magazines were actually carrying advertisements on the opening of a Christian night club in Detroit, a Christian hotel in Miami Beach, and an exclusively Christian town for retirement in Arizona!

This cultural withdrawal is relevant to the formation of ego identity. The fundamentalist is taught that he is different, unique, superior, odd, a stranger in this world, a species apart from the child next door. Thus the fundamentalist child is deprived of the recognition of self in others and deprived of the use of others to test the nature and reality of himself. Further, since others cannot be trusted, the child cannot test out the reality and actual extent to which one can have trust, faith, hope, and love with other human beings. Again this correlates with the clinical observations on schizoid, aloof, paranoid social attitudes, the difficulty in forming trusting relationships with a psychotherapist, and the problem in achieving meaningful intimacy in marriage.

Subjugation of the world implies subjugation of the self that is part of the world—the trite phrase "the world, the flesh, and the devil" reflects all that is to be conquered. Here again a conceptual value reinforces self control, compulsivity, and rejection of the self.

Subjugation of others as part of the orientation plays into the need to control others as a means of controlling self. Hence the ego perception of others in terms of things, not persons. People are objects to be manipulated, not persons with whom to relate. For example, the four-year-old son of an evangelist proudly proclaimed: "I've told all the boys the right way to be and soon they'll be saved and just like me."

Another consequence for ego development is the lack of ability to empathize with others, particularly if they are dissimilar from self. For example, the fundamentalist just cannot understand why the alcoholic, the poor, the uneducated, do not "just decide to get right with God and live right like I do." Social deviancy is seen as merely a problem of individual will-power—you can overcome anything if you want to.

The subjugation orientation carries the leitmotiv of aggression, dominance, and hostility. The fundamentalist avers that he is "defending" the faith, and that he is "at war" with the world. Here there is cultural approval for the expression of aggressive energies via hostile mechanisms. Whereas in past centuries basic aggressiveness was channeled into culturally sublimated geographic, economic, and scientific worlds to conquer, there are now no such worlds available. So instead of the constructive elaboration of aggression, it is funneled into destructive hostility.

It would seem that the subjugation ethic plays a role in the formation of what Wilhelm Reich (1949) termed the character armor of the personality. In this case, the cultural mold stamps out a cluster of ego modes of dealing with the world that center around active aggression. This cultural cast interdigitates with a cultural situation that creates frustration and anger. Berkowitz (1962) has shown that behavioral hostility occurs only when there is a combination of basic aggressive "set," frustrating stimuli provoking anger, and a context that sanctions the release of the aroused hostility. We see all three conditions met here.

But fundamentalists do not get far attacking the culture, for that is only further frustration and demonstration of impotence. Instead they turn to compete with and attack each other. Trivial issues become a means of ego enhancement—a feature Freud (1955) described in group psychology as the "Narcissism of small differences." A fundamentalist theologian (Grounds 1961) gives this self-description: "It is hard to get them to work together. If one has nominal success and the evident blessing of the Lord, he wants to start something of his own. It may be a school, an orphanage, a paper, or a missionary society . . . we are wondering if sometimes this is not being overdone. . . . One great trouble with us . . . we have far too many chiefs and not enough Indians." Insofar as the function of the ego is concerned we can see that the group cannot be used as a source of ego support, but is merely another arena in the contest for some narcissistic food for each beleaguered ego.

In sum, the orientation that *man is to subjugate nature* was historically culturally syntonic, but now dystonic to a subculture which cannot involve itself in the conquest of a complex urban society. Ego identification processes are distorted by a process of withdrawal into an idiosyncratic subculture. Subjugation of the self, of others, and culture is part of an aggressive character structure which has no useful cultural sublimation available for the constructive use of aggression. As a result, aggression is channeled into hostility turned upon each other in a competitive attempt to retain necessary ego narcissism.

3. Time Orientation is Futuristic

At the onset it would appear that the fundamentalists are future oriented, and in a sense they are: yet in another sense they are committed to the past. The paradox is observed among the charismatic leaders of millenarian cults who call the people to a future millenium that will restore the values of the past (Faris 1955).

The lower-class sects with apocalyptic visions of a bountiful future life may in a sense live for the future as an adaptation to the deprivations of the present. However that is different from the orientation toward the future which has been part of the American Dream that has produced a working, striving, goal-seeking society—an even better future. In contrast, those groups who are economically deprived and seek solace in the millenium foresee a future which will magically restore them, not a future toward which they themselves can work (Dynes 1957; Holt 1940; B. Johnson 1963; Pfautz 1955; Wilson 1959). This is even more true for the middle- and upper-class fundamentalists who have turned to a millenial future because the present is so conflict-laden.

The pattern of acculturation in which the sect with millenarian preoccupation becomes a church with contemporary interests has been reversed in the fundamentalist movement in which the sociological structure of orthodox denominations have returned to sect type structure and the theme of the fundamentalists has increasingly turned from defense of the orthodox faith to an obsession with millenial theories. Among fundamentalists the nature of the millenium has become a subject of bitter debates and repetitive internal divisions. Since the future affords the only answer to cultural non-adaptiveness, interest in the millenium is not just idle speculation but is emotionally tied to one's personal survival. The personal and group arguments over the millenium are a "fight for life," to prove that one's escape route is the right one.

The relevance to personality dynamics lies in the paradox that for the fundamentalist his values are not ultimate, but penultimate and unattainable in actual life experiences. We have already seen that current material achievements with concrete gratifications are not accepted as legitimate sources of pleasure. One cannot find realizations of one's values in the actuality of life, only future values are real.

This has two effects on the functions of the ego: (1) it promotes magical phantasy and disregard for real life, and (2) it fosters a disinterest in really getting involved in living. The ego does not effectively cathect the real world of objects, and life energy remains bound in internal narcissistic contemplation of what might be rather than what is. The fundamentalist has a self-imposed block toward achievement and movement in the real world. He wonders if achievement in "worldly" terms is really worth consideration, since only "eternal" values count. For the ego, this view results in ego constriction and correlates with the observed lowered scholastic, social, and vocational achievement of fundamentalists.

The role of time concepts in personality function has received scant attention (Arieti 1947; Fraser ed. 1964). It is commonly assumed that distortions of time orientation are the result of psychopathology. However, the existentialists maintain just the opposite: time is a central proposition in personality organization. The basic disorder is the distorted sense of time, and it is the inability to "have" a future that gives rise to anxiety and depression. The frequency of depression among fundamentalists and the constriction of the ego involvement is well described by Kahn's (1962) discussion of the time distortion leading to depression: "the past is represented by feelings of culpability, the future by an expectation of imminent chastisement . . . the present is reduced to nothing."

In summary, the fundamentalist speaks of the future, but is committed to the past and is deprived of the present.

4. *The Valued Personality is Oriented to Action*

The action orientation is obviously related to the subjugation of the world and so much of the action orientation has been discussed. However one aspect of action merits attention. In the action-oriented person, the discharge of basic instinctual drives is fairly direct and without extensive elaboration through the secondary processes of the ego. In our society the opportunities for primary direct expression of instinctual drives are vanishing. In order to discharge drive tension, the individual must employ more complex ego-mediated mechanisms. Passive participation in sports replaces active participation, control of machines replaces direct labor, etc. In these instances the person must shift from active direct gratifications to passive indirect gratifications. Aesthetic sublimations in art, music, literature, and more general play activities, become important mechanisms for drive discharge in complex societies.

For the action-oriented fundamentalists, these more passive and aesthetic discharge mechanisms are not as readily available to the ego. Passive mechanisms are identified with sloth and failure—to be passive is to be sinful. But more importantly passivity is a basic motif in the character structure which is defended against by activity and aggressivity. As will be recalled, the fundamentalist personality is characterized by an overt aggressive stance underlying which are more basic feelings of dependency and passivity in relation to an all-powerful, all-giving, God-parent. Hence passive mechanisms pose a threat to an ego defending against passivity. Aesthetic mechanisms are not allowed because aesthetic gratification hinges primarily on non-utilitarian satisfactions—more purely self-satisfaction, which is proscribed as gratification of the sinful flesh of self. Thus an affluent society which creates abundant leisure provokes guilt for the fundamentalist who has no culturally acceptable way to use leisure and no necessary or meaningful work.

The action orientation also effects the ego mechanisms for handling other intrapsychic affects—particularly guilt. Although fundamentalists emphasize a theology of grace and forgiveness, they practice a theology of works and propitiation. It is noteworthy that the fundamentalist churches have dispensed with the confessional and other congregational affirmations of guilt, penitence, absolution, and acceptance of forgiveness found in the historic creeds and practices. Not only are group mechanisms for handling guilt ignored, but the individual is left to his own devices. As Flugel (1961) notes, the tyranny of the external superego of the Catholic church was replaced by the even greater tyranny of the individual Protestant superego. The fundamentalist cannot accept grace, but rather must demonstrate grace through his right actions- proving that he is right. Of course, such an individual is constantly goaded by his superego for there is no external reality by which to assess his state of acceptance. Thus, there is no grace for the fundamentalist—only the constant quest to prove himself acceptable to God, and never knowing if he has succeeded (Pattison 1965b).

Consequently, the ego is always under pressure from the superego. Further, guilt is handled through action rather than thought. The use of the secondary processes of the ego are minimally exploited by the action-oriented person and hence the ego does not develop mechanisms for the delay and neutralization of affect through the elaboration of thought. Aroused affect brings action or a rigorous defense against that affect. The rigid personality cannot allow any regression in the service of the ego (Rapaport 1951), no childlike play, no carefree moments of "just fun." Action orientation may hinder the development of these elaborate ego functions while providing no feasible direct action.

In sum, the action orientation of fundamentalism demands direct social action in a cultural context demanding complex indirect action.

5. *Interpersonal Relationships are Individualistic*

The norm of individualism has already been discussed in large measure in the first section of the nature of the person. Not only does the stress on individualism and personal responsibility tend to form a strong rigid superego, but it also fosters excessive narcissism. Interpersonal relations are thus fraught with two problems: superego rigidity leads one to control others with an intolerance of others' standards of behavior, and the narcissism breeds less concern for social welfare, less need for interpersonal awareness, and less sensitivity to interpersonal contact.

The emphasis on individualism also provides problems for the ego in terms of reality testing mechanisms. If one's culture does not affirm reality then there is ample opportunity to distort and misperceive the nature of other people's feelings. The projective mechanisms of hostility already discussed are augmented then by the refusal to test out the attitudes of others. It is already assumed that the world is hostile. So if one is deeply immersed in the fundamentalist subculture there may be serious paranoid type distortions of how the world views one that are much like the paranoid pseudo-communities that Cameron (1959) describes. There is fear of both rejection and attack from a hostile world. They interpret rebuff of their evangelistic efforts as the world's hostility, and in turn, like the paranoid, they see their task as a call to "conquer" the world.

Victor Sauna (1959) suggests that a critical problem in interpersonal relations is how to engage in complementary relationships where neither party is superior to the other, because gradients produce hostility. For the fundamentalist this is difficult because he already feels inferior and has no respect for himself. Hence he can have no respect for the other. Interpersonal relations then are based on defense and domination. The first defense is to be passive and meek, hence posing no threat to the other which would provoke attack. The second defense is to justify attack—"a holy war." There is no meeting ground for collaboration. In fact, the fundamentalists pride themselves on refusing to compromise with the world in any way. As Moberg (1962) points out, they need conflict to maintain identity.

A final problem in individualism is that in a complex society individual norms cannot be pursued in disregard of group norms. Effective social function requires that there be a mutual commitment to group norms which may at times take precedence over individual norms. Hence a highly individualistic ethic imposes limitations on the complexity which a society can attain, and perhaps the complexity which ego organization can attain.

Cultural and Cognitive Dissonance—The Fundamentalist Case

In classic psychoanalytic terms, personality distortions grew out of intrapsychic conflict between id, ego, and superego, so-called structural conflict. Now it is suggested that there is an additional source of conflict which may lead to neurotic personality distortion. This source lies outside the self in cultural conflict, and via the ego this cultural conflict leads to basic intrapsychic conflict. In this instance the intraorganismic struggle is not between ego and id, but between two incompatible orientations, two major ways of adapting to life. Gardner Murphy (1965) describes this as "cultural dissonance"—a conflict between individual and cultural norms, or between various aspects of cultural norms. He concludes that these conflicts may produce psychophysiological stress and psychological symptoms.

This view is supported by clinical data. In a study on dissonant religious contexts, M. Rosenberg (1962) found that children reared in social situations where they were defined as a religious minority with norms at variance with their peers experienced low self-esteem, high anxiety, psychosomatic symptoms, and depression. Christenson (1960) observed that 17 of 26 ministers with severe neurotic conflicts were fundamentalists from rural areas. Their religious beliefs were used in a manner that might be judged unrealistic, poorly adaptive, or defensive. The precipitating conflict occurred when these ministers came to the seminary and ran into conflict with beliefs and values. Another important observation was made by Robert Leon (1964) on dyscultural anxiety reactions among men from rural Texas. In these men a cultural deficit plus their own psychopathology increased the susceptibility to the pathogenic influences of changing cultural norms. Leon conceives of this as an extension of Freud's "Aktual" anxiety neurosis in which the cause of anxiety stems from threatening life situations.

Now, as noted earlier, the fundamentalists comprise two groups who share a contraculture, but with different social dynamics. The lower-class sect-type churches have been described as social institutions which compensate for and adapt to socio-economic deprivation. The sect churches provide immediate gains in terms of social cohesion and support, a social outlet for repressed emotions, and a belief system that justifies God's ways to men (Dynes 1957, Kiev 1964).

Perhaps more significantly Benton Johnson (1961) has shown that the ideologies of these sects tend to promote the values of the culture at large, and consequently the sects are actually a socializing medium for converting lower-class values to dominant middle-class values. In other words, many of the indigenous and pentecostal sects are a social mechanism for integrating a subculture into the culture at large (Wilson 1959). Indeed this trend can be observed in the recent drives for educational prestige and ecumenical acceptability among pentecostal denominations, and the emergence of the charismatic glossolalia movement where Pentecostals and Episcopalians become collaborators. Thus the sect type fundamentalists are involved in a culturally syntonic movement. The sect is a condensed social process of acculturation (Mead and Schwartz 1960).

In striking contrast, the mainline fundamentalists suffer from cultural deprivation, which Bram (1957) notes is not poverty but limited participation in the overall schema of success and its visible material rewards. Further, this cultural deprivation is self-induced, self-defined, and self-maintained. The fundamentalist ethic, or perhaps more accurately the Protestant ethic, was once culturally syntonic, the germinal bed for the growth of modern science, capitalistic economics, and the geographic expansion of western society. However, this value orientation became obsolescent and increasingly dystonic as social and economic change required a shift in one's orientation to the world. Hence people holding to the protestant ethic began to find themselves on the fringe of society with the loss of both real and phantasied status due to irrelevant and obsolescent social, economic, and intellectual roles. These people could have moved toward cultural innovation—the development of new roles and concepts in which theological concepts were coordinated in new ways to society, but this innovation was blocked by the commitment to alleged eternal truths that assertedly could not change with time. The alternative was "retreatism"—a retreat socially, economically, politically, and psychologically. Hence a religious group became a minority ethnic group, and fundamentalism as a contraculture was born. This was a "cultural regression" which grew out of the attempt to reduce "cultural dissonance."

It should be added that some intellectuals who were aware of this regression attempted to forge a return to the culture at large and restore what Carnell (1959) has called the decomposition of "orthodoxy gone cultic." But the fundamentalist community viewed such efforts as heretical and derided these efforts at creative rapprochement (Henry 1957; Lightner 1962; Nash 1963; Sterick 1964).

This cultural regression is not limited to fundamentalists however. E. E. Hagen (1962) has brilliantly argued that cultural retreat as a psychosocial phenomenon has occurred many times in history when the cultural roles of people become obsolescent due to socio-economic change and there is a loss of role-status. These people then become a minority subgroup and experience increasing alienation from their culture at large. The attempt to deal with this alienation often takes the form of retreat to an entrenched subculture at odds with the new dominant culture—a contraculture has been formed. This is the phenomenon observed in the mainline fundamentalist who covertly desires the dominant values of society yet overtly repudiates them because he cannot integrate the new cultural norms into his obsolescent norms. Their cultural deprivation is real, but the dissonance is one of their own making, and as society continues to change the mainline fundamentalists are becoming more alienated and live by an increasingly dystonic value orientation. Whereas the sect-type fundamentalists are moving toward society, and for them the fundamentalist value system is more culturally syntonic. A good example of this is found among the Appalachian mountaineers who hold to a rigid nineteenth-century orthodoxy yet have been isolated enough not to have gotten caught in the fundamentalistic reaction and regression. These mountaineers are now coming into contact with the dominant society and are rapidly becoming acculturated into the dominant orientation of our society (Ford 1960).

Thus what has been described is not just the effect of values per se but also the effect of a conflict in "value orientation." A cultural value orientation may indeed affect the personality, and evidence for that has been presented here. In addition, conflicts in value orientations may affect neurotic distortion of the personality. The difference is nicely put by Lowenfeld's (1944) observation that neurotic disturbances only occur when ideological concepts lose their integrating power.

In terms of our basic thesis, the protestant ethic once was a value orientation which provided the ego with a syntonic world view. This set of values played a positive role in the development and adaption of the personality. In contrast, the fundamentalist regression provides a dystonic world view to the ego. The attempt to reduce cultural dissonance via the contraculture leads to psychosocial situations that create cognitive dissonances which can be resolved only by distortions of ego adaptive mechanisms. In succeeding generations these maladaptive ego mechanisms affect child-rearing patterns and consequently the basic development and maturation of the ego.

The central intrapsychic significance of conflicts in cultural values is well stated by Arieti (1965): "Inner objects [also include] . . . representations of concepts and clusters of concepts. Concepts may be in conflict and may lead to psychological dissonance, that is the lack of internal mental consistency."

It is the intolerance of dissonance in the internalized ego concepts that is a crucial theoretical issue for psychoanalytic metapsychology, although Festinger (1956, 1957) has presented empirical evidence for this view based on the assumption that "the human organism tries to establish internal harmony, consistency, or congruity among his opinions, attitudes, knowledge, and values. That is, there is a drive toward consonance among cognitions." The evidence presented here argues for a sequence by which cultural dissonance leads to cognitive dissonance and then results in distortions in ego development and adaptive function.

In summary, I have presented a discussion of the fundamentalist value orientation profile, following the outline developed by Kluckhohn and Strodtbeck. The position taken in this analysis is that the fundamentalist value system was a functional value system in an expanding agrarian culture of frontier America. Indeed the fundamentalistic value system was the dominant value system of America. However, since the closing of the frontier, the industrialization and urbanization of America, this value system has become obsolescent. Rather than transform their value system, the fundamentalists have clung to their value system in the face of increasing social and psychological dissonance. The price they have paid is measured in terms of personal and social dysfunction in participation in the society as a whole.

In the subsequent discussion I shall present observations on rituals that have been widely incorporated into recent fundamentalistic practice. And I shall indicate how these rituals currently serve to reduce psychological and social dissonance for the fundamentalists, reinforcing their belief systems in the face of dominant cultural values that challenge the maintenance of the fundamentalist value orientation.

RITUAL SUPPORT OF IDEOLOGY

In the face of individual and cultural dissonance described, one can look at the role of ritual in the fundamentalist subculture. I shall briefly summarize my observations on glossolalia, and then elaborate more precisely the function of ritual from our studies on faith healing.

Glossolalia

The social function and psychological function of glossolalia would appear to vary with the particular social movement of which glossolalia is a part. Several examples can be given.

R. A. Knox (1956) has written the history of glossolalia in the eighteenth and nineteenth centuries. In traditional Christian groups the experiential component of religion had been replaced by intellectual religion. Here glossolalia was a means to reestablish an experiential base for religion. Concomitantly, this was during the age of the enlightenment, when rationalistic criticism of Christian faith was in vogue. Thus glossolalia was not only a religious experience but an experience that could not be gainsaid. The mysterious experience of speaking in tongues was personal living experiential "proof" of the existence of God and the validation of the believer's faith. This might be termed an "affirming" function of ritual.

Now I have observed the so-called charismatic revival develop in the United States over the past fifteen years. This revival is characterized by conversion of fundamentalists, and those of fundamentalist persuasion in the mainline denominations to the practice of glossolalia. As in past centuries, we find those who turn to the ritual of glossolalia to be engaged in an intellectual religion and in dissonance with their society. Interviews with these subjects have consistently revealed the same dynamics described by Knox. They find in glossolalia an infusion of experience into their intellectual religious life, and an undeniable affirmation of the "rightness" and validity of their fundamentalist belief system. These practitioners of glossolalia engage frequently in the ritual, and it plays a central role in their religious life activities.

This stands in stark contrast to the utilization of glossolalia in those pentecostal sects which have undergone acculturation and socialization into the American middle class. A good example is the Assemblies of God. This denomination began around 1900 as a typical migrant worker holiness sect. By the end of World War II the sect had become middle class; they established liberal arts colleges and disbanded their Bible schools, while their large churches conducted services indistinguishable from other middle-class denominations.

In such churches the ritual of glossolalia was still carried on. But as a rite of passage. Most members at puberty made a "decision for Christ," spoke in tongues once, but never practiced the ritual thereafter. Here the ritual serves as a technique for recruitment, a method of organization, and as a means of demonstrating the claims of the movement to change people's lives. The ritual does not occupy centrality in the religion.

A third alternative is found in the glossolalic practice of the new outcroppings of indigenous pentecostal sects. Here we find the classic description of the socially and economically deprived who find emotional release via the religious ritual. Here we find people in conflict, practicing not only glossolalia but also a whole gamut of dissociative and hysterical religiously sanctioned acting-out of repressed conflict in the religious ceremonies. In this case, the ritual appears to subserve primarily psychological needs.

Here I can only summarize my observations of the personalities of glossolalists made over the past twenty years, and supported by data reported elsewhere (Pattison 1968a; Pattison and Casey 1969).

In sum, in the mainline pentecostals who have successfully moved into the middle class I have observed little overt psychopathology. Participation in glossolalia is a perfunctory religious ritual and is primarily a social event. In these churches, those who do practice glossolalia frequently have quite obvious neurotic conflicts. Thus their glossolalic practice appears to subserve psychological needs.

In contrast, the lower-class pentecostal sect members have obvious real-life conflicts with their culture, and appear to gain considerable emotional release through the practice of glossolalia. Their glossolalia is not a culturally affirming experience but a personally satisfying experience. I have not been impressed by any manifest neurotic conflict in this constituency. Affirmation is not their major need.

Finally, in the fundamentalists who have converted to the glossolalic movement, we find a third permutation. Here we have people in conflict. Here the glossolalic ritual subsumes both cultural affirmation and release of psychological conflict via the symbolism and mechanisms of the ritual. In my observations, this constituency has widespread neurotic conflicts. Here the ritual is not a rite of passage but primarily an affirming rite that secondarily serves psychological needs.

These patterns are more clearly illustrated in our data on faith healing, which demonstrate how social and psychological needs are both met in the ritual of healing, providing necessary support for an ideology in conflict with the world.

Faith Healing

A sample of persons claiming faith healing experiences was sought from churches in the Seattle area who were known to emphasize and practice faith healing. The ministers of all such churches were contacted, their cooperation elicited, and permission sought to interview persons in their congregations who were publicly identified as "faith healed." It was anticipated that this maneuver would identify persons for whom faith healing had been a significant experience. The maneuver was justified in our field experience, for although the minister and perhaps most members of these congregations evinced belief in faith healing and had participated in many such rituals, only a very few members in any one congregation claimed to have actually experienced faith healing. The implications of this finding will be discussed later.

After identification of such persons, an interview was conducted in their own home, having informed the person that this study was sanctioned by their pastor, and was being conducted to learn more about faith healing, about which we realistically had little information. Following a structured interview guide, information was obtained in the following area: (1) the life pattern of the person in relationship to himself, his family, his work, and his social relations prior to the faith healing; (2) life pattern in the same area subsequent to faith healing; (3) medical history prior to and subsequent to faith healing; (4) the perceived importance and function of the faith healing experience in the person's life. In addition, personality status was assessed with the Spitzer Mental Status Schedule, a scaled self-report schedule, the Minnesota Multiphasic Personality Inventory, and the Cornell Medical Index.

A total of 43 subjects were studied. There were 19 men and 24 women. At the time of the interview their ages ranged from 16 to 80 years of age, an overall mean of 52 years old (S.D. = 17 years). All subjects were married or widowed, save for 1 man and 3 women. The mean educational level for both men and women was only partial high school, while almost all who had some post-high school education attended Bible schools or technical-vocational school, rather than colleges and universities. The occupational level is similar. The men were skilled blue-collar and white-collar workers, while the women were preponderantly housewives with little outside work experience.

For the most part, social life is religious life for this population. Their social life centered around the church and its activities. *Average* church attendance for this population was three times a week. Social relations were for the most part confined to fellow church members and relatives, with few instances of membership in community organizations and activities. Daily home Bible reading and home worship was reported by nearly every respondent. An ascetic style of life was followed, without use of alcohol or tobacco, no attendance at dances or movies. Most reported watching television, but with the stipulation that they did not watch it very much.

Most of the subjects had been Christians throughout their lives, although a number who had been reared in religious environments had not been "born again" (i.e. experienced religious conversion) until adulthood. However, only in two instances were the "rebirths" coincident with their faith healing, and here the healings were subsequent to their conversion, not preceding it. In all other cases of adult conversion, the conversion had preceded the healing by at least one year. Interestingly, all of the subjects reported speaking in tongues (glossolalia), save for 3 men and 1 woman. Most reported speaking in tongues on numerous occasions.

A total of 71 healings were reported, with 7 men and 11 women reporting multiple healings, the maximum being one man who reported 5 healings. The mean age at which healing occurred was 38. The mean interval between healing and interview was 15 years with a range of 2 weeks to 51 years.

The diversity of illnesses reported was considerable, with all body systems represented. Of the 71 healings, 12 were appraised as life-threatening, such as leukemia, cancer, terminal tuberculosis; 38 were appraised as moderately disabling, such as peptic ulcer, ruptured disc, heart disease; while 21 were appraised as minimal ailments, such as plantar warts, sprained ankles, backache.

In all but 9 of the 71 healings, the person participated in some kind of formal religious ritual which was credited with the healing. These rituals included formal prayer for the individual in front of the congregation of the church, anointing with oil and prayer, laying-on of hands, and bedside prayer by the minister or member of the congregation. The majority participated in only one such ritual before healing occurred. The small number who did not participate in a formal ritual did participate in prayers for healing by themselves.

The majority reported that although a doctor may have been consulted for diagnosis, no medical treatment was received. However, a substantial number of subjects received occasional or continued medical treatment *subsequent* to their healing ritual. Such treatment was regarded as being of secondary importance, and in fact not contributory to their healing.

Half of the subjects reported instantaneous healing, whereas the other half reported gradual healing. However, in both instances this was not based on the subject's observed disappearance of symptoms. Instead, he asserted that he had been healed, regardless of the state of his symptoms. Thus, the instantaneous healings often occurred in the face of a history which demonstrated continuing symptoms after the instantaneous healing, while the gradual healings were described in terms of being healed with the persistence of symptoms that were "left over" and would now take some time to disappear. This interesting observation was obtained by asking the subjects to carefully describe the time sequence and changes in symptomatology before inquiring about their faith healing. It became apparent through this device that the subjects' perception of healing was related to their participation in a healing ritual, *not a perception of change in symptomatology.*

Each respondent was asked to initially describe his own emotional functioning, his work functioning, and his relationships with people prior to his faith healing. Then each subject was asked to describe his life style in each of the above areas after the faith healing. And finally, each subject was asked to describe changes in each area after his faith healing.

No change was reported by our subjects, using either the indirect descriptive enquiry, or on direct questioning regarding change in life style.

The subjects reported that their life, work, and social relationships had always been serene and comfortable. Rarely were personal or interpersonal conflicts reported. In retrospect, even their illnesses, for which they had sought faith healing, were not seen as seriously disruptive events in their lives. Their faith healing was not seen as particularly significant, nor an eventful occurrence in their lives, but almost an expected event. Thus, their faith healing was no watershed that changed their lives. On the other hand, a number of subjects who had been "born again" in adult life did report that their lives had been disturbed prior to their religious conversion, but subsequent to their religious commitment life had become peaceful and satisfying.

The subjects were also questioned regarding change in religious behavior subsequent to their faith healing. As before, there was *no change* in church attendance, private devotions, Bible readings, or religious interest.

However, there was one major change noted by all respondents.

All reported that their *certainty* in their belief in God and their religious convictions was *markedly increased* after their faith healing experience.

Personality status was first assessed by the Spitzer Mental Status Schedule and by a clinical rating scale in which the interviewer rated each subject on self-reports of: (1) level of energy, (2) worry, (3) anxiety, (4) restlessness, (5) depression, (6) anger. The scores on both methods of rating were uniformly very low. The subjects reported themselves as having high energy, and rarely experiencing worry, anxiety, restlessness, depression, or anger. The standard attitude expressed was that God can take care of everything, and since they had placed their trust in God there was little about which to be concerned or get upset. Adverse emotional experiences were seen as "works of the devil." Hence, devout religious persons such as themselves would not experience such adverse feelings so long as they lived in the proper religious manner.

In contradistinction to the self-reports, the interviewer noted manifestations of anger, depression, anxiety, worry, during the course of the interview. However, the subjects would deny or minimize these emotions when questioned. It appeared that the subjects wished to see themselves and present themselves in a uniformly good light.

On the MMPI we found a combination of elevated K and Hy scores with depressed F and Sc scores. In a recent MMPI study on various scale combination patterns, Carson (1960) has described persons with this profile as follows: "They are *affiliative, constrictedly overconventional people.* These individuals show prominently in their relations with others an exaggerated striving to be liked and accepted. Characteristically they maintain an unassailable optimism and emphasize harmony with others, if necessary at the expense of internal values and principles. They are likely to become extremely uncomfortable in, and therefore to avoid, situations demanding angry responses, independent decisions, or the exercise of power. When such persons do end up in the clinic, which is infrequent, they are most resistant to considering that their difficulties may result from emotional conflict. It is also a remarkable fact that even in the face of catastrophic failure they often resolutely maintain that 'things are going fine'; defeated feelings seem to be intolerable to these people."

A high degree of congruence has been demonstrated from the history of life style, religious belief and behavior, clinical interview observations, subjects' self-reports, and psychometric analyses.

These subjects present psychological characteristics indicative of a strong need for social acceptance and social affiliation. This exaggerated need presents along with the extensive use of denial and repression as major coping mechanisms that are so pervasive that major disruptive events in their lives are ignored and interpreted as part of a normal, smooth, unruffled existence.

These psychological characteristics are consistent with the fact that these subjects do not perceive of illness as a major disruptive event, nor do they perceive of their faith healing as a major life enhancing event. Further, these psychological characteristics explain why the subjects perceive of their faith healing as a definite occurrence regardless of presence or absence of symptoms, and regardless of persisting symptoms, and with concomitant medical treatment.

Further, it is not surprising that no evidence for symptom alternation is found, for the subjects do not perceive of their illnesses as conflictual events. Thus, in a sense, their faith healing does not remove their symptoms. Remission of symptoms does not significantly affect their psychic balance of defenses, and therefore, emergence of alternate symptoms is not required to maintain psychic equilibrium.

The issue of whether the subject actually achieved symptom relief or remission of organic symptomatology was not investigated. This was deliberately omitted, since there is ample evidence from psycho-physiologic research, placebo research, etc. to provide explanations for perceived and actual change in illness. From the subjects' point of view, relief of symptoms is really a tangential issue. For them, faith healing reaffirms their belief system and their style of life. Faith healing serves to buttress their psychological style of life. From a scientific medical point of view, the question usually asked of faith healing is, "Does it cure the disease?" But that is not the question asked by the prospective applicant for faith healing. His question is, "Am I living in the right way?" Thus, faith healing is not an exercise in the treatment of organic pathology, but an exercise in the treatment of life style.

This data comports closely to recent studies on magical healing, supporting and corroborating certain theoretical speculations on the psychodynamic and socio-cultural functions of magical healing. We shall start at one end of a spectrum with primitive witchcraft healing, move through American faith healing, and on to the other end of the spectrum that is pure mentalistic healing, as exemplified by Christian Science. Our thesis will be that such magical belief systems may not represent psychopathology, but rather represent an ego integrative and socio-integrative system. Hazel H. Weidman (1968) has elaborated on the theoretical analysis of witchcraft beliefs and magical healing. Her views will be briefly summarized.

In a broad view culture is adaptive and the group is necessary for survival. If a group defines man as basically evil, unpredictable, and potentially harmful, then one has all the ingredients for necessary suppression of aggression. Since no individual can experience group life without frustration, the actual impulse to engage in prohibited indulgent or aggressive acts is more widespread than suggested by group norms. When group values sanction friendliness, cooperation, generosity, and amiability they also sanction suppression of aggression in the group, and we may expect concealed feelings of anger, envy, jealousy, resentment, etc. Hence, communication is always ambiguous for one can never know what one's own true intents are, nor know the intents of others. With ambiguity in social situations, anxiety, doubt, and distrust become integral parts of the social process. There is a diffusion of the sense of reality and there is no way to test reality. The only appeal is to immediate sensate experience. Thus, Wiedman notes: "In a way misfortune actually experienced represents a reality test in that it corroborates what one has sensed as 'reality' but has previously been unable to admit or to verify as such. In this act of confirmation, reality sense and reality testing are fused. Corroboration is achieved. . . . The true nature of previous experience has been established. There is conviction and, with conviction, the willingness to take action. This, in effect, means a degree of increased control in the experiencing of the self, and therefore, a greater degree of ego integration."

Seen in this perspective, the maladies which our subjects experienced served to provide validating sensate experience, and the healing (a mental operation) is a reflection of control over oneself and one's world that has been achieved. In this vein, it is remarkable to note the high incidence of speaking in tongues of our subjects. Again, this is another sensate experience that provides personal validation of oneself and one's belief system.

A further function of magical belief systems is that they provide a mechanism for externalization and explanation when anxiety, misfortune, illness, etc., occur. In fact, three psychologically integrative functions of magical belief systems can be defined: (a) denial of unpleasant reality with irrational belief that a change can be effected, (b) displacement of a threat from within to the outside, and (c) naming of something that was previously ill-defined, anxiety-arousing, and disruptive of the experiencing of reality.

The necessity for the utilization of such magical belief systems might be interpreted in psychiatric terms as evidence of psychopathology and weak ego strength. However, anthropologists have questioned a too ready acceptance of this interpretation. If we look at the fundamentalist subculture the anthropological corrective can be demonstrated. This subculture is first of all a beleaguered minority; they view themselves as alien in a hostile secular world. They are not merely a subculture, sharing some values of the dominant culture, but are a "contraculture"—their values are defined in terms of opposition to the values of the secular world. Their view of man is that he is basically evil and capricious in behavior, yet the cultural norm prohibits the expression of aggressive impulses, and strongly sanctions affiliative agreeable behavior. As this paper has shown, persons who grow up in this fundamentalistic milieu develop a different ego structure and cognitive structure than persons who grow up in the dominant American value system. Thus, to an extent, different ego defense systems must be employed to maintain a sense of well-being within this subcultural system.

In accord with the theoretical expectations then, our psychological data demonstrate the excessive use of denial, externalization, and projection, with the disregard of reality in our subjects, which reflects the necessary adaptive ego maneuvers required to exist and maintain oneself within this culture. Festinger (1957) has described similar distortions in reality assessment as a mechanism to maintain "cognitive coherence" of one's assumptive world view. Faith healing becomes one expression of this total ego-coping system.

As Anthony Wallace (1966) has pointed out, here we see the transection of individual coping requirements and socio-cultural coping requirements. As pointed out earlier, the entire congregation of each church we contacted shared the magical belief system, yet only a small number had experienced faith healing. An even smaller number of the "faith healed" demonstrated overt dysfunctional symptoms. We may look at this data as reflective of the variation in individual capacity to use effectively the ego-coping mechanisms provided and required by the culture. For the large majority of this subculture, they are able to maintain an adequate ego-coping system. For those who participate in faith healing we may suggest that the system is less functional and required reinforcement via the faith healing experience. Whereas in a very small number even this ego reinforcement does not suffice, and they present with persistent functional symptoms, i.e. they are sick.

Up to this point, we have suggested that in primitive societies the use of denial and projection results in the development of witchcraft and gross magical belief and healing systems. In American fundamentalists we see an attentuation of the process, although involving the same dynamics. In Christian Science we see the end-point of this process. Here, as Thorner (1950) observes, the ascetic Protestant ethic reaches its polar development. Its value message is that life has joy for all, with health, vanity, and prosperity; and the denial of the existence of sickness, loneliness, poverty, oppression, alcoholism, unhappy social and business relations. Wardell (1965) indicates that the Christian Scientist insists on his own inner perfection, goodness, and spirituality, while using massive denial and disregard of reality to maintain this view of himself and his world. Projection to the outside evil world is used to rid the self of all hostility, sickness, and evil. Wardell notes: "The mask-like composure of many Christian Scientists is perhaps related to such denial and projection . . . the tenuous psychodynamic 'solution' . . . needs continual reinforcement by repetitious denial of the reality of evil. . . . Christian Scientists intellectualize denial through an abstract and impersonal metaphysics." Wardell goes on to note the costs in terms of psychic function that are required to maintain repression and denial; for example, the high incidence of deaths from cancer reported among Christian Scientists may reflect the adverse effects of continued internalization of conflict (Greene et al. 1956). This suggestion is corroborated by recent research by Pattison et al. (1972), who have shown a high correlation between the incidence of psychosomatic complaints and active participation in fundamentalist religious groups.

To summarize these observations, American faith healing is shown to be part of a continuum of magical thought, belief, and practice. Such magical systems develop in socio-cultural contexts where man is viewed as basically evil and capricious, yet where group solidarity is tenuous and must be sustained by repression of aggressive behavior among group members and human relations are defined as always good. Individual participation in the magical belief system is required to participate in the socio-cultural group. However, participation in the magical belief system is also required to maintain individual psychodynamic equilibrium. The variations found between gross witchcraft, American faith healing in the fundamentalists, and the mentalistic healing of the Christian Scientist, are variations in the level of abstraction of the magical system, but with identical psychological and cultural dynamics. The role of individual psychological variations is demonstrated in our data, where most of the religious did not need reinforcement of their magical belief system; some did and consequently experienced faith healing; and for a very few even this reinforcement was not sufficient to maintain psychological compensation and integration.

Summary

This paper has presented data to illustrate a pattern wherein cultural dissonance in a religious subculture presents psychological dissonance to individual members of the culture, resulting in specific distortions in personality development. The rituals of glossolalia and faith healing serve to reduce both cultural and psychological dissonance, thus reinforcing the very ideologies that underlay the basic dissonance. Data from both rituals indicate that most members of the religious subculture are able to sustain their dissonant ideologies without ritual reinforcement. Thus only a very few members of the fundamentalist subculture actually engage in these rituals. For a very few, even such ritual reinforcement does not suffice. Rather than relinquish their ideology, it would appear that such members experience emotional disintegration, cannot maintain cognitive coherence, and manifest overt and disabling psychopathology.

Eastern Philosophies and Western Alienation: The Social Function of Imported Cults

Meher Baha and Hare Krishina are cults derived from India and introduced into the United States. To the casual passerby, the chanting youths in saffron robes and shaved heads seem to be unique in his experience of American religious traditions. It takes little thought, however, to connect them to the intense interest in the many yogis and masters of Eastern philosophies stemming from Japan to India that is now current in America.

To regard American interest in Eastern religions in any sense as new or as some passing fancy is to ignore our long-term fascination with them. Americans have studied and adopted branches of Hinduism and Buddhism from the middle of the nineteenth century to the present. Seen in this light, Hare Krishna and Meher Baba are the most recent forms of American attachment to non-western religions. The attachment was, however, much earlier and perhaps initially represented by the American Transcendentalists. Both Emerson and Thoreau were deeply interested in Hinduism, interest perhaps best seen in Emerson's poem, "Brahma." This poem is the distillation of Emerson's many years of study in the Oriental scriptures and aptly stands for the level of understanding nineteenth-century American religionists-philosophers achieved in seeking out Eastern, especially Indian, religions.

Orientalism was a response to overly rational religion in the nineteenth century, just as Anthony and Robbins suggest that Meher Baba is a response to overly liberal and desacralized Christianity today. However, between these two prominent manifestations of Oriental philosophy there are enough others to establish a convincing link that shows America has consistently derived spiritual succor out of the "mystic East."

It is possible to tie current revivals of Oriental religions to a historical interest in them in American religious life. It is also possible to show that their modern forms are an intimate part of the whole modern religious revival this volume is devoted to describing. Insofar as the modern Indian religions are concerned, there are some critical distinctions between what the Transcendentalists used in Hinduism and what people take from Hare Krishna and Meher Baba today. On the face of it, of course, today's Eastern imports appeal to a totally different group from their nineteenth-century counterparts. Emerson and his fellow Bostonians were middle-aged, aristocratic intellectuals; the modern followers of Krishna and the "Baba lovers" are in their twenties, come from the middle class, and are often anti-intellectual.

The points of similarity between the Hare Krishna and Meher Baba movements are the same points at which both of these differ from the Oriental philosophies adapted to American usage in the nineteenth century. Speculative philosophy is regarded as being a hindrance to the development of Krishna Consciousness, and Meher Baba is frequently quoted as saying, "I have come not to teach but to awaken." Neither movement is intellectual; in fact, both attract many college drop-outs, often intelligent people who see American intellectual and academic life as sterile and debased. Even though there is a marked level of anti-intellectuality among them, that is not to say that Hare Krishna and more specifically Meher Baba followers are completely tied to rote. "Baba lovers" spend large amounts of time discussing Baba, love, and colloquial metaphysics. This certainly differs from the Transcendentalists for whom the Orient provided an intellectualized mysticism.

Both movements socialize a believer into a group of like-minded people who become the chief reference group and supporters for the new member. Hare Krishna devotees "renounce all fruitive activities, give up the company of non-devotees and associate only with devotees." Hare Krishna followers often withdraw, at least temporarily, from the world. "Baba lovers" may also withdraw for a time from the world but return to normal activities after learning how to love, to perceive reality in a new and satisfying way, and to view normal living routines as enjoyable ways of offering love to others.

Krishna and Baba followers deplore drug use and encourage celibacy. There is a strong effort to discipline the mind, to curb bodily desires, and to turn one's thoughts continually to the love received from and to be returned to the individual representing the embodiment of all gods. The concern with one's thoughts as the ultimate mode of expression is a point Meher Baba and Hare Krishna followers share with the American Transcendentalists. The intense absorption and participation in diety, the manifestation of love, and the imminence of divinity are emphasized among the current followers as was the case among their nineteenth-century antecedents. The depth of modern feeling on these points is, however, probably greater and more widespread than in the mid-nineteenth century.

Meher Baba is the reincarnation of all the great masters who have visited the earth. He is God come once again among men. "Baba lovers" have deity in the flesh right now. Worshippers of Krishna do not have so close a visible relation to deity but have access through individuals who have received "enlightenment" as well as vicariously through their many rituals. Krishna is a personal deity with whom worshippers feel a close relationship. He is a transcendent personal leader. And the modern leader, Bhaktivedanta, is their absolute authority whom they trust implicitly as the living representative of deity. No such relations existed for the Transcendentalists. But such a relationship does exist in those religions that are part of the current revival.

The significance of these papers on Eastern philosophies lies in presenting the functions that these movements fill in contemporary society. They are in some sense social instruments providing answers for alienated youth. It is their instrumentality that is so attractive. They offer their memberships either a permanent life as if in a monastic order, or a rite of passage on the way to reintegration into conventional life styles. These movements are conversionary in the sense that they offer a means for complete personal transformation. Part of that transformation is accomplished through the manipulation of body imagery using ritual vestments, hairstyles, and so on; and the socio-political stance they maintain protects the individual from the larger society while his transformation is taking place. One of the questions such movements raise is: Who goes through them on the way to reintegration into society as opposed to who takes them as a final answer to life's problems?

Anthony and Robbins argue that the Meher Baba cult recruits young people who have been involved in psychedelic drug use and have participated in the "hippie, drop-out" milieu. They argue that the Meher Baba cult performs basic expressive and communal functions that the drug-oriented "psychedelic" milieu fulfilled inadequately. They see post-adolescents facing a problem as they begin to participate in an "adult" world. The alienation expressed in "dropping out," through drugs, or in hippie milieux, is the result of the conflict between childhood familial orientations based on particularistic, diffuse, affective, and quality-oriented relationships and adult occupational relationships. Post-adolescents feel a scarcity of emotionally gratifying relationships in the adult milieu, which they do find in the Baba movement. The Meher Baba cult ameliorates these feelings by cultivating a sense of togetherness, expressive spontaneity, and solidarity among its members. Meher Baba is viewed as a personification of the universal consciousness which embodies the latent identity of all persons. He is perceived as expressive and "loving." This in turn serves to legitimate and give meaning to similar relationships among his devotees.

The cult propounds an ethic of selfless service, discourages dropout life styles, and encourages reassimilation to conventional educational-occupational routines. Through the Baba Cult such routines have their value reaffirmed and become viable sources of gratification. They are no longer perceived as oppressive to the devotees.

Judah examines the Hare Krishna movement and how its principal beliefs, devotional practices, and style of living have often totally transformed the lives of its followers. The goal of the Hare Krishna movement is the complete surrender of the individual to Krishna, who is recognized as the highest personality of godhead. Through this devotion he will develop Krishna consciousness, which entails the expressing of one's love of God and man. The consequence of this belief system on the devotee is the entire sacralization of life.

The Hare Krishna Movement

The Hare Krishna movement,[1] more formally known as the International Society for Krishna Consciousness is a Hindu religious sect imported into the United States in its same form from India. Its unusual social composition here has been made strikingly evident by the appearance of its devotees on the streets of the major cities of the United States. Therefore, this paper will seek first to examine briefly the principal beliefs, devotional practices, and style of living which has often transformed totally the lives of its followers; and secondly, to attempt to delineate some of the dynamics of the religion in the needs that it fills. That it offers something lacking in our established denominations is made evident immediately by two factors: its rapid geographical expansion; and the age group which is most greatly attracted to it.

Although the Society in the United States dates only from 1966, it has already spread to twenty-two cities here, and has also placed centers recently in West Germany, Canada, Australia, Hawaii, Hong Kong, Japan, England, France, Holland, and Trinidad. This year it is entering Siberia, Mexico, and Spain. There are no known statistics concerning the number of adherents, but the fact that each separate temple is situated in a building where the devotees dwell together communally limits the size of most groups to between twelve and twenty-four devotees. Each, however, may have twice that many non-initiates attending its devotional services. When a group expands to its capacity, new centers are established elsewhere. The limit to the number that may occupy an individual commune helps account for the very rapid geographical expansion.

The present movement in the United States is composed largely of youth. Over ninety percent of its following have been estimated to be twenty-five years old or younger. This includes a number, both male and female, who have joined while still in their late teens. This

---

[1] The dictionary form, "Harā," should normally be expected in some cases. The use of the spelling "Hare," which is really the vocative case in Sanskrit used in forms of address, is so prevalent, e.g. in the name of the movement and in the *mantras*, that it has seemed less confusing to use the more prevalent spelling in all cases.

percentage distinguishes the sect radically from the established denominations, in which the youth are led into the faith of their parents. Therefore, it is not composed of families who often worship together for convenience or for other reasons than deep conviction. On the contrary, it contains unmarried, and recently married young people, who have left their homes and have joined this movement, because their surrender to Krishna was the dominating factor in their lives. Although the majority of the membership studied is composed of youth of middle-class families with a small minority of blacks and chicanos, it is taught that there is no distinction between persons of different races, nationalities, or color, high born, straight middle class, or hippie. Moreover, it practices this belief in a way that belies the hypocrisy of many in our Christian churches, and provides one visible reason for the revolt of youth against the churches of the establishment. In the Hare Krishna temples all races have seemingly the same place socially and the same opportunity for leadership and advancement.

Ā. C. Bhaktivedanta Swami Prabhupada, the present spiritual leader, first brought its teachings to the United States in 1965. When he arrived in New York he began chanting the names of Krishna to the rhythm of his *kartals* (small Indian cymbals), while sitting beneath a tree in Tompkins Park on the Lower East Side. Soon, however, he attracted many about him, a number of whom were hippies. The following year a temple was established in New York. Other centers soon appeared, close to the hippie community in the Haight-Ashbury of San Francisco, in Los Angeles, Berkeley, and elsewhere.

A. C. Bhaktivedanta Swami Prabhupada, né Abhay Charan De, was born in Calcutta in 1896. After his education in English, Philosophy, and Economics at the University of Calcutta, he served in a chemical firm until retirement in 1954. In 1959 he became a *sannyasi*, i.e., one who has accepted a renunciation of a worldly life in the search for spirituality. At the request of his master, he came to America to spread the same teachings and devotional practices (Bhaktivedanta 1968b: xiii). Prabhupada, as he is affectionately referred to by the devotees, is ostensibly only the latest in an unbroken line of spiritual teachers or *acharyas*, whose succession stretches back to the founder of this movement, Chaitanya Mahaprabhu. The latter was a Bengalese Brahmin, born in 1486, who was married and reputed to have been a scholar by the time he was fourteen or fifteen. After being spiritually initiated as a Vaishnava when he was sixteen or seventeen, he became a preacher of Vaishnavism. He then began dancing and chanting the name of Krishna in the streets of the city with others who had been attracted to him (Bhaktivedanta 1968b: xxvii-xxx), just exactly as the youthful exponents of Hare Krishna do here.

The Vaishnavas in India are divided into a number of sects, which follow various teachers, all of whom worship the diety Vishnu or one of his forms as the Supreme Personality of Godhead. They all have in common their reverence for the teachings of the *Bhagavad Gita,* a theistic philosophical text advocating devotional surrender to Krishna. As part of sectarian Hinduism, they also accept the teachings of the older Hindu Vedic texts, including the philosophical treatises, the *Upanishads.* The followers of Chaitanya in India and America give special attention to the *Isha Upanishad,* as well as to more popular religious literature, particularly the *Bhagavata Purana.* Although Chaitanya himself was responsible for only a few lines of writing, his followers during his lifetime and after have contributed texts, which are still of prime importance to his present-day devotees.

The goal of the Hare Krishna movement may be said to be two-fold: First, one is to surrender himself completely to Krishna, who is recognized as the highest personality of Godhead. Through this devotion he will develop Krishna consciousness, which entails the deepening of one's love of God and man. This "is the revival of the original consciousness of the living being—the conscious awareness that one is eternally related to God, or Krsna" (International Society for Krsna Consciousness 1970: 3). Secondly, one should endeavor to spread this knowledge of Krishna consciousness to all who are willing to learn it. Thus the Hare Krishna devotee lives an entirely sacralized life, in which all his waking hours are directed to no other purpose than to serve Krishna in these ways.

While philosophy is very important to the American devotee, he reflects the modern mood of many students as to what is relevant in knowledge. Here he is entirely utilitarian. The devotee is not interested in the many critical studies concerning Krishna or Hindu philosophy. Knowledge or speculative philosophy for its own sake is considered irrelevant. Knowledge of Krishna and his pastimes and man's relation to Krishna, however, is of highest importance, because it is a way to make more meaningful one's devotion and to deepen his Krishna consciousness. Therefore, there are daily classes in each temple in which the *Bhagavad Gita* and or the *Bhagavata Purana* and other philosophical or religious works are read and expounded by the devotees, as *devotional pieces.*

Teachings

The followers of Krishna, like those in other Hindu or Buddhist sects recognize this age as one of decline, a period in which one has difficulty discovering the truth because of the effects of his past deeds or *karma*. They believe that most people are consequently blind to reality and are involved in *maya*, the illusory material life of pleasure seeking. Therefore man's salvation lies in his purification through complete surrender in devotion to Krishna. Through a sacralized life, in which every action is performed for Krishna's pleasure, one's eyes will be opened to the transcendental reality of Krishna. As one's Krishna consciousness deepens, he will experience an increasing transcendental spiritual pleasure surpassing any found in the false world of materiality. To try to merge oneself with Brahman, as the Vedantists do, according to Bhaktivedanta, is to seek only eternity and knowledge, but at the same time to miss the absolute pleasure which is in Krishna. To realize Krishna consciousness, however, is to include the pleasure of Brahman realization (Bhaktivedanta 1970b: 190).

This transcendental reality, which one may come to know and experience, is the Brahman or spirit. It is a reality comprising the whole world and all living creatures. Krishna, the Supreme Personality, the Lord, is, however, the complete whole and is designated as the Absolute Truth. The impersonal Brahman is regarded as one subordinate part of the Complete Person (Bhaktivedanta 1970b: 28).

Because man is part of Brahman, and therefore forms part of the body of Krishna, the individual soul and the supersoul are qualitatively one, (Bhaktivedanta 1970b: 39) but Krishna is infinitely greater quantitatively. Thus one may classify this phase of the philosophy as a panentheism, and note that it differs from the Vedanta philosophy of Shankara, which is more commonly known in the West. The devotees of Krishna are very conscious of this difference, and take occasion to make it plain in almost every lecture. On the one hand, in Vedanta, or Mayavada philosophy, as they are inclined to call it, the individual may proclaim himself to be Brahman or God. He then seeks to experience union in this impersonal Absolute. On the other hand, the Krishna devotees put emphasis upon the eternal retention of their individual selves. Therefore, rather than a final merging into the Absolute, the followers of Bhaktivedanta look eschatologically toward a sportive transcendental love and fellowship with a very personal deity, Krishna, in one of his transcendental heaven worlds. Krishna is therefore not only inclusive of Brahman, which he still transcends, but he also dwells in the heart of man. Not only is he an amorous deity sporting in his heaven worlds, but he is likewise present in his temple shrines.

The all-embraciveness and attributes of Krishna have often been divided in Hindu philosophy among the deities, Brahma, Vishnu, and Shiva in their creative, preserving and destructive aspects. The followers of Chaitanya, however, consider these to be manifestations of

Krishna's nature, as are other forms in which deities have been depicted in India and elsewhere.

The philosophy of the total system has been designated in the *Chaitanya Charitamrita,* one of the early texts of the movement, as *achintya-bhedabheda,* or "incomprehensible dualistic monism" (Kennedy 1925: 93). Besides the monistic side, which we have briefly delineated, there is also a dualism. Although the entire cosmos is contained in Vishnu or Krishna, who at times appears in the material world, he is transcendental to matter and is unaffected by its laws (Satsvarupa das Adhikari 1970: 22–23). Krishna belongs to the spiritual world rather than to the material. While there is no difference between the body and soul of Krishna or Vishnu, the same is not the case with man. The former is entirely spiritual, but man has a material body, because of "his desire to lord it over matter" and to have material enjoyment. Thus, besides a spiritual nature like Krishna, man has also a material body, which is produced along with the entire cosmic manifestation by the supreme Lord's lower energy called Maya Shakti. Although separated from the spiritual nature of Krishna, the cosmic manifestation is not false (Bhaktivedanta 1968b: 183–185, 190). It is, however, a reflection of the spiritual world, a shadow in which there cannot be any substance (Bhaktivedanta 1970b: 33).

The followers of Chaitanya developed a concept of Krishna's appearances on earth which involve both Krishna and Chaitanya. They accepted the teaching of the *Bhagavad Gita* that Krishna appears on earth in every age. He assumed his original form as Krishna, the charioteer for Arjuna, as told in the Gita. To the latter, he revealed himself as the Lord, the Supreme Personality of God. Krishna has also assumed the forms of all the other *avatars,* or appearances of Vishnu. Most important, however, for the adherents of Hare Krishna is the belief that he appeared on earth as Chaitanya.

Unique but important to the Bhakti cult is the concept that the latter appearance included not only Krishna, but his consort, Radha, as well. According to the *Charitamrita,* Krishna desired to experience the feelings Radha felt for him. Therefore, he appeared in this combined form as Chaitanya (Kennedy 1925: 94–96). It is further explained: "When Krishna wanted to understand Himself through the agency of Radha, they became united—and that unification is called Lord Chaitanya" (Bhaktivedanta 1968b: 9).

A further extension of this doctrine is that Krishna is regarded as expanded also into the four close disciples of Chaitanya, so that the five together are taken as the One Absolute Truth. The only difference is that Lord Chaitanya is regarded as the Supreme Living Entity and Lord of all. This also explains why in the *aratrika* ceremony at the temple the disciples of Chaitanya as well as Chaitanya himself are invoked and praised.

The reason given for Krishna's reappearance as Chaitanya is that he was to teach fallen souls again the way to Krishna, and to re-establish the fact that there is only One Supreme Personality of Godhead predominating over all living entities.

In the literature of the Hare Krishna movement one may search in vain for an expression of systematic philosophy. These pandits may be defended, however, on two counts: First, they begin with the premise that theirs is an "incomprehensible dualistic monism," and, therefore supra-logical. The tenents of philosophy are to be *lived* and *experienced* rather than argued or debated. Secondly, Chaitanya and his followers to the present day have stressed and elevated the cult of devotion above philosophy. Speculative philosophy in itself is regarded as a hindrance to the development of Krishna consciousness.

One may also note that in the Hare Krishna movement, when emphasis is placed upon the devotional and experiential side, a type of fundamentalism occurs, and a tendency to accept literally the words of the scriptures. This is an analogue to a similar concomitance seen among the pentecostal Christian sects. It is even more noticeable among individual members of liberal Christian churches, if they themselves experienced *glossolalia,* speaking in tongues. In accepting one's own religious experience as meaningful, one tends to accept literally the scriptural context giving authoritative validity to it. Since this may involve a change in basic attitude, this is often extended to the interpretation of all the scriptures. Such an hypothesis may help explain the change in belief of some Christians after speaking in tongues themselves. I recall my puzzlement when I once heard of such a shift in attitude by a formerly liberal Christian seminary professor. After having this experience, he was able to testify publically that Biblical criticism was no longer important to him. The scriptures were now meaningful just as they were written. This points again to an important difference between the critical and devotional use of religious texts. Are not such people making a dichotomy between an objective world of logic and analysis and a subjective mystical realm of religious experience? They are seeing through the eyes of faith originating from the event.

In the Hare Krishna movement there is a literal acceptance of the stories of the appearances and pastimes of Krishna, which others inside and outside the Hindu world might explain as allegories or regard as myths. The words of the scriptures, e.g. the *Bhagavad Gita,* are to be accepted just as they are literally. "Whatever Krishna says, we accept. This is Krishna Consciousness" (Bhaktivedanta 1969: 5).

Two facts, are, however, important to remember. First, the primary purpose of the scriptures for devotees of Krishna is to support their devotion to him. The texts exist for them as devotional works. Secondly, the pastimes of Krishna, i.e. his amorous experiences with his consort, Radha, and with other *gopis* or cowherdesses, are considered as spiritual and transcendental rather than material. It is this transcendental experience of the deity which the devotee of Krishna seeks, not only as an eschatological event in the future, but also as a spiritual one in this present life. This is sought through the unfolding of Krishna consciousness, a product of his devotion.

Adhering to a literal interpretation of the scriptures tends also to keep the precepts of belief the same as originally conceived. Toward this end, one also sees the importance of the spiritual master. Bhaktivedanta is believed to be in direct line of authority back to Krishna himself. In order to understand the scriptures, one is enjoined to seek out such a *guru*. He alone should reveal their meaning. The spiritual master never contradicts scripture, and therefore is believed never to contradict Krishna. The adherents point to their unity of interpretation by recognition of his authority, while pointing to the divisions among Protestant denominations due to their departure from the authority of the Pope (Hayagrivadas Adhikari 1920: 10–11). Therefore, Bhaktivedanta is now the ultimate standard of Krishna consciousness.

In return for his responsibility to his devotees in guiding them back to Godhead, they must serve him twenty-four hours a day. They must give him the honor due to God, because "the *guru* is the transparent via media or representative of God and is distributing unalloyed love of God" (Bhaktivedanta 1970b: 5).

BHAKTI (DEVOTION)

As already noted, the whole purpose of philosophy and of one's action is devotion to Krishna and the development of Krishna consciousness. Although it is recognized that action is necessary for man, he is enjoined not only to dedicate it to Krishna, but also to have no thought of meritorious reward.

One is not only to chant the names and praises of Krishna, but also to be completely aware of him with all the senses. Therefore, in counting off the prayer beads daily with his fingers, the devotee is remembering Krishna with his touch. In listening to the reading and explanation of the scriptures, he is made aware of Krishna through the sense of hearing. When one partakes of the the *prasadam,* i.e. the love feast offered first to Krishna, he remembers him through the sense of taste. When he looks at the deities in the temple, he recalls Krishna's memory through sight. And finally, when he smells the fragrance of the incense in the temple or the flowers offered to Krishna, he remembers him through the sense of smell.

Krishna consciousness is, however, a matter of growth and therefore has five stages of development, corresponding to the different kinds of devotional feelings one may feeel toward the deity. *Shanta,* meaning peaceful, denotes the quietistic stage of fixing one's mind calmly upon Krishna. *Dasya,* or service, connotes a servial relationship to the deity. On attaining the *sakhya,* or friendship degree, one relates himself to Krishna as a friend. *Batsalya,* fondness, is the parental relationship, in which one has love toward Krishna as if he were his mother or father. The last, *madhurya,* expresses the conjugal relationship of a lover. Each progressive stage contains the attributes of those before it, and increases the delight with the addition of each new quality.

In the short time the movement has existed here in the United States, presumably none of the members has advanced to the fifth stage. It would be difficult to tell whether one had, however, since humility is a virtue practiced among the devotees, and to bragg of one's attainments in Krishna consciousness is regarded as a sign of his lack of advancement.

Looked upon in another way, Bhakti has been divided into two paths toward the fulfillment of love in union with Krishna. The first is the regular or *vaidhi,* which follows rules laid down in the scriptures. Although there are sixty-four in number, there are four minimal requirements: One must refrain from eating meat, fish, or eggs; must not gamble nor have illicit sex; must not take drugs or intoxicants; must chant sixteen rounds on his prayer beads daily.

The second way is the *raganuga,* or spontaneous type, which finally transcends the rules of the former, and is characterized by the passionate desire for mystic union with the loved one. In his meditation the devotee seeks to visualize the amorous sport that Krishna carries on with the milkmaids, and to take part himself in this transcendental experience. Lest one should think that he should look upon these loving exchanges entirely in a material way, he is reminded by Bhaktivedanta that they are on a spiritual plane, where there are varieties of reciprocal love, which are inconceivable in our present state of material life. To understand the transcendental loving service with Krishna, one must first become in touch with the pleasure potency of the Supreme Lord (Bhaktivedanta 1970c: 286).

He gives us a little more clarity in the following:

Actually, lust and the sex urge are there in spiritual life, but because the spirit soul is now embodied in material elements, that spiritual urge is expressed through this material body; and therefore it is pervertedly reflected. When one becomes actually conversant in the science of Krishna Consciousness, he can understand that his material affection of sex life is abominable, whereas spiritual sex life is desirable.

Spiritual sex life is of two kinds; one completely in the constitutional position of the self, and the other according to the object. When one has understood the truth about this life but is not completely out of the material contamination, then, although there is an understanding of spiritual life, he is not factually situated in the transcendental Abode, Vrindaban. When, however, one becomes free from all bodily sex urges, he is actually situated in the Supreme Abode of Vrindaban. (Bhaktivedanta 1968b: 270–271)

Although illicit sex is frowned upon, and celibacy is an ideal to be followed by some, the movement encourages its devotees to marry if they wish. In fact all women are enjoined to marry and form a cooperative effort with their husbands in deepening Krishna consciousness. Marriages of devotees are performed as a religious rite in the temple. This union is to be for life. Sex in marriage is permitted, but only for the purpose of having children, who will be raised in Krishna consciousness. When I compared this ideal with that of the Roman Catholic Church, one devotee reminded me: "Catholics are allowed to have sex at a time when they cannot conceive children; we are allowed to have sex only when we know we can."

The more one associates with the devotees, the more one must realize the power of their discipline, which is aimed to develop Krishna consciousness, and which is made so visible in the complete change of their lives. Not only do they have severe sexual restrictions, but they have for all intents and purposes given up their American way of life for one which faithfully represents the Vaishnava way of Chaitanya. Their shaven heads and saffron *dhotis* for men and *saris* for women are exactly like the Hindu counterpart. Their prayers and invocations are memorized and sung in Bengali and Sanskrit. Besides the Hindu dietary restrictions, the only food which may be eaten by the devotees is that prepared with Hindu recipes under strict dietary rules. This is the *prasadam,* which is first offered to Krishna. Devotees are under no circumstances to eat unoffered food. The Association's efficiency in getting youth off the use of narcotics, including marijuana, LSD, and others has brought plaudits from the mayors of both New York City and San Francisco. Its prohibition of gambling is extended even to "idle amusements" such as movies or television (International Society for Kṛṣṇa Consciousness 1970: 13, 16).

The devotees, living together communally, spend their lives entirely in deepening their own consciousness of God, and trying to instill it into others.

Prabhupada, the spiritual master, has given the American devotees a daily schedule patterned after that observed in India. The strict discipline is designed to engage all one's senses in the service of Krishna. Although every part of it is not mandatory, each is urged to follow it as closely as possible. The schedule begins at 3:45 A.M. when the devotee rises, takes a shower, and puts on the *tilak*, the white clay marks that signify his body is engaged in Krishna's service. Then personal reading of scriptures is performed and the counting off of prayer beads, while repeating the Hare Krishna *mantra*. Each devotee is required to do sixteen rounds of this *mahamantra* on his one hundred and eight prayer beads, as part of his private daily devotion. The first *aratrika* ceremony occurs between 4:30 and 5:00 A.M. This is for the purpose of greeting Krishna with chanting. Between 5:00 and 5:30 the devotees prepare the morning *prasadam* and straighten up the temple. From 5:30 to 6:15 is the class for the study of the *Srimad Bhagavatam*, which is followed by chanting of prayers to the spiritual master between 6:15 and 6:30. "After these prayers are done, the devotees are prepared to meet the spiritual master as if he were actually present in the temple at the time." From 6:30 to 8:00 the devotees and any others who are there have a round of chants to Krishna, while fixing their minds on the sound vibrations of the *mahamantra*. Between 8:00 and 8:40 some clean the temple, while others begin preparing food for the afternoon offering. *Prasadam* is taken from 8:40 to 9:00. Then after a brief meeting, the devotees go out on the streets to sell their magazine, *Back to Godhead,* and chant the *mahamantra*. Those who have been attracted by the chanting are invited to the temple to have a lunch of *prasadam* together, while they are told about Krishna consciousness. Between 2:15 and 5:30 in the afternoon they again take to the streets as in the morning. Upon their return to the temple they again take showers and prepare themselves for evening classes. They may then continue their private chanting or talk about Krishna consciousness to guests who may be there. At 6:30 they read and discuss the book entitled the *Nectar of Devotion,* written by Srila Rupa Goswami, one of the disciples of Chaitanya. Then follows another *aratrika* ceremony at 7:15 for thirty minutes. Between 7:50 and 8:10 there is a *Bhagavad Gita* lecture, followed again by *kirtana,* chanting to 8:40. The book entitled *Kṛṣṇa,* compiled and explained by Bhaktivedanta, is read finally from 8:45 to 9:10. The devotees now have free time to prepare for the next day, wash their *dhotis,* do personal reading, etc., until they retire at 10:00. If this is still not enough, there is an optional final *aratrika* ceremony beginning at 9:15, which a goodly number still attend.

The *aratrika,* the principal daily ceremony, is one in which the deities are presented food, incense, flowers, a fan, a waving handkerchief, and an offering of flames. The deities worshipped in the temples are either visible representations of Krishna and his consort, Radha, or Krishna in the form of Jagannatha-Swami standing together with Balarama and Subhadra, his brother and sister. Every temple also has a picture of Lord Chaitanya. During the ceremony the deities are offered food, and they are symbolically dressed and bathed.

It is taught that Krishna is able to incarnate into a figure of wood, stone, or metal, which has been formed according to authorized descriptions. Even though we are not able to see his original spiritual form, because of our materially contaminated eyes, he appears before us to worship in his *archa* incarnation. This form, however, is never to be understood as an idol or as a material object, since Krishna actually only appears on earth in spiritual form (International Society for Kṛṣṇa Consciousness 1970: 15–17).

It is also recognized that every one is not suitable by either desire or temperament to submit to the life of communal living in the temple building, nor to devote every waking moment to devotion of Krishna, in order to deepen his love of God, and help instill it into others. There are, moreover, members who are expected to follow normal secular pursuits. It is possible for one in any line of secular work to dedicate his activity to Krishna, to attend the temple ceremonies, and to make contributions of money to him. Again, it is recognized that all may not be able to follow every prescribed principle, nor even to accept all the various beliefs. No one is turned away, however, because of his particular life or belief, whatever it may be. All are accepted and welcomed to come and participate in the services, to chant the names of Krishna, and to dance in the temple before the deities and in the streets; to listen to the lectures and readings and to perform whatever service he can for Krishna, in order to develop Krishna consciousness and thereby his love of God.

If devotion to God is the underlying emphasis of the adherents of Hare Krishna, the summit of that endeavor is hearing about Krishna, listening to the sounds of the chanting, and then adding one's own active performance of *sankirtana,* chanting and dancing with the devotees before the deities. The most important chant is the *mahamantra:* "Hare Krishna, Hare Krishna, Krishna, Krishna, Hare Hare/ Hare Rama, Hare Rama, Rama, Rama, Hare Hare."

Since the being of Krishna includes his names and forms, he is believed to be immediately present to any who call upon him. Through this participation, piety and spiritual consciousness will result, it is said. As soon as *karma,* the results of our deeds, is gone, we are believed to acquire pure consciousness or Krishna consciousness (Bhaktivedanta 1970b: 10), the highest expression of which is our love of God. Bhaktivedanta teaches that every devotee, when perfected, has a spontaneous attraction to the Lord. This is interpreted as his excessive desire to serve Krishna, which is pleasing to the deity. Although one may appear desirous of enjoying God, Bhaktivedanta says that it is really only the endeavor to serve him (Bhaktivedanta 1970b: 125). It is taught that Krishna is the "supreme enjoyer," and one who serves him finds a more meaningful happiness and pleasure through this participation. Through one's love of God the devotee comes to love all people as brothers, realizing that they too are all parts of God.

The ethical import of the teaching is directly connected with the devotion to Krishna, but few precepts are cited specifically except those already noted above. Chaitanya taught that through *Bhakti* one would become so purified that he would hate to break a moral law. Therefore, it is believed that a moral life will follow the life of *Bhakti* without one having anything to perform as his duty. One should be able to transcend a moral code (Bhaktivedanta 1968a: 97).

Its social ethics are based on the idea that since the suffering of humanity is due to forgetfulness of Krishna, to work toward the revival of this consciousness is the highest welfare, and more important than temporary physical relief (Bhaktivedanta 1968a: 146).

One question remains. Why is the Hare Krishna movement appealing to many American youths? The answer is at least partly answered, I believe, in the way A. C. Bhaktivedanta has brought to them a practice which promises them a transcendental religious experience, a way of life, and a philosophy which is satisfying to their wills and minds.

As I have endeavored to demonstrate elsewhere, religion should have an appeal to the mind, will, and emotions of an adherent (Judah 1967: 391). American church history has borne witness to the need of many for some kind of religious experience, e.g., the religious revivals of the Great Awakening of the eighteenth century and the rise of the transcendentalism of Emerson, Alcott, and others of the nineteenth.

The nineteenth century was the period when Hindu philosophy first made its impact on America through translations of the *Bhagavad Gita,* the philosophical *Upanishads,* and some of the *Puranas.* This monistic philosophy affected not only the transcendentalists, but also their allies, the various progenitors of the metaphysical movements

(Theosophy, New Thought, the Unity School of Christianity, and others) who, like the transcendentalists were dissatisfied with Christianity and sought some type of religious experience. The first wave of Hindu influence was succeeded by the second, when Vivekananda came to the United States in 1893 and stayed long enough to found the Vedanta Society and add his influence to the philosophy of many Americans. More recently he has been followed by a whole host of Hindu teachers, such as Prabhavananda, the founder of the Self-Realization Fellowship; Sant Kirpal Singh, who is responsible for the Ruhani Satsanga; and Mahesh Yogi and his transcendental meditation. All of these, including the latest entry, the Hare Krishna movement, have one thing in common, the possibility of religious experience. All but the latter, however, have a philosophy closer to the traditional Vedanta of Shankara than the philosophy of Chaitanya, which proclaims a very personal deity.

In interviewing the youth of the Hare Krishna movement, it was discovered that most of them had belonged to one of the established churches. A number were also looking for a transcendental reality, which they had not been able to find. The experiential element was missing. Each devotee of Hare Krishna, however, attests to the value of Krishna consciousness as a valid experience, which has given him a happiness and joy he had not known before, and a new meaning to life.

On the one hand, the fastest growing Christian churches in America are the Southern Baptists and more conservative groups, which still find a place for religious experience and a vertical dimension.

On the other hand, the doors of many liberal churches are closing. Without depreciating the need for social change and the important role liberal churches are playing in this cause, many churches are being crucified slowly on the cross of their activism. Faced with a missing vertical dimension and experiential element, and having become too liberal to accept a Christian fundamentalism, many people are forsaking their former churches to become seekers after God in other religions. Some of the dissatisfied youth are joining the Hare Krishna movement.

A study of the needs and attitudes of the youthful members who have surrendered to Krishna point to further values of the movement, which have been important in their situation. In many cases they are youths who have left home feeling some doubt about their parents' ability to see their problems or give them guidance. They needed outside help but felt that what was given was not valid to their situation. Their parents belonged to the establishment, which included the government and their churches, and there was a gap between the establishment and them. There was in some cases a distrust of the established ways which their parents represented, and which was not felt to meet their needs. It involved the controversial Vietnam War, to which they were vitally related and whose issues were made plain through the television news media. There was in other cases the distrust of the established government which had involved us and which had been elected by their parents.

The greatly accelerated advances in science, technology, and medicine had moved more rapidly than one's capability of fitting the changes into a system of morals or ethics. This, therefore, added to the confusion and called into question the validity of our ancient moral code.

With distrust in the established ethical system, they began questioning the very meaning of their lives and goals. There was the problem of the relevance of education in the changing scene, and even the value of education at all, if it meant working long hours to give us a surfeit of material comforts, when people here were hungry. Some again saw the hypocrisy of racists in churches who professed brotherhood.

These are but a few of the problems which we recognize in our youth. No two individuals, however, have been alike, and each differs from another in assessing the relative importance of every factor. Without answers, however, there had been a consequent loss of meaning to life which often led to aimless drifting. Some became hippies and took to drugs in the hope of finding some transcendental experience to give new meaning and direction. The Hare Krishna movement is not, however, a hippie movement. It is rather a movement which is broad enough in its view to include all youth who have disagreed with the world which their parents have helped to create and, feeling frustrated, have sought for meaning in a subjective world transcending the material—a world of spirit.

It was to such youth that Bhaktivedanta first ministered in New York. Finding in his message something of value, they started a center in that city and then began spreading the movement in others. The following are values found in the Hare Krishna Movement which seem to have particular relevance to many of our youth, as shown by their membership in the Association:

(1) Many have felt that by obtaining Krishna consciousness they found more happiness than they had known before, and a greater pleasure than drugs had ever been able to supply.

(2) The philosophy directs their lives toward the attainment of what they believe to be spiritual things rather than the acquisition of material possessions.

As Bhaktivedanta said: "One who takes pleasure in chanting and hearing the transcendental glories of the Lord has already surpassed all kinds of material benedictions." Again he says: "The philosophy is to work hard, get dollars, and enjoy as you like. This is misguidance. Therefore the young are not happy" (Bhaktivedanta 1968b: 19). He then proceeds to give them a philosophy to change their direction and give them happiness.

(3) Bhaktivedanta, the spiritual leader in the movement, supplies the outside authority which they have wanted, and leads them in ways that seem valid to them. If they had felt alone before, the personal, ever loving, eternally young Krishna is a deity with whom they can easily identify and feel a close relationship.

(4) The continuous rhythmic chanting and the graceful movements of their dancing before the shrine of Krishna in the spirit of love and play permit the giving and losing of themselves, which has important transcendental values. This emptying themselves of their emotions in their complete surrender becomes a way of ridding themselves of normal aggressions and allows them to sublimate their physical sexual drives. As Thomas Merton so beautifully expressed it when speaking of their dancing: "Once we live in awareness of the cosmic dance and move in time with the Dancer, our life attains its true dimension. It is at once more serious and less serious than the life of one who does not sense this inner cosmic dynamism" (quoted in Bhaktivedanta 1968b: 19).

(5) For some youth a strain of anti-intellectualism occasionally displayed against materialistic knowledge, strikes a harmonious chord in their attitudes. In various places Bhaktivedanta emphasizes the importance of devotion over knowledge, and one of the former *acharyas,* Bhaktivinode, said, "The advancement of material knowledge renders a person more foolish because it causes him to forget his real identification by its glimmer. . . . By the advancement of material knowledge people are becoming more and more entangled in material existence" (Bhaktivedanta 1970c: 11–12).

(6) Its philosophy of non-violence is for many an important antidote to the question of the war in Vietnam. Moreover, its lack of demonstrable concern about political, social, and worldly matters must be indeed a respite from the frustration many youth had formerly felt.

(7) Probably one of the most important factors for youth who have been confused about what they should believe about so many questions is that it offers an absolute authority, Bhaktivedanta, in whom they have come to trust implicitly, and who as the living representative of their deity gives them answers to all of their questions. Moreover, his personal dynamic appeal as a living model for their action is

very powerful, and continues to grow. How many will find the discipline too rigorous over a long period of time is yet unknown. That some have already dropped out is also true. For others it will be a permanent fellowship as is found in the Christian religious orders; for still others it will undoubtedly be a rite of passage, through which they will pass to an adult life that will be better for having had this meaningful experience.

The Meher Baba Movement:
Its Affect on Post-Adolescent
Social Alienation

1. INTRODUCTION

THE Meher Baba movement recruits many young people who have been involved in psychedelic drug use and have been participants in expressive "hippie" or "drop-out" milieux. In the following paper we will argue that the Baba movement performs basic expressive and communal functions which are increasingly marginal in bureaucratized "adult" instrumental milieux. Moreover, we will argue, these functions were formerly inadequately performed for our subjects by drug-oriented "psychedelic" milieux. The following paragraphs summarize the basic argument and present an overview of the paper.[1]

Eisenstadt and other sociologists have suggested that the increasing differentiation and specialization of the family have produced a conflict between expressive role orientations stressed in the modern familial milieu and instrumental role orientations which increasingly dominate the bureaucratic occupational structure.[2] The growing disjunction between expressive and instrumental roles creates a problem of *community* among post-adolescents who experience socio-emotional deprivation arising from a relative scarcity of gratifying expressive relationships in the adult instrumental milieu. A frequent response to this problem involves "dropping out" of alienating instrumental routines associated with school or career commitments and

---

[1] This study was supported in part by United States Public Health Service Grant 1–RO3–MH20803–01. The grant and research were conducted under the direction of Thomas E. Curtis, M.D., Department of Psychiatry, University of North Carolina School of Medicine.

[2] Our analysis relies heavily upon Parson's (1937, 1961) and Eisenstadt's (1956) distinction between "expressive" roles and relationships and "instrumental" roles and relationships. Expressive or "personalistic" relationships are those which are (1) terminal values or ends-in-themselves, (2) diffuse, i.e. spilling over into many different sectors of the participant's life-space, (3) particularistic or idiosyncratic, and (4) emotional or affective. In contrast, instrumental or "impersonal" roles and relationships are (1) means to ends, (2) functionally specific, (3) performance or achievement oriented, (4) universalistic, or capable of application without exception, and (5) unemotional or affectively neutral.

479

E.K.C.C. LIBRARY

cultivating expressive relationships in communes, "street scenes," etc. An aspect of this strategy is the use of psychedelic drugs to cultivate a sense of togetherness and expressive spontaneity and solidarity.

Subjects whom we interviewed in this study became disenchanted with expressive and quasi-communal drop-out milieux because they perceived them as being inadequately legitimated in terms of the traditional work ethic. Moreover, heavy drug consumption tended to involve our respondents in instrumental roles and relationships which were perceived as exploitative and inconsistent with the ethos of expressive spontaneity which was used to legitimate this life-style. Finally, the psychedelic approach to *Gemeinschaft* encountered a fundamental problem of meaning in that drug-induced sensations tended to be perceived as ego-alien and could not be easily integrated into the self-concept. Subjects thus became disillusioned with what may be termed "psychedelic utopianism" and were available for conversion to a new perspective.

These respondents have become participants in the Meher Baba movement which provides a context for working out satisfying expressive and communal relationships. It *legitimates* such relationships by deriving them from each follower's perceived affective, diffuse, quality-oriented, and particularistic relationship to Meher Baba. Meher Baba is viewed as a personification of the universal consciousness which embodies the latent identity of all persons. He is perceived as having expressive and "loving" role-orientations which are thus universal and archetypal and operate to legitimate and confer meaning on "loving" relationships among devotees.

The doctrine of Meher Baba's immanence in *everyone* produces a certain tolerance towards those outside the movement, including "straight" people who formerly may have been viewed with some antipathy. The affective nature of the ideal Baba-follower relationship, combined with the doctrine of his immanence in everyone, implies a necessity to act lovingly in the world to draw oneself closer to Baba. Meher Baba propounds an ethic of "selfless service" which implicitly de-legitimates a "drop-out" life-style and tends to induce followers eventually to become re-assimilated to educational-occupational routines and career orientations. Such instrumental roles seem less oppressive to the devotee once he has achieved, through the Baba movement a viable non-vocational source of expressive gratifications.

In writing this paper we are building on the work of a number of scholars who have recently called attention to the upsurge of mysticism and unconventional religiosity among American youth (Greeley 1969;

E.K.C.C. LIBRARY

Gustaitis 1969; Robbins 1969; Needleman 1970; Baum 1970; Bell 1971). Some of the scholarly and journalistic discussions of this phenomenon have focused on the status of current youth-oriented mysticism as a "post-drug" phenomenon. These analyses contend that this "movement" recruits from persons who have been involved in "drug abuse" and facilitates the termination of involvement with hallucinogens, amphetamines, and/or opiates (Crenshaw 1968; Robbins 1969; Gustaitis 1969; Nolan 1971; Richardson and Harder 1971). A recent study by the present authors analyzed the capacity of the Meher Baba movement to "resocialize" deviant drug users and to resolve the tension between conventional and "hippie" values (Robbins 1969). The 1969 paper described the effect of the Baba movement in facilitating the termination of drug use among converts in Chapel Hill, North Carolina.[3] This study also described a tendency among these converts toward a more comprehensive "rehabilitation" in terms of re-entry into conventional career and educational patterns.

The Meher Baba movement is growing rapidly and is eliciting increasing attention from scholars and journalists (Robbins 1969; Gustaitis 1969; Dunn 1968; Needleman 1970; Rowley 1970; Townsend 1970; *The New Yorker,* June 21, 1969). In view of the increasing importance of spiritual movements as youthful "post drug" scenes (Richardson and Harder 1971; Adams and Fox 1972), the authors decided to conduct an intensive participant-observation study of the Meher Baba movement at its resident center at Myrtle Beach, South Carolina. The present study was thus designed as a more comprehensive follow-up of the original study. In it we intend to integrate an explanation of the consequences of involvement in the movement (e.g., "resocialization," termination of drug use) with analysis of its continuing growth and appeal.

2. Methodology

The present study was conducted during the summer of 1970. The second author spent most of that summer at the Meher Spiritual Center in Myrtle Beach, South Carolina. The study utilizes a participant-observation or "anthropological" approach, which emphasizes living within a culture until one assimilates its meaning system (Bruyn 1966). The meaning system is presumed to have been acquired when the investigator can participate in the symbolism, ritual, and

---

[3] The integrative impact of the new faith on the deviant subculture of Chapel Hill was widely noted at the time by concerned authorities and the local media (*Winston-Salem Journal Sentinal,* October 22–26, 1967; *Chapel Hill Weekly,* November 5, 1967; University of North Carolina *Daily Tar Heel,* November 7, 1968).

patterned interactions of the culture in a way that is deemed acceptable or "correct" by its members.

As an urban anthropologist has recently pointed out, "participant observation is the method par excellence for the empirical investigation of systems of meaning" (Schwartz 1970). The method is phenomenologically grounded and thus "participant observers hesitate to explain conduct in terms of analytic categories which violate or ignore the substance of the actor's social experience" (Schwartz 1970: 27). Following Schutz (1971), we consider our own theoretical framework to consist of "secondary constructs" which we infer from the "primary constructs" through which our subjects as social actors conceptualize their own experience. Our emergent categories are not the categories of the subjects, but they do not, in our opinion, violate or ignore these categories.

In this connection, it should be noted that both researchers are, in varying degrees "in" the movement which they endeavored to study. Both researchers are "involved" with the Meher Baba movement, and have been personally "interested" in the thought of Meher Baba for several years prior to embarking on the present study. Of the two researchers, Mr. Robbins has the more "academic" orientation, with a tendency toward reductionistic explanations. Mr. Anthony, on the other hand, is a committed devotee with a penchant for explanations based on the perspective of Meher Baba himself. The theoretical framework of the present study emerged in part from a dialectical interaction between the conflicting perspectives of the two researchers.

The present study is primarily based on intensive interaction with "Baba Lovers" at the Meher Center during the summer of 1970. Interviews were conducted during the later part of this research period. The generality of conclusions thus arrived at was confirmed through periodic attendance by both researchers at Meher Baba meetings in Chapel Hill, North Carolina, Berkeley, California, and New York City over a period of three years.

An initial period of intensive interaction with "Baba Lovers" resulted in a tentative phenomenological understanding of the meaning system and interpretive categories of the subjects. Through such interaction we achieved an intuitive feeling for cultic processes and cognitive style which enabled us to conduct, code and analyze meaningful interviews.

We then tape recorded interviews with persons who appeared to be representative of types active within the movement. These interviews were generally informal and involved the respondent's description of his life from his initial involvement with drugs until his drugless present. The interviewer asked questions clarifying various points or seeking responses which would enable him to compare features of the respondent's history to that of other followers of Meher Baba. The respondents were aware of the interviewer's role as researcher, but tended to perceive him primarily as a fellow participant in the movement. In addition, we taped various informal "talks" given by a Baba follower for other Baba followers in the Saroja Library at the Meher Center.

Each interview, in addition to answering various questions arising from prior interviews and observations, also raised new issues. Interviews thus served two functions: the first one of verification in confirming or contradicting hypotheses we had arrived at through prior interaction; the second an exploratory function in generating new concepts and categories which structured subsequent observations and interviews. In this way, a coding scheme was gradually elaborated, and grew more complex and differentiated with each interview. The relationship between emergent theory and data gathering processes was reciprocal. This was considered by the researchers to be an application of the method of "constant comparisons" (Glazer and Strauss 1967) to interview data.

The primary purpose of this study was to generate theory, through participant observation. This approach may be contrasted with one which seeks to verify deductive consequences of a previously existing abstract formal model. It was anticipated, however, that initial understanding of cultic phenomena in terms of empathy or *Verstehen* (Bruyn 1966) might subsequently be translated into the categories of formal theories and models operative in the sociology of religion, the sociology of youth, or the sociology of deviance. The authors were, of course, familiar at the beginning of the study with various models and perspectives, which directed their observations somewhat. The study was, nevertheless, in its initial phase primarily inductive. Some of those models, as well as others suggested during the course of the research, eventually proved useful in reconceptualizing our observations. Section 3 presents the formal concepts and theories which proved useful in this respect.

3. The Sociological Analysis of Youth Culture and Youth Movements

Recently, a sociologist has noted that "youth culture is located at the point of conflict between the bureaucratic ethos and the ethos of modern childhood" (Berger 1970: 34). The separation of family and childhood from the productive process, the shrinkage in family size, and the diminishing likelihood of death during childhood have converged to produce a contemporary middle class "childhood" which is "vastly more humane than it was before" and which "brings forth more humane individuals" (Berger 1970: 35). Continuity is disturbed, however, because the humanistic and personalistic values fostered by the milieu of modern childhood cannot be carried over into the instrumental processes of the adult occupational milieu. The bureaucratic aspect of many post-childhood occupational and educational milieux is in some ways the antithesis of the "humanistic" patterns of childhood.

> Modern childhood is marked by values and by a consciousness that are emphatically personalistic. Modern bureaucracy, by contrast, has an ethos of emphatic impersonality. Put simply, an individual shaped by modern childhood is most likely to feel oppressed by modern bureaucracy. Indeed, he is likely to have a very low "oppression threshold" when it comes to the impersonal processes of bureaucracy. Thus people today feel oppressed, "alienated" or even "exploited" simply by being subjected to bureaucratic processes . . . that a generation ago would have seemed pragmatic necessities. (Berger 1970: 37)

A number of empirical studies have documented the increasingly "humanistic" character of middle-class familial milieux (Flacks 1967, 1970), particularly with regard to the backgrounds of "alienated" youthful respondents. These studies and the analysis above recall S. N. Eisenstadt's earlier classical analysis of generational discontinuity in industrial society (Eisenstadt 1956, 1961) as a consequence of the increasing differentiation of the family from the occupational structure. As the family increasingly specializes in the function of providing emotional gratification for its members, it tends to stress roles and relationships which are diffuse, affective, particularistic, and quality-oriented. These attributes define expressive or personalistic relationships which have terminal rather than instrumental value for participants. In contrast, the adult occupational structure (including preparatory higher educational institutions) inrceasingly stresses roles which are functionally specific, affectively neutral, universalistic and performance-oriented, in short, "bureaucratic," and "impersonal" instrumental relations (Eisenstadt 1956). The transition between the familial milieu and the adult instrumental milieu thus beecomes increasingly difficult and young people experience sharp role-conflict. Within the terms of this analysis, youth movements, although they may have explicit anti-establishment overtones, can often be seen as devices to ease the tension of the familial-occupational transition.

They do this by constructing value orientations and normative frameworks which combine elements of both familial and bureaucratic role systems (e.g. bureaucratic universalism and familial diffuseness). Through youth movements, adolescents and post-adolescents work out roles and relationships consistent with *some* aspects of both "childish" and "adult" milieux.

Eisenstadt's analysis is relevant to recent discussions of the clash of the "counter-culture" with "technocracy" (Roszak 1969; Reich 1970). It should be noted, moreover, that Eisenstadt and Berger interpret youthful "alienation" as essentially a problem of *community*. There is a dearth of gratifying expressive-communal relationships and roles available for young people in the adult instrumental milieu. Such people face the prospect of being "love-starved." Contemporary youth movements will necessarily cater to these longings, and, moreover, can be expected on the basis of Eisenstadt's analysis to manifest an *integrative dimension* facilitating the working out of satisfying expressive patterns within the context of the larger society.

Various other writers have discussed the pervasiveness of alienation qua communal deprivation in American life. Like Berger and Eisenstadt, Slater (1970) has analyzed youth movements and the "counterculture" as responses to this malaise and the perceived marginality of expressive roles and relations in "technocratic" society. Slater has characterized American lifestyles as pervaded by a "pursuit of loneliness." He argues that the dominant American value orientation—the Protestant ethic—has always been potentially dehumanizing and alienating. This potential is implicit in its stress on individualism and competition and its consequent neglect of the affiliative "needs" of human beings and the basic necessity of human interdependence. Yet, as long as Americans actually lived in small, self-contained rural villages, the dehumanizing potential of the Protestant ethic was never actualized. The conjunction of urbanization and industrialization on the one hand, and a competitive individualist ethos on the other, has led to the pervasive "pursuit of loneliness" in American society.

Slater argues that communal themes, which have always been implicit in American culture, have now been suppressed in behalf of dominant individualistic and competitive motifs. He further argues that any "counterculture" will necessarily emphasize those values which are latent in the dominant culture but have been suppressed. He therefore considers the "love" emphasis of the youth culture to be a result of this tendency.

Slater also comments that although dehumanization and the "pursuit of loneliness" affect everyone, the present generation of affluent youth are less able than former generations to tolerate this dearth of community. This is so because they cannot relate experientially to the *scarcity* premises of the competitive individualist ethos. A primary assumption of this ethos is that there aren't sufficient material resources to go around. A subsidiary assumption is that we must compete with each other for survival and cannot therefore afford the luxury of noncompetitive interpersonal communion. People who have not actually experienced the struggle for socioeconomic mobility tend to perceive these meanings as abstract and unreal and are hence less willing to defer expressive gratifications in behalf of instrumental concerns.

Slater seems to be saying that because of rapid social change, dissonance currently exists between social needs (expressive gratification), institutions (adult bureaucratic instrumental milieu), and the ethic which heretofore rationalized their integration (the Protestant ethic). In such a situation, one adaptive communal response may be to select a new ethic or religion which more effectively integrates social needs and institutions. Baum (1970) has discussed the significance of the communal factor in Max Weber's comments on mystical currents in the post-World War I German youth movement. Weber considered these movements to be a protest against the bureaucratization of society and the rationalization of culture. Weber noted the interpersonal solidarity and strong bonds of friendship and brotherhood which developed within these movements. Youthful spiritual movements provided a context for expressive interpersonal relationships which young persons found it difficult to develop and legitimate in the conventional institutions of an increasingly bureaucratized and rationalized society. Weber further remarked that the meaning systems of these groups tended to *legitimate* these relationships by giving them a spiritual interpretation.

4. The Meher Baba Movement

Meher Baba is a recently deceased (January 31, 1969) Indian spiritual master who claimed to be the most recent manifestation of the avataric tradition. According to Baba, Zoroaster, Rama, Krishna, Buddha, Christ, and Mohammed were all human manifestations of the same divine being whose appearances on earth have punctuated humanity's movement through an "avataric cycle." Baba is the most recent manifestation of this being, and his advent closes the cycle.

> I am the Ancient One whose past is worshipped and remembered, whose present is ignored and forgotten and whose future (Advent) is anticipated with great fervor and longing. . . . God has come

again and again in various Forms, has spoken again and again,
in different words and different languages, the same One Truth—
The outer life and habits of an Avatar reflect in some degree the
habits and customs of the people of that time, and in his teachings
he stresses the aspects that call for improvement. In essence every
Avatar embodies the same ideals of life. . . . I have come to sow
the seed of love in your hearts so that, in spite of all superficial
diversity which your life in illusion must experience and endure,
the feeling of oneness, through Love, is brought about amongst all
the nations, creeds, sects, and castes of the World. (Meher Baba
1971)

Meher Baba has hundreds of thousands of followers in India. Until
recently, however, his American following had remained small and
predominantly middle-aged. Nevertheless, Baba made several trips to
the United States and established a spiritual sanctuary outside Myrtle
Beach in South Carolina.

In the middle sixties an interest in Meher Baba developed on the
part of American "hippies." Some of this attention arose in connection with the enhanced interest in "eastern" mysticism which accompanied the early "utopiate" psychedelic scene. On the other hand,
some of this sudden interest was related to Meher Baba's forthright
opposition to the use of psychedelic drugs. Meher Baba writes:

If God can be found through the medium of any drug, God is not
worthy of being God. . . . No drug, whatever its great promise, can
help one to attain the spiritual goal. There is no shortcut to the
goal except through the grace of the Perfect Master, and drugs, LSD
more than others, give only a semblance of "spiritual experience," a
glimpse of a false reality. . . . The experience is as far removed
from Reality as is a mirage from water. No matter how much one
pursues the mirage, one will never reach water, and the search for
God through drugs must end in disillusionment. (Meher Baba 1971)

One of the authors wrote in 1969:

Baba opposes the use of psychedelic drugs and other drugs as
physically dangerous and spiritually futile. Meher Baba has declared
"I am the highest of the high," a claim that naturally intrigues
persons preoccupied with the cultivation of "highs." As we stated
earlier, "eastern" mysticism has prestige among drug users. As a
recognized oriental spiritual authority, Meher Baba's forthright
denunciation of the drug medium was bound to produce a stir.
Currently, Baba is avidly adored by small groups of ex-drug takers.
He is admired and respected, by some hippie circles in which he may

not be loved or followed. He is known to wider hippie circles in which he may be neither loved nor respected. (Robbins 1969)

Since the publication of this author's initial article, the Baba movement has continued to grow, and has attracted the attention of various scholarly and journalistic commentators on the contemporary cultic milieu (Needleman 1970; Coty 1971; Rowley 1971). It should be noted that, although Meher Baba currently appeals primarily to youth, he does not appeal exclusively to bohemian or "hippie" youth. Many relatively "straight" youth have been recruited, although the bohemian contingent remains conspicuous and probably disproportionately large.

Rowley (1971) lists Meher Baba as currently having about 7,000 followers in America. Rowley's calculation of the size of various new religious movements in America is "based on information given me by their disciples, as well as my own observations" (Rowley 1971: 3). The Baba movement continues to grow, although it is not nearly as large nor expansive as the better known "Jesus Movement." Since "Baba Lovers" rarely engage in public proselytizing or "street scenes," as do "Jesus Freaks" or Krishna devotees, their visibility is reduced, and this may contribute to an underestimation of their size and influence. The Baba movement is thus probably significantly larger than the far more visible Hare Krishna movement. The Baba movement has, however, gained a certain visibility in the media from the adherence of several well-known musical performers including "Melanie" Safka and Peter Townsend (of the Who). Mr. Townsend recently related his personal experiences as a Baba Lover in an eloquent and perceptive article in *Rolling Stone* (Townsend 1970).

Attitudes toward proselytization vary among Baba Lovers. There is a pervasive tendency toward fatalism, e.g. "if Baba wants someone, he will lead him to the spiritual path," and "let Baba take care of it." This tendency is enhanced by the fact that the Baba meaning system is non-exclusivist and grants the legitimacy of other faiths and other paths to spiritual awakening (see below). Nevertheless, some followers are eager to proselytize and spread Baba's word. It is significant, however, that such proselytization is relatively informal and carried on through primary group processes (i.e., followers "turning on" their friends and acquaintances). Baba Lovers do not chant in the street as do Hare Krishna devotees, nor "witness" in the manner of "Jesus Freaks." When they do (infrequently) proselytize publicly it is usually done quietly by means of a booth or table on a college campus. Thus most followers have "come to Baba" through the influence of friends or acquaintances who follow Baba. There seems to be a frequent pattern whereby a community of Baba Lovers in a certain area will develop around a particular follower who is charismatic and who makes numerous converts through the force of his personality. The prevalence of this pattern may be related to the basic "charismatic" focus of the movement, which emphasizes the person and personality of Meher Baba more than substantive doctrines or practices (Coty 1971). There may be some tendency for persons to use Meher Baba to legitimate or redefine their fascination with specific living significant others.

Meher Baba has said "I have come not to teach, but to awaken," and he de-emphasizes the importance of formal principles and precepts. Nevertheless, he has produced numerous writings and discourses (Meher Baba 1967). His basic "message" emphasizes the metaphysical unity of all persons, summarized in the phrase "We are all one." Meher Baba is himself the personification of this latent unity; he embodies the universal soul which is the "real" or "higher" self of every individual. Baba places a large emphasis on *Love*, through which we can sense an essential oneness with others. As the "Divine Beloved," Baba is the source of all love, and his essence is "infinite love." Through loving Baba, "Baba Lovers" can learn to love others and to sense their oneness with others (see section 8). The highest form of love is Divine Love in which "the Lover has no being apart from the Beloved. He is the Beloved himself." When one attains this intensity with respect to a divine manifestation such as Baba or Christ, one also attains union with God ("God-Realization"). Thus it is through love that one attains spiritual awakening.

> The sojurn of the Soul is a thrilling divine romance in which the lover, who in the beginning is conscious of nothing but emptiness, frustration, superficiality and the gnawing chains of bondage, gradually attains an increasingly fuller and freer expression of love, and ultimately disappears and merges in the divine Beloved to realize the unity of the Lover and the Beloved in the supreme and eternal fact of God as infinite love. (Meher Baba 1967: *III*, 180)

Baba followers also believe in various "eastern" doctrines such as reincarnation, *Karma*, and the illusory nature of all sensate experience (Maya), which conceals the latency of Baba's universal consciousness. Further aspects of Baba's "message" and the beliefs and meanings of Baba Lovers will be discussed in sections 8 and 9. It should be noted, however, that the Baba movement is somewhat inclusive and nonsectarian. Baba followers believe that God takes many forms, and this belief confers a certain legitimacy on other religions which are viewed as varied modes of relating to Baba. Many Baba followers believe that Baba is behind the current reawakening of older religious traditions (Krishna, Buddha, Jesus). On the other hand, most "Baba Lovers" are somewhat alienated from *organized* religion—formal rituals and ceremonies—which Baba compares to the husk on the grain, the shell which surrounds the kernel of true spirituality.

> When the mind expresses itself in patterns of formal rites and rigid ceremonies, it is nothing more than an empty echo of the habit of countless generations, performed automatically without heart! (Meher Baba, 1971)

Moreover, Baba does not define spirituality in terms of any special *technique* such as a particular ritual chant, prayer or form of meditation. As one Baba Lover has recently written:

> The typical question is "What does Meher Baba give you to do?" such as Yoga, meditation, etc. I feel this falls short of the issue, since Baba's main statement is "I have come not to teach, but to awaken." Some people are not fitted to do Yoga, some don't take to meditation, others do not like chanting. The great majority of people are not receptive to these things at all. Everyone's structure and makeup is different and no one way will do. Each must be approached on his own level. (Twig 1972)

Thus, the relationship between Baba and his followers is not mediated by standardized uniform operations (e.g. the Hare Krishna chant), but is particularistic. Baba is viewed as ministering to the unique and special needs of each individual.

Meher Baba has said "I lay down no precepts," and, accordingly, there are few "rules" involved in being a follower of Baba. Indeed, there is a sort of built-in "antinomian" tendency in the movement whereby various life-styles are legitimated, via personalistic interpretations of Baba's teachings. Thus there are many Baba Lovers who "know" that Baba wants them to be celibate. Others appeal to Baba's teaching that "mechanical repression" of impulses is nearly as dysfunctional as uninhibited self-indulgence, since both have the effect of obsessively fixating the individual on the sensation which is being either indulged or repressed. There is a tendency for some followers to use this idea to legitimate hedonistic indulgence, although the majority of followers have changed their life-styles (since conversion) in the direction of greater stability and order. In general, it might be said that the charismatic focus of the movement on the *person* (rather than on the doctrines) of Meher Baba enables followers to focus upon those aspects of his "message" which are most relevant to their own needs and feelings.

The glaring exception to this non-prescriptive emphasis is the issue of drug use. All followers are aware of Baba's forthright views on this matter. Most committed followers have given up drug use. Some gave up drugs prior to becoming Baba followers, while others have given up drugs through Baba. A frequent intermediate pattern involves giving up strong drugs (LSD, amphetamines, opiates, etc.) prior to conversion, and giving up marijuana sometime after conversion. Since the Baba movement has no formal "boundaries" or membership criteria, there are always many persons with some degree of commitment to or interest in Meher Baba who still use drugs.

One of the problems of making generalizations about Baba Lovers is the lack of clear criteria for identifying precisely who is or is not a Baba Lover. Since Baba is viewed as immanent in all persons, "everybody is consciously or unconsciously a Baba Lover," as one devotee told one of the researchers. At one point, one of the researchers overheard an undergraduate doing a term paper on the Chapel Hill Baba group ask one member for a list of Chapel Hill Baba Lovers. The devotee replied that he would be happy to oblige, but that his list would probably differ from any other follower's list. The Baba movement does not have clear "boundaries." There are a huge number of people who are interested in Meher Baba and who manifest varying degrees of commitment. This produces a pattern of concentric circles of marginal membership. At the "center" are persons who are definitely "committed," i.e. are clearly "Baba followers"; but the criteria for identifying these persons are rather difficult to formulate. Anyone can come to Baba meetings or participate in various activities, and numerous people who are not heavily committed nevertheless own books by Meher Baba, hang Baba posters in their apartments, wear Baba buttons, etc.

Unlike the Hare Krishna movement or Scientology, for instance, the Baba movement has no clear or unified authority structure. Local Baba groups are more or less autonomous. Most of them are fairly egalitarian and "anti-structural." The newer and smaller groups are often dominated by a single charismatic leader who may have converted many of the members, but the larger groups are usually not dominated by any single devotee. The membership usually displays hostile attitudes toward any kind of formal ritual or procedure as well as any formal system of authority.[4]

Most local Baba groups meet one or two times a week to read and discuss Baba's writings, see movies of Baba, or listen to talks by older

[4] The authority structure of the Meher Baba movement has recently been analyzed by James Coty (1971).

or better known Baba Lovers. But many deeply commited followers rarely go to meetings and view their relationship to Baba as something deeply personal which cannot be collectivized. On the other hand, most Baba followers associate primarily (but not necessarily exclusively) with other Baba Lovers. Baba Lovers in a given area thus usually constitute a definite *community* and a context for close friendships and informal social associations.

At this point it should be mentioned that there are two formal associations of Baba Lovers, the Society for Avatar Meher Baba in New York City, and Sufism Reoriented in San Francisco, whose organizational frameworks differ from those we have been describing. The internal organization of these groups is more structured than other Baba groups, and the group boundaries are much more clearly defined. We will not discuss these special groups further except to caution the reader that descriptions of the authority structure of Baba groups contained in this paper do not necessarily apply to these groups.

5. An Expressive Community of Believers

Much of our research on the Baba movement was carried out at the Meher Spiritual Center near Myrtle Beach, South Carolina.[5] The Meher Spiritual Center was founded at Meher Baba's direction by western disciples as a place for "rest and renewal of the spiritual life." Situated on 500 acres of virgin forest and fronting on about a mile of ocean beach, it is intertwined with paths. There is a random grouping of 15 to 20 residential cabins and communal buildings of one sort or another near the center of the property. Because Baba spent much time there, his "presence" is generally considered by Baba followers to pervade the area. In addition, the two western disciples who manage the Center spent much time in India as his intimate companions. Their advice and counseling is much sought after by young devotees. A visit to the Center is frequently, therefore, a formative influence in the emergent life-style of neophyte Baba followers. Young Baba followers come there from all over the United States, and it has been the experince of the authors that styles of interaction inculcated at the Center reinforce and give authority to emergent expressive patterns in small groups of believers around the country.

These patterns seem to be a basis for "expressive community" within these groups, and seem to alleviate the "love-starvation" mentioned earlier. For this reason we shall list briefly characteristics of interaction

[5] A vivid journalistic description of the Meher Spiritual Center can be found in Dunn (1968).

at the Center which seem relevant to the expressive quality of these nascent "communities."

1. Organizational procedures at the Center are mostly informal and "personal." Group activities are more or less spontaneously arranged by the people who happen to be there at the time. For instance, dining takes place in communal kitchens, all cooking is done by visitors themselves, and whether this shall be done individually or by groups is left up to the individuals concerned. Resident supervisory personnel live at the edge of the Center, not in the central visitors' area, and are usually seen only by appointment. There are a few rules posted on the cabin walls, but most of these have to do with the exigencies of living in the woods, e.g. carrying a flashlight at night as protection from snakes. A significant exception is a rule against possession of illicit drugs.

2. There is a de-emphasis on formal proselytizing. The only entrance criterion is some interest in Baba or the "spiritual path." Formal or intellectual belief is not emphasized. Baba is quoted as saying "I have come not to teach, but to awaken." An interest in Baba is not considered inconsistent with other "religious" or "worldly" interests. Insofar as there is anything approaching "worship services" at the Center, they take the form of casually arranged get-togethers, e.g. to hear an older follower relate anecdotes of his experiences with Baba, to listen to music or sing, to watch movies of the Master.

3. Interpersonal style at the Center is markedly familial and intimate. Hugs and kisses are customary greetings, occasionally between people just being introduced. This sort of affectionate physical contact is common between people of the same sex as well as opposite sexes, and is not treated as primarily sexual in nature. There are no shibboleths of membership, and there is a lack of defensiveness toward newcomers. Intimate personal information is openly exchanged between relative strangers, and these exchanges cut across normal affinity boundaries, e.g. class, sex, age. People smile ecstatically at each other for no apparent reason. Occasionally someone cries without embarrassment. Although many converts come from "intellectual" backgrounds, most conversation is simple, concrete, and personal.

The impact that this environment can make on a newcomer can be seen in an excerpt from one of our interviews.

> I had my doubts. But as the people started coming in for breakfast and cooking their food, I started getting to talk with them more and more and I just started loving them and it just really sparked something in me to want to find out about Baba, seeing what Baba had done to these people. . . . I sensed a peace in them all. All

their eyes sparked and their faces seemed to have light in them. They were just so warm. No separateness, really. . . . It was just such a loving environment and they had such a love for Baba.

The Meher Center thus plays a central role in establishing the informal and expressive character of the movement. Followers from all over the country meet and lay the groundwork for longterm friendships. The researchers have observed new acquaintances at the Center eagerly writing down each others' addresses and making plans to visit each other. Thus one follower coming to the Center for the first time subsequently traveled north with two other followers from Miami (whom he had met at the Center) and visited other followers in Boston, Mass., and Yonkers, N.Y. (whom he had also met in Myrtle Beach). The nature of the Myrtle Beach Center plus the existence of Baba communities in a number of cities means that a follower who has visited the Center is likely to have friends and acquaintances in various places in which, were it not for his involvement in the movement, he would not know anyone. The authors have observed over the last three years that geographically mobile followers tend to resettle in places in which there are Baba communities.

It has been the authors' experience that social patterns observed at the Center tend to be mirrored within these communities. Like the Center, these groups, while having rather permeable boundaries and no formal membership criteria, seem to supply an expressive social cohesiveness which their members formerly have been unable to find.

A respondent describes a weekly meeting of one of these groups in Atlanta, Georgia:

They're very free and open meetings and very pleasant to attend. There's little routine. We read a little, you know, everybody brings in a little something to read, maybe five or six people bring in something to read. We do a few songs together and discuss this and that. After the meeting a bunch of us will just stick around and just chant things. Several times we stayed until four or five in the morning. We've gone over to our house and had tea and cakes that Jack made and just really had a good time.

In this connection the evolution of the Monday night Baba meetings in Chapel Hill, N.C., is instructive. Initial meetings in the summer and fall of 1967 were highly "theoretical," and were characterized by intense discussions of Meher Baba's cosmology and eschatology. Current meetings in Chapel Hill seem to have a much more relaxed atmosphere and increasingly take on the appearance of a social gathering with refreshments and gossip. The spiritual symbols and belief system of the movement are still objects of deep attachment, but they have become an implicit rather than an overt dimension of collective gatherings and social interaction involving followers. A shared spiritual meaning system operates as an underlying premise of movement-related social phenomena, but is often not the explicit focus of the gatherings. In the opinion of the authors, this does not imply "secularization" in the sense of diminished attachment to cultic symbols and perspectives. It is, however, indicative of the growing socio-communal dimension of involvement in the movement. Thus the "official" Monday and Saturday night meetings of various Baba groups in New York City (run by older followers) have recently been supplemented by "Baba House" in the West Village (run by younger followers) which devotes more attention to social and recreational activities and is currently (1971) sponsoring a sensitivity group and a theater workshop.

In a later section we will analyze the role of the movement's meaning system and of Meher Baba as a "love" symbol in providing the expressive basis for a community of believers. At this point, it will be briefly noted that the representation of Meher Baba within the communities we've visited is consistent with the overtly affectionate styles of interaction among his followers. In the stories told about Baba, and in movies shown of him, he is generally depicted as relating affectively, diffusely, and particularistically to others. Baba is portrayed as jolly, playful, and "loving." He appears to function as a *model* for relationships within the community. Thus the Baba movement can be seen as a vehicle for establishing an expressive basis for community for adults outside of conventional technocratic channels. This community provides continuity with the expressive nature of modern childhood and eases the transition to adulthood by alleviating the "love starvation" felt in bureaucratic vocational milieux.

6. Failure of a Prior Expressive Life-Style

The analysis of the Baba movement in the previous section, while adequate as far as it goes, requires further elaboration to explain certain features of the movement's success.

One such feature: Most of our respondents had been involved in other counter-culture expressive milieux prior to involvement with the group. And such involvement, while it alleviated certain problems, created others of even greater scope. Our interviews revealed that some degree of disillusionment with these milieux generally preceded involvement in the Baba movement. It will be useful, then, in refining our analysis, to compare the Baba movement to the followers' prior drug-oriented "drop-out" expressive milieux; understanding why these involvements "failed" may help us to understand why the Baba movement "works."

After an initial period of feeling pleasure in their release from bureaucratic educational or vocational milieux, many of our respondents began to feel that these drop-out milieux were not appropriate as permanent life situations for adults. These respondents had internalized residues of a middle-class "work ethic" such that prolonged "dropping out" ultimately engendered feelings of anomie. This development is illustrated by the case of one respondent who left school and joined a "clique of long haired freaks" who filled their days with drugs and sex.

> We had an idea of finding some paradise in the woods or some tropical island and just staying in this paradise forever eating acid [LSD] and smoking grass. . . . We thought that just doing what we were doing, taking acid, making love, making music and just trying to be happy all the time was really the free life, and we didn't want to get imprisoned in the life our parents were leading.

But the respondent was never entirely at ease in his psychedelic paradise. His gratifying expressive relations seemed somehow illegitimate because they were not linked to instrumental behavior from which the expressive gratifications could be seen to arise as a reward. The respondent felt guilty and parasitic.

> *Respondent:* I was a parasite. You see, I always felt guilty because I'd say all these things and yet I knew I was a parasite. I knew I was just sucking what I could out of it without doing anything for it. It gave me a few guilty feelings.
>
> *Interviewer:* So you got a feeling that somehow it couldn't be right to just sit around and trip and ball?
>
> *Respondent:* Yes. Exactly. Exactly. I think all through this trip that I knew deep down that it wasn't for me and I always had a hidden feeling that, you know, this is short lived. It's not going to last. But I just blinded myself, just to get away from the thought of ever having to face work and just getting involved in the whole [routinized, work-oriented] life-style.

The respondent's pre-cultic history resembled that of another respondent who, prior to becoming a follower of Meher Baba, had become friendly with Charles Manson (convicted mastermind of the Sharon Tate murders), and spent some time at his California commune. The respondent was initially fascinated and awed by the uninhibited spontaneity which characterized group relationships: "Everyone was real free. . . . These people are all stoned out on acid and really loose . . . and I thought their freeness, their looseness or uninhibited selves was a kind of trip, so I hung around for a while." Subsequently, the respondent became disillusioned and saw the commune members as "sad" and their existence as really "drab" because "They did nothing . . . they'd sit around all day long . . . they'd either ball or eat or take dope." Unable to succumb to the charismatic mystique of Manson, the respondent ultimately perceived the totally non-instrumental communal life-style as devoid of meaning.

The cases presented above indicate that a totally expressive "dropout" life-style may be perceived as conflicting with a conventional "adult" role-identity. Many otherwise "alienated" persons have internalized such identities to a degree that simply "dropping out" is not psychologically viable for them in the long run. For such people, "dropping out" *requires a special legitimating rationale*. What we will refer to as "psychedelic utopianism" appeared to be a common legitimating mystique or pre-cultic meaning system among our respondents. The inherent contradictions and ultimate failure of psychedelic utopianism as a legitimating mystique constitutes a second dimension of the failure of these respondents' pre-cultic expressive milieux.

Formulated by Timothy Leary, among others, psychedelic utopianism stressed the attainment of vital personal growth and expressive community through psychedelic drugs (Leary 1968). Later "hippie" versions of psychedelic utopianism stressed the role of drugs and a drug-oriented life-style in operationalizing universal Love (Yablonsky 1968). One difficulty with psychedelic utopianism for our respondents was that there are intrinsic potentialities in drug use which are inconsistent with the utopian rationales which they utilized to rationalize drug-oriented life-styles. These problems can be illustrated by the case of two individuals who related to one of the authors how they had at one time been very much involved in a sort of utopian mystique centering around the concept of "love." This "love thing" was conceived as a new "way to live, a philosophy to live by." The respondents had some difficulty verbalizing the precise content of the new philosophy-life-style, i.e. how "loving" people and a "loving" life-style differed from conventional patterns. On the other hand, it was generally agreed that one clear difference between loving and nonloving people was that the former used psychedelic drugs while the latter did not. Drugs, however, were not, at least initially, the essence of the "love" scene, drugs were "not really it, *love* was the message." Gradually, however, the respondents perceived that drugs were beginning to overshadow the other elements of the scene. Drugs were becoming the very essence of the scene, and if the respondents ceased to use psychedelic drugs, users would not associate with them and would perceive them as having deserted the scene. The interviewer inquired as to why, in the respondents' opinion, many of their friends eventually "begun to be very attached to drugs, and that became their main thing although it was originally just incidental to a loving philosophy." One respondent commented:

> With drugs the pleasure is so intense that all the senses seem to be dulled while not on drugs and so that becomes the most important aspect. The other things are *intangibles,* like "unity" is intangible but getting stoned and feeling stoned is a very tangible thing.

Drug use thus tends to become an end-in-itself rather than a device to accentuate a "loving" milieu. As such it takes on "non-loving" aspects. Interview data could be presented to illuminate each "anti-utopiate" aspect of heavy drug use. To conserve space this will not be done here. Below we will merely summarize some of the points of tension between drug use and "utopiate" mystiques.

1. Drug dependency often involves the proliferation of highly instrumental relationships with peers, which are treated not as ends in themselves but as means for obtaining drugs. Involvement in these instrumental relationships conflicts with the legitimating mystique of spontaneous, expressive, personalist relationships.

2. The contradiction is particularly sharp when the need for drugs instigates dishonesty—people are "burned" (sold bad drugs) and "ripped off" (stolen from or otherwise cheated)—all of which falls short of "love."

3. The illegal status of "drug abuse" tends to breed "paranoia" over the ever-present threat of a "bust." Persecution of drug users also elicits negative stereotypes and vehemently hostile attitudes toward authorities, parents, "straight" non-users, etc. Many utopiate drug users become aware that these orientations are "unloving" or "separa-. tive" and contravene the mystiques of universal love, unity, and oneness which legitimate deviant patterns.

The use of psychedelic drugs may also cause "intra-psychic" problems which limit an individual's capacity for the interpersonal communion and expressive spontaneity which they were initially intended to enhance. The aftermath of a "bad trip" can leave a user feeling utterly isolated and unable to relate to others (Keniston, 1968). A number of respondents reported traumatic experiences of this nature. One follower recollected:

I couldn't communicate. Like people would ask me questions and I'd completely blow it. Like I wasn't really aware of it at that time. I might say one word three or four times and then go back and ask what had happened, oh you know, "What'd you say?" and then try to figure out what response to make. I had a very difficult time unless it was something just very basic or it was someone I knew very well. . . . I wanted to return to normal. That was like a real driving ambition, the goal of my life.

There are also intrinsic problems of meaning associated with drugs. Drug induced sensations tend to be perceived as ego-alien. They cannot easily be identified with. A follower of Meher Baba has recently described this problem in a confessional article in *Rolling Stone:*

On the surface, then, it seemed I owed a lot to dope. It gave me confidence, it gave me beautiful girls, it gave me R & B. What it didn't give me was the feeling that any of the above were really *mine.* They were all thanks to dope. That's where the paranoia came in. If I hadn't been stoned that solo would have been a bummer. If I hadn't been stoned that chick wouldn't have wanted to know [me]. If I hadn't been stoned the sun wouldn't have come up. (Townsend 1970)

Or as one of our subjects put it,

You can't define on drugs any experience. That's the most important thing. Like I've taken something, and I've seen something, is it me? Is it my subconscious, is it my psyche, or is it the drug? And there's no way of defining what it is, so it's almost useless. . . . You have to say "This is what it is! It's me obviously!" . . . On drugs it can always be the pill, always be the grass. You'll never know.

The current decline of psychedelic utopianism is probably a consequence of the problems we have discussed above. Drug use continues to be a major social problem and a central feature of adolescence and youth. However, it has been observed by several writers that since the middle sixties youthful middle-class drug abuse has been "secularized" (Robbins 1970) in the sense that "it is no longer claimed that recreational drugs have extraordinary value for achieving higher social goals" (Schaps and Sanders 1970). Hence "psychedelic drugs do not now have the spiritual and mystical aura they had several years ago" (Robbins 1969). The "secularization" of drug use is the immediate sociocultural context of the growth of movements such as the Meher Baba movement. As drugs lose their potency as symbols embodying utopian "love" mystiques, other movements, which become increasingly dissociated from drugs, arise to perform their expressive and communal functions. The Meher Baba movement is one such source of expressive symbolism.

7. The Legitimacy Dimension of Expressive Youth Communities

The preceding section has suggested the importance of meaning or *legitimacy* in rendering an expressive milieu viable for its members. This brief section attempts to conceptualize the legitimacy factor, utilizing current theory from the sociology of religion to elaborate our initial formulation of the role-conflict dimension of youthful alienation.

People do not feel confortable in their roles without some rationale which "legitimates" or confers meaning on their experiences. The absence or inadequacy of such a legitimating framework of meaning engenders "anomie" (Berger 1967). In *The Sacred Canopy* (1967) Berger discusses the role of "religions" in legitimating actual social patterns by "locating" them in a "sacred cosmos," i.e. interpreting them as derivative from the inherent nature of things. Assuming the secularization of institutional Christianity, Berger (1965) and Luckmann (1967) have discussed various sexual, familist, or psychoanalytic mystiques which are currently employed to legitimate social experiences and individual life-styles. As these legitimating mystiques are notably "privatized" (Luckmann 1967), they are often inadequate to legitimate *communal* relationships.

Deviant roles and life-styles stand in particular need of special legitimating mystiques. Because the dominant ideology of a society often cannot be utilized to legitimate deviant patterns, there is frequently a liaison between deviant roles and deviant ideologies or religiosity (Peacock 1969).

The problem of legitimacy is particularly aggravated among contemporary American youth. Eisenstadt's analysis of the growing discontinuity between familial-expressive and adult-instrumental milieux implies an increasingly sharp segregation between roles and relationships viewed as appropriate for an "adult" and relational patterns perceived as pertaining exclusively to "childhood." Extra-familial affective, ascriptive, diffuse and particularistic relationships among adults are thus inadequately legitimated. Post-adolescents who "drop out" of conventional instrumental routines and revert to such "childish" patterns will sense the illegitimacy of their behavior and will feel uneasy until an effective legitimating rationale can be developed.

In this connection, both Berger and Weber (from whom Berger

derives his concept of legitimacy) tend to discuss legitimacy primarily in terms of *rationalizing suffering*—the "problem of theodicy" which Weber (1956) and Berger (1967) discuss at length. But gratifying or ecstatic experiences also require a legitimating mystique, as a follower of Meher Baba has recently pointed out in a confessional essay.

> When you begin to realize that your own suffering has a purpose, you can bear it with dignity and poise, admit defeat or admit that you were wrong, without feeling that your life is worthless. Just as human suffering can be borne without too much trouble, so can human ecstasy. (Townsend, 1970)

8. Meher Baba as a Universal Expressive Symbol

In previous sections we argued that expressive role patterns rendered most meaningful by modern childhood will be perceived as inappropriate for adults unless an adequate legitimating rationale is constructed. Given the current fragmentation of expressive and instrumental role systems, an effective strategy for legitimating post adolescent expressive roles is to *universalize them*. Such universalizing is essential to the transmutation of specific values into a "sacred cosmos" (Berger 1967). Moreover, universalized expressive values combine the universalism associated with "adult" instrumental roles with the diffuse solidarity of familial expressive milieux. This combination is a frequent characteristic of "youth movements" (Eisenstadt 1956).

Meher Baba is perceived by his followers as a *universal Saviour*. He is the "Avatar of the Age" and "The Highest of the High." He is a Messiah who incarnates on earth at crucial periods "when the earth is sunk in materialism and chaos as it is now," and who comes to inspire humanity and lead mankind to a higher level of consciousness (Needleman 1970; Robbins 1969). We shall see later that Meher Baba is "universal" in a special sense which involves his immanence in all persons.

The essence of Meher Baba's universal message is "love," which, in its purest form "arises in the heart . . . in response to the descent of grace from the Master" (Meher Baba 1967). Meher Baba descends to impart this grace and awaken love in humanity. In Baba's case, "the medium is the message," in the sense that he is viewed by his disciples as a quintessentially "loving" Master. One follower commented to a researcher: "You can look at Baba's picture and know that he loves you and that he'll never leave you." Baba is thus viewed as a personification of universalized expressivity. A respondent discusses his perception of Baba as an infinitely loving master, the very essence and embodiment of affectivity:

> To me Baba *was* love and with God and love and all, it just seemed a really groovy thing and why didn't somebody tell me about him before? . . . I remember reading, well, like he says, "I can love you more than you can love yourself." Well, I know a little bit about self-love, hassling with it, and like that really seemed incredible to me . . . that I was into a love thing and here it was.

Another respondent comments:

> Love *is* God and *love* is Baba. Baba is love. Baba is God, it's like each one of us—we've got it within us. It's just finding it and finding it through Baba is the best way.

Meher Baba's status as the personified embodiment of love manifests through his relationship with his followers. These role-orientations appear to follow the dimensions of expressivity articulated by Parsons and referred to by Eisenstadt (1956). They are: affective, quality-oriented, diffuse, and particularistic. Baba's "loving" relationships to people are depicted in movies of Baba shown regularly at the Meher Center. One such movie shows Baba tenderly washing lepers, whom Baba is said to have called "beautiful birds in ugly cages." Baba is thus perceived as responding *qualitatively* to persons rather than in terms of their apparent circumstances or attainments.

Although he is the universal savior, Baba is viewed as relating *particularistically* to persons. Followers tend to perceive their relationships with Meher Baba as idiosyncratic in the sense that Baba is perceived as deliberately manipulating their experiences and circumstances to confront them with important learning experiences, challenges, or opportunities. Followers frequently declare that they obtained their jobs through Baba's intervention (see section 9). Below a respondent relates how he feels Baba has subtly manipulated his experiences to help him overcome a neurotic inability to communicate with others.

> . . . it seemed like Baba was putting me in situations where I had to confront this fear of mine, and in confronting it he sort of made me aware, that like it wasn't a big thing. It was never too difficult. It was always a little bit of a time sort of thing so I gradually in a large sense worked out of it.

Thus Baba is perceived as intervening in the unique and particular details of each follower's life-history. He is seen as ministering to each person's distinctive spiritual needs and as aiding in the development of his human potential. This produces a master-follower relationship which is not only idiosyncratic but *diffuse:* Baba is perceived as treating each person differently according to his own distinctive spiritual needs; he is also perceived as controlling and pervading all aspects of one's existence.

The *diffuse* nature of the ideal role-orientation of the "Baba Lover" is expressed in the statement of the respondent below, who is describing his spiritual awakening.

> I understood why I was alive, why I had been born. I was born to love him. That's the only reason I'm here. My life had no other purpose. That's the way I feel. He's my master.

The relationship of the "Baba Lover" to the "Divine Beloved" also has a basic *ascriptive* dimension which derives from the immanence of Meher Baba within each lover as his "real" or "higher" self. Meher Baba is conceived as the personal embodiment of everyone's latent identity. Meher Baba's universal love is thus grounded in his universal identity; he loves everyone as he recognizes himself in everyone. A Baba Lover has recently written:

> Baba loved all kinds of people, he could see God in each and every one of them, the criminal, the prostitute, the beggar, the false saint, the vainly rich, the indulgent westerner, the poet, the drug addict, the pusher, the soldier, the Christian, the Mohammedan, the middle road rock star. (Townsend 1970)

Meher Baba's immanence and his universal identity convert his "loving" role-orientations into universal and archetypal patterns. As such they hold the key to overcoming the segregation and age-specificity of expressive role patterns, which we discussed earlier. Meher Baba's relationship to his followers becomes the basis for interpersonal relationships involving Baba Lovers.

The interview excerpt below expresses the premise accepted by Baba Lovers that loving interpersonal relationships between themselves are derivative from loving relationships to Baba.

> *Interviewer:* Why was it you felt good when you were at the Center?
>
> *Respondent:* Just because of the feelings. Just because of what people were expressing. I could feel Baba coming through these people. I even felt myself expressing these things which I never thought I would.

Thus, "loving" roles in the Baba community, "loving" relationships among Baba Lovers, and "loving" attributes or "vibrations" of a Baba Lover *are seen as emanations of Baba immanent within the lovers.*

In the passage below, the derivation of positive expressive qualities and expressive relationships from inner liaisons with Meher Baba is stated clearly.

> I don't see Charlie as Charlie. Really, I see Charlie as—I see Baba in Charlie. I see Baba in the people in the Center. I see Baba in you. I see Baba in so many of the people in the Center. And it's not the individual Charlie, no, I think it's Baba in Charlie.

Or as another "Baba Lover" commented at a meeting: "Any love I've expressed toward people is just a very very dim reflection of the love I've received from Baba."

Summarizing this section, we have seen that Meher Baba is perceived as having conspicuous expressive role-orientations which, by virtue of Baba's status as universal saviour and immanent divinity, become archetypal and universal. Baba's love is viewed as diffusing through loving relationships among Baba Lovers, which are viewed as derivative from the participants' inner expressive liaison with the Divine Beloved. *Expressive and affective relationships among followers are thus universalized and achieve a transcendental legitimization.*

9. The Problem of Work Roles

This paper has undertaken a functional analysis of the Meher Baba movement, which we have viewed in its integrative aspect as embodying an effective strategy for coping with "alienation." This analysis is still incomplete. Considering youthful "alienation" in Parsons-Eisenstadt role-conflict terms, no "resolution" of alienation is complete without resolution of the perceived tension between instrumental "Establishment" work roles (including preparatory educational roles) and expressive needs which allegedly cannot be satisfied by these roles.

The fact of the "integrative" consequences of involvement in the Baba movement has been cited earlier and is also discussed in an earlier paper by one of the authors (Robbins 1969). Numerous Baba Lovers have been led to give up illegal drug use (Robbins 1969; Dunn 1968; Needleman 1970; Townsend 1970) *and* either resume educational career preparation or exchange casual and primarily menial "odd job" patterns for long-term career involvements. This change usually involves a concommitant upgrading of social respectability. A former "speed freak," and college drop-out who had been convicted of illegal drug use describes his return to college in Chapel Hill after an extended stay at the Meher Center:

> The following year I went back to school. Give it one more try. When I left Chapel Hill, I had been thrown out. Like everybody

was just trying to do me in. The administration, the police. They took me down to a cellar, you know, interrogating me. It was really something. . . . So I went back up there, and I talked to the dean, who a year before had made very serious efforts to have me put in prison. He was shaking my hand, saying, "Oh, it's so good you're back, you're just the kind of boy we need." That was an experience! He did everything but give me a scholarship.

It is the authors' belief that this transition from social alienation to social integration is accomplished through the particular form of universalized expressivity utilized by the Baba movement, i.e. expressive immanence. As explicated in the preceding section, an expressive community of believers is legitimated by this means. As a result, its members no longer suffer from "love starvation," and thus no longer feel a need to rebel against the impersonal institutions of the larger society. In addition, the logic of Meher Baba being the "real" universal self of all people compels a certain tolerance for people who are not followers of Baba. A writer describes a couple of his acquaintances: "Even without knowing about Baba they live and breathe his love, as does everyone, I suppose, but in them it is a fairy tale of color and good vibes" (Townsend, 1970).

A respondent manifests this tolerance with distinct pro-social overtones:

I get along with people more. It used to be, I'd go into the street and I'd see some white collar cat walk down the street and right away he's "The Enemy." I wouldn't like so far as ask him what he thought, he just *looked* like that and I didn't want to have anything to do with him. Or some cat would drive down the street in a Cadillac or something. There'd be no way in the world . . . I didn't want to meet him. But now like I want to talk to people. Even people like that, especially. Go out and tell them about Baba.

It has been argued in this paper that the Baba movement legitimates gratifying expressive relations by building them into a sacred cosmos defined in terms of an immanent divinity (Meher Baba) and his universal prototypical role-orientations. A sacred cosmos operates to legitimate or confer meaning on social experiences (Berger 1967), but it must itself be validated by confirming social experiences. Unless it can be seen to be somehow socially *relevant*, its definitive premise of universality is imperiled.

The *affective* quality of the universal archetypal role-orientation of the "Baba Lover" implies that the worldly activities and relations through which one works out one's unique relationship with Baba and acts out, reaffirms, and ultimately validates one's meaning system must above all be "loving." Thus one demonstrates the social relevance and universality of the Sacred Cosmos by *acting lovingly in the world*.

The next excerpt shows that gratifying relationships between Baba Lovers and non-Baba Lovers are frequently interpreted as manifestations of one of the participants' loving relationship with Baba. The respondent is describing hitchhiking home from the Meher Center.

> Normally, when I'm hitchhiking, I just talk drab with people, but I was so turned on I was really seeing Baba's form everywhere. And I was so full of his love, I was passing it on. You know, Baba says love is self-communicating. It normally would be rare to find a truck driver and a longhair really getting along. But this guy wanted to adopt me and wanted to know all about Baba. And then I got out of his truck and into another truck, and the same thing happened. And it happened all the way back!

Given that Baba followers regard others as manifestations of Baba as an immanent deity, and given Baba's prototypical affective role-orientations, it is hardly surprising that the ethic used to implement the universality of their "sacred cosmos" is one of "selfless service." This orientation, which discourages a "drop-out" life pattern, whether hedonistic or quasi-mystical, can be seen below in an excerpt from a television interview with Kitty Davy, co-supervisor of the Meher Center.

> The Avatar is God in human form. He comes again at the right moment, when the world is in chaos and materialism as it is now, to live again the way of life which is expressed in selfless service, because love means action. Baba says the material and the spiritual must go hand in hand. You cannot stay in a spiritual retreat for your whole life and find God. God must be found in the world, through service, through selfless action.

It has been the authors' observation that most Baba Lovers who remain committed to the movement for any length of time are eventually influenced by this ethic (Robbins 1969). A follower discusses his return to an active routinized life-style:

> Without that [Baba's service ethic] it would have been very easy not to do anything. I still don't feel inclined to work, like I'm not into production. So without Baba's saying do something, I would have probably not done anything positive—I probably wouldn't have gone back to school, since I didn't think school was the answer to my problem or was going to save me in any sense.

There is in Baba's writing an emphasis on the integration of detachment and action. This approach facilitates a modification of the drug-oriented mysticism with which many followers have previously rationalized their drop-out life-styles. In his discourse on "The Dynamics of Spiritual Advancement," Baba advises acting in the world in such a way that one's action is dedicated to the Avatar and one is inwardly detached from the consequences of one's actions.

Acording to Meher Baba, "The object of spiritual advancement is not so much 'works' but quality of life free from ego-consciousness." Nevertheless, one "may have to take to the life of action to wear out the ego one has already developed." This places the spiritual aspirant in a dilemma; action is necessary to wear out his ego, but action can create new layers of ego, particularly if one is attached to fruits of one's action and takes pride in one's actions. Baba resolves this dilemma by advocating a kind of action in which the aspirant views his own actions as not his but Baba's; the aspirant thereby becomes detached from the consequences of his actions which are "in the Master's hands."

> To avoid inaction on the one hand and pride of action on the other, it is necessary for the aspirant to construct in the following manner a provisional and working ego which will be entirely subservient to the master. Before beginning anything, the aspirant thinks that it is not he who is doing it but the *Master* who is getting it done through him. After doing it he does not tarry to claim the results of action or enjoy them, but becomes free of them by offering them to the Master. (Meher Baba 1967: II, 179)

This rationale of inner detachment from the results of one's work makes the impersonality of "technocratic" vocational routines less oppressive. A "detached" resolution of the problem of alienation from work roles is congruent with the increasing tendency of middle class employees to segregate their personal identity from their occupational roles which has been noticed by a number of sociologists (Berger 1965; Luckmann 1957).

Below, a respondent discusses how this ethic of inner detachment mitigated the traumas associated with re-entering school in his confused, post-LSD state of mind.

> Anyhow, the idea of being in it but not of it, was of utmost importance because if I'd tried to go back into it and gotten into it, I really can't imagine being able to come out of my difficulties with as much ease and speed as it happened. Like I think I was in a state of mind that the school would have even reinforced some of that.

It can be seen how Baba's ethic of inner detachment, in conjunction with the expressive context of the "loving" Baba community, enables "alienated" individuals to accept work roles which are not in themselves perceived as intrinsically gratifying or expressive. Moreover, the ethos of "selfless service" actually appears to provide a basis for a limited renewal of personal involvement in interesting and exacting work roles. Some indications of this tendency can be seen in the interview excerpt below.

> The relationship any job brings to spirituality is simply to use what I've been given as selflessly as possible. That is to say, I don't think it's right that if I happen to be a very intelligent person for me to spend my life stringing beads or washing dishes. It has to be put to use and it has to be lined up with the fulfilling of my own *karma*. . . . I don't think from the point of view of God-realization that it matters whether one were a dishwasher or a great scientist, except that if I could have been a great scientist, then maybe I wasn't fulfilling my karma and that's the reason I won't wash dishes any more.

Thus, the "selfless service" ethos can eventually become a basic for renewed "motivation" and career orientation. A sort of mutual validation occurs between the emergent work roles of Baba Lovers and the cultic meaning system. The ethos of "selfless service" facilitates the crystallization of career involvements, which, in turn, act out the cultic "love" orientation and make it appear socially relevant. Baba Lovers thus strive to articulate their emergent work roles with their sacred cosmos. This striving is commented on below by a disillusioned former Baba follower interviewed in the present study.

> I have a job I really like, you know, working with kids. If I was still into Baba, I'd say "Oh, Baba found me this job," like people say, "Oh, it's because of Baba I found this house, oh he directed me to. . . ." That's what people do, say it's Baba. People have a way of fooling themselves . . . whenever they're going to do something, they say they're doing it for Baba. You know, I'm saving humanity . . . Baba has helped me to do this. Because of Baba I found this service. But if you really want something, it's there. You can say, "Well, Baba has helped me find it," or Jesus or anything.

The respondent's comments indicate the degree to which Baba Lovers continually strive to relate all their worldly activities to their religious involvement in such a way that the former is viewed as inspired by and derivative of the latter. A process of mutual or reciprocal validation appears to take place whereby the religious meaning system legitimates ("loving") worldly roles which in turn reinforce the meaning system.

10. Conclusion

In section 3 of this paper, we outlined arguments from Berger, Slater, and Eisentadt. Berger indicated that children raised in a modern technocratic setting would perceive themselves as affectively deprived when attempting to make the transition from the familial "expressive" milieu to the adult bureaucratic "instrumental" milieu. Slater described the alienation of modern youth from the "scarcity premises" which are typically used to legitimate participation in adult instrumental milieux. Eisenstadt has argued that *youth movements which seem to be attempting to perpetuate this expressive milieu in adult life often actually function to integrate the expressive and instrumental systems of role orientation.*

In this paper we have argued that the Meher Baba movement has chosen one of the role-orientations from the instrumental system, *universalism,* and integrated it with role-orientations from the expressive system. In this way they have *legitimated expressive role orientations for adults.* Universalism seems to be a particularly useful orientation for legitimating expressivity, as it allows the elaboration of expressive role-orientations into a "sacred cosmos." This sacred cosmos, which presents itself as reflecting the nature and purpose of the universe, naturally supersedes all merely conventional institutions if their mandates should happen to conflict. It is thus an effective device for legitimating structural social change, such as the ones arising from the fragmentation of modern society into a bureaucratic instrumental system, and an expressive familial system.

The traditional "work ethic," which rationalized the old small entrepreneurial instrumental-expressive synthesis of role orientations, derived expressive values from instrumental ones. Thus Parsons (1937, 1961), paraphrasing Weber, has pointed out that Calvinism viewed man as an instrument for enhancing God's glory. This instrumental concept of man legitimated the assimilation of one's identity to a specialized instrumental work role. The "sacred cosmos" of Baba followers supersedes that ethic, by deriving instrumental values from expressive ones. It thus reduces the tension between conditions of modern childhood and the instrumental roles rationalized by the old ethic.

Other modern youth movements can also be seen as attempting to legitimate expressive role-orientations as a basis for community in adults by universalizing them. Thus we described the "hippies" attempt to universalize their drop-out drug-oriented expressive life-style into an ethic of psychedelic utopianism. We saw that this attempt failed, at least for certain of our respondents, for two reasons: (1) the ethic led to behavior which was inconsistent with itself, e.g. use of drugs led to unloving behavior, and (2) it failed to include enough of the instrumental role-orientations in its synthesis, and thus never seemed quite legitimate to many of our respondents.

The Baba movement seems to have escaped these problems in that (1) its ethic does not produce consequences which are obviously in-consistent with it, and (2) it ameliorates the problem of "loveless" work roles in adult instrumental milieux by "deriving" instrumental role-orientations (qua "selfless service") from expressive ones, not by trying to eliminate them entirely. It could be argued that insofar as a modern youth movement violates the second requirement, it will inevitably violate the former. That is, certain instrumental functions are necessary for the perpetuation of a total culture. If a subculture attempts to legitimate expressive functions by universalizing them, without including vital instrumental functions, it cannot maintain itself except as a specialized subsystem of the larger society. It must then, by its own logic of legitimation, convince the larger society to support it, because its "expressive" values rather than the larger society's "instrumental" values are the truly "universal" ones. But if the larger society were to accept this logic, it would adopt the purely expressive values of the sub-culture, and instrumental functions neces-sary to its maintenance would disappear. Thus, in order to maintain itself, the adult society rejects the love ethic of the hippies, and an escalating conflict between "hippies" and "straight" society appears. "Hippies" thus become "Yippies," love-ins evolve into hostile con-frontations (with "Amerika"), and the love-ethic has become incon-sistent with itself.

The particular form of universalism the Baba movement has chosen to legitimate its expressive values—expressive immanence—seems to have allowed it to escape these problems. This doctrine, which pre-sents the same loving self as the "real" self of all, obviates "seeming" conflicts of opinion and belief. If one "self" is present in all, and that "self" is loving, then people who have "realized" this must act in a way consistent with this awareness.[6] They must attempt to act

6 It is not our intention to explain Baba's "worldly" service ethic and its integrative and "resocializing" consequences solely on the basis of Baba's im-manence. The usual consequences of immanentist doctrines are "retreatist," as they imply the possibility of making direct contact with God through intense spiritual endeavour (i.e. meditation) which usually involves social withdrawal. In the case of the Meher Baba movement, the key factor is the emphasis on

"lovingly" toward others, whether those others consciously accept their ethic or not.

In order to remain self-consistent, this form of universal expressivity is elaborated into a service ethic, which synthesizes expressive and instrumental role-orientations. The cult's ethic incorporates the instrumental values which allow it to perpetuate itself within the larger society, while maintaining the expressive emphasis which gave it birth.

"love," and Baba's archetypal "loving" role-orientations. In the context of this theme, immanence operates to facilitate social re-integration. One must love Baba and this involves loving others in whom Baba is immanent. In consequence, one best validates and operationalizes the movement's meaning system by acting lovingly in the world, which precludes retreatism.

Symbols and Innovation:
Belief Systems and Ritual Behavior

ONE of the characteristics of the newer, modern religions is their rejection of centralized bureaucratic structures. Stillson Judah (1967) noticed the trend to autonomous, lay-organized groups that stress maximum contact with and responsiveness to individual believers. Robert Bellah has discussed a set of stages for religious evolution which places "modern" religion as the most recent type of religious phenomena seen in complex societies. "Modern" religion is thought of by both these scholars as a highly individualized approach to the relationship between man and the supernatural. And this approach is generally assumed to preclude highly organized ecclesiastical church structures and all-pervasive leadership.

Most of the religious movements discussed in this book fall into this class of "modern" religion and yet, on at least one count each, both Mormonism and Scientology appear to be exceptions. Mormonism, on one hand, presents a public appearance of a hierarchical, highly centralized, and bureaucratized church. Scientology, on the other hand, is completely dominated by L. Ron Hubbard who is its founder, inventor, guide, and leading thinker. Scientology *is* L. Ron Hubbard and seems to be completely pervaded by him, and as a result it seems natural to ask where is the individualization of belief so characteristic of pragmatic religions. How then is it that these two movements find a home as "modern" religions, as movements allied to all of those others discussed in this book, when they are both so centrally and hierarchically organized, one by its bureaucracy and the other by its charismatic founder?

In the case of Mormonism, Dolgin points out that Biblical literalism and controlled hierarchical management hide a great diversity in doctrinal matters. While it is true that neither the scholarly world nor in some cases the Mormons themselves are aware of that diversity, it is nonetheless the case that Mormons have as much theological freedom as any of the American marginal churches. Dolgin points out that the degree of freedom enjoyed by Mormons in matters of belief is possible under the aegis of a stable social organization. The fairly tightly defined structure of the church provides a set of self-conceptions which give Mormons a secure place, in their own view, in the working of reality. It is this stable framework that outsiders view as the totality of Mormonism.

The doctrinal diversity that exists in Mormonism and which is one of the features linking it to "modern" religious phenomena is paralleled in Scientology. Most of the churches we have been dealing with offer not just close ties between adherent and the means of reaching the transcendent, but they cater to the practical problems the faithful bring to the church. The Mormon statement of that relationship is Brigham Young's famous quote, "That religion which cannot save a man temporally cannot save him spiritually." For Scientologists the contact linking the individual, his personal problems, and the transcendent is auditing of *engrams*. Engrams are crises that have occurred in the past to an individual and the examination of them is the process of auditing. During auditing, which is carried on individually with a professional Scientologist, a person becomes aware of the forces he was previously unaware of that guide his behavior and life.

While Hubbard himself continues to elaborate the beliefs and principles of Scientology, church members come into contact with these pronouncements by belonging to local groups called *orgs*. It is in these centers that the individual is audited, and here he ties this very personalistic process to the larger vision of reality supplied by Hubbard through his professionals and publications.

Most of the scholars in this book are concerned with the social or psychological consequences of a religious movement. Many describe the belief system of the churches they are concerned with, but Dolgin and Whitehead are in particular more concerned with the internal dynamics of belief systems. Dolgin examines the Mormon's view of his place in the universe, especially his view of his fellowmen. Her particular concern is how Mormon metaphysics is shaped and expressed through rituals. Whitehead builds a detailed and complex historical sketch of Scientology's intellectual foundations. She examines the intersection of science fiction, psychoanalysis, and occultism as they are combined under L. Ron Hubbard's direction to form Scientology. The most widespread activity of Scientologists is auditing and it is shown as the ritual manifestation of the basic belief system.

Dolgin focuses on the mode of articulation between the individual Morman and the organizational framework of the church. First, how does the highly-structured Mormon church sustain and foster creedal independence, and second, how do the members of the Church maintain their perceived unity as Mormons despite the wide diversity among individual Mormons' systems of belief? How do they decide what makes an individual Mormon and a Mormon an individual? By examining the Mormon ritual system in an effort to integrate these two problems, she indicates how the Mormon himself uses his culture's symbols to order and define his world.

Toward this aim Dolgin uses two models. First is David Schneider's model of American kinship which deals with the relationship between code for conduct and the idea of natural substance. She uses the Mormon concept of blood as natural substance. Mormons can see themselves as part of one family. In addition to the natural relation among Mormons as the members of one blood group, there are also certain behaviors which are associated with being Mormon. What the Mormon church manifests therefore is a unisubstantial universe, one that is explicitly unified by blood and often implicitly unified in behavior. It is the unisubstantial nature of the Mormon community that is at least partly responsible for the maintenance of the idiosyncratic belief systems among individual Mormons. Tolerance for diversity can emerge within a community where, at the very level of blood, the community is one. She concludes, using a structural model, by examining the Mormon ritual systems. These are composed of three ritual subdomains: temple ritual, church ritual, and civil ritual—and are used to define and structure attitudes to contemporary concerns, particularly those pertaining to relations between Mormons and non-Mormons.

A concern with how worldview is constructed and internally articulated is also one of the motivations behind Whitehead's treatment of Scientology. Scientologists share a belief with occultists that each group is on the way to the Truth, and in that sense no one is precluded from any of the alternatives offered to any and all who are "spiritual shoppers." Because of the intimate connection between Scientology, science fiction, and the standard Western scientific tradition, no conflict is felt with science, for each tradition is on the road to knowing the Truth in its own way. Whitehead links the growth of Scientology to the church's own claim that a deficiency exists in established Western styles of knowing and comprehending reality. Science has become so particularized and rationalized that it can no longer provide a coherent and emotionally satisfying view of all reality. Science has divorced itself from too many of the critical domains that a real natural philosophy would attend to. Consequently other traditions with a bolder and more vital outlook fill this gap, two of them being science fiction and the world of the occult. These two, coupled with a fascination for technology and an element of psychoanalysis, produced Scientology. The mystical and transcendent are introduced into it in part through science fiction. This literary genre, having developed from around the turn of the century, has produced writers, including L. Ron Hubbard, who fill a role not unlike that of the mystic and seer.

The science fiction writer, like the medieval magician and the modern Scientologist, bridges the gap between ordinary, mundane knowledge and the seemingly fantastic.

For both Dolgin and Whitehead, the interrelationships between belief and ritual are mediated by a structure of meanings called symbols. The problem for some recent theoreticians in religion has been reconciling the atomization and individuation of belief structures and the predicted but hardly universal decline of ecclesiastical institutions. It is to this area that Mormonism and Scientology have provided answers.

Latter-Day Sense and Substance

THE Church of Jesus Christ of Latter-Day Saints presents the analyst with a set of anthropological paradoxes. The Church is literalistic yet encourages creedal independence; it is authoritarian yet values individualism; and it is organizationally stable yet adapts to the vicissitudes of social reality.

Recent observers of contemporary Western religion have noted the modulation of conventional forms of worship and the decline of traditional sacred authority. Thomas Luckmann has depicted present-day religion as a "new social form of religion" (Luckmann 1967: 104), a "private" phenomenon, not mediated by primary social institutions. Luckmann's "invisible religion" shares certain important characteristics with Robert Bellah's (1970) delineation of "modern" religion—in particular, a radical attenuation of the role of traditional churches and a flexible, individualistic system of thought.

This paper will attempt to show how Mormonism is a "modern" religion. The argument will begin with a consideration of Robert Bellah's model of religious evolution. The paper will focus on the mode of articulation between the Mormon individual and the organizational framework of the Church. The issue will be approached from two directions. First, I shall attempt to show how the apparently authoritarian Mormon Church sustains, and indeed fosters, creedal independence. Then, approaching the problem from an opposite direction, I shall try to show how the members of the Church maintain their perceived unity *as* Mormons, despite the wide diversity among individual Mormon's systems of belief. Finally, I will examine the Mormon ritual system in the effort to integrate these two approaches by indicating how the Mormon himself uses his culture's symbols to order and define his world.[1]

[1] The National Institutes of Mental Health and Princeton University sponsored the study of Mormon communities in east-central Arizona. I owe a special debt to Professor M. P. Leone, who was the principal investigator for this research project. A major section of the paper (part IV) developed through discussions with Professor S. A. Barnett. I would also like to express my appreciation to Professors Alfonso Ortiz and M. G. Silverman and to Messrs. John Kirkpatrick and Richard Parmentier for critical comments and to Mr. A. L. Bush, Curator, Princeton Collections of Western Americana, for invaluable scholarly assistance.

519

II

Bellah's model is based on the notion of evolution as involving increasing differentiation and organizational complexity within the (religious) system (Bellah 1970). While acknowledging the unsuitability of a strict linear (i.e. historical) correspondence, Bellah posits five stages of religion, beginning with what he calls "primitive religion" and ending with "modern religion." The essential character of the evolution entails increasing "freedom of personality and society" in relation to the larger environment (Bellah 1970: 44).

Superimposed upon the general evolutionary scheme is a perceived alteration between world rejecting and world accepting religious systems. The "primitive" and "archaic" forms are world accepting. "Historic" religion (and here Bellah includes Buddhism, Taoism, Islam, Confucianism, Judaism, and Catholicism) express a devaluation of this world in relation to the transcendental realms of divinity. The last two stages in Bellah's scheme, "early modern" and "modern," are once again accepting of this world.

The early modern phase, of which the Protestant Reformation is the only fully adequate illustration, maintains the "historic" division between heaven and earth but declares earthly activity ("work") a necessary concomitant to ultimate redemption. Bellah views the "social implications" of the Reformation within a Weberian framework, seeing its causal interconnections with the advent of capitalist and democratic social forms. The most decisive attribute of the early modern stage (social as well as religious) is the institutionalization of a "self-revising social order" (Bellah 1970: 39). Change, itself, became the fundamental constant of the new social form.

It is, of course, Bellah's typification of the modern stage which is most pertinent to the present paper. It is the most difficult stage to decipher because its limits and potentialities can only be discerned through the hyperopic mirror of the moment. Significantly, it is to Kant, a philosopher—and not a theologian—to whom Bellah turns when tracing the intellectual origins of a modern symbol system. The vital innovation of the modern situation is the replacement of the dualistic universe of the historic religions by an "infinitely multiplex" world (1970: 40). Bellah's modern man is faced with both the chaos of a multiplex symbolic universe and the potential for seizing his own "fiction" and revising it in the name of his own salvation.

The consequence of the new modes of religious actualization is the preclusion of stable or authoritarian forms of religious organization. Small groups of concerned individuals may come together for the joint realization of social and personal goals, only to disintegrate as the relevant goals are redesigned. The role of traditional churches may not be absolutely lost but, at the very least, radically foreshortened. Churches may provide appropriate social settings for the (symbolic) quest, but they can no longer pose as guardians of the final treasures or, indeed, tell man what those treasures are.

Without presuming to enter the by-now classic discussion concerning "secularization"—what it means, where it exists, and why—it seems relatively certain that Bellah's modern symbol maker is *homo religiosus* without being a man with a religion.[2] In particular, "religion," (as opposed to "religious") seems to demand the manifestation of a concomitant organizational system beside its systems of action and symbolization. At the level of collective religious action Bellah can see little possibility for an (even relatively stable) system of religious organization in the "modern" period. At the level of the individual he recalls Paine's "My mind is my Church" and Jefferson's "I am a sect myself"; here, any distinction between "religious" and "religion" would merge with sophistry and semantics—a singularly unprofitable combination.

Given Bellah's religious individual—without a religion—(the man for whom "loss of faith" has meaning), is there an equally modern man who understands "loss of faith" but does not experience it?

The set of religions which J. Stillson Judah (1967) has identified as modern "metaphysical movements" (e.g. Spiritualism, Christian Science, The Unity School of Christianity) clearly manifest much of what Bellah has noted as the religious essence of twentieth-century man. Judah has delimited several themes which are especially characteristic of the metaphysical movements. In particular, one might note: "principles" without creeds which ordain the individual as the final reservoir of his own salvation, the collapse of a static transcendentalism, the identification of science and religion as complementary and mutually supportive modes of orientation within the world, and the psychotherapeutic approach to internal and external well-being (Judah 1967: 12–19).

There are a number of significant ways in which Mormonism is akin to the metaphysical religions. Some of the more obvious similarities will be noted below. Clearly, it would be nigh impossible to summarize a major synthesis such as Judah's without admitting some distortion. My aim here is not to suggest that Mormonism should be

[2] This assertion applies that much more forcibly with regard to Bellah's article on "Civil Religion in America" (1970). His delimitation of the obviously religious themes which reinforce the civic domains with the aura of sacred authority and acceptance is a profound insight into the nature of American society. A religious polity and a civil religion are not, however, synonymous.

viewed as a metaphysical movement. Rather, the comparison is intended to make obvious some of the more important divergences of Mormonism and the metaphysical movements, alike, from traditional Christianity.

The early metaphysical leaders, strongly influenced by the transcendental philosophers, rejected the doctrinal theology of traditional Christianity. In particular, the metaphysical movements do not endorse the notion that man is naturally a sinner, tend to discard or redefine the Christian concepts of atonement and grace, and profess a belief in the "inner, or real, self of man [as] divine" (Judah 1967: 13). In addition, these movements hold that religion has scientific uses, including the restoration of health and the improvement of material conditions.

Certainly, Mormonism divorced itself, both ideologically and socially, from Reformation Protestantism. The Mormon theological system, developed in large part during the mid-nineteenth century, rests on the notions of immediate revelation in this world and the "eternal progression" of "worthy" men toward godliness. Since every Mormon male has the potential to become a god, the insurpassable qualitative gap between God and man, assumed by Reformation Protestantism, is replaced in Mormonism by a bridgeable separation. In so far as God was once a man and men may become gods, there is no absolute boundary between the finite and the infinite. Within the Mormon theological system the atonement of Christ is viewed as having secured the possibility of salvation and resurrection for all men. Christ "undid" the sins of Adam, and this undoing was for the sake of all men.

The "psychological approach to reality" (Judah 1967: 16) and the need to "demonstrate the scientific validity of different kinds of religious experience" (15) which Judah observed among the metaphysical groups also find a place in Mormonism. The Mormon approach to healing, as presented in the Commentary on the *Doctrine and Covenants* (1965), Section 66, asserts:

> There are two kinds of healing. . . . Mental healing is done through "suggestion" or even "auto-suggestion." The spirit within is an intelligent being and is greatly helped, in its effort to repair tissue or withstand the attack of diverse agencies, by the suggestion of others who have great will-power. . . . Spiritual healing is by the Spirit of God, through the Priesthood. It is healing effected by the Holy Spirit imparting the strength necessary to overcome the causes of diseases, and it often operates instantaneously.

The Mormon constantly reaffirms the validity of his religion through experience. The authority to heal or to be healed (*Doctrine and*

Covenants 1965: 46, 4c), the attainment of prosperity (among the "worthy"), and successful prediction of future events through prophesy, all stand as witness to the "science" within "religion."

Mormonism differs from the metaphysical religions (and from Bellah's modern *homo religiosus*) in its stabilization of an inclusive social framework and its ostensibly authoritarian mode of religious association.[3] The basic characteristic which Bellah imputes to the man of modern religion and which Judah sees in the metaphysical movements is the "increasing privatization" (Bellah 1970: 224), the "universal freedom of belief" (Judah 1967: 22)—individualism, in short, and it is this very individualism which seems so antithetical to organized forms of authoritarian control. To be sure, the Mormon Church has repeatedly been typified as literalistic and dogmatic in its interpretations of the sacred scriptures (e.g. Brewer 1968; O'Dea 1957; Whalen 1964). In fact, the Church is both literalistic *and* individualistic, and it is the nature of this seemingly paradoxical combination which is primarily responsible for the phenomenal success, both qualitative and quantitative,[4] of the Mormon Church.

None of the movements about which Judah has written have managed to devise a system of organization and control even approaching the well-defined social structure of the Mormon Church. These movements are, in varying degrees, explicitly uncomfortable with institutionalized authority. Geoffrey Nelson, in his study of Spiritualism, notes an early and "strong element of resistance to formal organization . . . [with] suspicion to organization continuing to the present

[3] The Priesthood of the Church is composed entirely of laymen. It is divided into two orders, the higher order or Melchizedeck Priesthood and the lower order or Aaronic Priesthood. Each Priesthood is, in turn, segmented into three levels through which the individual male may move according to criteria of age and "worthiness." The First Presidency stands at the top of the Church organization and is composed of the Church President (the Prophet) and his two counselors. The "General Authorities" of the Church include the First Presidency together with the Presiding Bishopric, the Church Patriarch, the Council of the Twelve Apostles and the First Council of Seventy. The membership is divided, according to geography, into stakes which, in turn, are composed of several wards. A Stake Presidency and High Council have primary responsibility for activity within the stake. At the level of the ward the Ward Bishopric has prime authority within the local Priesthood. In addition, the Church contains a number of "auxiliary organizations" which are entrusted with various responsibilities such as the preparation of genealogical material, the operation of local Sunday Schools, and the provision of recreational activities. In particular, women and young children become active participants in the Church via the various auxiliary organizations (O'Dea 1957, Whalen 1964).

[4] Membership has increased consistently since the emergence of the Church in the early nineteenth century. Current membership exceeds two million (Jacquet 1970). A comparatively large number of nominal Mormons are also "good" Mormons.

day among certain sects of the movement" (Nelson 1969a: 102). This attitude is not atypical of the other metaphysical movements.

If Mormonism is truly a "modern" religion, how then to explain its secure system of authorized officialdom? Is it a fluke, the inexplicable exception which proves the rule? I think not. In fact, Mormonism's "modern" symbol system and apparently vestigial patterns of social organization are not precariously welded together in an unseemly, albeit ostensibly viable, social whole. The ideological and social forms are well integrated; it is no accident that Mormonism has survived.

III

Bellah sees in the modern religious forms the implications for "endlessly revisable" systems of culture and personality (Bellah 1970: 44). His model for the cultural and psychological flexibility in the modern period is the alterations which obtained in the social system during the early modern phase. Accepting a Weberian explanation of the interrelations between the Reformation and attendant political and economic changes, Bellah points to the early modern period as having witnessed the inception of a "built-in tendency [of the social system] to change in the direction of greater value realization" (1970: 39). In fact, the type of change which Bellah posits for the personality and cultural systems in the modern period is not fully analogous with the alterations during the early modern period in the social system. The particular innovation of the democratic social system is the fact that change becomes a constant; contingency is built into structure. It is, as Bellah notes, precisely the institutionalization of change (at whatever "level") which enables the preclusion of "pathological distortions" (1970: 44), which unstructured flexibilities can hardly avoid.

Mormonism, like Bellah's modern *homo religiosus,* has "ever-revising systems" of personality and culture, but unlike the modern religious forms which Bellah describes, Mormonism has "built change in" to its notions of man and of ideology.

At the level of personality and revising self-identifications, the Mormon is expected (and expects) to "progress" in the direction of godliness. Every individual has an essentially dynamic core; even the divinity began as a less than absolutely adequate personnage and progressed to his current state of godliness only through time. Thus the relationship between man and god is not static. For the Mormon there is, in this time, no attainable goal of perfect faith, work, prosperity, or knowledge. Because man is inherently capable of becoming a god, the Mormon notion of progress implies far more than the Christian (and, indeed, American) value of "doing the best one can." Built into each person is a dynamic relation between himself today, himself tomorrow (as a god) or yesterday (as an unembodied intelligence).

It is not unusual for Mormons to draw an explicit correlation between spiritual progress (toward godliness) and material prosperity on this earth. One Mormon informant in east-central Arizona told me: "We should work for spiritual progress, but material progress and economic success go with it. Work for spiritual progress and the rest will come later." This notion has found its way into some of the official Church commentary on sacred scripture. In *Doctrines of Salvation* Joseph Fielding Smith writes: "The Lord will bless Zion. He will pour out his Spirit upon the people. He will prosper them . . ." (J. F. Smith 1969: I, 245). The association between spiritual and material progress operates at both the level of the individual and of mankind in general. A particular man's economic prosperity is often taken as a sign of spiritual "worth." But on a more inclusive plane, the technological progress [5] of America may be equated with the approaching millennium.[6] For the Mormon the Celestial Kingdom and IBM are not mutually exclusive; in fact, each seems to reinforce the validity (and value) of the other.

More significant still than the notion of spiritual and material progress through time, with regard to the flexibility of Mormon symbolization, is that of the restoration of divine revelation. The actualization of a direct and immediate communicative link between gods and men is the cardinal (and innovating) neologism of the Mormon Church when compared with traditional Christianity. Through revelation the Mormon can receive the word of God on earth and thus procure the highest sanction for the certainty of his own knowledge. Joseph Smith was the first prophet in these "latter-days" (i.e. in these days of the restoration of God's Priesthood on earth); succeeding Smith, each president of the Church has been a prophet and a link between divine truth and the community of Mormons on earth.

The possibility of continual revelation has enabled Mormonism to propose and legitimize essential ideological and social adjustments in the community's theology and social organization. Mormons hold that God has attained absolute knowledge. Yet often the revelations given to one prophet seem antithetical with those obtained through another prophet. The revelations concerning polygamy are perhaps the most

[5] For example, "Yet I maintain that had there been no restoration of the gospel and no organization of the Church of Jesus Christ of Latter-day Saints, there would have been no radio, . . . no airplane . . . [no] wonderful discoveries in medicine, chemistry, electricity . . ." (J. F. Smith 1969: I, 182–183).

[6] The millennium in Mormonism is a 1,000-year period when the forces of good will overcome the forces of evil.

well-known case of this sort. In 1852 the revelation received by Joseph
Smith, which made the practice of polygamous marriage a divinely-
inspired form of family organization, was publicly read and accepted
by the General Conference in Salt Lake City. In 1890 President Wilford Woodruff issued a revealed "manifesto" declaring the proscription
of polygamous unions. The new revelation was "unanimously" sustained by the Mormons present at the 1890 General Conference. This
seeming uncertainty on the part of the Lord, Himself, does not pose
an ideological problem for the Church. What may seem to be conflicting messages received by the Prophet through divine revelation
only reflect, for the Mormon, altered conditions on earth.

The possibility of revelation from God has backed up fundamental
scriptural modifications. Despite the belief in an all-knowing God and
the acceptance of his laws in the form of a theology, the Church has
also become its own symbol maker and reformulator.

So far, however, it seems to be only the Church, in its role as admin-
istrator of sacred authority, which seems to be "capable, within limits,
of continual self-transformation . . ." (Bellah 1970: 42). The individual Mormon appears to remain as heavily dependent on "standards
of doctrinal orthodoxy" as any man of the early modern or historic
periods.

Yet, despite the explicit theological formulations of the official
Church, individual Mormons construct personal conceptions of
man and the world which are marked in their diversity.[7] Beneath the
"canopy" of a universal symbolic form, the interpretations of the
official theology by individual Mormons produce belief systems which
vary enormously from person to person.[8] The individual Mormon *is*
his own symbol maker, his "sect in himself."

Mormons themselves do not tend to explicitly acknowledge the
disparities between individual beliefs and standard theology. Yet
when discussing theological issues Mormons do exhibit a wide toleration for nonorthodox interpretations. The level of consciousness at
which these interpretations are *perceived* as non-standard is an important issue. I do not have the necessary data to fully analyze this
question. It is, however, significant to note that Mormons tend to
rely on official exegesis more often when they are aware of being in
the presence of non-Mormons. To use an extreme illustration, the
conversion lessons, which are provided for potential converts, present a

[7] For additional discussion of the wide variation in belief between individual
Mormons, see Leone (1969).

[8] Unfortunately, I do not have the data which would be needed to decipher
the structure of the ideological variation among the members of the Church.

uniform message which does not seem to be highly dependent on the particular belief system of the missionary-teacher.

In large part, the theological and social unity of Mormons in the face of non-Mormon Americans is precisely responsible for the maintenance and toleration of ideological diversity within the Mormon community. Relevant aspects of the manner in which Mormons perceive themselves in contrast to non-Mormons and the way in which those perceptions foster internal toleration will be discussed below.

The phenomenon of variant interpretations and conceptions from individual to individual is not completely devoid of sacred support. Within the Church each individual is capable of receiving revelations. The number of persons to whom a particular revelation applies varies according to the position of the receiver within the Church. Only the President (the Prophet) of the Church can receive revelations which have applicability for every Mormon; the bishop of a ward may be the recipient of revelations which pertain to the members of his particular ward; similarly, to the head of a household come revelations which are binding upon that family, alone; the implications of a revelation received by an individual woman or child do not extend beyond that particular person. There is, therefore, no member of the Church who does not, himself, have a potential communicative link with divine knowledge. Bruce McConkie, in his compilation of *Mormon Doctrine* writes, concerning revelation: "With reference to their personal affairs the saints are expected . . . to gain personal revelation and guidance rather than to run to the First Presidency or some other Church leaders to be told what to do" (McConkie 1966: 645).[9]

Within the Church there are at any one time a set of official exegeses about the Church's theological system. In addition, there are the divergent belief systems of the individual Mormons—based on the individual's relationship to both the sacred theology and the secular ideologies and social realities of the "everyday" world.

Application of Ferdinand de Saussure's (1959) model pertaining to the relation between the signifier and the signified can offer clarification as to the dynamics of Mormon belief(s). The Church provides its membership with particular signifiers (e.g. words, images, even concepts). Presumably (i.e. from the point of view of the official Church)

---

[9] For any individual, regardless of position, there is the possibility for personal delusion with respect to the validity of apparent revelations. The Mormon who questions the divine authenticity of a particular revelation he receives may ask the revealer to shake hands. If the revealer agrees to shake hands, but his hand cannot be felt, he is Satan, for Satan, unlike the divinity, does not have a body of "flesh and bones."

the signifiers relate to specific signifieds; there are, that is, official signs, or concepts (signifier (Sr)/signified (Sd). In fact, each Mormon has his own conceptual set ($Sr^{1, 2, \cdots n}/Sd^{1, 2, \cdots n}$) which is not necessarily isomorphic with that of the "Church" or of his fellow Mormon. Because these concepts tend to employ official signifiers in the service of idiosyncratic signifieds, the correspondence between Church theology and religious idiolects looks closer than it actually is.

In so far as Mormons profess the possession of a unified belief system, the relation between the official ideology and the actual assumptions of faith and value of particular Mormons is an opaque relation; that is, to the extent that Mormons are *not* conscious of the divergences between the official theology and individuals' belief systems, they are operating under the illusion that the signifier is truly the signified. Personal reinterpretation goes on all the time, but it goes on in such a way that the idiolects and the official theology often appear consistent. The non-isomorphism of the relation between the Church theology and the individual's beliefs is in part *the result of* asserted (i.e. perceived) isomorphism. A diagrammatic (and radically simplified) model of the relation between the standard ideology and individual Mormon's ideology might look like Figure I.

Often, the beliefs of a majority of Mormons will coalesce at a point which is blatantly inconsistent with the official theology. In such a case, the new (majority) interpretation can be reinserted into the Church

FIGURE I. Relation Between Church Theology and Individual Mormon's Beliefs

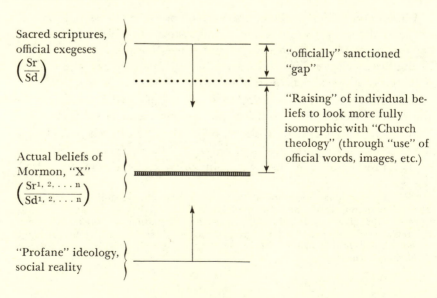

Sacred scriptures, official exegeses $\left(\dfrac{Sr}{Sd}\right)$

"officially" sanctioned "gap"

"Raising" of individual beliefs to look more fully isomorphic with "Church theology" (through "use" of official words, images, etc.)

Actual beliefs of Mormon, "X" $\left(\dfrac{Sr^{1, 2, \ldots n}}{Sd^{1, 2, \ldots n}}\right)$

"Profane" ideology, social reality

FIGURE II. RELATION OVER TIME BETWEEN CHURCH THEOLOGY AND INDIVIDUAL MORMON'S BELIEFS

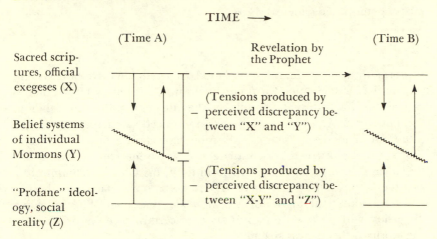

TIME ⟶

(Time A)

Revelation by the Prophet

(Time B)

Sacred scriptures, official exegeses (X)

(Tensions produced by — perceived discrepancy between "X" and "Y")

Belief systems of individual Mormons (Y)

(Tensions produced by — perceived discrepancy between "X-Y" and "Z")

"Profane" ideology, social reality (Z)

theological system through the mechanism of Presidential revelation. The divergence between official theology and individual interpretation is thereby kept relatively static over time. This adaptation can be diagrammed as in Figure II.[10]

Obviously, the relation between the Church theology and the beliefs of individual Mormons is not random. There are, in fact, a substantial number of core concepts which have remained in stable prominence since the early days of the Church, as well. This is surely a prerequisite of any discernible, and apparently coherent, cultural system.

Certain of these core concepts will be described and analyzed in the next section of this paper. The relation between core concepts and divine revelations vis-à-vis the remainder of the theological system (at any one time) is of utmost importance. It is hypothesized that certain core theological assertions must be upheld in order for the system as a whole to survive in its present form. I do not have the relevant data to support the following assertion, but it seems likely that revelations within the Church are responses to two rather different pressures: (1) revelations re-introduce isomorphism between the official theology and individuals' interpretations of that theology during periods when there are significant changes in social reality (e.g. alterations in United

[10] Richard Parmentier has pointed out to me that this model could be employed with respect to a primitive religion by obliterating the level of social reality. This is possible insofar as an "a-historical" religion does not experience the tensions produced by a perceived non-isomorphism between "social" and "sacred" fact.

States government laws or policies, in ecological conditions, in population distribution); (2) revelations serve to sustain core concepts in the face of potential ideological shifts.

IV

Mormonism does manifest a "modern" religious symbol system; yet, unlike Bellah's modern *homo religiosus,* Mormons have not discarded the institutional Church as the ultimate source of religious legitimization. While adapting to, and indeed participating in, the pluralism of modern America, Mormons maintain a unified stance *as* Mormons. In order to disentangle the apparent contradictions between the Mormons relationship to himself, his Church (community), and the larger society, it is necessary to turn to the native symbolism which embodies the modes of Mormon identification. The following discussion will be based on an analysis of certain core symbols within the Mormon theological system.[11]

The Mormon is a Mormon because he behaves like a Mormon— "relationship as code for conduct"—*and* because he is of "the seed of Abraham," a "descendant . . . of the House of Israel" (J. F. Smith, 1966–1970: 1, 140)—"relationship as natural substance." When the possible interconnections between Mormon blood and behavior are worked out, the system seems to offer a more obvious parallel to the structure, outlined by David Schneider, of the American kinship system than does Christianity, or indeed, Judaism. Schneider's intuition that: "The prevalence of the symbol of 'love,' in Christianity, the prevalence of the use of kinship terms in Christianity, the importance of such concepts as 'faith' and 'trust' and 'belief' all testify, to me at least, that the domain of religion may well be structured in the same terms as kinship . . ." (Schneider 1969: 123), becomes more apparent still, in Mormonism where the Judaic "act of birth" has been reinserted into the Christian "act of faith." (The nature of this transformation will be explained below.)

It is not surprising that Mormonism should structure its religious system in terms of the model of American kinship. Mormonism is, above all else, a product of nineteenth century America. In addition, the importance of the American continent and the American people is a constant theme in Mormon theology. This continent is a "chosen"

[11] The discussion of core symbols in Mormonism is based on David Schneider's *American Kinship* (1968). There are, however, certain important differences in the way the problem is approached here and the way Schneider deals with core symbols. My usage is similar to that employed by S. A. Barnett in "The Process of Withdrawal in a South Indian Caste" (in press).

continent; the Constitution of the United States is regarded as a divinely inspired document. It was on the American continent that God restored His Priesthood on earth; and the millennium, itself, will commence in Jackson County, Missouri.

The Mormon concept of blood entails the notion of a definitive substance which divides humanity into three broad groups; the blood of the House of Israel, the blood of the Gentile, and the blood of the Negro (*The Book of Mormon* 1961; Pratt 1855; J. F. Smith 1969, 1966–1970; Whitehead 1947). Mormons are "the descendants of the House of Israel who were scattered among the Gentiles to be a blessing to the Gentile nations . . ." (J. F. Smith 1966–1970: I, 140). Certain other groups, including the Jews and the "Lamanites" are also of the "seed of Abraham."

Through a "patriarchal blessing," generally received during adolescence, the individual Mormon may learn from which of the twelve tribes of Jacob he has descended. The patriarch, with the "right of inspiration" to guide him, is able "to *declare the literal descent* of the person receiving the blessing" (J. F. Smith 1969: III, 171; emphasis in original). A majority of Mormons are declared to be "of the lineage of Joseph through the loins of Ephraim and his fellows" (*Doctrine and Covenants* 1965: 113, 34). Those few Mormons who do not belong to the lineage of Ephraim are members of one of the other lineages which together form the House of Israel.

When a Gentile converts to Mormonism he is "adopted" into the House of Israel. The adoption involves a "literal change" in the blood of the convert (McConkie 1966: 390). It is the effect of the Holy Ghost which enables the appropriate alteration in the blood of the Gentile convert. Joseph Smith described this transformation of blood in the following manner: ". . . the effect of the Holy Ghost upon a Gentile, is to purge out the old blood, and make him actually of the seed of Abraham" (*Doctrine and Covenants,* 1965: 150).

Before the potential convert can undergo baptism, he must "believe in Jesus Christ and in the testimony of the apostle, or commissioned officer to whom he looks for the administration of these blessings" (Pratt 1855: 93)—"acts of faith." At baptism the convert is "buried" and then raised "from his watery grave" and conferred with the Gift of the Holy Ghost, "in reality a repetition of the natural birth" (Pratt 1855: 94)—"act of birth."

Unlike the Gentile, the Negro, who partakes of the blood of Cain, does not obtain House of Israel blood through the powers of the Holy Ghost. Negroes were cursed with a black skin "because of their iniquity" (The Book of Mormon 1961: Nephi 21:25) and "cursed has been the seed of him that mixeth with their seed; for they shall be cursed with the same cursing" (*The Book of Mormon* 1961: 2 Nephi 5:23).

All Mormons, therefore, are members of one family: Jesus Christ, "the literal son of God" (McConkie 1966: 129), is the elder brother. The integrity of natural substance within the Mormon community finds expression in everyday patterns of interpersonal reference and address. Mormons are siblings and address each other as "brother" or "sister."

Although the Mormon community is unisubstantial, particular Mormons may be relatively "good" or relatively "bad" Mormons according to individual adherence to the "code for conduct." Likewise, Gentiles and Negroes may be good or bad. Despite implicit suggestions (among individual Mormons and Church "authorities") that blood inheritance may involve a "predisposition" toward certain types of behavior, it is usually asserted that blood and behavior are independent in their relation to the individual.

In order to achieve a place in the Celestial Kingdom (the "highest" of the three kingdoms of glory) and the potential for becoming a god ("exaltation") one must have the "right" blood and exhibit the "right" behavior. Mormons who have not lived up to the "ordinances" of the Church and Gentiles who have lived "good" lives—"honest," "industrious," and "clean" (J. F. Smith 1969: 11, 29)—*but* heard *and* rejected the restored gospel (i.e. not become Mormons and obtained House of Israel blood) will have to settle for an afterlife in either the Terrestial or the Telestial Kingdom.[12]

The logical forms of the categorizations of blood—based primarily on a purity/impurity opposition—and behavior—based primarily on a good/evil opposition—are distinct. Blood is a discontinuous phenomenon, behavior continuous; that is, within the world of men each person has either Type A (House of Israel), Type B (Gentile), or Type C (Negro) blood (or, more succinctly, House of Israel blood or non-House of Israel blood). Any transformation of blood-type is an all or nothing matter; e.g. if a Gentile converts to Mormonism, his blood, and all of it, becomes House of Israel blood. Behavior, on the other hand, is not an all or nothing affair. The gradations between "good" behavior and "evil" behavior are infinite. Consequently, the possible permutations between type of blood and type of behavior are without end.

Within the community of Mormons, *as compared with* non-Mormon Americans, there is the implication that a broad range of behaviors—

---

[12] Only a few, particularly pernicious individuals, the Sons of Perdition, will, like Satan, be cast into the "outer reaches of darkness."

the worst behaviors—will not be evidenced. One finds, that is, an asserted likelihood for those with House of Israel blood to manifest appropriate (i.e. "good") behavior. Mormons view the interrelations between blood and behavior according to a "statistical model." Certainly, there are both good Gentiles and bad Mormons, for example, but in the main Morman conduct is superior to non-Mormon conduct.

To the degree that Mormons homologize the relation between (the individual and) blood and behavior, this is so only vis-à-vis, i.e., in the mental or physical context of, non-Mormons. Within the Church, itself, blood is unified, but behavior is variant. Those who are members of the Mormon Priesthood are "worthy"; those in the Melchizedek Priesthood are more "worthy" than those in the Aaronic Priesthood,[13] and so on.

Remembering the dimensions of the Mormon belief system outlined above, it now becomes possible to describe more adequately the mode of association within Mormonism of authoritarian officialdom and pervasive individualism. All Mormons have House of Israel blood and in this sense form a marked category within the larger category, "man." [14] The individual and the (Mormon) collectively are, explicitly in blood, often implicitly in behavior, one and the same. Both the individual Latter-Day Saint and the Church of Latter-Day Saints have "universal value" and are "a complete manifestation of the essence of man" (Dumont 1965: 9).

In so far as the Mormon individual and the collectivity are "naturally" inseparable, it is expected by Mormons that beliefs are also unified. In fact, however, Mormons are "modern" symbolizers, who are different and who think differently from one another. Each

---

[13] Age as well as behavior is a criterion for membership into the various Priesthood orders. To become a Melchizedek Priest, for example, one must be eighteen or more years of age. Yet there is an order of adult Aaronic Priests. The two factors of age and "worth," however, can be (conceptually) fused onto one scale. The notion of "eternal progress" also implies spiritual (and material) progression with advancing years, in this time, on earth.

[14] The other, but non-Mormon, members of the House of Israel (e.g. Lamanites) form a particularly ambiguous case. Mormons cope with this ambiguity in two distinct but interrelated ways. A significant part of the extensive Mormon missionary program is concerned with the conversion of Lamanites. Yet, Lamanites (both Mormon converts and potential converts) worship separately from the rest of the Mormon community (at least in east-central Arizona). Gentiles, on the other hand, even those who profess no intention of conversion, are welcomed in the Sunday Mormon worship services. This differential treatment of Gentile and Lamanite is explicable on several levels. It is not insignificant, however, that the Gentile—whether "good" or "bad"—has non-House of Israel blood and is, therefore, obviously and immediately apart from the community of Mormon worshipers and the sacrament which they share. Lamanites, however, have House of Israel blood but are not generally thought to have House of Israel behavior. Hence, spatial separation becomes important.

Mormon *uses* the official signifiers in his own way, and Mormons themselves are not entirely unaware of this fact. As described above, revelations through the President of the Church may decrease the distance between Church theology and actual beliefs. However, such revelations are not frequent occurrences and generally seem to take place during times of particular stress and potential crisis for the Church.

The psychological dissonances and social disturbances which might be created for the Mormon by the positing of a unified theology and the manifestation of ideological diversity are minimized in yet another way. A toleration for (and freedom to de-emphasize, if you will) variations in belief has been built into the belief system, itself. By stressing the difference between Mormons and non-Mormon Americans (through blood and behavior) the Church can maintain its unified stance vis-à-vis non-Mormon America *and* a toleration for ideological diversification among the members, themselves. Ideological and behavioral deviances can be sustained precisely because the individual Mormon actor and believer *should* not be distinguished from the larger whole. Of course, the potential for dissonance and disturbance, referred to above, could have alternatively been dealt with through enforced dogmatism and limitations on ideological freedom. Had the Mormon Church developed along this line, it would not be a "modern" religion.

It is pertinent at this point to underscore the dimensions, both stressed and unstressed, which make up the Mormon concept of being "worthy." In the selection of Mormon priests, bishops, etc., the stressed criteria relate to actual modes of individual behavior. A priest, for instance, obeys the Word of Wisdom by not smoking and not drinking coffee, tea, or alcoholic beverages. Similarly, the sorts of unorthodoxies which necessitate excommunication tend to be specific misconducts (e.g. adultery) rather than ideological heresies.

When one asks a member of the Mormon Priesthood why, in fact, he foregoes the drinking of coffee and alcohol etc., he generally responds by referring to Section 89 of the *Doctrine and Covenants,* which contains the "Word of Wisdom" revelation. But when one pushes him further and seeks an interpretation of the revelation itself it is no longer possible to predict the response. There is a broad spectrum of responses (from "it's bad for your health," to "it saves money" to "only the Lord knows")—almost as many explications as foregoers. The revelation, in short, has become a symbol which allows extensive liberty for individual interpretation while reenforcing the unity of the collectivity.

In brief, one might say: "good" Mormons seem to act alike far more than they actually think alike. Mormons themselves do postulate an interconnection between life style and spiritual essence, between action and belief. I have often heard Mormons infer that a "worthy" man (e.g. a stake bishop) is inwardly "spiritual." In fact, that bishop probably *is* spiritual, but not in exactly the same way as any other "spiritual" Mormon.

Indeed, with the exception of a few key prescriptions and prohibitions (e.g. paying one's tithing to the Church, foregoing liquor) Mormons "act" like "modern" symbolizers should. Mormons are boy scout leaders, relief society presidents, Sunday School supervisors; they are engineers, insurance brokers, and farmers. In all those domains the "search for adequate standards of action" (Bellah 1970: 43) is heavily dependent on the idiolect of the individual actor.[15] Idiosyncratic belief and action must be tolerated, short of excommunication, because at the level of its very substance (i.e. blood) the collectivity is identical with the individual.

V

In order to lessen the gap between the above analysis and the way the Mormon himself views his world, I shall now look at some aspects of the Mormon ritual system. The ritual domain seems appropriate for this purpose since it both reflects and is part and parcel of, both defines and structures, the larger world within which the dramas are enacted and the celebrations solemnized.

The Mormon ritual domain will here be conceived as consisting of three primary sub-domains: the Temple rites, weekly worship services held in local churches, and civil ritual. This division of the inclusive ritual system would almost certainly be acceptable to the "native" Mormon. Space and time, if nothing else, provide a sufficient basis for the categorization. It should not be assumed, however, that the three ritual spheres are comprehensible in isolation from each other, never mind from the wider theological and social realms. It is precisely the numerous modes of interrelation, the expressed and tacit patterns of symbolic reference, which imbue the "whole" with meaning and transmit that meaning across the boundaries of "person" and "event." A brief summary of each sort of ritual will be provided before the larger system is analyzed.

The Temple rites, instigated by Joseph Smith in the mid-nineteenth century, are unshared, exclusively Mormon events, only a good Mor-

---

[15] For a discussion of the evolution of predicated role-types within the Church during the past century, see Leone (1969).

mon being allowed admittance to the Temple.[16] The core of the rites involve a ritual drama. The creation of the world and the "Fall" of man in the Garden of Eden are enacted in the "Creation Room" and the "Garden of Eden Room," respectively. In the "World Room" Satan's preachers are ridiculed as they present their devilish opinions.[17] At this point the accounts differ slightly as to the order and character of the ritual events, but all imply (some state explicitly) that there is a recognition of the restoration of the "gospel" to earth through the Prophet, Joseph Smith. The culmination of the sacred dimension occurs in the "Celestial Room" ("heaven") which is entered through a sacred veil from the "Terrestial Room." This veil is the ultimate link, or alternately the boundary, between heaven and earth. The ritual concludes with the "sealing" ceremonies which join husbands and wives or parents and children for "time" and for "eternity." The rites may be participated in for the living (oneself) or for the dead, in which case an individual serves as "proxy" for a particular dead ancestor or friend.[18] At appropriate stages throughout the rites, the various "degrees" of the Aaronic and Melchizedek Priesthoods are conferred upon the participants, who recite oaths under specific penalties of bodily harm that will befall the unfaithful.

The following description of the Sunday church services is based on observation at a ward in east-central Arizona during the summer of 1970. The services consist of two parts, "Sunday School," held during the morning hours, and "worship service," held in the early evening. Sunday School begins with approximately a half hour of group devotion consisting of the singing of hymns, "talks" by members of the congregation,[19] and the "administration" of the sacrament. This de-

---

[16] Because only a faithful Mormon is allowed to participate in the Temple rites, both anthropological observation and native exegesis are precluded. Much of my information concerning the form and content of these rites comes from accounts written by apostate Mormons. There are, however, no striking discrepancies between the various accounts I have employed. Sources of data include: Beadle 1870; Brodie 1945; Coyner 1882; O'Dea 1957; Whalen 1964. It is assumed that the similarity of these accounts is not a result of the latter ones having drawn on the earlier ones; this possibility, however, cannot be ignored.

[17] The various parts in the ritual dramas are played by "Temple workers." The Temple workers are members of the Church who have volunteered to work in the Temple for a period of time. Often they are older persons who have retired from their secular jobs and businesses.

[18] The possibility for one to undergo this ritual as proxy for a dead person insures that even those people who died before the restoration of God's Priesthood on earth may achieve exaltation.

[19] The "talks" during the Sunday morning service are prepared and delivered by young persons (approximately between the ages of eight and sixteen) and are supposed to take "$2\frac{1}{2}$ minutes." Generally the "talk" relates an actual event which occurred in the life of the speaker to a moral or theological issue (e.g. honesty, friendship).

votional half-hour is succeeded by the separating of the congregation into small groups (based broadly on age) for "classes" where one is instructed in the gospel and Mormonism, generally. Mormons attend Sunday School throughout their lives. Each class is led by a teacher who has been appointed by the ward bishopric. In the Sunday School classes I attended in Arizona, the teacher selected a topic for each week's lesson (e.g. "equality," "magnanimity," "progress"). The classes took the form of discussion among all the participants (teacher and students) rather than a lecture by the teacher. The evening "worship service" is similar to the first part of the morning Sunday service and entails hymns, a second "administration" of the sacrament and talks by members of the ward and/or Mormons from other wards (e.g. missionaries stationed in the area).

The civil ritual—not so much a part of Mormonism, the "religion," as of Mormonism, the social community—involves the celebration of national, Mormon, and local holidays. The two ritual events which I shall deal with here were performed on the Fourth of July and July 24 (Mormon Pioneer Day) in two small towns on the Little Colorado River in Arizona. The core of the Fourth of July celebration was a program, enacted in the local Mormon Church, which consisted of a short play and the presentation of "Hall of Fame Awards" to two "worthy" local couples. The celebration of July 24 lasted two days; it included a parade, a rodeo, a fireworks display, athletic events, picnics, and a program in the ward chapel. Although both celebrations were expected to engage both Mormon and non-Mormon segments of the local communities, they were planned and executed by committees from the two respective Mormon wards.

The Temple rites and the weekly church services will now be considered in some detail. It will then be possible to indicate some of the ways in which the civil ritual makes sense in, and of, the more obviously "theological" messages of the first two ritual domains.

If one takes the Temple ritual as a linear whole and divides it into two halves, one finds a striking parallelism between the first and second halves of the rite (see Figure III). That is, if one starts at either end of the ritual (temporally, or spatially, as on Figure III) and moves inward toward the center, one notes (or undergoes) a similar series of ordered phases before one arrives at the middle.[20]

The first and last activities in which the participant engages involve the "recording" of individual identification. Before a Mormon can participate in the rites he must reaffirm his legitimate position (e.g.

[20] The division of the Temple rites into two halves is not a native classification. The accompanying diagram is intended to make clear the structure of the linear progression of the rites.

FIGURE III. Sequence of Events in the Mormon Temple Rites

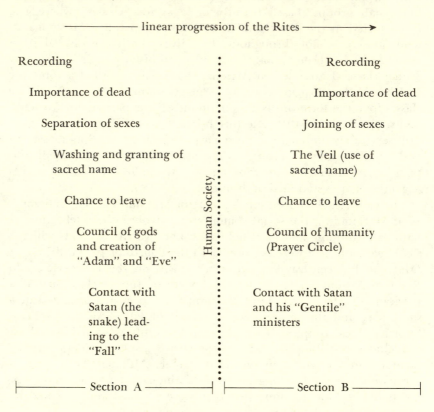

——————— linear progression of the Rites ——————→

Section A	Section B
Recording	Recording
Importance of dead	Importance of dead
Separation of sexes	Joining of sexes
Washing and granting of sacred name	The Veil (use of sacred name)
Chance to leave	Chance to leave
Council of gods and creation of "Adam" and "Eve"	Council of humanity (Prayer Circle)
Contact with Satan (the snake) leading to the "Fall"	Contact with Satan and his "Gentile" ministers

Human Society

├———— Section A ————┤ ├———— Section B ————┤

his name, parents' names, place of birth, and baptismal and tithing records) in the everyday world of Mormonism. Before he can re-enter everyday Mormondom, (after the ritual is completed) his status as a Mormon "sealed" for eternity to other Mormons is recorded. The second segment in the ritual (both forwards and backwards) relates to the importance of the dead. In section A (as specified in Figure III) this entails the ordination of those Melchizedek priests who are to undergo the endowment ritual in proxy for the dead, and in section B this involves sealing ceremonies performed for the dead. The next set of events concerns the non-identical nature of the two sexes. In section A the sexes separate (into the washing rooms for men and women, respectively), and in section B the sexes join in the sealing ceremonies for the living. In section A the separation of the sexes is followed by a cleansing of the body, an anointing with sacred oil, and the granting of a sacred, secret name. In section B the joining of the sexes is immediately preceded by the communication between man and heaven at which time the sacred name received during the washing ceremony is necessary for admittance into "heaven." In the next event in both sections the participants are offered the chance to curtail their ritual involvement. The subsequent set of events can be described as sacred council. In section A it is a council in heaven where the creation of the world is planned. In section B it is a council of humanity. The male participants congregate around an altar in a "Prayer Circle" to see the "tokens" of the two Mormon Priesthoods.

The line on Figure III labelled "human society" does not have a specific place within the linear sequence of the rites. It can, however, be broadly equated with human life on earth after the banishment of Adam and Eve from the Garden of Eden. Immediately before and after the scene depicting the "Fall" within the ritual the presence of "Lucifer" predominates: in snake form in section A and as gentile ministers (the "devil's advocates") in section B.

The stressed opposition in this rite is that between good and evil (and relates to "code for conduct"). Before Adam's Fall, there was no evil, after the millennium, Satan will be bound and the good Mormon will again inhabit a "Kingdom" devoid of evil. It was Eve who was responsible, but only indirectly, for the original Fall. Eve's role in the Mormon Garden of Eden is similar to that of the Judeo-Christian Eve. Satan (in the form of a snake) tempts Eve. Eve eats the forbidden. Adam concurs, and man is banished from the Garden. The Mormon Eve also holds responsibility, and again indirectly, for the inception of the millennium and the salvation of mankind. Mormons believe that through the procreative abilities of woman, the Mormon Priesthood (Mormon male) is created, and that it is this endowed Priesthood which shall enable the millennium to arrive. However, "Eve" (as the symbol for "woman") will only be able to (re-)enter paradise through her husband. Eve's relationship to Satan (all that is evil and dangerous) is precisely the inverse of her relationship to the Mormon Priesthood ("worthy" Mormon males).

Between the good and evil, therefore, one finds "woman," as an (overworked) Mormon mediator.[21] Of all persons in the Mormon

---

[21] The importance and ambiguity of the "woman" in the Mormon ritual system must be seen in the context of the radical shifts in the ideal marriage and family residence patterns which have occurred during Mormonism's one-hundred-fifty-year history. Initially Mormons were monogamous; then, ideally, polygamous. Within the polygamous family each wife maintained a separate residence for herself and her children. A man's chances of attaining exaltation were positively correlated with the number of wives and children to whom he stood as husband and father. Since 1890 only monogamous marriage is officially recognized, although small pockets of (excommunicated) polygamous Mormons do exist. After the millennium commences, "plural marriage" will again hold sway.

universe, it is the woman who is most capable of assimilating both good and evil equally well. She stands between and partakes of Man and the Fall, Man and his offspring, Satan and the Mormon Priesthood, Man and the millennium, and ultimately, human society and creation-redemption.

Unlike the Temple rites, within which the individual participates only irregularly, the services in the local Mormon churches are enacted on a weekly basis. The colorful and dramatic symbolisms of the Temple rites are not found in the weekly services; indeed, the traditional Christian sacrament is sensually weakened in the form of white bread and water. The tone of the services I attended in Arizona was one of relaxed, albeit "spiritual" communitas. The sharp dichotomies between good and evil present in the Temple rites are here minimized. The Mormon actor as "individual before God" is replaced by the unisubstantial community of fellow Mormons. Blood, in short, displaces behavior as the relevant core symbol.

The educational sessions, which immediately succeed the morning worship, are each presided over by a teacher. However, the participants are allowed a wide freedom of expression and interpretation. As M. P. Leone has noted, in Sunday School the Mormon appears to truly be his own exegete. Along with the reaffirmation of the unified collectivity (through blood) comes a pronounced tolerance for idiosyncracy and diversification.

The realm of civil ritual is in many ways the most significant and the most complex of the three types of ritual that are being considered here. Interrelations between the Mormon Church and America have varied through time from enmity and reciprocal hostility to mutual acceptance. Both conceptually and factually the Mormon is inextricably intertwined with the American continent and the sociopolitical forms of the United States. The conflicts engendered by this dual identification have been responsible for creating unending tensions for the Mormon, but these same conflicts have served to strengthen the very separation of the Church by "opposing it" (in "code for conduct" and in "natural substance") to non-Mormon America.

Indeed, the three ritual systems are all at least partially based on ritual models provided by non-Mormon America. The Temple rites take many of their symbolic elements from Masonic ritual (e.g. the hand grips and the design of the holy garment); the church services have a close (formal) affinity with traditional Protestant worship. The civil ritual is analogous with American commemorative ritual, but in addition, it employs (individually interpreted) messages and forms found in the Mormon Temple and weekly church ritual, to serve as "signifiers" of the "civil" "signifieds." That is to say, the messages of the civil ritual are in large part framed in the "language" of the Temple and Church ritual.

The symbolisms of the civil ritual bear primarily upon the association between the Mormon and the non-Mormon American. The (logical) relation (see above p. 530) obtaining between the Mormon "code for conduct" (of the Temple ritual) and the "natural substance" (of the church ritual) assures innumerable potential combinations of the two; this combination (in the civil ritual) can, consequently, form an infinity of messages about how Mormons and non-Mormon Americans are, in fact, associated.

Some historical material concerning the celebration of the Fourth of July and Mormon Pioneer Day in past years has been obtained.[22] This material indicates a marked variation from year to year in the way Mormons perceive themselves in the context of social and political America. In considering the 1970 celebrations of the two holidays, one is immediately struck by the prevalence of "Mormon" symbolisms (e.g. the singing of Mormon hymns; the use of Church liturgy) during the celebration of the national holiday and by the prevalence of "American" symbolisms (e.g. the wearing of red, white, and blue; the widespread display of the national flag) during the celebration of the Mormon holiday. The Fourth of July was, if you will, "Mormonized," and Mormon Pioneer Day, "Americanized." The boundary between the Mormon and the non-Mormon American was declared open and in that declaration the oppositions between good and evil and between purity and impurity were submerged, though not extinguished, beneath the concordant identities. Less than a decade ago, at a time when a majority of the local Mormon inhabitants disagreed with many of the national administration's policies, the rituals of July 4 and July 24 did not mediate the relevant oppositions but rather emphasized them.

Despite the apparent homogenization of Mormon and non-Mormon, which occurred in the 1970 rituals, the play presented during the Fourth of July celebration provides a fine illustration of the manner in which civil ritual may model itself on the ritual of the Temple and the Church.

The play in question was written and produced by local Mormons;

22 Such material is hard to obtain since the local Mormons tend not to save the written programs from year to year—and this, despite the Mormon proclivity for owning "Books of Remembrances" containing mementos and genealogical data. It is not, however, surprising that these programs should not be retained. Indeed, this very fact reaffirms the proposition that the civil rituals define and structure the social and political "present" with little regard for the "realities" of yesteryear.

the principal actors were "Liberty" and "Uncle Sam." The play opened with a proposal by Sam that the Fourth of July be celebrated. Liberty refused, saying that the "discontent in the land" made her unwilling to celebrate. Sam suggested that if Liberty would accompany him to some of the "small towns" on this July Fourth, she would feel much happier. Sam and Liberty stepped back and a dozen small children proceeded to express the patriotic sentiment of a "small town"—that in which the play was being performed—through song and rhyme. After the performance by the children, Liberty turned to Sam and declared, "Come, dear, I'm ready to celebrate."

The structure of this play is almost identical with the structure of the Temple rites; all of the relations, except the final one, have, however, been reversed. In the theological model presented in the Temple ritual the Mormon female mediates the good/evil opposition. In the Fourth of July play just recounted the (presumably Mormon) female (in the garb of the American "Liberty") mediates the opposition between the "good" Mormon and the "evil" American and thereby enables Mormon participation in American society and polity.

Fourth of July Civil Ritual	Temple Ritual
"Uncle Sam" proposes celebration (="good" thing)	"Satan" (i.e. snake) proposes that "Eve" eat the forbidden fruit (="bad" thing)
"Liberty" dissents	"Eve" concurs
Demonstration by children of "small town patriotism" (="good" thing)	Period of this-earthly time, entailing mortality and "evil" (="bad" thing)
Liberty agrees to celebrate the Fourth (="good" thing)	"Woman" produces Mormon Priesthood (="good" thing)

The presentation of "small town patriotism" falls at a point of structural similarity with "human society" in the Temple rites. By appropriating this structure from the Temple rites, but reversing its meaning—"evil" becomes "good"—the participants defined (and constructed) their perceptions of "everyday reality" in such a way that "human society" was stripped of some of its negative attributes (as evidenced in the Temple rites) and thus made to correspond more fully with the contemporary world-view of Arizona Mormons concerning their time and place.[23]

[23] Fawn Brodie (1945: 400) has attributed the survival of the Temple rites to the fact that they are and "were entirely extraneous to Mormon life." It is not the superfluity of the ritual content, but rather the fundamental appositeness of

The analytic distinction between "models of" and "models for" proposed by Clifford Geertz (1966) can be applied to the Mormon ritual system. Both the Temple rites and the church services furnish models for the civil ritual which, in turn, is a model of "everyday reality." By dealing more directly with immediate social reality than either the Temple rites or the church services, civil ritual may work to increase isomorphism between official theology and individuals' belief systems. Through civil ritual the official signifiers can be made relevant to changing political, economic, and social concerns. The civil ritual, fashioned anew each year according to the perceptions and conceptions of the "moment," relays the (re)newed messages (individual and collective) back into the forms and symbols of the Temple rites and weekly church services.

Civil ritual and revelations through the President of the Church can, in a certain sense, be viewed as working in inverse proportion to each other. In so far as the civil ritual succeeds, revelation is not needed. At the point where civil ritual can no longer extend the official theology to make sense of the world of everyday reality, revelation can change the theology, itself.

VI

In conclusion, I will return to a brief consideration of Robert Bellah's model of religious evolution in view of the social and ideological structures of Mormonism. The Church seems to present the anomaly of supporting "modern" men within the context of a "historic" form (The social organization of the Church is in several obvious ways more like Medieval Catholicism than Reformation Protestantism).

Bellah admits the possibility that "simpler form . . . [may] prosper and survive alongside more complex forms" (Bellah 1970: 21). Working within Bellah's model, two immediate possibilities arise with respect to Mormonism. Either it is a "simpler form" than the "modern" stage, in which case it becomes necessary to ask why and how it has achieved its apparent success in the "modern" world; or it is a more complex form. There is, however, a third possibility which stands alongside, rather than within, Bellah's model: Mormonism is both more "complex" and more "simple" than his characterization of the modern stage.

It is this third possibility which seems to characterize most aptly

---

the ritual structure (communicable in multifold contexts and designs) which is chiefly responsible for the continued viability of this ritual.

the Mormon who, while firmly embedded in the authoritarian structure of the Church, emerges to "take responsibility for his own fate" (Bellah 1970: 42). This third possibility throws light on a subtle shift in Bellah's model when he deals with the "modern" situation. In his characterization of the four earlier stages, Bellah is at least as concerned with (the evolution of) the pervasive institutional forms as he-is with the structure of their cultural analogues. It is, of course, one of Bellah's initial assumptions that the changes in "symbolization" from stage to stage are "systematically related" to changes in religious and secular forms. In the modern stage, however, the evolution which Bellah posits is almost entirely concerned with modes of symbolization. The institutional structures drop out at this point in the analysis and each man is left to evolve on his own.[24] Bellah intimates that suitable institutional forms may yet emerge in the modern period (Bellah 1970: 44).

One would certainly not, however, expect Bellah to posit an institutional form resembling that which has developed in the Mormon Church. Yet, this form is eminently well adapted to contain "modern" men, to enable ideological independence while providing social stability. Initially, the authoritarian organization of the Church is similar to the organizational systems which Bellah described for the historic period. There are radical, albeit subtle, differences, however, between the two structures. Most obviously, all Mormons are lay-men.[25] There is, therefore, no *a priori* religious elite. It has been noted that there is a correspondence between one's status in the Church and the number of persons to whom the revelations one receives may apply. However, the revelations received by the President of the Church are not qualitatively superior to the revelations received by a young boy. The prophet cannot become a repository for unmitigated truth. The Church structure *as a whole* may be as authoritarian as any structure extant during the "historic" period, but *no one* individual (or group of individuals) has unconditional social or theological authority.

[24] There is another problem which arises with Bellah's description of the modern stage and his implications for a post-modern stage. At that point when man becomes conscious of the processes of social and cultural evolution, it may no longer be possible to postulate evolutionary models. Here the problem is not specifically with Bellah's theory but with any evolutionary theory concerned with men who know they are "capable of self-transformation" and who can control that very process.

[25] M. P. Leone has pointed to the possibility that the presently lay Mormon Priesthood is evolving into a professional clergy. If this were to occur, Mormonism might quite possibly become another minor "Christian" sect—no longer able to offer its adherents a modern symbol system in combination with a stable organizational system.

In section III it was hypothesized that revelations received by the President of the Church occur at those historic moments when the core concepts of the Church are in danger and during times when significant alterations in social reality are increasing the non-isomorphism between Church theology and individuals' beliefs. It seems likely that a similar type of feedback is responsible for the timing of revelations received by individual Mormons. I have not seen a sufficient number of revelations received by individuals within the Church to test this hypothesis. If these hypotheses are valid, however, it becomes clear that the very authority of the institutional form allows the maintenance of a balance between ideological independence and social stability.

Bellah says of the early modern stage: ". . . . social flexibility was balanced against doctrinal . . . and characterological . . . rigidities" (1970: 44). He suggests that the modern stage will witness the decline of "doctrinal and characterological rigidities." It is not an untenable exaggeration to suggest that in Mormonism "doctrinal" and "characterological" flexibilities are balanced against "social rigidities"—or better, perhaps, against social stabilities. At critical moments the sources of authority (at the relevant level) can be called into play to prevent Mormons from escaping, as it were, to become absolutely independent men, evolving along independent paths, outside the network of an institutional structure.

It is the *use* individual Mormons make of the Church theology which makes them "modern" symbolizers. That use is made possible by the organizational structure of the Church and, in addition, is legitimized by the uni-substantial Mormon universe. It is the way the core symbols are structured which fosters both perceived unity and tolerance in the face of actual diversification at the level of individuals' definitions.

If the ideology which supports the unisubstantial character of the Mormon universe is, through individual reinterpretation, discarded, either explicitly or implicitly, by the Church of Jesus Christ of Latter-Day Saints, it would seem not unlikely that much of what accounts for the particular stability of the Church will be lost. This is not to say that particular aspects of the Mormon concepts of kinship and blood could not be altered. It is not unlikely that the revelations relating to the impossibility for Negroes to be ordained into the Mormon Priesthood may be changed through future revelation. In order to ensure the survival of the Church, this would, I propose, have to be done without subverting the uni-substantial universe within which the Mormon now thinks and acts and organizes.

Whitney Cross identifies the "assumption that sin must be attacked primarily in the individual, rather than in society" as having been finally responsible for the extinction of "enthusiastic religion" in Western New York (Cross 1950: 357). Among those religions which developed in what has come to be called the "burned-over district" during the early nineteenth century, Mormonism is unique in its enduring vitality. A major part of that vitality can surely be attributed to the (undeniably American) notions of "relationship as code for conduct" and as "natural substance" which developed in the Church of Jesus Christ of Latter-Day Saints.

Reasonably Fantastic: Some Perspectives on Scientology, Science Fiction, and Occultism

I~n~ the following essay, I have attempted to put into historical and cultural context a particular set of beliefs and practices that has arisen within contemporary society. These are the beliefs and practices of the Church of Scientology which came into being in the early 1950s.[1] While belonging, in a broad sense, to the growing collection of religious movements in this country that either stand totally outside of the Judeo-Christian tradition or constitute markedly unorthodox derivatives of the same, Scientology shares a kinship with certain of these "outsiders" that it does not share with others. Furthermore, many of its principles derive from such supposedly secular sources as the psychoanalytic tradition or the ideals of scientific and technological progress that continue to underlie much of the twentieth-century Western culture. In trying to place Scientology in proper perspective, to say more or less what it is in relation to surrounding belief systems, it became necessary, as is so often the case, to erase certain categories, to construct others, and to re-examine some that have been either neglected or over-used. In particular, a rather lengthy excursion has been taken through the world of American "Occultism" and the history of modern science fiction, as it is felt that an interpretation of these phenomena precedes an adequate understanding of Scientology. I have attempted to draw together all three subject areas— Scientology, science fiction and Occultism—under the notion that a deficiency exists, or is felt to exist, in the established Western styles of "knowing" or comprehending reality.

Scientology Organization and Personnel

Scientology, both as a system of ideas and as an organization, is the sole creation of one man, L. Ron Hubbard. Furthermore he is still in the act of creating it. At present, Hubbard spends most of

---

[1] Sources dealing specifically with Scientology, Dianetics, or L. Ron Hubbard are: Braddeson 1969; Gardner 1957; Hubbard 1940, 1950, 1958, 1964; Malko 1970; Moskowitz 1961; Van Vogt 1964; and Winter 1951.

547

his time on board the flagship of the Sea Org, a community of dedicated Scientologists, the some 300 members of which are distributed
among Scientology's upper-level land facilities and the six small craft
that serve as training bases for incoming Sea Orgers. Partly because
his "despotism" is for the most part benign but principally because of
his continuous intellectual productivity, Hubbard is able to maintain
virtually complete control of Scientology operations. No one is interested in killing the goose that still lays golden eggs. Every day new
data and policy notices leave the Apollo, or "flag," as it is called, and
find their way, in the form of books, mimeosheets, and tapes, into
the approximately 85 franchises (privately or corporately owned centers where introductory Scientology training is offered) and 14 Orgs
(Scientology-owned non-profit centers where advanced training is offered) of the United States. The United States contains the greatest
number of Scientology places of training, followed by the United
Kingdom. Centers and Orgs are also to be found in Canada, Australia,
South Africa, New Zealand, Mexico, Brazil, Spain, France, Denmark,
Sweden, Norway, and Germany. Scientology was incorporated as a
church in California in 1952, but because of the ambiguity as to
whether or not any of its monetary intake goes as profit to Hubbard
and his family, its tax-exempt status is still under adjudication.
Scientology sells its services in the form of auditing (to be explained
below) at a rate of $25 to $35 per hour, and training at the rate of
about $5 per day. However, the personnel of Centers and Orgs
receive much of their training free or at large discounts, and anyone
taking training receives a good deal of free "student" auditing. Anyone
wishing to become a full-time staffer at an Org can get the works for
nothing, provided he is able to find a means of supporting himself
and his family. Those entering the Sea Org receive all training and
processing free as well as board, lodging and some weekly pin-money.
Thus there is a good deal of incentive, especially among young members who have not yet established themselves in careers to become
professional Scientologists.

Speaking for this country only, my estimates of Scientology membership put the number of currently active Scientologists (professional
and non-professional) at around 30,000. The number of people who
have been "touched" by Scientology—to the extent of having bought
a book or put their names on a mailing list—is much larger, somewhere in the neighborhood of two million.[2]

---

[2] Exact figures are very difficult to obtain, so I have used the following indices:
(1) About 3,200 people attended the Grand National Convention at Long Beach,
July 1970. This was the largest Scientology convention to date. Almost all of
the attendees were currently active Scientologists. They came from all over the

Currently active Scientologists are predominantly urban, white, and middle class. The most heavily represented age-bracket is the 20–30 year olds; male and female membership is about even. The best description of educational background is some college and/or technical training, the nature of their education being weighted more heavily towards the sciences, business, and bureaucratic skills than towards the humanities. An exception must be made in the case of the graphic and performing arts. Scientology in Los Angeles and New York contains a significant number of artists and entertainers. Outside of artists and entertainers, those who enter Scientology from another career, or who maintain a separate career in the outside world, are generally in the white-collar professions. I have unfortunately very little data as yet concerning the religious backgrounds of Scientologists. The rather striking number of former Catholics among my small sample taken at Chicago can be accounted for by the fact that the Chicago population is about 50% Catholic, and at this point I will only hazard a guess that the distribution of religious backgrounds among Scientologists conforms to that of the population center in which they are located.

Scientology has been called variously a con game, a wacky cult, a type of psychotherapy, a sort of "scientific mysticism," an occult religion, and a spiritual discipline. Scientologists speak of it as an "applied religious philosophy." Attempts to describe its contents easily deteriorate into a chaos of minor concepts since Scientology lore covers everything from an explanation of the origins of the physical universe to a system for organizing one's business activities; and both the lofty and the trivial notions always turn out to be, on some level, inextricably connected.

Much of the confusion, as well as the almost uniformly vile press that

---

country and even from Britain and South Africa; the largest number, however, were from California. (2) The number of clears, those who have passed the major milestone in the training hierarchy, is just under 3,000, last count. This figure represents deeply committed Scientologists. (3) The number of names in the Central File of Los Angeles Org is 40,000. The files include everyone who has ever bought a book or paid for a service at L.A. Org. Since Los Angeles is a mecca for American Scientologists seeking advanced training, L.A. Org's files undoubtedly contain a great many "duplicates", i.e. people registered elsewhere as well (my own name is on file at six Scientology places of business). (4) A fairly prosperous franchise that I attended gave the introductory training course to approximately 360 people in 1969. Assuming that all franchises were as prosperous, which they are not, that all of the current franchises had been in business for 20 years, which they have not, and that the inflow of new people was as great in earlier years as it was in the late 60's, which it was not, this would put the number of rudimentary franchise-trained persons at just over a half million. (5) Hubbard's first book, *Dianetics: The Modern Science of Mental Health* (1950) has sold around two million copies.

Scientology, and its forerunner, Dianetics, have received ever since 1950 stems from the fact that Hubbard's creations have their closest cultural affinity to what is usually called the "Occult world," the "pseudo-sciences," and science fiction. The fact of the matter is that none of the latter are very well understood themselves, whether in respect to their basic principles, their inter-relationship, or their place in our culture. In the analysis that follows, it will be argued, first, that there is a basic "Occult" orientation, manifest in many earlier doctrines as well as in Scientology, and that given the history of Western religion this orientation occupies a logical position in our culture. I will try to bring out some of the ways in which science fiction, or the science fiction tradition, of which Scientology is a more immediate derivative, is related to Occultism. Lastly, I will suggest that it is the way in which Hubbard has made maximum use of the Occult orientation, giving it an intellectual and experiental coherence it has not enjoyed since the days of Alchemy, that accounts for much of Scientology's appeal.

Since the Occult deals, usually quite specifically, with the mysteries of the supersensible or "magical" realm, any discussion of its position in contemporary culture involves, inevitably, some reference to the concept of "secularization" or, to use Weber's terms, the "disenchantment of the world image." I do not wish to retread in any detail all of the arguments that have circulated through sociology concerning (a) the existence, and (b) the significance of this phenomenon; but it is important for present purposes to outline briefly what this author considers secularization to be, and to clarify certain ambiguities in Weber's original statement of the matter. It will also be possible, within the same context, to make some distinctions between the religious movements that are really quite new to the contemporary scene and the ones that have lingered in the background for decades. Let me turn then to the subject of contemporary religion.

Contemporary Religion

When I say "religion," I am using Robert Bellah's simple working definition: "A set of symbolic forms and acts which relate man to the ultimate conditions of his existence" (Bellah 1956b: 74). The anthropologist must note that there are certain things commonly associated with religion which are not a necessary part of this definition. For one, no line is drawn between those "symbolic forms and acts" which are widely entertained within a society and supported by definable groups and institutions and those forms and acts which are individual and idiosyncratic. If the social scientist prefers to study the former rather than the latter, he cannot argue that it is because the former is somehow more "religious," but only that the widely held symbolic forms and acts provide him with greater insight into the society, the sub-group, the class, or the era in question.

Another commonly associated feature of religions which is of more immediate interest to us here is that of conceptions of a transcendent or "supernatural" order—a higher level of reality—to which the mundane or commonsense order of experience is somehow meaningfully related. The question of whether religion—either societal or idiosyncratic—can truly exist in the absence of such concepts, remains moot. This is perhaps why simple, working definitions of religion "work" best when they sidestep the question. But arguments about "secularization" are often addressing this very point: has Western society, over the centuries, undergone a movement away from notions of the supernatural or transcendent? If so, does this mean also a movement away from "religion" itself, or are our definitions of religion misleading? Some clarification of this matter is necessary for the present discussion. Clearly something has been underway in Western culture, and if it is not a demise of religion per se, it is certainly a reshuffling of its ingredients.

"Secularization," on the personal level, is essentially an unconcerned this-worldly orientation. William James comments about one of the respondents to a religious questionnaire circulated by Professor Starbuck, that "His contentment with the finite incases him like a lobster-shell. . . ." To the question of what ideas came to mind in response to the words God, Heaven, or Angels, this man answered that "These words mean so much mythic bosh" (James 1961: 89). Such a personal orientation is, theoretically, possible for some individuals in any culture or during any era; it may even be prevalent. But when such an attitude came to be commonly accepted and in many circles even endorsed in the eighteenth, nineteenth and twentieth centuries, one is forced to ask whence this contentment with the finite?

Most sociological understandings of secularization derive from Weber's concept of "rationalization." This complex notion encompasses (a) the clarification and systematization of ideas, with an important emphasis upon the search for general principles and universals, and (b) the development of a methodical, pragmatic, and "sober" orientation in the patterning of the individual life style and in the patterning of institutions. In speaking of the cognitive-motivational dimension of rationalization, Weber says:

We have to remind ourselves in advance that "rationalism" may mean many different things. It means one thing if we think of the kind of rationalization the systematic thinker performs on the image of the world: an increasing theoretical mastery of reality by means of increasingly precise and abstract concepts. Rationalism means another thing if we think of the methodical attainment of a definitely given and practical end by means of an increasingly precise calculation of adequate means. These types of rationalism are very different, in spite of the fact that ultimately they belong inseparately together . . . (Gerth and Mills 1958 :293).

On a societal level rationalization is manifested in (c) the increasing functional differentiation of primary social institutions, and (d) the extension of normative control along the lines of precisely thought out and impersonal rules of law. Rationalization, while not an evolutionary principle per se, is a tendency present in all cultures and throughout history; furthermore, its cumulative effect is in an evolutionary or transformational direction.

The critical ambiguity in Weber's concept, from the point of view of the effects of rationalization upon religion, is the equation which he makes between increasing rationalization in a culture and the gradual elimination of magical, or in his words, "irrational" elements of the religious world-view. Since it is the fate of these "magical" or "irrational" elements that is the particular concern of this paper, let me clarify what is meant by these terms.

Weber begins his essay on "The Rise of Religion" by pointing out that while a significant portion of primitive magic can be viewed, in the light of present-day empiricism, as a pragmatically-oriented activity the chief peculiarity of which rests in the fact that the posited means-ends relationship is non-intrinsic, this is not the most productive approach to take to the "magical" element when we consider its place in the evolution of religious systems. He prefers to speak instead of that quality of "extraordinary power" that "inheres in an object or person simply by virtue of natural endowment." This he labels "charisma," although the terms "mana" or "orenda" could as well be used (Weber 1963: 2). From the concept of extraordinary power is derived the belief in spirits.[3] Weber deals with the charismatic primarily as an attribute or quality, one which commands a special sort of attention. Another way of looking at what is involved here is that the charismatic, and by extension the realm of the spirits, is a dimen-

---

[3] "A process of abstraction, which only appears to be simple, has usually already been carried out in the most primitive instances of religious behavior which we examine. Already crystallized is the notion that certain beings are concealed "behind" and responsible for the activity of the charismatically endowed natural objections, artifacts, animals, or persons. This is the belief in spirits" (Weber 1963: 3).

sion of experience. Attribute and experience are opposite sides of the same coin. I do not mean to imply that Weber was ignorant of this, merely that he chose to emphasize the one instead of the other. The trend in the literature on contemporary religious behavior, on the other hand, is to stress the experiential dimension and in speaking of "disenchantment" to address not just the elimination of magical attributes from the world order but the restriction on the accepted modes of experiencing that accompanies this. My own discussion will follow this trend.

Also, a common ambiguity in the use of the word charisma is of importance here. Both Weber and subsequent sociological writers use the term to cover a gamut of phenomena all of which properly fit the category of "extraordinary power" or a "sense of the extraordinary." The lowest level of this range is not, however, the notion of *mana* as it is exemplified in certain primitive cultures. One might speak of *mana* as itself being an abstraction of sorts from a lower level phenomenon, just as the belief in spirits is an abstraction of sorts from the notion of *mana*. When one speaks of the "charisma" of a political leader such as John F. Kennedy, one is speaking of a power that is even less articulated, less objectified, than is the power embodied in the primitive fetish or in the Polynesian aristocrat. The concept of charisma, then, is most useful if one recognizes within the broad category a gradient of abstractions upon, or objectifications of, extraordinary power. The transition from one level of abstraction to the next is of particular significance in considering cases in which, for instance, an unusually powerful personality begins to take on the qualities of a magician or god; or in examining, as I will below, the way in which the natural sciences came to be endowed, in the Positivist orientation, with a low-level, unarticulated charisma, whereas in the Occult orientation science is often connected with more objectified *mana*-like or spiritual phenomena.

The charismatic in general forms the basis of concepts concerning a transcendent order of reality. The process of rationalization, as it affects religion, is not simply one of the replacement of the magical (extraordinary power) with the scientific (ordinary power), as a simple-minded interpretation of Weber would have it. It is, on a more fundamental level, the transformations wrought upon concepts of the charismatic as man seeks to fashion from them an over-arching and universal system of meaning. In this process, the realm of the extraordinary is somehow inevitably "elevated" beyond the reach of human whim; it is rendered more abstract, more predictable, and at the same time less accessible. This is what is meant by the elimination of the "magical" or "irrational" elements from the world order. In fact, the charismatic is not eliminated; it is translated into the remote distance. There are various ways in which this can happen. The peculiar outcome of these transformations as they have occurred in the Western tradition is what Weber called "inner-worldly asceticism." Calvinism is the original case in point. What is important about Calvinism is not that a transcendent order of reality has been omitted—far from it: God is there and He has His plan for human beings. *But it is no longer very important that this transcendent order be the object of immediate or personal apprehension.* God's "plan" is that man turn his attention to the material world and assure his salvation by working appropriate changes upon it. It is this transformation which in some basic sense underlies the pervasive "contentment with the finite" which is not only associated with a trust in material progress and modern science but provides the atmosphere in which these reach their full flower. In other words, in Western culture, the restriction upon the accepted modes of experiencing began even before it became popular to question whether unusual experiences had any basis in the "real" world anyway.

To further this restriction, the excesses of Reformation off-shoots such as the Anabaptists and the last orgies of witch-burning left the saner and more ethically concerned thinkers of the West exhausted and morally repelled by supernaturalism, whether it be the immediate and spontaneous supernaturalism of the witch or the more abstract and derivative supernaturalism of his persecutor. This exhaustion paved the way for what might be called a "flight into empiricism." The paradox inherent in this solution did not go unnoticed. In 1786 John Wesley commented gloomily:

> It is true . . . that the English in general, and indeed most of the men of learning in Europe, have given up all accounts of witches and apparitions as mere old wives' fable. I am sorry for it, and I willingly take this opportunity of entering my solemn protest against this violent compliment which so many that believe the Bible pay to those who do not believe it. I owe them no such service. I take knowledge that these are at the bottom of the outcry which has been raised, and with such insolence spread throughout the land, in direct opposition, not only to the Bible, but to the suffrage of the wisest and best men in all ages and nations. They well know (whether Christians know it or not) that the giving up of witchcraft is in effect giving up the Bible. (Summers 1958: 169)

John Wesley notwithstanding, it happened that men could for both religious reasons and a-religious reasons find a common cause in devoting themselves to exclusively "this-worldly" matters.

The doctrine of Positivism bears witness to the fact that science served as a medium for the rechanneling of religious energies, for in it we recognize both an attitude of adulation toward technologic possibilities and an attempt at a comprehensive understanding of the human situation rather than the only partial understanding that science is legitimately able to provide. The sort of "secularization" that took place under the influence of Positivism is of a far different order from that which came into existence after this viewpoint had been discredited. In the former a "disenchantment" of the world and a restriction upon experience was not only a welcome relief but a positive value, in that hope for man's eventual mastery and comprehension of his situation was being vested *somewhere,* viz, in the scientific modes of comprehension and mastery. With the failure of science in the twentieth century to fulfill its promise of a better world, or a world more "humanly habitable" in both cognitive and emotional terms, one finds man's concern for the "ultimate conditions of his existence" in danger of being relegated, for the first time in history, to cultural limbo. The "God is dead" lament, the concept of the "existential vacuum," the rise of anti-utopian fiction in which man is depicted as being slowly devoured by a technological-consumerist society while he wallows in pleasure-saturated consent, and, on the sociological level, Marcuse's *One-Dimensional Man,* are all, in one way or another statements of the essentially religious impasse which modern man is felt to have reached.

There are essentially two ways of viewing what is going on now. One is that the contemporary disillusionment with the "inner-worldly" orientation has opened the doors for a fresh exploration of the charismatic realm. Most notably the door has been opened to that other common solution to a "disenchanted" world image, the one previously precluded by the inner-worldly stance, namely mysticism. I refer here to the invasion of the Eastern mystical traditions which has been recently superbly documented by Jacob Needleman in *The New Religions* (1970). The connection between this invasion and the liberating effects which the preceding invasion of hallucenogenic drugs has had upon the "modes of experiencing" has been treated at great length in other writings and in the popular media and requires no special comment here. On the evidence of drugs and Eastern mysticism alone, one may adopt Theodore Roszak's view of the current situation: that our culture is undergoing a return to the irrational, spontaneous, and anti-utilitarian (Roszak 1969). The Great Refusal is underway. Whether this is a direct response to the felt sterility of the technocratic (i.e. this-worldly) or a product of sociopolitical "stress" is a misleading question since the two have come in our times to be so intimately connected.

A fuller and, within a Weberian frame of reference, a more sophisticated view is the one foreshadowed by Robert Bellah in his treatise on "Religious Evolution" (1965b) and taken up by Gregory Baum recently in his article, "Does the World Remain Disenchanted?" (1970). Bellah proposes, tentatively, that modern religion be understood as a new stage in the rationalization process. He points to the movement of modern man's expression of ultimate concern out from under the control of those institutions and groups specifically labled "religious" and away from the attachment to concrete symbolism. Instead there is a "deepening analysis into the very nature of symbolization itself" (he notes in this respect that his own essay is as much a symptom of the modern religious situation as it is an analysis of it), and a turn toward an understanding of man's existential needs, or as he puts it, "the law's of the self's own existence" (Bellah 1965b: 84–85). In essential agreement with Bellah, Baum argues, I think convincingly, that certain trends in modern theology indicate a "functionalization of the sacred." This consists of the abstraction from the great religious traditions in general, but the Christian tradition in particular, of those elements which bespeak the deepest and noblest qualities of humanity: the quest for self-awareness, the sense of individual and collective responsibility, and the brotherly love which transcends all social divisions including the now fading "religious" divisions. These elements, then, are seen to constitute the truly religious dimension of human existence. Baum says, ". . . the line of separation introduced by the sacred is between the profound and the superficial, between the forces that promote life and those that destroy it; and this line passes, on different levels, through every person and every institution" (Baum 1970: 170–171).

The idea that this is the significant dimension of any religious system is not new in theological circles. But it has always struck the theologian that for man to embrace such virtues and insights unmediated to him by a compelling symbolic tradition was more than anyone could expect. Baum does not assert, however, that a totally cognitive step is being taken. Instead he sees the phenomena of drugs, mysticism and Occultism as symptomatic of a "prophetic breakthrough." Under Weber's concept of the prophetic breakthrough, a cultural advance in the direction of greater rationalism is ushered in by an upsurge of charismatic calling-to-order. In the modern example, the young are the prophets of the new order. Baum's chief concern—as was Weber's when faced with the religious experimentation of German students in the twenties—is that these newly released prophetic energies may become dissipated in a pursuit of the "gods of the moment," by which he may be taken to mean not just drugs but all those concretely symbolic, imminently distracting and divisionary dinosaurs of old-time religion and the Occult. He feels, in other words, that the fundamentally irrational source of prophetic energy and vision cannot help but overflow its banks, and there will be inevitably those who, in an effort to sustain the ecstatic state beyond the limits of its usefulness, become trapped in old tide pools of concrete symbolism.

There is much in Baum's argument to warrant attention. Were his "functionalization of the sacred" something that merely existed on the drawing boards of Christian theological seminaries, one might have reason to doubt. But one has only to visit Esalen, Kairos, or any of the personal growth institutes that dot the urban horizon, or read the works of the Humanistic Psychologists such as Maslow or Rogers who are guiding spirits in these movements, to realize that what Baum speaks of has already crystallized into an institutional form. Furthermore one will find the functionalization of the sacred coupled there with the practices, if not always the interpretive schemes, of the Eastern mystical traditions. I would probably not be the first to put forth the opinion that at Esalen one finds the quintessence of Contemporary Religion. This feeling has existed at Esalen almost from the start.

It is my purpose here to talk about one of the "old tide pools." Placed within the perspective of Baum's reasoning (and by extension Weber's), and contrasted with the culturally avant-garde Esalen, Scientology emerges as one of the "gods of the moment"—a not very old vessel, perhaps, but one into which new life has been poured from the recent overflow of the charismatic. There is no question that Scientology membership has benefited from what has been going on in the late 1960s. So, to some extent, has every marginal religion and spiritual methodology that has bothered to extend itself in the direction of the young. Yet many of these phenomena—and here I exclude Needleman's recent imports—were neither created nor imported in the '60s. Some have been with us for over a century, and no discussion of the counter-culture or the Great Refusal is sufficient to account for their earlier viability. These elements represent, instead, a longstanding "refusal," but one which is but poorly understood if it is designated simply "the irrational."

In his construction of the system of ideas which he has named Scientology, Hubbard owes an obvious intellectual debt to the psychoanalytic tradition. I will work reference to the latter into my discussion of the two other traditions that must be accounted for in order to place Scientology in its proper perspective: these are the Occult

World and the science-fiction world. I use the words "tradition" and "world" in the same way as one would speak of the Pop Art "tradition" or the surfing "world." What is meant by the latter is an area of specialized activity and interest characterized by a broad, if superficial, personal acquaintance among the more active participants and certain accepted styles of relating to their mutual interest; and by the former, a heritage of ideas, practices and lore.

The Occult World

"Occult" is not the only label given to the world I wish to deal with here. The "metaphysical world" has been employed as well. J. Stillson Judah (1968), in his study of metaphysical movements in America notes that two separate streams of thought blend together in these movements. The one has its immediate derivation from the notions of the New England Transcendentalists and the writings of Emmanuel Swedenborg. It's emphasis is upon an immanent rather than a transcendent God and upon man's participation in divinity. The other tradition comes to us by way of medieval Alchemy, the Tarot, the Qabbalah, the Gnostic doctrines of the early Christian era, and ultimately Egyptian magic. Its emphasis is upon the comprehension and pragmatic control of supersensible reality. These two streams of thought have, however, from the beginning fused together in American culture—the one comfortably accommodating the other. I will be using the term "Occult" as a cover for both, as it is often used in Occult/Metaphysical circles, and arguing too that the underlying orientation of this world is one which forbids firm doctrinal distinctions.

Before the youthful counter-culture and the co-optation of the counter-culture by the media made Occultism fashionable in contemporary life, there existed what Martin Marty has called the "Occult Establishment" and which he describes as a "safe and often sane 'above-ground' expression, whose literature gives every sign of being beamed at what is now usually called 'middle America,' 'the silent majority,' or 'consensus-U.S.A'" (Marty 1970). This form of Occultism got its foothold in America in 1848 when the mysterious rappings in the home of the Fox family of Hydesville, N.Y. precipitated the Spiritualist movement. It was reinforced in 1872 with the arrival in New York of Helena P. Blavatsky who became the guiding spirit of the Theosophical Society. The New Thought Movement, Unity, and Christian Science are somewhat more specialized manifestations of it. During the Depression, American Occultism sent forth a fresh burst of cultic off-shoots, notably Guy Ballard's "Mighty I Am" cult, Psychiana,

William Pelley's "Silver Shirts," and the Mankind United movement of California. Most of these Depression cults were frenzied, short-lived, and legally suspect. They did considerable damage to the Occultist's public image. They were not, however, the first of the "excesses" to which Occultism is susceptible; early American Spiritualism, in many people's minds, went off the deep end in some of its communitarian experiments (Nelson 1969: 21–23). In part because of its tendency to lapse into authoritarian-apocalyptic stances, in part too because of its basic style of comprehending human experience, Occultism in any of its forms has come to be viewed with almost uniform suspicion by the straight press, medical science, and the established churches.

The typical Occultist, however, is not single-mindedly an adherent of any of the specific forms nor do some of the older and more stable systems such as Spiritualism and Theosophy demand that he should be. This is for reasons that will become apparent. H. T. Dohrman, in his study of the Mankind United movement, found that many of his informants, in addition to their interest in Mankind United, knew something about "the Lemurians, the Rosicrucians, 'I Am,' New Thought, Unity, Theosophy, Yoga, Hermetics, Mentalphysics, pyramidology, Spiritualism, the Oahspe Bible, faith-healing, flying saucers, and the latest metaphysical innovations" (Dohrman 1958: 79). Any bookstore catering to Occult and Metaphysical interests—and these bookstores are to be found in any urban area—will feature the writings of Arthur Edward Waite, Emmanuel Swedenborg, Alice Bailey, Krishnamurti, Peter Ouspensky (the Interpreter of Gurdjeiff), and Count Alfred Korzybski, in addition to the major Theosophical, Spiritualist, and Christian Science publications. On the counters lie Tarot decks and copies of the popular Occultist magazines such as *Fate, Beyond, Astroview, Search,* and *Dreams.* Inevitably, too, there will be at least one or two paperback editions of *Dianetics: The Modern Science of Mental Health,* by L. Ron Hubbard (1950).

All attempts at a simple understanding of the Occult World have a tendency to leave something out. Journalists are inclined to treat it either as a sort of "refuge" for the irrational and zany elements in our culture, or as a rag-tag collection of "syncretic" or "eclectic" religions; or both. Neither picture does complete violence to the facts, for it is true that the commercial viability of many Occult publications and institutes is enhanced by cheap sensationalism and pandering to the gullible. Furthermore, concrete cults and doctrines which do emerge from the Occult milieu are invariably composed of elements selected from a great variety of religious traditions and practices. But to accept this ready interpretation of the Occult is to ignore the fact that underlying the syncretic results, and contradicting the image of gleamy-eyed emotionalism, is a process of sorting, surveying, analyzing and abstracting that in itself constitutes an intellectual style to which the Occultist is often deeply committed. The attitude that the Occult world offers to the individual a "free marketplace" of ideas is obvious in the Occult publications which characteristically provide a little bit of ESP research, some of the latest saucer sightings, personal accounts of communication with the dead, astrological analyses of the world situation, health food advice, and personal notes on famous psychics. That "no single group has a monopoly of the truth" was the creed propounded by many of Dohrman's Mankind United informants (Dohrman 1958: 98). What this resembles, and not by coincidence, is the intellectual democracy of the scientific or academic community. The result of this free-marketplace intellectualism is, on the whole, to militate against the formation of strict dogmatic belief systems, and to favor the emergence of generalized, non-dogmatic, "meta-religions" such as Theosophy, which command a very low quotient of personal faith or allegiance.

As to whether the Occultist is "religious," and if so what sort of religiosity he espouses—one runs into trouble in this quarter as well. Some Occultists will say they are religious; others see themselves as scientists, others as philosophers. Those who use the term "mysticism" are often guilty of offending true mystics as well as fellow Occultists.

The only two features that consistently mark the Occultist are (1) his interest in the more immediate forms of the charismatic, so long neglected in the Protestant West, and (2) the repugnance, both moral and intellectual, which he feels towards the personal God-Heaven-Hell theodicy of the established churches.

In regard to the first trait, it may be only one aspect of the charismatic that intrigues the Occultist: faith-healing perhaps, or communication with the dead. Even so, he is apt to feel that all such experiences have some validity. The rallying cry of the Occult world is this: that certain experiences do not cease to exist simply because there is no place for them in our customary order. Almost without exception the many lay publications devoted to the supernatural, ESP, ghosts, prophecy and matters smacking of the uncanny or fantastic, however sober the approach, are authored and introduced by men and women who have had such experiences themselves. An example is Eileen J. Garrett's crisp first paragraph to the introduction of Arthur Osborn's *The Future is Now:*

> I have been compelled by the unusual number of precognitive visions in my own life to give a good deal of thought to the subject of precognition, the significance of which the author, Arthur W.

Osborn, sets forth in this book. The Future is Now has the unique value of presenting a problem which is ever-present in our lives, but which modern civilization rarely recognizes. Modern materialism is, for the most part, satisfied to avoid all reference to the forces which would appear to influence our existence, but which do not fit readily into the picture of a purely material and causal universe. (Osborn 1961: 7)

In regard to the Occultist rejection of the established Christian Theodicy, it must first be noted that this does not imply a rejection of Christian morality. On the contrary, Martin Marty found, in his survey of contemporary Occultist publications, that a sort of "generalized" Christian morality seems to be assumed among the readership and no need is felt to spell out such matters (Marty 1970: 228). Articulations of this morality have not been lacking, however, especially in the nineteenth century. Charles Braden found in his investigation of both Theosophy and Spiritualism, as did Geoffrey Nelson in his more recent study of Spiritualism, that both of these doctrines explicitly accept the moral teachings of Jesus (Braden 1951: 245). What is being rejected is specifically the doctrine of atonement and the notion that the unrepentant are damned to eternal punishment. Dohrman found among his Mankind United informants who were like most Occultists of that day, from predominantly Protestant backgrounds, an inability to swallow the "Hell & Damnation" preachments of the churches (Dohrman 1958: 104). The punitive side of God is equally lacking in Christian Science, Unity, and the New Thought movement in general. It is not just the picture of a spiritually inadequate Man faced with a merciless and demanding God that seems to account for the Occultist's distaste. He complains too of what he perceives as the hypocrisy and insincerity of the average church-goer. In other words, under the orthodox Christian scheme, not only is any immediate experience with the transcendant order apt to be unpleasant, but nobody seems to take the possibility very seriously anyway.

We are back once again at what seems to be the raison d'être of nineteenth- and twentieth-century Occultism; it exists in reaction to the charismatic void left by the Protestant solution of "inner-worldly asceticism." The Occult world offers an alternative for those who, usually by dint of some uncanny experience in their own lives or their need for a more immediate and direct religious consolation, are not able to encase themselves in a "contentment with the finite," nor, on the other hand reconcile themselves to a concept of the infinite that seems (a) remote and (b) potentially hostile.

But just exactly what is it that these people embrace in turning to the Occult? Clearly, if charismatic immediacy is what they want they could turn to the emotionally charged atmosphere of the revivalist and the Pentecostalist churches. In fact, there is some trickling cross-over between the latter and the Occult world. But on the whole, the Occultist rejects the emotional sects because they do not meet his intellectual demands. Modern science, on the other hand, while strongly appealing intellectually, is charismatically sterile. "Materialism" is the Occultist's anathema.

An answer to what it is that the Occultist embraces is discernible if we examine the medieval and ancient roots of "pure" Occultism: the Tarot, Alchemy, Gnosticism, and the Qabbalah. In these the word Occult is synonymous with "magic." When we try to define what is encompassed by these "magical" traditions, we find that the Occultist (or the magician) seems to have his hands on a sliding scale of knowledge and practice which has mysticism at one end and the straightforward manipulation of events in the physical world at the other. The dynamic underlying this scale is not that of rational/irrational, for all mystical and magical lore as it has developed over the centuries, however rooted it may be in the "irrational" depths of the psyche, has acquired its highly "rationalized" expressions (see Weber's definition of supra) and it is these to which the modern Occultist, in his analytical style, is most partial. What seems to be involved instead is the degree of this-worldly vs. other-worldly orientation and, hand in hand with this, the degree of commitment to the charismatic. The usual distinctions made in the literature between the scientist, the mystic, and the magician are that the scientist is this-worldly oriented with no interest in the charismatic; the mystic is other-worldly oriented and by definition, accepting of the charismatic; while the magician is caught in between. He is concerned with the super-sensible dimension of experience while maintaining an essentially this-worldly orientation.

Let me exploit the usefulness of these distinctions before taking exception of them. The magician, by virtue of his position on the scale, is constantly being pulled in two—to him unsatisfactory—directions. On the one hand, the magic arts have an incorrigible tendency to "evaporate" into completely ordinary, i.e. non-charismatic, scientific knowledge or into the equally non-charismatic techniques of sleight of hand, or trickery. As long as it is not apparent to the magician's clientele, and to lesser extent not apparent to the magician, that this has happened, the illusion that he is manipulating events in the physical world by virtue of "extraordinary power" can be maintained. Once the ordinariness of his techniques is appreciated, however, he must move on to other things. By an understandable process both "magic tricks" as we know them today, and modern science are, in large part, derivatives of the Occult.

In a reverse process, and one which is a good deal less well understood, the magic arts experience a tug in the direction of mysticism. It is worth remarking that while Occultists do not always make a strong distinction between Occultism and mysticism, true mystics generally do. This point deserves some clarification. Any survey of the varieties of religious experience, or, if you will, the varieties of extraordinary experience, reveals an enormous heterogeneity. They range in mood from a sense of sublime serenity down to inexplicable terror, in mental content from a vision of God to a vision of an automobile accident that has not yet occurred. What they have in common is a violation of commonsense experience, suggesting thereby a dimension of reality other than that usually communicated to us by our senses. In addition they are, as events, very imperfectly distributed in the population or even in the psychic life of any one individual. Both features tend to link such experiences always, to some degree, to the realm of human subjectivity, however else they may be interpreted within a given culture. What seems to cause the mystic experience proper to stand out in this catalog of unusual experiences is both its profundity and its moral and emotional purity. Not only is it reported by those versed in spiritual matters to be the pinnacle of all that they have encountered, to carry with it an absolute conviction of its importance, but also to be experienced universally as good, "blissful," enriching and complete. No experience below it is quite able to command such unqualified acceptance. The reason for the true mystic's common devaluation of lesser charismatic experiences is that these are all in some way or other morally ambiguous. They may trick or reduce the recipient as well as enlighten or inform him, set him off in pursuit of evil ends as easily as stir in him a striving for the Absolute. Among the things to be especially devalued, if one is to believe the champions of mysticism, is the crass and worldly use to which the magician puts his spiritual awarenesses (Underhill 1955: 70–71).

The magician, on the other hand, has reason for more mixed feelings regarding mysticism and the mystic quest. Firstly, on the positive side, an association with mysticism lends a halo of sanctity to his worldly manipulations. Secondly, he takes knowledge of the fact that the mystic's devotion to a union with the Absolute and the disciplines which he employs in pursuit of this goal, often release in the devotee the same peculiar powers and states of mind which the magician wishes to harness to his own advantage. This phenomenon is explained (with a word of cautionary advice) by the Russian "Pilgrim" to his friend who has had a clairvoyant vision:

> "Love Jesus," I said, "and thank him all you will. But beware of taking your visions for direct revalations of grace. For these things may often happen quite naturally in the order of things. The human soul is not bound by place and matter. It can see even in the darkness, and what happens a long way off, as well as things near at hand. Only we do not give force and scope to this spiritual power. We crush it beneath the yoke of our gross bodies or get it mixed up with our haphazard thoughts and ideas. But when we concentrate within ourselves, when we draw away from everything around us and become more subtle and refined in mind, then the soul comes into its own and works to its fullest power." (Van Vogt 1965: 104–105)

To the magician, as well as the mystic, it is of paramount importance that the soul come into its own and work to its fullest power. The former's reasons for considering it important, however, are different from those of the latter. The final attraction of mystic consciousness, and one closely related to the above, lies in its noetic quality. The mystic experience carries with it, in the words of William James, "states of insight into depths of truth unplumbed by the discursive intellect" (James 1961: 300). The magician's passion is for knowledge: super-sensible knowledge, but at the same time practical knowledge. For him, the two need not be contradictory.

On the negative side, as far as the magician is concerned, the attainment of mystic consciousness seems to be inseparably linked to a renunciation of worldly interests. Furthermore, it is often experienced as a "loss of ego" or a complete surrender of self. Both attributes of mysticism constitute subversions of the magician's this-worldly, and thus inevitably egoistic, orientation.

The pull exerted on the magician by the mundane sciences on the one hand and mystical other-worldliness on the other is important for understanding the heterogeneity of the modern Occult world. Look at the various outcomes of the Spiritualist movement, for example. Both from the point of view of participants and observers, it has spawned for some a religion, for others an interesting piece of wizardry, for others another arena for charlatanism, and for yet others the stonecold sober Psychical Research societies and their scientists who have, indeed, produced evidence of a "psi" or ESP phenomenon. In the first case one is tempted to say "So *nu?*" and in the last case, "So what?" One is tempted, that is, if one takes any of these products in isolation from all the others. But the hallmark of the true Occultist is that he does not isolate them. This is why I must disagree with any attempts to categorically divide the magician from the mystic and the scientist, and speak instead of a sliding scale or a spectrum of knowledge.

I have found in the case of my own informants, and I observe it in the writings of other contemporary Occultists (see Pauwels and Bergier 1963), an ability to slip from the position of scientist to that of magician to that of mystic or back down again in reverse order with complete aplomb. What is of over-riding importance to them is that one is *not* confined to isolated, one-dimensional, segments of reality, but that the whole thing hangs together in one unified piece. A sliding scale does exist.

The ease with which the Occultist shifts from one dimension of reality into the next stems from an abiding sense that underlying all of the apparently diverse ways of comprehending the universe is a fundamental unity. The word "Truth" best articulates this feeling, and is a favorite Occult expression. Truth is what penetrates the mind and the heart simultaneously and a person can gain access to it from either direction. All ways of "knowing" lead there ultimately. The "contentless comprehension" of the mystic is on some level the same as the cognitive control of the intellect which is again on some level related to the orderliness and regularity of nature's most solid and material processes. Even though modern science has come to stand as a lion in a field of epistemological lambs, the Occultist finds no necessary distinction between the scientific way of knowing and the mystic. He views the stubbornly materialist bent of the modern scientist as more of a failure of insight or a moral sell-out. The scientist is not living up to his responsibility which is to unravel the riddles of the cosmos. If one examines the evaluations that have been made of medieval Alchemy, a subject which, while it still defies thorough decoding, is regarded with an understanding respect in contemporary Occultism, one senses that here is a system in which the practitioner could be simultaneously, or separately, a chemist, an Adept, and a mystic. The same sense of unity is betrayed in the definitions of Scientology which is defined, informally, as a "technology of the spirit" and, formally, as "the science of knowing how to know." It is part of Hubbard's genius to have invented a system which, like Alchemy, can move from the mundane to the mystical with a good long stretch of wizardry in between.

It is important to bear in mind this difference in epistemological orientation between the Occultist and the ordinary scientist when one assesses what impact, if any, the rise of the psychological and psychoanalytic sciences have had upon the Occult world. Whatever the philosophic preferences of the various Occultists, whatever schemes the different ones may be using to tie together the cosmic order, all are in essential agreement as to the enormous importance of the human psyche. (I refrain from saying either "mind" or "spirit" since these terms are both equated and opposed and variously disputed in the different schemes.) The latter is considered both much more sensitive than the normal man would give it credit for being and also, with the proper refinement, much more powerful. Evelyn Underhill remarks that "the ancient Occultists owed much of their power, and also their evil reputation, to the fact that they were psychologists before their time" (Underhill 1955: 161). It would seem then, that when Freud and his followers undertook a theoretical understanding of the total psyche, as opposed to a mere physiological tinkering with the brain, this would have had important repercussions in Occult circles. Initially, however, the intellectual threat, if one wishes to call it that, ran in the reverse direction. Freud recognized this danger. After his own brief infatuation with the numerological theories of Wilhelm Fliess whom he apparently mistook for a staunch materialist, he became very touchy about the subject of Occultism. Very revealing is Jung's recollection of his own encounter with Freud over this matter.

> I can still recall vividly how Freud said to me, "My dear Jung, promise me never to abandon the sexual theory. This is the most essential thing of all. You see, we must make a dogma of it, an unshakeable bulwark." He said that to me with great emotion, in the tone of a father saying, "And promise me this one thing, my dear son: that you will go to church every Sunday." In some astonishment I asked him, "A bulwark—against what?" To which he replied, "Against the black tide of mud"—and here he hesitated for a moment, then added—"of occultism." (Jung 1961: 150)

Jung adds that "This was the thing that struck at the heart of our friendship." While Freudian psychoanalytic theory went on to become respectably anti-charismatic and thus fiercely reductionist in its treatment of unusual experience, Jung remained throughout his own career a "covert" Occultist. By this I refer not just to his academic fascination with subjects occult but to the epistemological bias that underlay this fascination—an unwillingness to accept the confinement of "knowing" to the finite. It is only in his posthumous admissions that one reads of the great number of extraordinary experiences to which he himself had been subject.[4]

---

[4] The susceptibility of the psychoanalyst to an occult bias is also evidenced in the writings of Wilhelm Stekel, Nandor Fodor, and in the strange careers of Wilhelm Reich and Immanuel Velikovsky.

As to the ability of orthodox psychoanalysis to "reduce" the realm of the supernatural to what would appear to be an essentially organismic base, this can easily be viewed by the Occultist as again a simple failure of nerve, another materialist "sell-out." When, in the early fifties, Hubbard began to pull away from his own attempt at a materialist interpretation of the unconscious (Dianetics), he continued to acknowledge a debt to Freud; his complaint was that Freud did not go far enough.

THE SCIENCE FICTION WORLD

In turning to a discussion of science fiction, I am not altogether abandoning the Occult world for between these two fields there has always existed a natural affinity. It is necessary to explain this in order to avoid giving the impression that Scientology is either a direct purloining of Occult tidbits or that Ron Hubbard was a person who, before his appearance on the science fiction scene, steeped himself in the magic arts, plumbed the depths of astrology, or haunted the doorstep of the church of "divine science." In fact he did not. Before, and even after his literary debut, he could best be described as an adventurer.[5] His first literary endeavors were western and adventure stories and even after he progressed from these into fantasy and science fiction the element of high adventure retains an important position in his writing. His intellectual mentors are extremely heterogeneous. While one can find supporting evidence in both his fiction and his Scientology works for his claims to familiarity with Buddhism, the Vedic hymns, Taoism, Schopenhauer, Kant, Plato, Descartes, William James, Will Durant, Alfred Korzybski, Freud, and the fundamentals of physics and engineering, his main knowledge of magic and religion seems to come from early ethnographic accounts and *The Arabian Nights*. I find that all of these sources as well as the uses to which

[5] Beginning somewhere in his teens and continuing up into the present, Hubbard has managed to enliven his career with excursions into the South Seas, the West Indies, the Far East, Central America, Alaska, and the Mediterranean. He saw naval duty in both the Pacific and the Atlantic during World War II. In 1940 he was elected to the Explorer's Club of New York and has led expeditions flying the Explorer's Club flag in 1961 and 1966. He is an excellent mariner and in his youth acquired the reputation for being a daredevil glider pilot as well. Attempts to reconstruct the order of events in Hubbard's life (or even their facticity) before Dianetics are notoriously hard, and I will not undertake to do so here. The most exhaustive account to date, and the one from which I have taken some of this information appears in Malko (1970). Even this account is suspect partly because of the subject's elusiveness and partly because of Malko's obvious distaste for Hubbard and Scientology.

Hubbard has put them are best understood in the context of his literary profession.

Jules Verne, H.G. Wells, and earlier forerunners notwithstanding, science fiction did not really begin to emerge as a literary genre until the appearance of the "all-fiction" pulp magazines around the turn of the century. Besides featuring the early "western," the "adventure," the "detective," and the "fantasy" story, these periodicals discovered the enormous appeal of the type of tale which in Kingsley Amis' broad definition treats "of the kind of situation that could not arise in the world we know, but which is hypothesized on the basis of some innovation in science or technology, or pseudo-science or pseudo-technology, whether human or extraterrestrial in origin" (Amis 1960: 18). These were the first widely popular science fiction attempts.

Blending easily into the imaginative mixture that constituted the offering of the all-fiction pulps were themes and notions taken from the Occult world. One example of such a blend was a serial called "The Occult Detector," which ran in the Munsey pulps for over twenty years. The detective, "Semi Dual," was the creation of a Salt Lake City doctor, J. U. Giesy, and a Cincinnati lawyer, Junius B. Smith; he solved crimes through the use of astrology, chirography, handwriting analysis and various psychic skills (Moskowitz 1970: 338). Charles Hoy Fort, who became quite a favorite in both science-fiction and Occult circles because of his mammoth catalog of "facts" which science has been unable to explain, published some of his first satiric commentaries in the Munsey magazines. The appearance of Occult elements in the early all-fiction magazines is, at bottom, nothing to be wondered at. Obviously nothing that has been conceived or that is conceivable escapes the literary imagination once this imagination is given full scope and it was in the all-fiction press that full scope first came to be granted it. However, as different genres began to emerge from the mix—westerns, detectives, etc.—the two that maintained the greatest imaginative freedom were those of fantasy and science fiction. Their speculative permissiveness accounts in part for the fact that magic and Occultism came in the long run to be more wedded to these two literary forms than to any other.

Another and somewhat more obscure basis for the attraction of the science fiction mind to the Occult lies in the Positivism that was rampant in early science fiction circles. Sam Moskowitz remarks upon the strong mental bond that seemed to arise between otherwise total strangers once they had discovered each other's interest in science fiction. Science fiction fan clubs rapidly formed and these early fans felt themselves to be almost a race apart from ordinary man. "No one," they say, "has ever seen our visions, dreamed our dreams. Never before has man's brain reached out so far into the limitless stretches of the cosmos about him" (Moskowitz 1954: 1). Some of the spirit of these first enthusiasts is revealed in the letters sections of the first all science fiction periodicals which began to appear in the late 1920s. Moskowitz reports:

> In the Old *Amazing* (*Amazing Stories*) fans were ready and willing to discuss anything. The eagerness with which they prattled scientific talk was directly traceable to some scientific fact which had aroused their interest in its extrapolated counterpart in fiction. Be it astronomy, biology, physics or chemistry, they broached some query which coeval science could not answer, but which science fiction tried to. And the readers expressed their opinions on how logically it had been answered. (Moskowitz 1954: 5)

The unarticulated charisma with which the Positivist endowed science and technological achievement was but a hair's breadth away from the more expressly magical fantasies which the science fiction writer wove into it. In science fiction creations the Positivist could entertain himself by hovering on the brink of the fantastic while the Occultist could find in the same creations the possibility of bringing the supersensible realm down onto the plane of hard, commonsense factuality.

The affinity between the Occult and science fiction persists even to this day in spite of the fact that science fiction has itself become very diversified. Kingsley Amis, whose taste is clearly for "mature" sociological science fiction such as that which characterizes the works of Ray Bradbury, Phillip Dick, or Frederick Pohl, complains that a love of science fiction still carries the stigma of "an eccentric obsession probably connected with a belief in the validity of Rhine's experiments and in flying saucers operated by little green men from Venus . . ." (Amis 1960: 150). As the last phrase indicates, it was not just conventional Occult themes that provided the "wierd" material of science fiction, but all of the imponderables and improbables of the universe: life on other planets, death rays, healing elixirs, strange mutants, inter-galactic travel, "anti-matter," to mention just a few. Now these elements have drifted, not surprisingly, within the purview of modern Occultism—witness flying saucer clubs, anti-gravity societies, etc. The straightforward imaginative possibilities of such items cannot be dismissed as an insignificant factor in the drift. That both the science fiction writer and the Occultist traffic in the improbable, the charismatic, and the "unreal," is a principle reason for the attraction of each to the other's territory, and for the interchange of materials.

A final reason for the attraction of the two lies with the craft of science fiction writing itself. The science fiction writer, if he is good at his trade, has something special to return to his materials. For one, he articulates feelings and ideas latent in the culture concerning the unknown, the improbable and the magical, e.g. if there is life on other worlds it may be (a) monstrous, (b) superior to human life, (c) hostile, (d) benign, etc. Secondly he interprets in terms of modern conditions the significance of breakthroughs into the realm of what was previously felt to be the magical or, at the very least, the improbable. The moldy medieval "Adept," a being with superior mental powers, for instance, receives his modern or futuristic form in Van Vogt's *Slan* or Heinlien's *Stranger in a Strange Land*. Most importantly, the science fiction writer lends to his notions verisimilitude. An often quoted definition of science fiction bears repetition here:

> Science fiction is a branch of fantasy identifiable by the fact that it eases the "willing suspension of disbelief" on the part of its readers by utilizing an atmosphere of scientific credibility for its imaginative speculations in physical science, space, time, social science and philosophy. (August W. Derleth *in* Moskowitz 1961: 7)

The concept of verisimilitude was first seized upon and systematically exploited by Hugo Gernsback, who in 1926 put out *Amazing Stories,* the earliest all science-fiction periodical. According to Moskowitz,

> . . . he tried to lay down rules for science fiction. Primary among these was plausibility: nothing was to appear in the stories he published that could not be given logical, scientific explanation. To bolster this, ingenious photographs and related newspaper columns surrounded the tales until after a time it became difficult to differentiate the fact and the fiction. (Moskowitz 1954: 4)

I mention Hugo Gernsback in particular because he "externalized" a process which had been logically inherent in science fiction from the beginning, moreover one which is logically inherent in science itself. In fact, a chronicle of the uses and abuses of scientific verisimilitude would hardly begin or end with Gernsback. Martin Gardner has collected a number of the most famous—or infamous—cases in his *Fads and Fallacies.* One of the earlier American examples cited is that of the "Great Moon Hoax," perpetrated by the *New York Sun* in 1835. Richard Locke's articles, which recounted in vivid detail the physiognomy and habits of "moon men" as seen through a powerful new telescope by the British astronomer Sir John Herschel, were intended as satire; but thousands of New Yorkers continued to believe in "moon men" even after the reporter had disavowed their factuality (Gardner 1954: 66–67). While the establishment press of today has given up such pranks and become much more cautious in its scientific reportage, this did not prevent the *New York Herald Tribune,* the *New York Compass, Harpers,* and the *Reader's Digest* from giving credence in 1950 to Immanuel Velikovsky's *Worlds in Collision* in which the author uses astronomical theories to account for the great catastrophes and miracles of the Old Testament (Gardner 1954: 28–33). Velikovsky was neither a satirist nor a deliberate hoaxer. As are most of the thinkers dealt with in Gardner's book, he was an example of the serious "pseudo-scientist," a theorist who not only is convincing but personally convinced that through science he has managed to bridge the gap between the mundane and the fantastic. In the "pseudo-sciences" we recognize what is essentially the practice of the magic arts in modern form, for the pseudo-scientist, like the Occultist, finds it possible himself and makes it possible for others to cross over that thin epistemological boundary that separates the material and causal universe from the charismatic.

Gardner himself is an example of the opposite sort of mentality: the staunchly anti-charismatic determinist who is especially prone to lend his talents to the great American tradition of "debunking" which has grown up as a foil to the immediately charismatic elements in our culture, especially those embodied in the pseudo-sciences. H. L. Mencken was one of the most celebrated of its practitioners. Today the hand of the A.M.A. can be felt heavily in the same quarter.[6] These two inveterate foes, the Occultist and the debunker, point up the tension in our culture that has arisen in the wake of the Protestant solution. One of the places where this tension often came to a head was in the science fiction world; and it is very much in evidence in the early history of Dianetics and Scientology. The actual heyday of science fiction hoaxes and pseudo-sciences, like the heyday of overtly Occult uprisings, seems to have passed with the passing of the Depression era. A new sobriety and sophistication set in during the '40s and '50s; but the thrill of feeling that perhaps man's brain could, once again, reach out into the "limitless stretches of the cosmos" did not die. Those who, like Philip Wylie, deplore what he considers the

---

[6] The journalistic battle that the A.M.A. constantly wages against Occult "quacks" is well illustrated in the November 1970 issue of *Todays Health*—well illustrated in more ways than one. On the cover is a picture of a "Satanist" apparently in the act of "invoking," and the caption reads "Devil Doctors and the Gullible." Inside one finds that the cover character is not really a Satanist but instead Warren Albert, associate director of the A.M.A.'s Archive Library. Both article and cover, in terms of cheap sensationalism and bad research, easily rival the most inane piece of quackery. What may be betrayed in such examples is the A.M.A.'s fear that its own (unarticulated) charismatic currency will be devalued by Occult competition.

"psychologically toxic" effect of science fiction upon the public mind, a thing which made it possible for thousands of Americans to rush panic-stricken into the streets in 1938 on the occasion of Orson Welles' broadcast of "The War of The Worlds" (Wylie 1953: 235–236), might well ask themselves why these gullible souls didn't simply twist their radio dial to find out if the news was general and why some who did and found out that it wasn't believed the Welles broadcast anyway. Perhaps in their hearts they wanted to keep alive the possibility, even if it meant extermination, that there is more in heaven and earth than dreamed of in our philosophy. A little paranoia is the price one pays for letting the fantastic enter into the real.

One should not get the impression from the foregoing that the science fiction world is monolithic in its mental orientation—far from it. The average science fiction writer distinguishes himself from the true pseudo-scientist by keeping his tongue very firmly in his cheek, or by ignoring the magical dimension altogether. A secret yearning for the charismatic as well as Gernsback's editorial tradition cannot, however, be ignored when one turns to the subject of John Campbell Jr. It was John Campbell Jr. who, as editor of the immensely successful *Astounding Science Fiction,* introduced Dianetics to the world in 1950. Campbell's personal and professional orientation in many ways made this logical. Precociously intellectual as a child, Campbell became an enthusiast of science and science fiction in his teens and began his career as a science fiction writer while he was still a student at MIT in 1928. He had already made his name as a writer by the time he completed his degree, and he continued to write successful science fiction until 1937 when he assumed the editorship of *Astounding.* Although he launched his writing career at a time when the "super-science epic" (vast intergalactic plots, incredible weapons, thinking machines that take over civilizations, etc.) was just coming into its own and did his share in developing it to its finest peak, it is apparent from his later efforts and from the direction in which he was to carry the magazine, that for him, the fascination had begun to drain out of technological feats and into the area of the human mind and character (Moskowitz 1961: 26–46). In contrast to his early fantasies in which machines are seen as ultimately wiser and more "civilized" than their inventors, one finds Campbell's subsequent views of the scientific vs. the human expressed as follows:

> Man is not a realist; he's an idealist first, and a realist second. . . . The whole function of science, the magic that works, is lost if it does *not* serve to fulfill mankind's needs and dreams and to ward off fears. Yet the very nature of science is such that science, as

science, cannot recognize hope or fear or good or evil. . . . Science is . . . so inhuman, so utterly unsuited to mankind, that no human being can *be* a scientist; he can only set apart a certain section of his mind to think like a scientist. (Campbell 1953: 4–5)

The change from the Campbell of 1930 to the Campbell of 1953 was, of course, a change in the American Soul as well. After technological wizardry had given us Hiroshima and Nagasaki it became all too clear that the physical sciences, as such, were not going to be the heart's consolation. But Positivist yearnings were not entirely dead. In Campbell, as in many, they had simply taken an inward turn.

The atomic bomb seems powerful and impressive—but remember that it is merely an expression of human will and thought, that human beings control and direct it. Human thought, not atomic energy, is the most powerful force for either construction or destruction in the known universe. It is this aspect that science fiction is exploring today—the most dangerous and most magnificent of all *terra incognita* still lies a half inch back of your own forehead. (Campbell 1953: 20–21)

Campbell's movement toward the psychological and sociological was gradual. Beginning with his assumption of editorship of *Astounding*, he began to discover and cultivate new writers such as Heinlien, Van Vogt, Sturgeon, Asimov, Lieber, and Hubbard himself. All of these writers were strong on character-study, mood, and sociological speculation. In the cases of Hubbard, Lieber, and Van Vogt an interest in supernaturalism, mental powers, or peculiar mental states is dominant as well. Campbell's own leanings toward the psychic and uncanny did not in fact crystalize until the mid-fifties when he became openly absorbed with "psi" phenomena, at one point tinkered with a "psi" machine and elaborated a speculative science of "psionics" (Gardner 1957: 346–348). Before that, however, it might be said that while Campbell was in love with the fantastic he could not be wedded to it unless it appeared in the form of the materialistically reasonable. When in 1949 Hubbard came up with a new mental therapy called Dianetics, Campbell had found his psychic bridegroom.

DIANETICS AND EARLY SCIENTOLOGY

The original Dianetics consisted of a theory of the mind and a therapeutic technique. As to the theory, the psyche is divided into two strata: the Analytic Mind and the Reactive Mind. The Analytic Mind is operative in man's usual wakeful, fully conscious, "rational" state;

and it contains information and memories that are readily available to awareness. The only reason, Dianetically speaking, for the Analytic Mind to mislead an individual or cause him to act in an inappropriate manner, would be if the individual had acquired misinformation or false data. Inappropriateness or "mistakes" of an analytic nature are thus easily corrected by re-education. The Analytic Mind is a store-house for consciously acquired and accessible information and it operates upon this information by what is usually called the "reasoning" process; it discriminates, sorts, assesses, and explores and comes up with judgments, interpretations and decisions which are appropriate to the occasion at hand. Thus it serves in a very sophisticated and flexible fashion to aid the survival of the individual. The Reactive Mind, a more primitive level of the psyche, also acts to ensure the survival of the individual, but it does so through the much cruder device of "reflex"—or "reaction"—the underlying principle of which is simply that of equation. Fire for example may be equated, reactively, with getting burnt and thus "the burnt child fears the fire." [7] At the risk of some distortion, a parallel can be drawn between Hubbard's Analytic and Reactive Mind and Freud's Ego and Id. [8] The Reactive Mind is thus the part of the psyche that is subject to "conditioning" in the Pavlovian sense. The Reactive Mind is a storehouse for "conditioned" equations which are not, normally, accessible to awareness and which were not consciously acquired (Hubbard 1950).

Hubbard's theory of the mind shades into therapeutic technique via the concept of *engrams*. The Reactive Mind can only acquire its stored information during periods when the Analytic Mind is temporarily inoperative, i.e. during periods of apparent unconsciousness. In fact, in Dianetics, there is no such thing as true unconsciousness;

[7] Hubbard recognized a category somewhere midway between Analytic and Reactive which he dubbed the "Somatic Mind." The Somatic Mind consists of those behavior patterns and techniques which were *consciously acquired* but which have been reduced to the level of reflex or habit. Driving a car for instance is one such behavior pattern. In contemporary Scientology, these patterns are usually called "machinery" rather than Somatic Mind. It is recognized that many "machines," like driving, are useful. An effort however is made to "break down" the machinery that an individual has acquired in the social and interpersonal realm.

[8] The Analytic Mind serves in a way that is only ambiguously articulated to guarantee the survival of the "sense of self," while the Reactive Mind is more connected with the survival of the organism. Thus the two are often in conflict. Freud's concept of the Superego has no parallel concept in Dianetics or Scientology. Behavior and feeling which, from a Freudian point of view are to be considered Superego derived, are treated variously in contemporary Scientology. A Scientologist would hold that much of what a person calls his "conscience" is Reactive; the fundamentals of conscience, however, are not, but stem instead from the fact that man is basically good.

when the Analytic Mind is out of commission, the Reactive mind continues to record information. Furthermore, the information acquired during periods of unconsciousness does not become part of a reactive equation unless it is associated to some degree with pain. Thus the engram, which is defined as an incident containing pain and unconsciousness, is the basic building block of the Reactive Mind. All of man's apparently inappropriate or "irrational" behavior which cannot be explained on the basis of false analytic information and which does not clear up through simple re-education, stems from the engramic contents of the Reactive Mind. These engrams are stirred into action—"restimulated" in Dianetic terms—by any stimulus in the external world that resembles or is the same as something in an engram. When such a stimulus appears, the Reactive Mind "keys in," and causes the individual to react in a manner which would be appropriate were the present-time situation the same as the past-time situation of the engram, but which, since it most often is not, appears to be "irrational" or inappropriate. The contents of the Reactive Mind are responsible for neuroses, psychoses, and psychosomatic illness.

Early Dianetic theory also deals with a number of other things: the ways in which and the reasons why a person will, reactively, assume the identity of another; the way in which incidents of loss and painful emotion enter the Reactive Mind; the way in which people "dramatize" their engrams—that is, how they do unto others what has been done unto them, and so on. All of these additional bits helped to make Dianetics, even in its earliest stages, an intriguing and fairly comprehensive explanation of human behavior. This was part of the basis of its initial extensive appeal. For the sake of simplicity, I will confine most of the discussion for the moment to engrams.

Hubbard held that in order to "clear" a person of his irrationalities, psycho-somatic illnesses, etc. one had simply to dredge up into consciousness all the engrammic incidents and allow their emotional force to discharge itself, after which these incidents lost their influence. The way in which this was done was through "auditing." Auditing means, essentially, listening; but both in early Dianetics and in contemporary Scientology it includes special techniques, usually in the form of questions or commands, which aid the patient—or "pre-clear" as he is called—in looking for forgotten incidents. One such technique— now out of use—consisted of seizing upon any phrase that the pre-clear tended to overuse either in ordinary conversation or during auditing sessions and asking him to repeat it over and over again until some memory sprang to mind. Usually the over-used phrase would be found to be something heard during an engrammic incident (Hubbard 1950: 214–232). Another important consideration in auditing rests upon the fact that aberrative incidents are found to run in "chains." That is, one painful experience will be found linked to an earlier one by virtue of some similar element and so on down the line until one gets to the earliest on the chain. The earliest is called Basic and an incident's claim to the status of "Basic" is determined solely by the fact that it is the incident the discharge of which causes the aberration or illness to vanish. Part of the art of auditing then was an ability to get the pre-clear down to the "Basic" on any chain.

Originally Hubbard saw the Reactive and Analytic Mind in simple organic terms. Engrams were "cellular recordings;" memory itself could probably be explained, if one wanted to go to the bother, in bio-chemical terms (Hubbard 1950: 93). Really it did not much matter. He blithely audited his pre-clears through their automobile accidents, war injuries, operations, beatings by drunken fathers, falls from the crib in early infancy, the birth trauma, and back into such gruesome "prenatals" as attempted abortions and violent parental sex acts.

While orthodox science could, and did, question the *probability* of Hubbard's theory that there is no such thing as true unconsciousness, while it could, and did, question the probability that painful conditioning is the source of all aberration, and while it could, and did, question the probability that environmental influence begins before birth, it still could not say that Dianetics was anything other than utterly materialistic in its orientation. Where was the magic?

At first the sense of the fantastic spread only as far as those who had met Hubbard or been audited by him. An element of charisma comes with the man himself and has apparently been present from his youth: George Malko unearthed a racy little sketch of Hubbard that appeared in *The Pilot,* a west coast aviation magazine, in 1934. Hubbard was then 23.

> "Whenever two or three pilots are gathered together around the Nation's Capitol," the column's author, one H. Latana Lewis II, wrote, "whether it be a Congressional hearing or just in the back of some hangar, you'll probably hear the name of L. Ron Hubbard mentioned, accompanied by such adjectives as 'crazy,' 'wild,' and 'dizzy.' For the flaming-haired pilot hit the city like a tornado a few years ago and made women scream and strong men weep by his aerial antics." (Malko 1970: 32)

A. E. Van Vogt, who as a young science fiction writer met him eleven years later comments simply: "It was when I first met Hubbard that it suddenly dawned on me that all human beings do not have pedestrian-type minds" (Van Vogt 1964: 76–77). Scientologists and early

Dianeticists to whom I have spoken about him, whether they be pro or anti, always emphasize his commanding quality. "A very Big Being" is a common description. Others have remarked that he appears to look larger physically than he actually is. Even his detractors will say not simply, "He's a con man," but "the greatest con man of the century" (Gardner 1957: 263). What seems to stand out in Hubbard is an ability to enter into whatever he is doing and just carry it off whether it be to get into a sailplane, as the columnist of *The Pilot* describes, and perform feats that brought undertakers out onto the field (Malko 1970: 32), or to don a white sport jacket and stroll down the corridors of Oak Knoll Naval Hospital, where he was recovering from war injuries, and have everyone address him as "Doctor" (a trick he used to gain entrance to the psychiatric ward where he did some of his early observations of psychotics).

John Campbell, Jr., who was audited by Hubbard and relieved of chronic sinusitis (a condition into which he promptly relapsed after he became disillusioned with Dianetics), helped to spread Hubbard's magic. In 1949 he wrote to Dr. J. A. Winter, a medical doctor who had previously contributed articles to *Astounding,* touting Hubbard's new science. In response to Winter's request for further information, he supplied the following:

> There is only one important statistical fact that I think should be dealt with. This has been research; Hubbard has been working on it as a research program, trying to find out what causes what, and how to fix it. Therefore, with cooperation from some institutions, some psychiatrists, he has worked on all types of cases. Institutionalized schizophrenics, apathies, manics, depressives, perverts, stuttering, neuroses—in all, nearly 1000 cases. But just a brief sampling of each type; he doesn't have proper statistics in the usual sense. But he ·has one statistic. He has *cured every patient* he worked. (Winter 1951: 5)

Winter says, appropriately enough, "My first response to this information was one of polite incredulity" (1951: 5). Here then was a circumspectly materialist science, yet one which nevertheless seemed to be bridging the gap between the mundane and the fantastic.

When Hubbard's big book, *Dianetics: The Modern Science of Mental Health,* came out in 1950, it was hardly written in a tone conducive to dispassionate experimentation. Instead it explodes with declarative assertions. Early readers caught the spirit and promptly sat down and performed miracle cures on their friends and relatives using only the simple guidelines for auditing given in the book. This first book continues to have a charismatic impact upon many readers.

I have talked with a surprising number of Scientologists who entered Scientology as late as 1966 simply on the strength of having stumbled upon *Dianetics* and read it. One Scientologist who read the book in 1960 told me: "When I read *Dianetics: The Modern Science* I knew that this Hubbard was a man I could follow."

I am not arguing that there was no "science" at all to early Dianetics and that sheer enthusiasm alone was responsible for the cures that resulted. In fact, there was much in Hubbard's theory that warranted serious consideration, as Fritz Perls points out in his introduction to Dr. Winter's account. Even if the influence of early trauma on the development of neuroses and psychoses, or the possibility that seemingly unconscious persons do record the things that are done and said in their vicinity, were entirely ruled out by orthodox science—as they have not been—one would still find both in the early and the contemporary styles of Dianetic auditing a viable mundane notion at work, viz. that underlying most illness and somatic disturbance is an unconscious emotional "stance," the expression and objectification of which (either through recollection or fantasy) will alleviate the disorder. I only wish to make the point in passing that a strong appeal to the charismatic results in a much higher "cure rate" than viable scientific notions whether these be Hubbard's or anyone else's; and to go on to my main point which is that it was his interest in the charismatic dimension per se which caused Hubbard to scrap the early materialist version of Dianetics, and to be scrapped in turn by John Campbell, Jr., Dr. Winter, and orthodox science.

To return to the fate of early Dianetics: the impact of Hubbard's book and the enthusiastic backing of John Campbell, Jr. and Dr. Winter resulted in the setting up of a Dianetics Research Foundation in Elizabeth, N.J. in April of 1950. Its purpose was to disseminate information about Dianetics and to train people as Dianetic auditors. It boomed. Shortly thereafter a second Foundation came into being in Los Angeles under the guidance of Van Vogt, whom Hubbard had personally recruited to the cause. It also boomed. By Van Vogt's reckoning, the Los Angeles Foundation had taken in from two to three hundred thousand dollars before January of 1951. By then, however, it was in serious trouble, and by June 1951 it was closed. The Elizabeth Foundation seems to have followed a similar course.

A number of things had gone wrong, not the least of which was financial and organizational mismanagement. Hubbard apparently divided his time between his various groups and left control of the thing loose. At one point he appointed a Board of Directors, which included Winter, Campbell, and Van Vogt, to manage Foundation business while he devoted more time to lecturing and research. This did not seem to reduce the confusion but might well have heightened it. If Hubbard was, in the eyes of the orthodox, raking in hundreds of illicit dollars from the suggestible public, he was in turn being royally ripped off by his staff, some of whom, it is said, never showed up at the Foundations at all except on pay day. The telephone company and the government began moving in. To worsen the public image of Dianetics, Hubbard's wife, Sarah Northrup Hubbard, whom he had at one point pronounced "clear"—that is, a totally rational being—had him pronounced insane by some doctors she consulted and sued for divorce. In the same year, his attempt to present Dianetics to a large gathering at the Shrine Auditorium in Los Angeles failed disastrously. The whole organizational structure of the first Foundations, the public infatuation, and Hubbard's marriage, were over by the summer of 1951 and he fled in despair to Cuba. Within a month or so he was back for another round of very much the same thing. The second round was quieter, less in the public eye than the first; the new Foundations were in Witchita and Los Angeles; but again, within a year, bankruptcy threatened.

More significant than finances for the purposes of this discussion was the ideational split that began to brew within Hubbard's nascent organizations. Early in the game, Dr. Winter became distressed at what he considered the "unscientific" orientation that was starting to prevail in Elizabeth. Hubbard refused to pitch his approach to the professional or medical community and there was, even among the Board of Directors, a rather derogatory attitude towards the accomplishments of medical science. Winter disliked the idealistic and absolutist concept of the "clear" and the notion that anyone could become a Dianetic auditor. In October of 1950 he resigned (Winter 1951: 28–42). Something else had begun to happen which Winter does not mention but which was to result in the alienation of Campbell, Van Vogt, and a sizeable portion of Hubbard's followers. That was that pre-clears and auditors had started pursuing engram "chains" back past the prenatal stage and into past lives. I asked one early Dianeticist when "past lives" had first come up in Dianetic auditing. "Right away," he snapped, "That is, within the first six months." Another recounted to me the tale, which he concedes may be part legend, of how it first happened:

Before the conflict [over past lives] broke out, there were, as he recalled, two guys who always hung around the Foundation not ever really accomplishing much and tending to make snide remarks about the goings on there. In those days Ron apparently got things going by wandering around from room to room, setting up auditors with preclears, giving instructions, or sometimes starting a process himself and then leaving the auditor to complete it. So in effect there were little sessions going on all over the building all the time. Both of the two men in question had run lots and lots of engrams, but nothing seemed to work for them. They were turning into natterers; but no one paid them much mind. Then one day somebody opened a broom closet and found these two sitting there auditing each other on past lives. And having a marvelous time of it. [My informant's] interpretation of this was that both of these men were "pretty clean" on this lifetime, so the auditing didn't really start to "bite" until they went into earlier lifetimes. Hubbard's attitude was "Fine, as long as it works."

A reading of *Dianetics: The Modern Science* would suggest right away that Hubbard's commitment to a sober non-charismatic science, if it existed at all, was never very deep. Campbell and Winter, on the other hand, while they were as enchanted as the next person with Dianetic's "fantastic" results, could not bring themselves to take so raw a leap into the realm of the supernatural. In fact, it may have been Campbell's first inkling that he had been standing right next to it all along. Some say it was he, or he in combination with Winter, who led the "rebellion" against past lives that split early Dianetics ideologically down the middle. At any rate, Campbell dwindled from view somewhere around 1952 when the split became final.

In 1952 Hubbard left the Witchita Foundation in the hands of a former friend, Guy Purcell, who, having salvaged the Foundation from financial ruin, proceeded to denounce Hubbard's latest innovations and hold to the "scientific" line. Apparently many other early Dianeticists—like Campbell and Winter—felt scandalized when that which was implicit from the start in Hubbard's ideas began to emerge as the "figure" whereas what they had yearned for receded into the "ground." The "ground" stayed in Witchita with Purcell. The "figure" moved to Phoenix and became Scientology.

Hubbard was learning from his mistakes. Soon Boards of Directors, ill-regulated and salaried staffs, and irreverent wives were things of the past. He became a more honest man—in two ways. First, he left little doubt as to who was really in charge. He was. Secondly, he no longer felt the need to play upon the covert charismatic yearnings of frustrated Positivists such as John Campbell, Jr. Accordingly, he openly reversed his position on the material nature of the psyche and began to develop a set of ideas that would account not only for past lives and the wild assortment of incidents which people found in their earlier lifetimes, but also for the whole range of uncanny phenomena which have hitherto been relegated to the realm of the supernatural or passed off as unexplained "psi" factors. It is this set of ideas that he named Scientology. While the defection of the science-minded had cost him a goodly portion of his following and support, there were a number of the faithful remaining. They were the ones who found it quite a relief to be free of the onus of materialism, of being, as they put it, "just bodies." The notion that man is in some way, or on some level, a spiritual being, came to be refined into the concept of the Thetan, which is now the core concept of Scientology. Thetan is defined in Scientology as "The person himself—not his body or name, the physical universe, his mind, or anything else: that which is aware of being aware; the identity that IS the individual. (From Theta ⊙, the Greek symbol for 'thought' or perhaps 'spirit' ")" (Hubbard 1964: 34). The ego, or the perceiving Self, is "spiritual" in that it is not bound by the laws of the material/causal universe. In words vaguely reminiscent of those of the Russian Pilgrim, the first axiom of Scientology states: "A Life Static (Thetan) has no mass, no motion, no wavelength, no location in space or in time. It has the ability to postulate and to perceive" (Hubbard 1958: 2). In early Scientology, this concept was reinforced experientially not just by the recollection of past life incidents but also by the phenomenon of "exteriorization" (the sense of being outside one's body) which Hubbard and many of his auditors found they were able to produce in their preclears. Exteriorization was and still is one of the goals of Scientology auditing.

Scientology auditing took two basic directions, determined by the nature of the two sorts of experience just mentioned. On the one hand, his interest in exteriorization led Hubbard to concentrate upon a whole range of perceptual and character phenomena. What exactly was a pre-clear "doing" as he sat there before an auditor? Was his attention all there, and if not, why not? What exactly did he perceive/feel when told simply to "Look at that wall?" (Some pre-clears are unable to follow that command; others have exteriorized on it.) What ideas do people carry around concerning time, space, matter, or energy and how do these ideas affect their interaction with the environment? And so on. (In fact the nature of this sort of investigation and the insights Hubbard derived from it have parallels to the sorts of things dealt with in what is called "Existential Psychoanalysis.") This investigation resulted in many of the theoretical formulations that make up Scientology's vast inventory of psychological lore: the communication formula, the structure of understanding and how this relates to "upsets," the structure of "problems" and how they can be dispelled, the nature of devices people use to make themeselves "right" and others "wrong," etc. One of the things which came to be appreciated in Scientology was the enormous fragility of the ego (read Thetan) and the degree to which people must inhibit their attention, develop reflex "machinery" and erect barriers against sensory intake just to get through a normal working day. A stimulus-deprivation principle is at work in much of Scientology auditing and seems to be related in a way which is not well understood (in orthodox science that is) both to the phenomenon of exteriorization and to the experience of expanded awareness or heightened consciousness that makes Scientology so attractive to those experienced in drugs and meditation.[9] It is the movement of auditing in this direction too that causes Scientology to be sort of borderline mysticism.

The other direction auditing took was in the exploration of past lives. Hubbard put his followers to work "mapping" their Time Track. ("Track" is the expression used informally in Scientology to refer to past lives.) Since much of the recorded "Track" falls into the province of the Reactive Mind, he felt that if some sort of past history could be constructed from the immensely varied assortment of recollections people were coming up with, then a way could be found for ultimately subduing the influence of the Reactive Mind altogether. The types of past-life recollections that people had in common were a salient factor in this project. He did eventually arrive at just such a history. It is a history not just of the human spirit but of the entire universe that extends back into infinity. In "Track," Hubbard had finally found a place for the high adventure of which he was so fond and which figures so prominently in his fiction; for the spirit's previous existences comfortably encompass not only what we know of conventional history, and many of the things we don't know of conventional history, but also much of what is customarily assigned to the realm of myth and science fiction.[10]

[9] One scientological explanation for the relationship between stimulus deprivation and exteriorization is that it is sensation and the desire for sensation that chains us to our bodies in the first place. For the most part the psychiatric literature classifies exteriorization as a form of hallucination (which itself is not well comprehended). This is not surprising in light of the fact that psychiatrists most often encounter the phenomenon in cases where severe emotional stress or physical shock is present. This form of exteriorization—"forced exteriorization"—is recognized in Scientology but considered psychologically dangerous as it so strongly parallels the experience of dying. Another area in which exteriorization is reported is in the literature on sensory deprivation experiments. Sensory deprivation experiments precipitate in the subject a syndrome that begins with intellectual disorganization, proceeds into a free flow of fantasy, and often ends with an exteriorized or some other "hallucinated" state (see Cracke, 1967). It is of interest, in this respect, that in one of his early stories (1940) Hubbard anticipates the sensory deprivation experiment as well as its outcome.

[10] Hubbard is often quoted as having said that most of science fiction is just "track." People make the mistake of thinking that they are projecting something

The two lines of auditing exploration were reunited in the idea that the more of a person's Reactive Mind he sheds, by auditing out the really core (and unpleasant) parts of his Track, the more he will recover the spiritual abilities that have been lost over the eons as engrams piled up and man sank further and further down into the "rigid apathy" of the material universe. At the end of the auditing road lies total freedom, total awareness, total "knowingness."

To give an account of all of Scientology data, or even an account of the above in any sort of detail, would exceed the scope of this paper. What I have dwelt upon in this simplified rendition of the concept of the Thetan, exteriorization, and the Time Track would strike a Scientology reader as far too weighted in favor of the abstruse materials and too little weighted in favor of the every-day practical stuff which gives Scientology a broad, non-magical base and which is the basis of its approach to the man-in-the-street. But I have done so for a reason, which is to bring out the way in which Scientology employs and explains "unusual" experience. Given the above definition of a Thetan, phenomena such as out-of-body experience and clairvoyance become obvious. So too do the near-mystic states such as feeling that one's self encompasses the entire universe. Telepathy is accounted for in the Scientology theory of communication which puts it on the upper end of a gradient that covers all forms of exchange from the most material (like the exchange of bullets, warfare is a form of communication) to the most spiritual. The idea that one's self is not one's mind explains the way in which a person can operate above the level of thought and simply perceive and understand intuitively, or as they put it, on the level of "knowingness." *Déjà-vu*, fantasy, dreams, not to mention the elaborate visual imagery and the sense of racial memory encountered in drug-induced states, are accounted for through the concept of the Time Track which consists of "the consecutive mental image pictures or facsimiles (sense impressions) recording the consecutive moments of 'now' through which the individual has lived" (Hubbard 1964: 34). Aberration, psychosomatic illness, etc. have been dealt with above.[11] In the course of their auditing and training,

---

into the future whereas in fact they are dredging it up from the past. The story is told of Hubbard himself that he used to write his science fiction stories by sitting down in front of a blank wall and "just typing up the action as it came across the screen."

11 Psychokinesis and mysterious disappearances are also accounted for, but the explanation is too difficult to undertake here. The only unusual experience that Scientologists have some trouble with is precognition, as they do not hold to the notion of a predetermined future. All those with whom I have discussed it, however, are quite accepting of the phenomenon, and they manage to use speculative combinations of Scientology ideas to explain it.

Scientologists report a high incidence of such experiences in their personal lives, and they take it for granted that the incidence will increase as they progress up the training/auditing ladder. A not atypical "Success Story" is the following. The writer is an upper-level Scientologist. The excerpt comes from *Advanced Success Stories,* put out by the Advanced Org, L.A.

> I have rediscovered what telepathic communication really is. Knowing what someone is "thinking" before he says it has become part of everyday communication. I can sit at my desk and *fully* experience the reality of any place, from ocean to snow-capped Sierras. Always knowing who's calling on the phone before it rings, and being able to check the progress of my cooking hamburger without walking into the kitchen.

When I referred to the broad base of practical, non-magical techniques that make up lower-level, or everyday Scientology, this should not be taken to mean that there is some intrinsic division in Scientology between magic and non-magic, upper-level and lower-level. Such a division is easy for outside observers to create in their own minds; Scientologists often create it themselves in order to express what they have to say in a way that is comprehensible to the uniformed. These lower-level techniques include quick ways to alleviate the pain of a recent injury, step-by-step procedures for rehabilitating an area of one's life that is in trouble (one's job, one's marriage), methods of organizing groups of people and running a group project, study techniques, and many interpersonal "skills" which are usually thought of as half-conscious "arts" but which can in fact be consciously acquired, e.g. the "art" of getting and holding someone's attention, of creating a comfortable environment for someone who is in pain or emotional distress, of "listening," and of sizing up a person on the basis of minor cues so that one knows essentially where that person's "head is at." Many of these practices can be thought of and explained in quite mundane terms. But in an important sense they inevitably feed back into the higher level phenomena. There is a way in which the simple acknowledgement, "O.K." said by one Thetan to another *feels* differently from the same remark between two outsiders; a way in which looking at the chaos of papers amassed on one's desk and beginning to sort through them is a different experience for the Scientologist than for the non-Scientologist. The reason for this is two-fold. On a purely intellectual plane, the Scientologist says his "O.K." within the context of a communication theory that logically unites the exchange of bullets with mental telepathy; he sorts his papers within a frame of reference that unites the sorting of papers with the sorting of worlds and solar systems. At the same time—and here the connection between the lofty and the pedestrian is much harder to convey—the Scientologist is attuned to certain uniformities in his subjective experience. When receiving a verbal communication, for instance, he looks for the same sort of inner impact, the same subtle flash of knowing that one has picked up the communicator's intention, that one associates with those "wordless exchanges" of thought which are so common between people but so seldom remarked upon. To him, communication—good communication—is a quality of experience. Similarly, when sorting papers he is savoring an inner state—in this case the satisfaction of willing or predicting an event in the physical world, then accomplishing it; this same feeling that underlies the numerous acts of daily life may be found as well in the unusual Track memories of oneself as a "universe maker." Both on an intellectual and a subjective level, the Scientologist puts himself back once again on that sliding scale that extends from the mundane to the mystic. In effect the reorientation of the self wrought through Scientology may be no different from that achieved in any religious system; perhaps that is what is meant when the religious say that the tiniest event can be viewed *sub specie aeternitatis*. I only wish to bring out here the comprehensiveness of Hubbard's system. It is a comprehensiveness achieved in large part by his concentration upon all those intervening levels between mundane and mystical, those "unexplained" quasi-religious dimensions of reality that are skipped over in the highly transformed world religions. In articulating and making "rational" these levels, Hubbard has reintroduced the sense of a unitary Truth that is the Occultist's desideratum.

Scientologists, it should be pointed out, do make a number of distinctions between their philosophy and the ideas and practices of ordinary Occult World. One feature that is common in other metaphysical and Occult doctrines but notably absent in Scientology is, in fact, the emphasis upon "hiddeness." Judah points out that metaphysicians pay a good deal of attention to the symbolic value of words and images. They "have a belief in an inner meaning of words beyond their dictionary definition—a meaning that cannot be discovered empirically from the standpoint of usage or etymology, but that is revealed intuitively" (Judah 1968: 17). To the Scientologist, on the other hand, nothing is really hidden; it's all crystal clear once you understand the principles of the thing. Symbolism is of very little interest to them and they assign it to a level below that of ordinary (intellectual) thought, rather than, as is common in the rest of the Occult world, placing it just below the level of mystical insight. Students in Scientology training are encouraged to bring an English-language dictionary to class with them, and Scientology terms are catalogued and precisely defined in the Scientology Dictionary. Any student caught entertaining the impression that a word means something beyond its agreed-upon usages is quickly disabused of this notion. In this respect, Scientology may be the only "Occult" philosophy that actually carries through in practice the attitude that underlies the general Occult fantasy: that intuitive and rational knowledge are not, fundamentally, inconsistent.

It is the sense of a unitary "Truth" that makes Scientology, despite its hard-headed approach to the subject, a comfortable meeting grounds for both the old-style Occultist, the ex-"head," and the dissatisfied or unfulfilled mystic (a category that includes many ex-"heads"). In addition it reaches out to the many Americans who are fascinated with things psychological but either intimidated, disillusioned or repelled by the established psychological sciences. Scientologists acknowledge that whether one gets onto it by drugs, by dabblings in Occultism, by some peculiar experience in one's own life, or simply by a desire to understand humanity on a deeper level than that provided by the material sciences, one is all the same in touch with a sense of things that is essentially Scientological. In regard to those who dabble in other practices, or who have had some contact with Scientology but abandoned it, one man said, "Oh, they'll get there eventually. Maybe it won't be through Scientology, and maybe not in this lifetime, but they'll get there. Once you're on the road to Truth, you never get off."

Conclusions

What I have attempted to do is to lay the foundations for an understanding of Occultism, its place in American culture, and its relationship to Scientology, that goes beyond a simple play upon the words "rational" and "irrational" into which one is so easily seduced by a casual reading of Weber. It has been argued that the "rationalization" process that over the centuries has effected the great religious traditions is best understood as a transformation of charismatic elements into more and more abstract, and remote, formulations. This has had the result, in the Western tradition especially, of creating an experiential void in established religion, and a frustrating "gap" between the accepted modes of comprehending the universe and man's place in it. While the religious re-examination launched in the 1960s by the growing discomfort with our depersonalized social order and the impact of drug experimentation is doing much to fill this void in a way that transcends the adherence to specific traditions and concrete symbolic orders, earlier attempts at filling the void have been present in America, and indeed in Western civilization as a whole for several centuries. One of the products of this earlier attempt is the Occult World, and its style of comprehension still exerts a strong appeal today.

While American Occultism can be identified by its rejection of the established religious concepts of a remote and punitive divinity and its address to the more immediate and personal areas of charismatic experience, it represents neither a turning towards emotionalism and/or anti-intellectualism, nor is it definable as only one compartment of religious or worldly interests. The basis of Occultism in general, and American Occultism in particular, is a synthesizing orientation towards all the ways that man has found to "relate himself to the ultimate conditions of his existence." Occultism seeks to reunite the separate pieces of the intellectual, emotional, and apprehensional jig-saw puzzle by surveying and abstracting from all the traditions that address themselves to the task of *understanding* things, whether this understanding be directed at practical mastery or at passive acceptance. Occultism posits an underlying singular Truth, the search for which cannot be confined to a particular style and the content of which cannot exclude any dimension of human experience, however "irrational" it may seem.

When a group movement does arise in the American Occult world it generally does so on the basis of, first, strong leadership, and second, unusual achievements either in some area of charismatic experience (faith-healing for example) or in a more compelling intellectual formulation of the whole spectrum of knowledge—usually it is a combination of the two.

Scientology, which answers the above criteria almost to a fault, is the creation of a man whose intellectual background and style was— depending on the viewpoint taken—either strongly molded by or simply reflected in his vocation as a science fiction and fantasy writer, and his participation in the science fiction community of the '30s and '40s. It has been argued that the Positivist bias, the speculative style, and above all the skill with which science fiction integrates worldly knowledge with elements of the fantastic and the improbable, bring the science fiction world—or one might say the "science fiction mind"—into very close alliance with the Occult orientation. If Scientology has terms and concepts that sound more specifically like science fiction than like earlier Occultism, this is in no way inconsistent. Scientology defines itself as the "science of knowing," or the "science of knowing how to know," and its appeal is exactly commensurate with how well it fulfills this implicit promise.

Classificatory Approaches: Typologies in Historiographical and Sociological Analysis

THE authors in this section agree that traditional ways of classifying marginal religions are inadequate. They either hide more data than they reveal or answer problems that are no longer generally considered very important. John Wilson points out that historians of religion are only now becoming more aware of how social scientists treat religions of a non-mainline variety. Alan Eister agrees that the usual variables offered to explain marginal religions are often derivative rather than causal and suggests we look to disorganization in what he calls our orienting institutions for a possible explanation for the proliferation of religious groups. Marcello Truzzi uses characteristics of occult movements that the movements themselves provide to show the variety and non-threatening nature of most of these groups. Implicitly he emphasizes the ineffectual kinds of approaches usually applied to occult groups. Truzzi, since he is dealing with data so long and deeply misunderstood, brings home with unusual force the inadequacies of traditional analysis and classification of occult movements. And Virginia Hine in an exhaustive study evaluates several of the standard classificatory hypotheses for handling all these movements and churches. She shows systematically what data such hypotheses reveal in support of traditional explanations, and what ranges of data are left unaccounted for. The message that all the papers in the section offer with forceful uniformity is that the domain of marginal or splinter religious groups in America is ripe for new conceptualization and classification. This very healthy assessment is accompanied with a set of suggestions aimed at correcting the flaws in scholarship as it now stands.

Within the area of classification John Wilson deals with the attention historians have given to marginal religious movements. While there have been many historical studies of marginal groups, the groups have not been treated consistently in the historiography of American religions. This is the case even though such movements have been present in the United States through all its history. Furthermore, there have not been systematic efforts to place such movements in the context of religion in America. Wilson reviews available studies to see how marginal groups have been variously conceptualized in religious historiography. He shows the comparatively slight influence on historical studies of the sociological study of sectarianism, an area from which one might have expected significant cross-fertilization. Wilson then points to the kind of conceptualization that might allow historians to study both dominant traditions and marginal groups as well as the relationship of both to the common culture.

Wilson concludes that more attention was given to marginal groups in the nineteenth century than has been the case more recently. The earlier scholarly tradition took it for granted that sects were adequately explained as heretical deviation from orthodoxy. Late nineteenth- and early twentieth-century writers continued the basic pattern of interpreting sects and cults as anomalies and aberrations from the more consistent, unified Protestant tradition. The interpretations which ignored marginal movements thereby overlooked a significant range of religious variation, the interpretation of which is central to understanding religious development in American society.

Some social scientists have tried to explore different typologies. The most widespread approach to reaching more sophisticated explanations for these churches is that developed by Truzzi. It involved the use of categories and terms often used by the members of these groups to describe and explain their own churches. While ultimately native explanations are not always the most useful, they do however reveal the intricacies, variety, subtleties, and multiple meanings that religious systems contain. They represent more fully the reality of the believers and faithful. The fullness of native paradigms are presented by using this method, and its inherent descriptive advantages are manifest in many of the papers in this book.

Truzzi considers the importance of meaning systems in witchcraft and their relationship to science, religion, and magic. One criterion for dichotomizing between belief systems is the method of verification available to the believer. Any time we talk about phenomena over which there is no concensus or which can never be objectively verified, we are talking about what most people mean when they refer to the occult; if it is verifiable and validated it will be called science. But in their own eyes occult groups have come to see themselves as a type of science rather than as orthodox religion. Often they classify themselves as supernormalistic rather than supernaturalistic. Their magic has been secularized. Truzzi argues that the occult concern with things mysterious and inexplicable has always been intertwined with magic. Howover, occultism is so multi-dimensional that it does not necessarily include marginal social elements, nor does it always center its concerns about the supernatural. The sociology of the occult should be considered as a subdivision of the sociology of knowledge where it has important implications for its companion sub-fields, the sociologies of religion and science. This multi-dimensionality precludes our speaking of the occult as a single entity and points up the inaccuracy of the generic categories used by the public and older scientific analyses.

The problem of what set of categories to use to both describe and explain the rapidly growing religious movements in America has another dimension which is latent in several of the papers in this section. Classification ultimately depends on a problem, and problems are the product of a given culture at a specific time and place, and, consequently, classifications are relative. Because classifications and typologies exist to arrange data according to a set of more or less consciously understood criteria and exclude many other criteria, they are addressed to specific ends. They do not exist as eternally valid objects to be used by all investigators studying all problems. The criteria themselves stem from the problem a scholar wants to solve, and the origin of the problem, we must assume, stems ultimately from some aspect of the scholar's culture. Since all these things change—problems, criteria, classifications—we must assume that they can be readily discarded when they prove to be either misrepresentative or irrelevant.

To see this point from the perspective of a member of an occult group is to see why so many people in these religious movements are disillusioned with science and its academic home. They feel that what appear to them to be perfectly empirical things are either denied existence by the scientific world or are ridiculed. As a consequence many feel scientific categories are inadequate to handle a fairly large and certainly significant range of reality. Consequently the scientific world—and certainly some of its disciplines—are held to be unsatisfying, indeed bankrupt.

Science, however, has moved with extreme slowness to find new ways to deal with religious phenomena. Some current groups feel that they have extended the yardstick of knowing beyond that of science into the domain of the mystical and transcendent. None feels it is in conflict with science, although most feel science has abrogated its traditional task of providing universalistic explanations for incomprehensible or mysterious things. Most marginal churches think of themselves as necessary extensions of science.

Because traditional institutions like science have failed to some extent in our society at their task of orienting the individual, Eister suggests alternative institutions, sects and cults, are now popular. His basic hypothesis is that when the basic units of belief systems—meanings and orientations—are challenged, cult movements are stimulated. Dislocations in the orientational and communicational institutions of contemporary societies, e.g. artistic, literary, educational, religious institutions, should be regarded as a major factor in the current surge of interest in cults. Cults are freed from conventions of standard science and religion as well as from traditional ways of knowing and classifying reality. The usual rules are no longer in force and as a result cults are open to new beliefs and patterns of behavior.

Eister notes that the usual explanations of marginal religions no longer produce satisfactory results and criticizes them before setting out his own suggestions. Virginia Hine is also concerned with modes of describing and analyzing current religious movements. Here is an evaluation of the accuracy of traditional explanations in a systematic way. She looks at past scholarly treatments of these movements and says that most analyses of social, political, and religious movements are preoccupied with two questions: why movements arise, and why people join them. Movements are seen arising as a result of rapid cultural change, social disorganization, and dislocation of values. Deprivation arising out of the imperfections of the social matrix and tensions caused by the inevitable inequalities within the social system produce such movements. The second question usually leads to psychological analyses of maladjustments, pathologies, emotional inadequacies, or specific personality attributes which predispose an individual to seek a collective solution to private problems. The three ideas traditionally used to explain why people join these movements are the disorganization model, the deprivation model, and the deviant or defective individual model. She concludes the phenomena described by these models facilitate rather than cause these movements. They are derivative and correlative, not causal.

The whole notion of how to classify and create an accurate typology is complicated when dealing with marginal religions because they change so fast. The rapidity of change is caused by the speed with which these groups interact with external variables. There is a feedback relationship between faithful, institution, and the outside world. It is because of this relationship that Hine sees correlation, not cause, in models where others have seen prime movers. It is also because of the intersection of variables that all of the authors here have found a classificatory approach based on a few isolated criteria so inadequate. These churches have built their success on their quick response to pressure; they are built on their ability to change. A typology that focuses on isolated traits freezes a group into a typological category and consequently misrepresents its changeable nature. Typologies tend to obscure the observation that change in social composition or organizational structure may lead one of these groups to serve a different function for its members. Such static models have been particularly defective in categorizing Pentecostal and occult groups, presenting a view of their unity and disguising their internal diversity. Creating a picture of unity and masking internal diversity tends to hide the tension that often exists between some of these groups. Movements often identify themselves by opposing their chief attributes to some other similar church or movement, and an emphasis on static typologies tends to obscure the tension between the segments composing a movement.

The Historical Study of Marginal American Religious Movements

MARGINAL religious movements are so prominent in our own time that it should be unnecessary to demonstrate to the present generation their significance in the American past. In fact, myriad religious sects, cults, and movements have populated American society throughout its history. To be sure, specific groups have developed and declined; probably the relative number of them, and the proportion of the population identified with them, however, have remained virtually constant for the better part of three centuries. In what follows it will simply be assumed that there is no need to establish the reality of these phenomena in the society of the new world.

In certain respects American historians and students of literature have not neglected particular marginal religious phenomena. Sects, cults, and movements have been perceived, quite correctly, as thoroughly a part of social life in both colonial and national periods. At the hands of certain authors they have become an unusually effective subject matter through which to interpret broader cultural developments. Numerous studies could be cited to illustrate this point (e.g. Cross 1950; Meyer 1965).

If religious sects, cults, and movements have represented a continuing reality in American history, however, and if scholarly attention has been given to at least some of them, the *interpretation* of these groups as *religious phenomena* has not been consistent. In the historiography of American religion, marginal sects, cults, or movements have received remarkably little attention, and certainly there has not been effective explanation of them as religious phenomena. One of the primary intentions underlying this paper is to remark upon some of the major shifts in the interpretation of these phenomena as religious movements, for they have been variously perceived by those who have undertaken to interpret the history of American religion. Accordingly, the first section of the paper discusses the interpretations of marginal groups which have been developed by historians of American religion. Another basic purpose is to comment upon the influence of the sociological study of sectarianism upon the study of religious history. Finally, some attention will be given to the kind of historical study of marginal movements which seems to be appropriate in the light of present interests, especially among anthropologists.

The peopling of the English colonies in the New World, and especially in the New England colonies, was a highly self-conscious and concerted migration. Its origin and development can be studied in unparalleled detail. We know very well how it was interpreted (and freighted with religious significance) at the point of design and projection. Thus the religious interpretation of America originated in the early years of the seventeenth century, since the colonization was largely explained in religious terms. In this sense the first historical writings within the English settlements, e.g. the works of John Winthrop, Edward Johnson, or William Brewster, were done with religious purposes (among others) in mind. It is useful to draw a distinction, however, between general histories which are written in terms of specific religious views of history and attempts to interpret religious behavior, belief, and institutions as a separate class of phenomena (even if interrelationships with other classes are posited). In this perspective Cotton Mather, especially in his *Magnalia Christi Americana*,[1] represents the initial historian of American religion as distinct from and in addition to his work as a historian who made use of religious categories to interpret the American experience. Mather actually gave his major study the subtitle "The Ecclesiastical History of New-England."

The *Magnalia* is divided into seven books which severally chronicle the civil leadership of the colonies, pay tribute to the best known "divines," celebrate the "University" at Cambridge, preserve the "Acts and Monuments of the Faith and Order in the Churches of New-England," and recount "providences" of mercies and judgments which rendered the divine will intelligible to the settlement. The last of the books, militantly titled "The Wars of the Lord," is a "history of the manifold Afflictions and Disturbances of the Churches in New-England from their various adversaries. . . ." This is a major sustained interpretation of marginal social groups in the colonies from the point of view of a historian of religion at the turn of the eighteenth century. For Cotton Mather such phenomena were correctly understood as deviations from the orthodox churches of New England, ranged on the right hand and the left, and constituting the temptation wherewith the devil was assaulting the faithful. To frame an argument to suit his broader purposes, the author contended that virtually the

[1] The *Magnalia* was originally published in London (1702). Reference is to the edition published in Hartford (1820) and based on the London edition. On Mather as a historian, see Gay 1966.

whole morphology of religious deviance (to use modern terms) had been displayed within the New England wilderness.

In his analysis Mather undertook to identify the vexing sects under specific heresies by which they were identified. Thus Roger Williams (to whose stature Mather paid grudging tribute) and his followers stood guilty of "separatism." Samuel Gorton, who was likewise drawn to Providence Plantations (a cesspool of "exhorbitant novelties"), was damned as a "familist." Anne Hutchinson, that stubborn and gifted troubler of the New Israel, embodied in Mather's view both "antinomian" and "familistical" tendencies. "It is the mark of seducers that they lead captive silly women; but what will you say when you hear of subtil women becoming the most remarkable of the seducers?" (The male chauvinist in Mather would not be stopped: "Indeed," he opined, a poyson does never insinuate so quickly, nor operate so strongly, as when women's milk is the vehicle wherein 'tis given.") Anne was, in short, "a gentlewoman, of an haughty carriage, busie spirit, competent wit, and a voluble tongue." The seal of this interpretation of Anne as heretic was her alleged delivery of a monster with the assistance of a midwife who was herself "strongly suspected of witchcraft, and a prime familist." The point, of course, was the need to attribute deviance to Satan, a backhanded way of giving God glory. Indeed, Rhode Island became so exclusively a kingdom of Satan's that Mather doubted such a collection of religions had ever resided together on "so small a spot of ground": "Antinomians, Familists, Anabaptists, Anti-sabbatarians, Arminians, Socinians, Quakers, Ranters," etc.

Mather reserved his greatest contempt for the Quakers, "the worst of HERETICKS that this age has produced," and perhaps the worst of all time. An "upstart sect," its error was that of attending to "the mystical dispensations of the light within, as having the whole of religion contained therein." By comparison, Mather was quick to acknowledge Anabaptists (if they were so willing) to be his "brethren," though not failing to insist upon the "prodigious heresies that have been held, and actions that have been done by men so identified" (Mather 1820: II, 430–458).

In sum, Mather recognized marginal religious groups as very much a part of colonial life, and potentially a source of social disruption. From this point of view they were classical Christian heresies or deviations. Thus sectaries and fanatics were witnesses for the devil and a trial to the godly and through them the faith of the latter was exercised. "Fascination is a thing whereof mankind has more experience than comprehension. And fascination is never more notoriously sensible than in mens running after false teachers of religion" (Mather

1820: II, 470). In this sense it might even be thought that the sect was needed or required within the orthodox world view no less perhaps than the sect was derived from and depended upon orthodoxy.

As the first major historian to give attention to marginal religious groups in America Cotton Mather interpreted them under the rubrics of "heresy" and "sect." The next prominent student of the range of the religious life of the American people was Jonathan Edwards, who sought to make intelligible to himself and others the religiously expressed turbulence generally designated as the Great Awakening. " 'Tis no new thing, that much false religion should prevail, at a time of great reviving of true religion; and that at such a time, multitudes of hypocrites should spring up among true saints" (Edwards 1959: II, 85).[2] No less than Mather, Edwards viewed Satan as the author of heresies and the father of sects, and his own rather remarkable analysis of the "affections" was precisely intended to identify errors and, hopefully, to edify true religion (II, 88–93). With exquisite precision, Edwards defined false religions as based upon "impressions in the head" (not "a divine sense and relish of the heart") and attributed to them "the pretended high experiences, and great spirituality of many sects of enthusiasts." Through such false religions of the sects, he opined, Satan undertook "to confound hopeful and happy revivals of religion" (Edwards 1959: II, 286–287).

Both Mather and Edwards utilized the rubrics of heresy and sect to explain marginal religious phenomena. From this it may be inferred, and evidence of other kinds sustains the conclusion, that the marginal group was perceived as dangerous to colonial life. Theological and religious deviance served to identify and explain challenges to the society and its culture. Thus marginal movements were believed to be potent and direct threats to social order. Therefore civil and ecclesiastical authorities were necessarily concerned with them, and toleration, when granted, was out of necessity more than indifference. On this point a dramatic shift occurred in attitude and orientation toward marginal religious movements in the course of the next century.

Two important studies published at the end of the Jacksonian Era indicate the new perspectives on religion, and especially marginal religion, which had developed in the new nation (Baird 1856; Schaff 1961).[3] Both projects were initially undertaken to explain America to

---

[2] *A Treatise Concerning Religious Affections* was first published in 1746. On Edwards as a historian, see Gay 1966.

[3] Robert Baird, *Religion in America* (1856) was based on an earlier American edition of 1844 which was based on a Scottish edition of 1843. See condensed version, edited by Henry W. Bowden with introduction (1970). References to Philip Schaff, *America* cite the edition by Perry Miller (1961); the book first appeared in 1855.

Europeans; in each case, the studies were well received at home and provide useful analyses of ante-bellum society. Robert Baird was an American resident in Europe; Philip Schaff, a Swiss who had migrated to Pennsylvania. Each in his own way exhibits, rather incidentally, the change in perception of marginal religious groups and movements over the course of the preceding century. Neither speculated at length upon why these changed interpretations of American sectarian phenomena developed.[1] It is striking to observe how Baird and Schaff simply took for granted marginal religious groups as, so to speak, natural features in the landscape of a religiously complex society. While each remained committed to relatively "orthodox" perspectives, both abandoned the interpretation of "sects" as directly derived from "heresies." Heterodoxy might well characterize a marginal religious movement, but even if it were considered a "necessary cause," it was not viewed as "sufficient" in the manner of Mather and Edwards. Indeed, Baird and Schaff interpreted sects less as creatures of Satan than as created by excess human zeal in a largely unstructured environment.

Baird undertook to explain the "multiplicity of sects" to Europeans by emphasizing that the "evangelical sects," at least, were to be understood in terms of the factor of ethnicity in the migration which peopled the continent. Not "the indulgence of a capricious and sectarian spirit" but the "extension by emigration of a similar body in Europe" was the correct explanation for the multiplicity of evangelical communions. They "ought to be viewed as branches of a great body." Baird took pains to de-emphasize any "unseemly strife" among these groups, a feature of American religious life which had been widely reported in Europe (Baird 1856: 533–539). He also called attention to "unevangelical sects"—and a strange collection it turned out to be: Roman Catholics, Unitarians, Christians, Universalists, Hicksite Quakers, Swedenborgians, Jews, Shakers, and finally Mormons. Except for the first two enumerated, Baird believed that these sects were essentially "unstable." Beyond this he offered reasons for the interest of Americans in such sects: the fascination exercised by "novelty" in a literate country, the entertainment thus made available on Sundays (a day otherwise without activity), curiosity in the absence of an "evangelical ministry," and the positive advantages of member-

[1] One source lay in the migration and multiplication of population and in the consequent experience of expanding social space, a development which challenged all static institutions and ideas, e.g. authoritarian churches and orthodox theologies. Another related source was in the indigenous political tradition, explicitly formulated by James Madison, which limited the claims of governing institutions and permitted, indeed encouraged, the existence of "factions" or divisions in the society so long as the effects were not ultimately destructive.

ship in religious congregations under the conditions of religious liberty. Baird even identified a constructive way of viewing this confused religious picture; he opined that those who joined "un-evangelical sects" in the United States would have been stolidly indifferent to religion in another land, and thus they here benefited from partial truth which was preferable to none at all. Finally, sects rendered their members "more accessible to the faithful preaching of the Gospel, than others that are sunk in stupid indifference and infidelity" (Baird 1856: 579–580). Thus marginal religions, which for Mather were interpreted as challenges to the Godly since they served as displays of Satan's power, had become for Baird a secondary good within a society dominated by evangelical forces, virtual halfway houses to conventional religious practice.

Philip Schaff took a somewhat different ground in his analysis. Rather than emphasize the substantial identity of the evangelical communions he acknowledged outright that the "ecclesiastical condition of the country" was basically a "sect-system." By this he meant that "all religious associations, which do not outrage the general Christian sentiment and the public morality (as the Mormons . . .), enjoy the same protection and the same rights" (Schaff 1961: 96–97). While admitting certain difficulties with these arrangements, he nonetheless emphasized the positive aspects of this open market between religious groups. Schaff did nothing to paste over the reality of a "legion of smaller sects" to which he made explicit reference (104), but he urged his hearers (readers) to place this in perspective—and thus, like Baird, he laid great emphasis upon the numerically and culturally dominant "denominations." Especially for the benefit of his German audience, he stressed the transplantation of a few older European sects (Herrnhuters, Mennonites, etc.) more than the marginal groups native to the United States—except for the Mormons, for whom he reserved a special unsympathetic section (166 ff).

In effect both of these important mid-century studies placed emphasis on unitive interpretations of religion in America. The existence of marginal movements was acknowledged—but placed in a perspective which effectively served to de-emphasize them. Explained as accidents due to the conditions of American society, little interest or hostility attached to them—save perhaps to the followers of Joseph Smith, Jr. Otherwise, none possessed the fascination which so focused the attention of a Mather or drew the interest of an Edwards. Much the same view carried over into studies which followed the War between the States, e.g. Daniel Dorchester's *Christianity in the United States* (1888), which simply took note of "divergent currents" within broader patterns of "new life," "expansion," and "convergence."

Similarly H. K. Carroll's analysis of *The Religious Forces of the United States* (1893), which was based upon the 1890 census augmented with additional statistics, took note of "Non-Evangelical" denominations, "Non-Orthodox" bodies, and "Non-Christian" groups. Excepting the Jews and Unitarians from these totals, though retaining the "Latter Day Saints" and "Communistic Societies," Carroll identified fewer than 300,000 communicants organized into less than 2,000 units (1893: xlvii). From this perspective the marginal groups appeared to be minor anomalies within, or insignificant exceptions to, his general delineation of the religious life of the American people (a total of 20,600,000 communicants organized into 165,000 organizations). Carroll's book is significant because it was one volume of a multi-volume series on the subject, and the only one which made serious reference to marginal movements—excepting those groups which were clearly subdenominations within broader traditions.[5]

What strikes the modern reader of these nineteenth-century interpretations is the general disinterest in empirical accounts of, or first-hand reports upon, the marginal phenomena. Cotton Mather (perhaps from fascination if not fear) took sufficient interest in the sects to familiarize himself with them and to seek out additional information where such was lacking. Jonathan Edwards can be interpreted as a psychological student of Awakening deviance as well as a theological critic thereof. Baird and Schaff, by contrast, did little to inform themselves or their readers regarding the marginalia to which reference was made. Certainly there are available, e.g. with respect to the Shakers, comments by visitors to their communities, or, with respect to the Mormons, some materials which directly illuminate that movement in the period of its growth. But on the whole the students of religion in America did little to emphasize the place of religious deviance in the society or to analyze its significance.[6]

In many respects the same fundamental unitive interpretation carried over into twentieth-century studies of American religion, including those published up to the recent past. W. W. Sweet's (1930, 1942, 1952) many volumes at no point incorporated systematic and serious attention to marginal groups. Nor have the provocative essays by Sidney Mead (1963), or the essays and studies produced by others in this generation of interpreters of American religious history, e.g.

---

[5] The remaining volumes of the series were histories of denominations except for vol. XIII, *A History of American Christianity,* by L. W. Bacon (1897).

[6] For a discussion, among other matters, of the variety of religion in 19th-century America, see Tyler (1944). Milton Powell (1967) has edited excerpts from writings of European visitors to the new world who commented upon American religious life, including its diversity, between 1740 and 1865.

Winthrop Hudson (1953, 1965), Robert T. Handy (1963), Jerald C. Brauer (1953). The Princeton series on "Religion in American Life" devoted only a single essay (Jamison 1961) to the subject, although the extremely useful volume of critical bibliography compiled by Nelson Burr (1961) demonstrated the need for far more consideration. At the same time most of the secular historians who have turned to religious materials in recent decades, e.g. Henry F. May (1949) and Timothy L. Smith (1957), have directed little or no attention to the issue of marginal religious groups. (The Transcendentalists, eccentric in so many respects, count as a special case.)

In sum, the main tradition of American religious historiography from Mather to Mead exhibits a net decrease in interest with the marginal or the anomalous religious movement.* At least for Mather sects were distorted images of the true religion and direct challenges to it. In that sense the phenomena were considered socially functional, and in seeking to give an adequate interpretation of American religion he was required to come to terms with them. More recent interpreters have not believed themselves to be so constrained. Perhaps the chief reason for this pattern lies in the development within American society of virtually unlimited tolerance for ideas which are believed not to entail threatening behavior. Thus individuals and groups whose self-definition is given in religious terms within America experience widespread indifference to their beliefs. When antisocial activity ensues, however, even on the part of innocuous cults, toleration is no longer extended. The substance of religious freedom has thus become largely identical with the disinterest in ideas which is so endemic to American society.

Within the present century attention has been directly focused on religiously deviant groups and marginal movements not so much by historians of religion as by sociologists, and this development has a sufficient (although finally negative) importance for the historical study of American religion to warrant attention. Ernst Troeltsch first undertook initial systematic development of the concept "sect" which has since been widely utilized in sociological studies of religion. Troeltsch formulated this concept as a means of analyzing the differentiation of medieval Catholicism socially considered. In his view the church-type and the sect-type of Christianity coexisted within the medieval context, and the latter became especially important for understanding the history of Christianity in the modern period. Troeltsch used the

---

* Since this paper was written, Sydney E. Ahlstrom has published a major interpretation of religion in American history which devotes considerable attention to these phenomena. See *A Religious History of the American People* (1972).

term "sect" analytically. He carefully identified, and placed aside, the usual polemical and apologetic sense of the word, pointing out that such a meaning derived from "churchly" usage. Also, the term is not properly used to signify merely an "undeveloped expression" of a church. For Troeltsch the essential institutional principle of the sect type was that it is a "voluntary community whose members join it of their own free will." It is at base, therefore, a voluntary church (Troeltsch 1931: I, 331–339).

Troeltsch's study came down to the beginning of the twentieth century—at least in theory. Perhaps it would be correct to say that he interpreted the differentiation of Protestantism essentially within the terms which he developed to understand Christianity of the late Middle Ages, including the sixteenth century. Within the frame of reference of continental Christianity there may have been some merit in continuing to use a two-fold typology—church and sect—for understanding the social teachings of Protestant groups and Tridentine Catholicism (although Troeltsch supplemented it with a less well-developed third type, mysticism, which has received scant attention). The church-sect distinction could not illuminate the American Protestant story as adequately, however, and H. Richard Niebuhr significantly modified it in *The Social Sources of Denominationalism* (1929), the first sustained application to the American context. Niebuhr's study, it is important to note, was designed less to outline the social teachings of American religious communities (the underlying intention of Troeltsch's work) than to analyze the means through which social circumstances in their origins left indelible marks upon the "denominations" which were so derived. Thus the "denomination" came to be understood as a third type of organization peculiarly characteristic, perhaps, of Protestantism in America. Intermediate between church and sect, it was not especially distinctive in terms of its social ethic. Looked at from one point of view, denominations were simply Troeltsch's "voluntary churches" set in a social context which did not include church-type organizations and which was prepared to tolerate them.

To the degree that Niebuhr's study has had wide and continuing influence during the last four decades in studies of American religion it might be argued that social science perspectives have informed the study of marginal American religious groups. Two observations suggest why this has not actually been the case. In the first place, Niebuhr soon produced a companion study, *The Kingdom of God in America* (1935), which significantly qualified or modified the thrust of *The Social Sources of Denominationalism*. It shifted emphasis to a broader conception of Christianity (primarily Protestantism) in America as a social movement which, to be sure, passed through different stages or phases but which retained an identity through time.[7] The net effect of Niebuhr's work was probably to modify Troeltsch's categories for the American context so that the "social movement" corresponded to the "church" of earlier European society, and the "denomination" corresponded to the "sect." In each instance, there was absent the formal constituted social authority toward which the "church" had been oriented in a positive manner and the "sect" negatively. In general, historians have been informed by the whole of Niebuhr's work, and to this extent the direct influence of sociological analysis of sectarianism upon traditional study of marginal religious groups has been significantly diminished.

In the second place, refinement of the concept "sect" as a type of religious organization has become so much a sub-branch of the sociology of religion that there has not been present in the discussion that rich texture of historical analysis of the phenomena which was so distinctive in Niebuhr's original study—a characteristic in which he followed Troeltsch. (Perhaps the work of Bryan Wilson [1961, 1967, 1970] moves toward overcoming this fault.) Unfortunately, it is often the case that the more refined and potentially powerful a sociological theory becomes, the more remote it is from the very mixed data with which historians work because of their interests both in relatively large scale units and in social change through time.[8] For this second reason also, analysis of sects under the sociology of religion has not issued in a direct influence upon historiographical studies.

This paper does not represent a proper setting in which to give a detailed discussion of the development of the concept "sect" within the sociology of religion. The following brief comments are germane, however. Almost without exception the major contributions to the discussion of sectarianism have fallen into two groups. One set of studies has worked to refine the overall typology of religious institutions, often with an attempt to relate the types of institutions to other social factors. Within this group fall major studies like Werner Stark's *The Sociology of Religion* (1966–70), as well as numerous short essays (Johnson 1957; Goode 1967a, 1967b; Gustafson 1967).

The other group of studies has been primarily directed to the refinement of "sect" as a concept. The chief means has been in the elaboration of typologies of sectarianism. A frequent approach to this matter has been through straightforward classification of sectarian

---

[7] This interpretation was further reinforced by an essay written several decades later for the Princeton series "Religion in American Life" (Niebuhr 1961).

[8] See recent interesting comments by K. T. Erikson on the relationship between the methods of history and the presuppositions of sociology (Erikson 1970).

groups. Elmer Clark, as an early example, distinguished between seven kinds of sects in his widely utilized handbook, *The Small Sects in America* (1949). More recently Bryan Wilson has argued for a four-fold typology: *conversionist sects* are evangelistic, typically fundamentalistic or pentecostal within contemporary Christianity; *adventist sects* are "revolutionist" groups, proclaiming a new world order; *introversionist sects* focus on the claim to possess the spirit within the religious community; finally, *gnostic sects* emphasize esoteric teaching or knowledge (1967: 27–29). J. Milton Yinger argues for a three-fold analytic classification: *acceptance sects* are much like Wilson's gnostic sects; *progressive sects* are "power-oriented" whether in terms of Wilson's conversionist or adventist groups; and *avoidance sects* foster withdrawal into a pietist community, like Wilson's introversionist sects (1970: 275–278).

To some degree both of these enterprises (development of church-sect typology and refinement of the typology of sectarianism) have also led to a search for relevant variables. This has resulted in attempts to relate specific types of churches and/or sects to particular kinds of social contexts (Dynes 1955). A summary interpretation is offered by J. Milton Yinger in his recent *The Scientific Study of Religion*. There he proposes three critical variables: (1) inclusiveness of population, (2) degree of accommodation to the values of the world, (3) extent of organization and differentiation of the religious structure (1970: 260).

In one respect, it is unfortunate that more of the careful work on sectarianism which has been done by sociologists has not (to this point at least) contributed to the historical study of American religion. Application to historical materials of social scientifically-derived definitions and concepts does promise significant advances. A simple transference of developed theory, however, might prove to be both disadvantageous to historical studies and ironic as well. The disadvantage would consist in the reinforcement of the residual "church-sect" categories in American religious history (which we traced to Mather) even if they are present only in the more attenuated "movement-denomination" formulation. The irony would consist in the return to its initial religious context of a term indelibly stamped by its origin in traditional usage. In this sense the joke would be on the sociologists of religion who believed they were developing a concept which may actually turn out to have been insufficiently generic for their purposes.

Perhaps the most fascinating aspect of recent attempts to refine the concept of "sect" has been the disinclination to come to terms with a third type of religion in the modern world which Troeltsch termed—unfortunately perhaps—mysticism. He called attention to this phenomenon, identifying it as lay and personal religion, different from and not to be confused with sectarianism (1931: I, 376ff; II, 691ff, 729ff, 993ff). Whatever the adequacy of his discussion, by introducing it Troeltsch suggested that a shift of emphasis is required to understand marginal religious phenomena in the modern world. To this end, less stress should fall on comparison of institutional features, more on analysis of the *kind of intelligibility* brought to the world through the phenomena in question. In short, Troeltsch clearly recognized in his own work that a church-sect framework may not permit understanding of modern religious groups or movements, especially in terms of their genuine power to gain adherents.

Some older studies of marginal or eccentric religious movements have assumed something like this point of view more or less explicitly.[9] For theoretical purposes, however, an essay by Peter Berger is especially important (1954). In that discussion he shifted emphasis away from virtually exclusive attention to the social organization and the social function of the sect, and he argued for analysis of how adherents or members perceive, and are perceived by, the world. More recently, Geoffrey K. Nelson (1968, 1969) has proposed that the term "cult," generally subsumed under or conflated with "sect" in most sociological literature, is actually required to explain marginal groups which lack the precise structure of the sect, which prove to be extensive in space and resilient through time, and which often prove to be the matrix for a new religion. These recent perspectives upon marginal religious groups will certainly contribute to the historical study of American religion, and will prove more valuable in that context than the earlier work on sectarianism.

In light of the considerations suggested above, the interest in marginal groups displayed by anthropologists contributes very directly to the work of historians of American religion. In one respect there is simply the demonstration of richness and variety in the marginal religious phenomena within contemporary society. This presents the historian with a challenge to recognize similar religious diversity in the periods he studies. In addition the anthropologist's emphasis upon empirical data with respect to specific movements is a healthy corrective to the generalized analysis of sectarianism contributed by the sociological

---

[9] Charles Braden's work, for instance, embodied elements of such a perspective, although he never developed it, to my knowledge, beyond the point of a general sympathy for the groups under his discussion (1953). The numerous and at times engaging studies by Marcus Bach whatever their shortcomings, include aspects of this point of view as a positive virtue (1946, 1951, 1952, 1961, 1969). Frequent pieces by Edward B. Fiske in *The New York Times*, apparently part of a larger undertaking, certainly manifest a similar sympathy and interest. Also, the work of J. Stillson Judah (1967) ought to be mentioned favorably in this connection.

study of religion. The generalizing tendencies of historical studies must not obscure the importance of having adequate data—which can prove to be so elusive in the study of the past. Furthermore, the techniques developed within anthropology, for instance in the analysis of structures and symbols, suggest instruments and skills to augment more strictly historical techniques and procedures—especially with reference to the study of marginal cultural phenomena. In these ways, at least, anthropological study of marginal religious movements today will directly benefit historical studies.

To illustrate the above points we may take a cue from Cotton Mather and suggest a partial morphology of marginal religious movements in contemporary America. What follows is indebted to the anthropological investigations reported in this volume and depends rather less on the sociological study of sectarianism, although there are points of connection. At least three broad families of movements display rather different sets of characteristics, whatever the range of diversity within each one: *Occult groups* (e.g. Spiritualism, Satanism, Scientology), *Mystical or Transcendental movements* (e.g. Hare Krishna, drug-centered movements), and *Ecstatic or Enthusiastic movements* (Pentecostalists, Adventists, the incidence of glossolalia generally). Each of these families appears to have a typical constituency and to hold out or promise distinctive benefits or pay-offs to the adherents or believers. Furthermore, individual members seem to accomplish characteristically different purposes through these movements, and the collective effects vary from one "family" to another.

Occult groups seem to attract marginal middle-class individuals through the promise of a knowledge powerful in this world—even through the crass techniques of manipulation. The individual so involved ideally achieves reintegration (into middle-class society). Generally occult groups seem not to have explicit links with each other—although a fluid constituency held in common may effectively achieve this—and no consistent collective influence is apparent.

Mystical or Transcendental groups also appeal, it seems, to alienated but more often youthful members of the middle class. *Gnosis,* allegedly true knowledge of the world, is the benefit, and, in a relatively extended perspective, individuation and effective reintegration into society may directly result from participation in such movements. Transcendental groups may be bound together through a manifest collective commitment to at least a *vision* of a transformed society (as in the counter-culture or political radicalism).

Ecstatic or Enthusiastic movements find constituencies where there is emotional deprivation—most often among the lower and lower middle classes, and often within more-or-less alienated or blocked subgroups within society. The benefit to the participant is in immediate affective experience, in some manner shared with others. For the individual, participation in this type of movement creates or confirms an effective subculture, and thus there are deep links to conservative or reactionary political stances, and any collective expressions of such movements would be along these lines.

Insofar as such a morphology helps to clarify perception of modern American marginal religious movements, it may also illuminate in a fresh way the marginal religion of other eras, e.g. Jacksonian America, or American society of the late nineteenth century. To be more precise, the Second Great Awakening, a concept basic to most interpretations of religion in the early nation, is associated with and largely derived from unitive perspectives upon American religion. Use of the concept as a means to interpret the religious life of Jacksonian America works to synthesize rather than to analyze the variety present in the data. While the importance of the evangelical impulse should not be underestimated prior to and in the Jacksonian period, this three-fold morphology of marginal religious movements does suggest that evangelicalism may not be finally useful to explain, or to organize perception of, the diverse religious phenomena in the period. Thus early spiritualism, the Shakers and possibly some aspects of Millerism, to cite examples only, may appear in a rather different light, and even Brook Farm and the Transcendentalists may be perceived in a more adequate context. Similarly, the kind of morphology sketched above might enable a historian to turn his attention to the late nineteenth century with fresh eyes, a period which A. M. Schlesinger, Sr., some years ago labelled "A Critical Period in American Religion" because of its inherent diversity (1932).

In this and related ways anthropological study of marginal religion in modern America will significantly influence the historical study of American religion generally. Of course, other influences are also at work, for instance, the continuing decline in the cultural significance of the "mainline" Protestant denominations, and the dramatic display of diversity within the Roman Catholic tradition, both of which also render suspect and questionable unitive interpretations of religious history (Ahlstrom, 1970). In addition, the History of Religions (Religionswissenschaft) in the United States (primarily identified with the University of Chicago), is contributing to the formulation of new approaches to the study of Western religious materials. Application to religious subjects in American history seems especially promising (Brauer 1968).

Taken in conjunction with other considerations, the basic challenge posed by the marginal movements for the study of American religious history is the issue of defining religion for purposes of historical inquiry. The historian must recognize the importance of socially established as well as marginal religious phenomena. He cannot fail to account, at least implicitly, for both as well as the relationship between them. Clearly a supernatural premise cannot be considered necessary or sufficient, for it characterizes neither all marginal religious movements nor established ones. And traditional designations, such as those which came so easily to Cotton Mather in his orthodox orientation to the classical and heretical deviations, are quite inadequate for this purpose.

At this point the discussion carried on in sociology of religion may have special point and prove to be directly relevant for historians. A working definition of religion must be both adequately generic to subsume conventional and parochial instances, and sufficiently precise to exclude from consideration phenomena which may resemble religion but which should not be unambiguously so identified (e.g. political rituals). Peter Berger and Thomas Luckmann have formulated (related) concepts of religion in contemporary society which generally fit these criteria (Berger and Luckmann 1966; Berger 1967; Luckmann 1967). Their overall approach, which is not new, is more important than their specific theories. In general, they hold that religion provides a definition or definitions of social "meaning" so that, while not always recognized by individuals, "religion" nonetheless is necessary for all collective groups. Specific religions may be articulated more or less explicitly, their institutional expressions may be more or less highly developed, and they may possess a greater or lesser intellectual coherence. Whatever else is true, however, "religion" is at least residually instrumental in orienting members of groups and society generally toward collective values—thus directly contributing to patterns of behavior characteristic of a culture.

In terms such as these, the study of contemporary "established religion" permits analysis of the central social values or patterns of behavior and belief. "Established religion" means not only the dominant and differentiated conventional traditions—for instance, in American society, Protestantism, Catholicism, Judaism—but also those quasi-religious phenomena such as civic piety, and possibly it requires attention to substitute religions such as fraternal orders which may serve many of the same purposes. In this light the significance of marginal religious movements is clear. By definition on the edge of culture, they are in one way or another engaged in establishing the boundaries of the social order, and, as a consequence, they serve to indicate the points of uncertainty within, and the perceived borders of, a culture. In the American present this is manifest. It may be seen in terms of adult experience of frustration or anomie within contemporary society (glossolalia), or of attempts by youth to discover alternative life styles and belief styles (cults). Alternatively, it may be seen in terms of exploration by black Americans of the latitude available to them within the system (militant Black Churchmen), or the terrible burden borne either by those who have no access to, or by those who choose to reject, the dominant society (Black Muslims). With respect to the American present, marginal religious phenomena are important in refining our perception of the outer limits of contemporary society and the internal contours of our subcultures. Any serious study of religion in America which neglects the marginal movements is as fundamentally flawed as any which proposes that the established traditions have ceased to have religious significance within the whole (even though not, perhaps, in traditional terms).

No less needs to be said about the importance of marginal sects, cults, and movements for the historiography of American religion. We may find fascination with Anne Hutchinson, Kelpius, Jemina Wilkinson, Joseph Smith, Jr., John H. Noyes, Daddy Grace, Leonard Feeney, and a host of other figures who have deviated from conventional religion with sufficient power to draw followers and to create marginal movements around themselves. Chronicles of their lives and activities, insofar as we do not have them, are badly needed. Studies of the sects, cults, and movements which derived from these figures are also important. But such contributions will not achieve an adequate historical interpretation of religion in America. That will only come about when these figures, and the movements to which they are linked, are placed beside more established phenomena and in proper social and intellectual contexts as well. As a consequence the contexts and the phenomena will be more adequately illuminated. In a strange way this reaches toward a perspective in some respects like Cotton Mather's. Certainly it is not a return to the conviction that marginal movements serve as a trial to the godly. Nor is it a return to the formal "explanation" that sects derive from heresies. What is common to both is the assumption that the marginal as well as the central religious movements in American history are critically important elements within the whole, and further that an interpretation of the whole society and its culture requires that justice be done to both. In this respect the historical study of marginal religious movements will reach behind unitive interpretations of American religion and emphasize the great variety of religious behavior and belief which is so manifest within our present culture.

Culture Crises and New Religious Movements: A Paradigmatic Statement of a Theory of Cults

UNTIL very recently at least, the popularity of new religious movements of various kinds seems to have outrun the development of social scientific theories adequate to account for them (Glock and Stark 1965: 58, n. 49). This is evident, for example, in sociology where structural characteristics of new movements identifiable as cults have been only incompletely worked out—or where explanations to account for their rise and success have tended to rely heavily on rather limited ranges of variables.[1] The purpose of this paper,[2] however, is not to attempt to develop the fullest possible statement of a theory of cults but rather to sketch out, paradigmatically, a thesis which aims to relate the emergence—and the characteristic form or forms—of cult organization and cult movements to what have been called "culture crises." In the paper we shall argue that it may be analytically more fruitful to consider such crises more concretely as *dislocations* in the communicational and orientational institutions of advanced societies—dislocations which open the way for cults to flourish. We intend not to disparage social-psychological explanations for cult interest or for what can be called the "cult response" but to try to supplement these with additions from a theory of socio-cultural structures. At the end we shall suggest possible lines of inquiry for further testing of the thesis and of the general "model" that is being proposed.

The two basic "types" most commonly in use for describing new religious movements have been the *sect* and the *cult*—the former often described minimally as "a group formed in protest against, and usually separating from, another religious group" (W. J. Warner 1964: 624), the latter sometimes as "a loosely structured and often transitory and small voluntary association of people who share unique and generally

[1] See page 626 for a bibliographical note on the literature.

[2] An earlier version of this paper was read at an informal colloquium of British scholars at Trinity Hall, Cambridge University, in July 1967, and a slightly different version published in the December 1972 issue of the *Journal for the Scientific Study of Religion*.

world-denying religious values and/or who engage in bizarre religious rites . . ." (Hoult 1969: 90).

Numerous variations and extensions to these concepts exist in the literature, many of them devised without solid empirical grounding, sometimes merely rehearsing "armchair definitions" made decades ago and seldom tested against actual cases or even rigorously examined for their logical (or sociological) consistency.

Popular accounts of cults exist in great numbers—some dating back several years.[3] Some, but again relatively few, reflect the measure of sociological or other social scientific sophistication needed for full understanding of the phenomena.

Whereas sects have been examined in some cases in considerable detail, the *cult* remains a much more vague and unsatisfactory concept. An important distinction which further theoretical work seems likely to retain has been drawn by Charles Glock and Rodney Stark, for whom cults are "religious movements which draw their inspiration from other than the primary religion of the culture. . . . [They] are not schismatic movements in the same sense as sects, whose concern is with preserving a purer form of the traditional faith" (1965: 245).

One obvious response in the face of acknowledged deficiencies in the conception of the *cult* might be to try to remedy these shortcomings by systematically reviewing various definitions of the cult that have been used or proposed. Rather than doing this, however, and attempting thereby to reconcile variations in the definition of it, it is suggested here that we approach cults with the idea that any "ideal-type" structural characteristics we are able to identify—i.e. any "defining characteristics" of the cult as a concept—are likely to be closely tied to those kinds of factors and conditions which brought the phenomena of cult movements into existence or encouraged them. In other words, we shall assume that the *defining* of the *cult* ought not to be separated from theory or theories as to *why* cults exist.

Religion and religious movements, regardless of what else may properly be said about economic or political status-deprivation and other "factors" in their formation, development and structure, have always been tied to a very fundamental need in human beings, individually and in groups, for shared, "reliable" *meanings* in their life

---

[3] See, for example, Atkins (1923), Van Baalen (1938), Ferguson (1940), Bach (1946, 1961), Braden (1949, 1963), Mathison (1960). A quite different type of study of new religious movements, more interpretative in its approach, is J. Needleman (1970). An example of still another—and distinctly *un*sympathetic—account of cults, also written outside of the frame of reference of social science, is found in Roman (1970).

experiences. "Sophisticated man," John Plamenatz (1963: i, xix) asserts quite unequivocally,

> has a need to "place" himself in the world, to come to terms intellectually and emotionally with himself and his environment, to take his own and the world's measure. This need is not met by science. It is not enough for him to have only the knowledge which the sciences and ordinary experience provide. Or perhaps I should say, to avoid misunderstanding, it is not enough for him to have only . . . knowledge in the same sense [that what] they provide is so. . . . I have here in mind something more than the assumptions on which science and everyday experience themselves rest, assumptions which . . . must first be accepted before it makes sense to speak of verification.

"This need," Plamenatz added, "is not felt by all men; and it is felt by some much more strongly than by others; but it is a persistent need which can be met for some only by religion; but which for others can be met in other ways" (*ibid.*). In other ways, we might add, unless *any*—or *every*—set of orientations which meets it is to be called "religious," following a usage which some social scientists (not including the author) seem to prefer. Since several crucial issues are embedded in these assertions we shall have to return to them presently.

Meanwhile we should like to move directly to the central assertion of this paper which is that anything which disturbs or challenges not merely belief-systems but the fundamental elements or units of the frameworks in which belief-systems are formed—in which "meanings" are sought or orientations communicated—must be expected to have consequences of the most profound order, including among many others the stimulation or even provocation of cult interest, cult movements and cult activity. Such dislocations, we suggest, will have sociological consequences extending beyond those ordinarily comprehended by anomie or by secularism or by "unbelief."

Because of the breadth of the assertion and large number of questions it raises, it may be helpful to state it in careful formal fashion as a series of propositions and comment upon these before returning to the more specific thesis respecting cults. The argument is as follows:

(1) A "need for orientation" which includes, among other items, some definition of the "conditions of human existence," some basis for identifying and arranging values, etc. is assumed to be fundamental both for groups and for individuals.

(2) A significant aspect of this orientation is supplied by "religion" which explicitly, usually in the form of belief-systems, and im-

plicitly, in the form of rites, *cultus,* etc, profers explanations for evil, for death, suffering, that are acceptable *as explanations* to "the faithful."

(3) There are, in complex institutionally specialized societies, specific institutions which exist not only to promulgate or transmit or preserve particular orientations but, more fundamentally, to formulate, standardize, "authenticate," or "validate" words and other symbols in which beliefs and other modes of orientation are expressed. They also define norms of communication—norms which differentiate between sense and nonsense, etc.

(4) Both the once widely held orientations in contemporary societies (viz., religious belief-systems, norms of excellence in the fine arts, rules of grammar in literature and in general discourse) *and* the institutions which helped formulate these and other patterns have, through most of the past several decades, been undergoing unusually *severe disruption* or dislocation, amounting to what, in the opinion of many scholars, constitutes a "culture crisis" of major historical proportions.

(5) The resulting "confusion" in our orientations—not merely at the level of norms (and of "anomie") but at the more profound level of the *symbols* themselves and of the rules governing their use or defining the limits within which communication of "meaning" is possible (or desirable)—has "opened the floodgates" to (indeed may have helped to bring on) a large array of rival or of new "cultic" views of the nature of world and of man in relation to it and to other humans.

Functionaries who formerly acted as gatekeepers against the "invasion" of "the absurd"—or against loss of faith in the capacity to "communicate"—seem themselves, at times, to have become too demoralized or too scattered to halt the development. Some, indeed, may have opted to join one or another cult leaving a relatively leaderless population to find its own way. Rank and file members of a society who *might,* under other conditions (or in a different "climate of opinion"), have been constrained *not* to respond to cult appeals could find themselves more exposed or more open to them.

Ergo a major factor in the current surge of cult interest—and some clues to characteristic features of the ideologies and belief-systems of cults—may be identified.

Since the argument above is very elliptical and highly condensed, it requires some brief explication.

The first two of the five statements are in the nature of categoric assumptions, made as part of a general theory. The theoretically basic necessity of "orientation" in action has long been argued by social scientists—for example by Talcott Parsons and his associates (Parsons et al. 1951) and before them by Max Weber and others. Such orientation, however, should not be limited to *beliefs* or belief-systems which are highly verbalized or, in A.F.C. Wallace's terms, "intellectualistic" in character (Wallace 1961: 3–4); they are rather more inclusive in scope to the extent that they are implicit in sacramental rituals, in dance, in symbols and in myths. For even though the latter are usually conveyed in words, they are, as many scholars have suggested, a more fundamental expression of orientation to the world than are intellectualized belief-systems. Similarly, as the work of Evans-Pritchard (1965), Godfrey Lienhardt (1961), and others indicates, religion itself may be more usefully conceived as a mode of orientation to the conditions of human existence than primarily as "a set of beliefs, practices and feelings of Man with respect to a higher power" or to what is considered to be suprahuman or divine. Nevertheless, the propositions in the formal argument including the assumption that in modern societies the "orientations" will be expressed to a significant degree in verbal symbols—and their communication governed by verbalizable norms—seem justified.

As an aside it is interesting to note that a British sociologist who has written knowledgeably about the sociology of religion has recently asserted that the latter

> has tended during the past few decades to ignore the cognitive side of religion. . . . Where beliefs *have* been emphasized their structures have been relatively unexplored. Even more disconcerting, the kinds of religious belief which have been tapped have almost invariably been of the *surface, institutional* kind. That is, sociologists interested in *beliefs* have typically limited their analyses to the "official" beliefs manifested in organizationally promoted settings. (Robertson 1970: 116)

If this is correct, as we have no reason to doubt, a reaction to it may help to account for the recent and apparently rapid spread of interest in what has been called the "phenomenological approach to religion" among some sociologists.

The third formal statement introduces a somewhat less commonly held view; indeed, if there is an "original contribution" which this paper adds, it may well be at this point since very little mention seems to be made in the literature of the social sciences to the "orientational" or "communicational" institutions of modern societies in the sense here being proposed. It is a rather curious fact that in the lists of "major social institutions" with which social scientists work in describing the organizational structures of complex, advanced societies, there seems to be no separate category for designating those institutions—and the personnel and organizations which embody them in action—which are specifically concerned with supplying the society with its symbols, including its language and communication systems, and with the various kinds of norms upon which all orientations (whether they are "religious" or "secular" definitions of the conditions and meaning of human existence or some combination of these) depend.

To regard *society itself* as a system of communication (as was suggested by Charles Horton Cooley (1902, 1909) and some others)—or to assume that symbols, including words and language in the larger sense, simply arise in some general way out of human interaction—seems to miss the point that there are separable *norms* of communication and other institutionalized patterns that are not only enforced in every society (often by designated agencies) but often created *by* specialized institutions.

Although we shall probably not be able to anticipate all the questions which professional students of societal structure would raise, it might help to forestall some doubts about the worth—or the "reality"—of our "orientational" institutions if we were to cite four institutional functions which they perform. (That there are specialized personnel, organized in distinctive agencies, "chartered" and supplied with "apparatus" associated with the performance of these tasks—as Malinowski (1939: 938ff.) identified the minimum defining criteria of an institution—could probably be argued on similar lines.) The reason for considering these here, it should be kept in mind, is that, in accord with our central hypothesis, interference in the performance of these functions—from whatever source or on whatever grounds—would be expected to leave the way open for the "new" and variant orientations represented by cult movements, if not to invite such movements, possibly as a means of filling otherwise unmet needs.

The four "critical" functions we identify are:

(1) the task of ordering, identifying, or defining the *signs* and *symbols* to be used in communication. Included here are not only words but also non-verbal "units" which, if they are to serve as "building blocks" of meaningful discourse, need also to be specified and standardized in dictionaries, in lexicons and elsewhere.

(2) the task of establishing or clarifying the various kinds of rules of discourse, ranging from grammar and syntax through "style" to such matters as "good manners" in ordinary conversation. (There are many others besides—including, for example, rules for specify-

ing what is "decent" and what is not in mode as well as in content of communication.)

(3) the task of establishing norms or rules for reasoning—i.e. logic in one form or another—and the rules which guide the search for, or the "determination" of the truth-value of propositions. Societies differ in how or where they draw the lines between the "knowable" and the "unknowable," between the "credible" and the "incredible," the "intelligible" and the "absurd"; and they require norms to identify where the boundaries are. They need norms to guide the directions of investigations, to provide the "methods" that are acceptable and proper in that society for achieving verification or "proof" so that members of that society are able to decide when "knowledge" has "in fact" been attained—and when it has not. One might argue that even in cases where groups have concluded that "rational communication" of ideas about experience either is not possible or that there are no "meanings" to be conveyed (except perhaps the "idea" of meaninglessness itself) there still are norms guiding the process. Rejection of norms itself requires norms.

(4) the task of supplying one or more definitions of the conditions of human existence—i.e. the "terms" on which the human enterprise can or should be assumed capable of being carried on. (This, as we have argued before, presupposes clarity and reliability in the concepts or other units which are used in propositions about the meaning of existence, whether the propositions be "religious" or other.)

These tasks or functions, we suggest, are analytically separable—and different—from those performed by *either* religious *or* educational institutions. They have not been theoretically "allocated" (or even, by inference, attributed) to other among the so-called major institutions of modern society as these are usually listed; yet they point to a range of activities in the spectrum of institutions which are as much a part of the structures or "systems" of modern societies as are the economic or the political institutions, for example, and the norms, roles, and relationships which comprise the latter. The "personnel" of orientational institutions may include preachers or teachers; but one need not be either of these—or be employed within any religious or educational organization—in order to perform these vital tasks or interact with others in their performance. Painters, poets, editors, novelists, journalists, dramatists, composers and others are equally important participants. And the *organizations* in which they participate are often neither religious nor educational. Orientational institutions, in short, are a neglected category of social institutions.

The point to be reiterated here is that what happens within this area of institutions—whether or not they are to be specifically labeled the "orientational institutions" of the society—is of basic importance. It can as profoundly affect the operation of the society and of other institutions within the society as any change in the physical environment or in the forces or the relations of production, the level or pace of technological development, or in the political or other alterations in the social arrangements that may occur within or between societies.

It is just here—within the sector of communicational and orientational institutions and their functions—that we should be looking most closely for the "structural" sources of dislocation which lead, among many other possible consequences, to the proliferation of cults, which is the focus of our immediate inquiry.

Much more is involved here than is usually comprehended in discussions of "secularism"—or of secularity—or of the spread of skepticism or doubt—or of the rejection of traditional religious propositions and dogmas—allegedly engendered by science. Much more is involved, too, than dissolution of "normative consensus"—anomie—as even this important development has ordinarily been discussed in sociology or in the social sciences generally.

What is crucial, then, unless we are misreading the situation, is that in contemporary society the entire system of cultural patterns and of institutions for building and maintaining discourse (including the process underlying the construction of language itself) has encountered startling and possibly unexpected challenges and has been going through profoundly dislocative discoveries and innovations. Some of these may have had the appearance of "breakdown" or have been regarded as having produced pathological consequences. But, as we would argue, the latter position implies a value-judgment which, however warranted it may seem to be to some, seems unlikely to be helpful.

What has happened is that we have rather suddenly attained great sophistication about the nature of language, of communication, and about the processes or techniques of symbolization, of the standardization of meanings and of signs, and much more. The process underlying the construction of the rules of reasoning—if not the construction of language itself—has come to be seen as a *social* enterprise, occasionally quite arbitrary, in which the presence of "meaning" (or of reference to anything "ontologically real") is *in no way* guaranteed. And the import of this has come to be appreciated throughout broad new sectors of the society—perhaps by proportionately many more people in our society than in earlier less communication-rich societies.

Not just religious assertions or dogmas (or even quite different kinds of statements, such as scientific propositions) have been challenged. In philosophy—in logical positivism, for example—the fundamental processes involved in conceptualizing experience are now seen to be a matter of social invention, complicated by the presence of non-rational, irrational, and even anti-rational preferences and responses among humans. Although exceptional individuals throughout history, including philosophers, theologians, and others, have, apparently, as individuals, entertained serious doubts about the adequacy or reliability of concepts, the possibility of rational communication, and so on, there does seem to be something "new" and perhaps unique about the extent to which these understandings have spread among intellectuals and those who rely upon them.

Knowledgeable scientists, of course, have recognized all along that their vocabularies, their symbols, and perhaps even their methods are simply convenient tools by means of which trained and competent specialists can organize and communicate something about their experience with the objects of their study—that phenomena are empirical to the extent that they can be experienced in ways that can be "standardized" and shared—and that words may or may not point to anything "real" but may indeed be "heuristic devices." But even scientists may have, on occasion, slipped into tendencies toward reification of concepts or elevated methodological rules to the status of dogmas which, when challenged, can produce a sense of instability, loss, or dislocation. To the extent this happens, though probably not for this reason alone, even scientists might become candidates for conversion to cults. (Some, in fact, have been reported to have done so.)

It is amongst spokesmen for the humane arts and letters, however, that the evidences of "dislocation" we seek are probably most strikingly exhibited. Instances of deliberate abandonment of conventional language and of rules of grammar—of doubt or skepticism regarding older patterns and modes of disclosure, the possibility of finding meaning, and so on—abound in "modern" poetry and in other writing. Observing a trend that had begun some decades before, John H. A. Sparrow pointed out (1934: 4–6): "Writers of verse today are less concerned with meaning than was usual with writers in the past. . . . The revolution lies not merely in the exploitation of the powers of language other than meaning, but in the fact that in their exploitation, meaning itself is abandoned. . . ."

Among painters the underlying position and mood are almost equally explicit: "Every movement of the brush on the canvas," the contemporary painter, Francis Bacon, wrote in 1953, "alters the shape and implications of the image. That is why real painting is mysterious and a continuous struggle with chance. . . . I think that painting today is pure intuition and luck and taking advantage of what happens when you splash the bits down . . ." (quoted in the London *Sunday Times Magazine,* June 4, 1967: 26). Paul Klee had written somewhat more cryptically in 1919: "Art plays an unwitting game with ultimate things . . ." (*ibid.:* 24).

Painting—indeed, all forms of art—in the opinion of many spokesmen is not intended to convey meaning but to express feeling or mood within the artist, to evoke some expressive response from each individual in his audience. The latter responses may have meaning or they may not; and whether or not they, in turn, can be communicated is not really relevant.

That "meanings" cannot (or ought not to) be communicated literally—or the idea that human life is essentially irrational and, for some, preferably only minimally to be "standardized"—or that existence is best understood as absurd is not new. What does seem to be new, we have suggested, may be the numbers of people who share these views or who, directly or indirectly, are affected by opinion-leaders in contemporary society who do—by "intellectuals," for example, to whom they have looked for direction or guidance in "orientation" and in the ways of communicating.

The point to be emphasized here, however, is perhaps not so much the loss of confidence in the reliability of concepts or in the possibility of rational communication—or, conversely, the increased reliance upon luck or chance to "find" or convey meaning—as it is the general dislocations in orientations which were once thought to be stable and reliable. The crisis, to repeat also, need not be regarded as pathological, or even, in the long view, as dysfunctional. There has, however, been a profound "unsettling" of the foundations of contemporary thought related, we have argued, to sudden advances in knowledge about the nature of language and logic, about symbols and the symbolization processes, about the "social construction of reality," about the social contexts of knowledge.

For those who are able to cope with these discoveries, the impact would be expected to be less disturbing than for others. Intellectuals, for example, as experienced manipulators of symbols, might be more "accommodated" to the fact that concepts such as *space, time,* or *causality* are invented to help men come to terms with their experiences—that they are not now thought of as "standing for" anything in nature in any ways that are cosmically guaranteed. Intellectuals may even be better able to withstand "existential anxiety" and other stresses abetted by the dislocations we have cited without either feeling the need to abandon old affiliations or old beliefs in favor of new ones, without "losing faith" in whatever patterns of meaningful orientation, rules of reasoning, and so on they may have accepted, without, in short, becoming candidates for innovative, syncretistic cult appeals.

For others, however, dependent upon a stable cultural base, however indirectly, and accustomed to thinking of logic (if not of language) and of rules of discourse and of criteria of "meaningfulness" as more fixed than they are, the developments we have cited may leave many feeling literally "disoriented"—"abandoned" by their former guides or, for the more adventuresome, "set free" from conventional authority and erstwhile constraints. Either response, we are suggesting, could prompt increased interest in cults and in cult ideas which might otherwise have no special appeal. Some individuals might feel encouraged to create their own new "world views" or embrace those of others more imaginative or less intellectually "disciplined."

As sociologically perceived, not all cults are necessarily preoccupied with the occult, the esoteric or the arcane, a point which perhaps needs to be stressed in the face of popular stereotypes to the contrary. Some, like the Baha'i movement are deeply concerned with ethical ideas or ideals not thought to be adequately expressed or communicated in any one of several older traditions. Such a movement is syncretistic and innovative but not esoteric. Some, like various "New Thought" movements succeeded in combining elements of conventional religion, or religions, with ideas and practices that are essentially non-religious. Others, like Theosophy or the Universal Link Revelation Movement are more esoteric; while still others have directed attention toward the attainment of "self-awareness" or "self-realization," wisdom, insight or other primarily non-social objectives. Among the latter, Vedanta, the International Society for Krishna Consciousness, Subud, Soto Zen, the Human Potential Movement, and Transcendental Meditation come to mind. Others, like "The Process" are apocalyptic, but not after the manner of several of the well-known Christian sects.

Before attempting to designate structural characteristics which may be generalizable to *cults* as a major type of new religious movement, it may be useful to review the thesis as it has been developed up to this point and to consider the kinds of additional evidence from the historical record or elsewhere which might be required to buttress it further.

The central thesis, it will be recalled, is that dislocations in the orientational and communicational institutions of contemporary societies—and especially in the norms and elements of communication of "meaning"—should be regarded as a major factor in the current surge of interest in cults. We have not argued that the dislocations which we see as a basic part of the culture crisis are *of themselves* adequate to account for the existence of cult movements or their success in attracting members. Not all individuals aware of the situation we have described have been moved to join one or another of the cults; nor have cults been confined to contemporary societies.

Although we have argued that the conditions identified as fundamental dislocations in contemporary orientational institutions constitute a culture crisis that is, in fact, unique, "culture crises" and major social disruptions are not so. They *have* occurred in different ways in the past. Assuming that cults are often short-lived and somewhat "evanescent"—and the relevant historical documents therefore likely to be sparse—we think the historical record would show a rough correlation between the proliferation of cults or cult movements and the times and places of marked social and cultural change—for example, the Hellenistic and the late Greek and Roman periods, eighteenth-century France, twentieth-century Africa, Japan, Southeast Asia.[4]

Assuming the basic thesis is granted, we shall then turn to the question of what social scientists might theoretically expect in an array of possible responses to culture crises, including cult movements with ideological and organizational patterns which may generally characterize the cult as a type.

We have already noted that an effusion of belief-systems including some which would be highly unorthodox and even bizarre might be anticipated. Uncontrolled by rules, no longer generally in force, or freed from other conventions, cult innovators might be expected to create new patterns and new credos. Outside the confines of a single religious or other tradition, they could be eclectic or syncretistic—interested in putting together new formulations of truth or attempting to distill their truths from several sources rather than one. In short the cult would be ideologically more "open" in the sense of having fewer boundaries, guidelines or constraints. Unlike sects which expect to remain within the tradition they aim to improve or correct and which may be oriented toward a "purer expression" of the tradition believed to have existed in the past (or toward an "otherworldly" future), cults tend to look to the present and the future.

Being less inclined to set up rigid or sharply defined criteria of membership based on belief than sects, cults may be less tightly controlled by rank and file members holding each other "up to the mark." The

---

[4] See, for example, Murray (1925), Angus (1925), Nilsson (1925, 1943: 261ff.), Mathison (1961: 23–32), Baeta (1962: 6–7), Lanternari (1963).

general ideological character we have suggested for cults, in other words, may be expected to have its organizational counterpart in the form of movements which would tend to be "open" rather than "closed"—inviting all to come freely into them—or into the outer circles of membership—rather than admitting only a select few who could pass doctrinal or other tests or meet other demands for strict compliance. To pursue the point a bit further there might be less intra-group social control, not only less pressure exerted by the group on individuals but less strongly internalized controls exercised within the personalities of the participants—in part because it might be less clear to what, exactly, they are expected to adhere.

Different styles of leadership—more strongly charismatic in character—may be required than in other types of groups since more may depend upon the skills and the powers of attraction of the cult leader. Similarly different methods of recruitment and conversion might be anticipated where unorthodox and unusual orientations are being proffered. While individual cults might each be very demanding in its own terms, the basis of membership seems to be clearly different from that where, as in the case of sects, a particular item in an older tradition is elevated to special prominence. It has been suggested that cult members may expect to be drawn and held to movements or organizations more on the basis of affect and of immediate gratification than might be the case for other types of movements or organizations. Extending the thesis proposed in this paper leads to the hypothesis that cults meet needs which other types of religious organizations, under stress of contemporary cultural dislocation, would be less and less able to meet in any traditional or conventional idiom.

It should be said that the characteristics suggested above as those of cults are only *possible,* not necessary or inevitable, consequences of cultural crisis; and they are not conceived to identify phenomena as exclusively "religious." Cults could indeed be "secular" or could, without violation of the logical principles involved in defining the type, combine elements which *could* be defined as either.

Not all individuals in times of crisis join cults or perhaps even give them serious consideration; and other kinds of responses to dislocations in the orientational institutions of contemporary societies will be—or have been—made. Among the latter, for example, one might identify the "new theology" as one manifestation of this within the context of established churches; a new ideology within the context of Marxism would be comparable. Another, and nearly diametrically opposite response could be in the direction of ritualistic, occasionally shrill, re-affirmation of the old patterns—marked, for example, by enunciation of dogmas that place heavy strain on the credulity of the believer as though to challenge and "face down" skepticism and doubt by a strong show of authority.

Still another kind of response might be that of the "fundamentalist" or the "romantic reactionary" in and out of sects and other associations who would eschew cult patterns entirely. The cult as a manifestation of continuing interest in "meaningful" interpretation of the conditions of human existence in the face of major change in the orientational institutions of society is, in short, not the only form in which that interest is expressed; and it may not be the most popular one; but it *does* exhibit a distinctive and distinguishable type of group or of movement which can be derived theoretically from the crisis we have described.

There is, we think, no *a priori* ground for assuming in advance of further study of particular cult movements that the traits or characteristics which we have pointed to will necessarily be found together or that they will vary together in contrast with the characteristics of any other type. To the extent that the traits are theoretically derivable from the socio-cultural conditions we have described, they may indeed by linked; but the model itself is only a heuristic device at this point, not an empirical summation.

Because the "type characteristics" of the cult have been sketched out so briefly, there may be a need here to specify rather more precisely what some of the questions are that social scientists who wish to investigate cults from the theoretical perspective present in this paper might raise. Under the conditions we have already discussed, the "orientations" proffered by cults should be diverse and unconventional and they may be syncretistic, eclectic and perhaps esoteric and arcane as well. Appropriate questions about individual cults might include the following:

1. What interpretations, if any, of the "meaning" of human experience does the movement explicitly provide? How extensive are they?
2. How—in what form—are these cast? What kinds of symbols are used and how are their "meanings" communicated—if they are?
3. If the movements are self-consciously eclectic or syncretistic, how are these preferences justified?
4. Does leadership in the cult emphasize charismatic qualities of individual leaders?
5. Does the cult stress emotional gratification, immediate goals?
6. Do participants enter and leave the cult more freely than they move in or out of other types of groups or organizations?

7. What practices tie participants to the movement—and how effectively do they do this?
   etc.

The list suggests a possible agenda for further monographic studies.

It should be repeated, in conclusion, that it has not been the purpose of this paper to disparage analyses which have concentrated attention on socio-economic status, mobility, urban residence, and other social structural factors which have been reported to be operative in relation to new social movements. Rather it has been to argue that a wider and possibly deeper level of the socio-cultural structure of modern societies needs to be brought into the analysis and theory.

Clearly in approaching these problems we encounter an intricate web of interlacing factors which link religious, quasi-religious and other movements with the rest of the social system. In these circumstances, it is desirable to remain on guard against simplistic interpretations which emphasize only some or only certain kinds of factors to the neglect of others—and to the detriment of the comprehensive dynamic *and* structural analysis that is needed.

BIBLIOGRAPHICAL NOTE

Although sociologists have given attention to cults for several decades, much more work has been done on sects. Most sociological references to cults (as a kind of religious movement) seem to stem from the ideas of Howard Becker (1932). An early attempt to test out and amplify the concept was Eister's study of the Oxford Group Movement (1945, 1950). Other references to cults are found in Griswold (1934), Beynon (1938), Jones (1939), Klose (1940), Pfautz (1955), Mann (1955), Yinger (1957, 1970), Moberg (1962), Marty (1960), O'Dea (1968), Jackson (1966), Jackson and Jobling (1968), Demerath and Hammond (1969). Recent sociological studies of cults are represented by Lofland and Stark (1965), Lofland (1966), G. K. Nelson (1968, 1969), Babbie (1966), Robbins and Anthony (1972), Richardson (1970), and others.

Among anthropologists the literature on "cargo cults" as well as on "revitalization" movements and others (which seem to have features similar to those identified by sociologists as cult-like) is very extensive. See, for example, Guiart (1951), Berendt (1952), Simpson (1953, 1956), Firth (1955), Worsley (1957), Barnett (1957), Burridge (1960), Baeta (1962), Lawrence (1964), Smith (1959), Aberle (1965), LaBarre (1962), Gerlach and Hine (1969), Kitzinger (1969), and others. Cult for some anthropologists and other scholars is still sometimes identified less with movements as such and more with patterns of worship and of ritual sometimes spoken of as *cultus*. Examples are I. Kleivan (1960) and J. W. Fernandez (1964).

Social psychological studies of new religious (and other) movements, among which two well-known general works are Cantril's (1941) and Toch's (1965), have made little of the structural differences among different movements but have focussed attention primarily on personal needs met—or sought to be met—through participation in these movements. Festinger, Riecken, and Schachter (1956) was a study of an adventist sect rather than a cult. Although their primary affiliations are anthropological or sociological, Catton (1957), Lofland (1966), LaBarre (1962), Gerlach and Hine (1969), and others have tended to center their attention on the dynamics of movements they have studied.

Finally, there are many studies of movements such as the "new religions" of Japan which are difficult to classify either as sects or as cults or as to the social scientific affiliations of their authors. These studies are, nevertheless, valuable as case studies in many instances or as sources of information about movements, whether the latter are "religious," "philosophical," or "political" or some combination of these. A few of the many such works are D. B. Schneider (1962), Offner and Van Straalen (1963), Thomsen (1963), MacFarland (1967), Dator (1969).

Towards a Sociology of the Occult:
Notes on Modern Witchcraft

Multidimensional Occultism

THE occult, which includes all matters mysterious and inexplicable, has always been deeply intertwined with things magical.[1] However, occultism is broadly multidimensional and does not necessarily include magical elements nor need its concerns center about the supernatural. Basically, the sociology of the occult must be considered as a subdivision of the sociology of knowledge where it has important implications for its companion subfields, the sociologies of religion and science. Though most writers who have considered the sociology of the occult have concentrated upon its relations with the sociology of religion, many occultisms have no dealings with things defined as supernatural. The major concern of occultists is simply with the unknown, especially knowledge of that unknown to science. Since things unknown to science today can become known to it tomorrow, things occult can, and often have, been incorporated into science. Thus, the descriptive aspects of early astrology (as opposed to the predictive aspects) have become incorporated into modern astronomy, much of the herbal practices of witchcraft are now part of modern medicine, and ancient alchemy made its contributions to modern chemistry. Not only has

[1] For extensive bibliography on sociological studies dealing with the occult and witchcraft, see Truzzi (in press). Some relevant works dealing with general occultism include Marty 1970, King 1970, Greeley 1969, Staude 1970, Marwick 1970, Crow 1970, Levin 1968, Pileggi 1970, Sansweet 1969, and Spence 1960. For the works dealing with classical witchcraft, see Caro Baroja 1964, Hansen 1969, Murray 1921, Randolph 1947, Rose 1962, and Summers 1946. For works dealing with contemporary forms of witchcraft see Bloxham 1970, Bone 1964, Bracelin 1960, Gardner 1954, 1959, Glass 1965, Graves 1964, Holzer 1969, Huebner 1969, Huson 1970, Johns 1970, Klemesrud 1969, Kriss 1969, Leek 1968, 1970, Kobler 1966, Moore 1969, Martello 1969, Parrinder 1963, Paulsen 1970, Roberts 1971, Schurmacher 1970, Seabrook 1940, Smith 1970, St. Albin-Greene 1969, Thomas, 1966, Thomson 1859, Valiente 1962, Wallace 1967, and Weier 1970. For works on Satanism, see Burke 1970, Casey 1941, Cristiani 1962, Dodson 1969, Eckman 1969, Hartland 1908, Huysmans 1958, Kloman 1970, LaVey 1969, 1971, Lyons 1970a, 1970b, Rascoe 1970, Rhodes 1954, Robson 1969, and Steiger 1969. These works dealing with witchcraft and Satanism vary greatly in their reliability, but they are a good representative sample of this rapidly growing literature.

much of yesterday's occultism become part of today's science, but contemporary occultists often claim that their currently "illegitimate" views will be accepted by scientists of tomorrow. Thus, the definition of occultism is largely based upon what knowledge we view to be scientifically legitimate. In an important sense, occultism is often a kind of *deviant science*. Although much occultism stems from mysticism and anti-scientific philosophical premises, much of it is naturalistic and pragmatic. Thus, many occultists see themselves as properly scientific in the broad philosophical sense whereas the scientific establishment is seen as acting unscientifically in failing to give a fair hearing to the evidence allegedly being offered by the occultist. Occultists, then, often see their evidence as incompatible with the current paradigms present in the contemporary scientific world views (see Kuhn 1962).

Although most occult groups throughout history have been wrong in their assumption that the validity of their beliefs would eventually be accepted by all, it is also clear that many have been right about some of their "truths" becoming finally accepted. These groups, therefore, serve rather important functions for science. They often act as data repositories and reminders of the existence of anomalies for the expanding and adapting legitimated sciences. Thus, if it can be established that hexing works through as yet not fully understood psychosomatic mechanisms, we may have to turn to those who have been practicing such hexing rituals to understand the conditions of their greatest effectiveness, just as some pharmacologists have today begun to examine some of the old witchcraft remedies which apparently contained herbs with healing properties. Similarly, if a monster is ever actually found to be present in Loch Ness, the records of past sightings might prove valuable in tracing its history, and such records have primarily been kept by non-scientific (occult) organizations and individuals who have believed in the presence of the creature despite the debunking cries of legitimate biology. Thus, all such groups perform the valuable function of acting as storehouses for incongruous events. Finally, even if the alleged events never really existed, the records kept by these organizations may prove invaluable for more indirect scientific reasons. Thus, even if flying saucers are never proved to have existed, the data on sightings amassed by the many UFO Organizations should prove most important for later analysis by future students of collective behavior.

In general, occultists can be divided into three broad analytic categories or types. Though these can be found in pure form, most occult practitioners represent mixtures of the three types.

At the first level, we have the occultist who is concerned with a study of some anomaly or group of anomalies, usually of a physical sort. At this level, the individual concerned is only minimally involved with occultism, and he will not usually label himself as an occultist (though others, especially those who disagree with him, will do so). His concern is merely with explaining some mysterious phenomena, usually ones that fail to fit current scientific or accepted knowledge about the world. Typical examples might include persons claiming knowledge of flying saucers, abominable snowmen, sea monsters, or parapsychological events (this latter being the best example of a borderline case in that extra-sensory perception has some degree of acceptance among legitimated psychologists). While most groups in this category are concerned with particular, specific anomalies, some, like the International Fortean Society or the Society for the Investigation of the Unexplained, are general seekers after things anomalous.

At this level, there is often an absence of mysticism, supernaturalism or anti-scientific beliefs. Though some persons interested in these anomalies are involved in mystical belief systems (e.g. the flying saucer cult member who believes that they contain angels from heaven), many of these groups are highly interested in scientific validation of their alleged facts. Anomalies are, of course, relative to the beholder. Just as a scientists can understand some things mysterious to the layman, so can the scientist perceive mystery in that which the layman finds ordinary and non-problematic. One can differentiate between two types of scientific anomalies: *general* and *theoretical* anomalies. *General* anomalies are those which would appear abnormal not only to the scientists but to most laymen in their everyday lives given their general level of culture and common-sense expectations. Thus, patent violations of the basic laws of physics, a rain of "blood," or the sighting of strange creatures would be examples of such general anomalies. A *theoretical* anomaly, however, is an event which would appear anomalous only to one who had special knowledge or expectancies derived from scientific inferences. Thus, when Thor Hyderdahl and his crew on the *Kon Tiki* found a fish thought to be long extinct, this fish was not an anomaly to the surrounding natives who had been eating the fish for generations and were unaware of biologists' theories about evolution. It was, however a magnificent physical contradiction of expectancies based upon evolutionary theory which would deny the possibility of such a fish's contemporary existence.

Whereas our first type of occultist is concerned with the existence of some abnormal object or mysterious occurrence, the second level of occultism is concerned with some inexplicable relationship between events, both of which may themselves be rather "normal." Thus, the existence of an herb is not very mysterious nor is that of a healthy person. But if one believes that the herb brought about the health of the person, and if there is no scientific reason to think it should do so, this relationship would be an occult one. The existence of a deck of tarot playing cards is not inexplicable nor is the presence of a future set of experiences for some individual. But if the cards provide a prophetic reading of that future, this would suggest an occult relationship. This level of occultism, then, is concerned with mysterious causal relationships alleged to be present in the world but which are unknown to normal science. Practitioners on this level of occultism are usually concerned with it as a form of *extra-scientific technology*. One simply does X to obtain Y. The vast majority of things commonly labelled occult interests (e.g. palmistry, numerology, sun-sign astrology, love potions, hexing and spell casting, etc.) are on this level. Though persons do sometimes go beyond mere technological interest in these occultisms, developing elaborated belief systems around them, the majority of those dealing with them retain a superficial concern with them as mere instrumentalities towards particular sought after goals.

Although much (if not most) magical activity belongs at this level, much of it is not viewed as "magical" or "supernatural" by its practitioners. Thus, a love potion may be seen as effective not because of special "magical" but for "normal" reasons not yet fully scientifically understood (e.g. the mixture may have aphrodisiacal properties which today's pharmacology has not yet isolated and understood). Thus, the knowledge claimed is really *a*scientific or *extra*-scientific rather than *anti*-scientific. Thus, in a recent interview the High Priest of the Church of Satan, Anton LaVey stated that:

> I don't believe that magic is supernatural, only that it is super-normal. That is, it works for reasons science can not yet understand. As a shaman or magician, I am concerned with obtaining *recipes*. As a scientist, you seek *formulas*. When I make a soup, I don't care about the chemical reactions between the potatoes and the carrots. I only care about how to get the flavor of soup I seek. In the same way, when I want to hex someone, I don't care about the scientific mechanisms involved whether they be psychosomatic, psychological, or what-not. My concern is with how to best hex someone. As a magician, my concern is with effectively *doing* the thing not with the scientist's job of *explaining* it. (LaVey 1968)

The third level of occultism is concerned with more than the belief in and study of scientifically anomalous events or relationships. Here we are concerned with the development of complex belief systems which usually involve elements from the other two levels and which attempt explanations of them. It is these elaborated belief systems which usually come to our minds when we think of occultism. Here we find such things as Witchcraft, Satanism, systems of ritual magic, mystical traditions, etc. Though some of these occultisms are not anti-scientific, many of them are; for these systems often attempt to offer philosophical explanations of man's relation to nature in metaphysical and cosmological terms which are ultimately contrary to the scientific canons of validation in so far as they base their validity upon appeal to mystical sources, traditional authority, or other unfalsifiable criteria. Thus, this level of occultism is frequently a competitor with science not merely in the sense of claiming anomalous events or relationships which current scientific models can not fit, but in questioning or contradicting the basic philosophical principles of scientific validation (such as science's ultimate appeal to empiricism).

Given the above varieties of the occult (and it must be remembered that many are mixtures of these types), the multidimensionality precludes our speaking of a single world of the occult. Contrary to a recent argument that there exists a kind of Occult Establishment (Marty 1970), analytic subdivisions must be made for occultism to be properly examined. Before we can develop an adequate body of sociological theory to explain modern occultisms, we must have better descriptive information about that for which we seek explanations. This essay represents a start in this direction. We turn now to an examination of the forms and varieties of one type of occultism growing prominent in the United States today: Witchcraft-Satanism.

CONTEMPORARY WITCHCRAFT AND SATANISM

As with general occultism, modern witchcraft is highly differentiated. First of all, the contemporary forms of witchcraft (here including all types of occult witchcraft but excluding such non-occult groups using the name, such as the Women's Liberation group called WITCH) found in the United States and Western Europe have little connection either analytically or historically with the forms of witchcraft present in those preliterate societies which have carefully been examined by anthropologists (Parrinder 1958). Even about preliterate groups there has been growing dissensus about the possibilities of analytic and definitional equation of different forms of "witchcraft" found among them (Marwick ed. 1970), and serious questions can be raised about the theoretical value of the analytic construct *witchcraft* in light of its great cultural variations. In any case, most anthropological descriptions of witchcraft have little to do with what is today called witchcraft in the United States, and the numerous analytic distinctions made by them (e.g. that between witches and sorcerers) have little value for us in looking at modern urban forms.

SOME ANALYTIC DIMENSIONS OF MODERN WITCHCRAFT

Before looking at the varieties of witchcraft present in the United States, let us examine the major analytic dimensions along which they vary. All these dimensions tend to form continuums upon which we can place existing cases. It is probably the case that almost all variations and combinations can be found empirically, though, of course, in varying numbers. The dimensions to be outlined are certainly not exhaustive, and many others might be considered, but these differences seem to be among the most important and salient variations present.

The Source of Definition. The first dimension to be considered concerns the origin or source of definition of the practitioner as a "witch." The definition can be from an entirely external source. At some point, persons may label the subject as a witch. This might be due to knowledge or suspicion that the subject practices some occult "technology" such as those described earlier (e.g. reading fortunes, prescribing herbal remedies, etc.). This sort of external labelling was extremely common in the United States up to the middle of this century when fortune-tellers and other occultists who practiced the "crafts of witches" were frequently called witches by journalists and others (e.g. Thomson 1859).

The extreme form of such labelling, where the subject had really done nothing of a witchcraft-like character at all, has usually been the accepted picture of witchcraft held by the debunker who denied the existence of real witches. Thus, until recently (Hansen 1969) the well-known cases of Salem witchcraft were attributed primarily to hysteria and the scapegoating of innocent parties. In this form, witchcraft certainly has its parallels in preliterate societies where innocent persons are stigmatized by labelling them as witches. However, being labelled a witch today is hardly stigmatic. In much of today's middle-class society, a witch is viewed as a highly glamorous figure. Announcing that you are a witch today is more likely to get you invited to a party than burned at the stake! In fact, several nationally known witches, like Sybil Leek, have built highly successful careers around their public labels as witches, and one lesser known witch known to this writer is currently earning over $25,000 per year just through public lectures and paid participation as a guest at private social functions.

Probably largely due to the lack of negative stigma attached to the witch label today, this form of exclusive designation that one is a witch solely by others is growingly rare today among persons fully assimilated into American society. Nevertheless, this type of witch has had great historical importance and one still occasionally reads newspaper stories of such witch accusations among ethnic groups where the label is highly stigmatic.

A witch can also be defined as such by group membership. Thus, one can become initiated into a witchcraft coven or can be designated a witch through initiation by another witch, usually through some special kinship ties.

Finally, a witch can be totally self-designated. Thus, a person may simply announce that he or she is a witch without "proper" (i.e. traditional) credentials. Evidence would seem to indicate that the vast majority of practicing witches in the United States today are either self-designated or were designated by another self-designated witch.

Heretical Versus Non-Heretical Witchcrafts. A second major dimension concerns the origins of the witchcraft beliefs. Most people think of witchcraft in terms of Christian stereotypes, that is, of witchcraft as a form of devil-worship or Satanism. In fact, the majority of practicing witches, including many Satanists, would dispute this image. Many witches consider their beliefs to represent a pre-Christian, pagan, fertility religion (Murray 1921; Gardner 1954, 1959) which is in no way an heretical sect of Christianity (for a critical view of this position, see Rose 1962). These witches are concerned about their public confusion with Satanists. (Although Satanists will call themselves witches, these witches reserve that label for themselves and call Satanists things like *sorcerers, wizards,* or similar terms.) In fact, an organization called WICA (Witches International Craft Association) has recently been formed in New York City as a kind of witches' liberation movement to fight the negative public image of witchcraft and what they consider to be the slanders about their religion spread by Christianity.

At the other end of this dimension are those persons who truly represent the stereotyped Christian heresy of the devil worshipper: persons who, like Milton's fallen angel, have decided that it might be "better to rule in Hell than serve in Heaven." Although one encounters journalistic reports of such groups in modern times (e.g. Seabrook 1940), true examples of such groups are very rare today. Unlike the heretical or stereotypical Satanists, however, most Satanic societies throughout history have adopted a theological reconstruction of the Devil very unlike that of Christianity's Evil One. Satan is usually pictured as ruler of the earth rather than of Hell and is seen as without malice towards man. This form of Satanism has sometimes been called Palladism or Lucifierianism to distinguish it from the Christian variety (Hartland 1908).

The Moral Character of Witchcraft. Related to the above dimension is the witch's view of the nature of and the intentions behind the magical forces invoked. This has led to a common distinction made by occultists between so-called *black* and *white* magic. In part the view on this issue depends upon the witch's relation to Christianity. For a pure Satanist, the magic he practices is black in that its power supposedly derives from the forces of evil and darkness (though he may regard Christian miracles like transubstantiation to be instances of white magic). But for the witch who has no belief in the Christian's Hell or Devil, magic derives from special laws in nature. Because of the common public stereotype of the witch as Satanist, however, many non-Christian witches began to speak of themselves as *white witches* and began referring to magic they did as white or beneficial. But this reference to white and black magic was meant to refer to the intentions of the magician in its invocation, not to the character of the magic itself. Thus, magic itself is neither black nor white, just as a knife is neither good nor evil. In a similar manner, many Satanists (who we have noted are usually not pure Christian Satanists but might better be labelled Palladists) also deny any distinction between white and black magic, though not because they shun the label of being black (i.e. evil) magicians; rather, it is because they see all magic as equally black in that all magic (they claim) is used by persons for selfish goals, no matter what the stated intentions might be.

The Ontological Character of Witchcraft. The metaphysical nature of the magic used in witchcraft is another major dimension that must be considered. For some witchcraft practitioners, especially the more orthodox or traditional ones, magic is viewed as a supernatural phenomenon. The character of magic is such that it involves special spiritual agencies (e.g. elementals, demons, etc.) which are outside the natural physical order available for study by empirical science. Thus, for some witches, magical laws are not natural laws, and they can even contradict natural laws. Supernatural agencies and mechanisms are invoked, and these are beyond scientific explanation.

Most newer witchcraft groups, however, avoid supernaturalism and prefer instead to speak of *supernormal* or *paranormal* events. Magical laws are seen as effective and within the ultimate purview of scientific understanding, but their emphasis is placed upon pragmatic knowledge of such magical laws and not on their scientific validation or understanding. In this sense, it would appear that there has been a kind of secularization of magic in adaptation to the modern scientific and naturalistic world view. Thus, what were once described in the occult literature as supernatural psychic forces are now examples of extra-sensory perception of a kind basically examinable and potentially understandable in the psychologist's laboratory.

Finally, some note should be made of even greater secularization of the magical by some groups (e.g. the Church of Satan) who broadly define magic as the ability to obtain effects in accordance with one's will. Following this definition, even deceitful practices, including the artifices of the stage magician, can be used to obtain desired results under the label of *lesser magic,* reserving the term *greater* magic for the mysterious forces invoked through complex rituals. Thus, "artificial miracles" which are defined as magic by spectators unaware of the trickery may even qualify as a lower form of "magic."

The Legitimation of Witchcraft. The source of authority designating one a witch is highly important. Generally, we can speak of traditional and non-traditional forms of witchcraft. Basically, witchcraft constitutes a set of beliefs and techniques held in secret which the novice must obtain from someone familiar with them. The normal, traditional means for obtaining such information is through another witch who knows these secrets. Traditionally, this can be done through initiation into an existing witch coven or by being told the secrets of the Craft by an appropriate relative who is a witch. Any other means of obtaining the secrets of witchcraft, such as through the reading of books on the subject or obtaining a mail-order diploma, is not a traditional means and is not considered to be legitimate by traditional witches. Because most witches today have not been traditionally initiated into the Craft, they often create other links to the orthodox as a means of gaining legitimacy. Thus, many of today's witches claim hereditary descent from some ancient witch or claim to be the current reincarnations of past witches.

In general, ascertaining the source of legitimacy in witchcraft groups is very difficult, especially since almost all claim ancient, traditional origins. However, intensive investigation usually reveals that the group's secret sources are not as claimed. Thus, for example, many of the leading witches in the United States and England claim authority through alleged initiations via the coven on the Isle of Man headed by the late Gerald Gardner, probably the most important figure in the promotion of the contemporary revival of interest in witchcraft as a religion. Yet there is much evidence suggesting that Gardner concocted most of his rituals and legends from his own fertile imagination and that he promoted witchcraft for economic and sexual reasons (King 1970; Weier 1970). Since so many witches are the result of the diffusion of Gardner's exportations, any coven whose origin can not be traced prior to 1950 should be highly suspect in regard to its claims of earlier, traditional roots.

Though witchcraft groups most often legitimate their authority structure through appeals to tradition, the other forms of authority first outlined by Max Weber (Weber *in* Truzzi 1971: 170–179) can be found in witchcraft organizations, also. Thus, some groups base their legitimacy on the charismatic authority of their leader (e.g. the Satanic cult in Toledo, Ohio, around Herbert A. Sloane based upon his alleged revelations from Satan; see St. Albin-Greene 1969; Eckman 1969), while other Satanic groups (e.g. those following the teachings of the Church of Satan under Anton Szandor LaVey whose headquarters are in San Francisco) claim demonstrable evidence as their legitimation, thus invoking a form of rational-legal authority.

Individual Versus Group Witchcraft. A dimension of special concern to the sociologist is the number of persons involved in a witchcraft organization. The vast majority of non-traditional witches are individual or solitary witches. Nearly all the witches one is likely to hear about publicly are such individual practitioners. The most common case today is that of a young girl (witchcraft is still predominantly comprised of female membership) of high school or college age who has read some books about the subject, taken up some of its practices, and has been designated a witch either by herself or, probably more commonly, by her friends. However, there are traditional but solitary witches, especially in the southern mountains of the United States. These witches obtain their initiations into the Craft through an appropriate relative who passes family secrets on to them (Randolph 1947). Such individual practices probably stem from earlier covens forced to dissolve, largely due to the geographical emmigration of members to North America.

Though solitary witches in the United States probably number in the thousands (with only a few hundred of these being traditional or hereditary witches), group-affiliated witches (i.e. covens) are far more rare. Though there are reportedly about 300 covens in the United States (each of which contains from two to thirteen members), most of these are non-traditional ones resulting from the current revival. There are probably less than 100 traditional covens operating in the United States today (at least three of which exist in Michigan).

Instrumental Versus Consummatory Witchcraft. As we have noted, much interest in what is called witchcraft is merely an interest in certain divinatory and magical "technologies." Thus, some individuals and groups limit their activities and rituals to largely unrelated efforts to obtain specific goals through unorthodox means which they believe to be efficacious. Other witches, however, practice quite elaborate rituals for more general goals, sometimes bordering upon "ritual for ritual's sake" with the only justification given being an appeal to traditional authority. In these latter cases, the practices are primarily consummatory rather than instrumental, in the same sense that most religious ritual is not directly instrumental. Rather, such practices have important symbolic content and give the group its sense of definition. Since many witch groups accept the possibility that different witch groups can effectively work magic, it is these consummatory beliefs and practices that give the group its special character.

The public-private character of witchcraft seems unrelated to whether the witch is a solitary or group-affiliated practitioner. However, the maintenance of privacy about one's position as a witch seems more common among witches on the heretical, black magic, traditional, and consummatory end positions along the above dimensions of witchcraft.

These analytic dimensions of witchcraft are by no means exhaustive. Other relevant variables involved in modern witchcraft might include such things as sexual, racial, ethnic, and age composition of the witchcraft populations; geographical distribution of the various types of witches; the relation of the witch beliefs to other occult beliefs (e.g. astrology, astral projection, divination); and, possibly most important but most difficult to reliably obtain, typological groupings of the various types of witches according to the forms and methods used in magical and ritual practices. Unfortunately, information about these dimensions is extremely limited and presently forbids accurate generalizations. Having considered the more abstract and crosscutting characteristics of witchcraft, we turn now to an outlining description of the major witchcraft groups in their natural groupings.

THE EMPIRICAL FORMS OF MODERN WITCHCRAFT

Looking at the most common forms of public witchcraft (by its very nature, totally private witchcraft must be excluded in our discussion here) in terms of the most common phenomenological categories used by witches and occultists in their discussions of witchcraft, the general pattern of witchcraft groupings is outlined in Table 1. Broadly speaking, witches can be divided into those classed by most occultists as "white witches," ones who deal with beneficent magical forces, and those classed as "black witches," ones who allegedly deal with evil agencies. Within each of these categories, one finds both individual,

TABLE 1. THE VARIETIES OF MODERN WITCHCRAFT

I. "White" Witches
   A. Independent, Solitary Witches
      1. Traditional Witches
      2. Modern, Revival Witches
         a. Murrayite Witches
         b. Eclectic Witches
   B. Group-affiliated Witches
      1. Traditional Witches
      2. Murrayite Witches
         a. Gardnerian Witches
         b. Alexandrian Witches,
         c. Continental Witches
         d. Eclectic, Revival Witches
II. "Black" Witches (Satanists)
   A. Independent, Solitary Satanists
      1. Traditional Satanists (?)
      2. Acid-Culture Eclectic Satanists
      3. Psychotic Cases
   B. Group-affiliated Satanists
      1. Pure, Stereotypical Satanists
         a. Traditional Satanists (?)
         b. Acid-Culture Eclectic Satanists
         c. Sexual Satanisms
            (1) Sado-masochistic Satanists
            (2) Sexual-orgiastic Satanists
         d. Heretical, Anti-Catholic Satanists
      2. Non-Stereotypical Satanists (Palladists or Luciferians)
         a. Baphometists
         b. Idiosyncratic, Charismatic Satanists
         c. Church of Satan

---

solitary, and group-affiliated practitioners. And within each of these sets, one finds traditional and non-traditional types.

THE WHITE WITCHES

Looking first at the solitary, traditional, white witch, the most frequent ones encountered in the literature appear to have been initiated through family connections with another witch. These witches seem to most often be concerned with witchcraft as instrumental rather than consummatory. Their knowledge of witchcraft centers more around its applications than its religious content; thus many such witches are still members of the dominant religious church groups. The typical non-traditional, solitary, white witch usually also concentrates upon the instrumental aspects of the craft, but knowledge of witchcraft is most often obtained through a reading of books on and by witches on witchcraft (especially such how-to-do-it books as Leek 1970; Huebner 1969; Kriss 1970; and Huson 1970). Most such witches are eclectic witches since they must gather their knowledge of witchcraft from a wide diversity of sources on a largely "trial-and-error" basis. Some even obtain "certification" through some mail-order or local diploma source. Some solitary, non-traditional, white witches reject such sources and follow the form of witchcraft-as-religion first academically outlined by Margaret Murray (1921) and later elaborated by Gerald Gardner (1954, 1959). Such Murrayite witches (as they are called in England) are rarely solitary, however, since they normally form covens. However, some Murrayite coven members geographically move from their original coven areas and then may turn to solitary practice unless they can form or join a new coven. It should be noted, however, that most covens are strangers to one another; there is currently no established communication network for witches although several groups (including WICA and the Witchcraft Museum started by Gerald Gardner on the Isle of Man) have tried to put together such networks. Since many witchcraft groups and individuals are still sensitive about publicity, and since most groups do not fully recognize one another's legitimacy, such an enterprise is probably doomed to failure. Nonetheless, there is some communication between otherwise unrelated types of witches through a variety of semi-privately circulated newsletters. (Though many witches claim to be able to spot another witch through mystical means, no evidence exists that would convince the skeptical.)

Turning next to the group-affiliated, white witches, the less common traditional covens (operationally clearly all those with a history prior to the publication of Murray's first book in 1921, which was instrumental in creating the revival of witchcraft interest in England, and probably most groups existing in the United States prior to the publication of Gardner's first book in 1954, which had a similar effect in this country) are most clouded with mystery. Interviews with members of one such coven in Michigan indicate a great deal of doctrinal agreement with the portrait of witchcraft given us by Murray but much less so with that given us by Gardner, especially in his emphasis upon sexual rites and nudity. Such traditional covens are not only rare but have little interest in expansion. In order for a new coven to form, the original coven must allow one or two members to be "loaned out" to the new initiates who wish to form the new coven. The old members must help the new ones in the formation of their group. This may involve a great deal of time and trouble for the old members who are usually not anxious to do it, so this is not very frequently done. New traditional covens seem to result more often from the geographical movement of a coven member to a new locality when no other coven that can absorb the newly dislocated witch can be found, and the witch (under the proper conditions) then starts a new coven. However, it should be noted that since traditional witches need to get together with their full coven only for the four annual sabbaths (though some covens meet more often for the esbats which are largely social functions), most witches today—because of the ease of modern transportation—seem to make the necessary trips back to their covens for such meetings. Some, like Sybil Leek, even claim to make special trips to England from the United States for these occasions, but most witches do not need to go that far.

Far more common among the group-affiliated class of white witches are those newer witches—who might better be called revival witches—that, to greater or lesser degrees, pattern themselves after Murray's historical reconstruction of the alleged pre-Christian witchcraft religion. These witches fall generally into four categories. First, there are those who joined and followed the teachings of Gerald Gardner. Many of these Gardnerian witches exist in England, and several prominent witches in the United States are directly linked to his group. Second, and more recent, there are the followers of Alex Sanders (Johns 1970), the so-called "King of the Witches" who claims to have been elected head of several hundred covens, and who now reportedly sells mail-order certifications to would-be witches in the United States. Third, there are those who call themselves "Continental" witches and claim their legitimation to have originated from non-British groups such as those in Italy or France. Though varying greatly, the best obtainable reports would indicate that these groups still fall into the West European pattern of the witchcraft tradition described by Murray. Fourth, there are the eclectic revival witches. These, as with the solitary white witches, depend upon information, rituals, and doctrine from whatever sources they happen to have found useful. Finally, it might be noted that most of these Murrayite witches recognize their own non-traditional character, and many of them show great interest in joining a traditional coven if entry can be obtained. Thus, a traditional group-affiliated witch informant who gives classes on witchcraft in the Detroit area tells me that she is often approached by non-traditional witches who take her classes and who wish to join her own coven. She must consistently deny them since her own coven is filled and none of the members wish to take the time to help a new coven begin.

THE BLACK WITCHES (SATANISTS)

Among the so-called black witches, there seem to be fewer solitary cases. The existence of any traditional, solitary, black witches in modern times is highly questionable. There are individual occultists (such as gypsy fortune-tellers) who have fostered such an image of themselves for their clients who sometimes come to them for the casting of evil spells, but it is unlikely that these practitioners are sincere in their alleged Satanism. Such persons are most commonly actually involved in other forms of occultism than witchcraft, e.g. voodoo, spiritualism. Traditional Satanists seem to actually exist only in the mythological descriptions spread by Christians (Summers 1946; Cristiani 1962).

Much of solitary, black witchcraft seems to be connected with the narcotics culture. Hallucinogens and other narcotics have a long history of connection with witchcraft and many of the early witchcraft recipes contained herbs with narcotic properties that probably accounted for some of the visions and miracles claimed to have been perceived. Since interest in the occult has deeply entered into today's youth culture, and since narcotics have also, these sometimes come into conjunction. However, little is really known about such solitary uses of black magic by members of today's acid culture.

Finally, some mention needs to be made of the solitary, black witch who is truly psychotic. History is full of cases of persons who have claimed to see and make contracts with Satan. Though such persons surely exist today, cases are difficult to find. Most such persons encountered in the "world of witchcraft" seem to have been able to find followers with whom they can associate.

Turning to the group-affiliated Satanists, two basic varieties clearly emerge: those who are the Christian stereotype of the black witch and who are thus malevolent and evil-seeking, and those who really reconstruct Christian theology and Satanism into something quite different (the Palladists or Luciferians).

Looking then at the pure or stereotypical Satanists, we first have the alleged traditional Satanist pictured by the Catholicism of the Inquisition or the later Protestantism of the witch trials. All indications are that such groups have never really existed. Though similar groups have been reported by journalists (e.g. Seabrook 1940), and many such groups have been simulated for commercial purposes by those interested in selling jaded tourists in Paris and elsewhere tickets to see an "authentic black mass," there is little real reason to believe such groups have ever existed outside the romantic horror fiction of writers like Dennis Wheatley and others who have popularized the image of such Satanists in modern times.

More real are the acid-culture Satanist groups found in the drug culture and exemplified by such "hippy-witch" groups as that dominated by Charles Manson or those described by Arthur Lyons (1970a, 1970b) and many journalistic accounts (e.g. Burke 1970; Kloman 1970; Schurmacher 1970). These so-called Satanic groups are often not really Satanists at all but are merely described as such by journalists anxious to publish sensational stories. When these groups actually do exist, they are usually highly eclectic in their witchcraft, not even borrowing their doctrines but simply constructing them as they go along based on their experiences with the narcotics that guide their "visions." In these groups, witchcraft is really secondary to the interest in narcotics and merely forms a kind of setting or background for "trip-taking."

Highly publicized (Dodson 1969; Steiger 1969) and more common are sexual groups and clubs involved with Satanism. As with the drug-culture Satanists, witchcraft is usually quite secondary for such groups where it acts as a kind of backdrop for the primary sexual activities. Thus, black masses are important here not as rituals but as settings for orgies. It is important to note that among many more "legitimate" witch groups sexually significant activity (especially nudity and sexually symbolic activities of various characters) may play an important role, but in these groups, such sexual activity (which normally is never of a regular orgiastic variety) is primarily done for its religious or ritualistic significance, not merely as a sensual indulgence. The former types, because of their perverse character, are far more difficult to locate than are the latter, many of which advertise rather freely in the sexual "swinger" newspapers and magazines.

Finally, among the pure, stereotypical Satanists, we find the basically heretical groups. The primary concern of such groups seems to be anti-Catholic desecration. Such groups seem to be rare in the United States today, but one occasionally hears of a college-age group holding a black mass for such purposes. The major interest of such groups (as with the famous Hell Fire Club of the late eighteenth-century) seems to be the execution of what closely resemble cathartic socio-dramas in which Christian rituals are parodied and mockery seems to be a major goal, though also often mixed with sexual or other forms of indulgence. It is not uncommon for ex-priests to be found connected with such activities.

Turning now to the non-stereotypical, group-affiliated Satanists, three major varieties stand out. First, and historically most well known, have been those groups of heretical character that have in some way transformed Christian theology into a worship of Satan as Lord of this Earth. It is from this tradition that the black mass has emerged (Casey 1941; Rhodes 1954). A wide variety of groups and persons have been characterized as being this type of Satanist, including the Knights Templar and the followers of the late Baphomet-invoking magician, the "wickedest man in the world," Aleister Crowley. Many of these practitioners, like Crowley, would reject the description of themselves as Satanists, but they have been clearly labelled as such by many other witches and occultists.

Second, we have the occasional Satanic groups arising around some figure who has claimed direct communication with Lucifer. One such group, in the Gnostic tradition, is that around Herbert A. Sloane of Toledo, Ohio (St. Albin-Greene 1969; Eckman 1969; Roberts 1971: 200–216). These groups are highly idiosyncratic in their beliefs since they depend so strongly upon the "revelations" allegedly received and upon the charisma of the leader. But, as in Sloane's case, these groups are rarely the evil-seeking stereotype of the Satanist. Both these and the Baphometists above are best characterized as essentially heretical sects developing out of Christianity.

Finally, we come to the major Satanic society operating in the United States today. This is the international Church of Satan. This group is legally recognized as a Church, has a developed hierarchy and bureaucratic structure which defines it as no longer a cult, and claims over 10,000 members around the world. Most of these members are, in fact, merely mail-order and geographically isolated joiners, but there are clearly at least several hundred fully participating and disciplined members in the various Grottos (as their Fellowships are called) set up around the world. Grottos are growing up rapidly around this country with about a dozen now in operation. The Church's High Priest and founder, Anton Szandor LaVey, whose headquarters are in San Francisco, has written *The Satanic Bible* (LaVey 1969) which has already reportedly sold over 250,000 copies and is now in its third paperback printing. LaVey also publishes a monthly newsletter for those members who subscribe to it, conducts a newspaper column in which he advises those who write in questions, and he has recently written a book on man-catching for the would-be Satanic witch (LaVey 1971).

The Church of Satan is far from the stereotypical Satanic society. Its doctrines are primarily those of a materialistic (anti-mystical and anti-drugs) philosophy of anti-Puritanism and pro-indulgence coupled with a highly Machiavellian set of social ethics emphasizing success and survival by *any* means and a basically elitist political posture. This highly cynical and epicurean world view is coupled with a belief in the efficacy of magic and its ritual. However, magic is largely re-defined to make it compatible with science, and nothing is viewed as being truly supernatural.

Because of this emphasis on the natural world and the denial of the usual supernaturalism one might have expected to find in a Satanic organization, the Church of Satan's philosophical world view is really more accurately designated as an ideological than a religious one. The name "Satanism" and its other seeming relations to Christianity are actually somewhat misleading, for these are mainly used in a symbolic sense (thus, Satan is simply the symbol of The Adversary, in this case to the dominant belief system of Christianity). Thus, the Church of Satan is not really a sect of Christianity in the same sense as are most present and past Satanic groups.

Conclusion

In this brief survey, it has only been possible to present the bare outlines of even one type of major, contemporary American interest in the occult, that in Witchcraft. We see that both analytically and empirically, witchcraft is a highly multidimensional form of occultism and generalization is most difficult. In any case, it would certainly be premature, for much more research is needed into the basic ethnography of these groups before fruitful generalizations can be stated. It is hoped that this introduction to these social forms might help stimulate interest in this vital area and that more social scientists will turn their attention to these increasingly significant forms of marginal religious patterns in American life.

The Deprivation and Disorganization
Theories of Social Movements

Most analyses of social, political, or religious movements are pre-occupied with two questions: (1) why do social movements arise? and (2) why do people join them? The first question generally leads to the system-analysis approach. For the anthropologist who studies movements largely in situations involving culture contact and domination of a tribal society, movements are seen as results of rapid cultural change, social disorganization, dislocation of values, etc. For the sociologist who studies movements in complex societies, preconditions are seen in terms of deprivation arising from imperfections in the social matrix and tensions caused by inevitable inequalities within a social system.

The second question usually leads to psychological analyses of maladjustments, pathologies, emotional inadequacies, or specific personality attributes which predispose an individual to seek collective solutions to private problems.

The three models with which movements are generally studied by sociologists, anthropologists, or social psychologists are the *disorganization model,* the *deprivation model,* and the *deviant* or *defective Individual model.* This report summarizes literature supporting the first two, and presents our findings relevant to them. The third model and our findings relevant to it have been presented elsewhere (Hine 1969).

The research reported here was based on a study of the Pentecostal Movement in the United States, Mexico, Haiti, and Colombia. Data on glossolalia and movement involvement among American Pentecostals were collected by means of 45 case histories, 239 self-administered questionnaires, and participant-observation in over 30 Pentecostal churches and independent groups.*

SOCIAL DISORGANIZATION

The anthropological disruption-disorganization model of movements is classically associated with Ralph Linton's theory of "nativistic move-

* The research on which this report is based was supported by grants from the Hill Family Foundation, the University of Minnesota Graduate School, the McKnight Family Foundation, and the Ferndale Foundation.

ments," defined as "any conscious organized attempt on the part of a society's members to revive or perpetuate selected aspects of its culture" (1943). Clemhout (1964) develops a much more detailed and complex typology of movements in recently primitive ex-tribal societies, but is still concerned only with nativistic movements which "always occur from stress of culture contact." A.F.C. Wallace's analysis of revitalization movements expands Linton's typology into a processual model (1956, 1966). Again, the phenomenon is viewed largely in the acculturation context.

Melanesian cults are analyzed by Belshaw (1950) as results of the "halfway" position of Melanesian people between an old and a new way of living following European contact. Worsley (1968) analyses millenarian movements as "imperfect adjustments to contact with the West."

Anthropological studies of the spread of the Ghost Dance among American Indians classically point to the correlation between acceptance of the movement and the degree of cultural disorganization resulting from contact with and domination by Western culture (Barber 1941). Lanternari (1962, 1963) analyzes various types of religious movements in widely different areas of the world. He distinguishes between movements "generated by a conflict between societies . . . and those generated by dissensions within the pattern of one society." The latter he calls endogenous movements. His analysis, like those of others who use the social disorganization of deprivation models, is a systems analysis approach. He views religious movements as results of the "spontaneous inner processes" of religious traditions and the irreversible dynamic of history as it "obeys its own laws." The conditions out of which movements arise are always extreme distress, crisis, detribalization, deportations, catastrophes, conflicts with oppressive groups, or clashes of culture.

Sociologists frequently use the social disorganization models in explaining the appeal of movements within complex modern societies. Hadley Cantril prefaces his well-known study with the statement that "social movements flourish when the times are out of joint" (1941). Thomas Odea analyzes the response of Puerto Rican migrants in New York to the Pentecostal Movement as a function of Durkheimian anomie resulting from disruption of family and village social structures (Poblete and O'Dea 1960). He notes but does not attempt to explain the fact that Pentecostalism spreads in rural Puerto Rican communities where traditional family and village patterns are still providing social organization and solidarity.

Norman Cohn's analysis of millenarian movements (1957) incorporates the social disorganization theory. He stresses the breakdown of kinship and local groupings during historical periods when millenarian movements occurred and concludes that such movements do not appeal to those who are well-integrated into a kinship group or cohesive local community.

Nils Bloch-Hoell (1964) identifies Pentecostalism with the post-Civil War waves of immigrants in the United States and, after the turn of the century, with the process of industrialization and urban migrations. Holt (1940) noted the association between growth of Pentecostalism and geographical areas of population increase between 1890 and 1930. He utilizes the "culture shock" theory of Thomas and Znaniecki (1927), who define disorganization as that state in which a conflict of standards has arisen and new attitudes have developed leading to activities which do not comply with socially sanctioned behavior patterns. Holt saw Holiness and Pentecostal sects as a religious movement caused by the social disorganization, cultural conflict, and acute social maladjustment resulting from the farm to city migrations. Urbanization of a rural and religiously fundamentalist population, he contends, disrupts the stability, social control, personal relations, and status provided by traditional rural kin and community groups.

Holt's study explains the success of Pentecostal religion in terms of its function as the reorganizing mechanism of the migrants' social life. Heberle (1940) also presents the now widely accepted view that movements, political in the case of Heberle's study, may replace the *gemeinschaft* groups of a pre-industrial age, and attract persons who lack "inner resources or intimate social relationships." Borhek (1965) in an excellent analysis of the function of different role orientations in the sect-to-church development, identifies the evangelistic, committed type of recruiter with the rural-to-urban migrant.

That Pentecostalism provides a type of group involvement that is characteristic of closely-knit, supportive primary groups is apparent even in the kinship terms frequently used between members. Even the more sophisticated neo-Pentecostals are brothers and sisters in Christ. The fact that Pentecostalism spreads rapidly among the migrants, the dislocated, and the displaced in any society is irrefutable. Unfortunately, for this type of analysis, it also spreads successfully among life-long urbanites, particularly in the United States. Also unfortunately for the social disorganization model, our observations indicate that Pentecostalism in the United States and Latin America both, flourishes in small rural communities and villages where ties have not been disrupted, and among family groups whose very solidarity is one of the primary reasons for its "contagion." Lack of intimate social relationships or personal ties and disrupted families were *not* characteristic of the Pentecostal pre-converts in our study.

David McGavran reports the conversion of whole villages with family ties intact among a tribe of Otomi Indians in the mountains north of Mexico City. "Group decision by two or three families (and by twenty and thirty families, too) becomes an ordinary mode of conversion" (1963: 98). Observable social change would indicate that the group conversions are not purely superficial or syncretistic. (This area was visited by one of our researchers and his interviews and observations support McGavran's statements.) In this case it was the very functioning of the traditional tribal and village social structure, not its disorganization, that facilitated the spread of the movement.

A similar report comes from an isolated tribal group in the Argentine among whom a "spontaneous indigenous church" arose when a few of its men were converted to Pentecostalism while engaged in temporary wage labor in a quite distant city. Although the penetration of ideological and behavioral patterns associated with Pentecostalism follow slowly in this isolated and only irregularly contacted area, introduced changes are diffusing *through* family and tribal organization, not because of its disorganization (Loewen et al. 1965).

Malcolm Calley, in a thorough and well-documented study of West Indian Pentecostals in England (1965), clearly posits social disorganization as an explanation of the appeal of Pentecostalism. He describes the immigrant population as composed of isolated individuals. There are, however, several instances in which ties to the home sect in Jamaica are mentioned—leaders going back for extended holidays to Jamaica and taking an active part in the groups there, a young convert coming over to live with members of his home congregation who had migrated before him, recent migrants who get their jobs through fellow saints. Calley considers the church he studied most intensely "atypical" in this respect. Its nucleus was "largely composed of people who knew one another in the West Indies before coming to England." Other churches, he insists, show little continuity in personnel between Jamaica and England. In spite of this, "The typical congregation consists of two or three family groups of husband, wife and children, and a handful of people without close kin in England who very often rent rooms from one or another of the families." The use of these data in support of the social disorganization model would seem to raise serious questions.

In order to test the social disorganization model with our own data, we made some internal comparisons within our sample of two hundred and thirty-nine. As an indicator of depth of involvement in the movement, we used the frequency of interaction with other Pentecostals at church services, prayer meetings, and informal contacts. In order to classify individual respondents as socially organized or disorganized, we used the number of household members over twelve years of age who were also participants in the movement, and the type of relationship the respondent had with the person who recruited him to the movement. The first measure of social disorganization was based on field observation. Where there was family cleavage or disorganization, the commitment of one of its members to Pentecostalism did *not* usually heal the breach. In fact it often widened the split. On the other hand, where relatively close or well-adjusted family relationships existed, the involvement of one member of the household tended to draw the others in. The second measure, type of pre-existing relationship with recruiter, was based on theoretical considerations. If membership in the movement is a result of social disorganization and the Pentecostal group is a primary group substitute, those individuals most involved in the movement should have been recruited to the movement by someone other than a relative. For this reason, those respondents who had been recruited by a relative and all of whose present household members also participate in the movement were classified as socially organized.

Using these measures we found no correlation between social disorganization and involvement in the Pentecostal Movement (F-ratio .9555, 119 df, p < .33n.s.)

Approaching the analysis another way, we used frequency of glossolalic experience as a measure of involvement in the Movement. For these tests, social disorganization was measured by using three variables: (1) degree of participation in a church organization before commitment to the movement, (2) degree of participation in other types of community organizations—PTA, Scouting, clubs, drives, etc., and (3) number of household members over twelve years of age who were also involved in the movement.

The logic by which the first two of these measures were selected is based on the assumption that individuals who are active in church or community organization (attend regularly and hold some sort of office or chairmanship) are sufficiently integrated into the local community to escape classification as socially disorganized. Note also that church participation was that *before* commitment to Pentecostalism. For seventy-nine per cent of our sample, this meant participation in a non-Pentecostal church.

We found no correlation between any of these variables and participation in the movement as measured by frequency of glossolalic experience (see Table I).

There is no question but that the intimacy and emotional support provided by the Pentecostal type of group interaction is a highly successful solution for individuals experiencing social dislocation or family disruption. But the fact that Pentecostalism spreads as effec-

TABLE I. Glossolalia and Social Disorganization

Variable	F-ratio	X²	df	p value
Previous church activity	1.418		1+200	NS
Community participation		.40	1	NS
Family involvement		.31	1	NS
Spouse's involvement	1.558		1+200	NS
Crisis conversion	3.802		1+200	.05

tively among groups where family organization is strong would suggest that while social disorganization may be considered a facilitating factor on the spread of the movement, it cannot be viewed as necessary. Some other more determining factor or factors would seem to be in operation.

Another common assumption that is related in some ways to the social disorganization theory is that individuals become involved in movements under the pressure of personal crisis situations. We did find a significant correlation between conversion during crises and movement involvement as measured by frequency of glossolalia, *but in the opposite direction*. Frequent glossolalics were those whose conversion to Pentecostalism occurred *less* often at a time of personal crisis (Table I).

In summary, the social disorganization theory was not particularly useful in explaining our data on the spread of the Pentecostal Movement.

Deprivation

By far the most common explanation of the rise and spread of movements is that of deprivation. Where deprivation is not associated with the contact of cultures, the dominance of one society by another, or the processes of "acculturation," deprivation is generally traced to "imperfections in the social matrix" (Toch 1965). Originally the term "deprivation" had purely economic connotations. Sociological usage has stretched it to cover various other types of lacks or frustrations, and most recently David Aberle has stretched it even further by making deprivation relative to expectations (1965).

The view that movements of all types arise out of deprivation, however it is defined, is almost universal. The assumption is unquestioned when the movement is also a religious one involving ecstatic or highly emotional religious experience. J. Milton Yinger, in his widely accepted formulation of theories developed in the sociology of religion, states that such experiences are a temporary escape from "the hardships and humiliations of life" (1957: 187). Studies of Pentecostalism have consistently either assumed or been used to support the correlation between socio-economic deprivation and ecstatic or highly emotional religious practices (Boisen 1939; Pope 1942; Johnson 1961; Simpson 1956, 1957; Elinson 1965; Dynes 1955).

It should be noted that in all of these studies, no distinction is made between a sect and a movement. In fact the two terms are sometimes used interchangeably. It would be foolish to question the validity of these studies of the socio-economic correlates of sect-church member-ship as defined in the studies themselves. The problem lies largely in the confusion between the Pentecostal sects and the Pentecostal Move-ment, which represents many more bodies than just the Pentecostal sects. There has been a good deal of criticism recently of the classical church-sect typologies and we would agree that this approach has blocked good research and theory building on the processes and dynamics of religious movements (Eister 1967; Gerlach and Hine 1968).

Status deprivation is also associated with millenarian theology, reli-gious ecstasy, and rejection of the social values of the wider society. Emotionalism in religion is seen as an outlet for "the untutored" and "socially disinherited" (Niebuhr 1929) or as a means of substituting religious status for social status (Pope 1942). Sociologist Charles Glock goes so far as to apply this proposition not only to groups which value religious fervor but to the survival of churches in general, which he thinks is due largely to the persistence of social deprivation. Although he admits there is little empirical evidence, Glock asserts that the church functions "to provide individuals with a source of gratification they cannot find in society at large" (1964: 34). Such a view is based on the as yet unproven assumption that political, economic, or social rewards are more satisfying than religious ones.

Anthropologists have followed the deprivation model not only in their studies of movements and culture change but in their analyses of spirit possession phenomenon in stable societies. Socio-economic or status deprivation are shown to be correlates of dissociational behavior in a variety of societies (Goldschmidt 1944; Aberle 1966; Hamer 1966; Willems 1967). Self-enhancement for those of less privileged status is cited as a factor in pre-disposition to spirit possession (Messing 1958; Metraux 1959; Hogg 1960; Gerlach 1965b; Hamer 1966).

The deprivation model is not an unmixed blessing for students of modern Pentecostalism. Byran Wilson (1959, 1961) found his Pente-costal groups becoming disturbingly middle class and was forced to conclude that the relation between socio-economic circumstances and mode of religious expression no longer holds. He is left with "cultural lag" or an undefined "cultural deprivation" as explanation for the continued vitality of the sect. Malcolm Calley's study of West Indian Pentecostals in England 1965 was based on the theory that members of Pentecostal sects would be found in the more adverse social environments. He found, however, that not only are the West Indian Pentecostals economically better off in England that they were at home in Jamaica, but that the Pentecostal church he studied has "relatively more prosperous members holding permanent jobs than in the transplanted West Indian community generally." Pentecostals were also found to be better educated than other migrants, due, Calley believes, to their intense interest in and detailed knowledge of the Bible. The existence of West Indian Pentecostal groups in England, he concludes, cannot be attributed to economic deprivation. He turns for an explanation of Pentecostal activity to "the general difficulties experienced by migrants in settling down." Unfortunately this explains little as the non-Pentecostal West Indians experience the same general difficulties yet are not attracted to the movement.

Students of other movements have experienced similar difficulties with the deprivation model. Wesley Hurt (1960) found that he could not explain the differentiated spread of the Peyote Movement among American Indians in the Kalotas and Nebraska on the basis of either deprivation or socio-cultural disorganization. He found no correlation between relative income level of a reservation group and the success of the cult on the reservation. It was present at one and absent at one of the highest income level reservations and present at one and absent at one of the lowest.

David Aberle (1965) and Charles Glock (1964) have attempted to refine the concept of deprivation to make it more useful. Both make it clear that deprivation must be conceptualized as relative and that it must be perceived or felt. Aberle defines relative deprivation as "a negative discrepancy between legitimate expectation and actuality." Both identify four types of deprivation which coincide sufficiently to be useful as a combined typology: (1) economic deprivation or deprivation of possessions, (2) status or social deprivation, (3) behavioral or ethical deprivation, and (4) psychic or worth deprivation. Glock points out that economic and status deprivation tend to go together within a society but that they are sufficiently independent to be experienced and therefore become motivational separately. He also adds a fifth type of deprivation for which Aberle has no parallel-organismic, or physical handicap.

Aberle defines behavioral deprivation as "a pervasive feeling that people do not behave as they should." His concept of relative deprivation is largely based on his work with the Navahos where behavioral deprivation stems from the acculturative situation with the breakdown of old social structures and the introduction of a new value system. Navahos apparently feel themselves to be behaving inadequately either by traditional or by white American standards. According to Glock, a sociologist working within the context of American culture groups only, this type of deprivation, which he calls ethical, exists "when the individual comes to feel that the dominant values of his society no longer provide him with a meaningful way of organizing his life." Glock suggests that ethical deprivation is independent of other types and that it is, in fact, "more likely to arise when other forms of deprivation are not present" and is exemplified by the person "who becomes satiated with the economic and social rewards of life . . . and seeks some alternative system of value." This person would hardly fit Aberle's or any one else's concept of a deprived person. In refining the concept of deprivation, both Aberle and Glock seem at times to be going out of their way to avoid the possibility of positive motivation!

Psychical or worth deprivation is something of a residual category for both of them. Aberle refers to "a person's experience of others'" estimation of him on grounds *other than* characteristics of his economic, status, or behavioral situation." Glock defines psychic deprivation a bit vaguely and redundantly as a "consequence of severe and unresolved social (status) deprivation (in which) the individual is not missing the material advantages of life but has been denied its psychic rewards."

Aberle and Glock offer no objective measures of either of these last two types of deprivation. In attempting to review our data with respect to deprivation theory we could do only what these two analysts have apparently done—classify participants of the movements they were studying by subjective evaluation. We could find no reason to feel that psychic or worth deprivation was relevant to Pentecostals. Potential Pentecostal converts, except for those who are also American Indians or black Americans, do not suffer from others' estimation of them "on grounds other than economic, status or behavioral" considerations. Nor do they appear to have been denied anything that we could identify as "the psychic rewards of life."

There is no question but that Pentecostals seek an alternative system of values than that dominant in society. They also have "a pervasive feeling that people are not behaving as they should." This would indicate that they are behaviorally or ethically deprived according to Aberle and Glock. Several problems arise here, however.

In order to apply Aberle's concept of behavioral deprivation, one would have to identify Biblical standards of behavior with a past generation and then point to a shift within American society to a new value system by which potential converts measure themselves as inadequate. Alternatively, one would have to assume a breakdown of social structures which allowed them to behave according to older, presumably more Biblical, standards. There are some who suggest just this of fundamentalist, though not necessarily Pentecostal, groups. They suggest that there are groups who for some unexplained reason were by-passed as American culture moved into the twentieth century and became a "contra-culture" suffering from cultural dissonance in a sort of cultural cul de sac (Pattison 1965a). This suggests a parallel between the destruction of Navaho social structures and the destruction of nineteenth-century rural American society. This theory might explain the persistence of certain Holiness groups in rural areas. It does not explain why individuals who were socialized to and are adequately functioning in contemporary urban society are converted to Pentecostalism.

A second problem with this analysis is that Pentecostals, rather than being caught between two value systems by either of which they judge themselves to be behaving inadequately, appear to be particularly sensitive to the ideal-real gap that exists in any society. The standards by which they judge people in general to be behaving inadequately are ideal standards of the New Testament which never have been actualized in American or any other society. If this is ethical deprivation, all people are so deprived, and as any student of the social sciences knows, a constant cannot be used to explain a variable.

Thirdly, many of our informants reported the fact that they were perfectly satisfied with the dominant standards of society and with their own and others' behavior until a committed recruiter in a position to influence his thinking sensitized him to Biblical standards. In these instances perceived behavioral deprivation is an effect of movement dynamics, not a precondition, and we would be left explaining a phenomenon in terms of itself.

Testing our data for evidence of economic or social deprivation is easier because there are objective measures which, though crude, may be used.

There seems to be no question but that the first wave of the revival in the early part of this century attracted persons from the lower socio-economic income groups, immigrants, and migrant workers. The churches thus established have long been assumed to draw their membership from the same groups, although recent studies are beginning to show a shift in membership that carries long-established Pentecostal churches well into the middle class (Kendrick 1963; Muelder 1945; Wilson 1959). But the most interesting aspect of this change is that in the recent and still continuing wave of revivalism, the movement is spreading into upper-middle-class groups who are clearly not suffering economic deprivation. Furthermore, these groups are not just on the fringes of the movement but are at the heart of its new burst of growth. The dynamics of the early stages of movement growth are being manifested at present more within groups of economically successful Pentecostals than among those who are economically deprived. Those characteristics typically associated with the religions of the "economically disinherited" (emphasis on religious experience, lay leadership, confessional basis for membership, high degree of member participation, reliance on spontaneous leadings of the Holy Spirit in organizational matters, home meetings, etc.) are more in evidence among middle and upper class converts than in the established Pentecostal churches. The more routinized "church-like" Pentecostal groups are often those churches whose membership is characteristically drawn from the lower socio-economic levels.

This is not to say that the movement as a whole does not still draw from economically deprived groups. It is only to say that field observations in this and other cultures revealed too many active groups of Pentecostals who are not economically deprived to consider them a-typical of the movement.

We tested the theory of economic deprivation by using our data in three ways. First we compared socio-economic status with acceptance of the belief in the Second Coming of Christ. Second, we compared socio-economic status with frequency of interaction with other participants in the movement. Third, we compared frequency of glossolalic experience with six different measures of socio-economic status in order to define more precisely the type of deprivation involved.

In the first two tests, socio-economic status was determined by using income and occupational level. Income was coded according to the divisions used by the 1960 United States Census reports. Occupational level was coded according to groupings used by the Census report. A scale of nine ratings, based on W. L. Warner's Revised Scale for Rating Occupational Prestige (1960), was used to assign numerical scores.

The assumption that religious status is commonly substituted for socio-economic status was tested by comparing the socio-economic status of our respondents with their acceptance of the belief in the imminence of the Second Coming of Christ. This belief is typically attributed, by sociologists of religion, to a desire to withdraw from an unsatisfying social order and a perception of oneself as having a compensatory status in a new or coming order (Pope 1942). Theoretically, more Pentecostals of lower socio-economic status should hold this belief than those of higher socio-economic status. We found, however, using a multivariate analysis of variance that there was no correlation between low or "deprived" status and the Second Coming belief (F-ratio .0851, 1 and 119 df, p<.77 n.s.).

We then tested the deprivation theory by using these admittedly crude measures of deprivation and comparing this with frequency of interaction with other participants. We found the hypothesis supported by a significant correlation (F-ratio 6.8747, 1 and 119 df, p<.01).

In an attempt to pinpoint the type of deprivation more closely, we tested movement involvement against five separate measures of socio-economic status—income, occupation, education, age, and sex. We used frequency of glossolalic experience as the indicator of movement involvement as it was found to correlate significantly with frequency of interaction (F-ratio 4.4548, 1 and 200 df, p<.04). It also takes into account involvement in the type of religious experience that is characteristic of the movement and sets Pentecostal groups apart from other Christian sects or churches. If participation in the Pentecostal movement is to be explained in terms of relative deprivation, then those in the movement who speak with tongues more frequently should tend to experience more deprivation of some sort.

Again using the multivariate analyses of variance we found no correlation between frequency of glossolalia and annual income or educational level. We did, however, find a significant correlation between glossolalic experience and occupational status (see Table II).

TABLE II. Glossolalia and Deprivation

Measures of socio-economic status	F-ratio	X²	df	p value
Income	.016		1+200	NS
Education	2.915		1+200	NS
Occupation	3.993		1+200	.05
Age		21.9	1	.001
Sex		.38	1	NS

There were more high occupational ratings in our sample than there would have been in a statistically random sample of Minnesota urban residents as reported in the United States Census report (see Table III).

TABLE III. Comparative Distribution in Gross Occupational Categories

Occupation	Our Sample	Minn. Urban
Professional-managerial	43%	26%
Clerical, sales, and kindred	26%	18%
Skilled and unskilled labor	31%	56%

The mean occupational level of our particular sample is well above that of the average for the area, and surely above that of a statistically random sample of participants in the Pentecostal Movement. Within our sample, however, frequent tongue speakers tended to have relatively lower occupational ratings than non-frequent tongue speakers.

At first glance it seems difficult to reconcile this with the lack of correlation between glossolalic experience and income or education, both of which are also considered indices of socio-economic status in our society. If, however, we accept Glock's contention that economic and social deprivation, though linked, are sufficiently independent to be experienced and therefore become motivational separately, and if occupational status is a better measure than income or education for this variable, then our findings make some sense. Two of the most commonly used scales for social status use only occupation (North and Hatt 1947; Warner 1960). Hollinshead (1957) uses a two factor index assigning a factor weight of seven to occupation and four to education. He bases his weighting on the fact that, while education is an indication of knowledge and cultural tastes and therefore of behavior patterns, occupation is an index of power in the social structure. Our data, then, would point to a specific type of deprivation that is related to the find of religious experience involved in Pentecostal commitment. There is evidence of occupational, or status, deprivation or, if Hollinshead is right, of power deprivation.

This is consistent with the way in which Pentecostals characteristically describe the benefits of the Baptism with tongues. Again and again the concept of power is used. Spiritual power to overcome not only spiritual but temporal obstacles. The "power to witness for the Lord" is clearly a very real power to influence others. The power of prayer in personal, organizational, national and international situations is constantly cited. Healing power has obvious social benefits. As one of our informants put it, "You can get along without the Baptism, but it's like driving a car with six cylinders instead of eight." It is not surprising that desire for spiritual power would be associated with a *relative* and *perceived* lack of social power. Most Pentecostals would probably substitute the term "power in the natural" for "social power" and would agree that one must discover the limitations of living "in the natural" before one can accept God's invitation to "live in the Spirit" with access to spiritual power.

To further test the relevancy of status or power deprivation to involvement in Pentecostalism, we used the variables of age and sex which are usually associated with status and social power in this as well as in other societies. Frequency of glossolalia was again used as a measure of involvement in the movement.

Women in American society are usually assumed to be more religious because they wield less secular power than do men (Yinger 1957: 93). A similar explanation for women's participation in spirit possession phenomena in other cultures is common (Gerlach 1965; Hamer 1966). Not surprisingly there were more women than men in our questionnaire sample. A correlation between sex and frequency of glossolalia, however, showed that there was no significant difference between the sexes (see Table II).

Another charismatic experience that is usually attributed more to women than to men is faith healing. Calley reported his impression that women were more interested in healing rites than men among his West Indian Pentecostals (1965: 95).

We have statistics on whether or not those in our sample experienced healing at the time of their Baptism, on the frequency with which healings have been experienced since, and on the frequency with which the individual was used to heal others. When tested with the X^2 Test for k Independent Samples, none of these variables was found to be correlated significantly with sex (see Table IV).

TABLE IV. Sex and Faith Healing

Involvement in Healings	X^2	df	p value
At time of Baptism	1.51	2	NS
Since Baptism	3.86	3	NS
Healing of others	2.05	3	NS

In testing the effect of age on frequency of glossolalia, we found a very interesting and significant correlation. Six per cent of our sample were teen agers, twenty nine per cent were in their twenties, forty nine percent were between thirty and fifty, seven per cent were in their fifties and nine per cent were over sixty. One would expect, on the basis of social deprivation theory, that the older or younger groups with the least social power in our society might be found to seek religious status or dissociational experience more often. There was, however, a significant correlation in the opposite direction. The thirty-to-fifty age group were found to speak with tongues more frequently than any of the other groups at the .001 level of significance. This is the age group in American society who are in their "peak years" of productivity and social power.

To sum up, five different measures of socio-economic deprivation were used to test the relationship between movement participation and relative deprivation. Of these only one showed a significant effect. Deprivation theory was useful in pinpointing a particular type of status, or power, deprivation which seems relevant to involvement in

Pentecostal practices of glossolalia. It is also consistent with certain strands of Pentecostal ideology. This would tend to support Aberle's suggestion that an important analytical tool in studying movements is to find the relationship between the type of relative deprivation that is involved and certain characteristics of movement ideology.

It is important to stress the fact that a statistical correlation of the type we have found is in no way an indication of a causal relationship between two factors. It may be said that relative deprivation of status, or power as we have defined this concept, is associated with participation in the Pentecostal Movement. It would not be correct to assume that power deprivation is causal. We have, in fact, found that a far more satisfying explanation of an individual's conversion to Pentecostalism as well as to other types of movements can be found in a study of recruitment patterns. These and other factors internal to the movement have been discussed in detail in other publications (Gerlach and Hine 1968, 1970b). For the purpose of this report on Disorganization and Deprivation theories, it is sufficient to point out that while relative deprivation theory was useful in characterizing and analysing certain aspects of the movement, deprivation and disorganization should be considered facilitating rather than casual conditions of the movement.

Postscript

Since this analysis of the deprivation and disorganization theories, as they apply to the spread of the Pentecostal movement, was written, we have continued our research into other types of movements. The word "power" has become a key word in the rhetoric of movement spokesmen. We hear slogans like "Power to the People," "Black Power," "Red Power," and even "Power to the Biosphere."

Newspaper reports of polls and surveys carry headlines like: "Cynicism in U.S. Epidemic, Survey Shows" and "America the Beautiful: It's Here, Or Is It?" These characteristically document a growing sense of powerlessness over decisions that affect the lives of individuals in all walks of life. There is also important evidence of a significant decrease in faith in American political and economic institutions to solve the problems facing this country.

A more recent survey published in *Natural History* magazine (Gerlach and Hine 1970d) shows that nearly half of the five thousand respondents doubt the capacity of the "system" to cope with the environmental crisis. Again, consistent with our findings on the Pentecostal movement, occupational status is related to faith in the system. Men over thirty in business, government, and engineering occupations are significantly more likely to believe that environmental problems can be solved within the framework of existing political and economic institutions than are men over thirty in the professions or social service occupations. Again, there was no correlation with annual income, educational level, age, or sex.

We would suggest that what we have called power deprivation is related to the rise and spread of a wide range of movements committed to personal and social change. Further, as we have pointed out in our book on the structure and function of religious and social movements (Gerlach and Hine 1970a), participation in these kinds of groups enhances, quite realistically, a sense of social power.

This type of deprivation, then, must be set into the wider context of social change if its role in the spread of contemporary religious movements is to be properly understood.

Religious Innovation: Processual Considerations

Aₗₘₒₛₜ all analyses of religious innovation center on the change from the state of a society or an individual before the new religious phenomenon to the conditions brought about after the change. They are before and after sequences and they usually paint only a sketchy, half-remembered, and semi-mythologized picture of what the antecedents to change were. Not only are most such studies basically functional in outline but they fail, as a result, to capture the internal dynamic in a new religion. They fail to see that unlike many religious innovations in the past some new religious movements do not experience the "routinization of charisma." They do not plateau into some static, continuously harmonious equilibrium that continues on into the palmy future. The new religions emerging in America are built on an ability to allow their faithful to revise their lives continually and on an ability to revise themselves as religious movements.

Some of the current American religions handle change on a continual basis. In that way they may be sensitively tuned to the whole tenor of American society, but more certainly it means they are tuned to groups within our population who feel most acutely the problems stemming from successive, thoroughgoing change. There are two tangents along which the ability to deal with continual change can be examined. One is the life of the individual adherent and the other is the institution itself. Among the scholars involved in this volume, the former approach predominates. And within this section the chief contribution to this particular interest is to show that there is not just one change, a before and after sequence, but, on the part of the believer, a striving for continual change. There may be a single great transformation accompanied by conversion to the new movement. But the expectation is that the converted individual will be transformed again and again. This, of course, often refers to a continual renewal by the spirit but also includes the concrete improvements in worldly circumstances anticipated by believers and invariably reported by outside observers.

Anthropologists and other social scientists have usually supposed that movements of the type reported in this book were system-maintaining. That is, they helped keep the status quo and did not facilitate social change. That conclusion, at least on the surface, is directly contradicted by all three of the papers in this section. The authors all see the most radical changes occurring among adherents to a marginal church both when they first join and during the period of membership. In a material sense, this latter change is in an upwardly mobile direction and involves the observable improvement of one's life circumstances. In this sense the status quo *ante* is not maintained at all. People are changed spiritually and materially. But in another sense membership in modern marginal religious movements does reintegrate or move people for the first time into the middle class. In that sense these movements foster and even guarantee social change. Insofar as this achievement channels people into mainline society, these churches certainly do operate to maintain the system. None of these groups wants to tear down America; they want a more secure place in it as it is currently constituted. In that sense, they are conservative and system-maintaining.

In addition to transforming individuals into people who are equipped to continue transforming themselves, the churches are unusually amenable to change at the institutional level. Because these churches emphasize the importance of improving earthly circumstances now, and consequently adapt themselves to aiding with the practical problems of their followers, they are in close touch with pragmatic, everyday conditions. Since those conditions are subject to rapid and even unpredictable change, the religious institutions are called upon by their own members to adjust as rapidly as external reality changes. This may produce doctrinal changes, organizational shifts, or, more usually, decentralization allowing local units a free hand in addressing all manner of problems faced locally.

As Robert Bellah has suggested in his article "Religious Evolution," the "modern" religious system is one that absorbs and adjusts to continual change. It can do this since it is self-revising in a deliberate, usually conscious way. This would seem to be a way of keeping a "modern" religious movement always modern, or at least up-to-date. And, of course, this is the institutional dimension of what goes on within the life of the average believer in one of these movements as well.

The point of this assessment is to emphasize the need for models that are capable of describing the change inherent in the personnel and internal structure of marginal religions. If only from the believer's point of view, such models are required to account for the multiple manifestations of the Holy Spirit which are common to almost all these churches.

The most general model in this section is Gerlach's attempt to isolate the major factors that combine to produce a movement that attempts

to generate major change. To generate a movement involving fundamental change and the transformation of individual persons, a group
of people must be organized and have an ideology capable of motivating change. One of the manifestations of the motivation is the
active recruitment of others to the group. Adherents must also perceive the growth of the movement as occurring despite opposition from
the established order.

Insofar as members must continue to recruit other members as a
condition of membership, as Jehovah's Witnesses and Mormons must
do, and as long as the growth of the movement is regarded as a personal
responsibility in the face of opposition, then these churches are
continually confronted with unstable variables. With this dynamic
built into the definition of a believer, he or she is always facing active
definition of himself as a better or poorer member of the church.
With this continual change in one's personal status and with such
continual feedback from the world one proselytizes in, this adjustment
of the individual and the institution is guaranteed.

Gerlach's set of factors is offered to show the transformation of
persons in a movement and the transformation of the movement itself.
The more specific model suggested by Leone for Mormonism suggests
some of the economic conditions involved in an institution's internal
transformation. He points out that when the membership of a church
is composed of the economically disadvantaged, then the rapid economic shifts such people are often subjected to will result in the
decentralization of the way creeds are formed. There will develop an
increase in the means for personal definition of beliefs and behavior.
Such freedom in matters of belief of the kind pointed out for Mormons
is directly tied to the need of adherents to adapt to rapid and continual
economic transformation. Mormons and similar groups come from
economically strained regions. Their respective religious systems
actually give a competitive edge to the faithful caught in such a set of
economic circumstances. The case provided by Cooper's analysis
of Jehovah's Witnesses is an illustration of exactly that set of
conditions.

Cooper looks at Jehovah's Witnesses in the Philadelphia ghetto and
shows how that church transforms blacks from individuals who are low
on the social and economic order into individuals who are more competitive, mobile, and who have high self-esteem. The Witnesses
Cooper studies take people in the ghetto and turn them into the most
successful of all those living in that environment.

The notion of personal and institutional transformation is the key
to these papers whose theme is the process of change. But there is a
second area of shared assumptions as well. That is an attitude toward

cause derived from systems theory. Transformations are not to be explained in the light of a predominant variable, either religious, social, or economic. Rather, the interaction of these is considered the locus of cause. This makes any hypothesis both more complex and probably more accurate. The advantage of such an approach for the scholars in this section is that it allows a frank consideration of economic or material variables without any de-emphasis on social or ideological ones. Further, such an approach circumvents the failure of many older functional explanations. These assumed either univalent social or religious factors were behind such religious movements, and in addition assumed that once change was brought about there would result the same kind of stasis that characterized the period before change. A systems approach can be quite implicit and may ignore a formal consideration of cause, but it will use a series of variables which are examined for their feedback relationship to each other, thereby automatically building into any analysis consideration of change over time. This avoids the static trap of functionalism as well as the faulty conclusion that marginal religious movements operate only to maintain the changeless status quo.

Pentecostalism: Revolution or Counter-Revolution?

I. INTRODUCTION

A LOT of people have told me they don't find that their minister or priest is expressing their viewpoint in many sermons. . . . Maybe the (religious) leaders ought to realize that their total function is not only to enlighten their congregations but to live with their parishioners and serve them and be aware of the values that are inherent in the community they enter—instead of entering that community convinced of the need to instill a new set of values before they've even found out about the ones that exist."

Spiro Agnew said this in an interview with Catholic editor A. E. P. Wall (quoted in Wills 1970). Religion *should,* Agnew says, function to help maintain and integrate an ongoing sociocultural system. It *should not* be an agent of change, especially of radical change. Although couched in normative terms, the statement reflects the conventional view about what religion usually *does do.* If a classical structural-functionalist were to write an advice column for "social engineers," it is what he might well say. If A. E. P. Wall could interview Confucius, the prose might vary but not the sentiment.

Explaining religion as system sustainer, subsystem integrator, and people-pleaser is so much a part of the stock in trade of social scientists that it seems unnecessary to cite examples. Anthropologists do their thing by showing a culture-bound public how even the strangest appearing religious belief or practice can function importantly to keep the society running and its people mentally secure and ecologically adaptive. Sociologists assure their students that among ordinary middle class North Americans church attendance is more a function of social convention than real belief in the supernatural. Psychologists debate the therapeutic qualities of religious experience and ritual and formulate hypotheses which correlate deep belief in God with personality defect or socio-economic deprivation.

Advocates of "modernization" in the developing lands as well as proponents of fundamental change in the U.S.A. seem to share the view that religion normally functions to keep things as they are. But

669

of course instead of endorsing this, they attack it. Religion—particularly traditional religion—is decried as being a barrier to progress or an opiate to still the masses. Religious-inspired fatalism, for example, is often described as rationalizing *resignation* instead of motivating the revolutionaries' charge. Black militants criticize conventional Black Christian churches as blocking Black Pride, stifling the spirit of rebellion and causing blacks to be resigned to their subordinate status. Some may even feel ashamed of black Americans who participate in ecstatic religious services because establishment whites use this to reinforce traditional racial stereotypes.

Within this framework which portrays established religions as system celebrator, integrator, and maintainer, it takes but a quick sidestep to give the label of "sect," "cult," or ritual of rebellion to those religious activities which deviate from the norm—and the normative. And it is then part of scholarly convention to explain such deviations as ways in which an established order provides avenues of protest, release, or surcease for those who are troubled, misfit, deprived, or simply bored. In short, seemingly unusual religious activities are explained as providing havens and alternatives for those who have not yet made it into—or who have dropped out of, or who wish temporary escape from—the established order.

On occasion, however, social scientists do deal with instances in which most of the members of a society or a large social group become involved in religious change and often this religious change intersects with large-scale social, political, and economic change. Such events are usually labeled movements. A number of examples readily come to mind: the rise of Islam, the genesis of Christianity, the Reformation, the Ghost Dance, the Cargo Cult, Peyotism, and Madhist Movements. Terms like nativistic, revitalization, millenarian are used to encompass these and a host of other movements.

How are such large-scale instances of religious movement treated? For those who are still reluctant to examine such religious movements as producers of change there exist a number of standard defensive maneuvers. One is to de-emphasize the extent or depth of change. This is done by analyzing the movement as an example of syncretism and reinterpretation. As Wallace (1966) puts it: "Old religions do not die, they live on in the new."

Another tactic in the game of explaining (away) the significance of religious change is to describe it as a handmaiden of economic or political activity or a reflection of national character and basic personality. For example, we learn that seventh-century Islam functioned to facilitate the socio-political integration and centralization of segmented Arab society, and that in turn this centralization functioned to facilitate necessary trade and commerce (Wolf 1951). Behind this is the premise that it was to accomplish these political and economic ends that Islam was born, and furthermore, it is implied that political and economic growth is part of some grand and inevitable design. Muhammad becomes little more than an actor in a drama—and it appears that the script is not written by God but rather by the hand of evolutionary destiny.

Max Weber (1930) and Preserved Smith (1920) placed religious transformation at the center of a web of economic and political change which led to the rise of capitalism. But if one is looking for lineal cause-and-effect relationships it is indeed just as easy to postulate that religious change is the product of pragmatic, enterprising man looking for ways to justify his economic desires. Or, one can seek to reduce cause to a basic psychological dimension or "rebelliousness" and explain that "nonconformity in religion and economic activity were common results of their [the innovators'] personality traits" (Hagen 1962). Religious change remains a consequence of something else.

Yet another tactic in reducing the primacy of religion is to say that religious movements are but a reaction to radical change (Beals 1953). The proposition is made that the society in question has already changed—but changed for the worse. And its members can't cope with the changes. They have become disorganized, confused—their mental "mazeway" has become disoriented, devitalized. Indeed, their condition is so bad that to survive they require "revitalization" (Wallace 1956).

How do we know that people are sufficiently deprived, disorganized, devitalized, or defective enough to join or start a movement or a sect? Easy! You know that they have reached this condition after they do join or start this activity. Why do they join? Well, because they are deprived, disorganized, defective, devitalized. The trick in getting such tautology accepted is to separate statements about effect and presumed cause by pages of description. This game is facilitated by the commonly shared assumption of the social science community that there is in fact no "supernatural" or at least that we cannot use supernatural cause to explain events.

What, we can wonder, would happen if our scholarly paradigm was based on or at least admitted the existence of God, spirit forces, or the like? If an informant explains his religious behavior and the growth of the religious movement as the Will of God, the typical anthropologist smiles knowingly and searches for the "real reason." If the informant describes his religious experiences, his visions, the prophecies uttered through his lips and interpreted by his spiritual brothers, the anthropologist does not shout eureka! and write an

article explaining these activities as truly the workings of the supernatural. Instead, he happily continues the search for evidence of
psychological disturbance. And if he observes informants actually
having a religious experience, perhaps speaking in tongues, being
Baptized in the Spirit, dancing to the command of the spirits, he
becomes even more certain that this tells us much about their "real
world" problems. If the "subjects" of his study are those anthropology
once called primitive and now call peasants or "peoples of . . .," then
he displays commitment to cultural relativity, and explains their behavior as eufunctional or some such thing. If the "subjects" of his
study are North Americans, but are members of a racial minority
group or have not yet made it into "the middle class," then he explains
their behavior as a consequence of deprivation or disorganization. And
if they are "normal" middle class in all but religious behavior, then
he explains their behavior as a consequence of personality defect.

How different anthropological explanations of religion would be
if we could and did use supernatural cause. But then we would have
to decide "which" supernatural explanation to accept if we aspired
to take any sort of cross-cultural approach. So I suggest no such
revolutionary alternative to our present anti-supernatural paradigm.
All that I suggest is that for a moment we shift the center of our
emphasis: instead of examining religion as the consequence of or
reaction to change, consider that it may be a cause of change. Instead
of assuming that "strange religious behavior" by North Americans is
a consequence of deprivation or personality defects, examine such
behavior as commitment to religious movement and to change.
Instead of always searching for ways in which the seemingly new is
really a bit of reinterpreted tradition, look for the ways in which its
practitioners regard it as new. And if we learn about the preaching
and witnessing of evangelists and prophets, let us for the moment
consider the possibility that they did not simply arise spontaneously
because of pre-existing conditions of disorder and mazeway disintegration. It is possible that some converts to religious movements—or
other movements, for that matter—were reasonably satisfied with their
lives and the established order until the evangelist or prophet got to
them and made them feel dissatisfied with present conditions. Muhammad, for example, began his preaching by warning people of impending catastrophe if they did not change. He also was not content simply
to let his enemies collapse through their own disorganization. He led
raids to force their fall.

It is clear that the relationship between religion and social change
is very complex. In our analysis of subsystem interaction we are
limited by language and logic to the presentation of lineal cause-and-
effect relationships instead of being able to express a situation in

which everything is in fact cause and effect of everything else. Within this limitation, tradition has led us to evaluate religion far more as product than producer. In this paper I wish to reverse this pattern of analysis and to discuss two case studies in which it is necessary to consider how religion generates individual and social change.[1] One case study is that of neo-Pentecostalism in the U.S.A.; the other, the spread of Pentecostalism in Haiti.

In the study of Pentecostalism in the U.S.A. I will show how an activity which at first glance looks like therapeutic and system-maintaining spirit possession functions to generate personal transformation and social change. I will describe Pentecostalism not as a sect activity and an opiate for the deprived but as a far-flung movement of change. Finally, I will survey the spread of Pentecostalism in Haiti and propose that it also is best considered a movement of change rather than simply reinterpretation and maintenance of tradition.

II. The Pentecostal Movement in the U.S.A.

Conventionally, Pentecostalism in the U.S.A. has been evaluated as a religion for the economically deprived and disorganized, or a

---

[1] In other publications we have found it useful to distinguish between two magnitudes of change, developmental and revolutionary (Gerlach 1971; Gerlach and Hine 1973).

By "developmental" change I refer to change which adds to and enhances ongoing sociocultural patterns. Change continues within basic themes of the established system; indeed, such change helps to prevent more revolutionary change and perpetuate the established system, increasing its capabilities, reducing its limitations, helping it adjust to new conditions by patching, repairing, and re-forming. Some call aspects of such change "involution" (Geertz 1963; Service 1971: 12). New ideas and actions are modified as they are added to the ongoing system so that they conform to its basic paradigms, so that they blend with it and enhance rather than uproot and replace it. Syncretism and reinterpretation are common terms used in anthropology to describe this blending process. Trimmingham describes the Islamicization of Africans as essentially a developmental process (1962). From my research among the Digo of Kenya, I would describe their Islamicization as developmental and syncretistic. For example, to their established pantheon of spirits, they added Islamic spirits, Islamic ritual. It can be demonstrated that these Islamic additions "modernized" their religion sufficiently to help it resist the revolutionary impact of Christianity and Westernization.

By "revolutionary" change, I mean change which does overthrow established patterns instead of perpetuating them by "fixing them up." Revolutionary change refers to a fundamental and radical redesigning of the ongoing system and the creation of new guiding themes and actions. It means paradigm change (Kuhn 1962). I use the term personal transformation to refer to revolutionary change in the beliefs and actions of an individual. Smith (1920) describes the Reformation as revolutionary change.

Since completing this essay, we have elaborated in detail upon the difference between developmental and revolutionary change in our new book *Lifeway Leap: The Dynamics of Change in America* (Gerlach and Hine 1973), especially in chapter 2, "How Do You Spell (R)Evolution?"

religion for those seeking to cope with the effects of change or to resist change. Scholars have focused on its individual segments or congregations, and termed these "sects" or "cults" rather than the "churches" of a "denomination." Mention Pentecostal to the layman, describe Pentecostal religious behavior to him, and he will probably say most disparagingly, "Oh, you mean the Holy Rollers!"

A distinguishing feature of Pentecostalism is that its participants do seek to establish personal communion with the Holy Spirit or Jesus. In this process, they seek and have ecstatic religious experience, including trance and glossolalia, which they call "speaking in tongues," and which they regard as a "Gift of the Spirit." Pentecostals consider this an essential aspect of true Baptism, and conceive of it as part of the process through which a person is *transformed* or "born again." Some Pentecostals also seek gifts of prophecy and interpretation and exorcise demons. All of this is considered unusual enough in conventional North American society to lead people to regard its practitioners as persons suffering from some psychological failing, economic problem, or social stress. They explain the unusual behavior as some kind of defense or compensation mechanism, not as a transforming act. Scholars merely reflect this conventional wisdom.

These behaviors and beliefs looked like this to us when we began our research on Pentecostalism in 1965. I initiated the study primarily to provide field research experience for students. Its initial objective was only to study the phenomenon of "glossolalia" and to examine its social, economic, and biophysical correlates. Pentecostals seemed like just the kind of "subculture" which anthropologists could study— and right in their own backyard. We presumed that Pentecostals did not actually communicate with the Holy Spirit, and that their unusual religious experiences were "really" a product of some set of "natural" causes which could be determined.

I must add that I was led to this Pentecostal study by my interest in the phenomenon of "spirit possession," which in turn derived from my earlier field work in East Africa among the Bantu-speaking Digo. For the Digo it is easy to demonstrate that their spirit possession complex does function as system maintainer, and is an agent of therapy and product of development and syncretism. In the company of supportive kin, friends, and neighbors, "deprived" Digo experience trance, act as mediums for spirits, speak in the tongues of these spirits, and through this express their anxieties and anger. Persons the "spirits" identify as being responsible for causing their mediums such anguish promise to reform. These persons pacify the spirits by giving their mediums gifts, food, services, and attention. Through this activity wealth is shared, pushy entrepreneurs "leveled," family quarrels

subdued, and solidarity supported. My analysis of the system maintenance functions of this Digo spirit complex (Gerlach 1963, 1964, 1965a,
1965b, 1970d; Gerlach and Hine 1973) roughly parallels other cross-
cultural studies of trance and dissociation (e.g. Bourguignon 1965;
Bourguignon and Pettay 1964; Hamer 1966; Kiev 1962; Metraux 1959;
Mischel 1958), although these other writers focus more on the therapeutic value of the possession complex than on the economic impact.

Initially it appeared that we would with profit examine tongues
and trance among the North American Pentecostals as socio-psychological therapy. We sought ways in which this "spirit baptism" helped
the Pentecostals cope with the pressures of the world and was a
response to their deprivation, disorganization, or personality defect.
We hypothesized that the Pentecostal tongues, trance, and witnessing
(talking about experiences, problems, and prospects before fellow
church members) paralleled communication patterns in Digo ritual.
Pentecostals, we felt, could express their troubles in the sanctioned
atmosphere of witnessing and get support and release. In addition
to interview and observation we sought to measure psychological
correlates of trance and tongues (Palmer 1966) and to analyze personality of members (Sorem 1969). At first we studied only one congregation; the approximately 300 members of one established Pentecostal
church, comprising white, chiefly blue collar workers. We shall refer
to this as the United Brethren Church, a pseudonym.

With this group we found perhaps some support for our proposition
that relative economic deprivation was causally related to involvement
in Pentecostalism. But these Pentecostals were not using Pentecostalism as a refuge in the face of economic deprivation, but rather as a
launching pad to thrust into the middle class. Certainly, we found no
evidence to support our propositions that Pentecostalism was best
explained as a haven for the disorganized or confused. Members of
the church came from stable families. Many members were children
and grandchildren of the church founders. If anything, one could
explain the growth of the church as a consequence of recruitment
across generations, within tightly organized families. Personality
profiles corresponded to the range in most any church.

Furthermore, we found that the United Brethren Church was but
one of many Pentecostal groups in the urban area where we began
research. We included as "Pentecostal" those groups which accept
such identification and whose members seek or manifest "tongues" and
the other "charismatic" Gifts of the Spirit recorded in the New Testament as accompanying the emergence of the early churches. We
determined that there was sufficient variation in membership, structure,
and behavior across this range of groups to call for a new approach to

our study. We learned that the conventional therapy, equilibrium, and deprivation models could not account for Pentecostal growth, structure, or function. Accordingly, we shifted from the study of one church to the examination of the structure and function of the broad spectrum of Pentecostal groups as they interact to form a *movement* which generates change, transforms people, and challenges the established religious order. This led us to develop a general model of movements of change and to the study of the Black Power and Ecology movements. Elsewhere we detail how and why we took this approach (Gerlach 1968, 1970a, 1970b, 1970c; Gerlach and Hine 1968, 1969, 1970a, 1970b, 1970c, 1970d, 1970e, 1973; Hine 1969). Here I only summarize this. First I shall comment on the basic types of groups we observed in the Pentecostal spectrum. Then I shall indicate how they interrelate to comprise a movement. Finally I shall discuss the five characteristics of movement anatomy with particular reference to the role of glossolalia in generating *commitment* to the movement.

Types of Pentecostal Churches

Some of the Pentecostal groups we studied in several cities were like the United Brethren Church in organization and in socio-economic characteristics of members and in routinization of ritual and belief. Many members are the children or grandchildren of the founders. Only a few are new converts to Pentecostalism. On the basis of income, occupation, education, and area of residence, most can be classified as lower-middle to middle. Their religion helps them achieve a marked upward mobility. Our research indicated that Pentecostal churches of this type are found across the country. Many of these churches are now combined in 25 or 30 national or regional associations, of which the Assemblies of God is the largest. Such groups can best be termed the established Pentecostal churches.

In addition to these established, long-term, and routinized Pentecostal bodies, we also observed a number of smaller, quite new, and militantly independent storefront Pentecostal groups. Many members are new converts to Pentecostalism, but others are second or third generation Pentecostals who were recruited from the more established Pentecostal churches. With some notable exceptions, members of these storefront independents were lower in socio-economic class than those of the more established Pentecostal churches.

While most of the Pentecostal established churches and independent groups which we observed did have predominantly white membership, a few were integrated and some were totally or chiefly black. One integrated church which we studied was founded by a black minister after World War II. We refer to it as "The House of Deliverance."

About 80% of the congregation is black, the rest white. The minister is attempting to bring Indians into the fold but with little success. Most members, both black and white, would conventionally be labeled lower middle class. But the minister is trying successfully to recruit white students from the nearby university. They are initially attracted by the music of the church service, and in time by the message of the minister—a very dynamic and persuasive man.

To simplify matters, we can regard the above Pentecostal groups and churches as the often routinized descendants of a first wave of Pentecostal revivals which spread across the U.S.A. at the turn of the century and which, in turn, stem from that tradition in Christianity which some call "holiness religion." Some of these are indeed the groups which have traditionally been classified as sects by scholars and analyzed as appealing primarily to the socially, politically or economically deprived (Pope 1942; Johnson 1961; Harper 1963; Elinson 1965), to the socially disorganized (Holt 1940; Cohn 1957; Poblete and O'Dea 1960; Talmon 1962), and to the psychologically disadvantaged (Cutten 1927; Alland 1962). Furthermore, it is within the established Pentecostal bodies that scholars have identified the simple sect-church development (Wilson 1959).

But the Pentecostal movement as we describe it includes far more than these established groups. A second wave of "revivals," often called Neo-Pentecostalism or the Charismatic Revival, attained sufficient proportions to make newspaper headlines in the late 1950s and is still marching on. It is attracting people from a much wider range of socio-economic and educational backgrounds than the earlier wave. First it spread into the major Protestant denominations and then moved into Catholic religious and lay communities. As such it is recruiting from people of middle and upper-middle class backgrounds, people who by and large are well situated and not economically, socially, or politically deprived. Most recently, it is attracting young, white middle class youth, some of whom are turning to Pentecostalism as a way of casting off drugs. But this youth involvement is not simply explained as a consequence of "dropping into" religion after "dropping out of" society and then out of the drug cult. It is recruiting from a broad spectrum of young people, and its evangelistic endeavor is manned by otherwise conventional young adults who would easily be labeled "well-adjusted."

The spread of Pentecostalism across class lines into the middle and upper-middle economic strata and into the established religious order has resulted in the formation of many new independent groups of varying size. Some of these number in the hundreds, others consist of a few families. Some join with the established churches or old line independents mentioned earlier, many go on their own. Many are composed of individuals and led by ministers who have been asked to leave churches of the major denominations because they not only sought and obtained the Pentecostal charismatic gifts, especially tongues, but because they then engaged in the personal evangelizing which appears to be a natural aftermath.

In addition to these new independent groups, we observed yet another element within the Pentecostal movement, namely participants in the "tongues movements" who have remained within the Episcopal, Lutheran, Methodist, Baptist, Presbyterian, and Catholic churches. Enclaves of "spirit-filled" Christians who remain active in their non-Pentecostal churches meet regularly in a variety of settings, such as homes of participants, churches of sympathetic churchmen, rented motels and restaurants, or on campuses of colleges and universities where "there has been an outpouring of the spirit." We term such Pentecostals "hidden."

We have found it useful to range these diverse Pentecostal groups along an institutional continuum with the long established denominations at one end; the larger independent groups of some 15 to 20 years duration next; then the smaller, more recently organized independent groups; and finally the spirit-filled Christians still "hidden" in non-Pentecostal churches. We have described how these various groups are interconnected. In brief this is accomplished: (a) experientially, through the same Baptism of the Holy Spirit and manifestation of Gifts of the Spirit, particularly "tongues"; (b) ideologically, through a common interpretation of that experience as an empowering gift of God as recorded in the Acts and First Corinthians; (c) organizationally, in a network, accomplished through (1) overlapping membership in one or more of the various groups, (2) personal relationships or networks among members of the various groups, (3) exchange of leaders of various groups, (4) networks of the traveling evangelists who crisscross the country and the world, holding revivals and prayer sessions across the range of groups, (5) involvement of the various Pentecostal groups in one or more of the several national and international associations of Pentecostals, such as Full Gospel Businessmen's Fellowship International, which link organizational units within the movement much as Rotary Clubs link local business organizations.

So much for the description of the Pentecostal movement and the groups which comprise it. Certainly the range of variation among participants and groups was of such nature that nothing as simple as deprivation-disorganization models would suffice to explain the presence or growth of Pentecostalism or the appeal of Pentecostalism to its participants. In reality, the only thing which does distinguish

Pentecostals from the general American population is their specific religious practice and belief. This cannot then be used to prove them generally defective. The paper elsewhere in this volume by my colleague V. H. Hine speaks further to this point.

Before moving on we should consider the argument that for black Americans Pentecostalism and other Christian religions have served as an opiate to still their objections to American racism. No doubt it did have that function when blacks had no realistic hope for change. But while many "Negro" Pentecostal churches did preach resignation in the face of white power, most were quick enough to move to the offensive and press for change once Black Power gathered momentum. For another, black churches, some of them Pentecostal, often were the organizational base for civil rights protest when this was risky. It is clear enough that the pattern of resignation and acceptance of the status quo was a function of survival requirements, not an intrinsic characteristic of the Pentecostal religion itself. Indeed, the minister leading the House of Deliverance preached tolerance for existing conditions in the U.S.A. even while he preached a message of change in Haiti as he conducted his evangelical activities there several months each year. It is true that he did not preach against the political structure in Haiti, for this would have been suicidal. But he did preach militantly against Voodoo and this did bring him into conflict with Voodoo priests. In a society in which Voodoo has so much power, where people fear that its power can kill if it is challenged and where some Voodoo priests are also members of Duvalier's secret police, challenging it is dangerous.

As all of this became known to us, as our stereotypes of Pentecostalism proved defective, we had to change our approach. First of all, we had to change the level of our analysis from that of the single Pentecostal group (regarded as a kind of closed corporate community of "other peoples" appropriate to anthropological study) to that of the total spectrum of the many Pentecostal groups and to an examination of the ways in which they interrelated to form a movement. Second, we had to shift our focus from that of the ways in which Pentecostal belief and practice helped maintain the group and perpetuate convention and established order to the way in which the major thrust of Pentecostalism was to generate change. Third, we had to shift from a search for the causes of Pentecostal deviant behavior, using essentially deprivation, disorganization, and defective individual models, to an examination of the structure and function of Pentecostalism regarded as a system. And we found it necessary to examine Pentecostal tongues and trance as acts of commitment to the new rather than therapy to preserve the old.

Pentecostalism provided us with our first case study of what we came to term a movement of personal transformation and revolutionary change. Through this study we developed a model of the structure and function of such movements which we subsequently tested, refined, and applied in the study of the Black Power movement and the Ecology movement. Indeed, it was through this model that we anticipated the genesis and growth of the latter movement, which we call Participatory Ecology. The model identifies and describes five operationally significant factors in the movements we studied. These are factors of social organization, recruitment, commitment process, ideology and response to real or perceived opposition. We have discussed this model and its applications in our publications cited above. Let me now summarize the main characteristics of these factors, giving special attention to organization and commitment.

A. *Organization*

When Americans think of "organization" they often conceive of a pyramidal structure with central authority, leadership, and a clear channel of command. If they do not perceive such structure they may believe that the activity is a non-organization. Our research indicates a third structure. We propose that movements—certainly those we have studied, such as Pentecostalism, Black Power, Participatory Ecology—have the following organizational characteristics:

1. Movements are *segmentary*. That is, a typical movement is composed of semi-autonomous cells or segments. New cells are formed by a splitting of ongoing cells, by the formation of entirely new units, or by a combination of these two. Cells frequently overlap and intertwine in complex fashion so that movement participants are often simultaneously members of several cells. It is not unusual for a man to be a leader in one small group and a follower in another. Yet another characteristic of this segmentary structure is that there is considerable variation in the specific goals and means manifested by each cell. An individual cell is encouraged to do its own thing, perform according to its own special capabilities afforded by the qualities of its members.

2. A second characteristic of movement organization is that it is *decentralized* and *polycephalous,* or "many-headed." Movements do not have a single paramount leader who rules through a coordinated bureaucracy. Each cell may have its own temporary head, but such a man is no more than a *primus inter pares*, or first among equals. He can retain such leadership only by proving his worth. Any member of a small group is a potential leader and many indeed strive to be actual

leaders since they feel that they have a duty to help the group succeed. If an ongoing leader falters or fails, or appears to sell out to the establishment, he will quickly be replaced by another.

3. A third characteristic of movement organization is that it is *reticulate*. Reticulate means "network"; that the individual cells of a movement are tied into a loose and informal network of reticulate structure by the personal interaction of "cell" leaders, by overlapping membership as noted above, by the sharing of a common ideology, common cause, and common opposition. Traveling spokesmen or "evangelists" move across this network, contributing to its cohesion and ideological unity. This network also provides a very effective grapevine communication system and logistical financial support system.

Let us consider the functions of such organization. Observers or members generally regard such a loose structure to be defective and seek to centralize it, tighten its command structure, terminate "unnecessary duplication," and otherwise "rationalize" its organization and operation. Our research leads us to propose that such organization is highly adapted for exponential growth and for generating and promoting revolutionary change.

It is adaptive because: (1) It promotes effective coping in new environments. The injunction that each cell contribute in its own way, doing "its own thing," maximizes cellular variation, innovation, entrepreneurship, and trial-and-error experimentation and problem solving. The failures of one group do not cause the whole to fail, but the successes help the total movement. (2) It permits a movement to penetrate and recruit from a broad societal range. An individual who is attracted by what he perceives to be the general purposes of the movement can find within the myriad of movement cells a group of peers whose goals, tactics, personal life styles, and backgrounds appeal to him. (3) It prevents effective suppression or cooptation of the total movement through its redundancy, multiplicity of leadership, and self-sufficiency of local groups. (4) It generates an escalation of effort and forward motion through the rivalry and competition among its various segments and leaders.

B. *Recruitment*

Recruitment is essentially to a local group or cell of the movement rather than to the movement as a whole. New individuals are recruited to such cells primarily through face-to-face contact with members. That is, recruitment follows lines of significant pre-existing social relationships. Members recruit from family, friends, neighbors, associates, and colleagues. Recruiters use the capabilities, emotions, rights, and duties already existing in these relationships. The movement as a whole grows exponentially as each new recruit becomes in turn a recruiter of others. Such growth would not be possible if movement members recruited from loners or drifters. Pentecostals take pride in personally recruiting capable, effective associates.

Although it should be obvious that recruitment does proceed along these significant linkages, casual observers of movements assume that people are drawn to membership through exposure to mass media, advertising, large demonstrations, and the like, or to contact with a single charismatic leader. By the same token attitudes of members are changed through interaction with fellow cell members in the context of small group activities, not through large-scale "propaganda" or public information. In any event, such personal recruiting of effective people contrasts sharply with models which portray movements as a kind of giant magnet or vacuum cleaner which sucks up loosely articulated social particles.

C. *Ideology*

Movement ideology has a number of dimensions. On one level it provides a vision and master concept for the future, often presented in symbolic, easily communicated terms. On another level it affords to individual members a sense of personal participation in the shaping of this future. On yet another level, it affords individuals a feeling of personal worth and power; it contributes to the reshaping of individual self-image. Such ideology encourages individual and group persistence, risk taking, and sacrifice for the cause and the local cell. When striving in this way, movement participants do not easily perceive failure. Rather they reinterpret even what objectively *is* failure to signify either future success or a temporary testing of devotion and courage. Since the established order keeps score using a different set of criteria (theoretically more "rational," "objective" and "realistic") it characteristically misjudges the ability of the movement to persist in the face of setbacks.

D. *Opposition*

The participants in a movement characteristically perceive that they are facing opposition—*unjust* opposition. Opposition, either real or merely perceived, is necessary to promote the movement, to offer it a basis for its commitment process and a force against which to unite. Opposition optimum for movement growth is sufficient to be perceived as a threat and a challenge, but strong enough to be overcome.

E. *Commitment Process*

People can be committed to change their ways of living fundamentally and to strive to change others by a process which includes symbolic, emotional experiences and one or more "bridge-burning" acts, through which they identify with the movement of change as against the established order. We term this combination of identity-changing experience and act the commitment process.

Effective participation in a movement, such as Pentecostalism, Black Power, Ecology, involves just such a process. It sets the participant apart from the established order of things, it cuts him off from past patterns of behavior and often from past associations. It involves him with movement participants, and provides high motivation for changed behavior and for striving to accomplish group and movement objectives. In the commitment process individuals frequently must stand on the firing line to demonstrate their new identity and validate their faith. By taking risks they show "which side they are on." The term "radicalization" is now commonly used to describe the effects of commitment, particularly in reference to the ways in which individuals were changed during involvement in anti-war and Black Power demonstrations.

In American Pentecostalism, glossolalia is a phenomenon that does serve both as motivating experience and bridge-burning act. In a society where highly expressive religious practices are considered deviant, a new convert's ecstatic uttering of streams of unintelligible syllables and his demonstration of joyous enthusiasm and enraptured faith in the Glory and Power of God are enough to burn a great many bridges. Neo-Pentecostals, especially those who have been asked to leave their churches of origin, testify to this fact. They, however, characteristically press on with their belief and practice and give verbal witness to it in spite of the ridicule and scorn it generates among their "straight" associates.

It is because the Pentecostal acts of commitment do violate—and attack—convention and because Pentecostal experiences do transform people into changed "religiously radical" persons that members of the established social and religious order find it so tempting—perhaps so necessary—to explain it all away as the consequence of pre-existing defects in the Pentecostal.

We offer instead the proposition that participation in movements and involvement in its process of commitment turns "normal" persons into "abnormal" ones, ordinary persons into extraordinary ones, "straights" into "radicals," and the like. It generates and stimulates an enthusiasm and a power in participants to spread the word to others, to recruit and commit them to similar change. We see this repeated in movement after movement. The Mau Mau participant who engaged in terrible oath-taking rituals and then killed kinsmen, or the Melanesian Cargo Cult member who destroyed his property not only bound himself to the movement, he also committed himself to a striving for new ways of thought and action. For Mau Mau, rituals of de-oathing and of counter-commitment were apparently successful in breaking a convert from Mau Mau and turning him in new directions.

The violence associated with the Black Power and other "racial" and ethnic movements is usually viewed as a manifestation of explosive frustration resulting from deprivation. We suggest that it might be more usefully analyzed in terms of the evangelistic commitment and identity change that can be generated by such acts. The "new men" with new personal and social identity who emerge from effective bridge-burning acts of commitment are then deeply involved in their movement and leaders in its spread. It is at this point that conditions such as deprivation and disorganization, which may have been necessary conditions of its genesis, become merely facilitating and perhaps of little significance in the subsequent appeal or spread of the movement. While we are making such comparisons of various movements, we can but think of early Christianity and realize that Christ and his disciples seemed quite aware of the importance of symbol and risk in generating commitment. And of course from such perspective we can appreciate why American bombing in Viet Nam has not cowed the Vietnamese into submission but rather sparked them on to greater commitment, and the seemingly strange behavior of the Red Guards in China can be understood as Mao's attempt to rekindle the flagging flames of revolutionary commitment.

Interrelationship and Feedback

It is of course only for purposes of analysis that we isolate these factors. In the actual stream of events, they interact complexly. It is in their combination and interaction that these factors produce the energy and action that enables the movement to generate major change.

In summary, Pentecostalism can be described as a movement of personal transformation and revolutionary change; that is, as a group of people who are *organized* for and *ideologically* motivated and *committed* to the task of generating fundamental change and transforming persons, who are actively *recruiting* others to this group, and whose influence is growing in *opposition* to the established order within which it develops. It is true that, in the U.S.A. at least, the main focus of Pentecostal efforts is to transform persons, not to change the social order. But it is also true that social changes do follow upon the personal changes; in behaving differently, the committed individuals change relationships within their circle of kin and association, the committed individuals approach much of what they do in the social and economic spheres with positive fatalism and this has some effect upon these spheres. Certainly, what the Pentecostals and especially the Neo-Pentecostals are doing has an effect upon the established church structure. Some of the newer groups of independent Pentecostals, both young adult and adult, are establishing various experiments in communal living, often much to the chagrin of neighboring residents of the conventional society. In short, some Neo-Pentecostals envisage not only a new heaven, but also a new earth.

In other movements there may be a better balance between personal transformation and social change. This seems to be the case for Black Power. In others, such as the anti-war movement and perhaps ecology, there is more stress on social change than personal change.

The very characteristics of ecstatic religious behavior—ceremonial dissociation, decentralized structure, unconventional ideology, opposition to established structures—which might appear to be marks of a sect of misfits and dropouts, are indeed the features which combine to make Pentecostalism a growing, expanding, evangelistic religious movement of change. It is a movement which is likely to disturb those who wish religion to maintain established ways and values. Among our Pentecostal case studies are examples of men and women who certainly did open their neighborhoods, places of work, and churches to the winds of change—radical religious change. Some of these men are ministers or priests. Some of the women are nuns. And some could certainly be accused by Spiro Agnew of "not expressing conventional viewpoints."

It is interesting that some Catholics, both Pentecostal and non-Pentecostal, state that Pentecostalism is no more than enhancement of fundamental principles of the Church. They claim that the "Gifts of the Spirit" have always been recognized by the Catholic Church. They may agree that in recent years the Church has become so structured that deep personal religious experience has been somehow lost in the bureaucracy, but intrinsically it is all part of the real Church. They see Pentecostalism as but a movement of renewal and reaffirmation of fundamental meanings and principles. In our terminology, these Catholics see Pentecostalism as "developmental change" and not as "revolutionary change."

But even though this sounds very persuasive, there are cases where Catholic nuns, priests, and laymen have been heavily criticized by church officials, kin, neighbors, and colleagues for seeking Pentecostal experiences. Even where Catholic Pentecostals have been told by church officials that they can seek the Gifts of the Spirit, they have also been told that they should not allow this to lead them to beliefs and actions which conflict with the edicts of church superiors. Now this is all well and good for the officials to pronounce, but Pentecostalism does lead people into independent action. After all, the Holy Spirit can speak to or through people who have the "gift of prophecy." If the words of the Holy Spirit come in unknown tongues, others have the gift of interpretation to make all of this clear. Through these media, people can indeed be told or led to do things which established orders may not like. What "Word" should be followed if prophecy conflicts with the declaration of the Bishop—or the decree of the Pope? At some point Catholic Pentecostals either decide to go no further than developmental change, or they burn their bridges! Some realize indeed that "new wine cannot be put into old bottles."

Many Protestant denominations did not even attempt to accept a developmental version of Pentecostalism. They simply waged counter-insurgency against it. One case of such counter-insurgency effort is that of a Missouri Synod Lutheran minister who was expelled from the Synod and removed from his church building for speaking in tongues and persisting in a commitment to bring the Gifts of the Spirit to those of his congregation who wished this. Among other points Synod officials declared that his preaching had brought "deep division" into his congregation—some church members had changed and others had not.

We have thus far considered the two faces of religion: religion as stabilizing agent and as force for change. We have glanced at the spirit possession complex among the Digo as an integrator and maintainer of social structure and a product of syncretistic, developmental change. And we have examined Pentecostalism as an example of a religious movement which, in spite of conventional interpretations of its seemingly bizarre features, is in fact a movement for change, not a collection of sects, an opiate, or an anchor for tradition. Now we turn to the third and last part of our exploration and look at Voodoo and Pentecostalism in Haiti.

III. Haitian Pentecostalism and Voodoo

I have mentioned the House of Deliverance church as an example of an integrated but predominantly black Pentecostal church. Its minister and his wife also serve several months each year as evangelists in Haiti, where they spread Pentecostalism in opposition to Voodoo and establishment Catholicism. In 1967 and 1968 I conducted two brief studies of the evangelical activities of this minister and of the impact of Pentecostalism on Haitians living in and around Port-au-Prnce, Haiti.

My major concern was to estimate the extent to which Pentecostalism in Haiti acts as a religious movement to generate change, or exists as a syncretistic variant of the spirit possession system of Haiti, most commonly demonstrated in "Voodoo." I was also able to compare Voodoo with spirit possession among the Digo of East Africa. Voodoo, sometimes called *vodu, vodun,* or *ouanga,* has been well described by many scholars (Bourguignon 1965; Metraux 1959), and it is in many ways similar to Digo *uganga,* both in form and function. It has its practitioners or "priests," called *hungan* (who are much like the Digo *aganga*). A *hungan,* like the *muganga,* is assisted by musicians, aides, and apprentices. Patients, again chiefly female, are organized into graded guilds or associations (like the Digo *ateji*). Patients sing and dance in order to call up the spirits. While in trance, spirits speak through their voice and (as in the Digo case), they are thus able to assume the role of the spirit and in so doing speak and act in ways different from that possible in ordinary life. By being able to discuss their problems in front of sympathetic audiences and by achieving recognition of their new roles and support for their demands they can meet socio-psychological needs. This total complex does appear to contribute to community solidarity, or at least to blunt points of conflict. The *hungan,* by his control over these important areas of life, is in a good position to achieve social, political and economic power.

Haitians recognize, as do the Digo, the existence of numerous spirits of diverse type, origin, and behavior. Some of these appear to be chiefly of African origin, while others arise more clearly from the post-African experience of the Haitians and exposure to Catholicism and French culture. Generally, the belief and practice of Voodoo and the characteristics of the Voodoo spirits comprise a syncretistic blend of African and Catholic patterns, just as Digo *uganga* represents the blending of Islamic elements into traditional Digo religion.

The late ruler of Haiti, "Papa Doc" Duvalier, used Voodoo almost as a state religion. He had the reputation of using Voodoo beliefs and practitioners to support his regime, frighten or kill his enemies, provide him with information about plots against him. Indeed, some of the Voodoo priests and their assistants were in Duvalier's secret police and militia—I saw them come to rituals flaunting weapons. It was even asserted that Duvalier himself was a Voodoo priest.

Once Duvalier vigorously curtailed the operations and power of the Catholic Church in Haiti, perceiving it as a threat to his regime and as an ally of his foes. As a counter to Catholicism he not only encouraged Voodoo, but also permitted Protestant evangelism and missions. This contrasted sharply with the era before Duvalier when non-Catholics were suppressed by government and church. By 1967,

Duvalier relaxed many of his controls on the Catholic Church but continued to support Voodoo and also to permit the growth of Protestantism. Each religion counterbalances the others. Through this, Duvalier has divided his enemies, playing one against another to maintain his position. He did the same in political, economic, and social spheres.

This, then, is the situation within which Pentecostals in Haiti operate. As my observations and the comments of others indicate, they have been able to grow and spread on the island. Now let us consider if this growth is best explained as a consequence of deprivation, and if Pentecostalism in Haiti provides but another example of syncretism and reinterpretation whereby the life of the traditional, multi-spirit folk religion is maintained. Or is Haitian Pentecostalism better evaluated as a movement which does significantly change people, their religion and their way of life.

The 3-D Approach to Pentecostalism in Haiti

Most Pentecostals in Haiti are poor by North American standards, but so are most Haitians, Pentecostal or not. Some Haitian Pentecostals, especially the leaders, are economically successful relative to most Haitians, and if anything one could assert that the Pentecostal movement will contribute substantially to the growth of a Haitian middle class. To oversimplify, the traditional Haitian elite is Catholic, the masses are involved primarily in Voodoo and folk Catholicism, while increasingly the rising middle class is Protestant, especially evangelical Protestant and Pentecostal.

In any event, relative deprivation cannot by itself be used to explain Pentecostal growth because many Haitians who are equally "deprived" do not join Pentecostalism and the relative deprivation theory cannot explain this difference in reaction. Pentecostalism is not simply explained as an escape valve for frustration. Voodoo itself might better offer such opportunity and Pentecostalism stands as the foe of Voodoo. Since Voodoo was the religious system endorsed by "Papa Doc" Duvalier, one could better propose that Haitians can convert to Pentecostalism to demonstrate in some relatively safe manner their opposition to the rule of Duvalier and his supporters. But even relatively safe opposition to the established order may turn into a focus for more risky conflict. Also many Pentecostals expect that the day will come when they will again be persecuted for their beliefs and practices by a new government.

And certainly it is not feasible to explain the involvement in ecstatic religious behavior as simply the consequence of disturbed personalities.

Such behavior is characteristic of the rank and file of Haitian people as they participate in Voodoo.

Instead of focusing on pre-existing conditions which push Haitians into Pentecostalism, again we suggest that we consider how Pentecostalism functions to *recruit* Haitians to cells within its segmented *structure* and *commits* them to its purposes in *opposition* to the established order of Voodoo, and teaches them its *ideology*.

Let me now summarize these five factors as I observed them in Haiti, giving especial attention to commitment.

A. *Organization*

The Pentecostal organization is similar to that discussed for Pentecostalism and other movements in the U.S.A. It consists of tight-knit small local cells, each tied into a polycephalous network. As in the U.S.A. such organization is adaptive for survival, for multi-penetration of Haitian society, and for exponential growth. While segmentation in the U.S.A. appears to be chiefly spontaneous and a function of rivalry among leaders and the diverse striving of individual participants, in Haiti segmentation is also a function of design. When membership of some churches exceeds 100–150, some of the members living at greatest distance from the church are asked to found a new group. Yet other churches are founded when various members split off in consequence of disputes, frequently over means and ends in spreading the faith, but also over use of funds, personal and community issues and the like. It is the traveling evangelist, such as the House of Deliverance minister, who acts as the reticulator of these groups, helping to tie them together into an effective network, assembling them in the hundreds or thousands for revival sessions. But because each cell is small and self-contained, they seem like weak, unorganized, and varied religious groups. Perhaps because of this, the Haitian government does not feel threatened by the Pentecostals and even encourages more individual Pentecostal church growth to counter the Catholics. When I asked a government official, "Is Pentecostalism growing in Haiti? he answered, in effect, "Pentecostals, who are they? Oh, you mean those little churches up there?"

In short, Pentecostal groups had a low enough profile to escape massive repression, yet had a large enough presence to do their work well. Their cells continue to proliferate across the land, penetrating community after community.

B. *Recruitment*

Pentecostals in Haiti recruit participants primarily through face-to-face contact from among kinsmen, affines, neighbors. Their approach to this is illustrated by the response of one woman when I asked her why she sought to "bring others to Christ." She shook her head as if to show that my question was absurd. Then with a quick shrug she showed me the fruit and vegetables she had just brought back from market. Patiently, she explained that this was good food in the basket; she will give it to those she loves, because she loves them. In similar manner, she said, she and other Pentecostals in Haiti will bring those whom they love to hear the word of Christ and receive the Baptism of the Holy Spirit—simple, logical, and a far cry from explanations based on cognitive dissonance theories, in which it is asserted that the primary motive for recruitment to a religious movement is to find comrades to share your misery and help you escape the realization that you made a mistake. This woman felt that those who were not Pentecostal were making all the mistakes.

Yet other Haitian Pentecostals gave evidence that they sought to bring to Christ those who were competent enough to help their cause. They certainly did not go out of their way to recruit misfits, for they were more interested in gaining useful colleagues than in establishing a haven for those needing comfort. For example, the House of Deliverance evangelist concentrated on taking the Pentecostal message to influential government officials, while his Haitian counterpart prided himself on converting Voodoo priests and priestesses.

Pentecostals spend much time with a prospective convert, working with him, praying over him, testifying to the power that Pentecostalism can give to cure illness, defeat the power of Voodoo, and help the convert succeed economically and socially. Through this, prospective converts are led to accept the Pentecostal ideology, to struggle against the foes of Pentecostalism and to commit themselves to change.

C. *Ideology*

The ideology of Haitian Pentecostalism is very similar to that found in the U.S.A. and is communicated across cultures by traveling evangelists. It focuses on the conflict between Jesus and the devil (and his minions). This ties in nicely with the Haitian belief in Voodoo spirits. In preaching to their congregations, local Haitian pastors emphasize the conflict with Voodoo spirits even more than do the North American evangelists. The message is simple and powerful. Come forward on Altar Call, Be Saved, Get Jesus, Drive out the Devils, Become Baptized in the Holy Spirit, Gain Power over the Forces of Voodoo. God can punish those who oppose Him, just as He can reward those who put themselves in His hands.

D. *Opposition*

Pentecostals in North America feel opposed by officials of mainline churches and misunderstood by a "misled" general public.

American Pentecostal evangelists in Haiti and their Haitian brethren also feel that the mainline churches in Haiti oppose them. Probably correctly, they believe that while the Catholic Church is their chief Christian foe, orthodox Protestant churches also dislike them. Leaders of established churches accuse the Pentecostals of sheep stealing, and well they might for while Pentecostal numbers are growing, membership in the mainline churches is dropping.

Haitian Pentecostals and their American associates also feel that Voodoo is a deadly enemy. And, indeed, Voodoo practitioners do seek to curtail the Pentecostal advance. For example, I saw the House of Deliverance pastor confront a major Haitian Voodoo priest. Each called upon the supernatural to help him; the pastor proclaimed the power of Jesus while the Voodoo priest evoked various Voodoo spirits and "the devil." Pentecostals are sure that the pastor won, but unfortunately I have no reliable information on the reaction of the Voodoo priest's followers.

As I have noted, Duvalier and his government permitted the Pentecostals to compete with Voodoo and Catholicism and hence brake their power. By the same token, Duvalier would not permit the Pentecostals to become too strong. As long as this continues, Voodoo priests and their followers can threaten Pentecostals with supernatural or physical attack. But neither they nor the Catholics can mobilize a large-scale purge. Under these conditions, Pentecostals flourish. Their opposition is strong enough to be a challenge, but not strong enough to overwhelm them. This is opposition which will help a movement grow.

As in America, North American evangelists in Haiti say that nothing can stop them. They reinterpret what seems a setback to be but a testing of God, with victory around the corner. Negative feedback is converted into positive reinforcement (but Pentecostals are smart enough to know when finally to beat a strategic retreat or to change direction). To some degree this high sense of mission and confidence was also found among Haitian Pentecostal leaders and diffused among their followers.

Pentecostal evangelists, ministers, and participants exhibit more confidence than did personnel of mission churches of other denominations. Many other American missionaries of other denominations, for example, display disappointment and even hopelessness. They state that in most cases when a Haitian "native" acts as if he is converted to Christianity, this is only a superficial manifestation—he will quickly enough slide back into Voodoo.

In short, Pentecostals in Haiti have a message and conviction of victory, in contrast to the feeling of pessimism which marked the work of many other Protestant groups.

E. *Commitment Process*

Consideration of this process brings us to the very core of our concern. We have seen that in North America it is the Baptism of the Spirit, involving glossolalia and dissociation which distinguishes Pentecostalism from other Christian religious systems. It is this "Baptism" which identifies the convert as a member of the Pentecostal group and is seen as a sign of divine acceptance of the convert. It is this which sets the believer apart from conventional North American culture. It challenges tradition and "radicalizes" people in a movement of change.

But can this same process of tongues and trance radicalize Haitians and commit them to change since it is so much like traditional Haitian behavior in the Voodoo complex? It was in part to answer this that I conducted study in Haiti. I sought to arrive at an answer by investigating the differences and similarities between Voodoo and Pentecostal trance and tongues; by determining if Pentecostals in Haiti are committed by acts and experiences other than those involved in the Baptism of the Spirit, and by determining if the Pentecostals in Haiti did manifest changed patterns of behavior. I projected a number of alternative possibilities:

(1) Haitian Pentecostals experience no personal change and no process of commitment to change, and, indeed, Pentecostalism is but a *developmental* addition to the prevailing Voodoo complex. To their pantheon of African spirits, syncretistic blends of Catholic saints, and traditional spirits, Haitians now could add the Pentecostal Holy Spirit and/or Jesus.

(2) Haitian Pentecostals do experience the Pentecostal trance and tongues as sufficiently different from Voodoo and this itself can serve as a basis for fundamental change.

(3) Haitians engage in activities additional to trance and tongues which are different from Haitian religious tradition, which do burn Haitian bridges to this tradition, and which do commit them to changed patterns.

I anticipated that I would find the third alternative to be the case. I also considered two other possibilities: one, that Haitians do change markedly through involvement in Pentecostal groups even though they do not undergo a process which they experience as being different from and opposed to tradition; the other, that Pentecostals do become involved in bridge-burning acts and identity-transforming experiences, but in spite of this do not appear to be changed persons. Later I had to admit that there was yet another possibility which as an anthropologist I could not consider, namely that Haitians, like North American

Pentecostals, are really involved with the supernatural and that behavior, ritual and change are a function of the supernatural. Such a possibility would, of course, not simply change my anthropological game plan. It would lead me to play an entirely different game.

What *did* I find? First, I delineated the ways in which Voodoo ritual and related organization are like Haitian Pentecostal practice. To summarize:

(1) Leaders and followers in both Voodoo and Pentecostalism conceive of a world in which there are powerful supernatural forces, some evil, some good.

(2) In both instances the subject experiences dissociation and speaks in tongues. In both, dissociation is seemingly induced by religious ritual involving patterned singing, chanting, swaying, and dancing.

(3) The Voodoo priest, or *hungan,* is characteristically domineering and autocratic. He seeks to appear infallible and able to control or persuade supernatural forces as long as his clients follow his orders. The behavior of the Pentecostal minister and evangelist is not quite so stereotyped. But when in action, many Pentecostal evangelists, both Haitian and North American, also tend to act with great assurance and sense of power.

(4) The Voodoo priest is assisted by a number of male and female apprentices or practitioners; the Pentecostal minister is helped by a number of male and female aides, ministers, and evangelists.

(5) Both *hungan* and minister are also greatly assisted by musicians, who play their music throughout the period of inducement and dissociation, changing rhythm and song according to changes of pace in ritual, and often signaling changes by ringing bells.

(6) Both evangelist and *hungan* are assisted and followed by a large group of organized devotees.

(7) In both cases, the devotees seeking healing usually wear white.

At this point it would indeed be easy enough to analyze this Pentecostal growth within the usual framework of reinterpretation and syncretism, and to provide this as but another example of how alien culture patterns are selected and accepted because of their similarity to existing patterns. But although there are these similarities between Voodoo and Pentecostal ritual and structure, there are key differences, differences which are clearly recognized and emphasized by the Pentecostals, differences which may well relate to subsequent behavioral change. These include:

(1) Differences in the actual music which is played, in the style of dancing and singing, and in the musical instruments which are used. The drum, for instance, is the key to Voodoo, while for Haitian Pentecostals the piano, the trumpet, and in a few cases the organ are

vital. The tambourine, which is used in some Pentecostal groups in the U.S.A., is scarcely found in the Pentecostal services which I saw in Haiti—perhaps because it is so much like the instruments used in Voodoo?

(2) Differences in treatment of spirits. In Haitian Voodoo, as in Digo *uganga,* spirits are usually "brought to the head" of the person so that they can be controlled rather than exorcised. As among the Digo, it is unusual for the Haitian *hungan* to seek to drive out the traditional spirits. Control is more desired than exorcism. In contrast, the Haitian Pentecostals do wage war on these Voodoo forces and do seek to exorcise them. But then they seek to bring the subject of this exorcism to the Baptism of the Holy Spirit—that is, they replace the spirits they define as evil with the spirit force they define as good.

Haitian Pentecostals consider these differences of major import. To them, their Pentecostal religion is certainly not an extension of Voodoo, rather it is its implacable foe.

Bridge-burning Act

Most importantly, Haitian Pentecostals may participate in a ritual which does act as a significant bridge-burning experience and which is not simply an addition to Voodoo. They destroy their Voodoo amulets, spirit jars, and other Voodoo paraphernalia which they obtained at considerable cost over the years of their involvement in Voodoo and which are thought to confer power and good fortune on their possessors. Haitians feel that the Voodoo spirits will be so angered by this that they will not only attack the new Pentecostal convert who commits such sacrilege, but they may also strike out at the kinsmen and neighbors of the convert.

Ritual events occur pretty much as follows: First of all, the new convert experiences the Pentecostal ceremony of exorcism. The old Voodoo spirits are driven from him, and he receives the Baptism of the Holy Spirit. The elders of the Pentecostal church then assign a team of church members to continue to work with the convert and help him through prayer to find God and overcome evil. When they are sure that he is ready, they demand that he burn his Voodoo paraphernalia. When he agrees, they declare that a burning will be held. Together with many members of the congregation, often following a long religious service, they march off to the person's home, singing religious songs. They search his home, pulling out every sort of Voodoo object. They place these in a large pile and, accompanied by much music, singing, shouting, and hand clapping, they throw kerosene on them and burn them.

Typically, the kinsmen and neighbors of the new convert object to this burning, fearing the wrath of the Voodoo spirits or of the Voodoo priest. The new convert requires the support of his new Pentecostal brethren and may indeed find it necessary to move and live near some of them. On some occasions the new convert was once feared in his or her community as a noted practitioner of Voodoo, a possessor of great spirit power. Now that the convert has rejected such power, members of the community may breathe a sigh of relief. But in one case neighbors taunted and hit a former Voodoo priestess who had converted to Pentecostalism. Her husband also turned against her because she not only burned her Voodoo ritual objects but also burned some money she had earned through Voodoo. She first fled to a Pentecostal orphanage to live there in sanctuary. For reasons I had no time to ascertain she later returned to Voodoo practice and broke from Pentecostalism. Pentecostals now seek to reclaim her.

Undoubtedly there are other cases of backsliding, cases where Pentecostals return to Voodoo or simply to past patterns of behavior. And certainly some do practice both Voodoo and Pentecostalism in alternation. But as far as I could determine, most converts who do go as far as the ritual burning of Voodoo objects do change their ways of life in the direction of the Pentecostal ideal and do maintain these ways, particularly if they are supported through frequent prayer meetings with small groups of Pentecostal brethren. Haitians cite the case of the backsliding woman as a real novelty. I cannot, however, cite meaningful statistics on this and can only present impressions obtained through observation and interview. I must also add that my Haitian research was shorter by far than my research on North American Pentecostals and on the Digo. Much more research is now needed to test the above propositions.

Haitians told me of many cases where significant changes followed upon conversion and commitment to Pentecostalism. I would like now to summarize some of these changes, noting again that I can provide no statistics to support these impressions.

Changed Behavior

(1) Many Haitian Pentecostals either stop or try to stop drinking, smoking, gambling, and cock fighting.

(2) They move to terminate temporary consensual unions between man and woman such as placage and concubinage; they establish more binding church marriages, and modify family life in the direction of tighter and seemingly more lasting and harmonious relations among wife, husband, and children.

(3) They reject certain traditional festivities and rituals, such as Mardi Gras and Voodoo, and in their place turn to Pentecostal celebra-

tions. Not surprisingly, there is heightened Pentecostal church activity during Mardi Gras and in smaller communities during periods when especially important Voodoo ritual is conducted.

(4) Involvement in Pentecostalism does not noticeably increase the economic striving of participants, but it does appear to increase their ability to save what little income they have. The economic consequences of being Pentecostal may only be ascertained when and if economic opportunities increase generally in Haiti. The major barrier to economic development in Haiti is not low achievement orientation or low levels of entrepreneurship, but rather overall lack of opportunity and oppressive conditions. If conditions do improve, I would propose that Pentecostals will prosper economically more and faster than most other Haitians because they will more easily escape traditional demands on their income; they will work harder than others and save their income; they will have a more stable family and community base from which to launch their enterprise.

In sum, it seems reasonable to propose that the segments of the Pentecostal Movement which we observed in Haiti have characteristics of *organization, recruitment, ideology,* response to *opposition,* and, above all, *commitment* which permit or lead them to generate transformation in personal behavior. This, in turn, contributes to the generation of social change, perhaps revolutionary change.

IV. New Perspectives

Now let me present a further note on Pentecostal groups in the U.S.A. which have formed since we completed our basic research on the movement.

We terminated our intensive study of Pentecostalism in the U.S.A. in 1968, at about the time when the movement was beginning to spread among youth and young adults. This is now a chief area of Pentecostal growth, and has the reputation of appealing mostly to "dropouts" and drug addicts. It is seen as providing young people with an alternative to drug "abuse." This counter-drug approach has received national attention through the work of David Wilkerson, a New York Pentecostal evangelist who claims that through conversion to Pentecostalism and Baptism in the Spirit, he has saved many young persons from crime and addiction. National television and press have reported on Neo-Pentecostal type youth groups such as "the Children of God" and the "Jesus Revolution." But again these reports describe such groups as alternatives to the drug culture. The media refer to these groups as Jesus Freaks and note how young people are now "freaking out on Jesus instead of on drugs." In short, the primary concern of this has been to explain Pentecostal growth among young people as a consequence of social and psychological deprivation and personal disorganization. It is usually admitted that the young people who turn to drugs and then to Pentecostalism come from middle and upper-middle families and hence such involvement is not attributed to economic deprivation. Instead, it is argued that these young people have become so bored with affluence that they are seeking thrills, that they are the victims of permissiveness, or that they are simply unloved. The deprivation argument is still alive and well, it has simply taken a new turn. By now you know the usual message: "Pentecostalism is a strange activity, it must be appealing to misfits and the reason that people turn to it is because they are misfits. Poor people turn to it because they are poor; rich adults turn to it because they are psychologically disturbed; rich young people turn to it because they are unloved, misunderstood, dropouts from reality." The only new dimension is that now it is admitted that involvement in Pentecostalism does change people some-what—it takes a misfit on drugs and changes him to a misfit "freaked out on Jesus."

Instead of these approaches to the new wave of Pentecostal growth, we would suggest that this involvement of young adults and youth in Pentecostalism be examined as part of the present cutting edge of the Pentecostal movement. We would evaluate it according to the factors of its social organization, patterns of recruitment, commitment process, ideology and response to opposition. It appears that this youth "wing" itself is as segmented and polycephalous as the main body of Pentecostalism. The various youth segments do appear to interact in a local and national network, and furthermore they appear to interrelate with some adult Pentecostal groups. It would be important to gauge the extent to which these young Pentecostal segments also reticulate with the Ecology Movement or the anti-war movement or the Black Power or Chicano movements. We have some examples where traveling evangelists of the Children of God spoke strongly at Earth Day 1970 and at subsequent anti-war activities. But they always argued that these activities could be better served if the participants turned to God and put their faith in Jesus. On one campus students fought the construction of a Red Barn hamburger restaurant, declaring that it represented an invasion of their community by unfeeling business interests. The students constructed instead a "People's Park" on the site leased by the Red Barn. Members of the Children of God supported this action, advocating only that it remain non-violent. Indeed, they planted a cross in the center of the "Park." Ecology activists joined in and flew an ecology flag next to the cross.

Members of the "Children of God" or "Jesus Revolution" feel that they are opposed more by Establishment churches than by those avowedly anti-religious. Certainly they find little or no support from parents, shocked by this "over-zealous" display. Commitment for some involves protest against the religious hypocrisy of straight society. They also demonstrate commitment by going out into the established world to witness to their beliefs and to seek new recruits. It may be that among the young people in the new wave of Pentecostalism, tongues is less of a bridge-burning act than it is among establishment adults. Those who have experienced dissociation through the use of drugs and who have already learned how to demonstrate ecstatic experience might find that such religious demonstration is just a minor addition to "conventional behavior." They may be in a position similar to that of the Haitian to whom spirit exorcism and the Baptism of the Holy Spirit are too much like traditional behavior to provide bridge-burning and commitment to a new identity. "Turning from drugs and onto Jesus" may be an important first step. But then there must be something more—what will it be for the new youth wave of Pentecostalism? Perhaps the pain of withdrawing from drugs may be so intense that it does, indeed, provide sufficient basis for commitment and personal transformation. Clearly, this is an area for speculation and research.

V. Conclusion

Religion can serve as a force to generate personal transformation and revolutionary social change, or as a force to maintain the existing social order and provide therapy to reintegrate persons into this order or to rationalize their exclusion. Religion itself can change in slow, additive, syncretistic, reinterpretive ways, which we call developmental; or in revolutionary, decidedly different ways. Most studies of the function of religious systems examine religion in its role as conservator of tradition and therapeutic agent. My study of the Digo was of this type. Most studies of religious change stress reinterpretation and syncretism (as I also did for the Digo). Where the object of study is a group or movement which behaves or believes in ways which are fundamentally different from the norm, such behavior and belief are explained away as attempts by the deprived or defective to achieve therapy and some avenue of reintegration.

In our studies of the Pentecostal movement in the U.S.A. and Haiti, we have focused on religion as a force for fundamental personal and social change. From this type of study, we have also developed models for our later research on Black Power and Ecology movements.

We have proposed that the key to fundamental change is a social *organization* which is segmentary, polycephalous, and reticulate; a face-to-face mode of *recruitment* which follows along established lines of relationship; an *ideology* of change; perception of an *opposition* which challenges but does not crush; and a *commitment process*. For middle class, middle-aged North Americans, the manifestation of dissociation and glossolalia is a powerful bridge-burning act leading to commitment. For Haitians, this Baptism of the Spirit is perhaps a necessary first step, along with spirit exorcism. But it is too much like their traditional religious practice to generate a break with old ways. Full commitment requires an additional act of burning of the Voodoo ritual objects, often in confrontation with Voodoo priests and supporters. Young Americans of the counterculture are reported to be dropping out of drugs and into such Pentecostal groups as the "Children of God" and the "Jesus Revolution." But this requires more study, particularly to determine if this activity is simply a type of therapy or more significantly a generator of change.

"Publish" or Perish: Negro Jehovah's Witness Adaptation in the Ghetto

Every week in the United States over three hundred thousand followers of the New World Society of the Witnesses of Jehovah give three to six hours of their leisure time to systematic house-to-house visitation or "publishing" as it is known among Witnesses.[1] Supported in these persistent weekly contacts with non-Witnesses by their religious doctrine and particular life styles, Jehovah's Witnesses boast one of the steadiest growth rates among Protestant sect movements in recent decades. This growth has been particularly notable among certain segments of Negro population in metropolitan ghettos, the urban areas where opposing Black nationalist movements have also developed. Why are urban Negroes attracted to this millenial and authoritarian religious movement dominated by white American leadership? More specifically at the local community level, what do the Jehovah's Witnesses offer as a total life style for today's ghetto dweller that makes this sect movement attractive to growing numbers of Negroes?

Existing literature on the Jehovah's Witnesses gives very little help in answering these questions; a considerable part of it is polemical in approach and methodology, and the balanced historical and theological studies do not concern themselves with Negro participation.[2] To

[1] The Jehovah's Witnesses, as they are commonly known, always use a lower case "w" when printing the designation "witness" for a member of the New World Society, a practice they use to indicate that the "witnesses of Jehovah" are not another religion like the Christians or Buddhists nor another denomination such as the Baptists or Pentecostals. In this study, to differentiate the noun and verb meanings of the word "witness," I will follow the customary printing style of the secular press and use the majuscule "W" when referring specifically to the Jehovah's Witnesses.

[2] The literature on the Jehovah's Witnesses is small and written from a variety of viewpoints, not too many of which are helpful to the anthropologist interested in sect movements. William Schnell, an ex-Witness, has written a series of polemical attacks on the Witnesses (1956), largely with the intention of discrediting their doctrines and evangelizing them for conservative Protestantism. At the other end of the spectrum are Marley Cole's works (1955, 1957), which are essentially apologies for the Witnesses and, although never admitted, seem to be written by a practicing Witness. His is the only work Witnesses will encourage a newcomer to read; they do not know or do not approve of the balanced account by the ex-Witness Stevenson (1966), who writes only of English Witnesses.

understand this sect as it operates in an urban ghetto I spent eight months in 1968–69 with a Negro Jehovah's Witness congregation in North Philadelphia.[3] An analysis of Negro Jehovah's Witnesses as they interact in a hostile environment, including ghetto society and unsympathetic audiences of non-Witnesses, shows that their own shared definitions of reality and patterns of daily living, revealed in a "contract" of obligations and rewards, constitute a functionally adaptive way of life for certain segments of Negroes living in U.S. urban ghettos.

WITNESS AT WORK

It happens to hundreds of Philadelphians every Sunday morning: just when you've settled down with the newspapers the doorbell rings to announce two neatly dressed Negro visitors with briefcases in their hands. The man promptly but unhurriedly introduces himself.

"Good morning. My name is Mr. Jackson [4] and this is Mrs. Henry. We're calling on you today for the West View congregation of the Witnesses for Jehovah here in Philadelphia. We're concerned about how peace and order will be established in our city. Wouldn't you like to live in a Philadelphia where there would be no robberies or riots and where all the people lived together in peace?"

You smile. "Well, uh . . . sure, I'm for peace and order like everyone else, but this morning I . . ."

The one historical study that covers the Witnesses' recent history from 1942 to the 1960s under President Nathan H. Knorr is that by Timothy White (1968), a doctrinal history and sympathetic evaluation from exhaustive research in the New World Society's publications. The French Canadian Jesuit Hébert (1960) has a mixture of objective research combined with anti-Witness propaganda. For the history of the Witnesses under their second President, Judge Rutherford (1914 to 1942), Herbert Stroup's history (1945) is particularly useful; he documents the Society's recovery from the power and ideological struggles after the death of its founder Pastor Charles Taze Russell in 1914. It is now out of date because of numerous changes in doctrine and practice made under President Knorr. The book by the Negro theologian George McKinney (1962) is disappointing because it gives only a superficial theological analysis without any consideration of Negro membership. Pike (1954) and Whalen (1962, 1963) are general descriptions that do not help to understand an individual Witness's participation. Cohn's article (1955) is an attempt to typologize the Witnesses as another authoritarian proletarian movement.

[3] This study was done under the guidance of Ruben Reina at the University of Pennsylvania, and I am indebted to him for his interest and comments. A preliminary version of this paper was prepared for the Symposium on American Protestant Movements at the 69th Convention of the American Anthropological Association; to the organizers of that symposium, my editors Mark Leone and Irving Zaretsky, I am grateful for their support and suggestions. I particularly thank my colleague Michael Foster for his comments that helped me clarify my thinking during the different versions of this paper.

[4] All names and place designations, except for city locations, are pseudonyms.

Mrs. Henry adroitly resumes the conversation. "We're concerned because there don't seem to be any man-made solutions to our problems of living together peacefully. We know Philadelphia's police are doing a fine job, but the crime rates keep going higher and higher. Do *you* have any answers that will make Philadelphia a city of peace and order?"

Again, a question that startles. "Look," you say, "we both know how complicated the problem really is, and there just aren't any simple solutions or . . ."

Mr. Jackson interrupts your pause. "Well, Mr. uh . . . I'm sorry, I didn't catch your name . . . Jameson? Well, Mr. Jameson, we feel just like you do. We know that living in our city is getting worse and worse, and we don't have any answers of our own either. But we don't need man-made solutions because Jehovah has promised us that *He* will solve the evils of this world. Here in the Bible Jehovah has promised that soon he will rid our city and world of all wars, violence, crime, and injustice. In the coming battle of Armageddon, all evildoers will be destroyed. But those who are Jehovah's faithful will survive the destruction of this present system of things to live forever in Jehovah's new earthly paradise."

This time you interrupt. "Now we've been through this before, and I do not have . . ."

Mrs. Henry determinedly overrides your voice. "Jehovah tells us that these present evils of war, violence, riots, and crime are really signs that his long-promised kingdom will come very soon here on earth. All evil systems and people will be destroyed. But in Isaiah 32:18 Jehovah tells us that '. . . my people must dwell in a peaceful abiding place and in residences of full confidence. . . .' Mr. Jameson, wouldn't you like to live with Jehovah's faithful in that earthly paradise?"

Another question, but this time you try to make your reply a closing. "I'm sorry but I don't have time to discuss the subject this morning."

Mr. Jackson acknowledges your dismissal and continues. "We know you're a busy person, Mr. Jameson, and we don't want to bother you, but we have here our magazine *AWAKE!* that will tell you exactly how Jehovah plans to change this evil world. For only a contribution of ten cents to cover printing costs, you may have this copy to study. You'd like to know how you and your family can survive the destruction of this evil system of things, wouldn't you?"

Recognizing your hesitation Mr. Henry opens the magazine and thrusts it toward you. "I'm sure once you start reading this issue you will find it so interesting you will finish the whole magazine. See, here on page seventeen, there are pictures that illustrate Jehovah's new earthly paradise. For only ten cents to cover printing costs you can learn about life after Armageddon and how you can be a part of it with your family."

At this point you probably fish in your pocket for a dime, thinking it the best way to buy some peace on a Sunday morning. "Thank you for your contribution," says Mr. Jackson, "I'm sure you will learn a great deal from reading this issue of *AWAKE!* To show you our appreciation for visiting with us this morning, we want you to have this booklet titled "Would you like to understand the Bible?" It will explain to you how you can read and understand Jehovah's word. You will probably have some questions about this material so we will call back next Sunday morning to answer them. You wouldn't mind our visiting you next Sunday, would you?"

By this time if you aren't interested in their visit you are exasperated. "Well, uh . . . I'm not sure we'll be home next Sunday, but uh . . . thank you for your visit anyway . . ."

With a smile Mr. Jackson continues, "Well, I'm sure when you look at our magazine you will want to read it all the way through. Since we will be visiting in this neighborhood again next Sunday we'll just call back to see if you are home and we'll answer any questions you may have. Goodbye, Mr. Jameson, and thank you for talking with us this morning."

Mrs. Henry seconds his formal farewell, "Goodbye; we'll see you next Sunday. I'm sure you will learn much from reading our literature."

If you followed your two visitors you would notice them carefully writing your house number in the notebook where your name has already been recorded. Your purchase of *AWAKE!* is noted along with salient features of your conversation and your visitors' evaluation of your likelihood as a prospect. You are now on the Jehovah's Witnesses' official callback list, and even if you sounded unpromising to them they will probably pay you a return visit.

The Society and The Local Witness

With a multitude of variations this scene is duplicated thousands of times every weekend across the States and around the world. The callers are adherents to the religious movement called officially the New World Society of the Witnesses of Jehovah, a world wide organization which is controlled by the legal corporation called the Watchtower Bible and Tract Society of New York and Pennsylvania. In this paper reference to the "Society" means the world headquarters of this sect located at the huge publishing and printing plant in Brooklyn,

New York, where a volunteer religious community of trusted Witnesses, over five hundred in number, edit, print, and distribute the millions of pages of Witness literature that role off Society presses every year. The volume of the Society's two bimonthly magazines, *AWAKE!* and *The Watchtower* is staggering: every week a 32-page edition of one or the other of these magazines is published in over 6½ million copies, translated into 27 different languages, and sent into almost every country of the non-Communist world. *AWAKE!* is a general information magazine used both to attract outsiders and to inform local Witnesses of contemporary events as interpreted by the Society. *The Watchtower* is the organ for specific doctrinal instruction and news of the Society's mass meetings. Control of the total organization is concentrated in a small group of self-perpetuating officers and their aides who write and edit the publications, who appoint all supervisors and local congregational leaders, and who are the final judges for any appeals from members who have been excommunicated by local officials. As a "theocratic" organization all decisions and appointments handed down from the Society's headquarters are divinely inspired and therefore not open to question or interpretation. The top officers of the Society are aided in their tasks by an appointed hierarchy of middle-level supervisors called district and circuit leaders and by trained missionaries sent to local congregations. The supervisory officials have heavy administrative duties of biannual visits to each local congregation to instruct and inspire better methods of witnessing and to inspect and audit all local unit statistical records and finances. Not generally known among the members of the movement are the confidential progress reports on each congregation and the "Personal Qualifications Report" on every local and potential leader sent to the world headquarters after each supervisory visit.

Individual active members are called "publishers" by the Society, a functional title that emphasizes the most important work of the Witnesses, namely, proclaiming or "publishing" the news of Jehovah's impending New World through door-to-door visitation. The concept of "publishing" as the cornerstone of the Witnesses' life style is emphasized in the Society's basic training manual, *Qualified to be Ministers,* which says, "The Kingdom Work [read 'publishing'] then, is the [publisher's] primary occupation. It is his career, his life work" (Watchtower Bible and Tract Society 1955: 251). "Publishing" as the central activity of the individual witness is highlighted in this study of life styles of Negro Witnesses as observed in one congregation in North Philadelphia.

The basic success of the Society in motivating its adherents to "publish" can hardly be denied. In 1968 alone the Society claimed that its 330,000 "publishers" in the United States spent over 57 million hours in their Kingdom Work. This averages nationally nearly three hours a week per individual Witness for the year, a figure above the ten hours visitation per month required by the Society to remain a "publisher." In addition U.S. Witnesses averaged 7½ return visits per month per "publisher," a calculation from the Society's 21 million recorded backcalls. By keeping strict statistical control of those who spend ten hours a month or more as "publishers," the Society calculates its net annual growth, given as 4% in 1968, 6% in 1969. One might be skeptical of these figures printed by the Society but they also admit dropping ten thousand members from the Society in 1968 (a 3% loss) for disciplinary reasons. Further support for the above statistics is that they are in line with what was observed on a local level in the West View congregation.

There is no way to know precisely the number of Negro Witnesses in the United States as the Society doesn't reveal or encourage any knowledge about the extent of its Negro membership. Estimates of this membership in the early 1960s ran from 20% to 30% of the total Witnesses in the U.S. (Whalen 1962: 203). Such estimates would indicate a considerably higher proportion of Negro Witnesses than there are blacks in the general American population (10.6% according to the 1960 U.S. Census and estimated near 12% for 1970). In the Witnesses' circuit assemblies in North and West Philadelphia during the research period, each of which included more than 2,200 persons, 99% of the audience were Negroes, figures well above the 70% Negro population in North Philadelphia and 60% in West Philadelphia (Philadelphia City Planning Commission population estimates for 1964).

I have referred here to national statistics published by the Society, but this study does not presume to analyze Witnesses over the United States. It is a descriptive analysis of one Negro urban congregation in a northern black ghetto in 1968–69. Because the Society minutely prescribes all Witness activities, however, there is little chance that "publishing" can differ greatly from one congregation to another. What does happen as observed with the West View Witnesses is that a local group will apply the Society's teachings and practices so as to be relevant to their local setting.

It must also be noted that Witnesses are capable of change and are adapting to events as they perceive them so that an edict of the Society's can be modified within a year's time. An important limitation in any social analysis of the Witnesses is that the Society and the local congregation are closed to outsiders unless they come with a sincere desire "to learn the Truth." [5] The Society has dismissed most analyses of their movement because they have been written by renegade Witnesses or by non-Witness scholars who never really understood "the Truth" because they did not become Witnesses. What I did not understand until well into my study, when I thought some basis for friendship and trust had been established, was that my very presence as a social scientist constituted a spiritual and social threat to the families who opened their doors to me. The Society forbids any fellowship with outsiders that is not in the context of winning that person to become a Witness; if a "publisher" persists in an "outside" friendship, he is excommunicated from the Society. This restriction placed on West View families meant that I was not able to be with them informally as much as I would have preferred and that conversations almost invariably returned to what I thought about "the Truth."

In the context of these qualifications, my thesis is that the Witnesses' shared definitions of reality and of religious practice constitute, first, a coherent life style formed by a complex of obligations and rewards, and, second, that this pattern is a functionally adaptive alternative life style for certain segments of Negroes living in the urban ghettos of the United States. In a transformation of the academic slogan "publish or perish," the urban Negro Jehovah's Witness accepts that his life work will be to "publish" for the Society or he will die a social death now in being excluded from the elect community and a spiritual death at his life's end that precludes any participation in the Kingdom.

A "PUBLISHER'S" CONTRACT

The features of a "publisher's" life style can be seen in the following outline of the obligations and rewards expected by the individual Witness and by the Society:

---

[5] The Society's suspicion of outside investigators was a problem to consider in my approach to the West View congregation. I was fortunate to have a personal introduction to one of the local Witness families. At our first meeting I stated that I was an anthropolgist interested in learning why the Witnesses were strong and growing in numbers. The West View leaders accepted this approach, but it meant that throughout my presence with them, whether at group meetings or conversing in homes, I was asked to begin a "Bible study" with one of the leaders, an invitation I refused as politely as possible. This attitude meant that interviews with local Witnesses had to be done through informal questioning. I made no effort to contact supervisory personnel or the Society's headquarters because past experiences indicated that requests for information would be unanswered and might have adverse repercussions for research at the local congregational level (cf. Stroup 1945:22–24).

Obligations

1. "Publishing" work: magazine sales, backcalls, cell group study, and 4 weekly congregational meetings. Minimum of 16 hours a week.
2. Development of religious & social knowledge: doctrinal study, speech and interaction training.
3. Conformity to a moral code.
4. Acceptance of the Society as one's (a) absolute authority in religion and mortality, (b) status reference group.

Rewards

1. An assurance of earthly paradise.
2. Individual salvation by works.
3. A community of acceptance: local, international, and inter-racial.
4. A speech and interactional training program.
5. Moral guidance by an unambiguous code.
6. A degree of positive worldly recognition.
7. A new identity and self-respect.

The activities that make up "publishing" work demand a prodigious amount of weekly time from the individual Witness. Every "publisher" is expected to fulfill certain quotas for hours of weekly visitation and magazine calls, for numbers of backcalls and religious studies with prospective members, and for regular attendance at the weekly cell group study. To these basic obligations required of all "publishers," the West View congregation had added one additional demand: obligatory attendance at the four hours of weekly congregational meetings in the local Kingdom Hall. Including the amount of mandatory home study required to participate in most of these activities, a conservative calculation of the amount of time each "publisher" spends in these activities would be sixteen hours a week. The "publisher" receives no financial compensation for any of these activities, for the Witnesses do not have any local paid religious leaders. All "publishers" are called ministers, and they give of their time freely for spiritual and future material compensations.

The "publisher's" second major commitment is to his own religious and intellectual development which is guided by courses of study prescribed by the Society. Each "publisher" studies, first privately and then communally, with the other members of the congregation, two lessons a week: the hour-long Sunday *Watchtower* study and the midweek cell group lesson. In two additional hours of weekly congregational training each "publisher" enrolls in a speech course and visitation training. These sessions feature prepared talks on Witness doctrine given to the other members of the congregation, the performance of which is criticized for speech techniques by the training leader. Other techniques used are role-playing routines and audience participation quizzes about the Society's teachings and daily experiences of the Witnesses in their "publishing" work.

A commitment to a strict moral life as dictated by the Society is the third obligation of the "publisher." One non-Witness ghetto resident said of them, "They don't just talk about the hereafter, but they tell you how to live now." Admittedly some of the characteristics of Witness morality resemble traditional American middle class ideals, with their emphasis on the strong nuclear family, honesty, politeness in interaction, and an honest day's work. Although smoking is not permitted for reasons of health, drinking is not forbidden, only the excess consumption of alcohol and drinking with non-Witnesses. Dancing, watching television, and other forms of recreation are permitted as long as they are done in the company of other Witnesses, are not over-indulged, and do not interfere with reaching one's "publishing" quotas. Other regulations can be quite specific; since 1954, for example, Witnesses are specifically forbidden to hunt or fish for sport, laugh at dirty jokes, be sterilized, masturbate, go out on a date without a chaperone, throw rice at weddings, use profanity or do the twist (White 1968: 384–385).

Closely related to this role of following a strict moral code is the fourth obligation of all "publishers": to accept unquestioningly the New World Society as one's absolute religious and moral authority and as one's sole status reference group. Through its publications, its mass meetings, and its hierarchy of supervisory officers, the Society instructs Witnesses on all matters of daily living. There is no questioning of the Society's pronouncements; to do so is to question Jehovah's plan for mankind and to find oneself quickly expelled from the movement. On the local level the "publisher" commits himself to a new status reference group, his local congregation and the neighboring congregations which come to make up his spiritual "extended family." The new convert isolates himself from all former friends, renounces unsuitable leisure activities as he builds a new way of life focused on loyal participation in his new community of acceptance and status. As a part of his submission to the Society the "publisher" permits strict supervision of his life by his religious superiors who keep detailed records of his "publishing" work and confidential "personal qualifications reports" which are sent to the Society headquarters.

A "Publisher's" Rewards

This complex of obligations that are mandatory for the "publisher" exacts a heavy part of an individual's time and energies, but there is an accompanying set of rewards received by all Witnesses. Of primary importance is the assurance that the individual is now part of Jehovah's faithful remnant who will live through the impending battle of Armageddon when all evil systems and people will be destroyed. After being literally physically saved from destruction, the Witness and his family, if they are practicing "publishers," will live forever in the new earthly paradise that Jehovah will recreate. This is not a promise of "pie in the sky" after you die, but an event that Witness doctrine says will happen during the lifetime of the present generation of Witness leaders. Thus the individual Witness believes that within his lifetime he and his family will live in the new earthly kingdom of Jehovah. One father from the West View congregation stated his faith in this reward very simply. "You know," he said, "I just can't wait to live with my family in that peace of Jehovah's Kingdom after the battle of Armageddon. Everything'll be so wonderful."

This right to eternal life in a new earthly paradise is not just another other-worldly claim in the eyes of the Witness; he is convinced of its truth because of his second reward, namely that proof of his new birthright is verified by his "publishing" activities: door-to-door visitation, backcalls, magazine sales, and conducting religious studies with prospective members. One leader of the West View congregation repeatedly told his cell group unit, "By our good works of preaching we show that we are members of the faithful remnant. We do not want to let the number of hours we visit decrease in the least amount." Each Witness, then, proves his membership in Jehovah's elect by his good works for the Society, activities which are tangible and weekly reminders that you belong to the one select group of people worth belonging to—Jehovah's faithful remnant.

These first two rewards for the Witness would be difficult to sustain were it not for the third compensation of participation now in a new community of believers in which the individual finds acceptance and status. People who only come into contact with Witnesses at their door gain a decidedly warped view of this movement; in their own congregational life Witnesses form a genuine community of trust and acceptance. The small in-group feeling between Witnesses is facilitated by the Society rule that no local congregation can grow beyond 150 members; when that figure is reached the congregation splits into two new groups. Such a practice means that it is always possible to know group members by name.

The feelings of community are further strengthened by the Society's rule that Witnesses may have social friendships only with other Witnesses. In a real sense the local Witness congregation becomes a like-minded extended family which is a sustaining and compelling force to continue in the life style set forth by the Society.

BLACK AND WHITE TOGETHER

If we accept the views expressed by West View Witnesses, there is particular attraction for certain Negroes in that the Society is inter-racial, particularly in its regional and international Assemblies. Ad-mittedly the Society has no program to counteract residential segrega-tion as all social and political action are specifically forbidden, but West View Witnesses were proud of the lack of racial distinctions among the membership at large. An all-Negro group, in a year given to much rhetoric about "black power" and "white racism," West View believers spoke not one public word of bitterness toward whites. In the Circuit Assemblies scattered whites participated among many blacks with no indication that race was recognized; at baptismal services white and black converts were intermixed. West View Wit-nesses pointedly mentioned how "thousands of people, of all races and nationalities, eat and work together" during the week long Interna-tional Conventions. AWAKE! magazine (1969: 10) quoted the *Chicago Daily News* as saying, "The Witnesses don't seem to be conscious of race at all." The same article continues with testimonies from three Witnesses, a Mexican, an African, and a Japanese who told how the Society had taught them to regard race and nationality as unimportant. In 1968 *AWAKE!* quoted the St. Petersburg *Times'* (Florida) news story of a District Assembly: "Black and white together. Jehovah's Wit-nesses don't sing about it, they just practice it. Not only has the con-vention been a massive example of racial harmony with black and white worshipping together, but it has tucked some 700 Spanish-speaking Witnesses into its programs without a murmur." This is a distinct change from the practice of racially separate Assemblies under the Rutherford administration twenty-five years ago (Stroup 1945: 29).

There do not seem to be any Negroes in the higher echelons of the Society's hierarchy, although there are a good number of Negroes who participate in the Society's work force at the Brooklyn headquarters. The profusely illustrated *AWAKE!* and *The Watchtower* magazines do not carry many illustrations of Negroes; [6] when black people are portrayed they are often shown as Africans or Caribbean Negroes dressed in national costumes. In addition Negroes do not seem to have leadership roles in the Society's national leadership commensurate with their numbers in the movement. With these qualifications, the

---

[6] In the twenty-six issues of *AWAKE!* during 1969, the Society printed twenty-four illustrations of white families, none of a Negro family; twenty-three drawings of individual whites to one of a Negro; and eighteen illustrations of all-white groups to four mixed international groups that included black people, some of them obviously African by their dress. The 1969 *Watchtower* contained one illustration of a Negro family in its twenty-six issues.

degree of the Society's integration may be questioned, but as far as the West View Witnesses are concerned they belong to the only organization on earth that does not practice racial prejudice.

Training in Doctrine and "Publishing"

The fourth right of the "publisher" is that he will receive sufficient training before he begins his active visitation work and continued in-service training to improve his ideological competence and interactional ability. The increase in his religious knowledge is the aim of three of the five weekly meetings, namely the Sunday Lecture and *Watchtower* study, and the mid-week cell group study. The latter two are audience participation meetings with the leader posing the printed questions given with the assigned readings and the different members of the congregation or cell group responding by paraphrasing the information given in the assignment. Entire Witness families participate in these sessions; there is no Sunday School but a child is expected to answer his leader's questions as soon as he can read. Younger offspring who are non-readers participate by answering questions about the illustrations that accompany the weekly lessons. The Society carefully prepares these lessons to respond to the problems and arguments that "publishers" meet as they visit door to door. This ideological practicality plus the considerable familiarity with the Bible that a "publisher" acquires gives him a solid foundation for talking to others about his faith. But this ideological content is not enough to sustain Witnesses in the confrontations they face weekly in their "field" work; to give Witnesses confidence in their ability to handle conversations with all kinds of strangers the Society gives intensive speech and interactional training to all "publishers" in a mid-week two hour meeting.

The first hour of this training session is given to "The Theocratic Ministry School," a program of assigned talks, five to fifteen minutes long, given by different members of the congregation from eight years of age on up. Each member makes up his own talk following the outline distributed by the Watchtower Society; in his talk the Witness must show both good speech usage and effective organization of the Society's ideology. A typical assignment was that given to Brother McMillan of the West View congregation in January 1969; his was to be Talk No. 4 on the printed assignment sheet from the Society entitled "Jehovah sends a deliverer in his name." In addition the Theocratic Ministry School supervisor had given him two assignments from the Society's "Progressive Speech Training" course, Study No. 78: "Introduction to arouse interest, "and Study No. 84: "Develop Audience Contact, using only notes for talk." After Brother McMillan finished his speech, going a quick summary sentence beyond the alloted six minutes signaled by a bell timer, the Supervisor gave a short public criticism of the talk, called "speech counsel," a procedure followed for every speaker. He said that it had been "a very fine talk, and we all enjoyed listening to it," a formula he commonly used to introduce his speech criticism. Then he commended the introduction in which Brother McMillan had used a series of rhetorical questions as a good way to engage the attention of an audience, adding "We will mark him 'G' [meaning 'good'] for this part of his assignment." The supervisor noted that the religious topic had been presented in a logical progression making it easy to follow. The speaker had used good delivery, effectively pausing and modulating his voice to avoid monotony for his listeners. The supervisor then remarked that the speaker had seemed tied to his notes during the talk but that he had improved his audience contact from his previous speeches; "We will mark him 'W' [meaning 'work on this'] for this part of the speech lesson, but we will mark an 'I' [meaning 'improved'] for his overall talk." Observing that the talk had been longer than the allotted time, the supervisor counseled Brother McMillan to work to improve his timing so as to leave time for a strong conclusion. He summarized saying, "This is a good improvement for our student and we will look forward to more improvement next time"—again, a commonly used routine to terminate his speech criticisms. The impact of this speech training is not negligible. The Society is noted for taking people who are ill at ease in public and training them to be accomplished public speakers who have confidence and ability to articulate their faith to total strangers. The positive character of the speech counsel is noteworthy. Without subjecting the speaker to destructive criticism the Training Servant supports his ego while correcting his speech faults.

Special procedures have been developed to ensure the training of female members. Interpreting the Apostle Paul's New Testament teachings on the place of women, the Society does not permit women to teach or to lead men. Only a decade ago women were not allowed to speak in Witness meetings. Realizing the short-sightedness of such a policy, the Society changed their rules in 1958 so that now women do participate. They still may not directly address a congregation, but they can answer questions posed by a male leader and they can role-play life situations in front of the congregation (thereby indirectly teaching the males in the audience). One such assignment found Sister Perry and Sister Wright meeting as strangers in a bus queue. Sister Perry, acting the role of a "publisher" used the occasion to introduce Sister Wright, the non-Witness stranger, to the *AWAKE!*

magazine by drawing her attention to an article on how parents can prevent juvenile delinquency, a subject Sister Perry had introduced. Through the new policies of the Society, female Witnesses participate in training sessions and in return gain simulated experience in handling interaction "publishing" situations.

The second half of the mid-week session, the Service Meeting, is given to detailed training on how to be an effective "publisher." The Society prescribes every conceivable topic affecting the work of its members: ordering literature, placing magazines, visiting the elderly, holding daily family devotions, initiating a "Bible Study." Each weekly session, a series of talks and role-playing routines plus question-and-answer studies, follows the detailed monthly outline sent from the Society headquarters. Although the local congregation must adhere to the prescribed meeting plan, the ghetto illustrations used by West View Witnesses revealed how realistically they face their North Philadelphia environment. Brother Hill, for example, in a talk entitled "What it means to be honest," gave concrete illustrations of problems local Witnesses faced. He said:

(1) It is not honest when a mother, knowing that her daughter has bad friends, withholds this information from the father. When the daughter gets pregnant then the father is shocked.

(2) Wives are dishonest if they withhold excess grocery money from their husbands.

(3) Dishonesty among men begins when a man starts to flirt with other women beside his wife; this can lead to disfellowshipping [meaning excommunication].

(4) You cannot take towels from motels when attending Assemblies for that is stealing.

Although the Society's literature during the time of my study did not mention the issue of black identity, West View Witnesses were well aware of the problem, especially for their young people. The subject was touched in several role-playing routines and talks during these training sessions. In one routine a daughter asked her mother if she could join the Afro-American group at school, saying "they seem to want good things for all people." The mother gently but firmly forbade her participation saying that those people's actions and particularly their Afro hairdos and dashikis only call attention to themselves, something Witnesses do not do. The mother concluded her argument by saying that such movements only represented the last struggles of the evil systems of this world, and Jehovah would soon destroy them all. It is important to note that Witnesses are forbidden to participate in any voluntary associations, even such groups as the NAACP.

These training sessions are also noteworthy for the amount of freedom given for individual creativity in the role-playing routines. Although West View Witnesses withdraw from the street interaction of North Philadelphia, they create their own settings where verbal expressions, spontaneity, and humor are permitted and highly valued. One young Witness, Brother Grier, had the ability always to include humor in his talks and routines. At the conclusion of one routine his partner as the "publisher" asked Brother Grier as the non-Witness if he would like to continue their discussions by studying the Bible together. Brother Grier deadpanned back, "Okay, I think Wednesday night at 5:30 would be fine," and the congregation burst into laughter at the exaggeration. The teenage Witness sitting near me laughed and said: "It isn't ever that easy; most of the time they kick you out, swearing and cursing at you."

I have gone at length into this training program of the Watchtower Society as a right expected by every "publisher" in order to show the thoroughness with which the Society prepares its members for inter-actional situations and to show that realism, ingenuity, and humor when expressed in proper Witness channels are highly valued and constitute a basis for prestige and inceasing leadership responsibility within the Witness organization.

An unambiguous code for daily living is the fifth compensation for the Witness. This is, of course, the other side of his commitment to follow the moral code set forth by the Society. It is a compensation in the sense that all moral decisions are made for the "publisher." He does not have to choose between alternatives on ethical questions since the Society provides detailed guidelines for daily conduct whether it be the use of leisure time, how to be a good parent, or on-the-job behavior.

The sixth reward provided the individual "publisher" is a certain amount of recognition from the world outside the Society. Ghetto informants not religiously inclined have spoken of the Witnesses as "those crazy people," but they often add, "of all the religions in the ghetto, theirs is the best." Ghetto residents who are often in strong disagreement with the Witnesses do give positive recognition to them for their training to speak in public and for their reading ability to follow the Society's considerable literature. From mainstream America, too, comes qualified admiration. Witnesses often speak of their reputation for courtesy, organization, and cleanliness at their annual Assemblies. West View Witnesses remarked that even the *New York Times* recognized that Yankee Stadium is never so clean as when the Witnesses scour it for their conventions, a fact they had picked up from the *AWAKE!* magazine. As mentioned above, Witnesses are also proud of their record for racial harmony as recognized by the secular world.

Part of the reason Witnesses can sustain rejection and abuse from people to whom they preach is their new self-identity and respect, their seventh compensation. As a "publisher" in the New World Society they are convinced they are Jehovah's chosen people. One is no longer identified as Bill Green, warehouse clerk or shoe salesman, lower middle or lower class, Negro. As a "publisher" he is Brother Green, the West View Study Servant, one of Jehovah's elect. It is an identity impervious to outside opinion. By following the Society's rules for "publishing" and morality, thereby assuring his place among the chosen, Brother Green gains a sense of purity and superiority, factors of importance to an American Negro seeking, as Charles Keil says, a new image of self-esteem to overwhelm feelings of self-hatred (1966: 165).

POSITIVE ADAPTATIONS TO THE GHETTO: THE WITNESS ALTERNATIVE

With this description of the obligations and compensations for individual "publishers" the case can be presented that the Witnesses' life style has positive adaptive functions for certain segments of America's black ghetto population. When the religious, social, economic, and racial realities facing ghetto residents are considered, it can be understood how the Witnesses provide a viable alternative strategy of living which is coherent and which has functional significance.

It would be false, of course, to claim that the Witnesses appeal to all ghetto residents. We must consider the religious dimensions of ghetto dwellers' lives to gain an idea of what segment of the ghetto population is appealed to and what positive alternatives the Witnesses offer to that segment. Whether it be a W.E.B. DuBois writing in 1903 about the crisis in the Negro churches behind which "there still broods silently the deep religious feeling of the real Negro heart" (p. 168) or the poet Leumas Sirrah writing out of the Watts Writers Workshop in 1966 that "God is Infinite . . . A process, an effect, and a change causing . . . A process, an effect, a change" (Schulberg 1967: 236), the religious dimension in American Negro life has been a constant factor in understanding black existence in America. Drake and Cayton in their 1962 postscript to *Black Metropolis* tell us that twenty years after their original study Negro religious groups still constitute centers of stability and give a core of meaningful activities for some lower class residents, though not the masses of lower class society. Hannerz in his *Soulside* study of Winston Street in Washington, D.C., notes that among the shared perspectives of ghetto life is the influence of a common religious dimension; "soul, the essence of a human being, is a religious term, and fundamentalist religion continues to be an influence on the ghetto dwellers even as the institutional grip of black churches on them is loosening" (1969: 147).

Hannerz reveals more about what segment is church-going in the black ghetto population in his typology of four main life styles which he calls mainstreamers, swingers, street families, and streetcorner men. Although the boundaries between these ideal-type life styles are often crossed and although even the most specific ghetto-oriented behavior is influenced by a tradition of "that old-time religion," Hannerz indicates that in Winston Street the church-going population is largely composed of mainstreamers and older women of the street families (1969: 41, 46). My observations of the West View congregation support Hannerz' analysis. Of the twenty family groups represented in the West View congregation about one fourth were second-generation Witness families, one half were adults that had grown up in Baptist and Methodist lower middle class Negro churches, and the remainder were women with their children, some obviously from street families.

In spite of this evidence of religious institutional participation on the part of mainstreamers and some street families, both the Chicago and Washington studies indicate that there are strong criticisms of ghetto religious institutions by black ghetto residents of all life styles. Criticisms are leveled at the seeming greed for money, the round of social activities with little real religion being taught, the promises of a heaven after death without any help for the "here and now," the emotionalism of the "shake and shout" sects, and the hypocrisy of many church-goers. Preachers in particular are singled out for their worldly materialism and manipulation of their congregations to form a cult of personality around themselves. Many of them are seen as hustlers who have a good religious racket going for them (see Drake and Cayton 1962: 650–653; Hannerz 1969: 147; Rodgers 1969: 33). These may be unfair critical stereotypes of ghetto preachers and their churches, stemming perhaps in part from the influence of sentimental models of mainstream church life.

However stereotyped these criticisms, I heard them among Negro ghetto residents. It is to such critics that Witnesses offer an alternative. There is no paid, local clergy. In sharp constrast to the three or more average collections taken in many Negro churches the Witnesses never take a collection at any of their meetings. The minimum local budget for maintenance and rent or debt amortization is met by the Society's ten to twenty percent rebate on all literature sold by the local congregation. In addition, the Society permits "publishers" to keep ten cents of every one dollar annual magazine subscription obtained, and "publishers" invariably ask ten cents for every magazine placed in house visitations (the printed price is five cents, the subscription rate). In the West View congregational meetings and in house study groups it was occasionally suggested that "publishers" might contribute their magazine income to the small collection box placed on a side wall of the Kingdom Hall. The West View treasurer's quarterly report indicated that these voluntary contributions amounted to about ten percent of local receipts. The New World Society as well as its local units seems to be financed by its vast literature sales,[7] profitable because the Society's publishing operations are based on a communal workforce individually paid ten to twenty dollars pocket money monthly.

Witnesses emphasize that their religious faith and practices are based on rational thinking requiring reading ability and willingness to study. They are quick to point out there are no hypocrites in their ranks: anyone who breaks one of the Society's divine laws is quickly purged from the congregation by probation or "disfellowshipping," the latter being permanent exclusion. In spite of its hierarchical authority structure the Society does not permit a cult of personality to surround Society leaders or the local congregational leadership. To symbolize the equality among members, all Witnesses including Society leaders participate in "publishing" activities and the only titles of address ever used are "Brother" and "Sister."

The Witnesses offer an effective life style alternative when they make the local congregation the exclusive reference group for both men and women, and this group becomes a nearly full-time religious

---

[7] Financial reports of the Society are never published, but some idea of the financial base of its publishing operations can be calculated from a Society statistical report for November, 1968:

How did we do in November? A very fine report! Look at the results of our united efforts to place the "Truth" book with all whom we met. We placed 817,766 books! Marvelous, indeed! Obviously, placing books was not our only goal, for 2,398,497 back-calls were made. Yes, we wanted to cultivate the interest that persons showed in God's truth. Furthermore, consider that 307,331 Bible Studies were conducted in the homes of interested ones. Brothers, this represents a fine spirit and a commendable willingness to do more than the usual to help others gain eternal life. Keep up the very fine work! (from *Kingdom Ministry*, the Society's monthly newsletter to members, vol. XII, no. 1:2, Jan. 1969).

At a sale price of 25 cents per copy, the "Truth" book sales alone for November would amount to over two hundred thousand dollars ($204,441). Added to this would be the income from some six million *weekly* copies of the bi-monthly magazines *AWAKE!* and *The Watchtower,* a monthly sum approximating one million two hundred thousand dollars, an equal amount resting in the hands of the 338,663 "publishers" who had "placed" the magazines for ten cents a copy. On these two published items alone, the Society could well have grossed one million four hundred thousand dollars in one month (author's calculations).

subculture that reinforces mainstreamer aspirations for a strong nuclear family headed by the male. In a conversation about the Witnesses' model for marriage a wife confirmed her husband's description of his role as head of the family: "What's okay with him is okay with me; he makes the decisions in this family." If, as Hannerz suggests, the considerable degree of marginality to the household is a major reason for ghetto males to create ghetto-specific status patterns among street peers (1969: 89), then the Witnesses offer an alternative by giving the man the household leadership. The male Witness' status, then, comes from his membership in the New World Society and from his unquestioned position as family head.

A case can be made that the male Witness' roles in his religious reference group and family provides functional social alternatives to certain ghetto-specific male role requirements: concerns for toughness and ability to command respect, for personal appearance, liquor consumption, verbal ability, and sexual activity (Hannerz 1969: 79–87). Respect is considered especially meaningful when it comes from fellow Witnesses, although Witnesses are proud of their good reputation in American society at large. Natural respect accrues to their leaders who organize training sessions and visitation programs, who handle money and literature orders, and those supervisory leaders who make arrangements for the Circuit and District Assemblies.

Whereas respect for toughness in the ghetto-specific male role is related to the ability to appear or to be physically violent, the male Witness's "toughness" comes from his extraordinary ability to keep control of "publishing" situations in which he may take abuse and rejection from non-Witnesses. Witnesses enjoy recounting how they handled a difficult contact, how they contradicted arguments, how they went back after being kicked out the door. Even when they do not handle a situation adroitly, they may laugh at their predicament, usually vowing that the next visit they will know how to handle that person. "Toughness" is part of what it takes to be an effective "publisher," and the local male Witness who can both demonstrate and talk about his ability to handle difficult interactional situations is highly valued.

Although there is no emphasis on managing a smart impression through a display of expensive clothes, Witnesses take pride in dressing neatly and presenting an image of the well-dressed white-collar mainstreamer. Men wear white shirts, tie, and suit to all functions and especially when visiting door-to-door. Brother Leonard did not like his blue-collar job because it prevented him from wearing the suit and tie he felt necessary for home visitations or literature placements enroute to and from work.

Witnesses differ from the Protestant fundamentalist tradition in their moderate consumption of alcoholic beverages. Many West View males came from churches where there was preaching against "demon rum" but considerable tippling on the sly. Witnesses consider it natural to drink moderately in their own homes with fellow Witnesses.

The fourth characteristic of ghetto-specific male role, talking well and persuading others through speech, obviously is part of the Witness way of life. He may not participate in black patterns of expressive speech such as "jiving," "shucking," and "rapping" (see Kochman 1970; Abrahams 1962, 1964), but a skilled "publisher" is an accomplished verbal artist within his own religious domain. The difference between the Witness who gives a talk from rote memory at your door and the "publisher" who is capable of turning your conversation back to his religious orientation is immediately noticeable. As stated above, Witnesses relate their encounters with a keen sense of drama; a good storyteller who can also effectively speak to non-Witnesses gains local prestige and may be tapped for a more responsible post in the Society's organization.

A functional equivalent for the ghetto male's intensive concern with sex is more difficult to argue. Extra- and pre-marital intercourse or even joking about sex are forbidden to Witnesses. Exclusive sex relations with one's spouse are to be engaged in with moderation. If the ghetto-specific expectations of marriage infidelity and doubts that the husband can live up to a mainstream marriage model stem from the tensions between the roles of ghetto females and marginal males (Hannerz 1969: 89, 102), then the Witnesses' mainstreamer model of a male-headed stable nuclear family removes the need for a sexually exploitative male role.

The third adaptive factor in the alternative way of life offered by the Witnesses to the ghetto resident minimizes the hardships of living on a low income. Mainstream consumptive culture is denied as a pattern for Witnesses. In the Society's publications and in congregation talks they are reminded that they do not depend upon new cars, expensive clothes, or lavish living for their status. At the same time a Witness is to give a just day's work to his employer, be scrupulously honest, and not engage in union activities, though he may pay dues. Such traits make even a man without many skills a useful employee, and some Witnesses in North Philadelphia have moved up to positions of considerable job responsibility. Because they work steadily, do not have to contribute large sums of money to their congregation or the Society, and because they spend most of their leisure time in "publishing" activities which cost only transportation expense, most West

View families had enough money to buy a stereo-hifi and a TV, a few of the latter being color sets.

Faced with the facts of Negro job ceilings and career-deadend jobs, the economic advantages of the Witnesses' life style is further strengthened by ignoring the job status system of mainstream America. When I asked one West View Witness why he didn't accept a higher-paying job which had been found for him by a fellow Witness, he replied: "I need a job where I don't have to worry about it after I leave work; that way I can devote myself to Jehovah's way. Why should I spend more time getting ahead in this system when Jehovah will soon change everything?" Other West View members confirmed that this outlook was typical because when they talked of their life careers it was always in terms of their success as a "publisher," never in terms of their job career. Negro Witnesses can ignore the low status that mainstream America accords many of their jobs because they belong to an exclusive subcultural group that confers its own identity and status.

Lastly, and perhaps most important, the Jehovah's Witness life style is an adaptive strategy to cope with the racial prejudice experienced by American blacks. The clue to this possibility was stated by a black Philadelphia city government official responsible for social services in the ghetto: "Don't forget to put into your study what the Kerner Report says causes ghetto despair and responses—white racism. That's it, white racism. Understand that and you'll begin to understand your Witnesses." Social scientists are beginning to understand the depth of the race division that fragments our national life, and we are beginning to recognize what Negroes have long since known, namely, that racism is not a regional aberration but is built into the foundations of American society. The Negro Witnesses in the West View congregation are just as subject to these racial realities as any of the other black residents in the ghetto. By selectively withdrawing from both mainstream and ghetto culture into the movement of the Jehovah's Witnesses West View "publishers" have found psychic protection. As Negroes they are no longer dominated by the frustrating American socio-political scene. Now they are citizens of the one Society that assures them of an impending future earthly paradise, members of an international and interracial community. Racism does not exist in the New World Society or if it does it is not recognized by West View Witnesses. Equally important, through the cognitive filter inculcated by the Society's culture building processes, racial injustices experienced in the secular world are reinterpreted as signs that point to the approaching end of this present evil system.

CONCLUSION

In these religious, social, economic and racial dimensions the New World Society offers an adaptive life style to the Negro in the urban ghetto who is seeking a positive identity and an accepting community. Outsiders may object that Negro Witnesses pay a heavy price for such a way of life for in adopting it they lose most of any black cultural distinctiveness. That may be true, but as long as the societal structures and cultural values of the United States make the black man a marginal man, the Jehovah's Witnesses offer him an alternative life strategy that gives its adherents a way to find identity and self-respect, a community of acceptance, and hope for the future.

The Economic Basis for the Evolution
of Mormon Religion

THIS paper is a case study of specific evolution (Sahlins and Service 1960: 12–44). It is an examination of the changes one culture has undergone over the course of a century. It is not overtly comparative and as such does not aim at an explicit contribution to general evolution. I am interested in the adaptive modification of Mormon culture in a part of the Great Basin. Such an examination has as its explicit aim the elucidation of the means one culture used to meet the threats induced by a changing environment, both natural and superorganic. Such a treatment does not imply that nineteenth-century Mormonism is better or worse than twentieth-century Mormonism, only that it is different. Nor does it imply that either is more or less efficient than the other, only that each type of Mormonism is adapted to different environments and as such nineteenth-century Mormonism would not be efficient today and vice versa.

As a study in specific evolution I would like this presentation to serve as a test for a portion of Robert Bellah's scheme of general religious evolution (1970: 20–50). Bellah has created a typology of religious systems based on a series of linked criteria and postulates as the most recent type of religious phenomena, Modern Religion. Two criteria are most crucial here: that synthesis of religious belief in Modern Religion resides in the individual, and that continual self-transformation characterizes the synthesis. Bellah neither tests this category against ethnographic data nor suggests candidates for testing. Mormonism can serve the useful purpose of testing the validity of the type, as well as serving to disprove Bellah's hypothesis that such a religious type would take no institutional form. While Bellah has listed a few of the hypothetical criteria for his latest religious type, J. Stillson Judah in his *History and Philosophy of the American*

NOTE: Lack of space has made it impossible to present all of the data necessary for the full support of some of the hypotheses presented in this paper. That will be done in a monograph on the same topic now in preparation. It has also been impossible to become as familiar with Mormonism in the two-year period of this research as would be necessary to do full justice to that expanding and complex faith. This essay was written in February 1971 and revised in November 1971.

Metaphysical Movements (1967: 12–19) has constructed a catalogue of traits for the set of institutionalized religions that fit Bellah's category. Several of Judah's concrete characteristics can be used to be the measure of Bellah's more abstract points. Most metaphysical churches have a lay clergy and are officially creedless or de-emphasize institutional creedal statements. Such practices fit neatly as logical corollaries to Bellah's scheme since the individual would be his own priest holding a self-revising statement of beliefs, thus making a man his own theologian as well.

Both Bellah and Judah suggest that there is a class of modern religions which is oriented to change and as such is so in tune with the varying demands placed on adherents that the religious system changes as the rest of the culture changes. How does a religion keep itself practical without seeming opportunistic and without contradicting the revealed status of its knowledge? Part of the answer to that question resides in the nature of a religion's rituals. The hypothesis I would like to offer is that Modern Religion has a ritual system the efficacy of which depends on pragmatic content. The rituals of Modern Religion have systematic empirical effect on the natural world by making the content of the rituals the practical problems of the day-to-day world of adherents.

The systematic and empirical effect of ritual on the natural world has been thoroughly demonstrated by Rappaport (1967) and Meggett for agriculturalists of New Guinea. Rappaport has shown how ritual regulated relationships among human demography, garden produce, the population of pigs, the frequency and severity of warfare, and the exchange of some goods and personnel. And Meggett (personal communication) has demonstrated how ritual prestation maintains an elaborate kin and clanship network. These studies have shown that ritual is not merely a decorative, reinforcing subsystem of culture as has been claimed by some psychological anthropologists (Homans 1941: 172) and by evolutionists (White 1959). They lean far more toward Weber and his notion and demonstrations of systemic interdependence than they do to unicausal explanations or even to any consideration of cause.

Such an examination of the empirical effects of ritual has not been subjected to testing in a complex culture nor in one where a population had to depend on many natural zones for survival and where no one zone could support a population by itself. Rappaport's Tsembaga Maring and Meggett's Mae Enga are self-sufficient within their respective areas. None of the Mormon settlement on the Little Colorado River in nineteenth-century Arizona to be discussed here was self-sufficient. The theoretical interest of the Mormon case lies in the complexity of Mormon culture compared with the New Guinea agri-culturalists, and with the involvement of ritual in the redistribution of goods and services crucial to agricultural success. The difference between the New Guinea cases and the Mormon example is that in New Guinea the societies were pressing on the limits of the land and resources and were faced with overpopulation. In Arizona land was marginal for agriculture; it was underpopulated, and resources were scarce and unevenly distributed. Demographically, New Guinea was a closed system, Arizona an open one. And ritual played a central role in both.

Among nineteenth-century Mormons on the Little Colorado River in Arizona ritual affected the critical relationship between (1) the population and the products of the annual agricultural cycle and (2) the population and the irrigation system that enabled agriculture to work. I will consider only the critical relationship between ritual and the irrigation network here for lack of space. Following Rappa-port (1968: 1–2) ritual is taken to be, "conventionalized acts directed toward the involvement of non-empirical (supernatural) agencies in human affairs." Through ritual the following aspects of the irrigation system were affected:

1. Dams and canals were built or rebuilt. The technical advice, labor, and capital needed to construct or reconstruct this essential piece of technology were directly regulated by rituals.

2. Food distribution to a town stricken with a washout and to laborers on a dam was provided.

3. The presence of high level ritual functionaries, Church General Authorities who organized local and central Church aid, and who set up a plan of action in the field, was assured.

4. Ritual organized areal cooperation during a dam disaster and unified the Little Colorado area through reciprocity between towns when disasters hit.

5. Rituals communicated the interpretation of the disaster as a trial of the Saints, an effort on God's part to test the endurance of his latter-day chosen. The notion of the trial, or continual testing, geared the population for coping with repeated disasters.

6. Dams brought into existance by religious beliefs organized through ritual operated (1) to raise a pool of water for gravity flow through canals, (2) to store some water, and (3) to form a settling pond for silt before water flowed through the canals and onto the fields.

These and some lesser, correlated functions characterize the jobs that were accomplished either directly or were facilitated when Mormon rituals interacted with the operation of the irrigation network.

Among both the Mae Enga and the Tsembaga Maring a regulatory ritual cycle is set off by a set of natural timers such as overpopulation of pigs and humans which seem to have no positive value. Various types of constraints on the environment reach the limit of the system's tolerance and trigger corrective mechanisms. The ritual system operates as the trigger for the correctives which are pig slaughter, warfare, and so forth. There is essentially a single regulator, one timer that acts to keep the system in balance by keeping out upsetting variation.

The Mormon irrigation system is a variant of this classic description in that there are two timing devices in the system instead of one. Whereas various kinds of overpopulation in New Guinea have little or no inherent value, the collapse of a dam on the Little Colorado was essential to the system's maintenance. Collapse of a dam, in addition to maintaining part of the irrigation in functioning form, was periodic. Dam washouts tripped the ritual cycle into operation on behalf of the stricken town, just as overpopulation of pigs and people seems to in New Guinea, but in addition dam bursts themselves regulated a portion of the irrigation system, as pig and human overpopulation in New Guinea did not seem to.

When a dam washes out:

1. The silt and sand aggraded and settled behind a dam are flushed out, thus both recreating the settling pond and, more extensively, maintaining the elevation of the river bed constant. The more a stream bed aggrades or raises, the higher above a town a canal has to begin to take out water to maintain flow by gravity.

2. The unusual flood of water stays in the river channel instead of flooding the town, rushing through the canals eroding them, and depositing silt over the fields and damaging crops.

The aggrading of silt behind a dam is regular. If a dam is low and the river not constrained in a canyon, the capacity of a dam to hold water is compromised in the area closest to it by aggradation. And, during flood, water will tend to run around the ends of the dam eroding new channels and carrying away part or all of the dam. In these terms, dam washouts are somewhat predictable affairs and can be seen, in part, as self-regulating insofar as the destruction of a dam has the functions listed above. Aggradation makes a dam both progressively more useless to the irrigation system and progressively more susceptible to washouts. This outline needs some qualification and certainly does not mean that every dam disaster served these positive functions.

We are dealing, then, with a system in which the initial upsetting event is itself crucial to the survival of the whole system. Risking overstatement, I will say that for equilibrium to be maintained the system must be disturbed by a dam disaster. Those disasters were built into the system by the level of technology used to harness river flow. Second, a dam washout tripped the ritual cycle into action, and that cycle provided the organization to get the dam rebuilt and back into operation. These two sets of events will serve to illustrate the extent to which ritual is embedded in ecology and facilitates the distribution of resources critical to survival. It will also serve to show the nature of Mormon adaptation in late nineteenth-century Arizona and will serve when used in the second half of this paper to point up the differences between Mormon culture then and Mormon culture now. Further, nineteenth-century Mormonism provides the basis for testing the notion that by closely harmonizing ritual and the concrete problems of adherents, Mormonism laid the foundation for becoming a Modern Religion, in Bellah's terms. I do not think Mormonism was a Modern Religion, I think it has become one in the twentieth-century. But the basis for the rapid adjustment to and incorporation of change into religion was established in nineteenth-century circumstances like those existing on the Little Colorado River in Arizona, other areas in the Great Basin, and even before Mormons got to the desert West. Mormonism has changed its characteristics by being in close contact with the circumstances Mormons lived in, and it has changed as those circumstances have changed. In that sense Mormonism has evolved. Mormonism as such is a case of specific evolution. Nineteenth-century Mormonism also represents the early development of some of the forms found in Modern Religion, and insofar as that is so it begins to represent a new stage in the general evolution of religious systems. Twentieth-century Mormonism fully illustrates this new religious form, but the foundations of that form are a hundred and more years old in a kind of Mormonism that was not Modern.

The area that provides the empirical data for this presentation is east-central Arizona, along the drainage of the Little Colorado River. The area was settled by Mormons in the late 1870s and 1880s. The data for both nineteenth and twentieth centuries are drawn from there and at the lowest level of inference represent only that particular area of Mormonism. I would obviously like what is demonstrable for that area to stand in microcosmic fashion for what went on contemporaneously in Great Basin Mormonism as a whole. That is a more general level of inference and as such must be subject to further testing than is provided for here. This is also not a history, nor am I a historian. The region's history is well controlled (Peterson 1967) and serves to provide the data for testing more general ideas about ritual regulation of ecology and the adjustment of religious cultures to change.

About a hundred years ago Mormons in Arizona began settlement of a semi-arid area that required irrigation if agriculturalists were to survive. Dam building was the key to irrigation agriculture and was a cyclical activity that involved washouts and rebuilding (Fish and others n.d.; Hilton 1968; Peterson 1968). The Little Colorado River is the key to agricultural success in the area and is like most streams in arid and semi-arid lands. It is not even and constant but subject to sharp, wild rises during the spring when snows melt and during the thunderstorm season of July, August, and September. It is otherwise often sluggish, laden with silt, and capable of nearly drying up. This is the type of river that had to be blocked and the type of river that overcame one dam after another by washing them out with sudden torrential floods.

Dam building began in the 1870s and 1880s at the dozen or so Mormon towns that were deliberately established along the Little Colorado and its tributaries by the Church leaders of Salt Lake City. Dams were originally made of brush, stones, and mud and were more for diversion than for blocking a body of water for storage. Later dams were made of sandstone blocks and cement and became huge affairs, 30 to 40 feet high, 60 to 70 feet across, and 20 feet thick. These were all built with iron and steel tools, horse-team labor, and human muscle. No power machinery was involved. The process of dam washout and rebuilding ends in the mid-1920s when permanent reinforced-concrete dams were placed by the towns and still remain.

Not all Mormon towns in the Little Colorado area depended equally heavily on dam-controlled irrigation. Totalled, there were about 18 towns in this area with a total population of around 3,000 varying from several hundred in some towns to a few families in others. The process of washout and rebuilding was not equally regular in all. Roughly half depended on irrigated farming and so had dams.

As a technological event, a dam washout was usually caused by heavy rains falling or snow melting unseasonably fast in the head waters of the Little Colorado, a hundred or so miles above the farming towns. Water volume would increase as a flood moved down the river and would spill over a dam and undermine the footings on the dam's dry side or run around one end and carry off part of a dam. When undermined, the dam would collapse, releasing both the flood and the pond. These events, which occurred fourteen times at St. Joseph and twelve at Woodruff, Arizona over a forty-year period, were regarded as rather straightforward disasters by the Mormon population. And demographically, ecologically, sociologically, and spiritually they were. In the short run, the local view was correct. But technologically, even in the short run, washouts were often a prerequisite for the system's survival (interview with Gilbert Sullivan, water control expert, U.S. Department of the Interior, Holbrook, Arizona). The washing out of a dam prevented flood waters from pouring through the irrigation system and depositing silt over the land at the same time that it eroded the canals. Also, the bursting of a dam flushed out the silt piled up behind it. The Little Colorado is especially silt-laden, and the pond behind a dam served initially not to store water but to settle the soil particles suspended in the water. The ponds, none of them large, filled rapidly with silt, thus lessening capacity while forcing water more quickly into the irrigation system. A dam burst washed out the accumulated silt and reestablished the basin for a new pond. A washout, while a destructive event, was the basis by which a primitive irrigation system regulated and maintained itself in operation. In support of this, it is to be noted that once permanent dams were installed, the ponds silted up quickly, making some of the dams useless even for diverting water. This forced the area to abandon river water irrigation in favor of well water drawn from the water table with motor-driven pumps.

Apart from the technological readjustment derived from what was otherwise a disaster, the effects of a washout can be seen throughout the whole system. Washout often occurred during the agricultural season, thus either ruining the harvest or vastly reducing it. Automatically a washout in the growing season would compromise the potential stored resources for the local population. The economic base would be in a state of imbalance as a result, since farmers would have to resort to alternative employment to earn a living, at least until the dam could be reconstructed. Since the level of predicted surpluses was compromised, the carrying capacity of the area was automatically changed and overshot with the dam burst. The washout lowered the food supply, lowered the carrying capacity of the land, and created a population excess and a consequent need for migration. Washouts, usually occurring in a few hours, were quite unpredictable, and could occur any year over an area where any of a dozen and more towns could be hit on an almost random basis. It was an event that most towns shared to some extent, and it affected all towns when it occurred in any one.

In addition to the effect of a washout within the Mormon community, the disaster changed Mormon relationships with those outside. This area of Arizona was not wholly Mormon but also had a Gentile population, some of whom were engaged in farming and stock raising. Many non-Mormons were engaged in small businesses, especially after the railroad was constructed through the region in 1881. The Gentile population was located near the rail centers, when it was grouped at all. An agrarian disaster such as a dam burst sent members of Mormon families into these non-Mormon settlements to seek temporary work. Contact with the Gentile world was not encouraged in the course of living one's day-to-day life nor were many of the forms of business that Gentiles carried on seen as fit for the Saintly way of life. Mormonism up to this time was a religion for farmers, and farmers gathered up into special kinds of communities.

The flux to which the agricultural life-way was subject put Mormons into contact with non-Mormons and with the business world. The consequences of this were a familiarity with working for wages and a preadapting of the Saints to full dependence on the integration with the Gentile world. The immediate aim of wage work was to supply capital for dam rebuilding and to maintain the local Mormon population intact. To some degree it succeeded in providing the capital needed for rebuilding a dam. In addition, wage work at neighboring towns helped to keep the population from deserting the washed-out community. But the major effect of such wage work among non-Mormons is seen when self-sufficient families and even whole towns were bound into the regional secular network. The eventual effect was to short-circuit the purely Mormon network that was to link individuals and towns and gradually substitute the secular one. Involved here are such fundamental activities as types of employment and sacred versus secular schooling (Nelson 1959). Mormons were to be farmers, not wage laborers, and Mormon children were to be educated by Mormons, not by Gentiles. These were essential if Zion were to be truly independent. When such prerequisites to Mormon culture began to break down, a new level of integration was initiated with the outside world. The cycle of dam catastrophes began this level of integration and should be seen as extending its effects to aspects of social relations.

Demographically, dam rebuilding stabilized the resident population by supporting the economic base. Through donated supplies derived through the communal storehouses from all neighboring towns and later through the usual operation of the irrigation network, subsistence was guaranteed. The elaborate network of storehouses in each town was maintained through tithing and was operated by a bishop (Snowflake Stake Funds 1882–1901). These placed a minimal guarantee under every local population. Communal stores underwrote every experiment, every difficult season, and the effects of seasonal variation on every family in a town. They underwrote the future of neighboring towns and played an important role in an event like dam rebuilding. Not only could the extended presence of surpluses keep a population stable in a stricken town by equalizing carrying capacity but towns sufficiently well off would act as magnets to migrating segments of the population. The whole of the nineteenth century in this area of Arizona showed a pattern of high mobility. Families shifted from town to town following a pattern dictated by varying abundance. Dam rebuilding, then, had two demographic effects. It stabilized a portion of the local population and siphoned off a portion to towns that had more accumulated wealth or more opportunity to collect it. Since the area had few towns that were completely stable, the entire area gave rise to a population fragment that was unusually mobile. Since many of the migrating families had skilled members, this spread those areas of expertise around the entire region and more or less as a town could afford to support them. In ecological theory, this process of population movement is preliminary to niche specialization. It is analogous to adaptive radiation where new inhabitants in an area adapt themselves through time to the existing variation.

By the time a dam was rebuilt, in a season or sometimes over two seasons or years, the technological systems operated efficiently again. A raised pool of stored water was provided for the agricultural system. Since the irrigation system worked on gravity flow, it was essential to raise a body of water at a place where it could be imprisoned conveniently and let flow at a regulated rate over the irrigated fields. A dam also provided a pond behind it for settling silt, or alternatively, settling ponds connected to a diversionary dam allowed the silt to settle before the water flowed through the ditches and over the fields. In any case, the system in operation accomplished these two prerequisites.

It has never been seriously doubted that a people's belief system affected certain of its day-to-day economic tasks. What I should like to show is not so much how the ritual system of Mormonism is geared to an aspect of its economic-ecological base but how those two sub-systems are completely embedded in each other. Mormonism's unique survival value resides in its ability to impose the religious system on, to sacralize, all day-to-day activities and, by doing this, to so key itself to those activities that it sacralizes whatever its people touch. The religious system is given added efficacy through exposure to economics and, on the reverse, the ecological balance is maintained through religious activities. This is a theoretically standard case from systems theory of "deviation-counteracting feedback networks" (Maruyama 1968: 304). The elements in such a system influence each other reciprocally (Maruyama 1968: 305–6).

Nineteenth-century Mormonism created a state, even a small empire, in the Great Basin. The state was authoritarian and completely hierarchical, but it was also totally sacred. It was a new Zion and, like the old, it was completely convinced it did the will of God, largely because God pointed out his will rather unambiguously. He did so in hierarchical fashion, the President of the Church being chief confidant of the Deity. The Authorities in Salt Lake City managed their domain with elaborate care. The enormous system created in Utah and parts of surrounding states by Brigham Young and his fellow churchmen has been superbly described (Arrington 1968). Part of the system of governance which communicated the centralized opinions and solutions, as well as discovered grass roots needs, was a set of visiting officials working out of Salt Lake. Visiting General Authorities served as a base for part of the ritual system. The visits from hierarchs coincided with the various events in the ritual calendar, principally Quarterly State Conferences. Visits were tied to the Church calendar. The calendar governed the ritual cycle. And this cycle happened to mesh with two major ecological processes: agricultural redistribution and repair of the irrigation network.

The Church has organized its populations into a number of spatial subdivisions since shortly after it was founded in 1830. The basic unit is called a *ward*, which consists of several hundred people but rarely over 600 or 700. Wards are presided over, as in the whole Church, by a lay clergy, men who are essentially engaged in earning a living in some ordinary way but who are coincidentally clergymen. A group of wards is called a *stake* and is presided over by its own hierarchy that is more or less directly responsible to and is in frequent touch with the central bureaucracy and leadership in Salt Lake City. Wards and stakes are geographic units. Nineteenth-century Arizona wards were coterminous with towns, and stakes with the region.

Four times a year stakes have conferences that bring together all the faithful within the stake's wards in a central place. At such times, geared coincidentally to the beginning, middle, and end of the agricultural cycle, a member of the governing board of the Church, the Twelve Apostles, or one of their administratively close colleagues, visited the gathered stake, thereby providing the visible, knowledgeable link to Salt Lake headquarters. Such officials had power, brought the latest word from the center, and as a result could serve as catalysts in local difficulties if Salt Lake or local people wanted them to. Visiting officials were ever present in any Mormon area on a regular and recurring schedule. And drawing them automatically was an event such as a dam washout in one of the communities that the Church leadership carefully tended on the Little Colorado. A dam washout was instantly turned into a ritual event by the presence of visiting hierarchy. Since the scheduling of stake-wide ritual activities would never have been more than a month or two removed from a dam disaster one event automatically became subject to the other. Stake Conferences served as timing devices in the cycle of agricultural redistribution. But they also served as scheduling devices in the washout-rebuilding cycle. The coincidence of the cycles was not deliberate. It was inevitable that quadriannual events would intersect with some part of the agricultural round and with dam disasters.

Visiting officials attracted by any kind of crisis had at their command the schedule of Church meetings that could draw as large or small an audience as an official felt it was necessary to have. He could meet only with High Priests and thereby meet only with town leadership. He could preach at a Sacrament Meeting and thereby reach the whole town. Or he could urge a Stake Conference and gather all the faithful on the Little Colorado, an area of two dozen towns over several hundred square miles. These are all ritual activities but this is by no means a complete list, and these could be made to serve any economic function without losing the religious nature of the occasion.

Ritual activity usually has an immediately sacred end, and for Mormons all pragmatic matters aimed at redeeming and building up the earth were sacred by definition. Given this view there is hardly a Mormon gathering that is not a ritual. The most straightforward of these are Sacrament Meetings, Sunday Schools, Primary, Priesthood Meetings, and Quarterly Stake Conferences. The format of all is the same and does not vary through time. Rituals open with hymn singing, extemporaneous dedicating prayer offered by one person, more hymn singing, a statement of the reason for the meeting, generalized discussion of how the issue at hand can be solved, the relationship of proposed issues and solutions to Church teachings, hymn singing, and closing prayer. The format is invariable, as nineteenth-century records show, and remains much the same today. God is invoked in a general way in the hymn singing and called into the specific problem in the prayer. Divine agency is appealed to at least implicitly and often explicitly when an individual relates to the group how such-and-such a problem can be solved by employing such-and-such an example or principle out of the *Book of Mormon* or *Doctrine and Covenant,* these being revealed documents.

Visiting officials using the ritual calendar spoke in all surrounding towns urging the population to contribute goods and, more likely, labor and equipment to the task of dam rebuilding. Stake officials as well as those from Salt Lake could shift stored tithing from surrounding towns to the stricken one. Tithing was in kind and produced the range of goods that could bolster the subsistence base of a town stricken by a calamity. Stake officials could direct surplusses to any one town in the stake, and higher Church officials had authority to send in produce from anywhere in the Church's domain. Such officials could and often did provide the link whereby Church headquarters capitalized local economic ventures such as dam rebuilding and the maintenance of the local population until the agricultural cycle was back in operation. The ritual calendar should then be seen as having brought organizing officials together, as having tied them to a particular crisis, and as regulating the stages in solving the crisis.

The ritual cycle combined technical know-how in the hands of Church leadership with tithing in labor. Just as Brigham Young built some of the furniture in his own house, so did his fellow leaders possess the empirical knowledge to make agriculture work. High Priests, Bishops, and Stake Presidents were also surveyors, construction experts, and financiers. Their organizational skill was not least among these. Existing simultaneously with these skills was a population bound to give to the Church one-tenth of its annual income. One way to discharge a tithe was in donated labor. The labor of the faithful could be counted on in this way and furthermore could be quantified. This was combined under the knowledgable direction of dam-building priests. The activity of both groups was initiated and coordinated by the ritual cycle and was increased or decreased by fluctuations in that cycle. Labor and knowledge could be reinforced by major ritual events at least four times in the annual cycle. And the calibrations broke down so finely that the day itself provided ritual regulators in the form of men, women, or children meeting in various combinations, all aiding rebuilding through joint activities that although pragmatic were also sacred. The Ladies' Relief Society distributed resources to the needy, a meeting of the Aaronic Priesthood (young men and boys) chopped wood or tended livestock, or the Melchizedek Priesthood (adult men) might meet with visitors from the Stake Presidency to plot reconstruction strategy. In all these ways, the ritual round could be geared precisely to ecological and economic exigency when it was necessary to do so. And when this was done, the ritual system ameliorated the force of ecological stress. The following set of events describes the fifth dam of a total of twelve built at Woodruff (Fish et al. 1870–1912: 63–64):

After a little delay the labor on the dam commenced on the second day of January 1884 and was continued until near completion when a flood came down and took the work all out again. They immediately commenced work again and had got the damage nearly repaired when a second flood came down and took it out again. The work was now abandoned for a time, many feeling quite discouraged.

At the General Conference of the Stake held at St. Johns in May

President Smith called on all the brethren of the Stake to donate one week's work each on the Woodruff dam.

The work on the dam commenced on the 2nd day of June 1884. The brethren from all parts of the Stake coming in made about an average of 45 men at work which moved the work very fast. Pres. Smith came in person and labored for some three or four weeks. The brethren of this Stake in this movement donated about $3,000.00 in work. The dam was nearly complete when a heavy body of water came down cutting over it and soon went out leaving it about as it was one year before. This was a heavy blow to the people for the season had been quite dry and the little grain that had been put in had completely dried up and was not worth harvesting.

Not withstanding all the misfortune that the place had met with it continued to improve.

Finally, at the level of belief or world view a washout produced, in order: a sense of shared tragedy, a sense of cooperation, a trial as a result of being elect of God, a chance to demonstrate worthiness for the true Church, and an ability to endure for the truth. Rebuilding a dam reaffirmed this set of doctrinal principles. All dam building activity was regarded as the building up of Zion, of making the earth bloom through a special stewardship entrusted to the Saints. All was a preparation for a very proximate Second Coming of Christ, the often heralded and continually prepared for Millenium. The work and tasks of the Saints were the preparation of the planet for the reign of Christ on earth from a kingdom prepared for him by his elect. This is the religious rationale under which dams were built and rebuilt. Under this rationale the whole area of Mormon towns participated in rebuilding a dam. A disaster that would under ordinary circumstances in the frontier West bring only some assistance from surrounding towns, brought, under the aegis of Mormon religious orchestration, full participation in rebuilding. Such cooperation insured rebuilding, a task otherwise impossible given the resources of one town. In this way manpower, tools, horsepower, capital, know-how, and the resources to feed the labor and the population of the stricken town were provided. All communities invested materially in all others, thus guaranteeing their own future by rebuilding an economic base that would one day reciprocate in concrete, predictable ways. Cooperative rebuilding acted as insurance for the entire area. Reciprocity was guaranteed and balance for the whole set of communities resulted. In addition, a portion of the earth was permanently "redeemed."

Religions concerned with the explanation of suffering in this life have sometimes employed the idea that God tests out or tries his people so that they can demonstrate their worthiness in this life for the one to come. The idea has been used with varying intensity in different types of Christianity. It is not unlike the Calvinistic notion of the calling. Among Calvinists one is called continually to perform and demonstrate actively one's merits, but the trial calls upon the individual to endure the constraints imposed from the outside and then to prove worthiness through mastering them. For Calvinists a call is personal and requires action rather than endurance. For nineteenth-century Mormons in Arizona a trial or testing by God was communal as much as it was individual, and had a passive aspect to it. It was to be endured. From a brief talk given at the Quarterly Stake Conference March 1887, George H. Crosby of the Union Ward is recorded as feeling, "Trials are the common heritage of the Saints. I made a contract with the Lord that if wealth would injure me, to keep it from me; have lost all I had by fire on two occasions but have not lost any sleep over it" (Snowflake Stake Historical Record 1886–1889: 106). Similarly,

> . . . some are tried with wealth, this is the case with some in Salt Lake City and Ogden: some there who have a small piece of land . . . soon find themselves in possession of property to the amount of $100,000., still the taxes on this property are so high they are unable to pay them. Some in certain districts find themselves stripped of all they possess by floods. We see occasionally a person who raises their hand against their own life but as long as the feeling of hope remains in the breast the clouds do not look so black; possessing the bright ray of sunshine gladdens our hearts. What is a boy or girl worth who has continually basked in the sunshine, who has always been pampered; there are few of this class who have made their mark. Those who have toiled and battled their way step by step and struggled on to the topmost round of the ladder, those who struggled up this way learning to avoid extremes are the ones in whom confidence can be placed. When we look at this condition seeing those who are buffetted (?) become strong making each failure a success. There is no one prominent among the Latter-Day Saints who has not struggled with poverty. . . . The decree has gone forth that we will receive our reward in our Father's kingdom. (From a talk given by Apostle John Henry Young, Quarterly Stake Conference, March 2, 3, 1890; Snowflake Stake Historical Record 1890–1892: 4–6)

The idea of the trial is twofold. One side is that a Saint will be tested before being rewarded, the other is that testing will be repetitive. As the quote from the Snowflake Stake Historical Record shows, Mormons used the idea of being tried as an explanation for continual failures and as motivation for continually renewed efforts. The notion is not a prominent part of current Mormon thought. But neither are the "trials" of the nineteenth-century frontier part of modern Mormon experience. The idea of a trial is not unique to Mormons in Arizona and logically it would seem to predate Mormon entry into the Great Basin. That it was reinforced by conditions throughout the Great Basin is clear enough and clear also is the tie between the idea of the trial and the repetitive failures Mormons faced from Ohio to Illinois as well as the difficulties of the desert West. Settlement in Utah and surrounding territory repeated the problems of settlement every time a new town was founded. And the annual agricultural and irrigation cycles in a semi-arid area not especially suited to agriculture guaranteed its share of periodic events that were rather straight-forward tests of endurance.

Every level of culture is affected by what might be looked on in some lights as only an ecological event. That the washout-rebuilding cycle is not merely an ecological matter illustrates the close coincidence of all aspects of Mormon culture. Such functional coincidence between ritual and ecology is not random nor the product of accident, neither is it a sometime affair. The interrelationships are systematic, thoroughgoing, and serve to regulate each other. The model that should be kept in mind is one of a double-timing or scheduling mechanism that acts to keep these irrigation-based agrarian villages in equilibrium, or stable. The unit that is being kept in equilibrium is not the village but the whole collection of Mormon towns operating under similar conditions in the same area. The two scheduling or timing devices acting reciprocally to maintain equilibrium, or a balance between population and resources, are periodic dam washouts and the ritual cycle.

The scheduling works in the following way. Dam washouts at any one town were themselves spaced to some degree by the amount of sedimentation behind a dam. Unless a flood were unusually ferocious, a newly-built dam with its deepened pool was more likely to contain the season's torrents than would a dam with fully silted pond. This spaced or timed disasters at a town to some degree and, to some degree as well, disasters were timed at other towns since rarely were several towns hit at the same time with the same disaster. Therefore, dam washouts were to some degree self-scheduled and although they appeared to occur at random were in fact ordered with some periodicity within any one town. By virtue of that ordering, a larger regional schedule was created that timed disasters so that they were rarely simultaneous in several towns. Put grossly, there was therefore a schedule for a town and one for a region. When the two schedules are looked at as a single set of disasters, the pattern appears to be random. When the schedules are isolated, they can be seen to act like thermostatic controls regulating a segment of the agricultural system, population movement between towns, cooperation between the towns, contact of Mormons with non-Mormons, as well as ritual activity of several specific kinds.

The schedules of dam washouts fit within the cycle of ritual activity, the most significant form of which is the Quarterly Stake Conference. Such conferences occurred four times annually, but within a season fluctuated with some freedom. The minutes of these conferences reveal them to be a means for passing along information on every conceivable activity and problem resident in the local region. All aspects of the Saintly life-way were discussed. All was public and there was no distinction between what was sacred and what was secular. All parts of the conference were internally scheduled. There was, for example, an opportunity for every bishop to report on the condition of his ward and flock. This was usually done in detail including economic as well as spiritual assessments. This ritual event with its pragmatic business formed a scheduling cycle which fitted within the agricultural and irrigation cycles. The three formed a series of regulators that allowed irregularity in any one system to be smoothed out or controlled by the "thermostats" of all the others (Ashby 1968: 296).

The theoretical lesson to be learned from the Mormon arrangement lies in the coincidence of two sets of regulators: self-cleaning dams and periodic rituals facilitating rebuilding. Such a coincidence guaranteed successful adaptation. Neither regulator alone was responsible for the success of the system. Ecological balance was maintained because (1) primary religious orientation was to this life, not the next, (2) progressive mastery over the environment was seen as an ultimate goal, and (3) the ritual activity resulting from these ideas had precise demographic and economic effects. On the other hand, ritual and credal balance were maintained because (1) the irrigation network was itself regulated and consequently provided a pragmatic basis for the ritual round, and (2) ecological variation provided a basis for verifying doctrine. A washout represented a trial; rebuilding represented redeeming the earth. These two mutual causal processes, self-scheduled washouts and use of the religious-ritual system for rebuilding, reinforced one another. For a series of decades, they produced a balance or homeostasis. What is unusual here is the remarkable interdependence of the two sub-systems, rather than the clear causal nature of either ecology or ritual.

But the more critical point arises from the mutual causality involved in these sub-systems. Mutual cause existed in the Arizona towns because of the rapid reciprocal nature of events. Reciprocal alternation between the two sub-systems led to an amplification or change in the religious system. Maruyama (1968: 304) has characterized deviation amplifying processes. The idea is that a cause and effect relationship may not always be a stable one but that some effects, once caused, like ecological upset, may amplify themselves causing the entire nature of a system to change. In view of this idea, the Mormon case is more adequately represented. From its founding, Mormonism as a religion was in close touch with the economic base of its adherents. That base was unstable. The effect was to create a religious system that adapted readily to change: witness the frequency and alleged contradictions of some of Joseph Smith's revelations (Brodie 1963). But in the process of adapting to change, the religion was amplified so that it internalized and institutionalized its ability to absorb change and socialize adherents for it. Through its experience in the nineteenth century, Mormonism became a religion that existed and was successful because it fostered and handled variability, not in spite of it.

The Church is a this-worldly, non-world-rejecting faith that concentrates its action on improvement and progression in this as opposed to the next life. Mormons are of course concerned with the next life, but just as much with this one. Indeed, as Bellah has pointed out, the latest stage in religious evolution is one geared to the present, not to a rejection of this life in favor of primary concentration on eternal reward. Mormonism is but a specific example of this characteristic. It was possible, as a result, to ordain a Saintly life-way in which successful adaptation—or progression, as a Mormon would call it—was a holy activity unifying all others and thereby eliminating any discrepancy between religious goals and economic or ecological ones.

The specific case of the dam washout-rebuilding cycle serves to illustrate one of the general conditions in the development of the religious systems being considered here. As a causal element in the chain, dam washouts result in the destruction of a dam, the lowering and washing out of the reservoir, the lowered carrying capacity of the town, which in turn causes migration and half a dozen other technological, economic, and demographic effects. The washout also jogs the ritual calendar into action on behalf of the town. Visiting officials are attracted, aid is sent, and so on. A unified sense of tragedy is laid over the region which is translated into the belief system and is expressed positively as another chance to demonstrate Saintly endurance and negatively as a possible case of the Lord's displeasure with the Saints. Not only must a dam disaster be seen as setting off action through all sub-systems but, because such disasters befell Mormons all over the

Great Basin in one form or another to one degree or another, these events should be seen as active ingredients in the formation of the Mormon religious system. Notions like progression, the gathering and building up of Zion, economic independence, and the earth as a living force (Arrington 1958: 24–28) have to be seen as created and defined under the bulk of their agrarian experiences in Ohio, Missouri, Illinois, as well as in the Great Basin.

The idea of temporal, as well as eternal change, growth, and perfection is not common to all Christians. But it is common to all of those sects (Judah 1967: 16), including Mormonism, founded either as the Industrial Revolution or the frontier placed groups of people in circumstances that were flexible, changeable, and often fragile. A belief system built along side these economic and ecological facts was influenced by them and as a result enabled a population to adapt better. For the Mormons, the economic pattern influencing them was agriculture in ever more difficult and ever more marginal ecological zones. For Mormonism's kindred sects, the pattern often involved the economically marginal classes created in the northeastern United States by the enveloping Industrial Revolution. For all of them, the problem was adjusting and adapting a group of people to economic marginality so that the condition could be lived with and even lived off. As a result of this type of economic condition, one of permanent changeability, a whole new religious stage came into existence. It is what Robert Bellah characterizes as Modern Religion (1970: 39). The stage would seem to be based on two economic conditions: rapid economic change (and its agricultural corollary, existence in fragile and marginal ecological zones) and the inevitable existence of groups who are at a disadvantage in such circumstances. It is under such conditions that religions developed that were geared to change and changeableness. Such religions had two effects. They allowed populations to adjust successfully to rapid change and they produced people who could facilitate and contribute to change. This is the basis for Mormonism's ability to live with, absorb, and even cause change. And, by extension, it is the basis for a similar ability on the part of all or most members of the American metaphysical movement.

It is an open question as to whether Mormonism as the Prophet Joseph Smith conceived it was to be as responsive to the temporal needs of its people as it became in the late nineteenth century when Brigham Young could be heard to say, "That religion which can not save a man temporally can not save him spiritually." Whatever the historical case, Mormonism became a very flexible faith, one which has revised its institutions and even some of its beliefs since its founding, as it has encountered circumstances requiring pragmatic action. Since its rituals were often concerned with pragmatic issues, the affairs of the world were directly harnessed to the Church. In such a circumstance what I would suggest happens is a specific example of a deviation amplifying mutual causal process. One process is obvious: Mormons as farmers were continually adjusting to new and different environments. The empirical world of Mormons shifted rapidly and presented tremendous problems for survival. These shifts and problems entered the Church through its rituals. The second part of the process involves Mormonism's attempt to free its faithful from what it called Babylon: the early grips of exploitative capitalism institutionalized in the Industrial Revolution. It did that by inventing a sacred, egalitarian society in which at first all property, and then one-tenth of one's property, was communal. As a member of the nineteenth-century American utopian communal movement the Prophet Joseph wanted a reasonable form of salvation in the present for those who joined his Church. He employed the principle of continual revelation in the course of founding the Church and as a result Mormonism was continually elaborated throughout Joseph's life in what amounted to a process of continual experimentation. Revelation continued with Brigham Young, second President of the Church. The two interacting processes here were the continually changing and ever more stringent ecological circumstances Mormons found themselves adjusting to, and the steady elaboration of Mormon beliefs and institutions as Mormons fought ever harder to free themselves from the grips of competitive capitalism. The two simultaneously changing variables operated on each other. As a result, the ecological adjustment of Mormons is as much a product of Mormonism as Mormon beliefs and institutions are a product of the ecological circumstances they were elaborated in. Neither could exist without the other and they are the products of each other. Whether they are equally the product of each other is a question I do not know how to answer now. It should be clear that in addition to mutually causal relationships these two processes were themselves dynamic: called "deviation amplifying." Neither ecological adjustment nor religious elaboration was static. Both were deviating, changing, from what they had been, and the changes in each system were amplified, increased, by the changes going on in the other. The more marginal the ecological circumstances, the more novel were the religious and social solutions called for. The more novel the religious and social experiments, the more the Saints were forced into marginal ecological circumstances by the reactions of the larger society. And so the process was repeated from Ohio in the early 1830s to the Great Basin throughout the rest of the nineteenth century.

The vast majority of churches founded in the United States during the nineteenth and twentieth centuries are the results of similar circumstances. A religion founded among a group of economically exploited and marginal people adjusted to empirical circumstances, and because those circumstances were subject to continual flux, the religion and its church remained inductive: free of creed, clergy, and, theology and as a result continually open to experimentation and incorporation of change. These, with one additional criterion, are the institutional forms of Robert Bellah's Modern Religion.

If it can be argued that certain sets of economic and ecological events contributed to the formation of some elements in Mormon religion and similar American sects, then it may also be the case that Mormonism becomes the agent for a series of activities having fundamental connections with the economic and ecological adjustment of its adherents. In the case of building and rebuilding a dam on the Little Colorado, Mormonism may be said to have caused the dams to be there in the first place. However tenuous that point may be, what is not so tenuous is that specifically Mormon principles operated to found agricultural towns on the Little Colorado, to dictate the economic independence of the whole region, and to guide their technological efforts at water control. Rather more specifically, the ritual system organized the labor, capital, and stored resources needed to put a dam together or back together. Ritual events communicated the need for money and tithing relief to Salt Lake City headquarters and to surrounding communities which contributed goods and labor that had been stored up in the first place under tithing to a Church-run storehouse. The priesthood planned the new dam, coaxed and demanded its construction from pulpits, and oversaw its construction in the field. The whole affair was a sacred activity. Even the water impounded and canalized was sacralized to represent one of the distinctive features of a Mormon town. Today, as in the nineteenth century, water flowing through irrigation ditches tells a Mormon, and anyone else who cares to discover it, the efficacy of the true Church. That Mormonism and specifically its ritual round caused dams, irrigation, and dam rebuilding to take place is as justifiable as saying that dams, washouts, and rebuilding caused parts of Mormon rituals to occur.

As suggested earlier, the existence of marginal Christian churches is a function of groups who are either in marginal economic or ecological zones or in economic classes subject to rapid change. Such churches would be created when established churches serving such groups are oriented to permanence and the next world. When considering the first condition of the hypothesis, marginal economic or ecological zones, these religious systems will be tied to the economic base through a system of regulators against disturbances. These have the effect of meshing together the economic base and religious system, thus keeping the sub-systems in constant tune with one another. This has the effect of making all activities sacred affairs and is doubly effective because the objects of the technology automatically become concrete, reified expressions of the supernatural. The agrarian metaphors used in the *Book of Mormon* to describe the ideal and future life are enforced through the matching of those metaphors with the then current reality. Dams don't just stand for an aspect of the divine, they are a manifestation of it. Mormonism and its kindred churches worked by tying the economic and the sacred and tying them permanently.

The pattern of material objects that is a dam and its connected irrigation system is both passive and active. It is produced by Mormonism and produces parts of it. In operation, it is a passive model showing how the system operated but it also, in operation, caused stability in the town and region. When destroyed, it became an active agent in mobilizing the religious system and reinforcing all the Mormon principles that were brought to bear explaining the disaster as well as those used in rectifying it.

The irrigation system can be seen as one of the prime factors causing a certain level of population, stratification, social control, and regional cooperation. It has certain deterministic properties and is an apt case of technological determinism. A system like the Mormon one is itself endowed with meaning for the users and builders. The items become symbols in the standard sense that they come to mean things they are not inherently. The system and its component parts are given meaning; that much is obvious since they become part of a culture. But the elements of this system are also given religious significance. A block of stone is automatically an artifact and a cultural item as a result, but it is also a religious object in that it plays a part in redeeming the earth for the Lord and his elect. A dam, therefore, by having sacred properties operates in several sub-systems and becomes a piece of uniquely *Mormon* technology. As a result, Mormonism can be called to account for the dam's existence and maintenance. As a result, too, Mormonism created the dam. The object causes and is caused by. Certainly it is necessary for technological determinists and their opposites to come to grips with the dynamic connection between the two halves of any piece of technology. This is especially true when examining the connection between technology and belief.

On the Little Colorado, Mormon towns were founded in an environment that had not supported a population of any size since A.D. 1000.

From about A.D. 700 to 1000 the largest human population in the area's history, possibly excepting the present, coincided with a climatic variation characterized by increased rainfall and a longer growing season (increased number of frost-free days) to make agriculture a viable economic base (Martin et al. 1964). Human occupation began in this area by 4000 B.C., and there is some likelihood that there was a Paleo-Indian occupation as well. That would push initial occupation to 10,000 or so years ago. Systematic intensive use of domesticated plants as the major part of the economy did not begin until A.D. 700 and peaked, together with maximum population growth, around A.D. 1000. By 1400 the area was depopulated until the arrival of Athabascan hunter-gathers around 1500. Since the introduction of agriculture, the largest and most stable population was the prehistoric variant of the modern Pueblos. Aside from the modern population, which is probably but not decisively larger and less permanent than the prehistoric agriculturalists, only the Mormon population has had the adaptive traits capable of producing stable, long-lived towns each supporting a few hundred to a thousand people. The details of the prehistoric adaptation are only becoming clear, but one specific principle that is established is that the resources needed for population maintenance and expansion are a function of exploiting new ecological variation. Through a series of innovations, use of domesticated plants and animals, pottery, the bow and arrow, and so on, the environment capable of sustaining larger populations was expanded. Technological innovations underwrote population expansion. This coupled with high migration rates served as regulators over the carrying capacity of the land in its prehistory (Plog 1969; Zubrow 1971: 127–138).

We have a good measure of the variation of temperature and rainfall for almost the entire prehistoric era through the palynological record (Martin 1963). The variation is extraordinary and varies closely with measures of population density as well as with the changing ratio of domesticates to hunted-gathered foods (Schoenwetter and Dittert 1968: 41–66). It should be concluded that as with most balanced societies the prehistoric agricultural population, which lasted in the Little Colorado well over a millenium, contained a series of regulators or scheduling mechanisms. These mediated between environmental exigencies on one side and demography, settlement pattern, technological innovation, aspects of social organization, and religious matters on the other.

The Mormon population is not so long-standing nor much more populous, but the regulators against external variation are even clearer. The condition of the Mormon adaptation does make it one of the most successful modern cultural variants in the area. Its success is a function of its ability to harness the region's seasonal variation between localities in such a way as to exploit enough for survival while isolating the destructive remainder. These regulators, the dam washout-rebuilding cycle and the ritual round, served to maintain the agricultural system in self-regulating homeostasis while filtering out irregularities that upset the equilibrium. The filter provided by these coinciding timers or regulators leveled off population, kept dams from becoming useless through silting up, kept ritual in tune with economic reality, and prevented the regional fission that would have resulted from the Mormon plan to set up self-sufficient independent towns. These last are processes that are latent in the nineteenth-century Mormon agrarian strategy and were filtered out or controlled by the regulators within the system.

It is through the regulators that Mormonism produced one of the most viable cultures in the area by adapting its people to the ecological frailty of the nineteenth century. That same frailty was to become the economic instability of the twentieth century.

> With the triumph of eastern competitive capitalism, the . . . economy tended to become more and more unstable. More and more, the economic fortunes of Utah [and the Great Basin] came to depend upon decisions and centers of control that lay far outside the confines of the state. The state's economy became "provincial," where it had been "metropolitan"; that is, it came to be peripheral to the core economy of the nation rather than being the core of its own regional economy. Many of its basic enterprises were absentee-owned. Its exports consisted increasingly of raw materials and semi-processed goods destined for the East. The rate of growth in manufactures tended to slow down, and the state increasingly imported from the East the semi-processed and finished goods it required. (Arrington 1961: 17)

The system that has been described for Mormons in a part of Arizona began in the 1870s and closed in the 1920s. After the mid-1920s, permanent dams were installed, rapidly silted up, and became increasingly less useful. The agricultural system switched to wells for water but continued to survive. Throughout the late nineteenth century and until the Great Depression, the federal government made an active attempt to squash Mormon economic independence. In Utah, the Church was forced to dissolve its many holdings in a move that was ultimately calculated to make the Great Basin Kingdom fully dependent or at least fully integrated into the larger American economy. Brigham Young, following Joseph Smith's lead, had sought to free the Saints from the constraints the larger society had continually placed upon them. Geographic isolation and economic independence were used with no small amount of genius to set up what could be regarded from a federal viewpoint as an independent state.

That the Mormon kingdom in the Great Basin strove for economic independence is indisputable. But it should be thought of as independence at the level of the Mormon farming communities as well as, and almost instead of, independence for an integrated empire. Both levels were aimed at, and neither was ever achieved completely or even for long. At the level of economic independence for the integrated Mormon area on the Little Colorado, the efforts and achievements were extensive and partly successful. At the level of the many small agrarian communities scattered over the Great Basin, economic independence was probably never really attained, although, of course, this has to be a relative statement. The cooperation and mutual dependence dictated by the agricultural conditions in the semi-arid regions contradicted any real self-sufficiency aimed for. Witness the areal cooperation needed in dam construction. It is hard to measure the degree of interdependence as opposed to self-sufficiency of the Arizona communities, but beyond argument they could not have existed by themselves individually.

Regardless of Mormon economic reality, the degree of independence that had been achieved throughout Mormondom constituted a basis for federal interference of a more emotional sort. The issue of curbing Mormon independence took the public form of political debates over polygyny. While the motivation for this major fight has its obvious aspects, it also had solid economic foundations. After the polygamy-statehood-for-Utah issue was settled, the disenfranchisement of the Church took place. Systematically eviscerated was the whole series of economic institutions the Church had built up as a superstructure to support its farming population (Arrington 1958: 353–412). The ecclesiastical banks, boards of trade that had set universal prices, the mercantile institutions acting as wholesalers and retailers were simultaneously secularized and decentralized. Zion's Savings Bank and Trust Company, Zion's Board of Trade, and Zion's Commercial and Mercantile Institution were decentralized, diffused, and began to serve in a less sensitive way as balances to the exigencies of an agrarian economy. Robbing Utah of this closely integrated and responsive set of institutions had the ultimate effect of decimating Utah in the Great Depression. "The culmination of this trend was the Great Depression of the 1930s, from which Utah suffered relatively more than almost every state in the Union; the only candidates for worse states were Oklahoma and Colorado. Certainly, the expenditures for public assistance in relation to income were higher in Utah than for almost every other state" (Arrington 1961: 17). The national gain for all of the tribulation was the full commitment of the Great Basin to the national economy and polity.

The destruction of the economic superstructure of the Mormon domain and the full integration of that domain into the national economy had one important and measurable effect. It tied the economic bases of the Mormon farming towns to the national economy at the same time that it removed the economic cushion the financial machinery of the Church provided for the towns. It transformed a fragile ecological domain into a fragile economic one over a period of three decades. During the period, self-sufficient farmers became like all other American farmers, producers for a market over which they had no control. Their ecological condition improved somewhat through the use of a more sophisticated technology introduced mainly through governmental agencies. But this positive change which ameliorated ecological frailty was more than upset by the towns' being subject to market conditions that automatically placed them in as fragile an economic status as they had endured in the days of dam disasters.

For the Mormons of the Little Colorado towns and generally for the Great Basin as a whole, the twentieth century provided a different economic base but one with essentially the same qualities of unpredictability, marginality, and frailty. In examining the qualities of Mormon adaptation in the twentieth century, I would like to carry forward the principal hypotheses that guide this paper. They are three. (1) Mormonism is a reflection of and agent for the economic changes its adherents undergo. As a result, (2) Mormonism is in a state of perpetual innovation having institutionalized devices for continual absorption of change. And (3), Mormonism is neither authoritarian, hierarchical, nor literalistic but, in matters of doctrinal interpretation at least, is diffuse, egalitarian, and loose-constructionist. It is this last hypothesis that describes the chief trait of Bellah's Modern Religion: the self-revising synthesis of religious principles and religious action resides in the individual, not in an institution. This last hypothesis does not characterize nineteenth-century Mormonism in which the foundations for Modern Religion were laid, but which itself was not Modern. The foundation was the incorporation of pragmatic affairs, and hence change, into the religious system. This was done through the processes of continual revelation, the content of rituals, and the this-worldly emphasis on concrete improvement of the earthly Kingdom. These three hypotheses are closely related, but are also closely connected to the larger hypothesis that the nature of marginal Christian movements generally can be specified and more clearly understood by examining the economic base underlying their memberships. That base is basically the same for these many churches as it is for Mormonism: insecure, changeable, and unpredictable.

To examine the kinds of changes Mormonism and the Mormon towns of east-central Arizona have undergone since the 1920s, I would like to present two sets of quantitative data. These will come later in the paper and will attempt to present coordinate measures of economic and religious change. What the rest of this paper attempts to do is to measure from roughly 1920 to 1960 a set of variables in the Little Colorado area of Arizona in which Mormons form a major sector of the population. The aim is to assess the responsiveness of the system of Mormon values to the changing economic circumstances to which the Mormons find themselves subject. The assumption behind this is that values are the concrete portions of more general Mormon beliefs and principles. They are the action-oriented, motivating portion of the religious system and are viewed specifically as rules for behavior. I would also like to present some data on the institutions Mormons use to continually adapt themselves to change.

In order to address the issue of change within Mormonism, I would like to set the basis for change in the economic pattern of the twentieth century. The change in the area of Arizona I have used as a laboratory can stand for that happening in the Great Basin as a whole, and possibly even for most of agrarian America and Canada (Bennett 1969). For the Mormon villages along the Little Colorado, the basic shift in the economic pattern between the nineteenth and twentieth centuries involved a shift away from agriculture and a proliferation of other kinds of activities. This is reflective of the decline in use of agricultural labor and a spread of labor over many other categories. However, instead of proliferating economic options through the expansion of types of employment, the real effect of this economic change was to force individuals to hold many different jobs for a short period of time. Over a ten-year period in the twentieth century, a man might do a half-dozen tasks. Before, if a man were born into farming circumstances, those were the circumstances in which he died. For most of the twentieth century, the economy has been frail enough to provoke such changeable conditions. A man could never be sure of his means of employment and such insecurity had patterned effects on the religious system of such individuals.

The nineteenth-century economy was generalized in the Great Basin insofar as it was basically agricultural. It is not that farming does not call for the performance of many tasks, as much as it is that all of those tasks become familiar to a boy in the course of growing up in agrarian circumstances. A man may move into a new area, but the range of tasks does not proliferate. Further, the range of industries fundamentally different from agriculture was few and limited in the Great Basin, and non-existent in Arizona. A specialized economy of the sort that exists today involves disparate, unrelated tasks which a person is not so readily initiated into as he grows up. As a result in the nineteenth century, Mormon farmers were generalists in a generalizing economy, and in the post-World War I economy, Mormons in Arizona have remained generalists in a specializing economy. Generalists in the sense that they shift from task to task, but not necessarily with the prior training and exposure to those many tasks a farmer would have had in the nineteenth century. This is not the normal or expected pattern of employment in industrial areas, but it is the pattern among the unemployed and the economically marginal.

Table 1 is drawn from data representing the employment patterns from one of the small towns of the Little Colorado. It is almost a

TABLE 1. Percentage Distribution over Occupations
Joseph City, Arizona 1920–1965

Occupation	1920–1929	1930–1939	1940–1949	1950–1959	1960–
1. Professional, technical	7.35	10.48	14.89	16.50	18.29
2. Farmers	45.58	32.14	23.40	24.27	18.29
3. Managers, Proprietors (ex. farmers)	4.41	11.90	13.82	15.53	14.63
4. Clerical	2.94	3.57	3.19	5.83	7.31
5. Sales	1.47	2.58	2.12	2.91	7.31
6. Craftsmen	13.24	10.48	14.89	15.53	14.63
7. Operatives (mineworkers, etc.)	14.70	21.42	22.34	14.56	15.85
8. Private Household Workers	0.0	0.0	0.0	0.97	1.22
9. Service Workers (ex. 8)	8.82	10.48	4.25	2.91	1.22
10. Farm Laborers	1.47	.0.0	1.06	0.97	1.22

purely Mormon community. The data are given by occupation category. The categories themselves are derived from the Arizona State Employment Service (1950–1968). The data are divided by decades so that trends are more easily discerned. The graphs display many micro-changes. There are, however, several larger trends that are useful for the hypothesis considered here. The first is that farming represents 45% of the employed in the 1920s and decreases steadily to 18% in the 1960s. The second trend is that there is a far more even distribution of the population among the employment categories.

The third trend is that during these five decades, and especially during those most economically upset, individuals held more jobs, seriatim, and for a shorter length of time than in the more fully agrarian era. This particular observation is drawn from life histories recorded in a chronicle from the particular town (Westover and Richards 1961). These last data do not show up on the table. Complementing these trends while expanding their effects are two other statistical observations drawn from the same data. Women, who were almost totally unemployed until the decade beginning with 1910, enter employment categories in the 1920s, and in large numbers in the 1930s and 1940s. There is some decline in working women in the 1950s to the present, but the observation that remains is that economic conditions were so dire for a major portion of the twentieth century that Mormon women were forced to take employment outside the home. This pattern is noteworthy since the place of Mormon women is traditionally in the home with their generally large families. The second supporting line of evidence for the consistency and severity of economic change is the pattern of people leaving the community. During the 1920s and 1930s the number of people leaving more than tripled over the decade of 1910. In the 1940s, the number increased six times over 1910, and by the more stable 1950s was still twice as high as in the 1910s.

These economic indices are cited to witness two trends. The first is the change in kinds of jobs the population experienced between the nineteenth and twentieth centuries. The second is that while employment became more diverse, it also became less secure. A man not only was not usually to become what his father had been; he often had no firm guarantee that any one type of employment would remain a viable support for any length of time. The economy had become very unstable. Whereas for nineteenth-century Mormons the environment had been an unpredictable factor in an otherwise predictable life, the twentieth century eliminated environmental variation but replaced it with a degree of economic fluctuation that dissolved the predictability of the future. One set of variability had replaced another; one source of instability supplanted another having the effect of continuing the insecure, unpredictable subsistence base.

Mormonism has met this change of conditions with inventiveness and resilience. It has adapted some of its organizational principles so that the faithful are actually pretrained for rapid job turnover. Within the local Church there are wide opportunities for involvement in dozens of different activities all connected with Church membership. Training within the Church through its activities preadapts an individual for the changes the outside world often faces him with.

Inside the Church a man is not trained for specific tasks but for flexibility. He is processed through dozens of positions with the vaguest of expectations for skilled conduct. It does not matter if a person is inexpert at a specific job he is appointed to. What matters is the service, flexibility, endurance, cheerfulness, and inventiveness that he brings to the performance. Specific techniques and precise knowledge are picked up in the course of serving at a task. They are secondary to and are expected to be facilitated by the primary qualities brought to the job. The adjustment that an individual makes under these conditions fits him ideally for rapid economic flux. He is better adapted to switching jobs, to gaining new skills, to upward or downward mobility—in short, to doing a succession of different kinds of jobs in a more or less incoherent order at a rate of change that cannot be predicted.

Since no professional clergy exists at most levels—Mormons would say at any level, but I suspect that is becoming incorrect—the community of faithful must organize the whole ecclesiastical setup itself. Mormons are widely noted for their action-oriented life. Action within the Church is maintained through membership in the broad selection of sodalities and leadership positions available in every ward. There are hundreds of positions in each ward. This basic organizational unit contains 600 to 800 people. As a result, a large part of a ward is either leading, has led, or soon will lead. The principle of active membership is realized in a standard congregation through association with a scale of groups which encompasses all age grades and status groups. Such groups meet with a frequency involving a Mormon on a daily basis with his fellow faithful. There are, in addition to the head of the ward, a three-man bishopric, organizations like Sunday schools, which Mormons attend throughout their adult lives, Primary, which is a weekly religious instructions class for youngsters, Mutual Improvement Associations for young men and women, the Ladies' Relief Society, Boy Scouts, choirs, and so on. There are also quorums of the priestly divisions that have duties requiring organization. These and more organizations absorb the membership into a round of activity but provide positions of leadership for a large cross-section in the ward. The degree to which Mormons are involved in these activities is greater than that in the average mainline Protestant congregation, and it bears no resemblance at all to a Catholic's activities in his parish. Among marginal Christian groups, such high lay participation is not uncommon, however, and it obviously guarantees loyalty through action.

Mormon activity in leadership positions and sodalities has some effective consequences for the economic conditions in which they live.

A Mormon changes sodalities as he grows older, and since he may belong to several simultaneously he is passed successively through a complex chain of groups all arranged to do slightly different tasks. Every group mirrors central Church organizational principles with president, advisors, assistants, and so on. Significantly, tenure in any leadership position today is short. There is rapid rotation through positions of responsibility. This obviously guarantees a chance for everybody to lead, as well as to be led by his peers. Effective leadership and participation are supposed to be characterized by enthusiasm, resourcefulness, willingness to serve, flexibility, a weighted balance between attention to group needs and episcopal desires in favor of the latter, and abilities like persuasion, fund-raising, earnestness, and so on. Leadership does not have skilled training as a prerequisite. A man does not bring skill to his post; he brings a set of qualities that allows the position to fit him, not so much for the specific job but for the whole run of jobs and tasks he will face in the next several decades of Church service. He like every other Mormon is fitted to serve organizational variability within the Church.

I would like to suggest that the kind of ecclesiastical program just described, which is a product of twentieth-century Mormonism, is a mirror image of the economic position many Mormons throughout the church live in. Since my data come from a small part of Arizona and I have only imprecise or, better, impressionistic knowledge of conditions in the rest of the Church's domain, I cannot be sure of verifying the hypothesis. I suspect on local evidence from Arizona that it is nonetheless accurate. Economic conditions in east-central Arizona have forced individuals to change jobs often at the same time that the economic base has been diversified. There are therefore more kinds of jobs to be held more frequently. This is clearly opposed to the condition of the agricultural nineteenth century. But it is not so remarkably different from much of the United States. It is different in degree, however, since the Arizona part of Mormondom is more marginal economically than much of the rest of the country.

This one limited example serves to illustrate how Church social organization has been adjusted to equip its membership with experiences and predispositions to match conditions found in the world outside the Church. Since such training for changeableness begins early in life, an individual is fully socialized for flexibility in performance by the time he is a young adult. Therefore, a Mormon who falls away from the Church in early adulthood is still equipped with a range of attitudes that adapt him to external conditions.

Along with organizational adaptability, I think Mormons are accompanied by adaptability in their value system as well. Under the guise of strict literalism exists a diffuseness, individual inventiveness, and variability through time that contradicts usual views of the Mormon belief system. Judah characterizes metaphysical churches as creedless, as investing the member with powers of revelation superior to those of established dogma. Principles of faith are very much an individual's concern, not the business of church organization. As Bellah says (1970: 43–44):

> . . . the fundamental symbolization (set of meanings) of modern man and his situation is that of a dynamic multidimensional self capable, within limits, of continual self-transformation and capable, again within limits, of remaking the world, including the very symbolic forms (meanings) with which he deals with it, even the forms that state the unalterable conditions of his own existence. [There is] increasing acceptance of the notion that each individual must work out his own ultimate solutions and that the most the church can do is provide him a favorable environment for doing so, without imposing on him a prefabricated set of answers.

O'Dea takes Mormonism at its word in matters of dogma. The Church has a set of Articles of Faith, but more importantly it has notions of doctrinal orthodoxy absent in metaphysical churches. The tradition of prophesy and revelation within Mormonism would seem to dictate ways of maintaining consistency through time, and among the faithful at any one time in matters of belief. If Mormonism is to be considered a metaphysical church or a Modern Religion, there must be a degree and level of interpretive freedom that is not allowed for at the most explicit level. If Mormonism is an example of Bellah's Modern Religion and has an ability to absorb change, then that ability must be demonstrable and there must be institutions within Mormonism to foster it. The presentation of data that follows is directed at two aims just outlined. The first is to show the variation that does exist in the use of points of belief, and the second is to attempt a correlation of that variability with economic conditions. It is an attempt to demonstrate one of the ways Mormonism maintains consistency while promoting diversity.

All of the data used below come from the same area used for that part of the paper devoted to the dam washout-rebuilding cycle. The data are attitudes or values expressed in newspaper editorials or commentary columns. The data exhibit the public citation and invocation of basic principles of behavior by which the community is supposed to be guided from problem to problem. Data on frequency of citation of a set of values were recorded from the county newspaper from 1910 to 1966. There were 63 values determined inductively from the editorials. The categories were expanded from a core of two dozen presented in one editorial and said to represent basic virtues. As the initial set proved inadequate when measured against other editorials, the list was expanded. As it finally stood, the list represented a nearly complete set of values expressed both by name and by inference for the communities served by the newspaper. Some of the most common values are service, economy, self-sufficiency, reciprocity, loyalty, education, and so on. Paradigms were not constructed for the values, and some overlap exists as a result. Meaning drawn from contextual use was not recorded each time a citation was found and counted. The meanings I attached to the values are derived from contextual use but represent common denominator meanings rather than the range of variation in meaning any one value showed through time. In any year, a 25% sample of editorials was taken. Each calendar month was used in the sample, but within each month the week was chosen randomly. The sample was stratified first into months and then made random within a month.

A taxonomy of the 63 categories based on frequency of co-occurrence was created using a factor analysis. This was done using a canned computer program, PSTAT, developed at Princeton for use on data from the social sciences. That factor analysis yielded seven categories. These demonstrated a high degree of internal coherence and have been given labels drawn from two studies of Mormon values that isolate essentially the same few basic principles (Arrington 1958: 22–28; Fluidus 1963). The seven categories—equality, economic independence, progression, unity, stewardship, system, and redeeming the earth—coincide with major portions of Mormon doctrine. Each factor contains a group of the original 63 values, and again the factors are based on the frequency with which groups of the 63 values occurred together through 56 years. The 63 values should be seen as representing the public recitation in concrete, problem-solving contexts of parts of the Mormon system of beliefs. Mormons as the major segment of the population served by the newspaper, as the dominant political figures, as the biggest landowners, and as owners of the most important businesses can be assumed to have had their ideological stance represented in the public press. In addition, for a considerable period a Mormon owned the newspaper the data are drawn from. To the extent that standard, rural, modernizing, agrarian values are also represented in the paper, they usually coincide with Mormon values and represent notions evolved under circumstances close to or identical with Mormon values. It does not hurt the argument here to identify the values as rural, agrarian, and modernizing in addition to being

Mormon, especially since Mormonism is a product of such circumstances.

The frequency of use of each of these seven categories was then plotted against an economic indicator, percentage annual change in tax income to the county government (State Tax Commission of Arizona 1917–1966). County taxes are the product of multiplying annual tax levy with assessed valuation. Both are under the control of locally elected boards, and are subject to rapid adjustment and vary sensitively with economic change. Since until very recently most people owned property, this particular measure represents most of the population. Since private ownership is almost always the case for Mormons, they are more or less completely represented in the tax data. And since Mormons own a large share of property, their contribution is heavily represented in annual tax income to the county and they can be expected to provide rapid and pointed pressure on local tax adjustment boards depending on economic circumstances.

To discover whether any relationship existed between taxes and values, a correlation matrix was created. A small part of the results are reported below. The aim of such a correlation analysis is to discover what percentage of the variation in one variable, values, is accounted for in the variation of another variable, taxes. The result of the analysis shows that three of the seven factors covary closely with tax changes. Stewardship, redeeming the earth, and unity are accounted for to a significant degree by tax changes. Only stewardship and redeeming the earth are discussed here. To be more precise, the annual differences in frequency of citations were matched against the annual differences in tax changes to achieve the results that follow. Rate of annual tax change accounts for 45% (.5 level of significance) of the variation in the factor stewardship, and 57% (.1 level of significance) in redeeming the earth. One way to express this result is to say that 45% of the time a change in taxes governs the way stewardship is used in the public press. The same is true about redeeming the earth 57% of the time. By implication the rest of the variation in these values is accounted for by some other variable or set of variables and these other variables may be economic or social, or even ideological.

Stewardship in the nineteenth century was a major Mormon principle that meant that a "man must consider his rights to land as derived (from) and subject to church disposition. This principle assured primacy of group interest over individual interest and every man was to consider his property as consecrated to the Lord for the building of the Kingdom" (Arrington 1958: 25). As the notion of stewardship is carried over into the twentieth century, its concern is not so much with land which has less direct value for individuals now but with the general resources, including time, available to individuals. The primacy of group interest over individual interest is still a dominant value in Mormon culture. The resources open to an individual are the gifts of God and as such are subject to his Church. There is still a very close tie between the Church and earthly goods, and it is presumed that the individual uses those goods for the benefit of the collectivity before he uses theem for himself. The correlation analysis shows that 45% of the time when stewardship is used its use is a product of the economic situation and specifically of given tax factors. In prosperity it is frequently stressed, in economic decline it is not.

Any one of the seven major categories or factors of values can be broken down into components. Stewardship consists of self-reliance, vigilance, self-sufficiency, individuality, and service. These are part of the 63 values combined into one factor on the basis of their statistical co-occurrence. The label "stewardship" is my choice and points out the single Mormon principle that unites meanings of the constituents of the factor. The changes in the major category, stewardship, are made up of the cumulative changes of its components. The component values are not synonymous but serve to address sets of problems that are diverse in actual subject matter but are structurally similar in economic terms. In other words, every major category has a series of more specific referents connected with it that allow the factor to be used in a wide range of situations.

The following editorial from the *Holbrook Tribune* of December 2, 1932 illustrates the juxtaposition of values and taxes. The editorial is explicitly concerned with tax reduction, but clearly it is a response to the overall effect of the Great Depression which had just begun to hit this area. No explicit reference to Mormonism is made and the owners of the newspaper were not Mormon themselves. The town nonetheless had a significant Mormon population and was the commercial center for the almost purely Mormon hinterland of smaller towns. The Church general store was also located there at this time. Note, that the fight for lower taxes—a fight that was quickly won—starts with a hint of optimism, a value that rises in frequency of citation as economic conditions decline. The individual, "Every citizen," is responsible for acting in concert wth the whole for the greater good at the local level. The individual is stressed in the context of serving more than himself. The piece ends with a pitch for sufficient foresight, or vigilance, to act for the general good and to act now.

MUST FORCE TAX REDUCTION

One of the most encouraging phases of the late campaign was the attitude taken by most of the candidates for public office toward the the cost of government and the need for tax reduction. President-elect Roosevelt has stated that a 25 per cent cut is essential and has pledged his efforts toward achieving that. Those elected with him have echoed his views.

If such a reduction is made it will have an amazingly fine effect on the country—not only in the money that will be saved, but in psychological result. There is no question but what the spector of still higher taxes frightens thousands of investors and shoves money into safe-deposit vaults and tea pots; that it prevents business from going ahead and expanding; that it discourages home building and savings; that, in time of unemployment, it creates more unemployment, more hardship, more distress.

Every citizen should demand a sound program to lower taxes. We can do this by not asking for expenditures that touch only a small part of the country at the expense of the whole; by taking the broad, rather than the local view. We can follow up federal reductions by forcing state, county and municipal governments—which are the most expensive of all—and public officials, to observe the example. In short, the time and the opportunity for tax reduction are here—and it must be had (December 2, 1932: 2)

The peak of the Depression hit this area in the second half of the 1930s and in 1932 the economic index still had a long way to drop. This accounts for the continued use of stewardship and its component factors which decreased in use as the economy deteriorated. The general pattern revealed in the analysis is that 45% of the variance of local property taxes is accounted for by variation in the use, i.e. public citation, of five values. As taxes vary, the use of these five values varies. When taxes rise, so does citation of this cluster of values; when taxes decline, so does citation of the set of values.

The cluster of five values composing stewardship—self-reliance, self-sufficiency, individuality, vigilance, and service—are not synonyms nor do they cover identical situations nor are they used to provoke similar behavior. The editorial cited above stresses broad rather than local concern and action. It stresses service. An article in the very next column of the same issue stresses self sufficiency, seemingly an antithetical value.

BLANKET MINERAL LAND WITHDRAWAL NOT HELPFUL
TO GOVERNMENT WARDS

Attention has been called by Charles A. Mitke, a consulting mining engineer . . . with a mining experience in three continents, to a matter which should enlist the attention of Chamber of Commerce, boards of trade and generally the citizens of Arizona. It is the recent withdrawal by the government of approximately 1,000,000 acres of land in the Papago Indian reservation.

This withdrawal, like so many actions taken in the name of solicitude for the welfare of the government's wards . . . is condemned. (*Holbrook Tribune,* December 2, 1932: 2)

This is the ethic of economic self-preservation. It favors the community and presumably takes the "local" as opposed to the "broad view," or at least favors private interests over Indian interests. Here is self-sufficiency—and the supposed means to obtain it—competing with the simultaneous use of service in the editorial cited earlier. These seem to conflict yet co-occur through fifty years with significant frequency. However, the concept of stewardship unifies them: God has presented his abundance to men; if they do not safeguard it, He will not renew it. Very different actions—even in possible conflict— can be handled simultaneously using the different components of a single general principle.

Redeeming the earth, a value consisting of fellowship, intention, purpose, respect, and aggression has a correlation of 57% with percent annual change in tax income to the county. Such a notion is clarified with the following quotes, "Man must assist God in the process of regeneration and make the earth a more fitting abode for himself and for the Redeemer of Man" (Arrington 1958: 25–26). "The earth, as the future abiding place of God's people, had to be made productive and fruitful" (Arrington 1958: 25-26). "It is our business," Arrington quotes Brigham Young as saying, "to mould these elements to our wants and necessities, according to the knowledge we now have and the wisdom we can obtain from the Heavens through our faithfulness. In this way will the Lord bring again Zion upon the earth, and in no other" (Arrington 1958: 25-26). Today as in the nineteenth century redeeming the earth means spreading the Gospel. In addition, today as opposed to the nineteenth century there is a conscious notion about the Mormon role in saving the United States as a political entity. The notion of redeeming the earth has purposive and aggressive qualities to it. The idea strongly suggests an obligation to one's fellow man and that obligation is fulfilled through an active intent at redeeming him. Redeeming the earth is a doctrinal point supporting Mormon expansion—spatial expansion in the nineteenth century, expansion of membership of the twentieth. This idea of going beyond the established frontiers, of experimentation and investing in the uncertain seems to be very closely tied to economic conditions. Prosperity brings active stress on redeeming; an economic slump brings retrenchment. Stress on redeeming the earth is governed to a significant degree by very pragmatic concerns. There is a high degree of flexibility, changeableness, and match with economic conditions. These are some of the more obvious responses tax changes elicit in the values system. That the system of values represents undeviating adherence to dogmatic principles is patent nonsense. Adherence to dogma is a meta-value, but dogma itself is unspecified (Roy Rappaport, personal communication). That the values are flexible and sensitive to basic changes like economic disruption and prosperity is clear and stands as illustrating one of the ways Mormonism attunes itself to its faithful and maintains its own resilience.

Not only does this pattern represent flexibility but it does so at the local level. Such changes may be keyed into Salt Lake City headquarters, but the ties are not so close as to prevent sensitive reaction to economic conditions by the local Mormon community. Although the Church is hierarchical, authoritarian, and literalistic in matters of doctrine as O'Dea and other scholars have correctly observed, there is a level of activity in affairs of belief that has none of those characteristics. This level involves the use of a whole and inclusive network of values. These are used in local public contexts and reorganize a portion of the belief system depending on the circumstances a community faces.

Up to this point, the results of one factor analysis have been the basis for conclusions, but several such analyses have been performed. One particular analysis is judged more appropriate than another on the basis of applicability to a problem, not because one of them is somehow in closer tune with ultimate reality. Major groupings of the 63 values can be accomplished in several different ways. Raw data or percentage data can be used. The number of final categories, or factors, can be specified or not. In one arrangement tried in the course of this research, the values data were represented as percent of total citations in any one year and were then factored into ten categories. If service accounted for 10 of a total 100 citations for all 63 values for 1927, then it was represented as 10%. These factors were then run against the total range of tax changes using a multiple regression analysis. Such a method is designed to discover how closely related one variable, in this case tax change, is with a set of variables, not just one against one as in a correlation matrix. The set of variables that taxes are run against is a group of ten factors representing the thirty most frequently used values. The results of the analysis showed that 35% of the variation in the most frequently used values could be accounted for by changes in tax income to the county. It further showed that the reliability of that correlation was at the .05 level. Initially, 34% is not considered much of a correlation. Inferentially, it means that other variables also influence the changes in value use. That conclusion is obvious in terms of theory alone. The real result of this multiple regression is to assess how responsive values are to taxes. The conclusion is that values respond to tax changes about a third of the time.

Tax change predicts value change with 34% accuracy. That degree of accuracy is sufficient to demonstrate the link between an aspect of Mormon belief with the economic conditions one group of Mormons finds itself subject to. Values are ideas, guides for action when used in a concrete context, which are intermediate between the ultimate notions about existence that a people may have, and specific activities necessary to everyday life. Values are the transformation that is made between those notions, or ends, and actions. Further, those ultimate notions are related to the variations in daily activity through the value structure (Parsons 1951: 30–31). The sensitive tie that Mormonism developed with the economic base of its adherents in the nineteenth century has been maintained through the twentieth century. The measures I have used are fairly crude, but they are suggestive enough to demonstrate not only systematic responsiveness to economic conditions but also local control of part of the religious beliefs. Here is one of the ways Mormonism has developed and maintained its capacity to absorb change.

For Mormonism, an essential part of its ability to absorb change is maintaining a posture of unchanging interpretation of basic texts and truths. The church is literalistic, as any institution headed by a Prophet, Seer, and Revelator should be. How then to allow the diffuseness that exists and maintain literal consistency? One means by which the aura of literalism has been maintained is the continued use of the same sets of words. Over a period from 1910 to 1966, not more than 10% of the value lexicon was added or fell out of use. The words and phrases underwent relatively little change in expansion or contraction. The lexicon of values is stable, but the diversity that it permits is systematic, diffuse, and guided by factors quite outside of itself. The literalism and consistency Mormons claim for their Church is a reality linguistically. It also is real insofar as the corpus of value words—cooperation, self-sufficiency, vigilance, for example—is concerned. The corpus is fairly constant over 50 years. The words and allied phrases seem to be one of the consistent levels that support rapid and evidently unseen flexibility.

The quantitative analysis aimed at discovering the flexibility of that part of Mormonism represented by its value system. It indicated regular changeability depending on econoimc circumstances. It did not demonstrate individual variability since the analysis was not set up to accomplish that. The suggestion I would like to continue with is that just as flexibility in belief exists for the community as a whole over time, the same flexibility exists for the individual as well. And it is on this basis, finally, that Mormonism can be placed with that range of churches that is egalitarian, democratic, and diffuse in matters of doctrine. Although the degree of individual variability concerning values has not been measured, Mormons can be seen to be preadapted on an individual basis for the same kind of flexibility in belief that this community as a whole demonstrates. That they should be so is congruent with the hypothesis that the Church preadapts its faithful to the changeableness of the economic base, and allows individuals to adjust and survive successfully in the kind of economic conditions described earlier.

Through the 1880s Mormonism was an actively revealed religion. Joseph Smith, Brigham Young, John Taylor, and Wilford Woodruff, all Chruch Presidents, actively promulgated revelations. In addition, the chief leadership of the Church was actively involved in continual theological and philosophical debate with itself. Mormonism was actively being formed and applied through the '80s and the formulation was centralized in the hands of the President and Church leaders. On the Little Colorado the records of Sacrament Meetings, Quorums of various sorts, and Stake Conferences show that almost all the preaching and instructing was done either by visiting General Authorities or local leaders. The average Mormon rarely spoke. The very reverse is true today. In fact, today a good bishop is instructed to occupy the stand before his ward in preaching as little as possible. In the dozens of services I have seen in Arizona, most of the talks have been given by members of the ward, not by higher Church officials. To some extent I can make the same observation about ward meetings in Salt Lake City today. This is the very reverse of what happened in the nineteenth century. The leadership, be it local or from Salt Lake, dominated the pulpit and defined the meaning of the faith. The religion founded by the Prophet Joseph was doctrinally very experimental, incorporating doctrines, thoughts and practices from a broad range of sources. But that incorporation was done by very few men. It was not a universal process, and in fact the Prophet had to squash several attempts by others to proliferate the power to expand Mormon doctrine. My hypothesis is that the process of defining Mormonism which was centralized in the hands of a very few in the nineteenth century, has been decentralized so that it resides in the hands of the vast bulk of the faithful in the twentieth century. This process is latent and not recognized or labelled as such by the Church or the faithful.

Sunday School is one of the means of training individuals toward interpretive flexibility. The adult Sunday School sponsors the development of individual paradigms of belief that are more congruent with the idiosyncratic conditions an individual might face rather than the doctrinal purity traditional analyses would lead one to anticipate. All Mormons regardless of age attend Sunday School as a part of Sunday activities. Classes are age-graded and each class has a head approved by the bishopric. Classes for adults are small, averaging a few dozen people. Manuals with weekly lessons are provided and serve as the explicit guide to organize the class. The hour-long period is a formal occasion for the kind of discussion of points of Church doctrine that Mormons frequently engage in, and Sunday School provides a model that is structurally similar to usual Mormon discussions. The approach is inductive in fact, deductive in theory. A week's lesson revolves around a point of doctrine, the role of the Holy Spirit, eternal progression, the Millenium, or one of the Beatitudes, e.g., "Blessed are the meek. . . ." A concrete situational example based on the use of the principle or event is given, and then some questions of a what-would-you-do-if sort are asked those in attendance. The Church position is made clear as it applies to the doctrinal point, but the wider implications are rarely covered. Who progresses to the next life, who doesn't, who is saved and to what degree and by what means? All these proceed from a discussion of eternal progression. When a discussion involves the Beatitudes, the room for extension into all ranges of concrete application is as wide as the range of worldly variability that the members of the Sunday School class bring with them.

Typically, the Sunday School classes I attended in east-central Arizona were in fact, if not in theory, very wide-ranging. Although the lesson is prescribed by a manual prepared at church headquarters, the frank discussions usually consist of personal interpretations based on experience offered by the class membership. There is a lot of quoting textual evidence from the Bible, *Book of Mormon,* and *Doctrine and Covenants* to support differing interpretations. The amount of personal freedom an individual brings to exegesis is large, and not once in attendance at many sessions under a succession of teachers did I hear the teacher or a member of the class give what was declared to be an authoritative pronouncement on the debated issue. Discussion and interpretation were concluded when time ran out and not by a quote from a primary theological source aimed at harmonizing any disparity in the discussion. The Sunday School is a forum where literalism and doctrinal authority are present in text and language. But it is also where diversity is fostered through free use of sacred texts for justification of opinion and absence of assertive, officially authoritative resolution of issues.

Mormonism of course supports no official class of theologians or even a widely accepted exegetical tradition (Brewer 1968: 518). There is no official tradition of systematic theology. These matters, insofar as they are dealt with at all, are done by a myriad of individuals often "as the Spirit moves" them. There is a tradition of democratic and, hence, lay theology and exegesis within the Church. Exegeses produced by Church leaders, the General Authorities, or those approved by that body do have a status as more authoritative than others, but these are only coming into wide use now and even officially do not represent much more than the personal opinion of the author. At best they are the considered opinions of powerful men in the Church, at worst, amateur inductive theology based on vignettes. The absence of a theological tradition has allowed Mormonism the flexibility and consequent strength it has consistently demonstrated in dealing with pragmatic conditions. There is no burden of sanctified interpretation; doctrinal flexibility has been the fact that might seem to contradict the Mormon claim to ongoing prophesy and revelation. The absence of systematized theology and exegesis is a prerequisite for the kind of changeability the Little Colorado area demonstrates in its value system, and is a prerequisite for the personal and often idiosyncratic interpretations the faithful invent to accompany the rest of their life-way.

The conditions of idiosyncratic interpretation that exist for Spiritualists and other metaphysical groups certainly do not exist for Mormons. Mormon faithful are constrained by an extensive series of checks on doctrinal diffuseness. Mormon leaders have no intention of permitting schisms to the point where unity is threatened. The church membership does contain numbers of self-appointed doctrinal authorities who are willing to pronounce on the appropriateness of nuances of interpretation. This is a built-in check against diffuseness and proceeds again from lack of a professional body whose task it is to interpret and unify doctrine. But in the Arizona towns, which at this point can represent only themselves in this hypothesis, the unrecognized credal flexibility permits an individual freedom to define the message of the faith for himself. This is done in such a way that it provides belief-paradigms specific to personal needs and to personal changes at the same time that (1) it is unrecognized and (2) does not get so out of bounds that it is recognized as deviant and therefore threatens both Church unity and an individual's membership.

Of the three issues that this paper has been devoted to, the relationship between economics and religion has been developed to show the mutual, rather than primary, causal nature of the two sub-systems. The relationship between the two domains of culture is hardly a new idea; I have simply tried to specify it more closely for the case of Mormonism. That specification has, however, led directly to the second idea developed here, the hypothesis that Mormonism has developed a capacity to absorb change and exist in a condition of continual renewal. The condition is the result of Mormonism's close tie to the economic needs of its membership and occurs through the principle of the regulated use of a deviation amplifying mutual causal process. Mormon religion is sensitive to changes, can pick up indices from its membership, can respond to the changes by amplifying an appropriate segment of belief and ritual, and in so doing can accomodate its membership to the change. By doing so, of course, it simultaneously reinforces that change. In Mormonism, unlike most mainline churches but like the metaphysical movements, the alternation between causal factors is rapid. This is, of course, why there is no established body of protected dogma and exegesis. Within Mormonism, unlike most metaphysical churches, there is a set of regulators or, in systems theory, deviation-counteracting devices that preserve the unity of the organization. These give Mormonism the appearance of being hierarchical, authoritarian, and literalistic, and allow for the confusion that scholars have had in placing Mormonism either with orthodox churches or marginal movements. Mormonism's growth is so rapid today as a result of the existence of both deviation amplifying and counter-balancing processes in the Church. The former affect change while the latter mask it. Some would say the latter process prohibits change, but for the moment I would disagree. Most orthodox Christian churches are top-heavy with deviation counter-acting mechanisms, while most metaphysical churches suffer the consequences of unchecked deviation amplifying mechanisms. The former suffer from rigidity, the latter from schisms. By combining the two, Mormonism suffers only success. As a result, Mormonism becomes a Modern Religion absorbing and causing change. The regulators, both amplifying and counter-acting, are, however, part of a larger system of regular changes discussed next and last.

I have tried to avoid segmenting this presentation into distinct considerations of nineteenth- and then twentieth-century Mormonism. This has been done to highlight the processes of change that Mormonism has been subject to. These are more than a historical succession of events that this single religion exhibits, but rather a regular and predictable relationship between economic and religious conditions. I think those conditions co-occur in the following way. When Brigham Young and later Church leaders founded the towns on the Little Colorado, an attempt was made to provide each community with the complement of specialists needed to make a farming enterprise work. Church leaders called to the Arizona towns men who possessed either organizational abilities or technical know-how. Blacksmiths, master carpenters, brickmakers, surveyors, water control experts, and so on were placed there along with a few men with native financial and managerial genius to get things together. Although most men could farm and raise cattle, it was still a community of specialists who had spent the major portion of a lifetime training in their tasks. Today most men in these same towns are not life-time specialists but possess a common-denominator educational background which allows them to go from task to task picking up a specialty as they have to. Since rate of job turnover is high and moonlighting is common, individuals are not specialists in fact. Unlike the nineteenth century, men now become duplicates of each other insofar as their chief trait is the ability to switch jobs and pick up new skills. The economy has produced assembly-line men in two senses. Their basic skill is interchangeability and their skill allows them to revolve through the exigencies of the economic cycles with flexibility.

The economic transformation from nineteenth-century conditions to those of the twentieth century, a transformation from an undifferentiated economy with differentiated tasks to a differentiated economy with undifferentiated tasks, has been accompanied by religious changes. Authority in religious belief has been decentralized to a degree. In the nineteenth-century, doctrine was centrally defined by the process of ongoing revelation. Stability of economic task performance was matched by stability in definition of belief. In the nineteenth-century, stability in economic matters was a direct consequence of central direction and guidance in all pragmatic matters. The Church provided against all disturbances to the system. Today economic instability, in the sense of rapid shifts and changes in means of employment, is quite out of the Church's hands. It has been accompanied by a democratizing and decentralizing in some matters of belief so that the individual is allowed to construct his own code for behavior and justify it with an individualistic set of meanings, built onto doctrinal principles. An individual is allowed the kind of flexibility in belief that rapid, contradictory, and unstable economic patterns require if a man is not to find himself either without guidance or in conflict at every shift required for his own survival. Generally stated, this suggests (1) rapid economic shifts and (2) undifferentiated and revolving tasks are accompanied by decentralized formation of creeds and an increase in means for personal definition of paradigms for belief and behavior. This tendency accompanies the shift from economic independence to economic subordination. Mormonism represents the successful institutionalization of the change. And marginal Christian churches or metaphysical movements are the more general case of which Mormonism is an unusually successful example.

The question naturally poses itself: What has evolved? Obviously Mormonism has, but what part of it? There are specific items of belief that have been redefined, the concept of Zion, for example. There are points of doctrine that no longer receive the emphasis they did, the gathering of the elect and the immediacy of the Millenium. But the major change is not doctrinal, it is structural. Those who define belief have changed. The people do it now, the leaders did it then. And this change has occurred not in theory but in practice. The President is still Prophet, Seer, and Revelator. Interpretation, however, once in the hands of a few, those who also safeguarded the economy, is now in the hands of all. And that is what makes Mormonism a Modern Religion, something it was not during the first 80 years of its existence. This does not mean that the core of Mormon doctrine itself has undergone radical alteration. But given the broad base of exegesis, wide differences in the meaning of doctrine are bound to exist, and given the way meaning is arrived at, differences are also bound to go unrecognized.

ACKNOWLEDGMENTS

This research was initiated under the aegis of the Southwest Archaeological Expedition of the Field Museum of Natural History. I am grateful to the late Paul S. Martin, Expedition Director, for his support. The work reported here has been supported by research grants from the National Institute of Mental Health (MH 19116–01) and from Princeton University. I am happy to acknowledge their support.

The Office of the Church Historian, Salt Lake City, provided generous help. For assistance in the domain of scholarship on Mormons, I am indebted to Alfred Bush, Curator of Western Americana, Firestone Library, Princeton University; the late Lafe S. Hatch of Holbrook, Arizona; Albert Levine of

Snowflake, Arizona; Charles S. Peterson, Professor, Utah State University; Melvin T. Smith, Director, Utah State Historical Society; and John L. Sorenson, Professor, Brigham Young University. George S. Tanner of Salt Lake City guided me to many historical documents I would not otherwise have found.

The extensive and thoughtful comments of several people have made a significant difference in the substance of this paper. I am particularly grateful to Hildred Geertz, Thomas F. O'Dea, Sherry Ortner, Roy A. Rappaport, and Irving I. Zaretsky.

Robert Gutierez and Joel Klein were indispensable aids in research, and Janet Dolgin provided scholarly and intellectual assistance. Douglas Miller did the computer analysis. To them, I am particularly grateful.

Perspectives for Future Research

THE explicit assumption in the structure of this volume is that studies of contemporary religious groups need to take a more comprehensive view of the material, a kind of holistic approach, and attempt to understand religious innovation from more than one point of view. Indeed, we are going to have to address both the theoretical issues confronting our respective disciplines and, probably to a greater extent than in the past, issues in national life. One of the problems we face in this field is that many of the generalizations currently available about the development and spread of religious groups are often based on native familiarity with a movement rather than on careful study and verification of ethnographic detail. We carry a great deal of cultural information in our heads about such movements, and it is difficult to distinguish clearly conclusions based on investigation from those based on stereotype and prejudice.

To address this problem we need to examine more comprehensively individual religious groups. Rather than relying on general observations of the larger culture and then offering tautological explanations that religious groups are there because the culture lacks something, we might look within these groups themselves to discover how they define their role within our social system. Such an orientation would allow us to see how factors within these movements and from the external social environment combine to influence one another and produce particular institutional forms. This would result in tying together disciplinary domains through the focus on a specific unit of analysis.

A more unified view of church institutions also implies a broader view of the participants in these groups. For example, it will be harder for scholars to view a Pentecostal in his church experience in isolation from his experiences in the community. The emphasis will, hopefully, not be on fragmenting the roles of individuals, but on viewing them in their many roles, interacting with their religious and secular communities. Essentially, there is a need to move away from presenting analysis of religious institutions only within their religious activity. Rather, we need to see how religious activity is affected by the daily life experience of the adherent and the secular social institutions of the community.

It is in light of these observations that the approach we feel would produce clear empirical information and more realistic theoretical orientation is the one we choose to call the "ethnography of church institutions." More specifically, it is the ethnography of building church institutions. The specific unit of analysis would be a particular church. Our efforts would be toward understanding how a church is founded, maintained, and dissolved. So many contemporary churches are established and last for only a short period of time, ranging from a few weeks to several months to a year or two. It is feasible for a researcher to do field work with a group and observe its development from onset to end. The important point here is that it is not a question of witnessing the development of the church from beginning to end, its life cycle, for its own sake, but of being aware of the issues and forces that are involved at each stage of development. By viewing the church through the vantage point of its organizers or founders one comes face to face with important theoretical questions that are posed by various disciplines which attempt to study these institutions.

When religious innovators build a church they invariably hope that it will be tolerated by the community and that the church will enjoy some stability and permanence. The survival of a church depends on its leaders' knowledge of and ability to secure the proper certification for the organization and its practitioners; the design of rituals and belief systems that can withstand community antagonism and attract adherents; the ability to find a location for the church that would make it accessible to those sectors of the population most likely to attend; and the creation of an economic base upon which to exist. These are some of the issues that are significant in the building of church institutions. These issues also match the disciplinary interests in churches such as law, psychology, economics, anthropology, and so on.

In the past when scholars from these fields have studied a church they have been primarily interested in it as an example with data for certain purposes in their respective professions. For example, in scholarly writings about church-state cases the issue is not what happens to a given church as a result of a court's decision, and how it lives with it, is changed by it, etc. Rather, legal studies are interested in court decisions in terms of the legal issues and legal thinking in general. The church as an institution remains essentially unimportant, and falls into the interstitial spaces between various disciplinary concerns.

By focusing on comprehensive descriptive studies we do not minimize the importance of solving theoretical problems within the various disciplines. It is only a question of relating various domains to one another through more complete and comprehensive empirical observation.

Within the framework of the ethnography of church institutions there are several kinds of data that we sorely need. There is a need for long range, longitudinal studies that test and examine our generalizations, and give us some time depth as verification of our findings. The impact of longitudinal studies would not only give us information on the changing social organization of these churches, the kind and type of migration between them, the kind of order in which "seekers" travel from religion to religion and what features they look for in each one; it will also allow us to know whether there is a pattern to the kinds of innovations individuals are receptive to and seek out. Such studies will allow us to trace the direction of the population movement between churches and the conditions responsible for them. The longitudinal study is a way of cutting through the uniqueness of each group at a moment in time and is thus a research tool showing how groups are similar and different over time.

We also lack substantial quantitative and statistical data on these groups. There have been studies that have relied on sampling, but we need more quantitative material that describes the characteristics of these movements. Long-term studies and increased quantitative material are not desirable solely for their own sake; their main purpose is to allow comparative work. One area badly in need of comparison is how various groups deal with the range of human problems brought to them and their respective success in handling them. Further comparisons can be made with the many such movements in other societies. We need to look comparatively at the social conditions that generate certain religious innovations and the consequences these movements produce. We could then include data about our own society in cross-cultural comparisons with data from developing countries.

One paramount area of neglect and yet a crucial building block of these movements is the kind of function they perform for their adherents. We claim that people bring personal problems to these churches and that the groups offer them some kind of help or cure. Just what are the problems? How are they conceptualized by the adherents, how are they redefined by the church, and what kind of help is offered? This is still an area of fundamental ignorance. We always use functional models that show how these movements help orient people and describe the kind of therapy these groups offer, but can we point to specific numbers of people, what they suffered from, and what specifically was done for them, with what results? These data could be gathered by focusing on individuals as they migrate from group to group as well as by studying individual groups longitudinally.

What this suggestion is really aiming at is evaluating these groups in terms of their actual impact on their members. We often speak of these groups as alternative forms of rehabilitation or mental health care in a community. Yet few of us are really in a position to point out the specific area that these groups are competent in, not only in our analytical terms, but even in their own terms. How do they define problems and solutions, and how do they define cure and relapse? Such evaluation is of course one of the hardest tasks in social science. There is no way of avoiding such questions as long as we seek to verify our functional models scientifically and to escape circular arguments.

In essence, the role that the social scientist will continue to play in this area is explaining American society to his fellow countrymen. Many people feel that we should not allow prejudice or our own religious or social beliefs to interfere with studying a currently vibrant and important area. The religious movements discussed here grew out of the soil of this country, and they will probably be incorporated into the system in a way that will render them part of the established order. There should be neither exasperation with diversity nor fear of pluralism, but a realization that these groups and their incorporation into mainline society are the very tradition of this country. The only source for exasperation is that all too little is known about this major constituent of the American experience.

Aberle, David F. 1965. A note on relative deprivation as applied to millenarian and other cult movements. In *Reader in comparative religion*. W. A. Lessa and E. Z. Vogt, eds. New York: Harper and Row.

———. 1966. The peyote religion among the Navahos. Chicago: Aldine.

Abrahams, Roger D. 1962. Playing the dozens. *Journal of American Folklore* 75:209–220.

———. 1964. *Deep down in the jungle: Negro narrative folklore from the streets of Philadelphia*. Chicago: Aldine.

Adams, Richard N. and Arthur J. Rubel. 1967. Sickness and social relations. In *Handbook of Middle American Indians*, Vol. 6. Roger Wauchope, ed. Austin: University of Texas Press.

Adams, Robert, and Robert J. Fox. 1972. Mainlining Jesus: the new trip. *Transaction Society* 9(4):50–55.

Adelson, Daniel. 1970. A concept of comprehensive community mental health. In *Community psychology and mental health*. Daniel Adelson and Betty Kalis, eds. Scranton, Pa.: Chandler.

Adler, Nathan. 1966a. Campus drug culture. *Per Se* (Fall):38–41.

———. 1966b. The use of drugs and the manipulation of the self. *Issues in Criminology* 2:125–136.

———. 1968. The antinomian personality: the hippie character type. *Psychiatry* 31:325–338.

———. 1970a. Ethics, ethos, and actualization: the paradigm of the antinomian therapies. *Issues in Criminology* 5(1):85–89.

———. 1970b. Kicks, drugs, and politics. *Psychoanalytic Review* 57:432–441.

Adorno, T. W. 1957. The stars down to earth. In *Amerikastudien Jahrbuch*, Vol. 2. Heidelberg Universitats Verlag.

——— and others. 1950. The authoritarian personality. New York: Harper.

Ahlstrom, Sydney E. 1970. The problem of the history of religion in America. *Church History* 39:224–335.

———. 1972. *A religious history of the American people*. New Haven: Yale University Press.

Alberts, W. E. 1963. Personality and attitude toward juvenile delinquency: a study of Protestant ministers. *Journal of Social Psychology* 60:71–83.

Alland, Alexander. 1962. Possession in a revivalistic Negro church. *Journal for the Scientific Study of Religion* 1:204–213.

Allport, Gordon. 1955. *Becoming*. New Haven: Yale University Press.

American Law Review. 1967. Provision of religious facilities for prisoners. Vol. 12:1276 (third series).

————. 1969. Drug crime defense—religious freedom. Vol. 35:939 (third series).

Amis, Kingsley. 1960. *New maps of hell.* New York: Harcourt, Brace.

Anderson, E. 1958. Messianic popular movements in the Lower Congo. *Studia Ethnographica Upsaliensa,* Vol. 14. Uppsala.

Andrews, Edward D. 1963. *The people called Shakers: a search for the perfect society.* New York: Dover.

Angus, Samuel. 1925. *The mystery religions and Christianity.* New York: Scribner.

Arieti, S. 1947. The processes of expectation and anticipation, their genetic development, neural base and role in psychopathology. *Journal of Nervous and Mental Diseases* 106:471–481.

————. 1965. Contributions to cognition from psychoanalytic theory. *Science and Psychoanalysis* 8:16–35.

Arizona Basic Economic Data. 1950–1968. Arizona State Employment Service. Phoenix, Arizona.

Arrington, Leonard J. 1958. *Great basin kingdom.* Cambridge: Harvard University Press.

————. 1961. *From wilderness to empire: the role of Utah in Western economic history.* Institute of American Studies Monograph 1. Salt Lake City: University of Utah Press.

Ashby, W. Ross. 1968. Regulation and control. In *Modern systems research for the behavioral scientist.* Walter Buckley, ed. Chicago: Aldine.

Atkins, Gaius G. 1923. *Modern religious cults and movements.* New York: Fleming H. Revell.

AWAKE! 1969. Bi-monthly magazine of the New World Society of Jehovah's Witnesses. September 22, p. 10.

Babbie, Earl. 1966. The third civilization: an examination for Sokagakkai. *Review of Religious Research,* 7:101–121.

Bach, Marcus. 1946. *They have found a faith.* Indianapolis: Bobbs-Merrill.

————. 1951. *Faith and my friends.* Indianapolis: Bobbs-Merrill.

————. 1952. *Strange altars.* Indianapolis: Bobbs-Merrill.

————. 1961. *Strange sects and curious cults.* New York: Dodd, Mead.

————. 1969. *The inner ecstasy.* New York: World.

Bacon, Leonard W. 1897. *A history of American Christianity.* New York: The Christian Literature Company.

Baeta, C. G. 1962. *Prophetism in Ghana.* London: S.C.M. Press.

Baird, Robert. 1856. *Religion in America.* New York: Harper.

Balandier, G. 1948. Femmes possédées et leurs chants, *Présence Africain* (Paris) 5:749–754.

Bandura, A., E. B. Blanchard, and B. J. Ritter. 1969. The relative efficacy of modeling therapeutic approaches for producing behavioral, attitudinal, and affective changes. In *Behavioral approaches to abnormal psychology.* L. Ullman and L. Krasner, eds. Englewood Cliffs: Prentice-Hall.

Barber, Bernard. 1941. A socio-cultural interpretation of the peyote cult. *American Anthropologist* 43:673–675.

Barnett, H. Garner. 1957. *Indian Shakers: a messianic cult of the Pacific Northwest*. Carbondale: Southern Illinois University Press.

Barnett, S. A. 1971. Approaches to caste and change in South India. Unpublished paper, Princeton University.

————. in press. The process of withdrawal in a South Indian caste. In *Entrepreneurship and occupational diversification in the modernization of South Asian societies*. Milton Singer, ed.

Barrows, John Henry, ed. 1893. *The world's parliament of religions: an illustrated and popular story of the world's first parliament of religions, held in Chicago in connection with the Columbian Exposition of 1893*. Two Volumes. Chicago: The Parliament Publishing Company.

Bascom, W. 1944. The sociological role of the Yoruba cult group. *Memoirs of the American Anthropological Association*, Vol. 63.

————. 1951. The Yoruba in Cuba. *Nigeria* 37:14–21.

————. 1952. Two forms of Afro-Cuban divination. In *Acculturation in the Americas*. Sol Tax, ed. Chicago: University of Chicago Press.

Bascom, W. 1969a. *Ifa divination*. Bloomington: University of Indiana Press.

————. 1969b. *The Yoruba of Southwestern Nigeria*. New York: Holt, Rinehart, and Winston.

Bastide, R. 1967. *Les Amériques Noires*. Paris: Editions Payot.

Bateman, M. B., and J. S. Jensen. 1958. The effect of religious background on modes of handling anger. *Journal of Social Psychology* 47:113–141.

Bateson, M. C. 1968. Linguistics in the semiotic frame. *Linguistics* 39:5–17.

————. 1970. *Structural continuity in poetry: a linguistic study of five early Arabic odes*. Paris: Ecole des hautes études.

Baum, Gregory. 1970. Does the world remain disenchanted? *Social Research* 37(2):153–202.

Bax, Ernest B. 1903. *Rise and fall of the Anabaptists*. New York: Macmillan.

Beadle, J. H. 1870. *Life in Utah*. Philadelphia: National Publishing Company.

Beals, Ralph. 1953. Acculturation. In *Anthropology today*. A. L. Kroeber, ed. Chicago: University of Chicago Press.

Beattie, John, and John Middleton, eds. 1969. *Spirit mediumship and society in Africa*. New York: Africana Publishing Company.

Beeson, Paul B. 1968. Review of *Sickness and society*. Hollingshead and Duff. *Yale Journal of Biology and Medicine* 41:226–241.

Bell, Daniel. 1971. Religion in the sixties. *Social Research* 38(2):447–497.

Bellah, Robert N. 1965a. *Religion and progress in modern Asia*. New York: The Free Press

————. 1965b. Religious evolution. In *Reader in comparative religion*. W. A. Lessa and E. Z. Vogt, eds. New York: Harper and Row (second edition).

————. 1970. *Beyond belief*. New York: Harper and Row.

Bellak, Leopold, ed. 1964. *Handbook of community psychiatry and community mental health*. New York: Grune and Stratton.

Belshaw, C. S. 1950. The significance of modern cults in Melanesian development. *The Australian Outlook* 4:116–125.

Bem, D. J. 1967. Self-perception: the dependent variable of human performance. *Organizational Behavior and Human Performance* 2:105–121.

Bender, L. 1953. *Aggression, hostility and anxiety in children.* Springfield, Ill.: Charles C. Thomas.

Bendix, R. 1960. *Max Weber: an intellectual portrait.* New York: Doubleday.

Bennett, John W. 1969. *Northern plainsmen.* Chicago: Aldine.

Benson, Larry D. 1966. The literary character of Anglo-Saxon narrative poetry. *Publications of the Modern Language Association* 81:334–341.

Berendt, Ronald M. 1952. A cargo movement in the Eastern Central Highlands of New Guinea. *Oceania* 23:40–65.

Beres, D. 1965. Psychoanalytic notes on the history of morality. *Journal of the American Psychoanalytic Association* 13:3–37.

Berger, Peter. 1954. The sociological study of sectarianism. *Social Research* 21:467–485.

———. 1965. Towards a Sociological Analysis of Psychoanalysis. *Social Research* 32(1):26–41.

———. 1967. *The sacred canopy.* New York: Doubleday.

———. 1970. Between System and Horde. In *Movement and Revolution.* Peter Berger and R. Neuhaus. New York: Doubleday.

——— and Brigette Berger. 1971. The eve of the bluing of America. *New York Times,* February 15, p. 23.

——— and Thomas Luckmann. 1966. *The social construction of reality.* New York: Doubleday.

Beringer, K. 1927. *Der Meskalinrausch.* Berlin: Springer Verlag.

Berkowitz, L. 1962. *Aggression.* New York: McGraw-Hill.

Berlin, Brent. 1968. Tzeltal numeral classifiers: a study in ethnographic semantics. *Janua Linguarum* 70 (Series *Practica*). The Hague: Mouton.

Bernstein, B. 1958. Some sociological determinants of perception: an inquiry into sub-cultural differences. *British Journal of Sociology* 9:168–174.

Berreman, Gerald D. 1966. Anemic and emetic analysis in social anthropology. *American Anthropologist* 68:346–354.

Bertalanffy, L. von. 1958. Comments on aggression. *Bulletin of the Menninger Clinic* 22:50–58.

Bettelheim, B. 1954. *Symbolic wounds: puberty rites and the envious male.* Glencoe, Ill.: The Free Press.

Beynon, Edmann D. 1938. The voodoo cult among Negro migrants in Dttroit. *American Journal of Sociology* 43:894–907.

Bhaktivedanta, A. C. 1968a. *The Bhagavad Gita as it is: with introduction, translation, and authorized purport.* London: Collier-Macmillan, Ltd.

———. 1968b. The teachings of Lord Chaitanya: a treatise on factual spiritual knowledge. New York: International Society for Krishna Consciousness.

———. 1969. *Śrī Īsopanishad: the knowledge that brings one nearer to the supreme personality of godhead, Kṛṣṇa, with original Sanskrit text, Roman transliteration, English equivalents, translated and elaborate purports.* Boston: ISKON Books.

———. 1970a. The highest love. *Back to Godhead* 35:4–8.

———. 1970b. *Krsna: the reservoir of pleasure and other essays.* Boston: ISKON Books.

———. 1970c. *The nectar of devotion: a summary study of Srila Rupa Gosvami's Bhaktirasamrta-sindu.* Boston: ISKON Books.

Blackwell, Anna. 1875. Translator's preface to *The spirit's book.* Allan Kardec. Boston: Colby and Rich.

Blau, Joseph L. 1964. *Cornerstones of religious freedom in America.* New York: Harper and Row.

Bloch-Hoell, Nils. 1964. *The Pentecostal movement.* Oslo: Universitetforlaget.

Bloxham, Peter. 1970. The devil and Cecil Williamson. *New York Times,* April 19, Section 10, p. 5.

Blunsdon, Norman. 1963. *A popular dictionary of Spiritualism.* New York: Citadel Press.

Boddington, Harry. 1947. *The university of Spiritualism.* London: Spiritualist Press.

Borgoras, W. 1967. *The Chukchee.* New York: American Museum of Natural History.

Boisen, Anton T. 1939. Economic distress and religious experience. *Psychiatry* 2:185–194.

———. 1955. *Religion in crisis and custom.* New York: Harper.

Bolman, William. 1968. Cross-cultural psychotherapy. *American Journal of Psychiatry* 124(9):1237–1244.

Bone, Ray. 1964. We witches are simple people. *Life* 57:55–62.

The Book of Mormon. 1961. Salt Lake City: The Church of Jesus Christ of Latter-Day Saints.

Borhek, J. T. 1965. Role orientations and organizational stability. *Human Organization* 24:332–338.

Bourguignon, Erika. 1965. The self, the behavioral environment, and the theory of spirit possession. In *Context and meaning in cultural anthropology.* M. Spiro, ed. New York: The Free Press.

———. 1968a. *A cross-cultural study of dissociational states.* Columbus: The Ohio State University Research Foundation.

———. 1968b. Divination, transe et possession en Afrique Transsaharienne. In *La divination.* A. Caquot and M. Leibovici, eds. Paris: Presses Universitaires de France.

———. 1970. Ritual dissociation and possession belief in Caribbean Negro religion. In *Afro-American anthropology: contemporary perspectives.* N. Whitten and J. Szwed, eds. New York: The Free Press.

———. 1972. Dreams and altered states of consciousness in anthropological research. In *Psychological anthropology.* F.L.K. Hsu, ed. New edition. Cambridge, Mass.: Schenkman.

————, ed., 1973. *Religion, altered states of consciousness, and social change.* Columbus: The Ohio State University Press.

————. 1974. *Culture and the varieties of consciousness.* Reading, Mass.: Addison-Wesley Module in Anthropology, No. 47.

———— and Lenora Greenbaum. 1973. *Diversity and homogeneity in world societies.* New Haven, Conn.: HRAF Press.

———— **and Louanna Pettay. 1964. Spirit possession, trance and cross-cultural research. In *Symposium on new approaches to religion*. J. Helms, ed. Proceedings of the Annual Meeting of the American Ethnological Society. Seattle, Washington.**

Bousefield, W. A., and B. H. Cohen. 1955. The occurrence of clustering in the recall of randomly arranged words of different frequencies of usage. *Journal of General Psychology* 52:83–95.

Bowen, E. 1964. *Return to Laughter.* New York: Doubleday.

Bowers, M. K. 1963. *Conflicts of the clergy.* New York: T. Nelson.

Bowers, M. K., B. Berkowitz, and S. Brecher. 1958. Therapeutic implications of analytic group psychotherapy of religious personnel. *International Journal of Group Psychotherapy* 8:243–256.

Boyer, L. B. 1961a. Notes on the personality structure of a North American Indian shaman. *Journal of Hillside Hospital* 10:14–33.

————. 1961b. Remarks on the personality of shamans. *Psychoanalytic Study of Society* 2:233–254.

————. 1964. Further remarks concerning shamans and shamanism. *The Israel Annals of Psychiatry and Related Disciplines* 2:235–257.

———— and others. 1964. Comparison on the shamans and pseudoshamans of the Apaches of the Mescalero Indian reservation: a Rorshach study. *Journal of Projective Techniques and Personality Assessment* 28 (2):173–180.

Bracelin, J. L. 1960. *Gerald Gardner: witch.* London: Octagon Press.

Braddeson, Walter. 1969. *Scientology for the millions.* Los Angeles: Sherbourne Press.

Braden, Charles S. 1953. *These also believe.* New York: Macmillan.

————. 1963. *Spirits in rebellion: the rise and development of new thought.* Dallas: Southern Methodist University Press.

————. 1969. *Christian Science today.* Dallas: Southern Methodist University Press.

Braden, W. 1967. *The private sea: LSD and the search for God.* Chicago: Quadrangle Books.

Bram, J. 1957. Jehovah's Witnesses and the values of American culture. *Transactions of the New York Academy of Science* 19:47–54.

Brancato, John R. 1968. Characterization in religious property tax exemption: what is religion? *Notre Dame Lawyer* 44 (1):60–80.

Brauer, Jerald C. 1953. *Protestantism in America: a narrative history.* Philadelphia: Westminster Press.

————. 1968. Changing perspectives on religion in America. In *Reinterpre-*

tation in American church history. Jerald C. Brauer, ed. Chicago: University of Chicago Press.

Brenman, M. 1954. On teasing and being teased: and the problems of "moral masochism." In *Psychoanalytic psychiatry and psychology.* R. P. Knight and C. R. Friedman, eds. New York: International Universities Press.

Breton, André. 1969. *Manifestos of surrealism.* Ann Arbor: University of Michigan Press.

Brewer, David L. 1968. The Mormons. In *The religious situation: 1968.* Donald Cutler, ed. Boston: Beacon Press.

Bro, Harmon H. 1970. *Edgar Cayce on religion and psychic experience.* New York: Paperback Library.

Brodie, Fawn M. 1945. *No man knows my history.* New York: A. A. Knopf.

Brodman, Keeve, Albert J. Erdmann, Jr., and Harold G. Wolff. 1949. *Cornell medical index health questionnaire manual.* New York: Cornell University Medical College.

Bronner, A. 1964. Psychotherapy with religious patients (a review of the literature). *American Journal of Psychotherapy* 18:475–487.

Broom, Leonard, and John I. Kitsuse. 1955. The validation of acculturation. *American Anthropologist* 57:44–48.

Brown, O. G., and W. L. Lowe. 1951. Religious beliefs and personality characteristics of college students. *Journal of Social Psychology* 33:103–129.

Brown, Roger. 1965. The authoritarian personality and the organization of attitudes. In *Social psychology.* New York: The Free Press.

Bruce, David. 1956. Effects of context upon the intelligibility of heard speech. In *Information theory.* Colin Cherry, ed. London: Butterworths.

Bruyn, Severeyn T. 1966. *The human perspective in sociology.* Englewood Cliffs: Prentice-Hall.

Buber, Martin. 1958. *I and thou.* New York: Charles Scribner's Sons.

Buck, John, and Emmanuel Hammer. 1969. *Advances in the house-tree-person techniques: variations and applications.* Los Angeles: Western Psychological Services.

Bucke, R. M. 1901. *Cosmic consciousness: a study of the evolution of the human mind.* Philadelphia: Innis and Son.

Burke, Tom. 1970. Princess Leda's castle in the air. *Esquire* 73:104–109, 181–182.

Burkholder, J. R. 1969. Religion in the first amendment: a social theory approach to constitutional interpretation. Unpublished Ph.D. dissertation. Harvard University.

Burling, Robbins. 1964. Cognition and componential analysis: God's truth or hocus pocus. *American Anthropologist* 66:20–29.

Burr, George L., ed. 1914. *Narratives of the witchcraft cases, 1648–1706.* New York: Charles Scribner and Sons.

Burr, Nelson R. 1961. *A critical bibliography of religion in America.* Princeton: Princeton University Press.

Burridge, Kenelm. 1960. *Mambu*. London: Methuen.

Cabrera, Lydia. 1957. *Anagó*. La Habana: Ediciones C. R.

———. 1968. *El monte*. Miami: Rema Press (second edition).

———. 1969. *La sociedad secreta Abakuá*. Miami: Ediciones C. R.

California Law Review. 1968. January issue.

Calley, Malcolm J. C. 1965. *God's people: West Indian Pentecostal sects in England*. London: Oxford University Press.

Cameron, N. 1951. Perceptual organization and behavior pathology. In *Perception: an approach to personality*. R. Blake and G. Ramsey, eds. New York: Ronald Press.

———. 1959. The paranoid pseudo-community revisited. *American Journal of Sociology* 65:52–59.

Campbell, John W. 1953. The place of science fiction. In *Modern science fiction*. Reginald Bretner, ed. New York: Coward-McCann.

Cannon, Walter B. 1942. The "voodoo" death. *American Anthropologist* 44:169–181.

Cantril, A. Hadley. 1941. *The psychology of social movements*. London: Chapman and Hall.

Capron, W. E. 1855. *Modern Spiritualism*. Boston: S. Marsh.

Carey, J. T. 1968. Marijuana use among the new bohemians. *Journal of Psychedelic Drugs* 2:79–92.

Carrington, H. 1930. *The story of psychic science*. New York: Psychical Research.

Carmichael, L., H. P. Hogan, and A. A. Walter. 1932. An experimental study of the effect of language on the reproduction of visually perceived form. *Journal of Experimental Psychology* 15:73–86.

Carneiro, Edison. 1964. *Ladinos e Crioulos*. Rio de Janeiro: Editôra Civilização Brasileira S. A.

Carnell, J. E. 1959. *The case for orthodox theology*. Philadelphia: Westminster Press.

Caro Baroja, J. 1964. *The world of witches*. Chicago: University of Chicago Press.

Carroll, H. K. 1893. *The religious forces of the United States*. New York: The Christian Literature Company.

Carson, R. C. 1960. An introduction to MMPI interpretation. Unpublished manual. Duke University (revised 1969).

Carter, Huntly, ed. 1920. *Spiritualism, its present day meaning: a symposium*. Philadelphia: Lippincott.

Carvalho-Neto, Paulo de. 1965. *El Negro Uruguayo*. Quito.

Casey, Robert P. 1941. Transient cults. *Psychiatry* 4:525–534.

Castenada, Carlos. 1968. *The teachings of Don Juan: a Jacqui way of knowledge*. Berkeley: University of California Press.

Catton, William R. 1957. What Kinds of People Does a Religious Cult Attract? *American Sociological Review* 22:561–566.

Cawte, J. F., and M. A. Kidson. 1964. Australian ethnopsychiatry: the Walbiri doctor. *Medical Journal of Australia* 2:977–983.

Cerletti, V. 1950. Old and new information about electro-shock. *American Journal of Psychiatry* 107:87–94.

Charlton, D. G. 1963. *Secular religions in France, 1815–1870*. London: Oxford University Press.

Chomsky, Noam. 1957. *Syntactic structures*. The Hague: Mouton.

———. 1965. *Aspects of a theory of syntax*. Cambridge: M.I.T. Press.

Christensen, C. W. 1960. The occurrence of mental illness in the ministry: family origins. *Journal of Pastoral Care* 14:13–20.

———. 1961. The occurrence of mental illness in the ministry: psychotic disorders. *Journal of Pastoral Care* 15:153–159.

———. 1963. The occurrence of mental illness in the ministry: personality disorders. *Journal of Pastoral Care* 17:125–135.

Clark, Elmer T. 1949. *The small sects in America*. Nashville: Abingdon.

Clark, H. H., and E. V. Clark. 1968. Semantic distinctions and memory for complex sentences. *Quarterly Journal of Experimental Psychology* 20: 129–138.

Clark, Margaret. 1959. *Health in Mexican-American cultures*. Los Angeles: University of California Press.

Clark, R. W. 1968. *The Huxleys*. London: Heineman.

Clark, Uriah. 1863. *Plain guide to Spiritualism*. New York.

Clark, Walter H. 1969. *Chemical ecstasy: psychedelic drugs and religion*. New York: Sheed and Ward.

Cleaver, Eldridge. 1971. In *Good Times* (weekly newspaper). San Francisco, February 5.

Clemhout, Simons. 1964. Typology of nativistic movements. *Man* 64 (7): 14–15.

Cohen, Mabel. 1952. Countertransference and anxiety. *Psychiatry* 15 (3): 231–243.

Cohen, Norman. 1957. *Pursuit of the millennium*. New York: Essential Books.

Cohen, Werner. 1955. Jehovah's Witnesses as a proletarian movement. *The American Scholar* 24:281–298.

Colby, B. N. 1966. Ethnographic semantics: a preliminary survey (with comments). *Current Anthropology* 7:3–32.

Colby, K. M. 1955. *Energy and structure in psychoanalysis*. Nwe York: Ronald Press.

Cole, Marley. 1955. *Jehovah's Witnesses: the new world society*. New York: Vantage Press.

———. 1957. *Triumphant kingdom*. New York: Criterion Books.

Conklin, Harold C. 1955. Hanunoo color categories. *Southwestern Journal of Anthropology* 11:339–344.

———. 1962. Lexicographical treatment of folk taxonomies. In Problems in lexicography. F. W. Householder, ed. *International Journal of American Linguistics* 28 (2):119–141.

Conn, Charles W. 1955. *Like a mighty army*. Cleveland, Tenn.: Church of God Publishing House.

Cooley, C. H. 1902. *Human nature and the social order.* New York: Charles Scribner.

————. 1909. *Social Organization.* New York: Charles Scribner.

Corbin, Henry. 1969. *Creative imagination in the Ṣūfism of Ibn 'Arabī.* Princeton University Press.

Coty, James F. 1971. Guru authority and its implications for social organization. Paper presented at the annual meeting of the Society for the Scientific Study of Religion. Chicago.

Cowley, Malcolm. 1934. *Exile's return: a literary odyssey of the 1920's.* New York: Viking Press.

Coyner, John M., ed. 1882. *Handbook on Mormonism.* Salt Lake City: Handbook Publishing Company.

Cox, Harvey. 1970. *The feast of fools.* New York: Harper and Row.

Cracke, Waud H. 1967. The maintenance of the ego: implications of sensory deprivation research for psychoanalytic ego psychology. *British Journal of Medical Psychology* 40:17–27.

Crawford, Frederick. 1961. *The forgotten egg.* Austin: Texas Department of Health.

Crawford, J. R. 1967. *Witchcraft and sorcery in Rhodesia.* London: Oxford University Press.

Cristiani, Leon. 1962. *Evidences of Satan in the modern world.* New York: Macmillan.

Cronshaw, James. 1968. The hippies: beyond pot and acid. In *Maharishi the Guru.* Martin Ebon, ed. New York: New American Library.

Cross, Whitney R. 1950. *The burned-over district.* Ithaca: Cornell University Press.

Crow, William B. 1970. *A history of witchcraft, magic and occultism.* North Hollywood, Cal.: Wilshire Book Company.

Culten, George B. 1927. *Speaking with tongues.* New Haven: Yale University Press.

Curry, Donald. 1968. Pentecostalism in Brazil. Unpublished Ph.D. dissertation. Columbia University.

Custance, J. 1951. *Wisdom, madness, and folly: the philosophy of a lunatic.* London: Gollancz.

Damboriena, Prudencio. 1969. *Tongues as of fire: Pentecostalism in contemporary Christianity.* Cleveland: Corups Books.

Darton, Robert. 1970. *Messmerism and the end of the Enlightenment in France.* New York: Schocken Books.

Dator, James A. 1969. *Soka Gakkai: Builders of the Third Civilization.* Seattle: University of Washington Press.

Deese, James. 1970. *Psycholinguistics.* Boston: Allyn and Bacon.

De Félice, Philippe. 1936. *Poisons sacrés, ivresses divines: essai sur quelques formes inférieures de la mystique.* Paris: Editions Albin.

Demerath, N. J. and P. E. Hammond. 1969. *Religion in social context.* New York: Random House.

Denison Alumnus. 1970. April, p. 15.

De Ropp, R. S. 1957. *Drugs and the mind*. New York: St. Martin's Press.

Dillenberger, John. 1960. *Protestant thought and natural science*. New York: Doubleday.

Doctrine and Covenants. 1965. Cambridge: University Press, Inc.

Dodson, Victor. 1969. *Devil sex*. North Hollywood, Cal.: Barclay House.

Dohrman, H. T. 1958. *California cult: the story of mankind united*. Boston: Beacon Press.

Dohrn, Bernadine. 1970. New morning—changing weather. *The Berkeley Tribe*, December 18.

Dollard, J., and N. E. Miller. 1950. *Personality and psychotherapy*. New York: McGraw-Hill.

Donovan, Robert K. 1954. The ultra-violet world: Spiritualism in Great Britain, 1852–1898. Unpublished honors thesis. Harvard University.

Dorchester, Daniel. 1888. *Christianity in the United States*. New York: Phillips and Hunt.

Douglas, Mary. 1966. *Purity and danger*. London: Routledge and Kegan Paul.

————. 1967. Witch beliefs in Central Africa. *Africa* 37:72–80.

————. 1970. *Natural symbols*. New York: Pantheon.

Doyle, Arthur C. 1926. *The history of Spiritualism*. New York: George H. Doran.

Drake, St. Clair, and Horace R. Cayton. 1962. *Black metropolis: a study of Negro life in a northern city*. New York: Harper Torchback.

Draper, E., and others. 1965. On the diagnostic values of religious ideation. *Archives of General Psychology* 13:202–207.

Dreger, R. M. 1952. Some personality correlates of religious attitudes as determined by projective techniques. *Psychological Monographs* 66 (335).

Du Bois, W.E.B. 1903. *The soul of black folk*. New York: Simon and Schuster.

Dumont, Louis. 1965. The modern conception of the individual: notes on its genesis. *Contributions to Indian Society* 8:13–61.

Dumont, Matthew. 1968. *The absurd healer*. New York: Science House.

Dunn, J.A.C. 1968. Don't worry, be happy—I will help you. *Red Clay Reader*, pp. 71–80.

Dynes, Russell. 1955. Church-sect typology and socio-economic status. *American Sociological Review* 20:555–560.

————. 1957. The consequences of sectarianism for social participation. *Social Forces* 35:331–334.

East Village Other, The. 1971. Open letter from the Panther 21 to the Weathermen underground. February 23, pp. 3, 19.

Eaton, K. W., and R. J. Weil. 1955. *Culture and mental disorders*. Glencoe, Ill.: The Free Press.

Eckman, Beverly. 1969. Witch sounds his trumpet for Satan. *Detroit News*, October 19, 18-B.

Edwards, Jonathan. 1959. A treatise concerning religious affections. New Haven: Yale University Press.

Eisenstadt, S. N. 1956. From generation to generation. New York: The Free Press.

———. 1961. Archetypal patterns of youth. In *The Challenge of Youth*. Erik H. Erikson, ed. New York: Doubleday.

Eister, Allan W. 1949. The Oxford Group Movement: a typological analysis. *Sociology and Social Research* 34:116–124.

———. 1950. *Drawing-room conversation: a sociological account of the Oxford Group Movement*. Durham: Duke University Press.

———. 1967. Toward a radical critique of church-sect typologizing. *Journal for the Scientific Study of Religion* 6:85–90.

Eliade, Mircea. 1959. Cosmos and history. New York: Harper Torchback.

———. 1964. Shamanism: archaic techniques of ecstasy. New York: Pantheon.

Elinson, Howard. 1965. The implications of Pentecostal religion for intellectualism, politics, and race relations. *American Journal of Sociology* 70:403–415.

Engel, G. L. 1962. *Psychological development in health and disease*. Philadelphia: W. B. Saunders.

Erikson, E. H. 1966. The ontogeny of ritualisation. In *Discussion on ritualisation of behavior in animals and men*. J. Huxley, ed. London: Royal Society of London Philosophical Transactions, Series B, Vol. 251.

Erikson, Kai T. 1970. Sociology and the historical perspective. *The American Sociologist* 5:331–338.

Erikson, M. H. 1965. A special inquiry with Aldous Huxley into the nature and character of various states of consciousness. *American Journal of Clinical Hypnosis* 8:17–33.

Evans, W. N. 1943. Notes on the conversion of John Bunyan: a study in English Puritanism. *International Journal of Psychoanalysis* 24:176–184.

Evans-Pritchard, E. E. 1937. Witchcraft, oracles, and magic among the Azande. Oxford: Clarendon Press.

———. 1964. Zande theology. In *Social anthropology and other essays*. Glencoe, Illinois: The Free Press.

———. 1965. *Theories of primitive religion*. Oxford: Clarendon Press.

Fairfield, F. G. 1875. Ten years with spiritual mediums: an inquiry concerning the etiology of certain phenomena called Spiritualism. New York: D. Appleton.

Ferguson, Charles W. 1940. *The confusion of tongues*. Grand Rapids, Michigan: Zondervan.

Fernandez, J. W. 1964. The idea and the symbol of the Savior as a Gabon syncretistic cult. *International Review of Missions* 53:281–289.

Ferreira, A. 1951. O Maracatú. In *É de Tororó*. Rio de Janeiro: Editôra da Casa do Estudante do Brasil.

Festinger, Leon. 1957. *A theory of cognitive dissonance*. Evanston, Ill.: Row, Peterson.

————, H. Riecken, and S. Schacter. 1956. *When prophecy fails.* Minneapolis: University of Minnesota Press.

Fick, Luise. 1939. *Die Deutsche Jugend-Bewegung.* Eugen Diederich Verlag.

Firth, Raymond. 1955. A Theory of "Cargo Cults." *Man* 142:130–132.

Fischer, Roland. 1970. Ueber das Rhythmisch-Ornamentale im Halluzinatorisch-Schöpferischen. *Confinia Psychiatrica* 13:1–25.

Fish, Joseph, and others. n.d. Snowflake stake: history and settlement of the Snowflake area 1870–1912. Manuscript. Office of the Church Historian, Salt Lake City, Utah.

Fitzgerald, D. 1970. Prophetic speech in Gâ spirit mediumship. Working paper of the Language Research Laboratory. Berkeley: University of California.

Flacks, Richard. 1967. The liberated generation: an exploration of the roots of student protest. *Journal of Social Issues* 23:52–75.

————. 1970. Social and cultural meanings of student revolt: some informal comparative observations. *Social Problems* 17 (3):340–357.

Flugel, J. C. 1961. *Man, morals, and society.* New York: Viking Press.

Fluidus, Neil J. 1963. Latter-day prophets and present-day curriculum. Unpublished M.A. thesis. Provo: Brigham Young University.

Fodor, J., and T. Bever. 1965. The psychological reality of linguistic segments. *Journal of Learning and Verbal Behavior* 4:414–420.

Fodor, Nandor. 1958. People who are Christ. *Psychoanalysis and Psychoanalytic Review* 45:100–119.

Ford, Arthur, and Marguerite Bro. 1958. *Nothing so strange.* New York: Harper and Row.

Ford, T. R. 1960. Status, residence, and fundamentalist religious beliefs in the Southern Appalachians. *Social Forces* 39:41–48,

Foster, George M. 1960. *Culture and conquest: America's Spanish heritage.* Chicago: Quadrangle Books.

————. 1967. The dyadic contract. In *Tzintzuntzan: Mexican peasants in a changing world.* Boston: Little Brown.

Fox, Standord J. 1968. *Science and justice: the Massachusetts witchcraft trials.* Baltimore: Johns Hopkins Press.

Frake, Charles O. 1961. The diagnosis of disease among the Subanum of Mindanao. *American Anthropologist* 63:113–132.

————. 1962. The ethnographic study of cognitive systems. In *Anthropology and human behavior.* Washington: Anthropological Society of Washington, D.C.

Frank, Jerome. 1961. *Persuasion and healing: a comparative study of psychotherapy.* Baltimore: Johns Hopkins Press.

Frankl, V. E. 1962. *Man's search for meaning: an introduction to logotherapy.* Boston: Beacon Press.

Fraser, J. T., ed. 1964. *The voices of time.* New York: George Braziller.

Frazer, James G. 1922. *The golden bough: a study in magic and religion.* New York: Macmillan.

Freud, Anna. 1949. Aggression in relation to emotional development: normal and pathological. *Psychoanalytic Study of the Child* 3/4:37–42.

Freud, Sigmund. 1955. *Group psychology and the analysis of the ego.* London: Hogarth Press.

Fromm, Erich. 1941. *Escape from freedom.* New York: Farrar and Rinehart.

Fromm-Reichmann, Frieda. 1949. Introduction to psychotherapy of manic-depressives. *Confinia Neurologica* 9:150–164.

Furniss, N. F. 1954. *The fundamentalist controversy, 1918–1931.* New Haven: Yale University Press.

Galanter, Marc. 1966. Religious freedoms in the United States: a turning point? *Wisconsin Law Review* 1966 (1):217–296.

Gardner, Gerald. 1954. *Witchcraft today.* London: Rider.

———. 1959. The meaning of witchcraft. London: Aquarian Press.

Gardner, Martin. 1957. *Fads and fallacies in the name of science.* New York: Dover.

Garrison, K. C. 1962. The relationship of certain variables to church-sect typology among college students. *Journal of Social Psychology* 56:29–32.

Garrison, Vivian. 1972. Espiritismo: implications for provision of mental health services to Puerto Rican populations. Paper read at the Eighth Annual Meeting of the Southern Anthropological Society. Columbia, Missouri.

Gauld, Alan. 1968. *Founders of psychical research.* New York: Schocken Books.

Gay, Peter. 1966. *A loss of mastery.* New York: Vintage Books.

Geertz, Clifford. 1957. Ritual and social change: A Javanese example. *American Anthropologist* 59:32–54.

———. 1963. *Agricultural involution.* Berkeley: University of California Press.

———. 1966. Religion as a cultural system. In *Anthropological approaches to the study of religion.* M. Banton, ed. London: Tavistock.

Gerlach, Luther P. 1963. Traders on bicycle: entrepreneurship and cultural change among the Digo and Durma of Kenya. *Sociologus* 13:32–49.

———. 1964. Sociocultural factors influencing the diet of the northeast costal Bantu. *Journal of the American Dietetic Association* 45:420–424.

———. 1965a. Nutrition in its sociocultural matrix: food getting and using along the East African coast. In *Ecology and economic development in tropical Africa.* D. Brokensha, ed. Berkeley: University of California, Institute of International Studies.

———. 1965b. The spirit possession complex of the Digo of Kenya, East Africa. Paper presented at the Annual Meeting of the American Anthropological Association. Denver, Colorado.

———. 1968. People, power, change: a study of movements of revolutionary change. 16mm sound/color film produced in association with the University of Minnesota Audio-Visual Service. Minneapolis.

———. 1970a. Corporate groups and movement networks in urban America. *Anthropological Quarterly* 43 (3):123–145.

———. 1970b. Eco-Gemini: two for the teach-in. *Natural History* (May): 10–15.

———. 1970c. People eco-action. 16mm sound/color film produced in association with the University of Minnesota Audio-Visual Service. Minneapolis.

———. 1970d. Zanji-Africa. 35mm sound/color multi-media kit. St. Paul and Hollywood: EMC Corporation.

———. 1971. The ecology revolution. *Spirit Magazine* (June/July):10–15.

Gerlach, Luther P., and Virginia Hine. 1966. The charasmatic revival: processes of recruitment, conversion, and behavioral change in modern American religious movement. Paper presented at the Annual Meeting of the American Anthropological Association. Pittsburgh, Pennsylvania.

———. 1968. Five factors crucial to the growth and spread of a modern religious movement. *Journal for the Scientific Study of Religion* 7:23–40.

———. 1969. Participatory ecology: the genesis of a social movement. Paper presented at the Annual Meeting of the American Anthropological Association. New Orleans, Louisiana.

———. 1970a. Many concerned, few committed. *Natural History* (December):66ff.

———. 1970b. *People, power, change: movements of social transformation.* Indianapolis: Bobbs-Merrill.

———. 1970c. The social organization of a movement of revolutionary change: case study, black power. In *Afro-American anthropology, contemporary perspectives.* N. Whitten and J. Szwed, eds. New York: The Free Press.

———. 1970d. Wit, wisdom and woe: a preliminary report on replies to *Natural History's* questionnaire, "You and the ecology movement." *Natural History* (October):2–24, 5off.

———. 1970e. You and ecology: a questionnaire on attitudes toward the environment. *Natural History* (June/July):27–29.

———. 1973. *Lifeway Leap: The Dynamics of Change in America.* Minneapolis: University of Minnesota Press.

Gerstner, Jean. 1960. *The theology of the major sects.* Grand Rapids: Baker Book House.

Gerth, H. H. and C. Wright Mills, eds. 1958. *From Max Weber.* New York: Galaxy Books.

Giannella, Donald. 1967. Religious liberty, nonestablishment, and doctrinal development: Part One, the religious liberty guarantee. *Harvard Law Review* 80 (7):1381–1431.

Gillin, John. 1948. Magical fright. *Psychiatry* 11:387–400.

Glass, Justine. 1965. *Witchcraft: the sixth sense and us.* London: Neville Spearman.

Gloch, C. Y. 1964. The role of deprivation in the origin of evolution of religious group. In *Religion and social conflict.* R. Lee and M. W. Marty, eds. New York: Oxford University Press.

———— and Rodney Stark. 1965. *Religion and society in tension.* Chicago: Rand-McNally.

Gluckman, Max. 1955. The logic of witchcraft. In *Custom and conflict in Africa.* Glencoe, Ill:. The Free Press.

————. 1965. *Politics, law, and ritual in tribal societies.* Oxford: Blackwell.

Goldschmidt, Walter. 1944. Class denominationalism in rural California churches. *American Journal of Sociology* 49:348–355.

Goldstein, Arnold, Kenneth Heller, and Lee Sechrest. 1966. *Psychotherapy and the psychology of behavior change.* New York: John Wiley.

Goldston, Stephen, ed. 1965. *Concepts of community psychiatry.* Washington: U. S. Government Printing Office.

Goode, Erich. 1967a. Further reflections on the church-sect dimension. *Journal for the Scientific Study of Religion* 6:270–275.

————. 1967b. Some critical observations on the church-sect dimension and comments thereafter. *Journal for the Scientific Study of Religion* 6:69–77.

Goodman, Felicitas. 1968. Speaking in tongues in four cultural settings. Paper presented at the Annual Meeting of the American Anthropological Association. Seattle, Washington.

————. 1969a. Glossolalia: speaking in tongues in four cultural settings. *Confinia Psychiatrica* 12:113–129.

————. 1969b. Phonetic analysis of glossolalia in four cultural settings. *Journal for the Scientific Study of Religion* 8 (2):227–239.

————. 1971. The acquisition of glossolalia behavior. *Semiotica* 3:77–82.

————. 1972a. *Speaking in tongues: a cross-cultural study of glossolalia.* Chicago: University of Chicago Press. (Forthcoming)

————. 1972b. The Apostolics of Yucatán: a case study. In *Religion, altered states of consciousness, and social change.* E. Bourguignon, ed. Columbus: The Ohio State University Press. (Forthcoming)

Gould, R. E. 1971. The marginally asocial personality: the beatnik-hippie alienation. In *World biennial of psychiatry and psychotherapy.* S. Arieti, ed. I:258–290.

Graves, Robert. 1964. Witches in 1964. *Virginia Quarterly Review* 40:550–559.

Greeley, Andrew W. 1969. There's a new-time religion on campus. *New York Times,* June 1, p. 14ff.

Greeley, Andrew. 1970. Superstition, ecstasy, and tribal consciousness. *Social Research* 38 (2):203–211.

Greenbaum, Lenora. 1970. Evaluation of a stratified versus an unstratified universe of cultures in comparative research. *Behavior Science Notes* 5:251–290.

Greene, W. A., Jr., L. E. Young, and S. N. Swisher. 1956. Psychological factors in reticuloendothelial disease: Part Two, observations on a group of women with lymphomas and leukemias. *Psychosomatic Medicine* 18:285–303.

Greenland, C. 1965. Richard Maurice Bucke, M.D., 1937–1902: psychiatrist, author, mystic. In *Personality change and religious experience.* R. Prince, ed. Montreal: R. M. Bucke Memorial Society.

Greenson, Ralph. 1967. *The technique and practice of psychoanalysis,* Vol. 1. New York: International Universities Press.

Gregory, W. E. 1957. The orthodoxy of the authoritarian personality. *Journal of Social Psychology* 45:217–232.

Grimes, Alan P. 1964. *Equality in America.* New York: Oxford University Press.

Grinker, R. R., Sr. 1962. "Mentally healthy" young males (homoclides): *Archives of General Psychology* 6:405–453.

Griswold, Alfred W. 1934. New thought: a cult of success. *American Journal of Sociology* 40:309–318.

Grodzins, Morton. 1949. *Americans betrayed: politics and the Japanese evacuation.* Chicago: University of Chicago Press.

Grounds, V. 1961. Correcting the fundamentalist corrective. Paper presented at the Conservative Baptist National Convention. Portland, Oregon.

Guiart, Jean. 1951. Cargo cults and modern political evolution in Melanesia. *Mankind* 4:227–229.

Gumperz, J. 1962. Types of linguistic communities. In *The sociology of language.* J. Fishman, ed. The Hague: Mouton.

———. 1964. Linguistic and social interaction in two communities. In *The ethnography of communication.* J. Gumperz and D. Hymes, eds. *American Anthropologist* 66 (6), part 2.

———. 1967. On the linguistic markers of bilingual communication. *Journal of Social Issues* 23:48–57.

———. 1969. Communication in Multilingual Societies. In *Cognitive anthropology.* S. Tyler, ed. New York: Holt, Rinehart, and Winston.

——— and J. B. Blom. 1972. Social meaning in linguistic structures: code-switching in Norway. In *Directions in sociolinguistics.* J. Gumperz and D. Hymes, eds. New York: Holt, Rinehart, and Winston.

Gustafson, Paul. 1967. UO-US-PS-PO: a restatement of Troeltsch's church-sect typology. *Journal for the Scientific Study of Religion* 6:64–68.

Gustafson, Marlin. 1970. The religious role of the President. *Midwest Journal of Political Science* 14 (4):708–722.

Gustaitis, Rasa. 1969. *Turning on.* New York: Macmillan.

Hagen, Everett E. 1962. *On the theory of social change: how economic growth begins.* Homewood, Ill.: Dorsey Press.

Hall, David, ed. 1968. *The antinomian controversy, 1636–1638: A documentary history.* Middletown, Conn.: Wesleyan University Press.

Hallowell, A. I. 1967. The backwash of the frontier: the impact of the Indian on American culture. In *Beyond the frontier: social process and cultural change.* New York: The Natural History Press.

Hamer, John and Irene. 1966. Spirit possession and its sociopsychological implications among the Sidamo of Southeast Ethiopia. *Ethnology* 5 (4): 392–408.

Hammer, Emmanuel. 1958. *The clinical application of projective drawings.* Springfield, Ill.: Charles C. Thomas.

Hanawalt, N. G. 1963. Feeling of security and of self-esteem in relation to religious belief. *Journal of Social Psychology* 59:347–353.

Handelan, D. 1967. The development of a Washo shaman. *Ethnology* 6 (4):444–464.

Handy, R. T., H. S. Smith, and L. Loetscher. 1963. *American Christianity,* Vol. 2. New York: Charles Scribner's Sons.

Hannerz, Ulf. 1969. *Soulside: inquiry into ghetto culture and community.* New York: Columbia University Press.

Hansen, Chadwick. 1969. *Witchcraft in Salem.* New York: George Braziller.

Hardinge, Emma. 1970. *Modern Spiritualism in America.* New Hyde Park, New York: University Books.

Harmann, William C., ed. 1927. *Who's who in occultism, new thought, psychism, and spiritualism.* New York: Occult Press.

Harper, Gordon P. 1963. The children of Hipolito: a study of Brazilian Pentecostalism. Unpublished paper. Harvard University.

Harris, Marvin. 1968. *The rise of anthropological theory.* London: Routledge and Kegan Paul.

Hartland, E. Sidney. 1908. Satanism. In *Encyclopedia of religion and ethics.* J. Hastings, ed. New York: Scribner.

Hartmann, H. 1964. *Essays on ego psychology.* New York: International Universities Press.

Harvey, O. J., D. E. Hunt, and H. M. Schroder. 1961. *Conceptual systems and personality organization.* New York: John Wiley.

Haugen, E., H. H. Dixon, and H. A. Dickel. 1958. *A therapy for anxiety tension reactions.* New York: Macmillan.

Hayagrivadas Adhikari. 1920. The guru: via media to God. *Back to Godhead* 34:10–11.

Heberle, Rudolph. 1940. Observations on the sociology of social movements. *American Sociological Review* 14:346–356.

Hébert, Gérard. 1960. *Les témoins de Jéhovah: essai critique d'histoire et de doctrine.* Montreal: Editions Bellarmin.

Heinlien, Robert. 1961. *Stranger in a strange land.* New York: Putnam.

Helwig, Werner. 1960. *Die blaue Blume des Vandervogels.* Gutersloh: S. Mohn.

Henney, Jennette H. 1973. The Shakers of St. Vincent. In *Religion, altered states of consciousness, and culture change.* E. Bourguignon, ed. Columbus: The Ohio State University Press.

Henry, C. F. 1947. *The uneasy conscience of fundamentalism.* Grand Rapids: Eerdmans.

Herskovits, M. 1937. African gods and Catholic saints in New York Negro belief. *American Anthropologist* 39:639–643.

———. 1966. *The new world Negro.* Bloomington: University of Indiana Press.

———. 1971. *Life in a Haitian Valley.* New York: Doubleday.

Hilton, Ruth Savage, ed. 1958. Lorenzo Hill Hatch journal. Mimeographed by Brigham Young University Adult Education and Extension Services. Provo, Extension Publications.

Hine, Virginia. 1969. Pentecostal glossolalia: toward a functional interpretation. *Journal for the Scientific Study of Religion* 8:211–226.

Hockett, C. F. 1958. *A course in modern linguistics.* New York: Macmillan.

Hogg, Donald. 1960. The Convince cult in Jamaica. In *Papers in Caribbean anthropology.* S. W. Mintz, ed. Yale University Publications in Anthropology, Vol. 58.

Holbrook Tribune-News. 1910–1966. Holbrook, Arizona.

Hollender, M. H. 1965. On perfectionism. *Comprehensive Psychology* 6: 94–103.

Hollingshead, August B. 1957. Two factor index of social position. New Haven: privately published.

——— and Raymond S. Duff. 1968. Sickness and society. New York: Harper and Row.

Holmes, Ernest S. 1942. New thought terms and their meaning: a dictionary of the terms and phrases commonly used in metaphysical and psychological study. Dodd, Mead.

Holmes, M. B. 1960. A cross-cultural study of the relationship between values and modal conscience. *The Psychoanalytic Study of Society* 1:98–194.

Holmstedt, B. 1967. Historical survey. In *Ethnopharmacological search for psychoactive drugs.* D. H. Efron, ed. Washington: U. S. Public Health Service Publication No. 1645.

Holt, John B. 1940. Holiness religion: culture shock and social reorganization. *American Sociological Review* 5:740–747.

Holzer, Hans. 1969. *The truth about witchcraft.* New York: Doubleday.

Holzman, P. 1963. Repression and cognitive style. *Bulletin of the Menninger Clinic* 26:1–6.

Homans, George C. 1941. Anxiety and ritual: the theories of Malinowski and Radcliffe-Brown. *American Anthropologist* 43:164–172.

Hoult, T. F. 1969. *Dictionary of modern sociology.* Totowa, New Jersey: Littlefield, Adams.

Howard, J. 1967. *Drums in the Americas.* New York: Oak Publications.

Hubbard, L. Ron. 1940. The ultimate adventure. In *Unknown.* Chicago: Smith and Street Publications.

———. 1950. *Dianetics: the modern source of mental health.* New York: Paperback Library (1968 edition).

———. 1958. *Axioms of scientology.* East Grinstead, Sussex, England: Hubbard College of Scientology.

———. 1964. *Scientology abridged dictionary.* East Grinstead, Sussex, England: Hubbard College of Scientology.

Hudson, Winthrop. 1953. *The great tradition in the American churches.* New York: Harper.

———. 1965. *Religion in America.* New York: Charles Scribner's Sons.

Huebner, Louise. 1969. *Power through witchcraft*. Los Angeles: Nash Publishing Company.

Hunt, J. McV. 1965. Traditional personality theory in light of recent evidences. *American Scientist* 53:80–96.

Hurt, Wiley. 1960. Factors in the persistence of peyote in the northern plains. *Plains Anthropologist* 5 (9):16–27.

Huson, Paul. 1970. *Mastering witchcraft: a practical guide for witches, warlocks, and covens*. New York: Putnam.

Huxley, Aldous. 1944. *Time must have a stop*. New York: Harper.

———. 1945. *The perennial philosophy*. New York: Harper.

———. 1954. *The doors of perception*. New York: Harper.

Huysmans, Joris Karl. 1958. *Down there*. New Hyde Park, New York: New University Books.

Hymes, Dell. 1962. The ethnography of speaking. In *Anthropology and human behavior*. T. Gladwin and W. C. Sturtevant, eds. Washington: Anthropological Society of Washington, D. C.

Ilfeld, Fred, and Roger Lauer. 1964. *Social nudity in America*. New Haven: College and University Press.

Inkeles, A. and D. J. Levinson. 1954. National character: the study of modal personality and sociocultural systems. In *Handbook of social psychology*, Vol. 2. G. Lindzey, ed. Reading, Massachusetts: Addison-Wesley.

International Society for KRSNA Consciousness. 1970. *The KRSNA consciousness handbook*. Boston: ISKON Press.

Isherwood, C. 1965. *Ramakrishna and his disciples*. New York: Simon and Schuster.

Jackson, John A. 1966. Two contemporary cults. *Advancement of Science* 23 (100):60–64.

——— and R. Jobling. 1968. Toward an analysis of contemporary cults. In *A sociological yearbook of religion in Britain*. David A. Martin, ed. London: S.C.M. Press.

Jacobson, Edith. 1964. *The self and the object world*. New York: International Universities Press.

Jacquet, Constant H., Jr., ed. 1970. *Yearbook of American churches*. New York: Council Press.

James, William. 1882. The subjective effects of nitrous oxide. *Mind* 7:186–208.

———. 1961. *The varieties of religious experience*. New York: Collier Books.

Jameson, A. L. 1961. Religion in the Christian perimeter. In *The shaping of American religions*. J. W. Smith and A. L. Jameson, eds. Princeton: Princeton University Press.

Jansma, T. 1962. *Failure in Christian nurture*. Proceedings of the Christian Association for Psychological Studies. Holland, Michigan.

Jarvis, J. 1970. Quoted in *Stanford Daily*, January 8, p. 1.

Jilek, W. G. 1967. The image of the African medicine man. In Contribu-

tions to comparative psychiatry. N. Petrilowitsch, ed. *Bibliotheca Psychiatrica et Neurologica* 133 (6):165–178.

Johns, June. 1970. *King of the witches: the world of Alex Sanders.* New York: Coward-McCann.

Johnson, Adelaide. 1951. Some etiological aspects of repression, guilt, and hostility. *Psychoanalytic Quarterly* 20:511–527.

Johnson, Benton. 1957. A critical appraisal of the church-sect typology. *American Sociological Review* 22:88–92.

———. 1961. Do Holiness sects socialize in dominant values? *Social Forces* 39:309–316.

———. 1962. Ascetic Protestantism and political preference. *Public Opinion Quarterly* 26:35–46.

———. 1963. On church and sect. *American Sociological Review* 28:539–549.

Johnson, Harry. 1960. *Sociology: a systematic introduction.* New York: Harcourt, Brace.

Joint Commission on Mental Illness and Health. 1961. *Action for mental health.* New York: Basic Books.

Jones, A. M. 1955. *African rhythm.* International African Institute Memo 27. London.

Jones, E. 1951. The God complex. In *Essays in applied psychoanalysis,* vol. 2. London: Hogarth Press.

———. 1957. *The life and work of Sigmund Freud,* vol. 3. New York: Basic Books.

Jones, Raymond J. 1939. *A comparative study of religious cult behavior among Negroes.* Washington: Howard University Graduate School.

Judah, J. Stillson. 1967. *The history and philosophy of the metaphysical movements in America.* Philadelphia: Westminster Press.

Jung, C. G. 1961. *Memories, dreams, reflections.* New York: Vintage Books.

Kahn, E. 1962. *The past is not past.* Springfield, Ill.: Charles C. Thomas.

Kail, J. 1889. Über die Parallelstellen in der angelsächsischen Poesis. *Anglia* 12:21–40.

Kamiya, J. 1969. Operant control of the EEG alpha rhythm and some of its reported effects on consciousness. In *Altered states of consciousness.* C. Tart, ed. New York: John Wiley.

Kaplan, Berton H. 1965. The structure of adaptive sentiments in lower class religious groups in Appalachia. *The Journal of Social Issues* 21:126–141.

Kardec, Allan. 1875. *The spirits' book.* Boston: Colby and Rich.

———. 1960. *Coleccion de oraciones escogidas.* Mexico, D.F.: El Libro Español.

———. 1963. *El libro de los mediums.* Mexico, D.F.: Editorial Diana, S.A.

Kauper, Paul. 1964. *Religion and the constitution.* Baton Rouge: Louisiana State University Press.

Kautsky, Karl. 1897. *Communism in Central Europe at the time of the Reformation.* London: T. F. Unwin.

Kay, Paul. 1970. Some theoretical implications of ethnographic semantics. *Bulletin of the American Anthropological Association* 3 (3):19–31.

Keil, Charles. 1966. *Urban blues.* Chicago: University of Chicago Press.

Kellaway, P. 1946. The part played by electric fish in the early history of bioelectricity and electrotherapy. *Bulletin of the History of Medicine* 20: 112–137.

Kelly, Isabel. 1965. *Folk practices in North Mexico.* Austin: University of Texas Press.

Kelly, M. W. 1955. *The psychology of personal constructs.* 2 vols. New York: W. W. Norton.

———. 1961. Depression in the psychoses of members of religious communities of women. *American Journal of Psychiatry* 118:423–425.

Kelsey, Morton T. 1964. *Tongue speaking: an experiment in spiritual experience.* New York: Doubleday.

Kendrick, Klaude. 1963. The Pentecostal movement: hopes and hazards. *Christian Century* 80:608–610.

Keniston, Kenneth. 1968. Heads and seekers. *American Scholar* 38:97–112.

Kennedy, Melville T. 1925. *The Chaitanya movement: a study of the Vaishnavism of Bengal.* New York: Oxford University Press.

Kiev, Ari. 1962. Psychotherapy in Haitian voodoo. *American Journal of Psychotherapy* 16 (3):469–476.

———. 1964. Psychotherapeutic aspects of Pentecostal sects among West Indian immigrants to England. *British Journal of Sociology* 15:129–138.

———. 1964. *Magic, faith, and healing: studies on primitive psychology today.* New York: The Free Press.

Kimber, J.A.M. 1947. Interest and personality traits of Bible institute students. *Journal of Social Psychology* 26:225–233.

Kincheloe, Samuel C. 1928. Major reactions of city churches. *Religious Education* 23:868–874.

King, Francis. 1970. *Ritual magic in England: 1887 to the present day.* London: Neville Spearman.

Kingdom Ministry. 1969. Monthly newsletter of the New World Society of Jehovah's Witnesses 12 (1):2.

Kirkpatrick, C. 1949. Religion and humanitarianism: a study of institutional implications. *Psychological Monographs* 69 (9).

Kitzinger, Sheila. 1969. Protest and mysticism: the Ras Tafari cult of Jamaica. *Journal for the Scientific Study of Religion* 8:240–262.

Kleiner, R. J., J. Tuckman, and M. Lavell. 1962. Mental disorder and status based on Protestant subgroup membership. *Journal of Social Psychology* 58:345–348.

Kleivan, I. 1960. *Mitartut: vestiges of the Eskimo sea-woman cult in West Greenland.* Copenhagen: C. A. Reitzel.

Klemesrud, Judy. 1969. Some people take this witch business seriously. *New York Times,* October 31, p. 50.

Kloman, William. 1970. Banality and the new evil. *Esquire* 73:115–117, 182–184.

Klose, L. V. 1940. The cults and sects in the Los Angeles area. Unpublished thesis. University of Southern California.

Kluckhohn, Clyde. 1967. *Navaho witchcraft*. Boston: Beacon Press.

———— and D. Leighton. 1962. *The Navaho*. Garden City, New York: Doubleday.

Kluckhohn, F., and F. L. Strodtbeck. 1961. *Variation in value orientations*. Evanston, Ill.: Row, Peterson.

Kluver, H. 1928. *Mescal: the divine plant and its psychological effects*. London: Kegan Paul.

Knox, R. A. 1950. *Enthusiasm: a chapter in the history of religion*. London: Oxford University Press.

Kobler, John. 1966. Out for a night at the local caldron. *Saturday Evening Post* 239:76–78.

Kockman, Thomas. 1970. Toward an ethnography of black American speech behavior. In *Afro-American anthropology: contemporary perspectives*. N. Whitten and J. Szwed, eds. New York: The Free Press.

Kohler, Wolfgang. 1947. *Gestalt psychology*. New York: The New American Library.

Kohut, H. 1966. Forms and transformation of narcissism. *Journal of the American Psychoanalytic Association* 14:243–272.

Konvitz, Milton. 1968. *Religious liberty and conscience*. New York: Viking Press.

Koss, Joan. In press. Social process and behavior change in Puerto Rican Spiritualist cults. In *Caribbean cults: individual and social change*. D. Hogg and J. Koss, eds.

Krippner, Stanley, and Don Fersh. 1970. Paranormal experience among members of American contra cultural groups. *Journal of Psychedelic Drugs* 3(1):109–114.

Kriss, Marika. 1970. *Witchcraft past and present for the millions*. New York: Award Books.

Kroeber, A. L. 1952. Psychosis or social sanction. In *The nature of culture*. Chicago: University of Chicago Press.

Kubie, L. 1950. Neurotic potential and human adaptation. In *Cybernetics: circular and feedback mechanisms in biological and social systems*. H. V. Foerster, ed. New York: Josiah Macy, Jr. Foundation.

Kuhn, Thomas S. 1962. *The structure of scientific revolutions*. Chicago: University of Chicago Press.

Kurkland, Philip. 1962. *Religion and the law*. Chicago: Aldine.

La Barre, Weston. 1962. *They shall take up serpents: psychology of the southern snake-handling cult*. Minneapolis: University of Minnesota Press.

————. 1970. *The ghost dance*. New York: Doubleday.

————. 1971. Materials for the history of studies of crisis cults: a bibliographic essay. *Current Anthropology* 12:3–44.

Lacan, Jacques. 1968. *The language of the self*. Baltimore: Johns Hopkins Press.

La Moreaux, Karen. 1970. Drug use at Denison. Unpublished paper. Denison University.

Lampl-de-Groot, J. 1962. Ego ideal and superego. *The Psychoanalytic Study of the Child* 17:94–106.

Lanternari, Vittorio. 1963. Messianism: its historical origin and morphology. *History of Religion* 2:52–72.

———. 1963. *The religions of the oppressed: a study of modern messianic cults.* New York: A. A. Knopf.

Lashley, K. S. 1951. The problem of serial order in behavior. In *Cerebral mechanisms in behavior.* L. A. Leffress, ed. New York: John Wiley.

Laski, Marghanita. 1961. *Ecstasy: a study of some secular and religious experiences.* London: The Cresset Press.

La Vey, Anton S. 1968. Tape-recorded interview in the collection of Marcello Truzzi.

———. 1969. *The Satanic Bible.* New York: Avon Books.

———. 1971. *The compleat witch.* New York: Dodd, Mead.

Lawrence, Peter. 1964. *Road belong cargo.* New York: Humanities Press.

Lawton, George. 1932. *The drama of life after death: a study of Spiritualist religion.* New York: Henry Holt and Company.

———. 1930. Spiritualism: a contemporary American religion. *Journal of Religion* 10(1):37–54.

Leary, Timothy. 1964. How to change behavior. In *LSD: the consciousness-expanding drug.* D. Solomon, ed. New York: Putnam.

———. 1970. *The politics of ecstasy.* London: Paladin.

Leek, Sybil. 1968. *Diary of a witch.* Englewood Cliffs, New Jersey: Prentice-Hall.

———. 1970. *Cast your own spell.* New York: Bee-line Books.

Leighton, D., and others. 1963. *The character of danger.* New York: Basic Books.

Lenski, G. 1961. *The religious factor: a sociological study of religion's impact on politics, economics, and family.* Garden City, New York: Doubleday.

Leon, R. L. 1964. Dyscultural anxiety reaction. *Psychiatric Quarterly* 38: 271–277.

Leone, Mark P. 1969. Modern cultural patterns in east-central Arizona. Unpublished paper. Princeton University.

Leslau, W. 1949. An Ethiopian argot of people possessed by a spirit. *Africa* 19(3):204–212.

Leuner, Hanscarl. 1969. Guided affective imagery (GAI): A method of psychotherapy. *American Journal of Psychotherapy* 23:4–22.

Levin, D. C. 1969. The self: a contribution to its place in theory and technique. *International Journal of Psychoanalysis* 50:41–51.

Levin, Jay. 1968. The magic explosion. *Eye* 1:24–29, 80–81, 84.

Lévi-Strauss, Claude. 1966. *The savage mind.* Chicago: University of Chicago Press.

———. 1967. The sorcerer and his magic. In *Structural anthropology.* New York: Doubleday.

Lewin, L. 1924. *Phantastica.* Berlin: G. Stilke.

Lewis, I. M. 1966. Spirit possession and divination cults. *Man* 1:307–329.

———. 1971. *Ecstatic religion*. Baltimore: Penguin Books.

Lewis, Oscar. 1951. Urbanization without breakdown: a case study. *Scientific Monthly* 75:31–41.

———. 1965. *La vida*. New York: Random House.

Lhermitte, Jean. 1963. *True and false possession*. New York: Hawthorne Books.

Lichtenstein, Heinz. 1964. The role of narcissism in the emergence and maintenance of a primary identity. *International Journal of Psychoanalysis* 45:49–56.

Lienhardt, G. 1951. Some notions of witchcraft among the Dinka. *Africa* 21:303–318.

———. 1961. *Divinity and experience*. Oxford: Clarendon Press.

Lightner, R. 1962. *Neo-evangelism*. Findley, Ohio: Dunham Press.

Lincoln, Eric. 1961. *The Black Muslims in America*. Boston: Beacon Press.

Linton, Ralph. 1943. Nativistic movements. *American Anthropologist* 45:230–240.

———. 1956. *Culture and mental disorders*. Springfield, Ill.: Charles C. Thomas.

Loewen, Jacob A., Albert Buckwalter, and James Kratz. 1965. Shamanism, illness, and power in Toba church life. *Practical Anthropology* (November/December):250–280.

Lofland, John. 1966. *Doomsday cult*. Englewood Cliffs, New Jersey: Prentice-Hall.

——— and Rodney Stark. 1965. Becoming a world-saver: a theory of conversion to a deviant perspective. *American Sociological Review* 30:862–875.

Lomax, A. 1966. Special features of the sung communication. In *Essays on the verbal and visual arts*. J. Helm, ed. Proceedings of the Annual Meeting of the American Ethnological Society. Seattle: University of Washington Press.

———. 1970. African-Afro-American musical style. In *Afro-American Anthropology*. N. Whitten and J. Szwed, eds. Glencoe: Free Press.

Lorand, S. 1962. Psychoanalytic therapy of religious devotees. *International Journal of Psychoanalysis* 43:50–58.

Lord, Albert B. 1965. *The singer of tales*. New York: Atheneum.

Lowe, W. L. 1954. Group beliefs and socio-cultural factors in religious delusions. *Journal of Social Psychology* 40:267–274.

———. 1955. Religious beliefs and religious delusions: a comparative study of religious projections. *American Journal of Psychotherapy* 9:54–61.

Lowenfeld, H. 1944. Some aspects of a compulsion neurosis in a changing civilization. *Psychoanalytic Quarterly* 13:1–15.

Loyd, F. Glen, and Theodore Irwin. 1970. How anarchy thrives on the occult. *Todays Health* 48(11):21.

Lubchansky, Issac, Gladys Egri, and Janet Stokes. 1970. Puerto Rican Spiritualists view mental illness: the faith healer as paraprofessional. *American Journal of Psychiatry* 127(3):312–321.

Lubin, A. J. 1959. A boy's view of Jesus. *The Psychoanalytic Study of the Child* 14:155–168.

Luckmann, Thomas. 1967. *The invisible religion.* New York: Macmillan.

Ludwig, Arnold. 1968. Altered states of consciousness. In *Trance and possession states.* R. Prince, ed. Montreal: R. M. Bucke Memorial Society.

Lyle, N. H., Jr., and E. E. Levitt. 1955. Punitiveness, authoritarianism, and parental discipline of grade school children. *Journal of Abnormal and Social Psychology* 51:42–46.

Lyons, Arthur. 1970a. *The second coming: Satanism in America.* New York: Dodd, Mead.

————. 1970b. Violence and the occult. Unpublished paper.

MaCabe, Joseph. 1920. Spiritualism: a popular history from 1847. London: T. F. Unwin.

McConkie, Bruce R. 1966. *Mormon doctrine.* Salt Lake City: Bookcraft (second edition).

McCarthy, T. J. 1942. Personality traits in seminarians. *Studies in Psychology and Psychiatry of the Catholic University of America* 5:1–46.

MacFarlane, M. G. 1967. Witchcraft persecution in Essex, 1560–1690. Unpublished Ph.D. dissertation.

MacFarland, H. Niell. 1967. *The rush hour of the gods.* New York: Macmillan.

McGavran, Donald. 1963. *Church growth in Mexico.* Grand Rapids: Eerdmans.

Macklin, June. 1967. El niño fidencio: un estudio del curanderismo en Neuvo León. *Anuario Humánitas,* pp. 529–563. Centro de Estudios Humanisticos, Universidad de Nuevo León.

————. 1974. Folk saints, healers, and spiritist cults in northern Mexico. *Revista/Review Interamericana.*

————. 1973. Structural development and conservation in three North Mexican folk saint movements. *Comparative Studies in Society and History* 15:98–105.

McKinney, George. 1962. *The theology of the Jehovah's Witnesses.* Grand Rapids: Zondervan.

McLoughlin, William. 1967. Is there a third force in Christendom? *Daedalus* 96(1):43–68.

McLuhan, Marshall. 1962. *The Gutenberg galaxy.* Toronto: University of Toronto Press.

McPherson, Aimee S. 1946. *The foursquare gospel.* Los Angeles: Echo Park Evangelistic Association.

Maddox, J. L. 1923. *The medicine man: a sociological study of the character and evolution of shamanism.* New York: Macmillan.

Madsen, Claudia. 1966. A study of change in Mexican folk medicine. *Middle American Research Institute Publication* 25:89–138. New Orleans: Tulane University.

Madsen, William. 1955. Shamanism in Mexico. *Southwestern Journal of Anthropology* 11:48–57.

———. 1964. *The Mexican-Americans of South Texas.* New York: Holt, Rinehart, and Winston.

———. 1967. Religious syncretism. In *Handbook of Middle American Indians*, Vol. 6. R. Wauchope, ed. Austin: University of Texas Press.

Magoun, Francis P., Jr. 1953. Oral-formulaic character of Anglo-Saxon narrative poetry. *Speculum* 28:446–467.

Maharishi Mahesh Yogi. 1966. *The science of being and the art of living.* London: International SRM Publications (revised edition).

Mair, Lucy. 1969. *Witchcraft.* New York: McGraw-Hill.

Malinowski, Bronislaw. 1939. The group and the individual in functional Analysis. *American Journal of Sociology* 44:938–964.

———. 1968. The problem of meaning in primitive languages. In *The meaning of meaning*. C. K. Ogden and I. A. Richards, eds. New York: Harcourt, Brace, and World.

Malko, George. 1970. *Scientology: the now religion.* New York: Delacorte Press.

Mann, J. 1964. Clinical and theoretical aspects of religious belief. *Journal of the American Psychoanalytic Association* 12:160–170.

Mann, W. E. 1955. *Sect, cult, and church in Alberta.* Toronto: University of Toronto Press.

Mannheim, Karl. 1936. *Ideology and utopia: an introduction to the sociology of knowledge.* New York: Harcourt, Brace, and World.

Mannoni, O. 1956. *Prospero and Caliban: the psychology of colonization.* New York: Praeger.

Manwaring, David R. 1962. *Render unto Caesar: the flag salute controversy.* Chicago: University of Chicago Press.

Maple, Eric. 1962. *The dark world of witches.* New York: Pegasus.

Marcuse, Herbert. 1964. *One-dimensional man: studies in the ideology of advanced industrial society.* Boston: Beacon Press.

———. 1970. *Five lectures: psychoanalysis, politics, and utopia.* Boston: Beacon Press.

———. 1971. Quoted in *San Francisco Examiner*, February 4, p. 18.

Marsh, P. M. 1967. *Comparative sociology: codification of cross-societal analyses.* New York: Harcourt, Brace, and World.

Martello, Leo L. 1969. *Weird ways of witchcraft.* New York: H. C. Publishers.

Martin, C., and R. C. Nichols. 1962. Personality and religious belief. *Journal of Social Psychology* 56:3–8.

Martin, Paul S. 1963. *The last 10,000 years: a fossil pollen record of the American Southwest.* Tucson: Univ. of Arizona Press.

——— and others. 1964. *Chapters in the prehistory of Eastern Arizona II.* Fieldiana Anthropology, Vol. 55. Chicago: Chicago Natural History Museum.

Marty, Martin. 1970. The occult establishment. *Social Research* 37(2):212–230.

Maruyama, Magoroh. 1968. The second cybernetics: deviation-amplifying mutual causal processes. In *Modern system research for the behavioral scientist*. Chicago: Aldine.

Marwick, Max, ed. 1970. *Witchcraft and sorcery: selected readings*. Baltimore: Penguin Books.

Mather, Cotton. 1820. *Magnalia Christi Americana*. 2 vols. Hartford: Roberts and Barr.

Mathison, Richard. 1960. *Faith, cults, and sects of America*. Indianapolis: Bobbs-Merrill.

Matson, Floyd W. 1966. *The broken image*. New York: Doubleday.

May, Henry F. 1949. *Protestant churches and industrial America*. New York: Harper.

May, I. Carlyle. 1956. A survey of glossolalia and related phenomena in non-Christian religions. *American Anthropologist* 58:75–96.

Mayer, A. J., and H. Sharp. 1962. Achievement motivation and religious background. *American Sociological Review* 27:218–227.

Mead, George H. 1934. *Mind, self, and society*. Chicago: University of Chicago Press.

Mead, M. and T. Schwartz. 1960. The cult as a condensed social process. In *Group processes*. B. Schaffner, ed. New York: Josiah Macy, Jr. Foundation.

Mead, Sidney E. 1963. *The lively experiment: the shaping of Christianity in America*. New York: Harper and Row.

Meher Baba. 1967. *Discourses*. 3 vols. Ahmednagar, India: Adi K. Irani.

————. 1971. *Compassionate father*. Berkeley, Cal.: Meher Baba Information.

Mehler, J., and P. Carey. 1967. Role of surface and base structure in the perception of sentences. *Journal of Verbal Learning and Verbal Behavior* 6:335–338.

Merton, R. K. 1957. Puritanism, pietism, and science. In *Social theory and social structure*. Glencoe, Ill.: The Free Press (revised edition).

Messer, M. 1968. Running out of era: some nonpharmacological notes on the psychedelic revolution. *Journal of Psychedelic Drugs* 2:157–166.

Messing, Simon D. 1958. Group therapy and social status in the Zar cult of Ethiopia. *American Anthropologist* 60(6):1120–1126.

Metraux, Alfred. 1959. *Voodoo in Haiti*. New York: Oxford University Press.

Metzger, Duane, and G. Williams. 1966. Some procedures and results in the study of native categories: Tzeltal "firewood." *American Anthropologist* 68:389–407.

Meyer, Donald. 1965. *The positive thinkers*. New York: Doubleday.

Middleton, R., and S. Putney. 1962. Religion, normative standards, and behavior. *Sociometry* 25:141–152.

Miller, George A. 1967. *The psychology of communication*. Baltimore: Penguin Books.

———— and S. Isard. 1964. Free recall and self embedded English sentences. *Information and Control* 7:292–303.

Miller, William L. 1953. *Piety on the Potomac*. Boston: Houghton Mifflin.

Mischel, Walter and Frances. 1958. Psychological aspects of spirit possession. *American Anthropologist* 60(2):249–260.

Mishra, R. S. 1970. *Directory of light centres*. North Syracuse, New York: ICSA Press.

Mitchell, S. Weir. 1896. The effects of anhalonium lewinii (the mescal button). *British Medical Journal* 2:1625.

Moberg, D. 1962. *The church as a social institution*. Englewood Cliffs: Prentice-Hall.

Modell, Arnold. 1968. *Object love and reality: an introduction to a psychoanalytic theory of object relations*. New York: International Universities Press.

Moloney, J. C. 1954. Mother, God, and superego. *Journal of the American Psychoanalytic Association* 2:120–154.

Montejo, Esteban. 1968. *The autobiography of a runaway slave*. New York: Pantheon.

Montgomery, Ruth. 1965. *A gift of prophecy*. New York: Morrow.

Moody, Edward J. 1971. Urban witches. In *Conformity and conflict: readings in cultural anthropology*. J. P. Spradley and D. W. McCurdy, ed. Boston: Little, Brown.

Moore, Martin. 1969. *Sex and modern witchcraft*. Los Angeles: Enchelon Book Publishers.

Morris, H., and J. C. Whitcomb. 1961. *The genesis flood*. Philadelphia: Presbyterian and Reformed Publishing Company.

Moskowitz, Sam. 1954. *The immortal storm: a history of science fiction*. Atlanta: The Atlantic Science Fiction Organization Press.

————. 1961. *Seekers of tomorrow*. New York: World.

————. 1970. *Under the moons of Mars: a history and anthology of "the scientific romance" in the Munsey Magazines, 1912–1920*. New York: Holt, Rinehart, and Winston.

Muelder, Walter. 1957. From sect to church. In *Religion, society, and the individual*. J. M. Yinger, ed. New York: Macmillan.

Muller, Herbert J. 1963. *Religious freedom in the modern world*. Chicago: University of Chicago Press.

Murdock, George P. 1965. Tenino shamanism. *Ethnology* 4:165–171.

————. 1967. Ethnographic atlas: a summary. *Ethnology* 6(2).

———— and D. White. 1969. Standard cross-cultural sample. *Ethnology* 8:329–368.

Murphy, G. 1965. A cross-cultural view of ego dynamics. *Bulletin of the New York Academy of Medicine* 41:268–285.

Murphy, Gardner, and Robert O. Ballou, eds. 1960. *William James on psychical research*. New York: Viking Press.

Murphy, H. B. M. 1968. Cultural factors in the genesis of schizophrenia. In *The transmission of schizophrenia.* D. Rosenthal and S. Kety, eds. Oxford: Pergamon Press.

———, E. D. Wittkower, and N. A. Chance. 1964. Cross-cultural inquiry into the symptomatology of depression. *Transcultural Psychiatric Research Newsletter* 1:5–18.

Murphy, J. 1964. Psychotherapeutic aspects of shamanism on St. Lawrence Island, Alaska. In *Magic, faith, and healing.* A. Kiev, ed. New York: The Free Press.

Murray, Gilbert. 1925. *Five stages of Greek religion.* New York: Columbia University Press.

Murray, Margaret A. 1921. *The witch cult in Western Europe.* London: Oxford University Press.

Nadel, S. F. 1952. Witchcraft in four African societies. *American Anthropologist* 54: 18–29.

Nash, R. H. 1963. *The new evangelism.* Grand Rapids: Zondervan.

National Spiritualist Association of Churches of the United States of America.

———. 1948. *Centennial book of modern Spiritualism in America.* Chicago.

———. 1967. *Spiritualist* manual. Milwaukee (10th revision).

———. n.d. *Spiritualist hymnal: a revised collection of words and music for congregation.* Boston: R. D. Row Music Company.

Needham, R. 1967. Percussion and transition. *Man* 2:606–614.

Needleman, Jacob. 1970. *The new religions.* New York: Doubleday.

Nelson, Geoffrey K. 1968. The concept of cult. *Sociological Review* 16:351–362.

———. 1969a. *Spiritualism and society.* London: Routledge and Kegan Paul.

———. 1969b. The Spiritualist movement: a need for the redefinition of the concept of the cult. *Journal for the Scientific Study of Religion* 8:152–160.

Nelson, Pearl Udall. 1959. *Arizona pioneer Mormon: David King Udall.* Tucson: Arizona Silhouettes.

Newsweek. 1969. Digging the stars. January 13, pp. 54–55.

Nichol, John T. 1966. *Pentecostalism.* New York: Harper and Row.

Nida, Eugene A. 1964. Glosolalia: A case of pseudo-linguistic structure. Paper presented to the 39th Annual Meeting of the Linguistic Society of America, New York, Dec. 28, 1964.

Niebuhr, H. Richard. 1929. *The social sources of denominationalism.* New York: Henry Holt.

———. 1935. *The kingdom of God in America.* New York: Harper and Row.

———. 1961. Protestantism as a social movement. In *The Shaping of American religion.* J. W. Smith and L. Jameson, eds. Princeton: Princeton University Press.

Nilsson, Martin P. 1925. *History of the Greek Religion.* Oxford: Clarendon Press.

————. 1943. Problems of the history of Greek religion in the Hellenistic and Roman age. *Harvard Theological Review* 36:251–275.

Nimkoff, M. F., and A. L. Wood. 1946. Effects of majority patterns of religious behavior on minority groups. *Sociology and Sociological Review* 30:282–289.

Nketia, J. H. 1963. *Drumming in Akan communities in Ghana*. London: T. Nelson and Sons.

Nolan, James. 1971. Jesus Now: hogwash and holy water. *Ramparts*. August.

Nolen, William A. 1970. *The making of a surgeon*. New York: Random House.

North, C. C., and P. K. Hatt. 1947. Jobs and occupations. *Opinion News* 9(4):6.

Nunberg, H. 1938. Homosexuality, magic, and aggression. *International Journal of Psychoanalysis* 19:1–16.

Nunn, C. Z. 1964. Child-control through a "coalition" with God. *Child Development* 35:417–432.

O'Dea, Thomas. 1957. *The Mormons*. Chicago: University of Chicago Press.

————. 1968. Sects and Cults. *International Encyclopaedia of the Social Sciences* 14:13–135.

Offner, Clark B., and Henry van Straelen. 1963. *Modern Japanese Religions*. Tokyo: Rupert Enderle.

Oliver, Paul. 1970. *Savannah syncopators: African retentions in the blues*. New York: Stein and Day.

Opler, M. K. 1959. Dream analysis in Ute Indian therapy. In *Culture and mental health*. M. K. Opler, ed. New York: Macmillan.

Orozco, Jose Clemente. 1962. *An autobiography*. Austin: University of Texas Press.

Ortiz, Fernandez F. 1965. *La Africania de la música folclórica de Cuba*. La Habana: Editora Universitaria (second edition).

Osborn, Arthur W. 1961. *The future is now*. Wheaton, Ill.: Theosophical Publishing House.

Otto, Rudolph. 1917. *The idea of the holy*. London: Oxford University Press.

Padilla, Elena. 1958. *Up from Puerto Rico*. New York: Columbia University Press.

Palmer, Gary. 1966. Trance and dissociation. Unpublished M.A. thesis. University of Minnesota.

Parrinder, Geoffrey. 1963. *Witchcraft: European and African*. London: Faber and Faber.

Parry, Milman. 1930. Studies in the epic technique of oral verse making. *Harvard Studies in Classical Philology* 41:73–147.

Parsons, Talcott. 1937. *The structure of social action*. New York: The Free Press.

————. 1951. *The social system*. Glencoe: The Free Press.

————. 1961. An outline of the social system. In *Theories of society,* Vol. 1. T. Parsons, ed. New York: The Free Press.

————, Edward A. Shils, et al., eds. 1954. *Toward a general theory of action.* Cambridge: Harvard University Press.

Pattison, E. Mansell. 1963. Medical ethics and Christian values. *Christian Medical Society Journal* 15:12–16.

————. 1965a. The effects of a religious culture's values on personality psychodynamics. Paper presented at the Meeting of Section H of the American Association for the Advancement of Science.

————. 1965b. On the failure to forgive or to be forgiven. *American Journal of Psychotherapy* 19:106–115.

————. 1968a. Behavioral science research on the nature of glossolalia. *Journal of the American Scientific Affiliation* 20:73–86.

————. 1968b. Ego morality: an emerging psychotherapeutic concept. *Psychoanalytic Review* 52:137–182.

————, ed. 1969. *Clinical psychiatry and religion.* Boston: Little, Brown.

———— and R. L. Casey. 1969. Glossolalia: a contemporary mystical experience. In *Clinical psychiatry and religion.* E. M. Pattison, ed. Boston: Little, Brown.

————, T. Chinn, and R. Rhodes. 1972. Religious participation and psychosomatic illness. (Forthcoming).

Paulme, Denise. 1962. *Une Société de la Côte d'Ivorie: Les Bété.* Paris. (Cited in Mair 1969:162–163, q.v.)

Paulsen, Kathryn. 1970. *The complete book of magic and witchcraft.* New York: The New American Library.

Pauwels, Louis, and Jacques Bergier. 1963. *The morning of the magicians.* New York: Stein and Day.

Paz, Octavio. 1961. *The labyrinth of solitude: life and thought in Mexico.* New York: Grove Press.

Peacock, James L. 1969. Mystics and Merchants in Fourteenth Century Germany. *Journal for the Scientific Study of Religion* 8(1):47–59.

Pearl, D. 1954. Ethnocentrism and the self concept. *Journal of Social Psychology* 40:137–147.

Pearson, Leonard, ed. 1965. *The use of written communication in psychotherapy.* Springfield, Ill.: Charles C. Thomas.

Perls, Frederick. 1969. *Gestalt therapy verbatim.* Lafayette, Cal.: Real Peoples Press.

————, Ralph Hefferline, and Paul Goodman. 1951. *Gestalt therapy.* New York: Dell.

Peterson, Charles S. 1967. *Settlement on the Little Colorado 1873–1890: a study of the processes and institutions of Mormon expansion.* Ann Arbor: University Microfilms.

Pfautz, H. W. 1955. The sociology of secularization: religious groups. *American Journal of Sociology* 61:121–128.

Pfeffer, Leo. 1967. *Church, state, and freedom.* Boston: Beacon Press.

Phillips, John P. 1969. The free exercise of religion goes to "pot." In *The religious situation: 1969.* D. R. Cutler, ed. Boston: Beacon Press.

Photiadis, J. D. and A. L. Johnson. 1963. Orthodoxy, church participation, and authoritarianism. *American Journal of Sociology* 63:244–248.

Pike, James. 1968. *The other side.* New York: Doubleday.

Pike, Kenneth L. 1967. *Language in relation to a unified theory of human behavior.* The Hague: Mouton (second revised edition).

Pike, Royston. 1954. *Jehovah's Witnesses: who they are, what they teach, what they do.* London: Watts and Company.

Pileggi, Nicholas. 1970. Occult. *McCalls* 97:62–65, 140.

Plamenatz, John. 1963. *Man and Society.* 2 vols. London: Longmans, Green.

Plog, Fred T. 1969. An approach to the study of prehistoric change. Ph.D. dissertation, Department of Anthropology, Univ. of Chicago.

Poblete, Renato and Thomas F. O'Dea. 1960. Anomie and the "quest for community": the formation of sects among the Puerto Ricans of New York. *The American Catholic Sociological Review* 21(1):18–36.

Podmore, Frank. 1902. *Modern Spiritualism.* New York: Charles Scribner's Sons.

———. 1910. *The newer Spiritualism.* London: T. F. Unwin.

Pope, Alexander. 1931. *The complete poetical works of Pope.* Boston: Houghton Mifflin.

Pope, Liston. 1942. *Millhands and preachers.* New Haven: Yale University Press.

Powell, Milton, ed. 1967. *The voluntary church.* New York: Macmillan.

Pratt, Parley. 1855. *Key to the science of theology.* Liverpool: F. D. Richards.

Pressel, Esther. 1973. Umbanda in São Paulo: religious innovation in a developing society. In *Religion, altered states of consciousness, and culture change.* E. Bourguignon, ed. Columbus: The Ohio State University Press.

Prince, Raymond. 1962. Some notes on Yoruba native doctors and their management of mental illness. In *First Pan-African psychiatric conference.* T. A. Lambo, ed. Ibadan, Nigeria: Government Printer.

———. 1964. Indigenous Yoruba psychiatry. In *Magic, faith and healing.* A. Kiev, ed. New York: The Free Press.

———. 1968. Religious experience, youth, and social change. R. M. Bucke Memorial Society, *Newsletter Review* 3:1–3.

———. 1969. Psychotherapy and the chronically poor. In *Culture change, mental health, and poverty.* J. C. Finney, ed. Lexington: University of Kentucky Press.

———, ed. 1968. *Trance and possession states.* Montreal: R. M. Bucke Memorial Society.

——— and C. Savage. 1966. Mystical states and the concept of regression. *Psychedelic Review* 8:59–74.

Protestant Council of the City of New York, The. 1960. *A report on the*

Protestant Spanish community in New York City. New York: Privately printed.

Purdy, Beatrice, and others. 1970. Mellaril or medium, stelazine or seance? A study of Spiritualism as it affects communication, diagnosis, and treatment of Puerto Rican people. Paper presented at the Annual Meeting of the American Orthopsychiatric Association. San Francisco, California.

Rackman, S. 1966. Sexual fetishism: an experimental analogue. *Psychological Record* 12:293–296.

Ramos, Arthur. 1954. *O folclore Negro do Brasil.* Rio de Janeiro: Editôra da Casa do Estudante do Brasil (second edition).

Ramos, Samuel. 1938. *El perfil del hombre y la cultura en Mexico.* Mexico, D. F.: Editorial Pedro Robrido.

Randolph, Vance. 1947. *Ozark superstition.* New York: Columbia University Press.

Ranck, J. G. 1961. Religious conservatism-liberalism and mental health. *Pastoral Psychology* 12:34–40.

Rapaport, D. 1952. On the psychoanalytic theory of affects. *Journal of the American Psychoanalytic Association* 8:300–315.

———. 1958. The theory of ego autonomy: a generalization. *Bulletin of the Menninger Clinic* 22:13–26.

Rappaport, Roy A. 1967. *Pigs for the ancestors.* New Haven: Yale University Press.

Rascoe, Judith. 1970. Church of Satan. *McCalls* 92:74–75, 133–136.

Real, K. 1967. *O folclore no Carnaval do Recife.* Rio de Janeiro: Ministerio da Educaçao e Cultura.

Reich, Charles A. 1970. *The Greening of America.* New York: Random House.

Reich, Wilhelm. 1949. *Character analysis.* New York: Farrar, Strauss, and Cudahy.

Reisman, K. 1970. Cultural ambiguity in a West Indian village. In *Afro-American anthropoligy: contemporary perspectives.* N. Whitten and J. Szwed, eds. New York: The Free Press.

———. n.d. Contrapuntal communication. Unpublished paper.

Rhodes, H. T. F. 1954. *The Satanic mass.* London: Rider and Company.

Richmond, W. Edson. 1970. Review of *The art of the American folk preacher.* Bruce A. Rosenberg. *Georgia Review* 24:503–505.

Richter, Hans. 1965. *Dada: art and anti-art.* New York: McGraw-Hill.

Rickels,   and   Anderson. 1967.

Ricoeur, Paul. 1970. *Freud and philosophy.* New Haven: Yale University Press.

Robbins, C. 1970. A West African religious festival in New York City. Paper presented at the Conference on Continuities and Discontinuities in Afro-American Culture. Jamaica.

Robbins, Russell H. 1959. *The encyclopedia of witchcraft and demonology.* New York: Crown Publishers, Inc.

Robbins, Thomas. 1970. Characteristics of amphetamine addicts. *International Journal of Addictions* 5(2).

———. 1969. Eastern mysticism and the resocialization of drug users. *Journal for the Scientific Study of Religion* 8(2):308–317.

——— and Dick Anthony. 1972. Getting straight with Meher Baba. *Journal for the Scientific Study of Religion* 11:122–140.

Roberts, Susan. 1971. *Witches, U.S.A.* New York: Dell.

Robertson, Roland. 1970. *The sociology of religion: problems and desiderata.* Newcastle-upon-Tyne: Oriel Press.

Robson, Peter. 1969. *The devil's own.* New York: Ace Books.

Rodgers, Johnathan. 1969. The North: hustler, preacher, Panther. *Newsweek,* June 30, pp. 32–33.

Rogler, Lloyd H., and August B. Hollingshead. 1961. The Puerto Rican Spiriualist as a psychiatrist. *American Journal of Sociology* 67:17–21.

Rokeach, M. 1960. *The open and closed mind.* New York: Basic Books.

———. 1964. *Three Christs of Ypsilanti.* New York: A. A. Knopf.

Romm, Ethel G., ed. 1970. *The open conspiracy.* Harrisburg: Stackpole.

Rose, Elliot. 1962. *A razor for a goat.* Toronto: University of Toronto Press.

Rosenberg, Bruce A. 1970. *The art of the American folk preacher.* New York: Oxford University Press.

Rosenberg, B. G. and C. N. Zimet. 1957. Authoritarianism and aesthetic choice. *Journal of Social Psychology* 46:293–297.

Rosenberg, M. 1962. The dissonant religious context and emotional disturbance. *American Journal of Sociology* 68:1–11.

Roszak, T. 1969. *The making of a counter culture.* New York: Doubleday.

Rotnem, Victor, and F. G. Folsom, Jr. 1942. Recent restrictions upon religious liberty. *American Political Science Review* 36:1053–1068.

Rowley, Peter. 1971. *New gods in America.* New York: Donald McKay and Company.

Rubel, Arthur J. 1960. Concepts of disease in Mexican-American cultures. *American Anthropologist* 62:795–814.

———. 1966. *Across the tracks: Mexican-Americans in a Texas city.* Austin: University of Texas Press.

Rubin, Jerry. 1970. *Do it.* New York: Simon and Schuster.

Rusk, R. L. 1949. *The life of Ralph Waldo Emerson.* New York: Charles Scribners' Sons.

Sahlins, Marshall T., and Elman R. Service. 1961. *Evolution and culture.* Ann Arbor: University of Michigan Press.

Salisbury, W. S. 1956. Faith, ritualism, charismatic leadership, and religious behavior. *Social Forces* 34:241–245.

Samarin, William. 1968. The linguisticality of glossolalia. *The Hartford Quarterly* 8(4):49–75.

Sansweet, Stephen J. 1969. Strange doings: Americans show burst of interest in witches, other occult matters. *The Wall Street Journal,* October 23, p. 1.

Sanua, Victor D. 1959. Differences in personality adjustment among different generations of American Jews and non-Jews. In *Cultural and mental health*. M. K. Opler, ed. New York: Macmillan.

Sasaki, Y. 1969. Psychiatric study of the shaman in Japan. In *Mental health research in Asia and the Pacific*. W. Caudill and T. Lin, eds. Honolulu: East-West Center Press.

Satsvarupadas Adhikari. 1970. The prayers of Akrura. *Back to Godhead* 34:22–23.

Saunders, Lyle. 1954. *Cultural differences and medical care*. New York: Russell Sage Foundation.

Saussure, Ferdinand de. 1959. *Course in general linguistics*. London: Peter Owen.

Savin, H., and E. Perchonock. 1965. Grammatical structures and the immediate recall of English sentences. *Journal of Verbal Learning and Verbal Behavior* 4:248–353.

Schafer, Ray. 1968. *Aspects of internalization*. New York: International Universities Press.

Schaff, Philip. 1961. *America*. Perry Miller, ed. Cambridge: Harvard University Press.

Schaps, E., and C. R. Sanders. 1970. Purposes, patterns, and protection in a campus drug using community, *Journal of Health and Social Behavior* (June):134–145.

Scheuch, Erwin. 1968. *Die Wiedertäufer der Wohlstandsgellschaft: eine kritische Untersuchung der "Neuen Linker" und ihrer Dogmen*. Köhn: Markus Verlag.

Schlesinger, Arthur M., Sr. 1932. A critical period in American religion, 1875–1900. *Proceedings of the Massachusetts Historical Society* 64:523–546.

Schneider, David. 1968. *American kinship: a cultural account*. Englewood Cliffs: Prentice-Hall.

———. 1969. Kinship, nationality, and religion in American culture: toward a definition of kinship. *Proceedings of the Spring Meeting of the American Ethnological Society*. R. F. Spencer, ed. Seattle: University of Washington Press.

Schneider, Delwyn B. 1962. *Konkyoko: a Japanese religion*. Tokyo: International Institute for the Study of Religion.

Schnell, William. 1956. *Thirty years a watchtower slave*. Grand Rapids: Zondervan.

Schoenwetter, James, and Alfred E. Dittert, Jr. 1968. An ecological interpretation of Anasazi settlement patterns. In *Anthropological Archaeology in the Americas*. Betty J. Meggars, ed. Washington: The Anthropological Society of Washington.

Schulberg, Budd, ed. 1967. *From the ashes: voices of Watts*. New York: The New American Library.

Schurmacher, Emile. 1970. *Witchcraft in America today*. New York: Paperback Library.

Schutz, Alfred. 1971. *Collected papers*. The Hague: Martinus Nifhoff.

Schwartz, Gary. 1970. *Sect ideologies and social status*. Chicago: University of Chicago Press.

Seabrook, William. 1940. *Witchcraft: its power in the world today*. New York: Harcourt, Brace, and Company.

Seale, Bobby. 1970. *Seize the time*. New York: Random House.

Service, Elman. 1971. *Cultural evolutionism*. New York: Holt, Rinehart, and Winston.

Seth, Donald. 1968. *Witches and their craft*. New York: Taplinger.

Sherrill, John L. 1964. *They speak with other tongues*. New York: McGraw-Hill.

Shirokogorov, Sergiei Mikhailovich. 1935. *Psychomental complex of the Tungus*. London: K. Paul, Trench, Trubner and Company, Ltd.

Sidgwick, Emma M. 1887. Spiritualism. *Encyclopedia Britannica*, 22:404–407 (ninth edition).

Siegman, A. W. 1956. A "culture and personality" study based on a comparison of Rorschach performance. *Journal of Social Psychology* 44:173–178.

Siirala, Aarne. 1964. *The voice of illness: a study in therapy and prophecy*. Philadelphia: Fortress Press.

Simpson, George E. 1953. Political cultism in West Kingston, Jamaica. *Social and Economic Studies* 4:133–149.

————. 1956. Jamaican revivalistic cults. *Social and Economic Studies* 5(4):321–342.

————. 1957. The Ras Tafari movement in Jamaica: a study of race and class conflict. In *Religion, society, and the individual*. J. M. Yinger, ed. New York: Macmillan.

Slater, Phillip. 1970. *The pursuit of loneliness*. Boston: Beacon Press.

Slotkin, J. S. 1956. *The peyote religion*. Glencoe, Ill.: The Free Press.

Smith, H. S. 1955. *Changing conceptions of original sin*. New York: Charles Scribner's Sons.

Smith, Joseph Fielding. 1966–1970. *Answers to gospel questions*, 5 volumes. Salt Lake City: Deseret Book Company.

————. 1969. *Doctrines of salvation*, 3 volumes. Salt Lake City: Bookcraft.

Smith, Marian, W. 1959. Toward a classification of cult movements. *Man* 59:8–12.

Smith, Preserved. 1920. *Reformation in Europe*. New York: Henry Holt and Company.

Smith, Susy. 1970. *Today's witches*. Englewood Cliffs: Prentice-Hall.

Smith, Timothy L. 1957. *Revivalism and social reform in mid-nineteenth-century America*. New York: Abingdon Press.

Smith, W. Robertson. 1889. *Lectures on the religion of the Semites*. Edinburgh: A. & C. Black.

Snowflake Stake Funds. 1882–1901. Office of the Church Historian, Salt Lake City, Utah. Microfilm.

Snowflake Stake Historical Record. 1886–1889. Office of the Church Historian, Salt Lake City, Utah. Manuscript.

Snyder, G. 1969. *Riprap and cold mountain poems.* San Francisco: Four Seasons Foundation.

Sorem, Anthony. 1969. Some secular implications of the Pentecostal denomination. Unpublished M.A. thesis. University of Minnesota.

Sparrow, John H. A. 1934. *Sense and poetry: essays on the place of meaning in contemporary verse.* London: Constable.

Spence, Lewis. 1960. *Encyclopedia of occultism.* New Hyde Park, New York: University Books.

Spiegel, Leo. 1959. The self, the sense of self, and perception. *The Psychoanalytic Study of the Child* 14:81–109.

Spiro, M. E. 1967. *Burmese supernaturalism.* Englewood Cliffs: Prentice-Hall.

Spitz, R. 1953. Aggression, its role in the establishment of object relations. In *Drives, affects, and behavior,* Vol. 1. R. M. Lowenstein, ed. New York: International Universities Press.

Sprenger, Jakob, and Henricus Institoris. 1948. *Malleus malefarum.* London: Puskin Press.

Srole, L., and others. 1962. *Mental health in the metropolis: the midtown Manhattan study.* New York: McGraw-Hill.

Stace, W. T. 1960. *The teachings of the mystics.* New York: Mentor Books.

Stagg, Frank, E. Glenn Hinson, and Wayne E. Oates. 1967. *Glossolalia tongue speaking in biblical, historical, and psychological perspective.* Nashville and New York: Abingdon Press.

St. Albin-Greene, Daniel. 1969. There may be a witch next door. *The National Observer,* October 13, p. 24.

Stark, Werner. 1966–1970. *The sociology of religion,* 4 volumes. London: Routledge and Kegal Paul.

Starkey, Marion L. 1961. *The devil in Massachusetts: a modern inquiry into the Salem witch trials.* New York: Doubleday.

Starkie, Enid. 1954. *Petrus Borel.* London: Faber and Faber.

State Tax Commission of Arizona. 1917–1966. Biennial Reports.

Staude, John R. 1970. Alienated youth and the cult of the occult. Paper presented at the Annual Meeting of the Midwest Sociological Society. St. Louis, Missouri.

Stearn, Less. 1967. *Edgar Cayce: the sleeping prophet.* New York: Doubleday.

Steiger, Brad. 1968. *In my soul I am free.* New York: Lancer.

———. 1969. *Sex and Satanism.* New York: Ace Books.

Steiner, Lee. 1945. *Where do people take their troubles?* Boston: Houghton Mifflin.

Stern, G. G. 1954. Assessing theological students personality structure. *Journal of Pastoral Care* 8:76–83.

Stevenson, W. C. 1967. *The inside story of the Jehovah's Witnesses.* New York: Hart.

Stevick, D. B. 1964. *Beyond fundamentalism*. Richmond, Virginia: John Knox Press.

Steward, D., and T. Hoult. 1960. A socio-psychological theory of the authoritarian personality. *American Journal of Sociology* 65:274–279.

Stokes, Anson P. 1950. *Church and state in the United States*. 2 vols. New York: Harper and Row.

Stroup, Herbert H. 1945. *The Jehovah's Witnesses*. New York: Columbia University Press.

Sturtevant, William C. 1964. Studies in ethnoscience. In Transcultural studies in cognition. A. K. Romney and R. G. D'Andrade, eds. *American Anthropologist Publications* 66(3:2):99–131.

Sullivan, Gilbert. 1971. Personal communication. (Water control specialist for the U.S. Department of the Interior. Holbrook, Arizona).

Summers, Montague. 1926. *The history of witchcraft and demonology*. New York: University Books.

———. 1946. *Witchcraft and black magic*. London: Rider and Company.

———. 1958. *The geography of witchcraft*. New York: University Books.

Sundler, Bengt Gustaf Malcolm. 1961. *Bantu prophets in South Africa*. New York: Oxford University Press.

Sweet, W. W. 1930. *The story of religions in America*. New York: Harper.

———. 1942. *Religion in colonial America*. New York: Charles Scribner's Sons.

———. 1952. *Religion in the development of American culture, 1765–1840*. New York: Charles Scribner's Sons.

Szwed, John. 1970. Afro-American musical adaptation. In *Afro-American anthropology: contemporary perspectives*. N. Whitten and J. Szwed, eds. New York: The Free Press.

Talmon, Yonina. 1962. Pursuit of the millenium: the relation between religions and social change. *Archives Européenes de Sociologie* 3:125–148.

Thomas, Klaus. 1962. Ecclessiogenic neurosis. In *Handbook on suicide*. Berlin: Springer Verlag.

Thomas, Veronica. 1966. The witches of 1966. *Atlantic* 218:119–125.

Thomas, William, and Florian Znaniecki. 1927. *The Polish peasant in Europe and America*. New York: A. A. Knopf.

Thomsen, Harry. 1963. *The new religions of Japan*. Tokyo and Rutland, Vermont: Charles F. Tuttle.

Thomson, Mortimer N. (*alias* Q. K. Philander Doesticks). 1859. *The witches of New York*. New York: Rudd and Carleton.

Thorner, I. 1950. Christian Science and ascetic Protestantism. Unpublished Ph.D. dissertation. Harvard University.

———. 1953. Ascetic Protestantism and alcohol. *Psychiatry* 16:167–176.

Thrupp, Sylvia, ed. 1970. *Millenian dreams in action*. New York: Schocken Books.

Thurston, Herbert. 1933. *The church and Spiritualism*. Milwaukee: Bruce Publishing Company.

Toch, Hans. 1965. *The social psychology of social movements*. Indianapolis: Bobbs-Merrill.

Topitsch, Ernst. 1966. *Sozialphilosophie zwischen Ideologie und Wissenschaft*. Berlin: Herman Luchterhand Verlag.

Townshend, Peter. 1970. Loving Meher Baba. *Rolling Stone* (November 26):24–27.

Trevor-Roper, H. R. 1968. *The crisis of the seventeenth century: religion, the Reformation, and social change*. New York: Harper and Row.

Triandis, H. C. 1964. Cultural influences upon cognitive processes. In *Advances in experimental social psychology*, Vol. 1. L. Berkowitz, ed. New York: Academic Press.

Trimmingham, J. Spencer. 1962. *Islam in East Africa*. Edinburgh: Edinburgh House Press.

Troeltsch, Ernst. 1931. *The social teachings of the Christian churches*, 2 volumes. London: Allen and Unwin.

Truax, Charles, and Robert Carkhuff. 1967. *Toward effective counseling and psychotherapy*. Chicago: Aldine.

Truzzi, Marcello. 1971. *Sociology: the classic statements*. New York: Random House.

———. 1972a. The occult revival as popular culture: some random observations on the old and the nouveau witch. *Sociological Quarterly* 13:16–36.

Turner, Victor. 1967. *The forest of symbols*. Ithaca, New York: Cornell University Press.

———. 1969. *The ritual process: structure and anti-structure*. Chicago: Aldine.

Tussman, Joseph, ed. 1962. *The supreme court on church and state*. New York: Oxford University Press.

Twig (Richard Terwilliger). 1972. Meher Baba: messiah to millions. *Queens College Newsboat*. February 15.

Tyler, Alice F. 1944. *Freedom's ferment*. Minneapolis: University of Minnesota Press.

Tylor, E. B. 1871. *Primitive cultures: researches into the development of mythology, philosophy, religion, art, and custom*, 2 volumes. Gloucester, Mass. Smith Company.

Ullman, Leonard, and L. Krasner. 1969. *A psychological approach to abnormal behavior*. Englewood Cliffs: Prentice-Hall.

Underhill, Evelyn. 1955. *Mysticism*. New York: World.

———. 1972b. Definition and dimensions of the occult: towards a sociological perspective. In *The occult: studies and evaluations*. Robert Galbreath, ed. Bowling Green: Bowling Green University Popular Press.

U.S. Bureau of the Census. 1936. *Census of religious bodies*. Washington: Government Printing Office.

Valiente, Doreen. 1962. *Where witchcraft lives*. London: Aquarian Press.

Vanderveldt, R. and P. Odenwald. 1957. *Catholicism and psychiatry*. Boston: H. Regnery.

Van Baalen, Jan K. 1938. *The chaos of cults.* Grand Rapids, Michigan: Eerdmans.

van Gennep, A. 1960. *The rites of passage.* London: Routledge and Kegan Paul.

van Vogt, A. E. 1964. *Reflections of A. E. Van Vogt.* Compiled under the auspices of the Oral History Program, UCLA.

———. 1965. *The way of a pilgrim.* New York: Seabury Press.

Velikovsky, Emanuel. 1950. *Worlds in collision.* New York: Macmillan.

Verger, Pierre. 1957. *Notes sur le culte des Orisa et Vodun à Bahiá, la Baie de tour les Saints, au Brésil et à l'ancienne Côte des Esclaves en Afrique.* Dakar: IFAN Memoirs, Vol. 51.

———. 1969. Trance and convention in Nago-Yoruba spirit mediumship. In *Spirit mediumship and society in Africa.* J. Beattie and J. Middleton, eds. New York: Africana Publishing Company.

Vivier, L. M. van. 1968. The glossolalia and his personality. In *Beitrage zur Ekstase.* Th. Spoerri, ed. Bibliotheca Psychiatrica et Neurologica 134. Basel: S. Karger.

Von Wiese, Leopold, and Howard Becker. 1932. *Systematic sociology on the basis of the Beziehungslehre and Gebildelehre of Leopold von Wiese.* New York: John Wiley.

Waite, Edward F. 1944. The debt of constitutional law to Jehovah's Witnesses. *Minnesota Law Review* 28:209–246.

Wallace, Alfred Russell. 1875. *On miracles and modern spiritualism.* London.

Wallace, Anthony F. C. 1956. Revitalization movements. *American Anthropologist* 58:264–281.

———. 1961. Religious revitalization: a function of religion in human history and evolution. Paper presented at the Eighth Institute of Religion in an Age of Science. Star Island, New Hampshire.

———. 1966. *Religion: an anthropological view.* New York: Random House.

———. 1970. *Culture and personality.* New York: Random House (second edition).

Wallace, C. H. 1967. *Witchcraft in the world today.* New York: Award Books.

Wallenstein, J. S., and C. J. Wylie. 1947. Our law-abiding law breakers. *Probation* 25:107–112.

Walters, O. S. 1964. Religion and psychopathology. *Comprehensive Psychiatry* 5:24–32.

Ward Financial Record. 1901–1905. Joseph City, Arizona.

Wardwell, W. I. 1965. Christiance Science healing. *Journal for the Scientific Study of Religion* 4:175–181.

Warner, Wellman J. 1964. Sects. In *A dictionary of the social sciences.* J. Gould and W. W. Kolb, eds. New York: Free Press.

Warner, W. L. 1960. *Social class in America: a manual of the procedures for the measurement of social status.* New York: Harper and Row.

Warren, Donald, Jr. 1968. Spiritualism in Brazil. *Journal of Inter-American Studies* 10:393–405.

The Watchtower. 1969. Bi-Monthly study magazine of the New World Society of Jehovah's Witnesses.

Watchtower Bible and Tract Society of Pennsylvania and New York. 1955. *Qualified to be ministers* (revised 1967 edition).

Waterman, R. 1952. African influence on the music of the Americas. In *Acculturation in the Americas.* Sol Tax, ed. Chicago: University of Chicago Press.

Watts, A. W. 1957. *The way of Zen.* New York: Pantheon Books.

Weber, Max. 1930. *The Protestant ethic and the spirit of capitalism.* New York: Charles Scribner's Sons.

———. 1963. *The sociology of religion.* Boston: Beacon Press.

Weidman, H. H. 1968. Anthropological theory and the psychological function of belief in witchcraft. In *Essays in medical anthropology.* Athens, Georgia: Southern Anthropological Society.

Weier, W. Wilson. 1970. The new wave of witches. *Occult* 1:24–37.

Weima, J. 1965. Authoritarianism, religious conservatism, and sociocentric attitudes in Roman Catholic groups. *Human Relations* 18:231–239.

Weinser, W. W. and A. Riffel. 1960. Scrupulosity: religion and obsessive compulsive behavior. *American Journal of Psychiatry* 117:304–318.

Westover, Adele B., and J. Morris Richards. 1967. *Unflinching courage.* Publisher unknown.

Whalen, William L. 1962. *Armageddon around the corner: a report on the Jehovah's Witnesses.* New York: The John Day Company.

———. 1963. *Faiths for a few: a study of minority religions.* Milwaukee: The Bruce Publishing Company.

———. 1964. *The Latter-day Saints in the modern world.* New York: The John Day Company.

White, Leslie A. 1959. *The evolution of culture.* New York: McGraw-Hill.

White, R. W. 1963. Ego and reality in psychoanalytic theory. *Psychological Issues* 3(3), Monograph 11.

White, Timothy. 1968. *A people for his name: a history of Jehovah's Witnesses and an evaluation.* New York: The Vantage Press.

Whitehead, Earnest L. 1947. *The house of Israel.* Independence: Zion's Printing and Publishing Company.

Whorf, B. L. 1956. *Language, thought, and reality: selected writings of Benjamin Lee Whorf.* Cambridge: MIT Press.

Wilgus, D. K., and Bruce Rosenberg. 1970. A modern medieval story: the soldier's deck of cards. In *Medieval literature and folklore studies.* B. Rosenberg and J. Mandell, eds. New Brunswick, New Jersey: Rutgers University Press.

Wilkerson, David. 1963. *The cross and the switchblade.* New York: Random House.

Willems, Emilio. 1967a. *Followers of the new faith: culture change and the rise of Protestantism in Brazil and Chile.* Nashville, Tennessee: Vanderbilt University Press.

———. 1967b. Validation of authority in Pentecostal sects of Brazil and Chile. *Journal for the Scientific Study of Religion* 6:253–259.

Williams, George H. 1962. *The radical Reformation.* Philadelphia: The Westminster Press.

Williams, Gertrude. 1964. *Madame Blavatsky: priestess of the occult.* New York: A. A. Knopf.

Wills, Gary. 1971. Syndicated column (UP). *Minneapolis Star,* March 2.

Wilson, Bryan R. 1959. Role conflicts and status contradictions of the Pentecostal minister. *American Journal of Sociology* 64:494–504.

———. 1961. *Sects and society: a sociological study of the Elim Tabernacle, Christian Science, and Christadelphians.* Berkeley: University of California Press.

———. 1967. *Patterns of sectarianism.* London: Heinemann.

———. 1970. *Religious sects.* New York: McGraw-Hill.

Winter, J. A. 1951. *A doctor's report on dianetics.* New York: Julian Press, Inc.

Witmer, S. A. 1962. *The Bible college story: education with dimension.* Manhasset, New York: Channel Press.

Wolf, Eric R. 1951. The social organization of Meccas and the origin of Islam. *Southwestern Journal of Anthropology* 7:329–356.

Wolfe, Tom. 1968. *The electric kool-aid acid test.* New York: Farrar, Strauss and Giroux.

Wolpe, J. 1954. Reciprocal inhibition as the main basis of psychotherapeutic effects. *AMA Archives of Neurology and Psychiatry* 72:205–266.

———. 1958. *Psychotherapy by reciprocal inhibition.* Stanford: Stanford University Press.

Wolpe, J., and A. A. Lazarus. 1966. *Behavior therapy techniques: a guide to the treatment of neuroses.* New York: Pergamon.

Wood, William W. 1965. *Culture and personality aspects of the Pentecostal Holiness religion.* The Hague: Mouton.

Worrall, Ambrose, and Olga Worrall. 1965. *The gift of healing.* New York: Harper and Row.

Worsley, Peter. 1968. *The trumpet shall sound.* New York: Schocken Books.

Wylie, Phillip. 1953. Science fiction and sanity in an age of crisis. In *Modern science fiction.* R. Bretnor, ed. New York: Coward-McCann.

Yablonsky, Lewis. 1968. *The hippie trip.* New York: Pegasus.

Yalom, Irwin. 1970. *The theory and practice of group psychotherapy.* New York: Basic Books.

Yinger, J. Milton. 1957. *Religion, society, and the individual.* New York: Macmillan.

———. 1960. Contraculture and subculture. *American Sociological Review* 25:625–635.

———. 1963. *Sociology looks at religion.* New York: Macmillan.

———. 1970. *The scientific study of religion.* New York: Macmillan.

Zablocki, Benjamin D. In press. The social structure of drug based communes. In *Drug abuse and drug subculture.* Washington: U.S. Government Printing Office.

NATHAN ADLER, Attending Staff, Department of Psychiatry, Mt. Zion Hospital, San Francisco; (formerly) Lecturer, Department of Psychology and School of Criminology, University of California, Berkeley. He conducted extensive clinical studies of drug users in the San Francisco Bay area between 1965 and 1970. His recent publication is *The Underground Stream: New Life Styles and the Antinomian Personality*, Harper and Row, 1972.

DICK ANTHONY, Research Associate, Department of Psychiatry, School of Medicine, University of North Carolina at Chapel Hill. He has published studies on language patterns in schizophrenic families and on the relationship between emotional disorder and metabolic disturbance. Since 1969 he has been working with THOMAS ROBBINS on a long-range study of the rehabilitation of psychedelic drug users by counter-culture religions. Publications with Dr. Robbins include "Getting Straight with Meher Baba," *Journal for the Scientific Study of Religion*, June 1972; "On the Limits of Symbolic Realism," *Journal for the Scientific Study of Religion*, September 1973; *The Meher Baba and Jesus Movements: A Comparison of "Post-drug" Spiritual Movements*, a monograph in Contemporary Religious Movements: A Wiley Interscience Series, John Wiley and Sons (in press).

MARY CATHERINE BATESON is Associate Professor in the Department of Sociology and Anthropology, Northeastern University, Boston, Massachusetts. She conducted research on glossolalia in urban New England in 1966, and developed the theoretical model used here during her research on mother-child communication at the Massachusetts Institute of Technology between 1969 and 1972. Her publications include *Approaches to Semiotics* (ed. with T.A. Sebeok and A.S. Hayes), The Hague: Mouton, 1964; *Structural Continuity in Poetry: A Linguistic Study of Five Pre-Islamic Arabic Odes*, Paris: Écoles des Hautes Études, 1970; *Our Own Metaphor: A Personal Account of a Conference on Conscious Purpose and Human Adaptation*, New York: Knopf, 1972.

ERIKA BOURGUIGNON, Professor and Chairman, Department of Anthropology, The Ohio State University. She conducted field work in Haiti in 1947-48, and was Director of the Cross-Cultural Study of Dissociational States between 1963 and 1968. Her recent publications are "Divination, Transe et Possession en Afrique Transsaharienne," *in* A. Caquot and M. Leibovici, eds., *La Divination*, Presses universitaires de France, Paris, 1968; "Trance Dance," *Dance Perspectives 35*, Dance Perspectives Foundation, N. Y., 1968; "Ritual Dissociation and Possession Belief in Caribbean Negro Religion," *in* N. E.

Whitten, Jr. and J. F. Szwed, eds., *Afro-American Anthropology: Contemporary Perspectives*, N. Y., Free Press, 1970; "Afro-American Religions: Traditions and Transformations," *in* J. F. Szwed, ed., *Black America*, New York: Basic Books, 1970; "Dreams and Altered States of Consciousness in Anthropological Research," *in* F. L. K Hsu, ed., *Psychological Anthropology*, new ed., Cambridge, Schenkman, 1972; *Religion, Altered States of Consciousness and Social Change*, editor and contributor, Columbus: Ohio State University Press, 1973; with Lenora Greenbaum: *Diversity and Homogeneity in World Societies*, New Haven, Conn.: HRAF Press, 1973; *Culture and the Varieties of Consciousness*, an Addison-Wesley Module in Anthropology, #47, Reading, Mass.: Addison-Wesley Publishing Company, 1974; "Psychological Anthropology," *in* J. J. Honigmann, ed., *Handbook of Social and Cultural Anthropology*, Chicago: Rand McNally, 1974; *Possession*, San Francisco: Chandler and Sharp, (in press) ; "Foreword," *in* F. D. Goodman, J. H. Henney, and E. Pressel: *Trance, Healing, and Hallucination: Three Studies in Religious Behavior*, New York: Wiley Interscience, 1974.

JOHN RICHARD BURKHOLDER, Professor of Religion, Goshen College, Goshen, Indiana. His recent publication is *Can the Courts Define Religion?* Contemporary Religious Movements: A Wiley Interscience Series, New York, John Wiley and Sons, Inc. (in press) .

LEE R. COOPER is an instructor in anthropology at Temple University, Philadelphia, and a doctoral candidate in the Department of Anthropology, University of Pennsylvania. In 1968-69 he did field work in a Negro Jehovah's Witness congregation and in Witness District Rallies in North and West Philadelphia. He is currently completing his dissertation on the social significance of speaking in urban Guadeloupe, French West Indies, based on field research he conducted from 1970 to 1972.

JANET DOLGIN, Assistant Professor, Department of Anthropology, University of Maryland; (formerly) NEH Post-Doctoral Fellow, Department of Anthropology, University of Chicago. She conducted field research with Mormons in Arizona in 1970. Her dissertation, a study of the Jewish Defense League, was based on a year of field work with that group on the east coast of the United States and in Israel.

ALLAN W. EISTER, Professor of Sociology, Chairman of the Department of Sociology and Anthropology at Wellesley College and a former Visiting Fellow, All Souls College, Oxford. He conducted field research with the Oxford Group Movement (Moral Re-Armament) in the United States during the 1940s. From 1962 to the present his research has included informal interviewing of members of sect groups in the United States, Great Britain, and Israel. He has authored *Drawing-Room Conversion: A Sociological Account of the Oxford Group Movement*, Durham, Duke University Press, 1950; "H. Richard Niebuhr and the Paradox of Religious Organization," Chapter 8 in Charles Y. Glock and Phillip E. Hammond, eds., *Beyond the Classics?: Essays in the Scientific Study of Religion*, New York Harper & Row,

1973. He is editor of *Changing Perspectives in the Scientific Study of Religion,* Contemporary Religious Movements: A Wiley Interscience series, John Wiley and Sons, Inc., New York, 1974.

VIVIAN E. GARRISON, Senior Research Associate, Department of Anthropology, Columbia University. Dr. Garrison conducted field work in the South Bronx, New York City between 1966 and 1969 and between 1972 and 1974, studying 87 religious organizations in a ten-census-tract area, with particular emphases on Pentecostalism and Puerto Rican Spiritism. The study was conducted while Dr. Garrison was affiliated with the Lincoln Hospital Mental Health Services, a Division of Albert Einstein College of Medicine and was analysed and written up while she was Assistant Professor of Psychiatry in the Yale University School of Medicine and staff member of the Program Information and Assessment Section of the Connecticut Mental Health Center, New Haven, Connecticut. Her publications include "Espiritismo: Implications for Provision of Mental Health Services to Puerto Rican Populations," *in* H.E. Hodges and C.M. Hudson, eds., *Folk Therapy* (forthcoming) ; "Supporting structures in a 'disorganized' Puerto Rican migrant community," *in* D. Raphael, ed., *Supportive Behavior* (forthcoming) ; (with G.L. Tischler, J. Henisz, and J.K. Myers) "Catchmenting and the Use of Mental Health Services," *Archives of General Psychiatry,* 27 (1972) :389-392; "The Impact of Catchmenting," *Administration in Mental Health* 1(1972):22-29; and "Social Areas Analysis in Matching Populations for Comparative Study," Yale University Institute for Social and Policy Studies, Health Services Research Program, WP #26; and (with P.R. Goldblatt, L.D. Brauer, J.E. Henisz, and M. Malcolm-Lawes) "A Chart-review Checklist for Utilization Review in a Community Mental Health Center," *Hospital & Community Psychiatry,* 24(1973):753-756.

LUTHER P. GERLACH is Professor in the Department of Anthropology at the University of Minnesota. In 1971-72 he was Visiting Associate in Anthropology and Environmental Quality at the California Institute of Technology, and in 1972-73 he continued on leave as a senior staff member of the Aspen Institute of Humanistic Studies, helping develop an Institute for the Analyses of Public Choices. He has conducted field work on social organization and change among the Digo, Duruma, and Shirazi people of the Kenya coast (1958-1960) ; on neo-Pentecostalism in North America and its spread to Haiti and Colombia (1965-1969) ; and again in North America on such movements of change as Black Power and the Ecology movement (1966-1971). He is currently researching citizen and established order response to limits of growth, energy, and other shortages. He is co-author with VIRGINIA H. HINE of *People, Power, Change: Movements of Social Transformation,* Bobbs Merrill, 1970; and *Lifeway Leap: The Dynamics of Change in America,* University of Minnesota Press, 1973; as well as "The Social Organization of a Movement of Revolutionary Change: Case Study, Black Power," in N. Whitten Jr. and J. Szwed, eds., *Afro-American Anthropology,* Free Press, 1970. Additionally, he is author of many articles on social movements and social change, including "Movements of Revolutionary Change; Some Structural Characteristics," in a special issue on General Systems Theory edited by Bertram Gross, *American Behavioral Scientist,* 1971. Additionally, he has published articles and chapters resulting from his African research, including "Traders on Bicycle: Entrepreneurship and Cultural Change among the Digo and Duruma of Kenya," in Stanley Davis, ed., *Comparative Management,* Prentice-Hall, 1971. He has filmed and produced three films and two filmstrip kits paralleling the above research and writing on movements and change, and has also collaborated with Encyclopedia Britannica on two similar films. Furthermore, he has filmed and produced a movie about some Jamaican lifeways and a filmstrip kit about ecological adaptations and change along the Kenya coast.

FELICITAS D. GOODMAN, Assistant Professor, Department of Sociology and Anthropology, Denison University, Granville, Ohio, has conducted field work among various Apostolic congregations in Mexico City and Yucatán, Mexico. Her publications include *Speaking in Tongues: A Cross-Cultural Study of Glossolalia,* University of Chicago Press, 1972; "Disturbances in the Apostolic Church: A Trance-Based Upheaval in Yucatán," in Felicitas D. Goodman, Jeanette H. Henney, and Esther Pressel, *Trance, Healing, and Hallucination: Three Field Studies in Religious Experience,* New York, Wiley-Interscience, 1974.

VIRGINIA H. HINE, Instructor, Department of Anthropology, University of Miami. She has conducted five year field research with groups identified with the Pentecostal Movement or the "Charismatic Renewal," and for three years has worked with conservation and ecology groups. She has published several articles on Pentecostalism and other movements and is co-author, with LUTHER P. GERLACH, of *People, Power, Change: Movements of Social Transformation* Bobbs Merrill, 1970; and *Lifeway Leap: The Dynamics of Change in America,* University of Minnesota Press, 1973.

J. STILLSON JUDAH is Professor of the History of Religions and Head Librarian at the Graduate Theological Union, Berkeley, California. Supported by a Sealantic Fund grant in 1957-58, he conducted field research with metaphysical religious groups in various parts of the United States. That research culminated in 1967 with his publication, *The History and Philosophy of the Metaphysical Movements in America,* Westminster Press, 1967. For the past three years he has conducted research with the Hare Krishna Movement in Berkeley, San Francisco, and Los Angeles. His publications include *Index to Religious Periodical Literature, 1949-1952* (compiler and editor), The American Theological Library Association, 1952; *Hare Krishna and the Counterculture,* Contemporary Religious Movements: A Wiley Interscience Series, New York, John Wiley and Sons, Inc., 1974.

ROGER M. LAUER, M.D., Lecturer, Department of Psychiatry, University of California School of Medicine, San Francisco; and Assistant Chief, Acute Treatment Service, Langley Porter Neuropsychiatric Institute, San Francisco.

(Formerly) Staff Psychiatrist, Mental Health Study Center, National Institute of Mental Health, Adelphi, Maryland. He conducted field research with metaphysical practitioners in a West Coast urban area and a mid-Atlantic urban area between 1969 and 1972. His publications include *Social Nudism in America* (with F. Ilfeld), New Haven, Conn.: College and University Press, 1964; "Masters of Metaphysics" in R. Cox, ed., *Religious Systems and Psychotherapy*, Springfield, Illinois: Charles C. Thomas, 1973; "Urban Shamans," *The New Physician*, August 1973.

MARK P. LEONE is Assistant Professor in the Department of Anthropology, Princeton University. He conducted several field tours among Mormons in Arizona and Utah between 1969 and 1972. A volume, *The Evolution of Mormonism,* resulting from this work is in preparation. His articles on Mormonism have been published in the *Utah Historical Quarterly, Dialogue, A Journal of Mormon Thought,* and in *Archeology Today* (1973), ed. C. L. Redman. Other publications include *Contemporary Archeology,* Southern Illinois University Press, 1972, and articles on neolithic agriculture.

JUNE MACKLIN, Professor and Co-Chairman, Department of Sociology and Anthropology, Connecticut College, New London, Connecticut. She has gathered data on Spiritism and Spiritualism while conducting field work projects in Indiana and South Texas (1964 to the present), Northern Mexico (1965 to the present), Argentina (1968), and New England (1969 to the present). Her publications include "El Niño Fidencio: un Estudio del Curanderismo en Nuevo León," *Anuario Humánitas 1967,* Universidad de Nuevo León; she is co-author of *The Human Nature Industry,* Doubleday and Co., 1973; "Structural Development and Conservatism in Three North Mexican Folk Saint Movements," *Comparative Studies in Society and History,* 1973; "Sacred Ritual vs. the Unconscious: the Efficacy of Symbols and Structure in North Mexican Folk Saints' Cults and General Ceremonialism," in Ino Rossi, ed., *Structuralism in Perspective,* New York, Dutton & Co. (in press); "Folk Saints, Curanderismo, and Spiritist Cults in Mexico: Divine Election and Social Selection," *Revista/Review Interamericana* (forthcoming).

MORTON A. MARKS, Assistant Professor of Anthropology, City College of New York. He conducted field work between 1965 and 1972 in the west and east coasts, Puerto Rico, and Brazil on a variety of subjects dealing with ritual behavior and linguistic and musical forms. He is currently preparing for publication *Crossing Over: Sound and Meaning in Ritual Music.*

EDWARD JAMES MOODY, Lecturer, The Queen's University of Belfast, Ireland. For two and a half years he was a member of the First Church of Satan in San Francisco doing participant observation; and for four years he conducted research with individuals practicing various forms of magical ritual. Part of 1972 was spent researching exorcism in London, England. His recent publication is "Urban Witches" in *Conformity and Conflict: Readings in*

Cultural Anthropolgy, James P. Spradley and David McCurdy, eds., Little, Brown, 1971.

E. MANSELL PATTISON, M.D., Associate Professor and Vice-Chairman, Department of Psychiatry and Human Behavior, University of California, Irvine. He has served as consultant to the National Institute of Mental Health and to the National Council of Churches in its Missionary Orientation Program: Religion and Mental Health in the Community Task Force; and Task Force on Clinical Pastoral Education. He conducted field interviews in Appalachia (1961-1964); Pacific Northwest Indian Communities (1967-1970); and Seattle (1966-1970). He has published widely in scientific journals. His recent publications include "Social and Psychological Aspects of Religion in Psychotherapy," *Journal of Nervous and Mental Disorders,* 1966; "A Critique of Alcoholism Treatment Concepts," *Quarterly Journal of Studies On Alcoholism,* 1966; "Psychiatry and Anthropology: Three Models for a Working Relationship," *Social Psychiatry,* 1967; "Ego Morality: An Emerging Psychotherapeutic Concept," *Psychoanalytical Review,* 1968; "Change in Public Attitudes on Narcotic Addiction," *American Journal of Psychiatry,* 1968; "Group Psychotherapy and Group Methods in Community Mental Health," *International Journal of Group Psychotherapy,* 1971. He is editor of *Clinical Psychiatry and Religion,* Little Brown, Boston, 1969.

LEO PFEFFER, Professor of Constitutional Law and Chairman of the Department of Political Science, Long Island University, The Brooklyn Center. He is widely recognized for both his legal work and academic research in matters of church and state. He is author of *Church, State and Freedom,* Boston, Beacon Press, 1953, rev. ed. 1967; *The Liberties of an American: The Supreme Court Speaks,* Boston, Beacon Press, 1956, 2nd ed. enl., 1963; *Church and State in the United States* (with Anson Phelps Stokes) revised one-volume edition, New York, Harper & Row, 1964; *Creeds in Competition: A Creative Force in American Culture,* New York, Harper, 1958; *This Honorable Court: A History of the United States Supreme Court,* Boston, Beacon Press, 1965.

RAYMOND H. PRINCE, Research Director, Mental Hygiene Institute; and Associate Professor, Department of Psychiatry, McGill University, Montreal. He is President and one of the founders in 1964 of the R. M. Bucke Memorial Society for the Study of Religious Experience, Montreal. He has conducted field research in Nigeria (1957-1959 and 1961-1963), where he was affiliated with the Nigerian Institute of Social and Economics Research, Ibadan. Among his publications are "Indigenous Yoruba Psychiatry, in Ari Kiev, ed., *Magic, Faith, and Healing,* Glencoe Free Press, New York, 1964; and "Mystical States and the Concept of Regression" in J. White, ed., *The Highest State of Consciousness,* Anchor Books, Doubleday, New York, 1972.

THOMAS ROBBINS, Assistant Professor in the Sociology Department, Queens College, City University of New York. He has research interests in the fields of deviance and the sociology of religion and has published studies on the characteristics of amphetamine addicts as well as on the rehabilitation of psychedelic drug users by counter-culture religions. Since 1969 he has been engaged in a long-range study of such movements with DICK ANTHONY. Publications with Mr. Anthony include "Getting Straight with Meher Baba," *Journal for the Scientific Study of Religion*, June 1972; "On the Limits of Symbolic Realism," *Journal for the Scientific Study of Religion*, September 1973; *The Meher Baba and Jesus Movements: A Comparison of "Post-drug" Spiritual Movements*, a monograph in the Wiley Interscience Series: Contemporary Religious Movements, John Wiley and Sons, Inc., New York (in press).

BRUCE A. ROSENBERG, Professor in the Department of English, The Pennsylvania State University. He has conducted research on the preached sermon in fundamentalist churches in southern and central California, central Oklahoma, Virginia, and North Carolina between 1966 and 1970. His primary research area is medieval English literature, and his attention is drawn to the American preached sermon to gain a comparative and methodological perspective on the nature of spontaneous composition. He is author of *The Art of the American Folk Preacher*, New York: Oxford University Press, 1970, which was awarded the James Russell Lowell prize in 1970 and second place in the Chicago Folklore Competition.

E. FULLER TORREY, M.D. is Special Assistant to the Director for International Activities at the National Institute of Mental Health. He has conducted extensive field research with indigenous therapists in Ethiopia (1964-1966) and for briefer periods in Sarawak, Bali, Peru, and among subcultures in the United States, especially Mexican-Americans. He has authored many journal articles; his most recent publications include *Ethical Issues in Medicine, The Role of the Physician in Today's Society* (editor), Little, Brown, 1968; *The Mind Game: Witchdoctors and Psychiatrists*, Emerson Hall, New York, 1972; and *The Death of Psychiatry*, Philadelphia, Chilton, 1974.

MARCELLO TRUZZI, Associate Professor of Sociology at New College, Sarasota, Florida. He has conducted field research in California, Michigan, and Florida with witch covens and Satanic grottos. He is editor of *Sociology and Everyday Life*, Prentice-Hall, 1968; *Sociology: The Classic Statements*, Random House, 1970; *The Humanities As Sociology*, Charles Merrill, 1973; and *Sociology for Pleasure*, Prentice-Hall, 1974. He is currently completing two books on the occult, *The Sociology of the Occult in America* and *Science and the Occult Today*. He is editor and publisher of *Exploration*, a newsletter of academic research into the occult and occult movements.

HARRIET WHITEHEAD, doctoral candidate, University of Chicago, conducted field research with Scientologists in the Chicago and Los Angeles area between 1969 and 1971.

JOHN F. WILSON, Professor in the Department of Religion, Princeton University. He is the editor of *Church and State in American History*, Boston, Heath, 1965; and author of *Pulpit in Parliament: Puritanism during the English Civil Wars, 1640-1648*, Princeton University Press, 1969; as well as numerous journal articles.

IRVING I. ZARETSKY is a Russell Sage Fellow in Law and Social Science at Yale Law School and Lecturer at Yale College. He has worked with Spiritualist churches in California and the mid-Atlantic states from 1966 to the present. His publications include "The Language of Spiritualist Churches" in James Spradley, ed., *Culture and Cognition: Rules, Maps, and Plans*, Chandler Press, 1972; *Bibliography on African Spirit Possession and Mediumship*, Northwestern University Press, 1967; "Jesus in Jerusalem 1973: Mission Impossible?" in B. Z. Sobel, *Hebrew Christianity: The Thirteenth Tribe*, New York, Wiley-Interscience, 1974. He is Series Editor of Contemporary Religious Movements: A Wiley-Interscience Series, John Wiley and Sons, Inc., New York.

Tʜᴇ general headings in the index (e.g. religion, ritual, belief) are not exhaustive; the reader is encouraged to consult the entries for specific religious movements for more complete coverage. The index does not include references to deities, geographical locations (with some exceptions), mainline denominations, or bibliographical material. The cross-idexing system should alert the reader to the extensive overlapping of terms used by the various movements.

Library of Congress Cataloging in Publication Data

Zaretsky, Irving I.
    Religious movements in contemporary America

    Bibliography: p.
    1. United States—Religious life and customs
2. United States—Religion—1965-   I. Leone,
Mark P., joint author.   II. Title.
BR516.5.Z37   200'.973   73-39054
ISBN 0-691-07186-1